ACCOUNTING FOR LAWYERS

■ ■ ■

Steven J. Willis

Professor of Law
University of Florida College of Law

Member, Florida Bar Association
Member, Louisiana Bar Association (in-active)
Certified Public Accountant (Louisiana, in-active license)

WEST ACADEMIC

© 2024 LEG, Inc. d/b/a West Academic
    860 Blue Gentian Road, Suite 350
    Eagan, MN 55121
    1-877-888-1330

West, West Academic Publishing, and West Academic are trademarks of West Publishing Corporation, used under license.

Published in the United States of America

ISBN: 978-1-68467-564-7

SUMMARY OF CONTENTS

TABLE OF CONTENTS

TABLE OF CASES

The principal cases are in bold type.

ACCOUNTING FOR LAWYERS

LESSON ONE

WHY LAWYERS NEED TO UNDERSTAND ACCOUNTING

■ ■ ■

Lesson Objectives

1. Student will learn what this course concerns.

2. Student will learn some brief examples of accounting used by lawyers involving:

   a. Family law.

      i. Property division.

      ii. Alimony.

      iii. Child support.

   b. Bankruptcy law.

      i. Chapter 7 liquidation.

      ii. Chapter 11 insolvency restructure.

   c. Estates and trust law.

      i. Income beneficiary rights.

      ii. Principal beneficiary rights.

   d. Corporate law and corporate finance.

      i. Distributions and dividends.

      ii. SEC reporting and compliance.

      iii. Mergers.

      iv. Liquidations.

   e. Tort law.

      i. Damages for lost wages.

      ii. Valuation of other damages.

   f. Contract law.

      i. Accounting or financial triggers of contract provisions.

      ii. Compensation as a function of income.

    g.   Tax law.

        i.   Measuring income and expenses.

        ii.   Accounting for assets and liabilities.

    h.   Employment law.

        i.   Compensation negotiations.

        ii.   Percentage of income compensation arrangements.

    i.   Environmental law.

        i.   Cost/benefit analysis.

        ii.   Trend analysis.

    j.   Criminal law.

        i.   White collar crimes.

        ii.   Tax crimes.

    k.   Sports and entertainment law.

        i.   Team/movie investments and valuation.

        ii.   Percentage of income contracts.

3.   Student will learn some instances in which everyone needs to know basic accounting:

    a.   Applying for a loan.

    b.   Preparing tax returns.

    c.   Budgeting for a household.

    d.   Saving for a purchase.

4.   Student should end the lesson convinced of the *practical* need for this course.

Terminology Introduced

- Insolvency.
- Balance sheet.
- Income statement.
- Statement of cash flows.
- SEC.
- Ratios.
- Cost/benefit analysis.
- GAAP.
- IFRS.

- Going concern.
- Present value of an annuity.

———

Having taught this course for 40 years, I've learned that most law students, as well as most lawyers and judges, understand too little about accounting . . . and "know" too much about accounting that is not so. Reported cases abound which misuse accounting terminology such that an expert in the area will have difficulty understanding the decision.

Similarly, legislators (and members of Congress) who draft statutes all-too-often use accounting terms incorrectly or inconsistently. As a result, many resulting laws are vague, inconsistent, or even meaningless.

This course focuses on basic accounting concepts, as well as terminology. If law students, lawyers, judges, and legislators better understand the purposes (and limitations) of accounting, they will perform much better. The course will not turn anyone into an accountant: that is a task that takes four or five years of instruction and study. But this course can help the uninitiated learn some basics.

LESSON ONE illustrates that knowledge of accounting is important for all lawyers, not simply those who practice tax law or corporate law.

1. FAMILY LAW

Much of family law involves allocating limited resources. This may arise in the division of property, the awarding of alimony, or the determination of child support.

If faced with dividing property—whether in a community property or an equitable distribution state—a lawyer and judge must first determine which assets and which liabilities are separate (non-marital or non-community). That requires an understanding of assets and liabilities, which necessarily involves accounting terminology and at least a basic balance sheet. The second step will be to prepare the marital balance sheet, comprising marital (or community) assets and liabilities. As students will learn, the exercise of considerable judgment goes into balance sheet preparation. If a lawyer (or judge) mistakenly considers "book value" as shown on a typical balance sheet to be a fair representation of the assets and liabilities, the result will typically be inequitable. Similarly, if a lawyer or judge (as is all-too common) uses a tax-law based balance sheet (one prepared using tax laws and principles), the result will likewise typically be inequitable. LESSON ONE makes these points. Later lessons illustrate them in greater depth.

If faced with determining alimony or child support, a lawyer or judge must necessarily deal with income statements. Ideally, this will involve statements for multiple periods. Correctly viewed, neither alimony nor child support is function of past income; instead, they are each a function of future projected income. But, to project income, the decision-maker must look at the only evidence available: the past. As the student will quickly realize, the exercise of considerable judgment enters income statement preparation. All-too-often, lawyers and judges unwisely rely on tax returns as proper measures of income. LESSON ONE introduces the idea of how dangerous this can be, while later lessons illustrate the point in greater depth.

2. BANKRUPTCY LAW

Students of bankruptcy quickly learn of two main bankruptcy types: Chapter 7 and Chapter 11. Chapter 7 involves a liquidation: selling assets and paying creditors. Chapter 11, in contrast, involves a "work out" or continuation of a business under temporary court supervision. This may involve selling some assets and paying some creditors, as well as the discharge of other liabilities.

Both bankruptcy types focus on the balance sheet: the assets and the liabilities. With a Chapter 7, the equity portion of the balance sheet is likely very much negative—a type of insolvency. Although a Chapter 11 "work out" also focuses on the balance sheet, it must more carefully consider the income statement and the statement of cash flows. Why? Because it deals with a different view of the term "insolvent." In the Chapter 7 sense (the balance sheet view of insolvency) liabilities exceed assets and equity is negative. In a Chapter 11 sense, that may or may not be true. Importantly, in a Chapter 11 matter, the entity has hope for the future, after some creditor protection. This requires an income statement focus to ensure adequate future income will occur. It also requires an understanding of the statement of cash flows is adequate cash coming in such that creditors can be paid as the liabilities come due. That focuses on the cash flow concept of insolvency: the lack of liquidity and the inability to pay what is currently due.

LESSON ONE only introduces these concepts. Later lessons consider them in more depth. But the student should end with an understanding that bankruptcy law requires significant knowledge of accounting.

3. ESTATES AND TRUST LAW

Many legal issues arise in trust law: how to form the trust, what and where to file, fiduciary duties, and tax implications. Ultimately, however—as with family law—the matter boils down to who gets what. Does the cash flow or appreciation in value create "income" that inures to the income beneficiary? Or does it "belong" to the principal beneficiary? Which "expenses" must the income beneficiary suffer, and which must the principal beneficiary suffer? A trustee cannot properly allocate income and expenses between the beneficiaries unless he properly understands the concept of "income," which necessarily involves accounting. When do we recognize the income such that it inures to someone? How do we measure it? What duties does a fiduciary owe in choosing investments that create large cash flows as opposed to those that create little cash flow but larger appreciation?

LESSON ONE, as an introductory lesson, will not answer those questions; instead, it begins to raise them. Students should end the lesson with an understanding that knowledge of accounting is essential for the proper management of a trust, as well as for the proper crafting of a trust agreement.

4. CORPORATE LAW

The relevance of accounting to corporate law is extensive and, at times, intricate. State law, for example, controls the authority of a corporation to distribute assets via a dividend. Typically, that authority is a function of either "earned surplus" or "current earnings." Those terms which vary from state to state, are inconsistent with traditional accounting terminology. Generally accepted accounting principles use the terms "retained earnings" and "current profit" to roughly approximate the corporate law terms. Later lessons expand on these differences. For now, students should understand that accounting is important to an understanding of corporate law, even if the terminology is often different.

5. TORT LAW

Accounting and finance are relevant to tort law in many ways. Financial calculations are essential for determining the present value of future lost earnings. Accounting is essential for determining the "earnings" aspect of the calculation. For example, an injured person may have operated a business, which either suffers or fails because of the victim's absence. Accounting principles will measure the effect the person had on the earnings as well as the projected lost impact. Or a tortfeasor's actions may have damaged a business's reputation or viability. Once again, accounting—through an analysis of both the balance sheet and the income statement—will be critical in evaluating the damages.

6. GENERAL LITIGATION AND CONTRACT LAW

Contract law is a common area of accounting relevance. Often, parties share profits. That necessarily requires a definition and a determination of profits, which is the province of accounting. As students will learn in later lessons, accounting involves a great deal of judgment; hence, if one party to a contract defines the term "profits," his incentive will be to define it in a manner beneficial to his side and detrimental to the other. Thus, a lawyer drafting a contract that uses the term "profits" or "share of profits" must understand the varying meaning of those terms.

Also, many contracts have "trigger" provisions that cause a contract provision to become applicable or "active" upon the occurrence of a defined condition. Often, the condition is a function of an accounting term or ratio (the subject of LESSON TEN). For example, a lender may insist that a term loan become due and payable if the borrower's "current ratio" drops below 1.5/1. LESSON TEN covers such ratios and their uses. Earlier lessons cover the more fundamental accounting terminology that forms the various aspects of financial or accounting ratios.

7. TAX LAW

The study of tax law does not require an accounting background; however, an understanding of basic accounting clearly helps with the study of taxes. Fundamentally, an income tax is a function of "income," which is an accounting concept. Financial accounting defines "income" quite differently than does tax accounting; however, the concepts and terminology are similar. As a result, understanding one aids understanding the other. Other aspects of tax law—for example, an estate tax—necessitates an understanding of balance sheets. Once again, the tax law definitions of assets and liabilities may be different from the financial accounting definitions, but the understanding of one still aids understanding the other.

8. LABOR AND EMPLOYMENT LAW

Labor negotiations—between management and workers—involves workers' needs and management's ability to pay. Both fundamentally require an understanding of the financial statements for each. Employment law may involve a claim for lost wages, either past or future. That necessitates an understanding of "income," "expenses," as well as "opportunity costs," each of which is an accounting concept.

9. ENVIRONMENTAL LAW

Environmental law often involves an "impact study" that measures the costs and benefits of a proposed action or regulation. Such studies necessarily involve accounting concepts. Measuring costs involves accounting. Allocating costs to the appropriate period and activity also involves accounting. As students will learn in later lessons, much of accounting involves the exercise of judgment—often whether a cost has been incurred currently versus in the future, as well as well the cost best "matches" with one activity or division versus another. As students learn in LESSON TWO, the "matching principle" is the most important principle of accounting: it matches income with the costs of producing that particular income. That principle—and the accounting skills required to apply it—are critical to a valid cost/benefit analysis.

10. CRIMINAL LAW

A significant portion of criminal law involves "white collar" crime, such as embezzlement or securities fraud. Necessarily, prosecution and defense of such crimes requires an understanding of the underlying accounting consequences the crimes caused.

11. SPORTS AND ENTERTAINMENT LAW

Sports and entertainment clients often enter contracts that provide for compensation as a function of various activities or profits. Such contracts necessarily use accounting terminology. Litigation involving such contracts, as a result, will necessarily involve expert accounting testimony regarding the meaning of terminology, the measurement and timing of profits, as well as the proper allocation and timing of expenses. If the client allows management or the team owner to define the terms and to make the allocations, the client's share of profits is likely to be small because the "profits," as defined will be small. That situation, as students will learn in later lessons, results from accounting judgment: to which year or activity do we allocate the income and to which year or activity do we allocate the costs. Although the exercise of the judgment may be incremental, it can cumulate to material amounts. Anyone who represents sports or entertainment figures should, as a result, have a good understanding of both accounting and finance.

12. PERSONAL MATTERS

If for no other reason, law students need to understand basic accounting for their own purposes. Throughout their lives, each will need to prepare personal budgets, as well as personal income statements and balance sheets when applying for loans. They will all want (or should want) to plan for their own retirements, which necessitates some knowledge of accounting (one must know what one earns and spends, as well as what one owns and owes) and finance (FINANCE FOR LAWYERS is a separate but related course.)

LESSON TWO

ACCOUNTING IS NOT A SCIENCE

■ ■ ■

LESSON TWO continues the introduction to accounting and breaks into three parts:

- Part A illustrates many ways in which financial statements involve "soft numbers." Those are ones that result from estimates and choices, and the exercise of judgment. within the framework of accounting principles and assumptions.

- Part B covers accounting principles and assumptions.

- Part C works through a beginning problem designed to illustrate practical examples of "soft numbers" and the points made in Part A. This PROBLEM is one that flows through many later lessons.

LESSON TWO-A

TERMINOLOGY, ESTIMATES, CHOICES, AND JUDGMENT

■ ■ ■

Lesson Objectives

1. Student will learn that accounting is not a science; instead, it involves much imprecision:

    a. Estimates.

        i.   Estimates of value.

        ii. Estimates of useful life.

        iii. Estimates of future costs.

    b. Choices.

        i.   Choice of depreciation method.

        ii. Choice of inventory method.

         iii.   Choice of accounting method.

   c.   Judgment.

         i.   When is a transaction complete?

         ii.   Distinguishing a repair from an improvement.

   d.   Principles and assumptions.

         i.   Historical cost assumption.

         ii.   Going concern assumption.

         iii.   Periodic assumption.

         iv.   Materiality.

         v.   Separate entity assumption.

         vi.   Monetary principle.

         vii.   Conservatism principle.

         viii. Matching principle.

2.   Student will learn that clients often have multiple sets of books for legitimate reasons.

Terminology Introduced

Later lessons cover these terms in greater depth; however, because this lesson introduces them, the student should review the definitions in the GLOSSARY.

- GAAP.
- IFRS.
- Cash method.
- Accrual method.
- Hybrid method.
- Accounting principles.
- LIFO.
- FIFO.
- Depreciation.
- Materiality.
- Capitalize.
- Expense.
- Pass-through entity.

1. GENERAL POINTS AND SOME TERMINOLOGY

Although a basic accounting degree probably always[1] involves either a Bachelor of *Science* or a Master of *Science*, the profession is more of an art than a science. Indeed, it involves the application of many rules; however, those rules provide many opportunities for judgment calls. As a result, the resulting numbers—and thus the resulting financial statements—are no better than the judgments exercised.

That is really the point of LESSON TWO: lawyers must understand the large amount of discretion necessarily exercised in the preparation of financial statements and their underlying numbers. This point is not meant as a criticism of the profession; indeed, generally accepted accounting principles [GAAP] are well-designed. Nevertheless non-accountants must understand the financial statements are never perfect and can never provide a guarantee, particularly if parts of them are viewed in isolation. That is a risk lawyers face: the natural temptation (or legal reality) of viewing only parts of a person's or entity's financial picture (whether it be only some assets or some liabilities or some time periods).

LESSON TWO-A refers to two critical terms: GAAP and IFRS. Students should always refer to the GLOSSARY for new or unfamiliar terms.

The GLOSSARY definition of GAAP is:

> **GAAP: Generally   Accepted   Accounting   Principles.** [pronounced gap]. These rules form the basis of public accounting. In the United States, audited financial statements must conform to GAAP for them to receive an unqualified opinion of the auditors. Departure from GAAP is sometimes permissible—or even advisable; however, it will always raise a red flag of concern and thus necessitate a convincing justification.
>
> Unaudited financial statements need not conform to GAAP. Publicly traded companies must issue financial statements consistent with the Securities and Exchange Commission [SEC] accounting rules, which may differ from GAAP in some instances. They must also issue GAAP conforming statements
>
> Most nations other than the United States follow International Financial Reporting Standards [IFRS].

The GLOSSARY uses the term GAAP several dozen times, so students may want to search for the term so they can see it used in context. LESSON THREE covers the sources of GAAP authority in considerably more depth. The GLOSSARY definition of IFRS is:

---

[1]   I must hedge that statement: perhaps some institution offers an accounting degree as a B.A. or M.A., but I am unaware of any.

IFRS: International Financial Reporting Standards: [pronounced I-fers]. IFRS are issued developed by the International Accounting Standards Board [IASB]. Generally, they are less specific and more open to the judgment of the auditor than are GAAP. Generally, GAAP is a more "rules-based" system of accounting, while IFRS is a more "principles-based" system. Most nations, other than the United States, follow IFRS rather than GAAP. The SEC has, for many years, studied whether the U.S. should switch to IFRS rather than GAAP.

Multinational entities ultimately must conform to both systems, depending on where and why the statements are issued and used. This course—ACCOUNTING FOR LAWYERS—focuses primarily on U.S. GAAP. The United States may someday adopt IFRS but that does not appear likely soon. The differences between the two systems are sufficient to justify a single system of accounting, or greater ease of comparison. Thus, efforts to unify them will likely continue.

A. FOUR REASONS ACCOUNTING IS NOT A SCIENCE

Four reasons accounting is not a science are:

- Estimates.
- Choices.
- Judgment.
- Principles and assumptions.

1) Estimates

Accounting inevitably involves at least some estimates, if not many. This is true both for audited and unaudited financial statements. Often, estimates result from an experience-based framework; however, sometimes (perhaps many times) they are not much more than a "best guess" of some underlying unknown (and probably unknowable) fact.

Three examples of "estimates" involve value, useful life, and future costs.

a. Value

The "historical cost assumption" of U.S. GAAP requires the use of the actual "cost"[2] of an asset for reporting purposes. But the "conservatism

---

[2] As covered in LESSONS FIVE and SEVEN, the "cost" of an item is not clearly defined, as it may include some related "costs" such as delivery, set-up, or even over-head. Also, an entity may have one "cost" for GAAP reporting, another for tax law, and a third for internal cost accounting, as covered in LESSON SEVEN.

principle" requires a reduction in value if a clear and permanent loss of "value" occurs.

EXAMPLE 1

JOE'S BAR & GRILL and Expensive Wine

JOE'S purchased a bottle of wine for $1,000. The wine—a particularly rare vintage—appreciates in value to $50,000.

In the alternative, the wine loses its popularity and drops in value to $100, which appears to be a permanent decrease.

GAAP would not permit JOE'S to increase the value of the wine; however, it would *require* JOE'S to decrease the value under the alternative facts. In that situation, JOE'S would recognize a $900 loss.

In EXAMPLE 1, JOE'S BAR & GRILL purchased a bottle of rare wine for $1000. It would list the wine on its balance sheet as an asset using the number $1000, the historical cost. Even if the wine appreciated to $5,000 or $50,000, JOE'S BAR & GRILL would not increase the number above $1,000 because the historical cost assumption, as well as the revenue recognition principle would forbid it. In some cases, involving marketable securities,[3] JOE'S would report increases in value, but a bottle of wine would not qualify.

In contrast, if the wine clearly and permanently lost value to $100, JOE'S would have to recognize the $900 loss. EXAMPLE 1, however, *assumes* JOE'S BAR & GRILL follows GAAP. If audited by a C.P.A., the example is correct; however, most entities are not audited, which means JOE'S may prepare its financial statements however it wishes, subject only to state and federal laws (*e.g.*, fraud prohibitions, family law definitions of assets and liabilities, state law trust accounting rules, or tax law). As we cover throughout the course, many areas of law use accounting terminology (*e.g.*, assets, liabilities, income, expenses, balance sheet); however, many lack accounting principles and assumptions—a framework for those terms—or they lack definitions of the terms. Statutes may define the terms inconsistent with GAAP. As a result, in many legal areas *fair market value* accounting may control rather than GAAP. For example, this would likely be the case for family law and the division of property (it would generally be a function of value rather than historical cost).

The "value" of an asset—rather than its cost—is also relevant for internal "cost accounting" and planning (covered in LESSON SEVEN).

---

[3]   Per FAS 115 and Codification Topic 320, marketable securities held for sale or "available for sale" must be listed at "fair value." Per IRC § 475 U. S. tax accounting requires securities dealers to use "mark to market" accounting and thus list marketable securities at fair market value.

Management likely wants to know the current value of all material items so that it can properly plan for the future and set current prices. For example, if the $1,000 bottle of wine would produce 5 glasses, JOE'S may set the price at $300 per glass: a 50% mark-up. However, if the "value" rose to $50,000, JOE'S would likely charge more than $10,000 per glass, and likely much more. Assuming it only has one bottle of wine, accounting for this item would be simple; however, in reality, JOE'S would have considerable inventory and many varied assets (tangible and intangible) that continually appreciate or depreciate as the economy and the market for them changes. JOE'S may desire "fair market value" financial statements, at least for internal use. If so, someone with accounting skills will need to prepare them. If your client has a legal action with JOE'S, you may want to see them, as well as any GAAP-based statements.

The GLOSSARY definition of "fair market value" provides:

Fair Market Value: FMV: What a willing buyer would pay to a willing seller, neither under any special compulsion to buy or to sell at that time. For tax purposes, the amount realized in a taxable transaction includes the fair market value [FMV] of any property or services received. At least a few lower court opinions have defined FMV in a personal sense, *i.e.,* at least partially as a function of the individual recipient's circumstances. For example, a person who won a first-class trip to Brazil—but who seldom travelled and never first class—might have a FMV in the trip which is significantly less than would a more worldly winner. While authorities supporting such a viewpoint are few, lawyers should be aware of the potential "personal" nature of *Fair Market Value. See Turner v. Commissioner, 13 T.C.M. (CCH) 462 (1954).*

b.   Useful Life

Financial statements inevitably involve assets with useful lives greater than one year. For example, a truck may last 7 years, a refrigerator 10 years, and a building 40 years or longer. As we will learn, the matching principle requires GAAP-based financial statements to "match" income with the costs of producing that income. That necessitates a variety of accounting rules we cover in subsequent lessons. In LESSON FIVE, we cover depreciation and amortization, which allocate the cost of multi-year assets over their "useful lives."

Consider EXAMPLE 2. We cannot know how long the truck will last. We can predict 7 years, though it may ultimately last only 5, or it may last 10. Without a crystal ball, we inevitably must estimate the useful life for every asset we acquire, including intangible assets such as trademarks, copyrights, patents, and goodwill.[4]

EXAMPLE 2

JOE'S BAR & GRILL Buys a Truck

JOE'S purchased a new truck for $50,000. It must allocate the historical cost over the "useful" life of the truck via depreciation, as covered in LESSON FIVE.

How long will the truck last? Experience may suggest 5 to 10 years, but the answer is not much more than an educated guess.

PROBLEM 1 in LESSON TWO-B contemplates, for example, employee and manager training costs of $20,000 for JOE'S BAR & GRILL. This could involve, for example, required training for operating a franchise. Whatever it entailed, that large expenditure would likely benefit the entity for multiple years. The impact would likely be negligible 50 years from now; however, the training will likely result in a better-run business this year and next year and probably the year after. Whether it will be useful for 3 years or 5 or 7 is where the speculation really breaks down. Perhaps the franchiser (or some other authority) has statistical information based on actual experience that can help us; but, more likely it does not. Whichever, even that information is an estimate because we can never know how it applies to a particular business in a particular locality. Similarly, we may know that the average lawyer uses his or her legal education for 40 years, but that does not mean that _you_ will use yours for 40 years. Perhaps you will quit practicing law after 10 years, or perhaps you will work until you are 90. If you attempt to compute the expected return on your legal education (or to amortize JOE'S BAR & GRILL employee training costs over their "useful life") you will need to have a time period to represent the useful life.

That future period is inherently speculative. You may base it on solid information, or it may be a guess. Accountants inevitably face both situations: those in which they have solid experiential information on which to base an estimate, as well as those in which they have less reliable information. In both cases, however, someone must decide: 1 year, 2, 5, or 20. They must then base the depreciation or amortization deduction on that estimate. The result will almost never be perfect. We hope the errors will cancel each other, at least in part: we may estimate 6 years for something that lasts 5, but we may also estimate 4 years for some other machine that turns out to last 5 as well. The two errors (which turn out to be hundreds

---

[4]   Patents generally have a legal life of 20 years, while copyrights last for the life of the author plus 70 years; however, their economic lives may be much shorter. For tax purposes, they each have a life of 15 years. IRC § 197.

of errors involving myriad estimates of useful lives) ultimately tend to average out to something that is not material.

That last statement, however, deserves some thought: if all the estimates are honest and there are many of them over many years, they will probably average out. But, if we have only a small number of items about which we "estimate" lives or values, or if we focus on only a small number of years, the chance of the cumulative error rate being immaterial is no longer large. Further, we must—especially as lawyers who deal with contract breaches, dissembling, and a general lack of trust in others— recognize the incentives for manipulation.

EXAMPLE 3

JOE'S *Manager* Swayed by Self-Interest

JOE'S incurred $20,000 of employee training costs and the manager must determine the "useful life" of the training.

She considers using one year, which results in a $20,000 current expense. In the alternative, she considers using ten years, which results in a $2,000 current expense. Her bonus is 20% of JOE'S profits.

As illustrated in EXAMPLE 3, if you are the manager who decides the useful life of the employee training, you will be interested in how your decision impacts you. Perhaps, it has no impact at all, in which case you will provide your best estimate. But your bonus may be 20% of JOE'S BAR & GRILL "profits" for the year, as posited in the example. If you allocate the training costs to one year, then "profits" this year decrease by $20,000 and your bonus drops by $4000 (20% of $20,000). You thus have a personal incentive to estimate a longer useful life. A 10-year amortization would result in a $2000 per year deduction and a drop in your bonus of only $400. A 10-year life for employee training is implausible and would unlikely satisfy an auditor; however, JOE'S likely is not audited. If the owners assign such authority to the manager, then they need to understand the consequences and temptations that may result.

Imagine you have responsibility for making 10 or 50 or perhaps 2000 such "estimates." You can see how temptation might affect *your* ability to properly estimate. Morally and contractually, you should use your best judgement, of course. But, without an external auditor, what you should do may differ from what you do, especially if the temptation/incentive is large. Further, you may not be so egregious as to estimate a 10-year life. A 2-year life would surely be defensible. That would result in a $10,000 current expense and thus an extra $2000 for your bonus.

Consider EXAMPLE 4: JOE'S owner, Scott, is getting a divorce and expects to pay child support and alimony, and to equitably divide the business. As a business owner, he has a powerful incentive to understate income for the current year. One way to do that is by estimating asset useful lives such that they result in more expenses for relevant years.

In EXAMPLE 4, a 1-year life for the training decreases JOE'S—and almost certainly Scott's[5]—current income by $20,000. In contrast, a more reasonable 3-year life reduces income by only $6,666.67. The $13,333.33 difference likely affects the Scott's child support and alimony obligations as well as his obligations for marital or community property division. The present value of the reduced child support resulting from the $13,333.33 "income reduction" could easily be $15,000.[6] The present value of reduced alimony could easily be $50,000.[7] Further, the reduced obligation under equitable distribution or community property law could easily be over $65,000.[8] Thus, that one decision might save Scott $130,000.

EXAMPLE 4

JOE'S *Owner* Swayed by Self-Interest

JOE'S incurred $20,000 of employee training costs and the owner, Scott, must determine the "useful life" of the training.

Scott considers using 1 year, which results in a $20,000 current expense. In the alternative, he considers using three years, which research suggests is more reasonable. He is getting a divorce this year and his ex-spouse's lawyer wants to know JOE'S current profits.

If Scott manipulates his income in that manner, he inevitably will have higher income in later years because he deducted the costs earlier and can only deduct them once; but that is plausibly post-divorce and irrelevant. Will his ex-spouse be aware of the future income? Will she have the funds to file a new action for a modification of alimony and child support in a future year? Will she be able to prove the future income increases? Even if she can prove this in the future, Scott has the ability to

---

[5] JOE'S would likely be a "pass through entity" such as a partnership, an S corporation, or an LL.C. As a result, the entity income would—at least for tax purposes—be taxed to the owner as if the entity and the owner were the same.

[6] Child support obligations can be up to 9.5% of income. See F.S. 61.30(6) (for three children and combined income over $100,000). $13,333.33 times .095 equals $1,266.67. The present value of $1,266.67 per year, using a 2.25% nominal annual interest discount rate for 14 years, is approximately $15,000.

[7] Alimony is typically a function of the recipient's needs and the payor's ability to pay, which is essentially his/her income. For a long-term marriage, an award equal to 20% of the payor's income would not be high. Twenty percent of $13,333.33 is $2,667.67. An award of permanent periodic alimony could plausibly last for twenty-five years. The present value of $2,667.67 per year for 25 years, discounted using a 2.25% rate is approximately $50,000.

[8] The value of a small business is plausibly 4 or 5 times average annual earnings. If earnings drop by $13,333.33, the business value would arguably drop by about $55,000 or 5 times the earnings decrease. In a dissolution, the business-operator spouse would likely receive the entity and the other spouse would receive an amount equal to the value.

play similar "games" with myriad estimates and choices and judgment calls in the future to manipulate his income for those years.

If JOE'S financial statements are audited by a CPA and are thus subject to GAAP, Scott will have to convince an independent auditor that his assumptions, estimates, choices, and judgment calls were valid and fair. That still leaves considerable leeway. In EXAMPLE 4, the 1-year life may be unreasonably short in the opinion of an auditor; however, the CPA would likely consider either 2 or 3 years to be reasonable. If so, even if the CPA preferred a 3-year period, he or she would very likely defer to the owner/manager's choice.

In any event, most businesses are never audited, so relying on outside auditors is not a realistic solution to the potential for manipulative estimates. The only real solution is knowledge: you as a lawyer must be aware that many of the numbers on a financial statement are the result of judgment calls. That alone is inevitable and does not mean the net of all the various judgment calls (and the numbers they affect) is anything other than zero. But you must be aware that the person exercising the judgment may be on the other side of the table from you and may have an incentive to have exercised his or her judgment in a manner that is not favorable to you.

You Are Responsible

Because most businesses are never audited, <u>you</u>, as a lawyer, must be aware of the impact of various judgement calls. <u>You</u> must be able to recognize the issue, communicate with an expert, and explain the issue to a judge or jury.

c.   *Future Costs*

Future costs are important for many reasons. Some examples are:

- Setting the price for a service or warranty.

- Valuing an investment.

- Determining alimony needs.

- Valuing lost net income in a tort case.

Accountants often speculate about future events, such as repairs on an airplane, cleanup costs at the end of a mining operation, dismantling of an oil rig at the end of production, or expected pay-outs from a pending tort case involving a slip-and-fall this year. In each case, the matching principle requires (for GAAP-based statements) someone to estimate the costs of maintaining the airplane (which might be done every three years) to the extent the repairs are attributable to this year's flights. Someone must estimate the cost of cleaning up the strip-mining operation at the end of the mine and then allocate some portion to match with this year's income.

Or, perhaps because of poor management, someone left a banana peel on the floor of JOE'S and a customer was injured, but no suit has been filed, or it was filed but not yet settled or tried. See EXAMPLE 5. Someone must estimate the present value of the expected negligence claim. Whether that amount would be accrued as a current expense is a topic for LESSON SIX. Accrual will largely hinge on whether liability is clear and whether the amount can be determined with "reasonable accuracy," at least per GAAP.[9] Some legal areas may consider unclear or "contingent" liabilities using a different standard.[10]

EXAMPLE 5

JOE'S Banana Peel

Suppose a customer slipped on a banana peel at JOE'S this year. Negligence is clear and the amount of the injuries is estimable, though the case is unsettled.

How would you match the cost of the negligent operations this year with the income those operations produced? You would estimate the present value of the expected future pay-out. As an attorney you may need to disclose information regarding the contingency in a "response letter" to an auditor, as discussed in LESSON THREE-B.

Without such incurred[11] but deferred _future_ costs, the current income would be over-stated. We will likely have useful information on which to base the predictions; however, the predictions are still predictions and no more accurate than the person making them. As discussed above, the person making the predictions may also have an incentive to over-state or to under-state the amounts.

Consider this: a person making predictions (whose income is affected by the prediction) may be contemplating a divorce and thus tempted to _overstate_ the current value of the expected future cost. But, another person (in relation to another business) may seek a loan and thus be tempted to

---

[9] As covered in LESSON THREE, an auditor will request information from an entity's counsel regarding the existence of contingent liabilities, such as from possible litigation. The attorney's "response letter" is one fraught with issues of privilege and confidentiality.

[10] _E.g.,_ Florida Family Law Rules of Procedure Form 12.902(c), Financial Affidavit (Long Form). The instructions provide: "If you have any POSSIBLE assets (income potential, accrued vacation or sick leave, bonus, inheritance, etc.) or POSSIBLE liabilities (possible lawsuits, future unpaid taxes, contingent tax liabilities, debts assumed by another), you must list them here."

[11] The airline maintenance, mining clean-up, and oil rig dismantling costs would likely be "incurred" because liability is certain. The banana peel matter might be less clear and thus potentially not incurred, as covered in LESSON SIX.

understate costs so as to overstate income. As a lawyer, you need to be on the look-out (or your forensic accountant needs to be) for unintended incentives that may sometimes be positive and sometimes be negative.

2) Choices

Accounting involves many choices, each of which can have a substantial impact on the numbers presents. LESSON TWO-A illustrates this point by focusing on three choices most businesses must make:

- Depreciation Method.
- Inventory Method.
- Accounting Method.

As with estimates, the choices can appear arbitrary, they can have a material impact on the numbers, and they can be subject to manipulation by the person making the choice.

a. Depreciation Method

LESSON FIVE covers this choice in some depth. For now, you should understand the available choices are usually all legitimate: none is right or wrong ... they are just different. Depreciation may be straight-line (treating every year the same), or it may be accelerated (allocating more cost to early years and less cost to later years). No one ever "knows" in advance how quickly or evenly a machine or other asset loses value (let alone *whether* it will lose value in the future). Nevertheless, someone must choose not only the useful life of the asset, but also whether to treat each year in the life the same (straight-line depreciation) or to treat them differently (typically allocating more to the early years).

For example, life experience may tell you that a new car loses 5 to 10% of its value the minute you drive it off the lot. It then loses another 5 to 10% during the rest of the first year. In contrast, it will not lose much value between the 10th and 11th year of its life (assuming you keep the car that long). Thus, *your* own experience probably supports accelerated depreciation, but you are also surely aware of the lack of precision.

b. Inventory Method

LESSON SEVEN covers inventory accounting. For now, you should understand accountants have choices among the inventory system used regarding when to count inventory as well as the inventory system used for valuing inventory.

As explained in the GLOSSARY:

Inventory: Inventory refers to merchandise held for sale to customers. Businesses that hold inventories must follow "inventory accounting" methods or systems. This involves deciding when to count inventory as well as how to value inventory.

For example, for financial accounting, a business with inventories must count the items either periodically or perpetually to keep track of them. Generally, a periodic system counts inventory once per period (generally a year). In contrast, a perpetual system keeps track of each item sold (often with a bar code or UFID tag).

Businesses must also determine how to value inventory—both that which was sold and that which remains unsold. Often, inventory is fungible; for example, a grocery store may have 100 cans of green beans, each of which is the same, but which it purchased at different times and with different costs. Deciding which can was sold and which remain involves last-in-first-out [LIFO] versus first-in-first-out [FIFO] systems. That affects the entity's cost of goods sold [COGS] and can have a large impact on income for a particular period.

Inventory accounting for United States tax purposes is a specialized field. The internal revenue code [IRC] distinguishes between "stock in trade," "inventory," and "property held primarily for sale to customers in the ordinary course of a trade or business."[12]

As Lesson Seven will explain, the choice of accounting system for tracking inventory—periodic or perpetual—will affect the "quality" of the information provided: perpetual inventory systems are more accurate, although they are also more expensive to maintain. Also, the valuation method—FIFO, LIFO, or average cost—can have a material impact on cost of goods sold. For now, GAAP permits each of the methods, though they may produce significantly different income and asset numbers.

c. Accounting Method

Lesson Six covers the accrual method of accounting, which both GAAP and IFRS require. Most people and a great many businesses, however, use the cash method of accounting because it is far simpler. The two methods are very different.

Under the accrual method, a person has income when he or she has earned it, regardless of whether anything has been received. Likewise, under the accrual method, a person recognizes an expense when all events have occurred such that the amount is owed, and it can be determined with reasonable accuracy. Again, payment is irrelevant. The accrual method of accounting is usually essential to a fair statement of income.

In contrast, most people use the cash method. They recognize income when they receive something. Similarly, they recognize expenses when

---

[12] *See* IRC §§ 1221, 1231.

they pay them. This very simple accounting method works acceptably well for the average person's budget. It does not, however, clearly reflect income—at least not in most cases. For example, a lawyer using the cash method could work 100 hours on a legal matter during the last quarter of the year (October through December). He could, however, delay billing the client until January of the following year, and thus delay collecting any revenue. Under the accrual method, the lawyer would have income as he earned it in October through December. In contrast, under the cash method, the lawyer would have income when he ultimately received payment from the client.

In the long run, the two methods of accounting produce the same income: eventually the earner is paid and thus recognizes the income under both the accrual and cash methods. But *when* the earner recognizes the income can vary a great deal under the two methods. Lawyers should be very wary of that timing issue. For example, if the lawyer who delays' billing is amid a divorce, his obligation for alimony, child support, or property division may be a function of when he recognized the income. In the family law arena, state laws and cases tend to insufficiently address the effect and accounting method can have. Because a divorce matter may look at only a few years of financial information, the differences between the cash and accrual method can be profound. Hence, recognizing that the two methods—in the long run—eventually produce the same numbers is of little solace to a lawyer who only looks at the information for the short run.

Thus, at this point, you should understand the chosen method of accounting can have a huge impact on the resulting numbers. Although both GAAP and IFRS require the accrual method, state and federal law, or a particular contract, may either be silent on the issue, or they may permit the cash method. Indeed, the law may permit a person to choose among accounting methods; if so, the person with the power to choose will have an incentive to choose a method favorable to him or her.

3) Judgment

Management must often exercise judgment regarding important issues that directly affect the financial statement numbers. If the financial statements are audited, a CPA will render an opinion regarding the "fairness" or "reasonableness" of any material exercise of judgment. Inevitably, many matters are subjective; hence, precision is impossible. LESSON TWO-A provides two examples in which someone must exercise judgment.

For example, is a transaction complete? Under the realization principle of accounting, we do not recognize income until it has been sufficiently "realized." That requires some sort of event, such as a completed sale or the performance of services. But "completion" of a transaction can be a subjective call. Arguably, an estate plan is not "complete" until presented to and approved by the client. Just as arguably, the plan is complete when substantially all the work has been completed; after-all, the lawyer will likely charge the client even if the client ultimately declines the recommended plan. Is the building of a house complete when the last drop of paint goes onto the wood; or, is it effectively complete at some earlier time? The answers to these questions are judgment calls. In many cases, the issue is irrelevant for example if completion occurs either on June 10th or June 15th, the realization of income is almost certainly the same as both dates occur within the same year. But, if completion is arguably on December 30th versus January 5th, the difference in timing can be dramatic.

As posited before, the person who makes the decision regarding "completion" may be amid a divorce and thus have an incentive to recognize income earlier or later. Or the decision maker may be applying for a loan and thus have an incentive to report income for a particular period. Or, I may have agreed to pay you 25% of the profits from projects "completed" during 2022, but nothing for projects "completed" in some other year. In that case, you and I may have very different views regarding when a particular project was "complete," as well as the meaning of "completion."

Because financial accounting inevitably functions around an arbitrary period—a year or a quarter or a month—it also inevitably relies on someone's judgment regarding when various transactions are sufficiently "complete."

The other example in LESSON TWO-A involves the judgment of whether a transaction involves a repair, as opposed to a capital expenditure. The GLOSSARY uses the term "capital" in many ways. You should examine the various uses. For now, consider the term "to capitalize."

> **Capitalize**: For both tax law and accounting purposes, "to capitalize" an expenditure means to add it to an asset account. For example, if expenditure is for an asset or service with a life greater than one year—and if it is material—one would typically add the cost to an asset account via a debit. The corresponding credit would be to cash or a liability. The resulting asset would be "amortized" over its useful life (typically straight-line) or "depreciated" over its useful life. Capitalization furthers the matching principal of accounting by ensuring costs properly match with the income they produce. One would "expense" short-term or immaterial expenditures.

Later lessons explain this in greater depth. For now, consider a simple example. You are a lawyer who owns a building. A windstorm blows off a single shingle from the roof and breaks a single pane of glass in one window. Both items are relatively small, and both are the type of thing that occurs periodically in every person's life. Repair of each item does not extend the life of the building; instead, it merely puts it back into a usable condition. As a result, you would easily classify both as repairs and you would recognize the resulting expense in the year or period in which the storm occurred (assuming you use the accrual method of accounting per GAAP and IFRS).

But the storm may, instead, have more severely damaged the roof, requiring the replacement of many shingles, or perhaps the repair of a large section, or perhaps even an entirely new roof. You may even, in that case, choose a new and better type of shingle, which results in a longer projected useful life for the roof. Similarly, the storm may have damaged multiple windows; as a result, you may decide to replace them all with new, expensive architecturally designed windows with multiple panes for energy efficiency. Such major changes would not be small or immaterial and they would likely extend the useful life of the building or otherwise affect income in multiple years (perhaps your clients like the new look better and you, as a result, get more clients in the future). Thus, you would likely "capitalize" such major expenditure so that you could spread the costs over a period of years. LESSON FIVE covers depreciation and Amortization of such costs.

Or the storm damage could be somewhere in between. One shingle is clearly a repair. Likewise, changing two or three shingles is also a repair that results in a current expense and no "capitalization." But, what about 100 shingles or 1,000? At what point does a repair become a "capital expenditure"? No clear answer exists to that question, but the question inevitably arises in the normal operation of every business: accidents happen, damages occur, repairs and improvements are required. Accounting for them requires judgment: do we account for the cost this year or over a period of multiple years? As explained above, the consequences are irrelevant if we look at the long run, perhaps 50 years. But lawyers tend not to look at 50 years; instead, they isolate the 2 or 3 years before a divorce, or the single year involved in compensation under a contract. In such isolation, the judgment calls of whether to classify a cost as a repair rather than a capital expenditure can have a large impact.

A caution deserves re-stating: if you let me decide how to define income or expense (or _when_ to report it) I will have the natural temptation to decide in a manner that favors me. Lawyers must understand how to determine whether my decision is appropriate, what impact it has (on me and on you), whether an alternative decision might be more appropriate, whether legal procedures of discovery allow you to even determine whether and who made any such decision, whether applicable law or contracts allow you to challenge the decision, and who has the burden of proving the propriety of the decision.

To summarize: accounting is filled with estimates, choices, and the exercise of judgment. You as a lawyer must understand that. You must also understand how great an impact those estimates, choices, and judgments can have on your client. Ultimately, you may want to plan for them in the negotiation of contracts, or you may need to deal with them in litigation if they impact your client negatively.

LESSON TWO-B

ACCOUNTING PRINCIPLES AND ASSUMPTIONS

■ ■ ■

Lesson Objectives

1. Student will learn that all accounting systems, whether for financial or legal purposes governed by a particular statute *should* have a framework and rules.

2. Student will learn about Accounting Principles and Assumptions.

GAAP has 13 fundamental principles and assumptions. Lawyers, legislators, regulators, and judges should heed the caution below.

Accounting Systems Must Have Rules

An accounting system without fundamental principles and basic assumptions lacks a sufficient framework and is thus inherently flawed.

This includes legal and contractual accounting systems for family, trust, or tax law, as well as compensation or income-sharing arrangements.

For example, lawyers often refer to income or profits in a contract or other legal document. Unfortunately, many fail to define those words adequately or by reference to adequate standards, principles, and assumptions. Similarly, many statutes or court decisions use terms such as income, assets, profit, losses, expenses, and liabilities along with definitions. Often, however, they do so without reference to any fundamental standards, rules, principles, or assumptions. State family law references to income and assets for alimony, child support, or property division are a common and unfortunate example. The results are often unfair, subject to manipulation, wasteful in terms of unnecessary litigation, and distorting in terms of the economic impact they have on decision making.

The point is not that family law, trust law, tax law—or any other area of law—should use GAAP or IFRS principles and assumptions; instead, the point is that some defined set of rules must apply to reduce inconsistencies and ease of manipulation.

Each principle, test, and assumption has its own GLOSSARY definition:

- The *Matching Principle.*
- The *Historical Cost Assumption.*
- The *Going Concern Assumption.*
- The *Monetary Unit Assumption.*
- The *Consistency Principle.*
- The *Revenue Recognition Principle.*
- The *Expense Recognition Principle.*
- The *All Events Test* (formerly the revenue recognition and expense recognition principles).
- The *Materiality Principle.*
- The *Separate Entity Assumption.*
- The *Time Period Assumption.*
- The *Full Disclosure Principle.*
- The *Conservatism Principle.*

1. THE MATCHING PRINCIPLE

Ultimately, the matching principle is the most important principle of accounting. It provides:

An income statement must match income with the costs of producing that income.

Without proper matching, an income statement would provide misleading information. For example, management may need to know whether a particular division is worth keeping, expanding, reducing, or eliminating. To evaluate the division, the manager would want to know how much income it produces. For that to be a meaningful number, the periodic revenue must match with (be reduced by) the direct and indirect costs of producing that revenue. Similarly, costs must match with the income they produce; otherwise, management could not evaluate whether the costs were justifiable.

The *accrual method* of accounting (covered in LESSON SIX) rests on the *matching principle*: income is recognized when *all events* occur such that the item has been earned and the amount can be determined with reasonable accuracy. The conditions of the all-events test temper the *matching principle* of accounting with the conservatism principle: do not recognize income before it is earned *and* reasonably determinable. Thus, an entity may accrue income in a period even if it has received nothing. Similarly, it will defer advance receipts to the proper period in which they are earned. Also, an accrual entity will accrue expenses (costs) when they are incurred, regardless of whether they have been paid.

In contrast, the *cash method* of account does not follow the matching principle. Instead, a cash method user recognizes income upon receipt and expenses upon payment. This risks matching income from one operation with expenses from another. Neither GAAP nor IFRS permits the *cash method* because it violates the *matching principle*.

EXAMPLE 5 posited a slip-and-fall injury at JOE'S because of inadequate managerial oversight. To be accurate, the income the manager helped produce must be reduced by the costs of the manager's negligence, at least to the extent the injury is clear, and the amount is reasonably determinable. This process necessitates an estimate of the costs as well an evaluation of liability. Postponing the incurred but deferred cost (the tort liability) to a later year would match the cost with income it had nothing to do with. Poor management may have resulted in more revenue this year, at the cost of the slip-and-fall injury (perhaps too many customers). Perhaps JOE'S fired the manager as a result. Assigning the cost to next year would then penalize the new manager and would distort next year's income because the cost belonged in the current year.

A reasonable criticism of statutory accounting in many legal areas is that it fails to provide basic principles,[13] including the matching principle. For example, in family law, both alimony and child support are functions of income; however, most (perhaps all) state statutes defining income for alimony or child support fail to require adherence to the matching principle. Unless the parties or the court imposes matching—which would tend not to be the case—the resulting numbers risk being inaccurate, perhaps to a very large degree. Of course, a person who works for a regular salary, paid frequently, and who has few employee expenses or other accessions to wealth would provide similar numbers under both the cash and accrual methods of accounting. But that scenario is probably a small percentage of the populace. For example, many salaried employees accrue deferred compensation, bonuses, overtime, and various fringe benefits that may be irregular or easily advanced or deferred. They also typically have a

---

[13] Steven J. Willis, *Family Law Economics, Child Support, and Alimony: Ruminations on Income, Part I,* 78 FLA. B. J. 34 (No. 5 May 2004); *Family Law Economics, Child Support, and Alimony: Ruminations on Income, Part II,* 78 FLA. B. J. 34 (No. 6 June 2004) [WILLIS I AND II].

variety of employee and other business expenses, which are also subject to timing choices.

2.   THE HISTORICAL COST ASSUMPTION

The historical cost assumption is another critical component of both GAAP and IFRS, although IFRS deviates from it somewhat. As illustrated throughout this course, the historical cost assumption ignores appreciation in assets and thus often results in understated value. As a result, the "book value" of a business is frequently less than its fair market value. EXAMPLE 2 illustrated this.

Per the assumption, a business must record assets at their cost. It will reduce the recorded cost for depreciation or amortization (LESSON FIVE) but will never[14] increase the value except for the cost of improvements.

The GLOSSARY explains book value with the following caution:

Book Value: This represents the value of an entity for financial reporting purposes. Because accounting uses several significant and conservative reporting principles, *book value* is not generally representative of *fair market value*. For example, accountants generally record items at historical cost and do not change that number unless the item has clearly lost value. Rarely would an accountant increase the value. Hence, *book value* is generally much lower than *fair market value*.

Book Value Is Likely Understated

Lawyers should pay special heed to *book value*. Lawyers should not take numbers on financial statements literally without understanding the context of the numbers, the method of accounting used, and the various assumptions made, as well as the auditor's opinion.

3.   THE GOING CONCERN ASSUMPTION

The going concern assumption is another important rule for both GAAP and IFRS. As explained in LESSON THREE, an important part of an

---

[14] Per FAS 115 and Codification Topic 320, marketable securities held for sale or "available for sale" must be listed at "fair value." Per IRC § 475 U. S. tax accounting requires securities dealers to use "mark to market" accounting and thus list marketable securities at fair market value.

audit is the CPA's evaluation of whether the going concern nature of an entity is impaired.[15]

EXAMPLE 6

JOE'S Assets in Liquidation

Suppose JOE'S purchased substantial specialty equipment in its kitchen—things suited for JOE'S but far less suitable for other bars and restaurants in the area.

If JOE'S is a going concern, listing the specialty assets at historical cost less depreciation is useful. Perhaps that amount is $100,000. But if JOE'S is *not* a going concern, the value of those items may be $10,000 if they must be sold *now* in a liquidation.

This rule assumes the business will continue operating for the foreseeable future. With that assumption, the book numbers on the balance sheet and income statement are both informative and predictive within the framework of all the principles and assumption. If the assumption, however, is invalid, the validity of the numbers change. Asset values likely drop as a non-going concern will need to sell them to liquidate obligations, as illustrated in EXAMPLE 6. That can result in "fire sale" prices, which may be substantially lower than book value. Income, likewise, will drop as sales decrease and customers become concerned about future service. Suppliers will be wary to provide inventory except on a cash basis, so working capital will evaporate.

4. THE MONETARY UNIT ASSUMPTION

The monetary unit assumption is important because some items are not subject to valuation in monetary terms although they have substantial non-quantifiable value to people. This important principle or assumption requires the use of a monetary unit—such as the dollar—to represent assets, liabilities, and equity. The assumption has two important consequences:

- Non-quantifiable items—such as emotional value—may be disclosed in footnotes; however, they cannot be disclosed directly on financial statements.

- The monetary unit has a constant meaning; hence, a dollar in 1950 is the same—for financial reporting purposes—as a dollar in 2023. Inflation and deflation are generally irrelevant

---

[15] Going concern doubt is a significant reason an auditor may issue *other than* an unqualified opinion.

for financial reporting, although their impacts may be discussed in footnotes and *pro forma* statements.

5.   THE CONSISTENCY PRINCIPLE

The consistency principle is arguably the second most important accounting principle: it requires a person to be consistent from year-to-year in whatever choices, assumptions, and judgments he or she makes. Students should realize that isolated financial statements for a given period are not nearly as useful as statements in the context of many years. With multiple years, one can detect trends and can predict the future, which is often what lawyers attempt to do: predict future lost wages in tort or future income to determine alimony or child support obligations.

Accounting statements must rest on consistent principles, assumptions, estimates, choices, and judgments from period-to-period. Such matters may include depreciation methods, inventory methods and valuation techniques, cost-segregation rules, capitalization rules, timing-of-income recognition rules, and similar decisions as discussed in LESSON TWO-A. As explained in relation to the conservatism principle, accounting is not a science. Lawyers who view it as a guarantee of precision do so at their peril.

Comparative financial statements are essential for financial analysis. They illustrate increases and decreases in profit or losses as well as changes in specific items over time. Without such comparisons, management and investors will be hard-pressed to make informed decisions. If those comparative statements do not rest on consistent principles, any comparison of them risks being misleading.

Because most people and most entities do not have an annual audit, they are free to be inconsistent in their accounting choices. Viewed in isolation, such inconsistency is unwise as it impairs the validity of year-to-year comparisons. While such inconsistency-created comparisons may be *useless* for internal purposes, they may be *beneficial* for illicit external uses: they may materially distort income and equity, particularly in terms of how those items appear on a trend graph. Most people would view the presentation of such distortions in legal matters as dishonest; nevertheless, such inconsistencies may not be illegal or unethical or even a breach of contract. Lawyers should thus be very careful in viewing multi-period un-audited financial statements.

6.   THE REVENUE RECOGNITION PRINCIPLE

The revenue recognition principle used by GAAP encompasses what this course often refers to as the "all-events test." United States tax law uses a modified form of the all-events test.[16] The accrual method of accounting—the topic of LESSON SIX—rests on this principle for purposes of income, along with the expense recognition principle for deductions. Lawyers must understand that most people do not use accrual accounting; instead, they use the cash method, which does follows neither the revenue nor the expense recognition principles. If you, as a lawyer, examine a statute or contract that refers to "income," "revenue," "expense," or deductions," you should question how the statute or contract defines those terms. Standing alone—without principles defining them—those terms have little meaning and thus allow much room for mischief.

The principle has 4 elements:

- Has delivery occurred or the service been rendered?

- Is the price fixed or determinable? [Arguably this has a "reasonable" element to it].

- Is collection reasonably assured?

- Is there persuasive evidence of an arrangement, *i.e.*, that a transaction has taken place?

7. THE EXPENSE RECOGNITION PRINCIPLE

Per GAAP, an entity recognizes expenses when incurred. Payment is irrelevant. Expenses break into three types:

- Expenses recognized when revenue is recognized because the two are directly associated. An example would be the cost of goods sold.

- Expenses that benefit multiple years. These must be capitalized and amortized over the relevant years. Depreciation and amortization are examples of the annual expense.

- Expenses that will benefit the business over a short period or which provide no *discernable* future benefit. Research and development expenditures are often a good example. If management discerns a specific future benefit regarding specific elements (such as a building or equipment) capitalization is appropriate. Otherwise, research expenditures are expensed. This is a substantial deviation from IFRS.

---

[16] IRC § 461(h). Steven J. Willis, *Show Me the Numbers, Please* 93 TAX NOTES 1321 (2001); Steven J. Willis, *It's Time For Schlude to Go,* 93 TAX NOTES 127 (2001) [WILLIS II AND IV].

8. THE ALL EVENTS TEST

This is one of the fundamental accounting principles and assumptions. It applies to the accrual method of accounting and is the cornerstone of the matching principle. Still part of common accounting and tax vernacular, it is largely replaced by the revenue recognition and expense recognition principles. Historically, the test had two parts:

- *Income recognition* is appropriate when *all events* have occurred such that the earner has a right to the item and the amount thereof can be determined with reasonable accuracy.

- *Deductions* are appropriate when *all events* have occurred such the obligor must incur the item and the amount thereof can be determined with reasonable accuracy.

The *all-events test* is irrelevant for the *cash method* of accounting. For U.S. tax law, the following rules apply:

- Income occurs at the earliest of it being due, paid, or earned,[17] with "earned" essentially comprising the all-events test. This test combines elements of both cash and accrual accounting, which can be very misleading, though it raises more revenue.[18]

- Deductions are appropriate at the later of all events or economic performance. This, too, is distorting and effectively increases the earner's tax rate.[19]

9. THE MATERIALITY PRINCIPLE

The materiality principle of both GAAP and IFRS is one non-accountants often struggle with. All too often, non-accountants view financial statements with a false sense of precision. After all, the numbers balance and appear precise. An official "opinion letter" accompanies them if they are audited. LESSON TWO-B should disabuse you of this false sense.

An additional reason to overcome that temptation to being lulled by a sense of precision involves the concept of materiality: if it doesn't matter, it doesn't matter. Accountants ultimately only deal with what matters. Small amounts—which is a relative term—should be ignored. Exactly what constitutes a material amount is situational. For example, for a small business, $1,000 may be a material amount, while it may be irrelevant for a large international firm.

---

[17] IRC § 451(c); Schlude v. Comm'r, 372 U.S. 128 (1963).

[18] See WILLIS III AND IV, *supra* note 16.

[19] *Id.* IRC § 461(h) imposes the later of "all events" or "economic performance" for accrual method taxpayers.

Accountants and courts have strived to avoid a percentage test for materiality, although the relative importance of an item is a factor. Also, materiality has an absolute concept in that some amounts are material despite the size of the entity. While $1,000 may be immaterial for many, $1,000,000,000 is surely material for all.

10. THE SEPARATE ENTITY ASSUMPTION

One of the fundamental principles of accounting, this assumes an entity is separate from its owner. Hence, the entity has a set of books and financial statements, as does the owner.

The assumption may appear self-evident to lawyers who have studied corporate and trust law, which are separate artificial legal entities. Nevertheless, it deserves some thought because, while it makes sense for accounting, it may not make sense for some legal matters. For example, in family law, a court may want to look through the separate entity to combine a person's share of corporate, trust, or partnership income with that stated in his or her own name. Similarly, contractual arrangements may focus on "consolidated financial statements" that also ignore the separate legal entities involved.

11. THE TIME-PERIOD ASSUMPTION

The time-period assumption is another issue that may appear self-evident but is critical for lawyers to focus on. Financial accounting, as well as *income* tax accounting, functions based on time. The arbitrary period used is one year, although many interim statements appear based on quarters or months.

An alternative to the time period would involve transactional accounting. In such a system, one would report income, expenses, gains, and losses per transaction rather than per period. Many such systems exist:

- For *tax purposes*—at least from the consumer's perspective—excise taxes, sales taxes, VATs, gift taxes, estate taxes, and inheritance taxes are all transactional.

- For *financial accounting*, GAAP and IFRS require the time-period assumption for audited financial statements; however, cost accounting—particularly for internal reporting—often functions on a transactional basis, or at least for groups of similar transactions. Indeed, pricing a product properly often requires one to focus on transactions rather than periods.

- For *legal purposes*, many instances of transactional accounting exist. For example, a joint venture is often a single project or transaction. It would report financial operations for the venture, separate from activities and project involving other ventures. Similarly, partnership accounting has elements of transactional accounting, although it almost always is based on an annual period. Nevertheless, a partnership—which is not a typical legal entity—will prepare financial reports on a mixed annual and transactional basis.

- Family law also has elements of transactional accounting. While income for purposes of child support and alimony is typically based on a time period, financial reports for determinations of community property rules and equitable distribution rules are more transactional. That occurs because—in most jurisdictions—some transactions produce community or marital income while other transactions produce separate income. Oddly, under at least some regimes, some transactions that result in income from separate property affect marital property while those that produce losses from separate property do not.

Lawyers should be aware of the time-period assumption; however, they should also be aware that it is not universal. Entities and individuals frequently use the *calendar year*, which ends on December 31st. In contrast a *fiscal year* (FY) ends on the last day of a month other than December.

For non-human persons, *fiscal years* are often useful—particularly for cyclical business that have significant operations for part of the year and little for others. In such cases, a fiscal year ending during the slow season is sensible; indeed, splitting a normal business cycle between two years could be misleading. For example, many retail businesses have their dominant sales period between the U.S. Thanksgiving through Christmas, and then after-New Year's sales. Because such a business cycle fits together, the use of a *calendar year* for financial reporting would split the year in ways that generate distortions. Last year's after-New Year's sales would join with this year's before-Christmas sales, generating less than optimal information. A *fiscal year* ending in February or March would make more sense in terms of presenting annual operations. Generally, taxpayers who use a financial *fiscal year* for financial reporting must use the same year for tax purposes.

Cases in which a person controls multiple entities with different fiscal years are ripe for manipulation. Consider EXAMPLE 7: JOE'S WINE SHOP adopts a January 31st fiscal year and JOE'S BAR & GRILL adopts a February 28th fiscal year. The GRILL pays the SHOPPE $10,000 for services in February.

EXAMPLE 7

JOE'S BAR & GRILL and JOE'S WINE SHOP

Suppose Scott and Adrian, the owners of JOE'S BAR & GRILL, also own JOE'S WINE SHOP. The GRILL uses a February 28th fiscal year, while the SHOP uses a January 31st fiscal year. For this Example, both are "pass-though" entities.[1] Scott and Adrian each use a calendar year.

The GRILL pays the SHOPPE $10,000 in February for management services performed in February. What can go wrong?

The GRILL deducts the $10,000 cost for its fiscal year ending February 28, 2023. As owners of the GRILL, Scott and Adrian include their respective shares of the GRILL'S 2023 fiscal year income in their calendar year in which the GRILL'S fiscal year ends. Thus, each has $5,000 less income for calendar year 2023.

The SHOPPE includes the $10,000 income in its fiscal year ending January 31, 2024: it earned and received payment for the income in February, which was the first month of its fiscal year. As owners of the SHOP, Scott and Adrian include their respective shares of the SHOP'S 2024 fiscal income in their calendar year in which the SHOP fiscal year ends. Thus, each has $5,000 greater income for calendar year 2024. Effectively, they deferred $10,000 of income from 2023 to 2024.

Be Wary of Differing Years

The *calendar year* makes sense in most cases but can be distorting in others. But lawyers should be wary of related entities with differing years. Multiple entities with differing years present opportunities for manipulation of financial information.

For tax purposes, the different years would unlikely be permissible. A partnership must use the year used by its partners[20] and an S corporation[21] must use the calendar year. Under GAAP, the commonly-controlled entities would file consolidated financial statements[22] and would have to

---

[20] IRC § 706(b) requires a partnership to use a taxable year consistent with a majority of its partners. Per §§ 444 and 706(b)(1)(C), the partnership may elect a year different from the one required upon the showing of a business purpose. The government must approve the election.

[21] IRC § 1348 generally requires an S corporation to use a calendar year. The entity may elect, per § 444, to use a fiscal year with permission of the government and the showing of a business purpose. Deferral of income, as in EXAMPLE 7, is not an acceptable business purpose.

[22] Consolidated financial statements combine related entities, eliminating inter-company transactions.

use the same year. Nevertheless, if unaudited the entities and owners could adopt the differing years for financial purposes and thus create the deferral. Substantively, the deferral is not real because it merely involves moving income from one pocket to another. If done with the intent to manipulate a legal matter, the ruse is at best deceitful and arguably fraudulent. Unfortunately, it will work unless you, as the lawyer representing persons affected, stop it. That means you must notice it, understand it, and be capable of explaining it to a judge or jury.

12. THE FULL DISCLOSURE PRINCIPLE

The full disclosure principle is one many lawyers struggle with when they first learn about the role of a CPA. Lawyers tend to view their duty as one of "zealously" representing the client. They view the client as the person who hired them. In contrast, a CPA owes a much broader duty to the users of financial information and has no duty to "zealously" represent the person who pays for an audit. LESSON THREE covers the role of a CPA in greater depth. As explained in the GLOSSARY:

> **Full Disclosure Principle of Accounting:** This financial accounting principle—part of GAAP and IFRS—requires financial statements to disclose all material information, particularly negative information.

> For example, an auditor will traditionally request a statement from an entity's counsel regarding pending or possible litigation or liabilities. Counsel may be reluctant to provide such information, as it can be damaging from a litigator's perspective. Nevertheless, a CPA cannot say the financial statements fairly present the entity's financial condition if undisclosed liabilities exist. In many cases, such liabilities may be contingent or difficult to assess; nevertheless, proper and full disclosure requires the release of as much information as is fairly and reasonably available.

13. THE CONSERVATISM PRINCIPLE

The conservatism principle of accounting is one lawyers should always recall. Fundamentally, it leans toward understatement of income and assets and away from over-statement.

Under this principle, when given reasonable choices, an accountant will tend to choose the more conservative: the lower valuation for assets and receipts, and the higher valuation for obligations and expenses. Properly applied, this principle results in financial information such as income and net worth being more likely understated than overstated.

The mere existence of this principle illustrates an important point often missed by non-accountants:

Accounting is not a science. It is more art. Financial Accounting is filled with many legitimate but materially different choices, methods, assumptions, and rules.

LESSON TWO-C

INTRODUCTORY PROBLEM

■ ■ ■

Lesson Objectives

1. Student will learn how to prepare a simple balance sheet and income statement

2. Student will work a problem creating an entity.

Terminology Introduced

Later lessons cover these terms in greater depth; however, because this lesson introduces them, the student should review the definitions in the GLOSSARY.

- Debit.
- Credit.
- Double entry bookkeeping.
- Balance sheet.
- Income statement.
- Statement of cash flows.

---

1. TYPES OF FINANCIAL STATEMENTS

LESSON TWO-C introduces the three main types of financial statements:

- Balance sheet.
- Income statement.
- Statement of cash flows.

Later lessons cover each in greater depth. Mostly this course focuses on the first two.

A. BALANCE SHEET

This is one of three important financial statements, the other two being the *income statement* and the *statement of cash flows*. It presents a financial picture as of a particular date. Many users refer to it as a snapshot: it says a great deal about conditions at one moment.

The *balance sheet* lists assets on the left side and liabilities plus owner's equity on the right side. The two sides necessarily balance, as owner's equity results from the basic accounting equation:

$$(Assets - Liabilities) = Owners' Equity$$

or

$$Assets = (Liabilities + Owners' Equity)$$

A *single underline* on a *financial statement* indicates the column above it is being added or subtracted. A *double underline* indicates a sum. A simple balance sheet appears in this format:

Balance Sheet

Assets	Liabilities
	Owners' Equity
Total Assets	
	Total Liabilities plus Equity

B. INCOME STATEMENT

The income statement reflects a business' operation for a defined period—often a year, quarter, or month. It first lists income from operations. It then deducts expenses attributable to those operations, as well as overhead. It nets the items to determine the current net operational income.

The statement next lists extraordinary (unusual) income and expense items, as well as taxes. The bottom-line figure reflects the period's net earnings. A closing entry then adds the net to (or subtracts it from) retained earnings on the balance sheet. A traditional income statement, consistent with GAAP, uses the accrual method of accounting.

C. STATEMENT OF CASH FLOWS

Along with the income statement and balance sheet, the statement of cash flows forms a triad of fundamental financial statements. To a significant degree, the statement of cash flows is a cash method income statement with borrowing and retiring debt added in. It eliminates accruals on un-paid expenses and receivables, as well as non-cash items such as depreciation, amortization, and bad debt write-offs. The statement does not comport to show accurate income; however, it gives a picture of liquidity or solvency and the direction or trend of liquidity.

2. INTRODUCTORY PROBLEM

This lesson works through a problem intended to illustrate some simple notions about financial statements. The problem continues through later lessons.

You are asked to prepare a balance sheet and an income statement upon the opening of JOE'S BAR & GRILL, the name of the new business. You are told the start-up process takes four months and begins on August 1. Pay close attention to PROBLEM 1 terminology.

PROBLEM 1

JOE'S BAR & GRILL Start-up Costs

Scott and Adrian form a small business. The start-up period begins on August 1 and lasts four months.

1. They each contribute $250,000.
2. They purchase a liquor license for $75,000 plus incur attorney fees of $5,000. They acquire other local permits for $1,000.
3. They pay $30,000 for one year of rent in advance
4. They purchase machinery for $31,000.
5. They purchase inventory of $30,000.
6. They incur employee/management training costs of $20,000.
7. They incur trademark and signage costs of $10,000.
8. They earn interest income during start-up of $10,000.
9. During start-up, the liquor/wine inventory appreciates $5,000.

---

1. Scott and Adrian each contribute $250,000

Initially, we prepare the balance sheet on August 1, the date of creation. Notice in **Figure 1**, the balance sheet balances: *that is definitional*. It must balance. Assets equal $500,000 and liabilities (which are zero) plus owner's equity equal $500,000.

JOE'S BAR & GRILL Balance Sheet August 1			
Assets		**Liabilities**	
Cash	$500,000		
		Owner's Equity	
		Scott	$250,000
		Adrian	$250,000
Total Assets	**$500,000**	**Liabilities & Equity**	**$500,000**

Figure 1: Balance Sheet on August 1

Balance Sheets Balance by Definition

A balance sheet will always balance unless someone forgets to make part of an entry. Even a fraudulent balance sheet will balance.

You should *conclude nothing* merely because the "books balance" or the balance sheet balances

We could create a fraudulent balance sheet in which Scott and Adrian contributed $2,500,000 each. The cash would then be listed as $5,000,000 while Scott and Adrian equity accounts would each show $2,500,000. The total assets and the total liabilities plus equity would equal $5,000,000. The balance sheet would balance, but it would be fraudulent because they contributed only $250,000 each. That is a primary point of this lesson: the balance sheet balances by definition. That it balances does not mean it is honest or fair.

The remainder of the lesson discusses each of the start-up costs and purchases. Notice the inadequate terminology in PROBLEM 1. The first and third items involve a contribution and a payment, both of which necessarily involve a cash flow. The other items are not clear. JOE'S "incurred" various costs and "purchased" other items. Neither term is clear regarding whether JOE'S transferred any funds. That was intentional to see if you would notice. A bookkeeper would have to ask: did those involve payments (a reduction of cash) or promises to pay (an increase in liabilities)? Let's work PROBLEM 1 with the additional information that JOE'S paid for all items.

2. **They purchase a liquor license for $75,000 plus incur attorney fees of $5,000. They acquire other local permits for $1,000**

Each is an intangible asset with a useful life probably greater than one year; as a result, each must be capitalized (treated as an asset, not an expense). The best answer involves listing the liquor license at its historical cost of $80,000, which includes its $75,000 direct cost plus the $5,000 indirect cost of attorneys' fees. Per GAAP, the attorney's fees incurred to acquire the license are part of the cost. We list the permits separately because they likely have a shorter life (perhaps one year) while the liquor license may be perpetual.

Be careful, however, because the liquor license may only have a fair market value of $75,000. For example, if we were to sell the business immediately with the license, we may not be able to recover the attorneys' fees we expended to acquire it: the price would depend on what a buyer would be willing to pay. This is an illustration of how "book value" differs from "fair market value."

An important point made in recording these two assets is that they have no impact on owner's equity: we spent cash on the items, so we shifted assets from one asset to another. In doing so, we affected the left side of the balance sheet but not the right side.

3. They pay $30,000 for one year of rent in advance

We decide to capitalize the rent so that we can amortize it over its useful life. We learn they paid this on September 1 for September through the following August. We allocate $7,500 to the start-up period (three months) and then $22,500 to the remaining nine months at $2,500 per month. LESSON FIVE covers depreciation and amortization in more depth. GAAP would not require the monthly allocation; however it would require allocating a portion to the start-up period (September through November), one month (December) to year one and seven months (January through August) to year two. Scott and Adrian would likely choose to have monthly income statements and thus would make monthly allocations. Without monthly statements, they would be—as you see in later problems—unable to compute the manager's compensation which will be a function of monthly "profit." To be clear—the creation of such interim (non-annual) financial statements is not required and would not be audited even if JOE'S decides to have an audit (which is not generally required in the U.S.).

4. They purchase machinery for $31,000

The amount is sufficiently large that we must capitalize it: it is material. Recall the materiality principle: if it does not matter, it does not matter. Had JOE'S purchased a note pad for $2.00, it would surely "expense" it, rather than "capitalize" it. Thus, a single notepad which cost a trivial amount would not appear as an asset and its cost would not be spread over its useful life. The amount ($2.00) is too small to matter.

Acquisition of the machine probably included a delivery and an installation cost, which we would capitalize (add it to the historical cost of the asset) as part of the machine: without shipping and installation, the machinery would not be valuable to JOE'S.

Recall the historical cost assumption, the going concern assumption, and the conservatism principle. Scott and Adrian now have the machinery, which cost $31,000 to get it to where it is, but that does not mean it is worth $31,000. Indeed, if Scott and Adrian died the next day, or if they otherwise decided not to start the business, someone would have to dispose of the machinery. They would be unlikely to recover any shipping or installation costs unless they sold the business as a "going concern." If they had to sell the machinery (perhaps because someone died or someone was arrested and needed bail money) they might not receive any more than they could get from a pawnshop or at a garage sale. That could be only a few thousand dollars. Thus, listing the machinery at $31,000 does not mean JOE'S BAR & GRILL has assets worth $31,000; instead, it means the business has assets with an historical cost of $31,000 and we assume the business is a going concern such that it will use the assets for their expected useful lives. Those assumptions may—or may not—prove to be valid. Once again, the "book value" of the machinery may be very different from its fair market value.

5. They purchase inventory of $30,000

We capitalize it because we expect to sell it over time. The matching principle of accounting requires us to allocate the inventory costs to the revenue produced from selling the inventory during the appropriate time period, which will start in December. LESSON SEVEN covers inventory accounting in greater depth.

6. They incur $20,000 of employee/management training costs

The training costs present a real set of issue. These are essentially "sunk costs": Scott and Adrian will not be getting that $20,000 back. In contrast, if they close the business, they will recover something from selling the inventory and the machinery, even if it is at a large discount. But they have no plausible way of getting the training costs back. Nevertheless, the matching principle along with the going concern assumption require us to capitalize the costs into an intangible asset.

We will later (once operations begin) amortize the costs over their useful lives. Determining the useful life of training is speculative. We may have information from the provider of the training regarding how long it should last (when do we need to train new employees or re-train current ones), but even the best information can never be precise. Employees may quit tomorrow or turn out to be poorly trained. Nevertheless, we must come up with some method to allocate the costs. LESSON FIVE covers this in greater depth.

7. They incur trademark and signage costs of $10,000

The trademark and signage present some similar issues. First, we divide them into two assets based on their relative costs. Likely, the signs have a determinable useful life—information we can obtain from the manufacturer of the sign. The trademark has a legal life,[23] as well as a tax law life[24] which differ. As a result, the financial books and the tax books will differ because of these assets.

8. They earn interest income during start-up of $10,000

This raises another piece of missing information. I stipulated all costs and items were paid for but said nothing about receipts. The interest accrued, but that does not mean JOE'S received it, which illustrates a difference between cash and accrual. With accrual accounting, we would recognize the $10,000 income and a $10,000 asset (either cash or a receivable). But, with cash accounting, we recognize the income *only if* JOE'S received the funds. Let's stipulate the $10,000 was received and deposited into the bank account.

With the stipulation, we must recognize this as income. We also must add it to assets. As you see in **Figure 2**, to keep the balance sheet in balance, we add the $10,000 to owner's equity: ultimately Scott and Adrian (the owner's) own the cash resulting from the income.

9. During the start-up period, the liquor/wine inventory appreciates $5,000

This is irrelevant for bookkeeping and the *main part* of the financial statements. Per the revenue recognition principle and the conservatism principle (and the all events test), we would not recognize any income from *this type* of asset appreciation until disposition of the asset. We might, however, note the appreciation in a footnote to both the income statement and balance sheet.

The resulting balance sheet, as of November 30, appears in **Figure 2**. Retained earnings is the net of $10,000 interest income less $7,500 rent expense. This immediately becomes the starting balance sheet for the next day, December 1, when JOE'S BAR & GRILL begins its operations.

---

[23] Generally, a trademark has a 10-year renewable life. Under GAAP, it is amortizable over the initial 10 years on a straight-line basis; however, the owner may choose to classify it as having an indefinite life and thus not amortize the cost. In either event, the book value is subject to an impairment analysis.

[24] Per IRC § 197 the trademark would have a 15-year useful life for tax purposes.

JOE'S BAR & GRILL Balance Sheet November 30				
Assets		**Liabilities**		
Cash	$308,000			
Inventory	30,000			
Machinery	31,000			
Liquor License	80,000			
Local Permit	1,000			
Pre-Paid Rent	22,500	**Owner's Equity**		
Trademark	6,000	Scott	$250,000	
Training	20,000	Adrian	250,000	
Signs	4,000	Retained Earnings	2,500	
Total Assets	**$502,500**	**Liabilities & Equity**	**$502,500**	

Figure 2: Balance Sheet on November 30

LESSON THREE

AUDITS AND OPINIONS

Can We Trust the Numbers?

■ ■ ■

Lesson Objectives

1. Student will learn additional accounting terminology.

2. Student will learn some basic rules amount confidentiality and privilege in relation to accountants.

3. Student will learn:

   a. Requirements of an audit.

   b. Requirements of an audit opinion letter, including the types of opinions:

      i. Unqualified

      ii. Modified Unqualified

      iii. Modified

      iv. Adverse

      v. Disclaimer

   c. Requirements to be a CPA.

Terminology Introduced

- FASB.
- EDGAR.
- GAAS.
- PCAOB.
- AICPA.
- Codification.
- Audit.
- Internal controls.
- Going concern.
- *Kovel* letter.
- Response letter.

LESSON THREE covers three topics:

- The sources of accounting authority.

- CPA's and other professionals, including confidentiality and privilege.

- Auditor opinion letters.

LESSON THREE-A

SOURCES OF ACCOUNTING AUTHORITY

■ ■ ■

Just as lawyers deal with statutes, regulations and cases, accountants also deal with original authorities. Four of them are important for this beginning course:

1. GAAP: Generally Accepted Accounting Principles.

2. GAAS: Generally Accepted Auditing Standards.

3. IFRS: International Financial Reporting Standards.

4. PCAOB: Public Company Accounting Oversight Board.

1. GENERALLY ACCEPTED ACCOUNTING PRINCIPLES

GAAP forms the basis for accounting in the United States. Pronounced "gap", it includes the list of principles discussed in LESSON TWO-B, *e.g.*, the matching principle, the historical cost assumption, and the consistency principle. Audited financial statements must conform to GAAP; in contrast, unaudited statements need not conform and most likely do not conform to GAAP.

Under the Securities Acts of 1933 and 1934, the SEC has statutory authority to create accounting principles.[1] The SEC delegated that authority to the private sector, initially to the AICPA. However, in 1973, the FASB came into existence and the SEC delegated its authority to the FASB for the creation of GAAP.[2]

---

[1]   Section 10A of the Securities Exchange Act of 1934.

[2]   *Reaffirming the Status of the FASB as a Designated Private-Sector Standard Setter*, SEC Policy Statement, Release Nos. 33–8221 (May 1, 2003), 68 FED. REG. 23333, available at https://www.sec.gov/rule-release/33-8221. This policy continues through at least 2020. *See,*

Hence, in the United States, the authoritative body for creating GAAP is the Financial Accounting Standards Board [the FASB] (pronounced fazby). Established in 1973, it issues Statements on Financial Accounting Standards that cover specific issues. These accounting rules involve a great deal more than the list of broad principles: they include nearly 200 very detailed statements on particular issues. In a general sense, they are like statutes used by lawyers. Knowledge of them is far beyond this course other than their existence. In 2009, the FASB codified all existing opinions. The codification is available on-line (for a fee) and is now "authoritative" in that it replaces all prior opinions and statements.

The 2009 codification was not intended to change GAAP; instead it reorganized the many opinions and pronouncements, as well as SEC rules, into a more usable and electronic searchable body of information. Officially it is the FASB Accounting Standards Codification [the Codification].

The SEC has examined the adoption of IFRS for many years.[3] *Recent* public statements[4] suggest the adoption is no longer contemplated in the foreseeable future. Because the SEC has statutory authority to adopt U.S. accounting principles,[5] no additional legislation would be required.

2. GENERALLY ACCEPTED AUDITING STANDARDS

GAAS (pronounced gas) are the standards used in the conduct of an audit subject to GAAP for non-publicly traded entities. Part of the standard audit opinion letter attests to the CPA having conducted the audit in conformance with GAAS.

The Auditing Standards Board of the American Institute of Certified Public Accountants [AICPA] is responsible for creating and updating GAAS. In contrast, the Assurance Standards Board of the International

---

FINANCIAL REPORTING MANUAL, SEC Division of Corporate Finance (2020). While non-authoritative, the 370-page manual is an SEC guide to U.S. financial reporting. It cites heavily to the Codification. SEC adoption of the FASB and the Codification has been criticized by some. See, Wm. Dennis Huber, *The SEC's Ultra Vires Recognition of the FASB as a Standard Setting Body*, 19 RICHMOND J. LAW PUB. POL'CY 124 (2016).

[3] See, *Work Plan for the Consideration of Incorporating International Financial Reporting Standards into the Financial Reporting System for U.S. Issuers Final Staff Report* (July 2012).

[4] "Securities and Exchange Commission chief accountant James Schnurr is rethinking a proposal he made last December that the SEC allow U.S. companies the option of providing some information, such as revenues, using International Financial Reporting Standards as a supplement to U.S. GAAP without requiring reconciliation." ACCOUNTING TODAY (May 7, 2015), http://www.accountingtoday.com/news/audit-accounting/sec-chief-accountant-backs-away-from-ifrs-proposal-74553-1.html; "Kara Stein, a commissioner with the Securities and Exchange Commission, appeared to reject the need for convergence with International Financial Reporting Standards in a speech last week." ACCOUNTING TODAY (March 30, 2015) http://www.accountingtoday.com/news/audit-accounting/sec-commissioner-rejects-ifrs-74428-1.html.

[5] Section 10A of the Securities Exchange Act of 1934.

Federation of Accountants is responsible for creating and updating the International Standards on Auditing [ISOA].

Since 2002, for publicly traded entities, the Public Company Accounting Oversight Board [PCAOB] is responsible for auditing standards. Required by the Sarbanes-Oxley Act, these initially followed GAAS. Since 2002, they have become more and more detailed as they anticipate issues commonly faced by auditors of publicly traded entities.

Generally, auditing standards include three sets of rules, which comprise ten standards:

- General Standards.

- Standards of Field Work.

- Standards of Reporting.

As explained in AU 150[6]:

An independent auditor plans, conducts, and reports the results of an audit in accordance with generally accepted auditing standards. Auditing standards provide a measure of audit quality and the objectives to be achieved in an audit. Auditing procedures differ from auditing standards. Auditing procedures are acts that the auditor performs during the course of an audit to comply with auditing standards.

AU 150.01.

The *General Standards* are:

1. The auditor must have adequate technical training and proficiency to perform the audit.

2. The auditor must maintain independence in mental attitude in all matters relating to the audit.

3. The auditor must exercise due professional care in the performance of the audit and the preparation of the report.

The first standard essentially means the auditor and the persons conducting the audit must have sufficient technical training. Clearly the auditor must have a license as a CPA, as must much of the audit team. Others involved need sufficient training for their respective tasks.

The second standard involves independence—mentally and factually. The auditor must feel independent and must not feel pressured or financially (or otherwise) influenced by the "client." This is a very different mental state than faced by lawyers who typically have a duty to "zealously represent" their client. To the contrary, a CPA auditor owes more of a duty to the users of the financial statements being audited than to the entity

---

6   http://pcaobus.org/Standards/Auditing/Pages/AU150.aspx

paying for the audit. Importantly, no client should be so important to a CPA or CPA firm that loss of the revenue for the audit would materially affect the CPA or the firm. The CPA must feel the mental and actual ability to render an independent opinion regarding the financial statements. As a result, many accounting firms are very large, comprising tens of thousands of professional employees—far larger than the largest law firms. They must be that large to have the independent personnel who can form unbiased independent opinions about what are often very large, multinational clients.

The third standard—of professional care—also emphasizes independence. The auditor must be diligent and must report misleading statements. World-wide, this duty is one of "professional skepticism." The auditor must question information from the client, keeping an open mind and insisting on sufficient first-hand knowledge of the things he expresses an opinion regarding. For example, inconsistent evidence or responses require further inquiry.

The *Standards of Field Work* are:

4. The auditor must adequately plan the work and must ***properly supervise*** any **assistants**.

5. The auditor must obtain a **sufficient** understanding of the entity and its environment, including its **internal control**, to assess the risk of **material misstatement** of the financial statements whether due to error or fraud, and to design the nature, timing, and extent of further audit procedures.

6. The auditor must obtain **sufficient** appropriate audit evidence by performing audit procedures to afford a **reasonable basis** for an opinion regarding the financial statements under audit.

The fourth standard regarding supervision emphasizes the important of a CPA's responsibility. The CPA who signs the audit opinion letter is expressing an opinion on the whole financial statements hence, he or she must be informed as to the whole. This includes adequate supervision over employees who gather information or who confirm parts of the statements.

The fifth standard has several key words highlighted: the auditor must have a sufficient understanding of the entity: he or she will never know everything, but he or she must understand a great deal. "Know your client" is a key phrase among broker-dealers, but it is also key for CPAs. They must become familiar with the business of the client; otherwise, they cannot express an informed opinion. If not familiar with the business, its operations, its history, and its plans, the CPA is not going to understand what to question and what to investigate.

Another key word in the fifth standard involves "internal control" which refers to the procedural safeguards put into place by management to ensure its financial records and its assets are proper. We will cover internal controls later. For now, understand, they are very important. Also note the emphasis on "material misstatement." This is reminiscent of the materiality principle of accounting: if it does not matter, it does not matter. Accountants only concern themselves with material issues. Hence, be wary of a false sense of precision: financial statements may appear precise and give the impression of "perfection." But, as you learned in LESSON TWO, accounting is replete with estimates, judgments, and other subjective choices.

The sixth standard has two critical words. First, an auditor must obtain "sufficient" evidence. No audit can check everything: that would be very expensive and unlikely to be worth the trouble. Instead, an audit will be based on statistical sampling of many items such that the audit has sufficient evidence for his or her opinion. Further, the opinion must rest on a "reasonable basis," not some high standard of perfection. The auditor will not say he or she is "certain" the financial statements are fair; instead, he or she will express a reasonable basis for the opinion.

The *Standards of Reporting* are:

7.   The auditor must state in the auditor's report whether the financial statements are presented in accordance with ***generally accepted accounting principles***.

8.   The auditor must identify in the auditor's report those circumstances in which such principles have not been ***consistently*** observed in the current period ***in relation*** to the preceding period.

9.   When the auditor determines that informative disclosures are not ***reasonably*** adequate, the auditor must so state in the auditor's report.

10.   The auditor must either express an opinion regarding the financial statements, taken as a whole, or state that an opinion cannot be expressed, in the auditor's report. When the auditor cannot express an overall opinion, the auditor should state the reasons therefor in the auditor's report. In all cases where an auditor's name is associated with financial statements, the auditor should clearly indicate the character of the auditor's work, if any, and the degree of responsibility the auditor is taking, in the auditor's report.

The seventh standard requires the auditor's report (or opinion letter) to state whether the financial statements conform to GAAP. This is for

United States operations and reporting. International standards require conformity to IFRS.

The eighth standard requires disclosure of inconsistent application of GAAP in relation to the prior period. This relates to the Consistency Principle of Accounting: management can make many choices in the application of GAAP, but it must do so consistently. Without consistency, a comparison of numbers from one year to another would lose validity. Also notice the comparison element: financial statements in isolation are not nearly as useful as they are when compared to other periods.

The ninth standard requires the auditor to disclose the lack of reasonable disclosure of information from management. This is strikingly different from the role of an attorney, who must keep disclosure (or the lack thereof) confidential. Remember: the CPA/auditor does not zealously represent the client; instead, he or she expresses an independent opinion on the fairness of the financial statements prepared by management. The CPA's duty is more to the users of information than to the client who pays for the audit.

3. INTERNATIONAL FINANCIAL REPORTING STANDARDS

In 1973, the various accounting professional bodies in ten nations formed the International Accounting Standards Committee [IASC]. The nations were: Australia, Canada, France, Germany, Japan, Mexico, the Netherlands, the United Kingdom, Ireland, and the United States. The initial goal was to adopt international standards for cross-border entities. By 1993, the committee completed its initial set of standards. In 1996, it created the IAC, the Standards Interpretations Committee [SIC] with authority to issue interpretations of international standards.

In 2000, the IASC restructured itself into the International Accounting Standards Board [IASB], which became part of the IFRS® Foundation, a non-profit international organization which now has responsibility for appointing members of the IASB and for issuing IFRS.

In 2002, the European Commission issued a regulation[7] requiring listed companies on securities exchanges, as well as banks and insurance companies, to prepare financial statements consistent with IFRS. In 2007, the SEC adopted a regulation permitting non-U.S. companies to report financial statements to the SEC using IFRS.[8] As of 2021, the United States has not adopted IFRS. Efforts continue to bring U.S. GAAP and IFRS closer; however, a timetable for unification does not exist.

---

[7]   IP/02/799. EU regulations have the force of law.

[8]   17 CFR Parts 210, 230, 239 and 249.

4. PUBLIC COMPANY ACCOUNTING OVERSIGHT BOARD (PCAOB)

Congress created the PCAOB in 2010 as part of the Sarbanes-Oxley Act.[9] to oversee audits of publicly traded companies. Accounting firms that audit "publicly traded" companies must first be "registered" with the PCAOB. They must then perform the audit consistent PCAOB auditing standards. The PCAOB initially adopted GAAS as the "interim" set of rules. With more than 800 employees, it issues auditing statements [ASs] which form standards for public company audits.

The PCAOB has disciplined many CPAs and firms—some through hearings and some by consent. It generally appears to have taken over a role more traditionally left to state disciplinary agencies or to the SEC. "Non-U.S. accounting firms that furnish, prepare, or play a substantial role in preparing an audit report for any issuer, broker, and dealer also are subject to PCAOB rules."[10]

As stated on the entity's website:

The PCAOB is a nonprofit corporation established by Congress to oversee the audits of public companies to protect the interests of investors and further the public interest in the preparation of informative, accurate and independent audit reports. The PCAOB also oversees the audits of broker-dealers, including compliance reports filed pursuant to federal securities laws, to promote investor protection.[11]

LESSON THREE-B

CPAS AND PRIVILEGE

■ ■ ■

1. GENERAL

All fifty states issue licenses for CPAs. To become a CPA, a person must satisfy the requirements of the state in which he or she seeks a license. All states use the same Uniform CPA exam that the AICPA prepares. The exam comprises four parts:

- Auditing and attestation (AUD).

---

[9]   15 U.S.C. §§ 7211–7220.

[10]   http://pcaobus.org/Pages/default.aspx

[11]   *Id.*

- Business environment and concepts (BEC).

- Financial accounting and reporting (FAR).

- Regulation (REG).

Prior to 2004, applicants took all four parts in "paper and pencil" format at a single testing time (spread over fifteen hours and three days). The first-time pass rate varied from state-to-state, but generally ranged from three to fifteen percent. Applicants could pass part of the test, however, and then re-take only the failed sections.

In 2004, the testing format changed dramatically. Current applicants sit for a single section at a time and take it electronically. The total testing time is now fourteen hours. The pass rate for each part is now close to fifty percent for all takers (less for first-time takers). Preparation for each section is typically rigorous and most applicants take a CPA review course similar to bar review courses commonly taken by law school graduates.

In addition to passing the exam, all states have both education and experience requirements. Although none require an accounting degree, all jurisdictions require specific training in the various tested areas. In many states, an applicant effectively needs the equivalent of a master's degree because of the large amount of training required. States also vary in the work or experience requirement, which is commonly two years of practice under the supervision of a CPA. In some jurisdictions, an applicant must satisfy the work requirement prior to taking the examination.

Do not confuse the designation of a CPA with similar sounding designations. The GLOSSARY explains many other certifications used by various financial advisers, who may also be CPAs. For example, as explained in the GLOSSARY:

- **Chartered Financial Analyst: CFA**: This is a designation granted by the *CFA* Institute. It is _not_ a state license According to the Institute:

   > The CFA Program is a three-part exam that tests the fundamentals of investment tools, valuing assets portfolio management, and wealth planning. The CFA Program is typically completed by those with backgrounds in finance, accounting, economics, or business. CFA charterholders earn the right to use the CFA designation after program completion, application and acceptance by CFA Institute. CFA charterholders are qualified to work in senior and executive positions in investment management, risk management, asset management, and more.

   > https://www.cfainstitute.org/en/programs/cfa

The designation *CFA* is multi-national. The Institute and its predecessors have granted it since 1963. The three required examinations total 18 hours.

- **Forensic Accountant**: This is an accountant trained to reconstruct realistic financial statements. For example, a forensic accountant might work in marriage dissolution as an expert for a spouse who believes the other spouse has manipulated or wasted assets or income. Or, he might work in a labor law case for a union that believes management has understated its ability to pay higher wages. Just as forensic medicine focuses on the cause of death, forensic accounting focuses on the cause or reasons why a situation is what it appears to be.

Historically, the American College of Forensic Examiners [ACFE]:

The ACFE offered certification for *Forensic Accountants* through a program leading to a designation called Cr. FA®. This is not a state granted license.

Some forensic accountants specialize in fraud detection. Some seek the designation of Certified Fraud Examiner [CFE]. This is a designation offered through the Association of Certified Fraud Examiners [ACFE]. It is not a state granted license. According to the ACFE:

Globally preferred by employers, the Certified Fraud Examiner (CFE) credential denotes proven expertise in fraud prevention, detection, and deterrence. Members with the CFE credential experience professional growth and quickly position themselves as leaders in the global anti-fraud community.

http://www.acfe.com

- **Investment Advisor**: Defined in the Investment Advisors Act of 1940,[12] any person or group that makes investment recommendations or conducts securities analysis in return for a fee, whether through direct management of client assets or written publications. In contrast, a broker dealer is a person or entity that is in the business of buying and selling securities for itself or on behalf of clients. Often, an investment advisor is also a broker dealer.

2. CONFIDENTIALITY AND PRIVILEGE

Rules of confidentiality for accountants vary significantly from those applying to lawyers; however, they have some similarities. Understanding them requires an examination from three different viewpoints:

---

[12]   15 U.S.C. § 80b–2.

- The sources of the rules.
- The object of the rules: What is confidential or privileged.
- The inter-play of accountants and lawyers.

Three _sources_ of confidentiality and/or privilege rules exist:

- Tax law.
- State law.
- Ethics rules of the profession.

Confidentiality rules also break into two <u>categories</u>:

- Confidentiality of communication.
- Confidentiality of work product.

As with the attorney-client privilege, the rules and law affecting communications vary significantly from the rules affecting work product.

A third way of examining confidentiality in relation to accountants involves the inter-play of accountants and their work product with attorneys either in anticipation of litigation or in the normal course of providing legal services. This "third way" viewpoint has prompted conflicting court decisions and may be best described as evolving.

A. THE SOURCES OF THE RULES

1) Tax Law

A CPA, or any "federally authorized tax practitioner" giving tax advice in relation to the United States Internal Revenue Code is subject to IRC section 7525:

Sec. 7525 Confidentiality privileges relating to taxpayer communications

(a) Uniform application to taxpayer communications with federally authorized practitioners

(1) General rule. With respect to tax advice, the same common law protections of confidentiality which apply to a **_communication_** between a _taxpayer and an attorney_ shall also apply to a communication between a taxpayer and any federally authorized tax practitioner to the extent the communication would be considered a privileged communication if it were between a taxpayer and an attorney.

(2) Limitations. Paragraph (1) may only be asserted in—

(A) any *noncriminal tax matter* before the Internal Revenue Service; and (B) any *noncriminal tax proceeding* in Federal court brought by or against the United States.

(3)   Definitions. For purposes of this subsection—

(A) Federally authorized tax practitioner. The term "federally authorized tax practitioner" means any individual who is authorized under Federal law to practice before the Internal Revenue Service if such practice is subject to Federal regulation under section 330 of title 31, United States Code.

(B) Tax advice. The term "tax advice" means advice given by an individual with respect to a matter which is within the scope of the individual's authority to practice described in subparagraph (A).

(b) Section not to apply to communications regarding tax shelters.

The privilege under subsection (a) *shall not apply* to any written communication which is—

(1)   between a federally authorized tax practitioner and—

(A) any person,

(B) any director, officer, employee, agent, or representative of the person, or (C) any other person holding a capital or profits interest in the person, and

(2)   in connection with the promotion of the direct or indirect participation of the person in any *tax shelter* (as defined in section 6662(d)(2)(C)(ii)).

Several aspects of IRC section 7525 are noteworthy:

- The tax preparer privilege only applies to a person who is "federally authorized" to practice before the IRS, which would likely include many CPAs, but only those who register.

- The privilege only applies to *civil* matters. It *does not* apply to criminal matters.

- The privilege *does not* apply to participation in a "tax shelter."

- The privilege mirrors the traditional attorney-client privilege as it has traditionally applied in tax law.

The "civil matters" and "non-tax shelter" limitations are substantial restrictions that *do not* apply to attorneys covered by the attorney-client privilege. Whether an attorney communication with a client is covered by the attorney-client privilege for tax law is not an easy issue to resolve: it can be a function or whether the attorney was acting as an attorney and whether the matter involved legal advice.

2) State Law

Some states grant a CPA-client privilege _or_ an accountant-client privilege; but most do not. Common law also did not recognize the privilege.[13] But, sixteen states currently recognize an accountant privilege, though they vary significantly. Some apply the privilege to all accountants and some only to CPAs. The sixteen are:

- Arizona. A.R.S. § 32–749.
- Colorado. C.R.S. § 13–90–107.
- Florida. F.S. §§ 90.502; 90.5055; 473.316.
- Georgia. O.C.Ga. § 43–3–29.
- Idaho. I.R.E. Rule 515.
- Illinois. 225 IL. C.S. 450/27.
- Indiana. In. Code 25–2–1–23(b).
- Kansas. K.S. § 1–401.
- Louisiana. La. C. Evid. Art. 515.
- Maryland. § 9–110.
- Michigan. Mich. St. Ann. § 18.425 (713).
- New Mexico. N. M. Stat. Ann. § 67–23–2b.
- Ohio. Oh. Ad. Code § 4701–11–02(A).
- Oklahoma. 12 Okl. St. § 2502.1.
- Texas. Tex. O. C. § 901.457.

The relevant Florida Statutes are:

90.5055 Accountant-client privilege.—

(1) For purposes of this section:

    (a) An "accountant" is a certified public accountant _or a public accountant_.

    (b) A "client" is any person, public officer, corporation, association, or other organization or entity, either public or private, who consults an accountant with the purpose of obtaining accounting services.

    (c) A _communication_ between an accountant and the accountant's client is "confidential" if it is not intended to be disclosed to third persons other than:

---

[13] Mark Segal, _Accountants and the Attorney-Client Privilege_, JOURNAL OF ACCOUNTANCY (April 1, 1997).

1. Those to whom disclosure is in furtherance of the rendition of accounting services to the client.

2. Those reasonably necessary for the transmission of the communication.

(2) A client has a privilege to refuse to disclose, and to prevent any other person from disclosing, the contents of *confidential communications* with an accountant when such other person learned of the communications because they were made in the rendition of accounting services to the client. This privilege includes other confidential information obtained by the accountant *from the client* for the purpose of rendering accounting advice.

(3) The privilege may be claimed by:

(a) The client.

(b) A guardian or conservator of the client.

(c) The personal representative of a deceased client.

(d) A successor, assignee, trustee in dissolution, or any similar representative of an organization, corporation, or association or other entity, either public or private, whether or not in existence.

(e) The accountant, but only on behalf of the client. The accountant's authority to claim the privilege is presumed in the absence of contrary evidence.

(4) There is no accountant-client privilege under this section when:

(a) The services of the accountant were sought or obtained to enable or aid anyone to commit or plan to commit what the client knew or should have known was a crime or fraud.

(b) A communication is relevant to an issue of breach of duty by the accountant to the accountant's client or by the client to his or her accountant.

(c) A communication is relevant to a matter of common interest between two or more clients, if the communication was made by any of them to an accountant retained or consulted in common when offered in a civil action between the clients.

473.316 Communications between the accountant and client privileged.—

(1) For purposes of this section:

(a) An "accountant" is a certified public accountant.

(b) A "client" is any person, public officer, corporation, association, or other organization or entity, either public or private, who consults an accountant with the purpose of obtaining accounting services.

(c) A *communication* between an accountant and her or his client is "confidential" if it is not intended to be disclosed to third persons other than:

    1. Those to whom disclosure is in furtherance of the rendition of accounting services to the client.

    2. Those reasonably necessary for the transmission of the communication.

(d) A "quality review" is a study, appraisal, or review of one or more aspects of the professional work of an accountant in the practice of public accountancy which is conducted by a professional organization for the purpose of evaluating quality assurance required by professional standards, including a quality assurance or peer review.

(e) A "review committee" is any person or persons who are not owners or employees of an accountant or firm that is the subject of a quality review and who carry out, administer, or oversee a quality review.

(2) A client has a privilege to refuse to disclose, and to prevent any other person from disclosing, the contents of *confidential communications* with an accountant when such other person learned of the communications because they were made in the rendition of accounting services to the client This privilege includes other confidential information obtained by the accountant from the client for the purpose of rendering accounting advice.

(3) The privilege may be claimed by:

(a) The client.

(b) A guardian or conservator of the client.

(c) The personal representative of a deceased client.

(d) A successor, assignee, trustee in dissolution, or any similar representative of an organization, corporation, or association or other entity, either public or private, whether or not in existence.

(e) The accountant, but only on behalf of the client. The accountant's authority to claim the privilege is presumed in the absence of contrary evidence.

(4)   There is no accountant-client privilege under this section when:

    (a)   The services of the accountant were sought or obtained to enable or aid anyone to commit or plan to commit what the client knew or should have known was a crime or fraud.

    (b)   A communication is relevant to an issue of breach of duty by the accountant to her or his client or by the client to her or his accountant.

    (c)   A communication is relevant to a matter of common interest between two or more clients, if the communication was made by any of them to an accountant retained or consulted in common when offered in a civil action between the clients.

(5)   Communications are not privileged from disclosure in any disciplinary investigation or proceeding conducted pursuant to this act by the department or before the board or in any judicial review of such a proceeding. In any such proceeding, a certified public accountant or public accountant, without the consent of her or his client, may testify with respect to any communication between the accountant and the accountant's client or be compelled, pursuant to a subpoena of the department or the board, to testify or produce records, books, or papers. Such a communication disclosed to the board and records of the board relating to the communication shall for all other purposes and proceedings be a privileged communication in all of the courts of this state.

(6)   The proceedings, records, and __workpapers of a review committee__ are privileged and are not subject to discovery, subpoena, or other means of legal process or to introduction into evidence in a civil action or arbitration, administrative proceeding, or state accountancy board proceeding. A member of a review committee or person who was involved in a quality review may not testify in a civil action or arbitration, administrative proceeding, or state accountancy board proceeding as to any matter produced or disclosed during the quality review or as to any findings, recommendations, evaluations, opinions, or other actions of the review committee or any members thereof. Public records and materials prepared for a particular engagement are not privileged merely because they were presented during the quality review. This privilege does not apply to disputes between a review committee and a person subject to a quality review.

The italicized portions of each statute do not appear in the other; otherwise, the two are identical. The F.S. 90.5055 accountant privilege is part of the Florida Evidence Code. In contrast, the F.S. 473.316 accountant privilege is part of the Florida Code regulating Occupations and

Professions. It is part of the regulation of Public Accountancy. Of note, the privilege applies only to communications and does not apply, at least not facially, to work product or working papers. The regulatory privilege has additional provisions on "review committees" which apply to work product. Review committees exist to review accounting firms as part of the state regulation. Work product prepared *by the committee* for use in aiding the State to regulate an accounting firm—the object of the review—is privileged. That has nothing to do with the relationship between an accountant and his/her client.

No general accountant privilege exists in federal law; hence, federal courts, unless they are applying state law (such as in a diversity case) would not recognize the privilege.

3)   Professional Ethics Rules

The AICPA Code of Professional Conduct [CPC] governs most CPAs nationally. As stated in the CPC, it applies only to AICPA *members* who "should also consult the following, if applicable:

- The ethical requirements of the member's state CPA society and authoritative regulatory bodies such as state board(s) of accountancy.

- The Securities and Exchange Commission (SEC).

- The Public Company Accounting Oversight Board (PCAOB).

- The Government Accountability Office (GAO).

- The Department of Labor (DOL).

- Federal, state and local taxing authorities.

- Any other body that regulates a member who performs professional services for an entity when the member or entity is subject to the rules and regulations of such regulatory body."

The CPC includes extensive and detailed rules on confidentiality. The substance of those rules is far beyond the scope of this text; however, lawyers who deal with clients should be aware of the CPC and may need to consult it if accountant confidentiality issues arise.

B.   THE OBJECT OF THE RULES

Confidentiality rules affects two categories of information:

- Communication with a client.

- Work product.

Application of the rules to the two categories differs significantly. Communication with a client receives more protection than does work product or working papers. As illustrated above, the statutory accountant-client privileges tend to apply to communication and not to work product.

Typically, the "work product doctrine"—which protects the confidentiality of tangible work—applies only if the accountant prepared the "work product" in anticipation of litigation. Courts vary on what constitutes "work product" as well as what "in anticipation of litigation" means. Much of the litigation concerning those terms has arisen in relation to tax matters. Arguably, the IRS has been very aggressive in seeking to limit the "work product doctrine."

The issue often arises in relation to tax accrual working papers or memoranda. As explained in various lessons, tax accounting varies substantially from financial accounting and in particular from GAAP. Consistent with FASB 48, a CPA must identify "uncertain tax positions" or inconsistent tax positions so as to reconcile book and tax disparities.

First, consider a common inconsistent position in EXAMPLE 8. For example, an entity may report $1,000,000 of taxable income during a year, but also report $4,000,000 of "book" income consistent with GAAP. The disparity could result because of many reasons—as explained and illustrated in many lessons.[14] These might include different depreciation methods, different accounting methods for items of income or expense, and different capitalization rules. The differences are proper, common, and appropriate: they exist because tax accounting and financial accounting serve different purposes. Tax accounting, governed by tax laws, exists to measure "income" as defined by taxing authorities with an aim toward producing revenue or perhaps stimulating the economy. In contrast, financial accounting, governed by GAAP, exists to fairly represent economic income consistent with the historical cost assumption and conservatism principles.

---

[14] LESSON FIVE-D covers book/tax reconciliation.

> ## EXAMPLE 8
>
> ### Deferred Tax Liability and Expense
>
> Suppose JOE'S were to have $1,000,000 of taxable income for the year 2021. Using U.S. corporate tax rates, it would owe approximately $200,000 income tax. Suppose JOE'S, in contrast, had $4,000,000 of income per GAAP for financial reporting purposes.
>
> For financial reporting, JOE'S would accrue a tax expense of $800,000—the expected 20% rate on the full $4,000,000. Of that, $200,000 would be paid with its tax returns and the remaining $600,000 would be a deferred tax liability. Computation of these amounts would be part of the "tax accrual work papers." They may be non-controversial, or they may involve opinions JOE'S would prefer to keep confidential.

In EXAMPLE 8—where book income exceeds tax income by $3,000,000—the CPA will need to accrue (for book purposes) a deferred tax expense. This will be an estimate that will be a function of when the book income will eventually result in tax income as well as a projection of the future tax consequences. Under the matching principle, the estimated future tax expense attributable to the extra $3,000,000 of book income must be accrued during the period the income accrued—2021 in the example. If, for example, the estimated tax rate is 20%, the entity would accrue a "deferred tax liability" of $600,000 on the extra $3,000,000 of income. If, instead, the predicted tax rate was 35%, the accrued expense and corresponding deferred tax liability would be $1,050,000. This is not—at least not yet—a liability to the government because the $3,000,000 of financial income is not considered "taxable income" under the law. Eventually it will be income because whatever caused the item to escape tax currently will cause it to be subject to tax in a later period.

In contrast to inconsistent positions, which naturally result because tax and financial accounting have different rules and definitions, uncertain tax positions result because tax law is itself complex and often uncertain. The entity may take positions on its tax returns that its attorney and CPA believe to be appropriate. Indeed, if the advisors consider the positions inappropriate, they should probably withdraw from the representation. In preparing a financial analysis or an opinion on audited financial statements, a CPA will commonly review tax returns. Often, he or she will find some positions taken to be controversial and potentially subject to challenge. If so, the CPA will likely comment on the risk of a challenge and will advise the client in relation to such "uncertain" positions. That is where the controversy over confidentiality typically arises. Understandably, the government would like to see the accountant's work product and opinion evaluating any uncertainties. Such work product is a perfect roadmap for a tax audit. But is such "work product" or "tax accrual working papers" subject to confidentiality? The answer is unclear and depends on who prepared them and why they were prepared.

> ## CPA Tax Accrual Workpapers Are *Not* Privileged
>
> CPA work product prepared for an audit, including opinions regarding controversial tax positions, is *not* privileged.

The Supreme Court considered the issue in the 1984 Arthur Young decision.[15] At the time, Arthur Young & Company was one of the "Big Eight" international accounting firms. It later merged with other firms and remnants of it are one of the current "Big Four"[16] firms. The case considered tax accrual work papers prepared by an auditor, such as the accrual work papers (estimates) in EXAMPLE 8. Pay attention to how the Court distinguished the attorney-client privilege from accountant-client privileges that exist under some state laws. Also pay attention to the Court's discussion of the CPA's role in an audit and his/her duty to users of financial statements rather than to the nominal "client" who pays for the audit.

UNITED STATES V. ARTHUR YOUNG & CO.
465 U.S. 805 (1984)

(Emphasis added and some footnotes omitted or renumbered.)

CHIEF JUSTICE BURGER delivered the opinion of the Court.

We granted certiorari to consider whether tax accrual workpapers prepared by a corporation's independent certified public accountant in the course of regular financial audits are protected from disclosure in response to an Internal Revenue Service summons issued under § 7602 of the Internal Revenue Code of 1954 [* * *].

---

15   United States v. Arthur Young, 465 U.S. 805 (1984).

16   The Big Four international accounting firms are:
- Ernst & Young (*aka* EY).
- PricewaterhouseCoopers (*aka* PWC).
- Deloitte.
- KPMG.

Respondent Arthur Young & Co. is a firm of certified public accountants. As the independent auditor for respondent Amerada Hess Corp., Young is responsible for reviewing the financial statements prepared by Amerada as required by the federal securities laws.[17] In the course of its review of these financial statements Young verified Amerada's statement of its contingent tax liabilities, and, in so doing, prepared the tax accrual workpapers at issue in this case. **Tax accrual workpapers are documents and memoranda relating to Young's evaluation of Amerada's reserves for contingent tax liabilities. Such workpapers sometimes contain information pertaining to Amerada's financial transactions, identify questionable positions Amerada may have taken on its tax returns, and reflect Young's opinions regarding the validity of such positions. [* * *]**

> Tax accrual work papers may have confidential financial information as well as tax advice.

Tax accrual work papers may have confidential financial information as well as tax advice.

The District Court found that Young's tax accrual workpapers were relevant to the IRS investigation within the meaning of § 7602 and refused to recognize an accountant-client privilege that would protect the workpapers. [* * *] Accordingly, the District Court ordered the summons enforced. [* * *]

The Court of Appeals majority agreed with the District Court that the tax accrual workpapers were relevant to the IRS investigation of Amerada, but held that the public interest in promoting full disclosure to public accountants, and in turn ensuring the integrity of the securities markets, required protection for the work that such independent auditors perform for publicly owned companies. Drawing upon *Hickman v. Taylor*, 329 U.S. 495 (1947), and Federal Rule of Civil Procedure 26(b)(3), the Court of Appeals fashioned a work-product immunity doctrine for tax accrual workpapers prepared by independent auditors in the course of compliance with the federal securities laws. [* * *]

Corporate financial statements are one of the primary sources of information available to guide the decisions of the investing public. In an effort to control the accuracy of the financial data available to investors in the securities markets, **various provisions of the federal securities laws require publicly held corporations to file their financial**

---

[17]   See, e. g., Securities Exchange Act of 1934, §§ 12(b)(1)(J)–(L), 48 Stat. 892, as redesignated, 78 Stat. 565, 15 U. S. C. 78l(b)(1)(J)–(L); Regulation S-X, 17 CFR § 210 et seq. (1983). *See also* n. 5, infra.

statements with the Securities and Exchange Commission.[18] Commission regulations stipulate that these financial reports must be audited by an independent certified public accountant in accordance with generally accepted auditing standards.[19] **By examining the corporation's books and records, the independent auditor determines whether the financial reports of the corporation have been prepared in accordance with generally accepted accounting principles.[20]** The auditor then issues an opinion as to whether the financial statements, taken as a whole, fairly present the financial position and operations of the corporation for the relevant period.[21] [* * *]

An important aspect of the auditor's function is to evaluate the adequacy and reasonableness of the corporation's reserve account for contingent tax liabilities. This reserve account, known as the tax accrual account, the noncurrent tax account, or the tax pool, represents the amount set aside by the corporation to cover adjustments and additions to the corporation's actual tax liability. Additional corporate tax liability may arise from a wide variety of transactions.[22] The presence of a reserve account for such contingent tax liabilities reflects the corporation's awareness of, and preparedness for, the possibility of an assessment of additional taxes.

The independent auditor draws upon many sources in evaluating the sufficiency of the corporation's tax accrual account. Initially, the corporation's books, records, and tax returns must be analyzed in light of the relevant Code provisions, Treasury Regulations, Revenue Rulings, and

---

[18] See Securities Act of 1933, Schedule A (25)–(27), 48 Stat. 88, 15 U. S. C. § 77aa (filing of audited financial statement prior to registration of new stock issue); Securities Exchange Act of 1934, §§ 12(b)(1)(J)–(L), 48 Stat. 892, as re-designated, 78 Stat. 565, 15 U. S. C. 78l(b)(1)(J)–(L) (filing of audited financial statement prior to listing securities on an exchange); Securities Exchange Act of 1934, §§ 13(a)(2), 13(b), 48 Stat. 894, as amended, 15 U. S. C. §§ 78m(a)(2), 78m(b); 17 CFR §§ 249.310, 249.460 (1983) (filing of annual reports); Securities Exchange Act of 1934, § 14, 48 Stat. 895, as amended, 15 U. S. C. § 78n; Schedule 14A, Item 15, 17 CFR § 240.14a–101 (1983) (filing of audited financial statement in connection with proxy and information statements).

[19] **Regulation S–X, 17 CFR § 210 et seq. (1983), prescribes the qualifications of accountants and the contents of the accountants' reports that must be submitted with corporate financial statements. In particular, 17 CFR § 210.1–02(d) (1983) requires that the financial statements of a public corporation must be audited by an accountant "in accordance with generally accepted auditing standards." "Generally accepted auditing standards" are promulgated by a committee of the public accounting profession's national organization, the American Institute of Certified Public Accountants (AICPA). See 1 AICPA Professional Standards (CCH) § 150.02 (1972).**

[20] See 1 AICPA, Statement on Auditing Standards § 110.01 (1972). Promulgated by the accounting profession's Financial Accounting Standards Board, "generally accepted accounting principles" are the conventions, rules, and procedures that define accepted accounting practices. See W. Meigs, E. Larsen, & R. Meigs, Principles of Auditing 25–26 (5th ed. 1973); H. Stettler, Auditing Principles 12–16 (5th ed. 1982).

[21] See 1 AICPA Professional Standards (CCH) § 509 (1974).

[22] For example, the characterization of the proceeds of a sale as capital gain instead of ordinary income, the claiming of an investment tax credit, and the attribution of a transaction to a future tax year are decisions requiring judgment calls in gray areas of the Code, any one of which might result in a re-computation of the corporation's outstanding tax liability.

case law. The auditor will also obtain and assess the opinions, speculations, and projections of management with regard to unclear, aggressive, or questionable tax positions that may have been taken on prior tax returns. In exploring the tax consequences of certain transactions, the auditor often engages in a "worst-case" analysis in order to ensure that the tax accrual account accurately reflects the full extent of the corporation's exposure to additional tax liability. From this conglomeration of data, the auditor is able to estimate the potential cost of each particular contingency, as well as the probability that the additional liability may arise.

The auditor's tax accrual workpapers record this process of examination and analysis. Such workpapers may document the auditor's interviews with corporate personnel, judgments on questions of potential tax liability, and suggestions for alternative treatments of certain transactions for tax purposes. Tax accrual workpapers also contain an overall evaluation of the sufficiency of the corporation's reserve for contingent tax liabilities, including an item-by-item analysis of the corporation's potential exposure to additional liability. **In short, tax accrual workpapers pinpoint the "soft spots" on a corporation's tax return by highlighting those areas in which the corporate taxpayer has taken a position that may, at some later date, require the payment of additional taxes. [* * *]**

> Tax accrual workpapers are a roadmap for an audit but prepared by the entity's CPA.

That tax accrual workpapers are not actually used in the preparation of tax returns by the taxpayer or its own accountants does not bar a finding of relevance within the meaning of § 7602. The filing of a corporate tax return entails much more than filling in the blanks on an IRS form in accordance with undisputed tax principles; more likely than not, the return is a composite interpretation of corporate transactions made by corporate officers in the light most favorable to the taxpayer. [* * *]

We are unable to discern the sort of "unambiguous directions from Congress" that would justify a judicially created work-product immunity for tax accrual workpapers summoned under § 7602. [* * *]

To the extent that the Court of Appeals, in its concern for the "chilling effect" of the disclosure of tax accrual workpapers, sought to facilitate communication between independent auditors and their clients, its remedy more closely resembles a testimonial accountant-client privilege than a work-product immunity for accountants' workpapers.

> The Court has _not_ recognized an accountant privilege.

But as this Court stated in *Couch* v. *United States*, 409 U.S. 322, 335 (1973), "no confidential accountant-client privilege exists under federal law,

and no state-created privilege has been recognized in federal cases." In light of *Couch*, the Court of Appeals' effort to foster candid communication between accountant and client by creating a self-styled work-product privilege was misplaced, and conflicts with what we see as the clear intent of Congress.

Nor do we find persuasive the argument that a work-product immunity for accountants' tax accrual workpapers is a fitting analogue to the attorney work-product doctrine established in *Hickman* v. *Taylor*, 329 U.S. 495 (1947). The *Hickman* work-product doctrine was founded upon the private attorney's role as the client's confidential adviser and advocate, a loyal representative whose duty it is to present the client's case in the most favorable possible light. **An independent certified public accountant performs a different role. By certifying the public reports that collectively depict a corporation's financial status, the independent auditor assumes a *public* responsibility transcending any employment relationship with the client. The independent public accountant performing this special function owes** ultimate allegiance to the corporation's creditors and stockholders, as well as to the investing public. This "public watchdog" function demands that the accountant maintain total independence from the client at all times and requires complete fidelity to the public trust. To insulate from disclosure a certified public accountant's interpretations of the client's financial statements would be to ignore the significance of the accountant's role as a disinterested analyst charged with public obligations.

> A CPA's duty is more to the public than to the entity being audited.

We cannot accept the view that the integrity of the securities markets will suffer absent some protection for accountants' tax accrual workpapers. **The Court of Appeals apparently feared that, were the IRS to have access to tax accrual workpapers, a corporation might be tempted to withhold from its auditor certain information relevant and material to a proper evaluation of its financial statements. But the independent certified public accountant cannot be content with the corporation's representations that its tax accrual reserves are adequate; the auditor is ethically and professionally obligated to ascertain for himself as far as possible whether the corporation's contingent tax liabilities have been accurately stated. If the auditor were convinced that the scope of the examination had been limited by management's reluctance to disclose matters relating to the tax accrual reserves, the auditor would be unable to issue an unqualified opinion as to the accuracy of the corporation's financial statements.** Instead, the auditor would be required to issue a qualified opinion, an adverse opinion, or a disclaimer of opinion, thereby notifying the investing public of possible potential problems inherent in the corporation's financial reports.[23] **Responsible corporate management would not risk a qualified evaluation of a corporate taxpayer's financial posture to afford cover for questionable positions reflected in a prior tax return.**[24] Thus, the independent auditor's obligation to serve the public interest assures that the integrity of the securities markets will be preserved, without the need for a work-product immunity for accountants' tax accrual workpapers.[25] [* * *]

Beyond question it is desirable and in the public interest to encourage full disclosures by corporate clients to their independent accountants; if it is necessary to balance competing interests, however, the need of the Government for full disclosure of all information relevant to tax liability must also weigh in that balance. This kind of policy choice is best left to the Legislative Branch. Accordingly, the judgment of the Court of Appeals is affirmed in part and reversed in part, and the case is remanded for proceedings consistent with this opinion.

---

[23] An *unqualified opinion*, the most favorable report an auditor may give, represents the auditor's finding that the company's financial statements fairly present the financial position of the company, the results of its operations, and the changes in its financial position for the period under audit, in conformity with consistently applied generally accepted accounting principles. See 1 AICPA, Statement on Auditing Standards §§ 510, 511.01 (1973). Alternatively, the auditor may give a *qualified opinion*, which states that the financial statements are fairly presented except for, or subject to, a departure from generally accepted accounting principles a change in accounting principles, or a material uncertainty. *Id.*, § 512. An *adverse opinion* is a reflection of the auditor's determination that the corporation's financial statements do not fairly present the financial position, results of operations, or changes in financial position of the company in conformity with generally accepted accounting principles; an adverse opinion is issued when the auditor determines that the corporation has materially misstated certain items or its financial statements. *Id.*, § 513. Finally, a *disclaimer of opinion* expresses the auditor's inability to draw a conclusion as to the accuracy of the corporate financial records. A disclaimer of opinion is generally issued when the auditor lacks sufficient information about the financial records to issue an overall opinion. *Id.*, § 514. See generally A. Arens & J. Loebbecke, Auditing: An Integrated Approach 643–660 (1976).

[24] **The inclusion in an audited financial statement of anything less than an unqualified opinion could send signals to stockholders, creditors, potential investors, and others that the independent auditor has been unable to give the corporation an unqualified bill of financial health. Such a public auditor's opinion could well have serious consequences for the corporation and its shareholders.**

[25] Indeed, rather than protecting the investing public by ensuring the accuracy of corporate financial records, insulation of tax accrual workpapers from disclosure might well undermine the public's confidence in the independent auditing process. The SEC requires the filing of audited financial statements in order to obviate the fear of loss from reliance on inaccurate information, thereby encouraging public investment in the Nation's industries. It is therefore not enough that financial statements be accurate; the public must also perceive them as being accurate. Public faith in the reliability of a corporation's financial statements depends upon the public perception of the outside auditor as an independent professional. Endowing the workpapers of an independent auditor with a work-product immunity would destroy the appearance of auditor's independence by creating the impression that the auditor is an advocate for the client. If investors were to view the auditor as an advocate for the corporate client, the value of the audit function itself might well be lost. See generally Arens & Loebbecke, *supra*, at 55–58.

Circuit Courts have split regarding the test for determining whether work product is "in anticipation of litigation. One approach is to apply a "because of"[26] test. The other involves a "primary purpose"[27] test.

C. THE INTER-PLAY OF ATTORNEYS AND ACCOUNTANTS

A *second type* of state law privileges involves the use of the attorney-client privilege. Application of the attorney privilege to encompass an accountant is fraught with nuances and frequent litigation. *Generally*, an attorney may employ an accountant or CPA to prepare an analysis of a matter in anticipation of litigation. This does not extend to someone to be used to assist the client; instead, it applies to an advisor who assists the lawyer. In 1961, the Second Circuit Court of Appeals rendered its opinion in *U.S. v. Kovel*,[28] which has helped spawn much of the analysis and law involving attorneys bringing accountants within their privilege. The Court emphasized that for the attorney privilege to reach an accountant, the advice being given must ultimately be legal advice, as opposed to accounting advice. The accountant role is more akin to an interpreter than as an accountant.

For Litigation, a CPA May Come Under the Attorney-Client Privilege

For this to work, be very careful. Follow the *Kovel* Letter format carefully.

The *Kovel* court was very critical of the lower court for inadequately developing the record, as was also critical of the parties for their harsh, if not dogmatic positions. Omitted parts of the opinion deal with burden of proof issues: ultimately, the matter involved criminal contempt because the accountant refused to answer grand jury questions; hence, the burden of proof fell to the government. Had the accountant answered, the court suggested the burden would have been on the accountant.

---

[26] United States v. Textron, Inc., 553 F.3d 87, 89 (3d Cir. 2009); Maine v. United States Dep't of the Interior, 298 F.3d 60, 70 (1st Cir. 2002).

[27] United States v. El Paso Co., 682 F.2d 530, 542 (5th Cir. 1982), cert. denied, 466 U.S. 944 (1984).

[28] U.S. v. Kovel, 296 F.2d 918 (2d Cir. 1961).

UNITED STATES V. KOVEL
296 F.2d 918 (2d Cir. 1961)

This appeal from a sentence for criminal contempt for refusing to answer a question asked in the course of an inquiry by a grand jury raises an important issue as to the application of the attorney-client privilege to a non-lawyer employed by a law firm. [* * *]

Kovel is a former Internal Revenue agent having accounting skills. Since 1943 he has been employed by [* * *] a law firm specializing in tax law. A grand jury in the Southern District of New York was investigating alleged Federal income tax violations by Hopps, a client of the law firm; Kovel was subpoenaed to appear on September 6, 1961 [* * *]. The law firm advised the Assistant United States Attorney that since Kovel was an employee under the direct supervision of the partners, Kovel could not disclose any communications by the client of the result of any work done for the client, unless the latter consented; the Assistant answered that the attorney-client privilege did not apply to one who was not an attorney.

[* * *] On September 7, the grand jury appeared before Judge Cashin. The Assistant United States Attorney informed the judge that Kovel had refused to answer 'several questions * * * on the grounds of attorney-client privilege'; he proffered 'respectable authority * * * that an accountant, even if he is retained or employed by a firm of attorneys cannot take the privilege.' The judge answered 'You don't have to give me any authority on that.' A court reporter testified that Kovel, after an initial claim of privilege had admitted receiving a statement of Hopps' assets and liabilities, but that, when asked 'what was the purpose of your receiving that,' had declined to answer on the ground of privilege 'Because the communication was received with a purpose, as stated by the client'; later questions and answers indicated the communication was a letter addressed to Kovel. After verifying that Kovel was not a lawyer, the judge directed him to answer, saying 'You have no privilege as such.' The reporter then read another question Kovel had refused to answer, 'Did you ever discuss with Mr. Hopps or give Mr. Hopps any information with regard to treatment for capital gains purposes of the Atlantic Beverage Corporation sale by him?' The judge again directed Kovel to answer, reaffirming 'There is no privilege—you are entitled to no privilege, as I understand the law.' Kovel asked whether he might say something; the judge instructed him to answer, saying 'I'm not going to listen.' Kovel also declined to tell what Hopps had said concerning a transaction underlying a bad debt deduction in Hopps' 1954 return, and whether Hopps had told him that a certain transfer of securities 'had no effect whatsoever' and was just a form of accommodation; the judge gave similar directions after the reporter had read each question and refusal to answer. Then the grand jury, the Assistant and Kovel returned to the grand jury room.

Later on September 7, they and Kovel's employer, Jerome Kamerman, now acting as his counsel, appeared again before Judge Cashin. The Assistant told the judge that Kovel had 'refused to answer some of the questions which you had directed him to answer.' A reporter reread so much of the transcript heretofore summarized as contained the first two refusals. The judge offered Kovel another opportunity to answer, reiterating the view, 'There is no privilege to this man at all.' Counsel referred to New York Civil Practice Act, § 353, which we quote in the margin,[29] and sought an adjournment until co-counsel could appear; the judge put the matter over until the next morning.

On the morning of September 8, the same dramatic personae, plus the added counsel, attended in open court. Counsel reiterated that an employee 'who sits with the client of the law firm * * * occupies the same status * * * as a clerk or stenographer or any other lawyer * * *'; the judge was equally clear that the privilege was never 'extended beyond the attorney.' In the course of a colloquy the Assistant made it plain that further questions beyond the two immediately at issue might be asked. After the judge had briefly retired, leaving the Assistant and Kovel with the grand jury, proceedings in open court resumed. The reporter recited that in the interval, on reappearing before the grand jury and being asked 'What was the purpose communicated to you by Mr. Hopps for your receiving from him an asset and liability statement of his personal financial situation?', Kovel had declined to answer. On again being directed to do so, Kovel declined 'on the ground that it is a privileged communication.' **The court held him in contempt, sentenced him to a year's imprisonment, ordered immediate commitment and denied bail.** Later in the day, the grand jury having indicted, Kovel was released until September 12, at which time, without opposition from the Government, I granted bail pending determination of this appeal. [* * *]

---

[29] 'An attorney or counselor at law shall not disclose, or be allowed to disclose, a communication, made by his client to him, or his advice given thereon, in the course of his professional employment, nor shall any clerk, stenographer or other person employed by such attorney or counselor * * * disclose, or be allowed to disclose, any such communication or advice.'

Decision under what circumstances, if any, the attorney-client privilege may include a communication to a nonlawyer by the lawyer's client is the resultant of two conflicting forces. One is the general teaching that 'The investigation of truth and the enforcement of testimonial duty demand the restriction, not the expansion, of these privileges,' [* * *]. The other is the more particular lesson 'That as, by reason of the complexity and difficulty of our law, litigation can only be properly conducted by professional men, it is absolutely necessary that a man * * * should have recourse to the assistance of professional lawyers, and * * * it is equally necessary * * * that he should be able to place unrestricted and unbounded confidence in the professional agent, and that the communications he so makes to him should be kept secret [* * *]. **Nothing in the policy of the privilege suggests that attorneys, simply by placing accountants, scientists or investigators on their payrolls and maintaining them in their offices, should be able to invest all**

> A CPA must be under the direction and control of the lawyer to come under the attorney-client privilege.

communications by clients to such persons with a privilege the law has not seen fit to extend when the latter _are operating under their own steam._ On the other hand, in contrast to the Tudor times when the privilege was first recognized, [* * *], **the complexities of modern existence prevent attorneys from effectively handling clients' affairs without the help of others**; few lawyers could now practice without the assistance of secretaries, file clerks, telephone operators, messengers, clerks not yet admitted to the bar, and aides of other sorts. 'The assistance of these agents being indispensable to his work and the communications of the client being often necessarily committed to them by the attorney or by the client himself, **the privilege must include all the persons who act as the attorney's agents.'** [* * *]

We cannot regard the privilege as confined to 'menial or ministerial' employees. Thus, we can see no significant difference between a case where the attorney sends a client speaking a foreign language to an interpreter to make a literal translation of the client's story; a second where the attorney, himself having some little knowledge of the foreign tongue, has a more knowledgeable non-lawyer employee in the room to help out; a third where someone to perform that same function has been brought along by the client; and a fourth where the attorney, ignorant of the foreign language, sends the client to a non-lawyer proficient in it, with instructions to interview the client on the attorney's behalf and then render his own summary of the situation, perhaps drawing on his own knowledge in the process, so that the attorney can give the client proper legal advice. All four cases meet every element of Wigmore's famous formulation, § 2292, '(1) Where legal advice of any kind is sought (2) from a professional legal adviser in his capacity as such, (3) the communications relating to that purpose, (4) made in confidence (5) by the client, (6) are at his instance permanently protected (7) from disclosure by himself or by the legal adviser, (8) except the protection be waived,' save (7); literally, none of them is within (7) since the disclosure [is not sought to be compelled from the client or the lawyer. Yet § 2301 of Wigmore would clearly recognize the privilege in the first case and the Government goes along to that extent; § 2301 would also recognize the privilege in the second case and § 2311 in the third unless the circumstances negated confidentiality. We find no valid policy reason for a different result in the fourth case, and we do not read Wigmore as thinking there is. Laymen consulting lawyers should not be expected to anticipate niceties perceptible only to judges—and not even to all of them.

This analogy of the client speaking a foreign language is by no means irrelevant to the appeal at hand. **Accounting concepts are a foreign language to some lawyers in almost all cases, and to almost all lawyers in some cases.** Hence the presence of an accountant,

> This court believed accounting is a foreign language to many, if not "almost all" lawyers.

whether hired by the lawyer or by the client, while the client is relating a complicated tax story to the lawyer, ought not destroy the privilege, any more than would that of the linguist in the second or third variations of the foreign language theme discussed above; the presence of the accountant is necessary, or at least highly useful, for the effective consultation between the client and the lawyer which the privilege is designed to permit. [* * *] By the same token, if the lawyer has directed the client, either in the specific case or generally, to tell his story in the first instance to an accountant engaged by the lawyer, who is then to interpret it so that the lawyer may better give legal advice, communications by the client reasonably related to that purpose ought fall within the privilege; there can be no more virtue in requiring the lawyer to sit by while the client pursues these possibly tedious preliminary conversations with the accountant than in insisting on the lawyer's physical presence while the client dictates a statement to the lawyer's secretary or in interviewed by a clerk not yet admitted to practice. What is vital to the privilege is that the communication be made in confidence for the purpose of obtaining legal advice from the lawyer. **If what is sought is not legal advice but only accounting service, as in Olender v. United States, 210 F.2d 795, 805–806 (9 Cir. 1954), see Reisman v. Caplin, 61–2 U.S.T.C. P9673 (1961), or if the advice sought is the accountant's rather than the lawyer's, no privilege exists.** We recognize this draws what may seem to some a rather arbitrary line between a case where the client communicates first to his own accountant (no privilege as to such communications, even though he later consults his lawyer on the same matter, Gariepy v. United States, 189 F.2d 459, 463 (6

Cir. 1951)),[30] and others, where the client in the first instance consults a lawyer who retains an accountant as a listening post, or consults the lawyer with his own accountant present. But that is the inevitable consequence of having to reconcile the absence of a privilege for accountants and the effective operation of the privilege of client and lawyer under conditions where the lawyer needs outside help. We realize also that the line we have drawn will not be so easy to apply as the simpler positions urged on us by the parties—the district judges will scarcely be able to leave the decision of such cases to computers; but the distinction has to be made if the privilege is neither to be unduly expanded nor to become a trap. [= * *]

Lawyers who seek *Kovel* protection should carefully draft a "*Kovel* Letter" or "*Kovel* Engagement". It should provide:

- The accountant works for the lawyer.

- The accountant reports directly to the lawyer or members of his/her firm.

- The accountant must keep all work papers, opinions, and information confidential. The work papers belong to the lawyer and will be turned over to the lawyer upon request, including all copies.

- The accountant will provide advice to the lawyer, and not to the client directly without the express permission from the lawyer. The accountant generally should bill the lawyer, not the client. The lawyer can then pass on the charge.

- If the accountant separately advises the client on other matters, the accountant agrees to bill the client separately. Generally, however, a lawyer may prefer to not use an accountant with either a pre-existing or other relationship to the client.

In recent years, the IRS has aggressively sought to limit the *Kovel* Doctrine, with some success, particularly in relation to tax accrual work papers[31] and in the preparation of tax returns.[32]

---

[30] We do not deal in this opinion with the question under what circumstances, if any, such communications could be deemed privileged on the basis that they were being made to the accountant as the client's agent for the purpose of subsequent communication by the accountant to the lawyer; communications by the client's agent to the attorney are privileged, 8 Wigmore, Evidence, § 2317–1. See Lalance & Grosjean Mfg. Co. v. Haberman Mfg. Co., 87 F. 563 (C.C.S.D.N.Y., 1898).

[31] See, United States v. Deloitte LLP, 610 F.3d 129 (D.C. Cir. 2010). *See also* FASB 48 relating to accounting for tax/book differences: tax accrual work papers arise from it.

[32] United States v. Gurtner, 474 F.2d 297 (9th Cir. 1973) (attorney sent client to CPA for preparation of tax returns. CPA did not come under the attorney's privilege.) *See*, Kossman, *CPAs and Privileged Communications*, THE TAX ADVISOR (Oct. 1, 2013), *See also*, Denzil Causey and

D. THE LAWYER WHO ALSO ACTS AS AN ACCOUNTANT

Many lawyers are also CPAs. In addition, many lawyers, especially tax lawyers, often do work more commonly performed by non-lawyers. For example, some tax lawyers also prepare tax returns. As the following decision illustrates, clients who hire lawyers to perform non-legal work may waive the attorney-client privilege not only as to the communications, opinions and work products performed in purely non-legal matters, but also in relationships involving mixed professional roles.

Legal Advice from an Attorney _May Not_ Be Privileged if in Relation to the Preparation of a Tax Return

This is astonishing but true. Some courts do not consider tax preparation to be legal work!

For example, a lawyer may be a skilled carpenter. Clearly, communications with him and his client purely related to carpentry work are not privileged. Similarly, as the Seventh Circuit explains, traditional accounting work performed by a lawyer does not have an umbrella of attorney-client privilege accompanying it. Thus, lawyers who perform tax return preparation work or financial statement preparation work should be careful in evaluating whether the attorney client privilege attaches to communications and work product in relation to the work. If the work is _clearly and solely_ in relation to litigation—perhaps a dissolution of marriage, a product liability case, or a claim for personal injury—the privilege likely attaches. If, however, the facts are less clear, or the use is mixed—perhaps the work product is useful in evaluating a claim, but it is also important in management decisions—the ambit of the privilege is less clear.

UNITED STATES V. FREDERICK
182 F.3d 496 (7th Cir. 1999)

POSNER, CHIEF JUDGE. These appeals challenge an order enforcing summonses that the Internal Revenue Service issued to Richard Frederick. **Frederick is both a lawyer and an accountant**, and **he both provides legal representation to, and prepares the tax returns** of, Randolph and Karin Lenz and their company, KCS Industries, Inc. The IRS is

Frances McNair, An Analysis of State Accountant-Client Privilege statutes and Public Policy Implications for the Accountant-Client Relationship, 27 AM BUS. L. J. 535 (1990).

investigating the Lenzes and their company, and the summonses directed Frederick to hand over hundreds of documents that may be germane to the investigation. Frederick balked at handing over all of them, claiming that some were protected by either the attorney-client privilege or the work-product privilege (or both). His refusal precipitated this enforcement proceeding. 26 U.S.C. § 7604(b). The district judge examined the documents *in camera* and ruled that some were privileged but others were not. The appeals challenge the latter ruling.

[* * * *] The presumption in this circuit is and we hope will remain that the clear-error standard is the proper standard for appellate review of determinations of mixed questions of fact and law. This presumption is a helpful simplification of the law of appellate review, with no downside that we can see; and there is certainly nothing in the circumstances of the present case, or the class of cases that it exemplifies (non-constitutional privilege cases), to rebut it.

Most of the documents in issue were created in connection with Frederick's preparation of the Lenzes' tax returns. They are drafts of the returns (including schedules), **worksheets** containing the **financial data** and computations required to fill in the returns, and correspondence relating to the returns. These are the kinds of document that accountants and other preparers generate as an incident to preparing their clients' returns, or that the taxpayers themselves generate if they prepare their own returns, though in the latter case there is unlikely to be correspondence. The materiality of the documents to the IRS's investigation of the Lenzes is not in issue.

There is no common law accountant's or tax preparer's privilege, *Couch v. United States*, 409 U.S. 322, 335, 34 L. Ed. 2d 548, 93 S. Ct. 611 (1973); *United States v. Arthur Young & Co.*, 465 U.S. 805, 817–19, 79 L. Ed. 2d 826, 104 S. Ct. 1495 (1984), and **a taxpayer must not be allowed, by hiring a lawyer to do the work that an accountant, or other tax preparer, or the taxpayer himself or herself, normally would do, to obtain greater protection from government investigators than a taxpayer who did not use a lawyer as his tax preparer would be entitled to.** *United States v. Lawless*, 709 F.2d 485, 487–88 (7th Cir. 1983); *United States v. Bornstein*, 977 F.2d 112, 116–17 (4th Cir. 1992); *In re Grand Jury Investigation*, 842 F.2d 1223, 1224–25 (11th Cir. 1987); *United States v. Davis*, 636 F.2d 1028, 1043 (5th Cir. 1981). **To rule otherwise would be to impede tax investigations, reward lawyers for doing nonlawyers' work, and**

> This court does not consider tax preparation to be legal work.
>
> If filing reports with the SEC or EPA is legal work, why would filing reports with the IRS not be the same?

create a privileged position for lawyers in competition with other tax preparers—and to do all this without promoting the legitimate aims of the attorney-client and work-product privileges. The attorney-client privilege is intended to encourage people who find themselves involved in actual or potential legal disputes to be candid with any lawyer they retain to advise them. *Upjohn Co. v. United States*, 449 U.S. 383, 389, 66 L. Ed. 2d 584, 101 S. Ct. 677 (1981). The hope is that this will assist the lawyer in giving the client good advice (which may head off litigation, bring the client's conduct into conformity with law, or dispel legal concerns that are causing the client unnecessary anxiety or inhibiting him from engaging in lawful, socially productive activity) and will also avoid the disruption of the lawyer-client relationship that is brought about when a lawyer is sought to be used as a witness against his client. **The work-product privilege is intended to prevent a litigant from taking a free ride on the research and thinking of his opponent's lawyer and to avoid the resulting deterrent to a lawyer's committing his thoughts to paper.** *United States v. Nobles*, 422 U.S. 225, 236–39, 45 L. Ed. 2d 141, 95 S. Ct. 2160 (1975); *Hickman v. Taylor*, 329 U.S. 495, 510–11, 91 L. Ed. 451, 67 S. Ct. 385 (1947); *id.* at 516 (Jackson, J., concurring).

Communications from a client that neither reflect the lawyer's thinking nor are made for the purpose of eliciting the lawyer's professional advice or other legal assistance are not privileged. **The information that a person furnishes the preparer of his tax return is furnished for the purpose of enabling the preparation of the return, not the preparation of a brief or an opinion letter. Such information therefore is not privileged.**

We do not, however, accept the government's argument that there is no issue of privilege here because the information was transmitted to a tax preparer with the expectation of its being relayed to a third party, namely the IRS. It **is true that "if the client transmitted the information so that it might be used on the tax return, such a transmission destroys any expectation of confidentiality."** [* * *] That is, the transmittal operates as a waiver of the privilege. But the tax preparer here was also the taxpayers' lawyer, and it cannot be assumed that everything transmitted to him by the taxpayer was intended to assist him in his tax-preparation function and thus might be conveyed to the IRS, rather than in his legal-representation function. [* * *]

We also reject the government's argument that numerical information can never fall within the attorney-client or work-product privilege. Cf. *United States v. Schwimmer*, 892 F.2d 237, 242 (2d Cir. 1989); *United States v. Davis, supra*, 636 F.2d at 1043; *In re Grand Jury Proceedings*, 601 F.2d 162, 171–72 (5th Cir. 1979). Such cases are rare, but they can be imagined. Suppose a lawyer prepared an estimate of his client's damages; the estimate would be numerical, but insofar as it reflected the lawyer's professional assessment of what to ask the jury for it would be attorney work product. Similarly, if the lawyer asked his client how much he had obtained in the theft for which he was being prosecuted and the client answered, "$10,000," the answer would be protected by the attorney-client privilege. But we do not agree with the appellants that the district judge based his ruling on the erroneous view that numbers can never be privileged. He found no basis for privileging these numbers, remarking, rightly, "It cannot be argued that numbers in the hands of the accountant are different from numbers in the hands of a lawyer."

Besides the information supplied to Frederick by the Lenzes, **there are the worksheets, which Frederick prepared and which doubtless reflect some of his own thinking.** But the Supreme Court has held that **an accountant's worksheets are not privileged**, *United States v. Arthur Young & Co., supra*, 465 U.S. at 817–19, and a lawyer's privilege, as we explained earlier, is no greater when he is doing accountant's work. A complicating factor is that when Frederick was doing these worksheets and filling out the Lenzes' tax returns, he knew that the IRS was investigating the Lenzes and their company, albeit in connection with different tax years, and he was representing them in that investigation. But people who are under investigation and represented by a lawyer have the same duty as anyone else to file tax returns. They should not be permitted, by using a lawyer in lieu of another form of tax preparer, to obtain greater confidentiality than other taxpayers. **By using Frederick as their tax preparer, the Lenzes ran the risk that his legal cogitations born out of his legal representation of them would creep into his worksheets and so become discoverable by the government. The Lenzes undoubtedly benefited from having their lawyer do their returns, but they must take the bad with the good; if his legal thinking infects his worksheets, that does not cast the cloak of privilege over the worksheets; they are still accountants' worksheets, unprotected no matter who prepares them.**

Put differently, a dual-purpose document—a document prepared for use in preparing tax returns and for use in litigation—is not privileged; otherwise, people in or contemplating litigation would be able to invoke, in effect, an accountant's privilege, provided that they used their lawyer to fill out their tax returns. **And likewise if a taxpayer involved in or contemplating litigation sat down with his lawyer (who was also his tax preparer) to discuss both legal strategy and the preparation of his tax returns, and in the course of the discussion bandied about numbers related to both consultations: the taxpayer could not shield these numbers from the Internal Revenue Service. This would be** not because they were numbers, but because, being intended

> This is astonishing.

(though that was not the only intention) for use in connection with the preparation of tax returns, they were an unprivileged category of numbers.

The most difficult question presented by this appeal, and one on which we cannot find any precedent, relates to documents, numerical and otherwise, prepared in connection with audits of the taxpayers' returns. An example is a memo from Frederick to a paralegal asking her for the amount that Mr. Lenz and his corporation had paid Frederick for legal services rendered personally to Lenz in 1992. The memo was prepared to help Frederick respond to questions raised in an audit of the Lenzes' and the corporation's tax returns. An audit is both a stage in the determination of tax liability, often leading to the submission of revised tax returns, and a possible antechamber to litigation. **When a revenue agent is merely verifying the accuracy of a return, often with the assistance of the taxpayer's accountant, this is accountants' work and it remains such even if the person rendering the assistance is a lawyer rather than an accountant.** Throwing the cloak of privilege over this type of audit-related work of the taxpayer's representative would create an accountant's privilege usable only by lawyers. If, however, the taxpayer is accompanied to the audit by a lawyer who is there to deal with issues of statutory interpretation or case law that the revenue agent may have raised in connection with his examination of the taxpayer's return, the lawyer is doing lawyer's work and the attorney-client privilege may attach. But the documents in issue do not, so far as we are able to determine, relate to such representation.

We should consider the possible bearing of a new statute, 26 U.S.C. § 7525, which extends the attorney-client privilege to "a federally authorized tax practitioner," that is, a nonlawyer who is nevertheless authorized to practice before the Internal Revenue Service. § 7525(a)(3)(A). Nonlawyers (including tax preparers, many of them accountants) have long been allowed to practice before it. 5 U.S.C. § 500(c);

> IRC § 7525 protects tax practitioner communications but not work product.

31 C.F.R. §§ 10.3, 10.7(c)(viii). **The new statute protects communications between a taxpayer and a federally authorized tax practitioner "to the extent the communication would be considered a privileged communication if it were between a taxpayer and an attorney." § 7525(a)(1). (It does not protect work product.)** Nothing in the new statute suggests that these nonlawyer practitioners are entitled to privilege when they are doing other than lawyers' work; and so the statute would not change our analysis even if it were applicable to this case, which it is not, because it is applicable only to communications made on or after July 22, 1998, the date the statute was enacted. See Note following 26 U.S.C. § 7525.

We have looked at all the documents that Frederick argues are privileged. Most are dual-purpose documents, about which no more may be said; some were not even submitted to the district judge for consideration of whether they might be privileged; in others as well, privilege was waived. We cannot find any clear errors in the district judge's rulings.

Affirmed.

LESSON THREE-C

AUDIT OPINIONS

■ ■ ■

---

1. AUDITOR ENGAGEMENT AND OPINION LETTERS

Arguably, the most important part of audited financial statements is the final auditor's opinion letter, which will appear at the beginning of the financial statements.

A. ENGAGEMENT LETTER

Prior to the audit, the auditor will issue an audit engagement letter detailing the responsibility of the auditor.[33] This will come from the auditor to management and to the audit committee of the Board of Directors. It, too, is a very important document. Lawyers who have serious questions or doubts about audited financial statements should seek the engagement letter. Notice several important aspects of the engagement letter:

- The objective of the audit is to express an opinion of financial statements prepared by management.

- The opinion concerns whether the statements conform to GAAP. A similar letter would apply for international audits in conformity with IFRS.

- The audit will conform to GAAS.

- The audit will *not* examine everything; instead, it will examine statistically significant sample of various documents, receivables, payables, and such.

---

[33] AUC section 210; SAS number 122.

- The auditor will request information from the client's counsel who will bill separately. This is essential: the client must authorize counsel to respond regarding possible litigation and other liabilities that may be privileged. Without that information, the auditor cannot express an opinion regarding whether the information in the statements is "fair."

- The auditor looks for "material" misstatements: immaterial items are not relevant.

- The auditor provides "reasonable assurance" of his/her opinion; hence, a risk exists that fraud or illegal acts will be undetected. A "fraud audit" would be far more intrusive and more expensive. A routine audit, with the assurance of adequate internal controls, is not designed to detect fraud.

- If the auditor finds evidence of insufficient internal controls, he/she will discuss that with management. Inadequate internal controls will likely result in other than an "unqualified opinion." But, per the following letter, the auditor has not been engaged to advise on changing or improving internal controls: that is a separate process and requires a separate engagement and fee.

- The auditor may inform management of problems involving some accounts or records. Management will have an opportunity to correct those problems prior to the issuance of the opinion.

- Auditors require unrestricted access to records, assets, and employees. Limitations on access will result in an opinion other than "unqualified" or will result in withdrawal from the audit.

- The audit fee is not contingent on the results of the audit, or the opinion expressed.

A sample engagement letter[34] follows, with annotations. Pay special attention to the highlighted and annotated portions.

[Date]

[Client Contact]

[Client Name]

[Client Address]

Dear [Client Contact]:

---

[34] *Id.* at 116–118.

This letter is to confirm our understanding of the terms and objectives of our engagement and the nature and limitations of the services we will provide.

We will audit the consolidated balance sheet of [Client Name] as of [Date], and the related consolidated statements of operations, retained earnings (deficit), and cash flows for the year then ended.

The objective of our audit is the expression of an opinion about whether your consolidated financial statements are fairly presented, in all **material** respects, in conformity with **accounting principles generally accepted** in the United States of America. Our audit will be conducted in accordance with **auditing standards generally accepted** in the United States and will include tests of your accounting records and other procedures we consider necessary to enable us to express such an opinion. **If our opinion is other than unqualified, we will discuss the reasons with you in advance.** If, for any reason, we are unable to complete the audit or are unable to form or have not formed an opinion, we may decline to express an opinion or to issue a report as a result of this engagement.

> The auditor will discuss the opinion in advance if it will be other than unqualified. That may give management a chance to correct a concern.

> The auditor will seek a "response letter" from counsel regarding contingent liabilities.

Our procedures will include tests of documentary evidence supporting the transactions recorded in the accounts, tests of the physical existence of inventories, and direct confirmation of receivables and payables and certain other assets and liabilities by correspondence with selected customers, creditors, and financial institutions. **We will also request written representations from your attorneys as part of the engagement, and they may bill you for responding to this inquiry.** At the conclusion of our audit, we will require certain written representations from you about the financial statements and related matters.

An audit includes examining, on a **test basis**, evidence supporting the amounts and disclosures in the financial statements. Consequently, our audit will involve judgment about the number of transactions to be examined and the areas to be tested. Also, we will plan and perform the audit to obtain reasonable assurance about whether the financial statements are **free of material misstatement**. Because an audit is designed to provide **reasonable, but not absolute, assurance** and because we will not perform a detailed examination of all transactions, **there is a risk that material errors, fraud, or illegal acts, may exist and not be detected by us**. In addition, an audit is not designed to detect immaterial

> Unless this is a "fraud audit" because of suspected fraud, the auditor may not discover fraud. Thus do not assume an unqualified opinion means the statements are not fraudulent.

errors, fraud, or other illegal acts or illegal acts that do not have a direct effect on the financial statements. **Our engagement cannot, therefore, be relied upon to disclose errors, fraud, or other illegal acts that may exist**. However, we will inform you of any material errors that come to our attention and any fraud that comes to our attention. We will also inform you of any other illegal acts that come to our attention, unless clearly inconsequential. **Our responsibility as auditors is limited to the period covered by our audit and does not extend to any later periods of which we are not engaged as auditors.**

Our audit will include obtaining an understanding of your **internal controls** sufficient to plan the audit and to determine the nature, timing, and extent of audit procedures to be performed. An audit is not designed to provide assurance on internal controls or to identify reportable conditions, that is, significant deficiencies or material weaknesses in the design or operation of internal control. Accordingly, **we have no responsibility to identify and communicate significant deficiencies or material weaknesses in your internal controls** as part of this engagement, and our engagement cannot be relied upon to disclose the same. **However, during the audit, if we become aware of such reportable conditions, we will communicate them to you.**

Prior to preparation and execution of this engagement letter, we discussed with you the fact that we provide clients with services specifically focused on identifying and addressing weaknesses in internal controls (internal control review), and on searching for the existence of fraud within your company (fraud audit). We further explained the additional costs associated with such different levels of service. After consideration of such services, you have informed us that you wish to retain us to perform only the audit services described in this letter.

You are responsible for adopting sound accounting policies, for maintaining an adequate and efficient accounting system, for safeguarding assets, for authorizing transactions, for retaining supporting documentation for those transactions, and for devising a system of internal controls that will, among other things, help assure the preparation of proper financial statements. You are also responsible for adjusting the financial statements to correct material misstatements and for confirming to us in the management representation letter that the effects of any uncorrected misstatements aggregated by us during the current engagement and pertaining to the latest period presented are immaterial, both individually and in the aggregate, to the financial statements taken as a whole. Furthermore, you are responsible for management decisions and functions, for designating a competent employee to oversee any of the services we provide, and for evaluating the adequacy and results of those services.

You are responsible for the design and implementation of programs and controls to prevent and detect fraud, and for informing us about all known or suspected fraud affecting the Company involving (a) management (b) employees who have significant roles in internal control, and (c) others where the fraud could have a material effect on the financial statements. You are also responsible for informing us of your knowledge of any allegations of fraud or suspected fraud affecting the Company received in communications from employees, former employees, regulators, or others. In addition, you are responsible for identifying and ensuring that the entity complies with applicable laws and regulations.

You are responsible for making all financial records and related information available to us and for the accuracy and completeness of that information. We will advise you about appropriate accounting principles and their application and will assist in the preparation of your financial statements, but the responsibility for the financial statements remains with you. **As part of our engagement, we may propose standard, adjusting, or correcting journal entries to your financial statements. You are responsible for reviewing the entries and understanding the nature of any proposed entries and the impact they have on the financial statements.**

> Management prepares the financial statements, not the auditor. The auditor may suggest changes, but management must decide whether to accept the suggestions.

In order for us to complete this engagement, and to do so efficiently, we require **unrestricted access** to the following documents and individuals within your company: _____.
We understand that your employees will prepare all cash, accounts receivable, and other confirmations we request and will locate any documents selected by us for testing. Any failure to provide such cooperation, and to do so on a timely basis, will impede our services, and may require us to suspend our services or withdraw from the engagement.

Our fees for this engagement are not contingent on the results of our services. Rather, our fees for this engagement will be based on our standard hourly rates, as set forth on the attached rate sheet. In addition, you agree to reimburse us for any of our out-of-pocket costs incurred in connection with the performance of our services. We estimate that our fee for these services will range from approximately _____ to _____. You acknowledge that this range is not a limit to the total fees we may charge for our services, and that our fees may actually exceed that range. However, in the event that we encounter unusual circumstances that would require us to expand the scope of the engagement, and/or if we anticipate our fees exceeding the aforementioned range, we will adjust our estimate, and obtain your prior approval before continuing with the engagement.

Prior to commencing our services, we require that you provide us with a retainer in the amount of _____. The retainer will be applied against our final invoice, and any unused portion will be returned to you upon our collection of all outstanding fees and costs related to this engagement. Our fees and costs will be billed monthly, and are payable upon receipt. Invoices unpaid 30 days past the billing date may be deemed delinquent, and are subject to an interest charge of 1.0% per month. We reserve the right to suspend our services or to withdraw from this engagement in the event that any of our invoices are deemed delinquent. In the event that any collection action is required to collect unpaid balances due us, you agree to reimburse us for our costs of collection, including attorneys' fees.

If we elect to terminate our services for nonpayment, or for any other reason provided for in this letter, our engagement will be deemed to have been completed upon written notification of termination, even if we have not completed our report. You will be obligated to compensate us for all time expended, and to reimburse us for all of our out-of-pocket costs, through the date of termination.

In connection with this engagement, we may communicate with you or others via email transmission. As emails can be intercepted and read, disclosed, or otherwise used or communicated by an unintended third party, or may not be delivered to each of the parties to whom they are directed and only to such parties, we cannot guarantee or warrant that emails from us will be properly delivered and read only by the addressee. Therefore, we specifically disclaim and waive any liability or responsibility whatsoever for interception or unintentional disclosure of emails transmitted by us in connection with the performance of this engagement. In that regard, you agree that we shall have no liability for any loss or damage to any person or entity resulting from the use of email transmissions, including any consequential, incidental, direct, indirect, or special damages, such as loss of revenues or anticipated profits, or disclosure or communication of confidential or proprietary information.

You are responsible to notify us in advance of your intent to reproduce our report for any reason, in whole or in part, and to give us the opportunity to review any printed material containing our report before its issuance. Such notification does not constitute an acknowledgement on our part of any third party's intent to rely on the financial statements. With regard to financial statements published electronically on your internet website, you understand that electronic sites are a means to reproduce and distribute information. We are not required to read the information contained in your sites, or to consider the consistency of other information in the electronic site with the original document.

It is our policy to retain engagement documentation for a period of seven years, after which time we will commence the process of destroying the contents of our engagement files. To the extent we accumulate any of your original records during the engagement, those documents will be returned to you promptly upon completion of the engagement, and you will provide us with a receipt for the return of such records. The balance of our engagement file, other than the compiled financial statement, which we will provide to you at the conclusion of the engagement, is our property, and we will provide copies of such documents at our discretion and if compensated for any time and costs associated with the effort.

In the event we are required to respond to a subpoena, court order or other legal process for the production of documents and/or testimony relative to information we obtained and/or prepared during the course of this engagement, you agree to compensate us at our hourly rates, as set forth above, for the time we expend in connection with such response, and to reimburse us for all of our out-of-pocket costs incurred in that regard.

In the event that we are or may be obligated to pay any cost, settlement, judgment, fine, penalty, or similar award or sanction as a result of a claim, investigation, or other proceeding instituted by any third party, then to the extent that such obligation is or may be a direct or indirect result of your intentional or knowing misrepresentation or provision to us of inaccurate or incomplete information in connection with this engagement, and not any failure on our part to comply with professional standards, you agree to indemnify us, defend us, and hold us harmless as against such obligations.

You agree that any dispute (other than our efforts to collect an outstanding invoice) that may arise regarding the meaning, performance or enforcement of this engagement or any prior engagement that we have performed for you, will, prior to resorting to litigation, be submitted to mediation, and that the parties will engage in the mediation process in good faith once a written request to mediate has been given by any party to the engagement. Any mediation initiated as a result of this engagement shall be administered within the county of [County and State], by [Name of Mediation Organization], according to its mediation rules, and any ensuing litigation shall be conducted within said county, according to [State] law. The results of any such mediation shall be binding only upon agreement of each party to be bound. The costs of any mediation proceeding shall be shared equally by the participating parties.

Any litigation arising out of this engagement, except actions by us to enforce payment of our professional invoices, must be filed within one year from the completion of the engagement, notwithstanding any statutory provision to the contrary.

This engagement letter is contractual in nature, and includes all of the relevant terms that will govern the engagement for which it has been prepared. The terms of this letter supersede any prior oral or written representations or commitments by or between the parties. Any material changes or additions to the terms set forth in this letter will only become effective if evidenced by a written amendment to this letter, signed by all of the parties.

If, after full consideration and consultation with counsel if so desired, you agree that the foregoing terms shall govern this engagement, please sign this letter in the space provided and return the original signed letter to me, keeping a fully-executed copy for your records.

Thank you for your attention to this matter, and please contact me with any questions that you may have.

Very truly yours,

[Firm Contact]

[Title]

ACCEPTED AND AGREED:

[CLIENT NAME]

_____   _____

By: [Name of Signatory]   Date

Its: [Title]

_____

B. OPINION LETTER

Audit opinion letters have six possible formats:

- Unqualified opinion.
- Modified unqualified opinion.
- Modified opinion.
- Adverse opinion.
- Disclaimer of an opinion.
- Interim opinion.

An unqualified opinion is what you as a lawyer should look for. Anything else is cause for concern. If you are not qualified to judge an opinion other than one that is "unqualified," you should seek expert advice.

Read the Opinion

Anything other than an unqualified opinion should concern you. Read it carefully.

An unqualified opinion should look exactly—*or very close to it*—like the samples.

The audit opinion appears at the beginning of the financial statements. A sample audit opinion letter for pre-2013 engagements follows. Traditionally, it contained the same three paragraphs and did not vary significantly; hence, reading an audit opinion letter is not complicated: the reader should look (pre-2013) for essentially what follows. Anything different would be a red flag, as discussed below. The post-2013 letter is similar.

Independent Auditor's Report

Board of Directors, Stockholders, Owners, and/or Management of ABC Company, Inc.

123 Main St.

Anytown, Anystate

We have audited the accompanying Balance Sheet of ABC Company, Inc. (the Company) as of December 31, 20XX and the related statements of Income, Retained Earnings, and Cash Flows for the year then ended. These Financial Statements are the responsibility of the Company's management. Our responsibility is to express an opinion on these financial statements based on our audit.

We conducted our audit in accordance with generally accepted auditing standards. Those standards require that we plan and perform the audit to obtain reasonable assurance about whether the financial statements are free of material misstatement. An audit includes examining, on a test basis, evidence supporting the amounts and disclosures in the financial statements. An audit also includes assessing the accounting principles used and significant estimates made by management, as well as evaluating the overall financial statement presentation. We believe that our audit provides a reasonable basis for our opinion.

In our opinion, the financial statements referred to above present fairly, in all material respects, the financial position of the Company as of December 31, 20XX, and the results of its operations and its cash flows for the year then ended in accordance with generally accepted accounting principles.

Signature

Auditor's Name and Address

1) Unqualified Opinion

A post-2013 sample unqualified opinion follows. It conforms with SAS 134 and SAS 137. The most important part is the final paragraph that should not deviate from that single sentence. As discussed below, some deviations are not overly alarming, but any deviation is cause for concern. As with the engagement letter, notice the emphasis on "materiality" and "fairness": the opinion is not a guarantee of perfection. Also notice the conformity to GAAP. For an international opinion letter, the auditor would require, instead, conformity to IFRS.

INDEPENDENT AUDITOR'S REPORT[35]

Board of Directors, Stockholders, Owners, and/or Management of ABC Company, Inc.

123 Main St.

Anytown, Any Country

---

[35] New format based on SAS 122 and SAS 123, which became AU–C § 700 in 2014 (and AU 700 in 2015) per the Clarity Project. Note: this document is copyrighted by the FASB and used with permission for educational purposes only. Emphasis added.

We have audited the accompanying financial statements of ABC Company, Inc. (a California corporation), which comprise the balance sheet as of December 31, 20XX, and the related statements of income, retained earnings, and cash flows for the year then ended, and the related notes to the financial statements.

Management's Responsibility for the Financial Statements

Management is responsible for the preparation and fair presentation of these consolidated financial statements in accordance with U.S. generally accepted accounting principles; this includes the design, implementation, and maintenance of internal control relevant to the preparation and fair presentation of consolidated financial statements that are free from material misstatement, whether due to fraud or error.

Auditor's Responsibility

Our responsibility is to express an opinion on these consolidated financial statements based on our audit. We conducted our audit in accordance with U.S. generally accepted auditing standards. Those standards require that we plan and perform the audit to obtain reasonable assurance about whether the consolidated financial statements are free from material misstatement. An audit involves performing procedures to obtain audit evidence about the amounts and disclosures in the consolidated financial statements. The procedures selected depend on the auditors' judgment, including the assessment of the risks of material misstatement of the consolidated financial statements, whether due to fraud or error. In making those risk assessments, the auditor considers internal control relevant to the entity's preparation and fair presentation of the consolidated financial statements in order to design audit procedures that are appropriate in the circumstances, but not for the purpose of expressing an opinion on the effectiveness of the entity's internal control. Accordingly, we express no such opinion. An audit also includes evaluating the appropriateness of accounting policies used and the reasonableness of significant accounting estimates made by management, as well as evaluating the overall presentation of the consolidated financial statements. We believe that the audit evidence we have obtained is sufficient and appropriate to provide a basis for our audit opinion.

Opinion

In our opinion, the financial statements referred to above present fairly, in all material respects, the financial position of ABC Company, Inc. as of December 31, 20XX, and the results of its operations and its cash flows for the

year then ended in accordance with U.S. generally accepted accounting principles.

AUDITOR'S SIGNATURE

Auditor's name and address

---

2) Modified Unqualified Opinion

A modified unqualified opinion may result for several reasons, including:

- A change in who did the audit.

- Something requires special emphasis.

- Some going concern doubt.

A _change of auditors_ is always a matter of concern, although the reasons may be innocent and the consequences immaterial. Entities change auditors for many legitimate reasons. Perhaps they grow too large for the old audit firm or expand operations to areas not convenient for the old firm. Or perhaps the old firm mergers with another or ends its operations. But a change can also occur for less legitimate reasons. Perhaps the auditor and management disagreed regarding the treatment of material items. Arguably, a regular change is helpful, as it provides a fresh perspective and reduces the chance for long-term collusion between management and the auditor.

When a publicly traded company changes auditors, it must file a Form 8-K with the SEC. Changing auditors (as opposed to the lead auditor) is not common; hence, it is a significant event when it occurs. Instructions to Form 8-K provide:

Section 4—Matters Related to Accountants and Financial Statements Item 4.01 Changes in Registrant's Certifying Accountant.

(a) If an independent accountant who was previously engaged as the principal accountant to audit the registrant's financial statements, or an independent accountant upon whom the principal accountant expressed reliance in its report regarding a significant subsidiary, resigns (or indicates that it declines to stand for re-appointment after completion of the current audit) or is dismissed, disclose the information required by Item 304(a)(1) of Regulation S-K (17 CFR 229.304(a)(1) of this chapter), including compliance with Item 304(a)(3) of Regulation S-K (17 CFR 229.304(a)(3) of this chapter).

(b) If a new independent accountant has been engaged as either the principal accountant to audit the registrant's financial statements or as an independent accountant on whom the principal accountant is expected to express reliance in its report regarding a significant subsidiary, the registrant must disclose the information required by Item 304(a)(2) of Regulation S-K (17 CFR 229.304(a)(2)). Instruction. The resignation or dismissal of an independent accountant, or its refusal to stand for re-appointment, is a reportable event separate from the engagement of a new independent accountant. On some occasions, two reports on Form 8-K are required for a single change in accountants, the first on the resignation (or refusal to stand for re-appointment) or dismissal of the former accountant and the second when the new accountant is engaged. Information required in the second Form 8-K in such situations need not be provided to the extent that it has been reported previously in the first Form 8-K.

The first opinion letter from the new auditor will normally be a modified unqualified opinion, noting the auditor change. Standing alone, an opinion for a set of financial statements could arguably be unqualified; however, when the statements are used to show comparisons with earlier years, the unqualified nature evaporates. Ultimately, auditors exercise discretion in how they conduct the audit as well as in how they apply GAAP; hence, statements certified by different firms are not fully comparable.

Occasionally, the auditor will be comfortable with the financial statements, but will want to _emphasize a particular point_. The modified unqualified opinion with thus contain an "emphasis paragraph" in which the auditor essentially says "Pay some extra attention to this issue. We think the statements are fair but pay attention." An example could involve important pending litigation with an unclear outcome. Or it might involve a change in a prior period opinion that affects how the user will compare current results with prior results. Or the company may have substantial transactions with related parties. In such a case, the auditor may believe the reported results are fair, but nevertheless also believe a user should be aware of and cautious regarding those matters.

Third, the auditor may have some _going concern doubt_ regarding the entity, though not so much as to justify an adverse opinion. Sample language for such an emphasis paragraph would be:

The accompanying financial statements have been prepared assuming that the Company will continue as a going concern. As discussed in Note (X) to the financial statements, the Company has suffered recurring losses and has a net capital deficiency. That raise substantial doubt about its ability to continue as a going concern. Management's plans in regard to these matters are also described in Note (X). The financial statements do not include any adjustments that might result from the outcome of this uncertainty.[36]

If you were to see this paragraph—or something similar to it—you should pay very close attention.

3) Qualified Modified Opinion

A qualified modified opinion follows the standard unqualified format; however, it conditions the opinion because of some irregularity. It does so in an "except for" paragraph explaining the condition. The irregularity is not one such that the auditor finds the statements to be unfair: that would result in an *adverse opinion*. Instead, the qualification may result from such things as:

- the inability of the auditor to examine a particular asset

- the necessity of the auditor's reliance on the opinion of another auditor not legally associated with the primary auditor, or

- a single deviation from GAAP, which does not affect the overall fairness of the statements.

Each of these might occur for innocent reasons, but they require attention. For example, the entity may have a material asset in a remote location the auditor (or auditor's representative) was unable to reach. Without specific knowledge of the asset's existence and condition, the auditor cannot render an unqualified opinion. Nevertheless, the auditor may believe from his/her relationship with management and indirect knowledge that the financial statements are nevertheless fair. Still, users should understand the lack of independent confirmation regarding the material asset.

Sometimes, a multi-national entity will have operations in an area not serviced by the auditor. In such cases, the auditor may need to engage the services of a local accounting firm to audit operations in that locality. If so—and if the auditor believes the outside firm is competent and trustworthy—the auditor can issue an opinion, albeit Modified to the extent of those operations auditor by another. This is not likely alarming; however, users must understand they are not relying solely on the reputation of the well-known auditor (perhaps a Big Four Firm), but also on a small, less well-known firm.

A third common reason for a qualified modified opinion results from a single GAAP deviation. Sometimes, despite the complexity and breadth of

---

[36] AS 2415: CONSIDERATION OF AN ENTITY'S ABILITY TO CONTINUE AS A GOING CONCERN at 13. (2002).

GAAP, a particular situation justifies a deviation. If so, the auditor cannot issue an unqualified opinion; however, the auditor can issue a modified opinion with an explanation regarding and justifying or explaining the deviation. Necessarily, the deviation cannot, in the opinion of the auditor, raise material doubts regarding the fairness of the statements.

4) Adverse Opinion

An adverse opinion is devastating. It essentially says, "In my opinion, these financial statements are unfair." As explained in AS 3105, "the opinion paragraph should include a direct reference to a separate paragraph that discloses the basis for the adverse opinion."[37] An example of the opinion paragraph provided by AS 3105 is:

> We have audited the accompanying balance sheets of X Company (the "Company") as of December 31, 20X2 and 20X1, the related statements of [*titles of the financial statements, e.g., income, comprehensive income, stockholders' equity, and cash flows*] for each of the years then ended, and the related notes [*and schedules*] (collectively referred to as the "financial statements"). **In our opinion, because of the effects of the matters discussed in the following paragraphs, the financial statements do not present fairly, in conformity with accounting principles generally accepted in the United States of America**, the financial position of the Company as of December 31, 20X2 and 20X1, or the results of its operations or its cash flows for the years then ended.[38]

5) Disclaimer of an Opinion

A disclaimer of opinion is similarly alarming. It can result from several causes:

- Lack of Independence (SAS 26).

- Substantial Limitations on Scope (SAS 58).

- Substantial Concerns about Going Concern (SAS 59).

- Substantial Contingencies and Uncertainties (SAS 79).

Recall, the proper title for a CPA is an Independent Certified Public Accountant. If the CPA is not independent, he/she cannot serve in the role and must disclaim an opinion regarding financial statements.

Sometimes a client will impose substantial limitations on the scope of the audit. Perhaps the client refuses access to important employees, or

---

[37] AS 3105, DEPARTURES FROM UNQUALIFIED OPINIONS AND OTHER REPORTING CIRCUMSTANCES at .43.

[38] *Id*. at 44 (emphasis added).

assets, or records. If so, the CPA cannot express an opinion about the financial statements.

Or the auditor may have substantial concerns about whether the client will or can continue as a going concern. This goes beyond what would justify a modified qualified opinion—which might involves suspicions about going concern viability—and reaches the point of serious doubt. In such a case, an opinion is inappropriate. If the entity continues, then the statements may indeed be fair; however, it the entity fails, the assets may have little value and creditors may accelerate debts. Because the auditor cannot predict what will happen, he/she must disclaim an opinion.

Or, the entity may face substantial, material contingencies and uncertainties. Perhaps pending litigation is potentially and plausibly devastating; or perhaps a project has such uncertain outcomes.

6) Interim Opinion

Often an entity will issue interim financial statements which are not fully audited. An auditor/CPA may comment on this but must do so using specific language. Sample language follows:

> We have reviewed the accompanying [describe the interim financial information or statements reviewed] of X Company as of September 30, 20X3 and 20X2, and for the three-month and nine-month periods then ended. This (these) interim financial information (statements) is (are) the responsibility of the Company's management.
>
> We conducted our review in accordance with the standards of the Public Company Accounting Oversight Board (United States). A review of interim financial information consists principally of applying analytical procedures and making inquiries of persons responsible for financial and accounting matters. It is substantially less in scope than an audit conducted in accordance with the standards of the Public Company Accounting Oversight Board, the objective of which is the expression of an opinion regarding the financial statements taken as a whole. Accordingly, we do not express such an opinion.
>
> Based on our review, we are not aware of any material modifications that should be made to the accompanying interim financial (statements) for it (them) to be in conformity with U.S. generally accepted accounting principles.[39]

---

[39] AU Section 722A Interim Financial Information at .30.

LESSON FOUR

THE ACCOUNTING EQUATION

*An Introduction to Double Entry Bookkeeping
and Fundamental Accounting*

■ ■ ■

Lesson Objectives

1. Student will learn additional accounting terminology

2. Student will learn:

   a. The Fundamental accounting equation.

   b. How to prepare a simple balance sheet.

   c. How to prepare a simple income statement.

   d. How to journalize entries using debits and credits.

   e. How and why to post journal entries to ledgers.

   f. How to close the books.

Terminology Introduced

- Debit.
- Credit.
- Books.
- Journal.
- Ledger.
- T account.
- Permanent accounts.
- Temporary accounts.
- Journalize.
- Post.
- Double entry bookkeeping.
- Going concern.
- Amortize or amortization.
- Equity.

- Inventory.

- Intangible.

- Capitalize versus expense.

- Adjusting entry.

- Non-operating income.

- Closing entry or "to close the books".

- Retained earnings.

- Income stream.

  LESSON FOUR comprises three parts. Part A covers bookkeeping basics:

  - The fundamental accounting equation.

  - How to prepare a simple balance sheet.

  - Some basic terminology, particularly debits and credits, ledgers and journals, and permanent versus temporary accounts.

Part B covers a closer look at financial statements, as well as bookkeeping entries. Part C covers a more structured look at the balance sheet.

LESSON FOUR-A

THE ACCOUNTING EQUATION AND BASIC TERMINOLOGY

■ ■ ■

Before you can understand financial statements, you need to first understand the basics of bookkeeping. We start with the fundamental accounting equation:

Assets = Liabilities + Owner's Equity

With the equation, the balance sheet _must always balance_. Essentially, owner's equity is a plugged figure: we should know what the assets comprise, and we should know what the entity or person owes as liabilities. Subtract the liabilities from the assets, and you get owner's equity, or net worth. It can really be that simple. Essentially, that is it, although we will add sub-categories later in this and other lessons (_e.g._, current assets and fixed assets, current and long-term liabilities and various forms of equity).

If, perchance, the balance sheet does not balance, that would not indicate fraud or some irregularity; instead, it would indicate a bookkeeper failed to make a needed entry. Essentially, a failure to balance results from a math error: someone added or subtracted incorrectly. It is a problem, but not an alarming one. Likewise, just because the statement balances does not indicate the balance sheet is accurate. Indeed, the numbers could all be fictitious, and it would still balance.

A typical balance sheet format is:

Balance Sheet Date	
Assets	**Liabilities** **Owner's Equity**
<u>**Total Assets**</u>	<u>**Total Liabilities & Equity**</u>

Figure 3: Basic Balance Sheet

Assets _always_ appear on the left. Liabilities _always_ appear on the upper right. Equity _always_ appears on the lower right. The two sides _always balance_ because the second form of the equation forces it to:

Assets – Liabilities = Owner's Equity

A helpful way of viewing a balance sheet involves who owns what if we must liquidate. From this viewpoint, the balance sheet indicates claims on assets—and someone must have a claim on everything: either your creditors have a claim, or you own it free and clear.

Balance Sheet Date	
Assets This lists what you have.	**Liabilities** This lists what you owe: the claims creditors have on your assets. **Owner's Equity** This lists what _you_ own: what would be left if you paid off all debts.
<u>**Total Assets**</u>	<u>**Total Liabilities & Equity**</u>

Figure 4: Descriptive Balance Sheet

At this point, we can prepare a simple balance sheet for a typical person using EXAMPLE 9. You should imagine your own assets and debts so that you can prepare your own personal balance sheet. EXAMPLE 9 uses some likely numbers and simply lists the items. It then applies the fundamental accounting equation: it subtracts liabilities from assets to determine Kyle's net worth (his equity). Do the same for yourself. As with Kyle, be neither surprised nor alarmed if you have negative equity: that is common with students. Eventually, at least one hopes, you will have positive equity.

EXAMPLE 9

A Simple Balance Sheet for Kyle

Kyle, a typical law student, has a car (worth $8,500), some personal items ($750), furniture ($800), and electronics ($2,500). He also has some short-term debts (utilities, rent of $1,500), a credit card ($800) plus student loans of $78,500.

Prepare his balance sheet.

EXAMPLE 9 uses fair market value for the assets. This is not consistent with GAAP, but that does not matter because Kyle (or you) is not being audited and neither of you is a publicly traded company subject to GAAP and SEC reporting (or IFRS for non-U.S. companies).

Kyle's balance sheet appears in **Figure 5**. Notice that it balances: it must. Kyle effectively owns $12,550 of stuff (his net worth) and he owes $80,800 of debts. Thus, his net worth is ($68,250):

Kyle Balance Sheet Today			
Assets		**Liabilities**	
Car	$8,500	Misc.	$1,500
Furniture	800	Visa	800
Electronics	2,500	Student Loans	78,500
Miscellaneous	750		
Total Assets	$12,550	Total Liabilities	$80,800
		Owner's Equity	(68,250)
Total Assets	**$12,550**	**Liabilities & Equity**	**$12,550**

Figure 5: Kyle's Balance Sheet

Assets – Liabilities = Owner's Equity

$12,500 – $80,800 = –$68,250

We show the negative number using parentheses. We could alternatively show it in red or with a negative sign. Four very important things should be evident from the EXAMPLE 9:

- The balance sheet has a _date_ on it: it is a snapshot of Scott's finance condition as of that date. It tells us nothing about the day before or the day after.

- The balance sheet balances because _equity is essentially a plugged figure_.

- Having _negative equity is permissible_ and not particularly unusual (although no one can exist for long with negative equity).

- We made up the numbers and _they still balanced_.

For example, Kyle could have lied to us about the student loans and claimed they did not exist. If so, he would have $10,250 of equity [$12,500 assets less $2,300 debts]. The total assets would still be $12,550 and the total liabilities & equity would also still be $12,550. The balance sheet would be fraudulent; however, it would balance. Thus, as explained in LESSON FOUR, never fall for the litigation trick in which a lawyer proves "the books balance" and hopes the judge, jury, and you conclude everything must be fine and dandy. For one thing, it's the balance sheet that we would be concerned with (although the books had better balance, too, as we see in this lesson). And for another, the books and balance sheet _always balance_— even if fraudulent—unless someone made a mere addition or subtraction error.

That simple example leads to some terminology: what are the books and how do the numbers get into them? Hence, we must define some terms. Remember, these terms are defined in the GLOSSARY.

The _books_ comprise the journals and the ledgers. The numbers are recorded into the journals and ledgers through a system of double entry bookkeeping: debits and credits. The GLOSSARY definition of a debit is:

A _debit_ is a bookkeeping entry on the left. It decreases liabilities and owners' equity on the _Balance Sheet_ and income on the _Income Statement_. It increases assets on the _Balance Sheet_ and expenses on the _Income Statement_.

Why _debits_ are on the left and _credits_ are on the right confuses many beginning accounting students. The answer is simple: that is how we define them. They have no other meaning. If one pictures a _balance sheet_ (which is merely a complete _ledger_) as a _T-account_, one can see how the two sides should balance. Hence, for every entry on the left (a *debit*), one must have an entry on the right (a *credit*).

Balance Sheet

Debit	Credit

Often, the actual number of *debit* and *credit* entries does not balance because the bookkeeper uses summations for one or the other. For example, one could *debit* cash deposits $10,000 (which increases cash) and correspondingly *credit* ten different customer accounts for $1,000 each, reflecting payments from each of them. The single *debit* of $10,000 would balance the ten *credits* of $1,000 each: the totals are what are important.

From the business's point of view, it would *credit* each customer account to reduce the respective asset accounts called *accounts receivable*. From the customer's point of view, they would each—on their own books (in their own journals and on their own ledgers)—*debit* their respective liabilities called *accounts payable*.

The term *credit* has two very different, but equally important (and related) meanings: one for bookkeeping and one more general.

A *credit* is a bookkeeping entry on the right. It increases liabilities and owners' equity on the balance sheet and income on the income statement. It decreases assets on the balance sheet and expenses on the income statement. *Credit* also refers to one's ability to borrow money. A person with good *credit* can borrow at a lower interest rate than can a person with poor *credit*. A person's ability to borrow is generally a function of their "credit score." The terms are related: for bookkeeping, a *credit* increases debt and in finance *credit* refers to debt.

Debits and Credits Are Not "Good or Bad"

Debits are on the left. Credits are on the right.

Avoid thinking of either as good or bad. Debts increase assets but also expenses. Credits increase liabilities but also income.

The following definition of the books is more detailed than immediately needed, but you should consider it:

For financial accounting, a set of books refers to:

- *Journals*: These are chronological entries of transactions. An entity may have a single journal. More likely, it will have multiple journals, including ones for cash receipts and disbursements, one for sales, one for inventory, and one for closing entries.

- **Ledgers**: These are topical entries of transactions. They include all journal entries, but in a different format. Often called *T-accounts*, ledgers group a period's transactions by type. For example, all debits and *credits* affecting cash will appear in the cash ledger. All *debits* and *credits* affecting supplies will appear in the supplies ledger.

Accountants maintain *journals* daily, as transactions occur. They then transfer the debits and credits separately to the appropriate *ledgers*. Both journals and ledgers provide important information. Journals show the timing of transactions while ledgers show the impact. Journals are continuous, although accountants separate them by periods. Some ledgers are continuous—those that are balance sheet items, such as assets, liabilities, and equity. Accountants net them periodically, but the ledgers and their balances continue from period to period. In contrast, some ledgers are temporary—confined to a particular period. These are the income, expense, profit, loss ledgers, which are income statement items.

At the end of each period, accountants close temporary ledgers to a single ledger that produces the income statement. Accountants then close this ledger into retained earnings. A periodic profit will have a credit balance in the income statement ledger. The final closing entry will be a debit to the ledger and a credit to retained earnings, a permanent ledger (account). A periodic loss will have a debit balance in the income statement ledger. The final closing entry will be a credit to the ledger and a debit to retained earnings.

Management is responsible for keeping an entity's books. Internal accountants supervising bookkeepers perform this task. From the books, management will prepare the entity's financial statements: the income statement, the balance sheet, and the statement of cash flows.

The external auditor—a *CPA*—will audit (check and verify, often using statistical samples), the financial statements. He/she will then issue an *auditor's opinion* regarding whether they are fair and consistent with *GAAP*. He/she will base the audit on GAAS. The auditor neither prepares the books nor the statements.

Most entities will have multiple sets of books. Contrary to popular wisdom, not only is this appropriate, but it is required:

- *Financial books*, consistent with *GAAP* for external reporting.
- *Tax books*, consistent with the *IRC* for tax reporting.
- *Internal books* for managerial and cost accounting.

- *Pro forma books*, for special circumstances that require adjustments to account for changed methods or assumptions. For example, a Bank may require special assumptions or depreciation or inventory methods. If so, the entity will re-state its accounts to conform to such contractual requirements.

Multiple Sets of Books Is Normal

Entities typically have multiple sets of books because they are subject to multiple sets of rules.

Lawyers need to see financial statements for each set of books, not just a single set.

Accountants must be able to reconcile the different sets of books. As one might suppose, this is not a simple process. Lawyers should be aware of the multiple sets of books and the multiple sets of financial statements that flow from them. Lawyers who need to know an entity's *income* or *equity* must realize that these are not terms of art. Accountants have many ways of presenting income, expenses, assets, liabilities, and *equity*. Lawyers who seek information about these should expect multiple answers which may appear conflicting, and which may be very different.

Also, too often lawyers accept a single set of financial statements, as if they are correct. An unfortunate example involves the common acceptance of tax returns as evidence of income for family law and other legal matters. Hence, lawyers who request, through discovery, financial information should request all of it, including tax statements, external accounting statement, internal accounting statements, and any *pro forma* statements used in loan or other applications or disclosures.

Before we examine the journal and ledger, you should notice several important points from that definition:

- The auditor issues an opinion on the financial statements, not the books, although he/she necessarily examines the books from which management prepares the statements.

- Management prepares and keeps the books, not the outside CPA. If the entity hires a CPA to prepare and to keep the books, that CPA is not independent and cannot render an opinion on his/her own work. Naturally, many entities hire persons licensed as CPAs to "keep the books" or to oversee the bookkeepers; however, such "internal accountants" are not acting as Independent CPAs when they perform those tasks.

- *Having multiple sets of books is common.* That results from having different rules for different audiences. For example, an entity must have a tax books to comply with tax laws. It may (or, if publicly traded, must) have a set of books and corresponding financial statements that comply with GAAP or IFRS. Contractually, it may need a third set of books and statements to comply with reasonable contractual obligations. Internally, it may have a fourth set for cost or managerial accounting.

Two other terms are also important. To <u>journalize</u> something means to record the debit and credit in the journals. To <u>post</u> something means to record the various journal entries in the appropriate ledger.

———————

LESSON FOUR-B

BOOKKEEPING ENTRIES

■ ■ ■

In LESSON TWO-C we worked PROBLEM 1 and prepared a simple balance sheet. At that point, we did not yet cover the journal entries or ledger postings; instead, we recorded directly to the balance sheet. We need to do things correctly now. Working PROBLEM 1 EXPANDED requires

---

PROBLEM 1 EXPANDED

JOE'S BAR & GRILL Start-Up Costs

Scott and Adrian form a small business. The start-up period begins on August 1 and lasts 4 months.

1. On 8/1, they each contribute $250,000.

2. On 8/15, they purchase a liquor license for $75,000 plus incur attorney fees of $5,000. They acquire other local permits for $1,000.

3. On 9/1, they pay $30,000 for one year of rent in advance.

4. On 10/1, they purchase machinery for $31,000.

5. On 10/15, they purchase inventory of $30,000.

6. On 11/1, they incur employee/management training costs of $20,000.

7. On 11/15, they incur trademark and signage costs of $10,000.

8. They earn interest income during start-up of $10,000.

9. During start-up, the liquor/wine inventory appreciates $5,000.

---

three steps:

- Create a set of journals and journalize the transactions.

- Create a set of ledgers and post the journal entries to the ledgers.

- Prepare a balance sheet and income statement from the ledgers.

1. JOURNAL ENTRIES

Typically, we would create a *general* journal for most entries and some *specialty* journals for important items such as cash receipts and disbursements. All of this is now performed with sophisticated electronic bookkeeping software, so handwritten paper journals (which I learned about in my first accounting school basic class) are mostly relics.

Figure 6 illustrates the general journal. Each entry has an equal *number* of debits and credits. That is why we call it <u>double-entry bookkeeping:</u> for everything that increases, something else happens as well: either something decreases (as in most of this example) or a liability or equity increases as well (as with the income in the last entry). Also, each entry has a brief explanation and a date. In each entry, the debit increased an asset account. In all but the last entry, the credit decreased an asset account (each time it was cash). In the final entry, the debit increases an income account—an issue we cover more in depth later.

Notice something else: entries are in chronological order as various events occurred. While a self-evident way of recording, as items occur, it provides little information because the entries involve many different events. A journal classifies only by date. This simple involves a small number of entries. Imagine the thousands of journal entries that must occur for even a modest business with hundreds of customers and employees. Accountants (bookkeepers, actually) also keep a set of ledgers *to which they post the very same entries*. Ledgers, however, are topical and thus provide useful information about the amount of cash, inventory, or other items. Keeping the journal chronologically is essential; however, keeping the ledgers topically is also essential.

We make an additional journal entry for amortization of the pre-paid rent. This introduces a concept discussed more in depth in LESSON SIX on accrual accounting: we must allocate the pre-paid rent over time, consistent with the matching principle. In **Figure 7**, that entry, on the last day of November (the relevant period) is an *adjusting entry*, one that adjusts for something that occurs over time. Thus, it involves a debit to rent expense of $7,500 and a credit to prepaid rent of the same amount. The credit reduces the asset (prepaid rent) and the debit increases the temporary account of rent expense. I allocated the prepaid rent over the four quarters of the one-year rental period: the initial start-up period of three months thus receives an allocation of one-fourth of the prepaid $30,000. Although we could allocate the rent daily, that would not typically provide any useful information: usually, an entity seeks monthly, quarterly, or annual reports, not daily. In future periods, we will allocate it monthly so that we can prepare monthly income statements.

As explained in the GLOSSARY:

Adjusting Entry: At the end of each period (which may be a month, a quarter, or a year) an accountant or bookkeeper makes a series of entries for non-transactional items. These include *depreciation* and *amortization*. In accounting parlance, they are *adjusting entries*, as they adjust for items that are not the result of events or transactions. Regular entries appear chronologically in the journal but *adjusting entries* and *closing entries* appear at the end of a period.

General Journal for JOE'S BAR & GRILL			
Date	Account	Debit	Credit
8/1	Cash	500,000	
	Capital Stock (Scott)		250,000
	Capital Stock (Ann)		250,000
	Contributions to Capital.		
8/15	Liquor License	75,000	
	Cash		75,000
	Liquor License	5,000	
	Cash		5,000
	License Purchase, atty fee cap.		
	Local Permit	1,000	
	Cash		1,000
	Local annual permit fee.		
9/1	Prepaid Rent	30,000	
	Cash		30,000
	One-year rent paid in advance.		
10/1	Machinery	31,000	
	Cash		31,000
	Machine; 10-yr. life; 1,000 salvage.		
10/15	Inventory	30,000	
	Cash		30,000
	Purchase of Inventory.		
11/1	Employee Training	20,000	
	Cash		20,000
	Capitalized training, one-year life.		
11/15	Trademarks	6,000	
	Signs	4,000	
	Cash		10,000
	TM; 15-yr life; sign 5-yr life.		
11/30	Cash	10,000	
	Income		10,000
	Interest income for startup period.		

Figure 6: General Journal Entries

Similarly, the **Figure 6** journal entry for the accrued interest income was an adjusting entry: recording it daily would not have been worth the effort. We did not make an entry for the appreciation to the inventory because of the historical cost assumption, as well as the conservative principle, and the income recognition principle. We will recognize any gain on the inventory when and if we sell it.

General Journal for JOE'S BAR & GRILL		Debit	Credit
Date	Account		
11/30	Rent Expense	7,500	
	Pre-paid Rent		7,500
	Adjusting Entry for Amortization.		

Figure 7: Final Adjusting Entry

That last point is worth pausing over. We know (or have good reason to know) the inventory appreciated a material amount ($5,000); however, for financial accounting purposes we largely ignore that information. We could disclose the information in a footnote, but it would not appear in the "books" or directly on the financial statements. For legal purposes, however, the appreciation may be significant. Perhaps, for example, one of the owners is involved in a dissolution of marriage: his or her spouse would be more interested in the fair market value of the inventory than the historical cost. Similarly, if a banker were considering a loan to the business, the bank would be more interested in the value of the assets rather than their original cost.

Remember Historical Cost Assumption

For GAAP, we ignore appreciation in inventory or similar assets, even if we are certain. The information may appear in a footnote. It can have significant legal consequences.

2. POSTING TO THE LEDGERS

Now that we have journalized the various transactions (and made two adjusting entries), we must post to the ledgers. Often accountants refer to these as T-accounts: they appear to form the letter T. **Figure 8** illustrates the cash ledger.

Cash Ledger for JOE'S BAR & GRILL		
Date	**Debit**	**Credit**
8/1	250,000	
	250,000	
8/15		75,000
		5,000
		1,000
9/1		30,000
10/1		31,000
10/15		30,000
11/1		20,000
11/30		10,000
11/30	10,000	
11/30	308,000	

Figure 8: JOE'S Cash Ledger

We copy each journal entry that affects cash into the cash ledger. We then draw a single line (which denotes the taking of a net figure) to provide the useful information that our cash balance on 11/30 is $308,000. Each journal account would have its own ledger; hence, we are not concerned with debits and credits balancing in a single ledger: they are not supposed to. Instead, debits and credits will necessarily balance when we view all the ledgers together: after all, they are merely copies of the various journal entries, which necessarily had a balance between debits and credits.

Ledgers have two large classifications with several sub-classes. The two large classes are:

- Permanent accounts.

- Temporary accounts.

A. PERMANENT ACCOUNTS

Permanent accounts comprise:

- Permanent asset accounts (a ledger for each asset or class of asset).

- Permanent liability accounts (a ledger for each liability).

- Permanent equity accounts.

The permanent *asset* accounts appear in **Figures 9 to 17**. The ledgers are in alphabetical order, not in the order of transactions. These permanent accounts will appear in the ledgers as long as these assets exist; thus, the dates are less unimportant than being able to find them.

Cash		
Date	Debit	Credit
11/30	308,000	

Figure 9: Cash Ledger

Employee Training		
Date	Debit	Credit
11/1	20,000	

Figure 10: Employee Training Ledger

Liquor License		
Date	Debit	Credit
8/15	75,000	
	5,000	
	80,000	

Figure 11: Liquor License Ledger

Employee Training		
Date	Debit	Credit
9/1	30,000	
11/30		7,500
	22,500	

Figure 12: Pre-Paid Rent Ledger

Inventory		
Date	Debit	Credit
10/15	30,000	

Figure 13: Inventory Ledger

Trademark		
Date	Debit	Credit
11/30		6,000

Figure 14: Trademark Ledger

Local Permit		
Date	Debit	Credit
8/15	1,000	

Figure 15: Local Permit Ledger

Signs		
Date	Debit	Credit
11/15	4,000	

Figure 16: Signs Ledger

Machinery		
Date	Debit	Credit
10/1	31,000	

Figure 17: Machinery Ledger

As of November 30, the entity has no permanent liability ledgers because it has no debts. LESSON FIVE will add that complexity. The permanent equity ledgers appear in **Figures 18 to 20**.

Capital Stock Ann		
Date	Debit	Credit
8/1		250,000

Figure 18: Capital Stock: Adrian Ledger

Capital Stock Scott		
Date	Debit	Credit
8/1		250,000

Figure 19: Capital Stock: Scott Ledger

Retained Earnings		
Date	Debit	Credit

Figure 20: Retained Earnings Ledger

For now, the $10,000 of interest income appears below in a temporary income ledger shown in **Figure 21**. Thus, the retained earnings account is currently blank because we have not yet closed the books. Eventually, the **Figures 21** and **22** ledgers will close to zero and the **Figure 20** ledger will have a $2,500 debit balance.

Permanent accounts carry-over from period to period as long as the relevant asset exists, the relevant debt is owed, or the relevant type of equity exists. These accounts form the balance sheet.

B. TEMPORARY ACCOUNTS

Interest Income		
Date	Debit	Credit
11/30		10,000

Figure 21: Interest Income Ledger

Rent Expense		
Date	Debit	Credit
11/30	7,500	

Figure 22: Rent Expense Ledger

Temporary accounts, in contrast, exist only for a particular reporting period—typically a month. They appear in **Figures 21 and 22**. Ultimately income accrues to the benefit of the owners who also suffer expenses. Income and expenses do not appear on a balance sheet; instead, they appear on the income statement. At the end of a period (typically a month), the bookkeeper will "*close*" the temporary accounts to retained earnings.

Temporary accounts comprise:

- Temporary income.

- Temporary expenses.

The two temporary accounts are interest income and rent expense. Pay close attention to them: the income ledger has a credit balance and the expense ledger has a debit balance. This is one of the more difficult issues for students new to accounting: it can appear counter-intuitive.

Ultimately, the income closes to retained earnings, which is part of equity; hence, it necessarily has a credit balance. Likewise, the expense is closed to retained earnings, but it reduces equity, so it necessarily has a debit balance. Thus, a debit increases an asset, but it also decreases equity because it increases an expense. A credit increases a liability, but it also increases equity because it increases income.

A few definitions and some review should be helpful:

A T-account is another term for a *ledger*. These are called T accounts because they look like the capital letter T. *Debit* entries are on the left side and *credit* entries are on the right. Asset and expense accounts/ledgers will normally have *debit* balances. Liability, equity, and income accounts will normally have *credit* balances. The aggregate *debits* will always equal the aggregate *credits*.

A *balance sheet* is one large *T-account* for all permanent accounts (plus all temporary accounts closed to *Retained Earnings*).

At the end of each period, accountants and bookkeepers *close* the books using *closing entries*. More specifically, they close all *temporary accounts*, which are the income, gain, loss, and expense accounts. An income account will normally have a *credit* balance. To *close* it, the bookkeeper *debits* the account for the periodic balance and credits another temporary account called profit and loss summary (or some similar name). The income *ledger*—or *T-account*—will then have a zero balance; hence, it has *closed*.

After similarly *closing* all income and expense *ledgers* to the revenue and expense summary *ledger*, the bookkeeper will then close that *temporary account*. If it has a credit balance, the entity had a profit for the period. If the account has a *debit* balance, the entity had a loss for the period. In either event, the bookkeeper will *debit* or *credit* the balance to cause the resulting balance to be zero. He/she will correspondingly *debit* or *credit* retained earnings for the profit or loss. As a result, all *temporary accounts* effectively transfer to the *balance sheet* in the form of an increase or decrease to *retained earnings*. From the profit and loss summary *ledger*, the bookkeeper and accountant can easily prepare the periodic *Income Statement*.

Remember: *Balance sheet* accounts are permanent accounts, and *Income statement* accounts are temporary accounts. By *closing* the books with such *closing* entries, the accountant keeps each period's operations separate. He or she also, by transferring those operations to *retained earnings*—either as an increase or decrease—maintains a proper snapshot of the entity's cumulative operations.

3. CLOSING THE BOOKS

To close the books, we transfer the temporary accounts to another temporary account called revenue and expense summary. Accountants use this temporary ledger to group all income and expenses into a single ledger. From that, we can easily net the numbers to show the amount of profit or loss. We can also more easily prepare an income statement from the grouping of accounts in a single ledger. We then close that ledger to retained earnings. **Figure 23** shows the initial closing entries.

General Journal for JOE'S BAR & GRILL			
Date	Account	Debit	Credit
11/30	Interest Income	10,000	
	Revenue & Exp. Summ.		10,000
	Close income ledger		
	Rent Expense		7,500
11/30	Revenue & Exp. Summ.	7,500	
	Close income ledger		

Figure 23: General Journal Closing Entries

The two temporary ledgers (**Figures 21** and **22**) are now closed with zero balances (**Figures 24** and **25**). These ledgers do not carry-over to the next month; instead, JOE'S will open new temporary ledgers for each type of income and each type of expense in December. At the end of December (in LESSON SIX) it will close those accounts to a new revenue and expense summary ledger, which will itself be closed that same day to retained earnings. The double line in the account indicates closure.

Interest Income		
Date	Debit	Credit
11/30		10,000
11/30	10,000	

Figure 24: Interest Income Ledger

Rent Expense		
Date	Debit	Credit
11/30	7,500	
11/30		7,500

Figure 25: Rent Expense Ledger

Retained Earnings		
Date	Debit	Credit
11/30	7,500	
11/30		10,000
		2,500

Figure 26: Rev. & Exp. Summ. Ledger

Figure 26 shows the new temporary ledger, revenue and expense summary, with a 2,500 credit balance, indicating a net profit for the start-up period.

Figure 27 shows the last journal entries for November. First is a debit to revenue and expense summary for $2,500, which closes it to zero. Next is a credit to retained earnings for $2,500, which adds the profit to equity, a permanent account that appears on the balance sheet. We have now "closed the books" for the start-up period. The revenue and expense summary ledger (**Figure 28**) has a zero balance. Retained earnings (**Figure 29**) has a $2,500 credit balance.

General Journal for JOE'S BAR & GRILL			
Date	**Account**	**Debit**	**Credit**
11/30	Revenue & Exp. Summ.	2,500	
	Retained Earnings		2,500
	Close R & E to Retained Earnings.		

Figure 27: Final Closing Entries for November

Revenue & Expense Summ.		
Date	**Debit**	**Credit**
11/30	7,500	
11/30		10,000
		2,500
11/30	2,500	

Figure 28: Interest Income Ledger

Retained Earnings		
Date	**Debit**	**Credit**
11/30		2,500

Figure 29: Rent Expense Ledger

The final step is to prepare the income statement (**Figure 30**) and the balance sheet (**Figure 31**). The income statement includes the temporary accounts (**Figures 21–22**), which have closed to zero (**Figures 24–25**). The balance sheet includes all permanent accounts (**Figures 9 to 19 and 29**), which carry-over to the next period.

JOE'S BAR & GRILL Income Statement Start-up Period Ending November 30		
Income:		
Operating Income:	$ 0.00	
Non-operating Income		
Interest	10,000.00	
Total Income		**10,000.00**
Expenses:		
Operating Expenses:	0.00	
Non-Operating Expenses	7,500.00	
Total Expenses:		**(7,500.00)**
Net Income:		**$2,500.00**

Figure 30: Income Statement

JOE'S BAR & GRILL Balance Sheet November 30			
Assets		**Liabilities**	
Cash	$308,000		
Inventory	30,000		
Machinery	31,000		
Liquor License	80,000		
Local Permit	1,000		
Pre-Paid Rent	22,500	**Owner's Equity**	
Trademark	6,000	Scott	250,000
Training	20,000	Adrian	250,000
Signs	4,000	Retained Earnings	2,500
Total Assets	**$502,500**	**Liabilities & Equity**	**$502,500**

Figure 31: Balance Sheet

Lesson Four-C

How Entries Affect the Balance Sheet

■ ■ ■

Lesson Four-C focuses on how the various entries affect various parts of the balance sheet. It places the ledgers within the balance sheet to help show what each section comprises. The lesson also introduces a list of 14 common bookkeeping entries. We have covered the first four. Later lessons cover the others. The number of possible bookkeeping entries is not large as **Figure 34** shows: a debit occurs to one of the accounts and a credit to another or the same account.

Joe's Bar & Grill Balance Sheet	

Assets			Liabilities	
Debit	**Credit**		**Debit**	**Credit**

Stock	
Debit	**Credit**

Retained Earnings	
Debit	**Credit**

Figure 32: Balance Sheet with Permanent Ledgers

Figure 32 is a balance sheet with ledger accounts superimposed into the statement. The balance sheet would have many different assets, many debts, and possibly multiple classes of stock (as covered in Lesson Nine). Of course, a real balance sheet would not have ledgers within it.

Figure 33 divides retained earnings into its component parts of income and expense, each with space for debits (Db.) and credits (Cr.). That helps illustrate why income is a credit (the same as a liability) and an expense is a debit (the same as an asset). Students must not think that somehow debits are "good" and credits are "bad"; instead, they are an arbitrary way of balancing the books. Income benefits equity, which is a credit, so income must also be a credit.

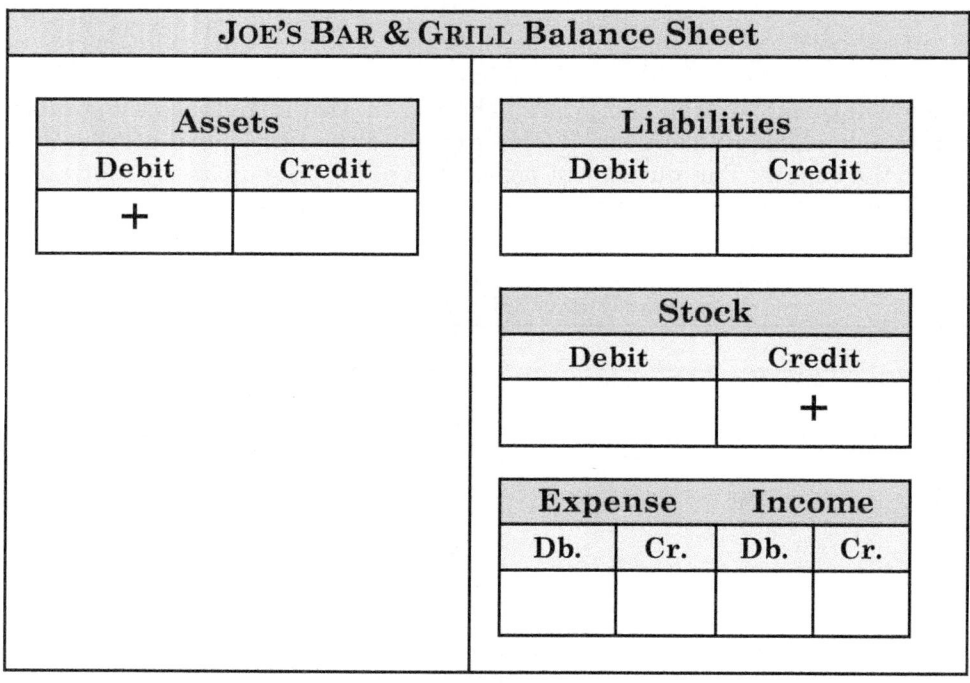

Figure 33: Balance Sheet with Permanent and Temporary Ledgers

Of all the concepts introduced in this course, this is—based on more than four decades of experience—the most difficult for non-accountants to grasp. Debits are not "good"; instead, they are merely on the left. Credits are not "bad"; instead, they are merely on the right. We increase income with a credit, and we also increase a liability with a credit. We increase expenses with a debit, and we also increase assets with a debit. Consider the fourteen *common* types of bookkeeping entries with this very odd balance sheet (with permanent and temporary ledgers in it).

This Is the Most Difficult Concept

Debits increase both assets and expenses. Credits increase both liabilities and income. Neither is good nor bad: they are merely left and right.

The 14 entries in **Figure 34** are not the universe of entries, they are merely the common ones. The number of possible entries is 25. Examine **Figure 33**. Consider a debit to an asset. It must balance with a credit to an asset, liability, equity, expense, or income, which makes 5 entries possible. Consider a debit to a liability which similarly could balance with 5 possible credits. The same is true of debits to equity, expense, or income. Some of those entries are uncommon.

Frequently lawyers must examine financial transactions, which are often complex and difficult to visualize. Remember the fourteen common entries and the twenty-five total possible entries. Whatever happens, however complex, it involves one of those twenty-five. Nothing else is possible. If you must draw a picture of what occurred, consider doing it with the balance sheet super-imposed with ledgers. No matter how complicated a set of transactions may be, they will fit in those twenty-five boxes, and they will balance.

14 Common Bookkeeping Entries:	
1. Debit Asset/Credit Equity.	Contribute capital.
2. Debit Asset/Credit Asset.	Buy something for cash.
3. Debit Asset/Credit Income.	Sell something or earn income.
4. Debit Expense/Credit Asset.	Pay an expense or depreciate.
5. Debit Asset/Credit Liability.	Borrow money or buy on credit.
6. Debit Expense/Credit Liability.	Charge an expense.
7. Debit Liability/Credit Liability.	Re-finance a debt.
8. Debit Liability/Credit Asset.	Pay a liability.
9. Debit Equity/Credit Asset.	Distribute to shareholders.
10. Debit Equity/Credit Liability.	Convert equity to debt.
11. Debit Liability/Credit Equity.	Convert debt to equity.
12. Debit Asset/Credit Expense.	Refund of expensed item.
13. Debit Income/Credit Asset.	Refund income item.
14. Debit Income/Credit Liability.	Agree to refund income item.

Figure 34: 14 Common Bookkeeping Entries

Complex Financial Transactions

No matter how complex, all transactions involve accounting and all fit into one or more of the 25 possible entries, with most being among the 14. *Nothing else is possible.* And they *always* balance.

1. INCREASE AN ASSET AND INCREASE EQUITY

JOE'S BAR & GRILL Balance Sheet	

Assets	
Debit	Credit
+	

Liabilities	
Debit	Credit

Stock	
Debit	Credit
	+

Expense		**Income**	
Db.	Cr.	Db.	Cr.

Figure 35: Type 1 Entry: Increase Asset/Increase Equity

For example, debit cash and credit stock to record a contribution to capital. This was the first entry in PROBLEM 1, when Scott and Adrian each contributed $250,000 to purchase stock in the new entity. Owners' equity, of which capital stock is part, necessarily has a credit balance. Thus, do not fall into the trap of believing debits are good because they increase assets and credits are bad because they increase debts. *Credits also increase equity.* Thus, the increase (+) to an asset balances with an increase (+) to equity in the type 1 entry illustrated in **Figure 35**. Picture it as a pair of scales evenly balanced. Add the same amount to both sides and it still balances.

2. INCREASE AN ASSET AND DECREASE AN ASSET

JOE'S BAR & GRILL Balance Sheet			

Assets	
Debit	Credit
+	−

Liabilities	
Debit	Credit

Stock	
Debit	Credit

Expense		Income	
Db.	Cr.	Db.	Cr.

Figure 36: Type 2 Entry: Increase Asset/Decrease Asset

For example, credit cash and debit machinery to record the purchase of equipment. This was the second (and several subsequent) entries when JOE'S purchased the liquor license, the permit, inventory, and equipment. The increase (+) to an asset balances with a decrease (−) to another asset in the type 2 entry illustrated in **Figure 36**. Picture it as a pair of scales evenly balanced. Add and subtract the same amount from one side and it still balances.

Thus, bookkeeping entries can affect only one side of the balance sheet. In **Figure 36**, neither debt nor equity changes. This entry can affect some liquidity ratios (discussed in LESSON TEN); thus, it can be very consequential.

3. INCREASE AN ASSET AND INCREASE INCOME

For example, debit an asset and credit income to record the earning of income from service or to record revenue from the sale of inventory. The asset could be cash, or it could be accounts receivable. This is the *effectively* same entry as entry 1: debit asset and credit equity because the proceeds of the income belong to the owners (equity). The increase (+) to an asset balances with an increase (+) to income, which is part of retained earnings and owner's equity in the type 3 entry illustrated in **Figure 37**. Picture it as a pair of scales evenly balanced. Add the same amount to both sides and it still balances.

JOE'S BAR & GRILL Balance Sheet			

Assets		Liabilities	
Debit	**Credit**	**Debit**	**Credit**
+			

Stock	
Debit	**Credit**

Expense		Income	
Db.	**Cr.**	**Db.**	**Cr.**
			+

Figure 37: Type 3 Entry: Increase Asset/Increase Income

Near the end of this lesson, we consider more family law examples. Indeed, many examples in this course involve family law, an important legal area greatly affected by accounting. Some unfortunate statutes refer to "income" as an asset to be divided (as in a dissolution of marriage). That terminology is disturbing because "income" is never an asset: it produces assets, but it is part of equity, which is on the opposite side of the balance sheet from assets. The assets produced may be cash or they may be something consumed and gone. Thus, if a statute instructs a court to divide "income," it presumes something exists to divide; however, that may not be the case.

4. DECREASE AN ASSET AND INCREASE EXPENSE

For example, credit an asset and debit expense to record the payment of an expense item. The decreased asset would be cash and the increased expense could be (as explained in LESSON SIX), one we do not capitalize and did not previously accrue. An example would the purchase of some pencils: the item is too small to capitalize as an asset that we would amortize over its life (see LESSON SIX). Another example involves depreciation (LESSON FIVE) in which we debit depreciation expense and credit accumulated depreciation (a *contra* asset).

The decrease (−) to an asset balances with an increase (+) to an expense, which is part of retained earnings and owner's equity in the type 4 entry illustrated in **Figure 38**. The increased expense reduces income and thus reduces retained earnings and thus reduces equity. Remove the same amount from both sides and the scales still balance.

JOE'S BAR & GRILL Balance Sheet	

Assets		Liabilities	
Debit	**Credit**	**Debit**	**Credit**
	−		

Stock	
Debit	**Credit**

Expense		Income	
Db.	**Cr.**	**Db.**	**Cr.**
+			

Figure 38: Type 4 Entry: Decrease Asset/Increase Expense

5. INCREASE AN ASSET AND INCREASE LIABILITY

JOE'S BAR & GRILL Balance Sheet				

Assets			Liabilities	
Debit	**Credit**		**Debit**	**Credit**
+				**+**

Stock	
Debit	**Credit**

Expense		Income	
Db.	**Cr.**	**Db.**	**Cr.**

Figure 39: Type 5 Entry: Increase Asset/Increase Liability

For example, debit cash and credit loan payable to record the borrowing of money. LESSON SIX adds this element to the PROBLEM. The increase (+) to an asset balances with an increase (+) to a liability, in the fifth entry in **Figure 39**. Picture the balanced scales. Add the same amount to both sides and it still balances.

As explained in this lesson and LESSON SIX, the type 5 entry has no effect on equity, which remains the same. However, the relative amount of equity versus debt changes, which is the topic of LESSON TEN: ratio analysis. That lesson looks at the relationship of various financial statement parts to each other to analyze the past and to predict the future. Also, the ratio of assets to income and equity has changed, which can be significant.

6. INCREASE AN EXPENSE AND INCREASE A LIABILITY

JOE'S BAR & GRILL Balance Sheet			

Assets		Liabilities	
Debit	**Credit**	**Debit**	**Credit**
			+

		Stock	
		Debit	**Credit**

	Expense		Income	
	Db.	**Cr.**	**Db.**	**Cr.**
	+			

Figure 40: Type 6 Entry: Increase Expense/Increase Liability

For example, debit expense and credit liability to record the accrual of an expense item not yet paid. LESSON SIX (accrual accounting) covers this type of entry. It might occur, for example, if the business receives an invoice for utilities but has not yet paid the bill. It would debit utilities expense and credit utilities payable. Because the liability exists, it must be recorded. The expense matches to the current period and thus must be recorded as well. The expense shows up on the income statement and eventually reduces owner's equity on the balance sheet. Picture the pair of scales evenly balanced. The increase (+) to a liability balances with an increase (+) to an expense (a decrease (−) in retained earnings), in the type 6 entry illustrated in **Figure 40.** Add an amount to one side but also remove an amount from the same side and the scales still balance.

This entry affects only the right side of the balance sheet: liabilities plus equity. Assets are unaffected (though later payment will affect them). Because assets remain the same, but liabilities increase owner's equity must drop, as it does through the expense and ultimate decrease in retained earnings. As explained in LESSON SIX, this is essential to accrual accounting (required by GAAP and IFRS) and the matching principle.

7. INCREASE A LIABILITY AND DECREASE A LIABILITY

JOE'S BAR & GRILL Balance Sheet				

Assets

Debit	Credit

Liabilities

Debit	Credit
-	+

Stock

Debit	Credit

Expense / **Income**

Db.	Cr.	Db.	Cr.

Figure 41: Type 7 Entry: Increase Liability/Decrease Liability

For example, an entity may owe short-term debt to a bank. It decides to re-finance the debt for a longer term. In the process, it pays off the old debt and enters a new debt contract with a longer term. Cash unlikely changes hands, so no entry would affect assets. Equity would also remain unchanged. The increase (+) to a liability balances with a decrease (−) to a liability in the type 7 entry illustrated in **Figure 41.** Add an amount to one side but also remove an amount from the same side and the scales still balance.

Although this entry does not affect assets or equity or even the total amount of debt, it affects important financial ratios as discussed in LESSON TEN. For example, by reducing short-term debt and increasing long-term debt, the entity will have a stronger "current ratio" because it will have a reduced expected cash out-flows in the near term because the longer-term debt will have smaller monthly payments.

8. DECREASE AN ASSET AND DECREASE A LIABILITY

For example, debit accounts payable and credit cash to record the payment of an invoice. LESSON SIX (accrual accounting) covers this type of entry. As illustrated earlier in **Figure 40**, it might occur because the business received an invoice for utilities but did not immediately pay the bill. That would have resulted in the type six entry. The liability existed and had to be recorded. The expense matched to the current period and thus was recorded as well. Later payment of the obligation results in the type eight entry. It does not affect expenses because the entity accrued the expense in an earlier period as shown in **Figure 40**.

The decrease (−) to an asset balances with a decrease (−) to a liability in the type 8 entry illustrated in **Figure 42**. Add an amount to one side but also remove an amount from the same side and the scales still balance. As explained in LESSON SIX, this is essential to accrual accounting (required by GAAP and IFRS) and the matching principle.

JOE'S BAR & GRILL Balance Sheet				

Assets

Debit	Credit
	−

Liabilities

Debit	Credit
−	

Stock

Debit	Credit

Expense		Income	
Db.	Cr.	Db.	Cr.

Figure 42: Type 8 Entry: Decrease Asset/Decrease Liability

9. DECREASE AN ASSET AND DECREASE EQUITY

For example, debit retained earnings (or dividends payable if a dividend was "declared" with a later "payment date") and credit cash to record the payment of a dividend. Dividend payable would be part of equity rather than liability. This entry is like the type 4 illustrated earlier in **Figure 38**: credit an asset and debit an expense. It differs, however, because it does not affect the income statement. Dividends are distributions to shareholders. They reduce retained earnings but are not an expense. LESSON NINE (capital structure) covers this type of entry.

The decrease (−) to an asset balances with a decrease (−) to equity in the type 9 entry illustrated in **Figure 43**. Notice the figure uses the balance sheet with only permanent accounts from **Figure 33**. Prior entries used the **Figure 34** balance sheet, which included both permanent and temporary accounts. Remove an amount from one side and remove an amount from the other side and the scales still balance.

JOE'S BAR & GRILL Balance Sheet

Assets		Liabilities	
Debit	**Credit**	**Debit**	**Credit**
	−		

Stock	
Debit	**Credit**
−	

Expense		Income	
Db.	**Cr.**	**Db.**	**Cr.**

Figure 43: Type 9 Entry: Decrease Asset/Decrease Equity

10. DECREASE EQUITY AND INCREASE A LIABILITY

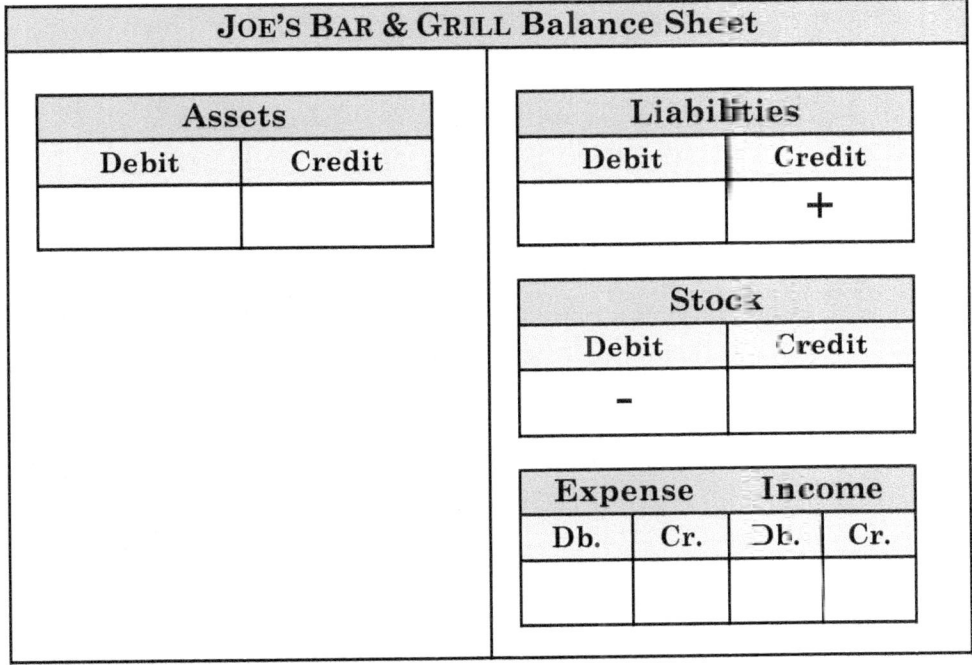

Figure 44: Type 10 Entry: Increase Liability/Decrease Equity

For example, debit preferred stock (covered in LESSON NINE) and credit bonds payable to record the conversion of equity to debt. LESSON NINE covers the capital structure of a corporation. An important feature is the (sometimes) right of some classes of stock to convert to debt (either a bond (secured) or a debenture (unsecured). Conversion rights affect earnings per share (covered in LESSON TEN (ratio analysis) thus, this is an important entry.

The type ten accounting entry affects only the right side of the balance sheet: it does not affect assets. It also does not affect the income statement (there is no entry to expense or income). The decrease (−) to equity balances with an increase (+) in debt in the type 10 entry illustrated in **Figure 44**. Remove an amount from one side but add an amount from the same side and the scales still balance.

11. DECREASE A LIABILITY AND INCREASE EQUITY

JOE'S BAR & GRILL Balance Sheet		

Assets

Debit	Credit

Liabilities

Debit	Credit
−	

Stock

Debit	Credit
	+

Expense   **Income**

Db.	Cr.	Db.	Cr.

Figure 45: Type 11 Entry: Decrease Liability/Increase Equity

This entry is the opposite of type eleven. Just as some classes of stock may have rights to convert to debt, some types of debt have rights to convert to equity. For example, debit bonds payable (secured debt) and credit common stock (*aka* capital stock) to record the conversion of debt to equity. LESSON NINE (capital structure) covers this type of entry. Debt conversion rights are sometimes an important feature of a particular issue of bonds (secured debt) or debentures (unsecured debt). Creditors may have contractual rights to convert their debt obligation into equity (either common stock with voting rights or preferred stock with preferences as to dividends and distributions). LESSON TEN covers earnings per share, which conversion rights affects.

Creditors might have such conversion rights which they can exercise on a stated condition, such as interest not being paid for a period or a particular financial ratio reaching an unacceptable level. LESSON TEN covers financial ratios.

The type eleven accounting entry affects only the right side of the balance sheet: it does not affect assets. It also does not affect the income statement (there is no entry to expense or income). The decrease (−) to a liability balances with an increase (+) in equity in the type 11 entry illustrated in **Figure 45**. Remove an amount from one side but add an amount from the same side and the scales still balance.

12. INCREASE AN ASSET AND DECREASE AN EXPENSE

JOE'S BAR & GRILL Balance Sheet					

Assets	
Debit	**Credit**
+	

Liabilities	
Debit	**Credit**

Stock	
Debit	**Credit**

Expense		Income	
Db.	**Cr.**	**Db.**	**Cr.**
	–		

Figure 46: Type 12 Entry: Increase Asset/Decrease Expense

For example, debit cash and credit repairs expense to record the refund of a payment for poor work. Although PROBLEM 1 featuring JOE'S BAR & GRILL does not include an example of this entry, it is common. Likely most people have paid for repairs or other items and later found them to be faulty.

As covered in LESSON SIX (accrual accounting) management would have decided whether to capitalize or to expense the "repair." The debit would be to cash (if refunded) or to accounts payable (if the item had not been paid and the entity received a price reduction). If it were capitalized, then the credit would be to the asset into which it had been capitalized; otherwise, the credit would be to an expense. If the refund occurs in a period later than the expense, the impact on the income statement would be as an "extraordinary item" so as not to affect "current earnings from operations." If material in amount, subsequent financial statements would have to note the earlier mistaken "expense." We would not make a prior period adjustment: *i.e.*, we would not re-state the prior income statement or balance sheet (although we might do so on a *pro forma* basis).

The type twelve accounting entry may affect both sides of the balance sheet or, perhaps, only the left side. The decrease (−) to an expense likely balances with an increase (+) in assets in the type 12 entry illustrated in **Figure 46**. Remove an amount from one side but add an amount from the same side and the scales still balance.

13. DECREASE AN ASSET AND DECREASE INCOME

| JOE'S BAR & GRILL Balance Sheet | | | | |

Assets	
Debit	Credit
	−

Liabilities	
Debit	Credit

Stock	
Debit	Credit

Expense		Income	
Db.	Cr.	Db.	Cr.
		−	

Figure 47: Type 13 Entry: Decrease Asset/Decrease Income

This is the opposite of entry 12: this time we did the faulty work. For example, debit revenue and credit cash to record the refund to a customer. If this also involved the return of inventory, the entry would be more complicated.

The type 13 accounting entry would affect both sides of the balance sheet. The decrease (−) to an asset would balance with the decrease (−) in revenue as illustrated in **Figure 47**. Remove an amount from both sides and the scales still balance.

14. DECREASE INCOME AND INCREASE A LIABILITY

Like entry 13, this too involves a faulty work on our part, but this time the customer had not yet paid. Thus, we reduce the amount the customer owes: debit revenue and credit accounts payable to record the agreement to refund money to a customer for faulty work. The type 14 accounting entry would affect both sides of the balance sheet. The decrease (−) to accounts payable would balance with the decrease (−) in revenue as illustrated in **Figure 48**. Remove an amount from both sides and the scales still balance.

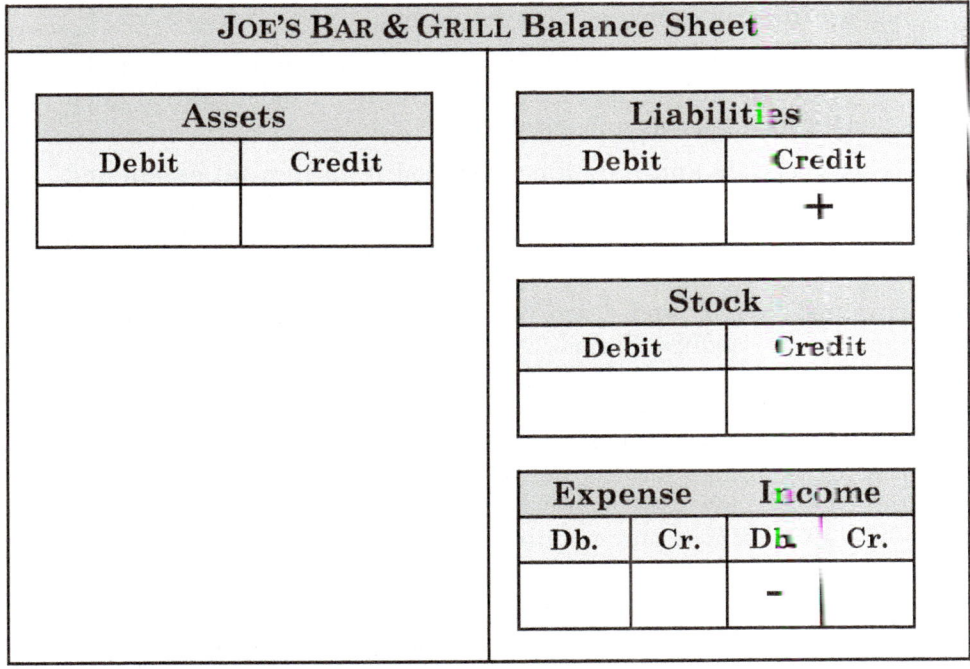

Figure 48: Type 14 Entry: Decrease Income/Increase Liability

15. FAMILY LAW EXAMPLE

Consider a family law application. All states have laws dealing with the division of property incident to a divorce or dissolution of marriage. Some involve community property, and some adopt what is generally known as an "equitable distribution" regime. In all states, issues arise regarding what is a marital or community asset versus what is separate because one or the other spouse brought the asset into the marriage. Typically, such rules are clear. But states also struggle with what to do with the income produced by or resulting from non-marital or non-community assets. Do the resulting assets produced by the income become marital/community or do they remain separate? The answers vary and are beyond this course.

But consider a Florida Statute addressing the issue in a very confusing manner: F.S. section 61.075(b) provides in part:

(b)   "Nonmarital assets and liabilities" include:

1.   Assets acquired and liabilities incurred by either party prior to the marriage, and assets acquired and liabilities incurred in exchange for such assets and liabilities;

2.   Assets acquired separately by either party by non-interspousal gift, bequest, devise, or descent, and assets acquired in exchange for such assets;

3.   All income derived from nonmarital assets during the marriage unless the income was treated, used, or relied upon by the parties as a marital asset;

4.   Assets and liabilities excluded from marital assets and liabilities by valid written agreement of the parties, and assets acquired and liabilities incurred in exchange for such assets and liabilities; and

Paragraphs 1, 2, and 4 are reasonably clear. The accountant in me questions what "acquired" and "incurred in exchange" mean. The word "acquired" has elements of the cash method, while "incurred" is more reminiscent of the accrual method. Certainly, if a spouse were to spend non-marital cash purchasing a valuable painting, the painting would be acquired in exchange for the non-marital cash and thus would be non-marital. Money, however, is fungible and exactly which funds might be used for which purpose may not always be clear. As a result, states tend to resolve any lack of clarity by placing the burden of proof on the spouse asserting an asset is non-marital.

But look at paragraph 3. Although "income derived from nonmarital assets" is clear by itself, how can income ever be part of a definition of "assets"? Accounting rules do not permit that. Income is never an asset; instead, it is income, and it belongs on an income statement. The assets which result from the income (the asset account that is debited to correspond with the credit to income) would be an asset; however, that prompts substantial ambiguity. Sometimes, no asset is debited because the item produced by the income is immediately consumed. Likely the original drafters were not accountants and were thinking of the assets corresponding to the income, if any.

Consider EXAMPLE 10. If a spouse owned a nonmarital bond, the interest income it produced would result in nonmarital cash. If the owner/earner spouse accumulated the nonmarital cash in a separate account, it would remain separate, as would the bond. That example is sufficiently clear to require no litigation.

EXAMPLE 10

Bond Example: Interest Used for the Family

Spouse A owned a bond prior to marrying Spouse B. The bond has a face value of $100,000, a 30-year life and pays $5,000 interest annually. A retains the interest (ignore taxes for this example) in a separate account.

But what does the remainder of the paragraph mean? If "the income was treated, used, or relied upon by the parties as a marital asset" apparently the income is marital. Once again, income cannot be an asset, so this must refer to the debited asset corresponding to the credited income. If that asset were used by the parties as marital, it appears to become marital.

Consider EXAMPLE 11. The owner/earner spouse uses the bond interest proceeds to purchase a new table and chairs which the family uses for meals. The table and chairs would be "treated, used, or relied upon" by the parties as a marital asset. Unfortunately, the statute suggests the "income" is the resulting marital asset, as opposed to the item purchased with the proceeds representing the income. Facially, the statute makes no sense; thus, it would surely be interpreted to refer to the table and chairs purchased with the income proceeds. Thus, the table and chairs would be marital, despite their origin as non-marital when the value used to acquire them was merely in the form of cash.

EXAMPLE 11

Bond Example: Interest Used for the Family

Spouse A owned a bond prior to marrying Spouse B. The bond has a face value of $100,000, a 30-year life and pays $5,000 interest annually. A uses the $5,000 to purchase a dining room table and chairs which the family uses daily. The parties are seeking a divorce.

Picture EXAMPLE 11 using debits, credits. Spouse A receives the bond interest in the form of a check and deposits it into a bank account. A debits cash and credits income for $5,000. At this moment, the cash is separate property if the account is in the name of Spouse A. A uses the cash as soon as the funds have cleared (been collected by the bank) to purchase the table and chairs. A would debit table/chairs and would credit cash. That—*if traceable to that extent*—makes the table and chairs marital. If not, then paragraph (b)(3) has no meaning. At this point in our examination of the statute it is adequately clear and arguably reasonable, albeit sloppily drafted.

That example, however, prompts some interesting questions and observations. The rule that treating a non-marital asset as marital converts it to marital applies only to paragraph 3 assets: those resulting from income from non-marital assets. It does not apply to paragraph 1 or 2 nonmarital assets.

Suppose Spouse B receives a gift of $5,000 from a parent. Spouse B would debit cash and credit gift income or something of the sort. The cash would be non-marital. If Spouse B then used the $5,000 to purchase bedroom furniture, that furniture would remain non-marital per paragraph (b)(2). The "treated, used, relied on" language applies to income derived from non-marital assets in (b)(3), but not to the assets themselves and especially not to (b)(2) gifts or bequests. Arguably, the difference between what Spouse A did and what Spouse B did is not significant. One used "income" and one used "principal"; but money being fungible, that difference is elusive. Had Spouse A accumulated funds for many years and later used them, one must at least ask whether the funds ever lost their character as "income." The question is odd because *no* asset, including money, is *ever* income. It is at best the *proceeds* of income.

Similarly, if Spouse A used cash brought into the marriage to purchase the kitchen table and chairs, that would remain separate under paragraph 1. The conversion-from-use rule applies only when the nonmarital asset is connected to income from nonmarital assets. Why the drafters would draw such a line is unclear.[1] Further, how the purchasing spouse would distinguish between using the *principal* brought into the marriage rather than the *income* it produced—interest, dividends, rents—is unclear. Money is fungible. Accounting traditionally treats all cash the same, regardless of source. The law, however, clearly does not. But the law often neglects to provide a "tracing" rule to help people understand which money is which. Ultimately, the burden will be on the one asserting an asset remains separate. That will require some non-typical accounting.

Another question involves a more literal reading of the statute. Perhaps instead of reading common-sense into the law and presuming the drafters intended to describe the assets corresponding to the income as the nonmarital assets . . . perhaps we should take the paragraph literally for what it says. Although income cannot be an asset, future income certainly can be. Consider EXAMPLE 12.

---

[1]   I testified regarding this and related issues in 1986 before the Florida Senate committee considering the proposed law (which it adopted as written above). I cautioned the members that income cannot be an asset and about the disparate treatment of assets, but they did not follow my advice.

EXAMPLE 12

Bond Example: Interest Used for the Family

Spouse A owned a bond prior to marrying Spouse B. The bond has a face value of $100,000, a 30-year life and pays $5,000 interest annually. A uses the interest to pay needed family expenses such as utilities, transportation, food, and rent. Without the $5,000, the spouses would have a noticeably lower standard of living. The parties seek a divorce, and the bond does not mature for another 20 years.

Spouse A regularly used the money received as interest from the nonmarital bond to provide for family support including utilities, transportation, food, and housing. Spouse A would be treating the "income" as a marital stream of income. The family would be relying upon the investment proceeds to live, both currently as well as their continued existence. Indeed, the statute is irrelevant if applied to current income because that is used for food and electricity and this produces no remaining asset to divide. Logically, that mean the future income is the asset the paragraph refers to. Did the reliance upon the income stream convert the income stream into a marital asset?

If so, then the remaining twenty years of future bond interest is the asset the spouses relied upon. Indeed, that seems to be the most "common sense" way of reading it. In EXAMPLE 12, the bond has a face value of $100,000. To analyze this, we need to know the current value of the bond. To keep the problem simple, let's assume the value is also $100,000. Using well-established and commonly-used methods to value the income stream (the remaining interest as opposed to the principle due in twenty years) the present value of the income stream—the future income relied upon—would be about $75,000. Under that view, by regularly consuming the income proceeds (as opposed to purchasing assets with it), Spouse A converted 75% of the bond value to marital.

If Spouse A were savvy in finance and accounting, he/she could have sold the bond and then invested the proceeds such that the principal remained separate from the income proceeds. Spouse A would use separate accounts as well as for accounting. Then Spouse A could regularly invade (spend) funds withdrawn from the principal account for family needs but would keep the income account separate and untouched but increasing regularly as both it and the principal account earned income, all of which would go into the income account. Nothing in the statute converts separate principal to marital even if treated, used, and relied upon as marital. Anything purchased with it would be irrelevant because it would be consumed: the food, cleaning products, utilities, and rent. Whether a court would collapse this scheme into EXAMPLE 11 is unclear. Facially, Spouse A could trace all reliance to principal and never to income. Spouse B would appear to have the burden of convincing the court to undue the scheme.

Or perhaps Spouse A would use the funds from selling the bond to purchase cattle or land. Spouse A could keep all calves born but sell part of the original herd for family needs. Or Spouse A could, from time to time, sell a portion of the land to satisfy family needs, keeping any rental income proceeds separate. Such examples remove the fungibility issue in the bond example and would seem far more difficult to collapse.

Why are such schemes possible, especially considering they lack any real substantive differences between them? They are possible because the legislature defined income as an asset. That facially makes no sense. It allows accountants to manipulate the facts the change the result without changing the substance.

I asked that question in 1986 to the Florida Senate committee considering the statute. The committee had no answer. Indeed, the committee chair chastised me because I called future income an asset after I'd previously said current income is never an asset. I tried, but I failed to explain the clear difference. Future income is an asset. It is what gives principal and everything value. In financial and economic terms, an asset is worth the present value of its future utility. Thus, an asset is always the present value of its future use. Future income is always an asset; however, as soon as it becomes current income, it loses its character as an asset. That occurs because the "income" creates a credit to a temporary account that ultimately appears on an income statement. The proceeds of the income may result in a related debit to cash, but the cash is not the income. The income is the income. Ultimately, that income becomes part of equity, which also is never an asset.

In 1986, I predicted the issue would remain unresolved for many years. As of 2022, Florida appellate courts have failed to address the issue.

LESSON FIVE

DEPRECIATION, AMORTIZATION, AND DEPLETION

Basics of Cost Allocation

■ ■ ■

Lesson Objectives

1. Student will learn that depreciation varies among GAAP, tax law, and internal accounting.

2. Student will learn how to compute depreciation under various methods.

3. Student will learn that depreciation is one of the most easily manipulated accounting factors.

Terminology Introduced

- Depreciation.
- Amortization.
- Depletion.
- Accelerated depreciation.
- Straight-line method.
- Declining balance method.
- Double declining balance method.
- Sum-of-the-years' digits method.
- Salvage value.
- Accumulated depreciation.
- Contra asset.
- Book value.
- Convention.
- Adjusted basis.
- IRC section 179.
- Cost segregation.

LESSON FIVE has four parts:

A: Introduction to depreciation.

B: Basis, salvage value, useful life, and conventions.

C: Methods of depreciation.

D: Reconciliation and recapture.

LESSON FIVE-A

INTRODUCTION TO DEPRECIATION

■ ■ ■

Cost allocation is essential for accrual accounting and fundamental for the matching principle: we match income with the costs of producing that income. To accomplish this, we must allocate many costs over multiple periods—the periods in which those costs help produce income. Accountants allocate costs using three broad techniques:

- Depreciation.

- Amortization.

- Depletion.

The first two—depreciation and amortization—are very similar. They primarily differ in what they affect: depreciation applies to tangible property and amortization applies to intangible property. Otherwise, they serve the exact same purpose: allocating depreciable or amortizable costs over the useful life of the asset. How they apply mechanically often differs: depreciation has multiple methods (straight-line, declining balance, usage) while amortization almost always involves the straight-line method. Depletion, in contrast, applies to minerals and is mechanically very different. This chapter focuses on depreciation.

1.   TERMINOLOGY

Let's review some important terminology:

- **Capitalize**: This is the process of adding costs (debiting them) to an asset account. It increases the basis of an asset. We capitalize costs we anticipate we will properly allocate over a period of years.

- **Expense**: We expense a cost we want to allocate to the current period. This may be the entire cost of the asset (such as a box of pencils with an immaterial cost) or it may be a portion of the capitalized depreciable basis of an asset.

- **Basis**: This is the historical cost of an asset.

- **Depreciable Basis**: This is the portion of an asset's basis that is allocable over its useful life. Generally, this is the historical cost, adjusted for capitalized improvements less the Salvage Value.

- **Adjusted Basis**: This is the current basis of an asset—its historical cost adjusted upward for capitalized improvements and adjusted downward for depreciation expense (and sometimes other expenses).

- **Useful Life**: This is the expected productive life of the asset for the owner.

- **Salvage Value**: This is the expected value of the asset at the end of its useful life.

- **Convention**: This is an arbitrary determination regarding the acquisition and disposition date of an asset.

2. WHY DO YOU CARE ABOUT DEPRECIATION?

Why does depreciation matter to a lawyer? It matters because it is easily manipulated and because it is material: in simple terms, it matters because it matters. Whoever makes the decisions regarding capitalization, useful life, convention, salvage value, and depreciation method has substantial power over an entity's *reported* income.

Depreciation Can Affect *You*

If your income is a function of another's income, then the other's depreciation decisions affect you, probably substantially.

If your compensation is a function of that income, then each of those decisions affects *your* income—and the effect can be large. If you let someone else make those decisions with no input from you, then you risk having all the decisions made in a manner that hurts you and helps the other person. Almost certainly, the various decisions—whether to capitalize, how long an asset lasts, what convention to use, what depreciation method to use—grant broad discretion to the decision-maker. That is true whether the standard is GAAP, IFRS, SEC rules, state family law, state trust law, or general contract law. If you want to control the decision-making, then you need to do so. But, to do so, you first need to understand the options. Then you must understand freedom of contract: you can define depreciation methods, conventions, and other variable in a contract however you wish, so long as the other parties agree.

Depreciation Does _Not_ Affect Cash

Another important thing to remember is this: depreciation has no impact on cash; hence, it does not affect the statement of cash flows. It is not an expense in the sense that it is costing you money on a current basis; however, it is a real expense in that the related asset is likely losing value over time and eventually will have to be replaced.

Why should you care about the depreciation in the EXAMPLES 11 and 12? You care because the cost of things—buildings, vehicles, tables, machinery, software, trademarks—is large. The expense or capitalization plus depreciation will affect:

- An entity's stock price.

- An entity's ability to get a loan.

- An owner's alimony or child support if a divorce is involved; or, the same issues for an employee whose salary/bonus is a function of entity income.

- Anything else that is a function of income.

Remember: the decision to expense something or to capitalize it and depreciate it is often a judgment call—particularly for tax depreciation— which means it can be manipulated.

Focus on each separate fact or scenario in EXAMPLE 13 as they are packed with ambiguity. We have a commonly used arrangement under which you receive 10% of my profits as a bonus. The word "profits" is itself unclear without a definition. Capitalization and depreciation are an important part of that word. If you let me define the word "profits," I am likely to do so in a manner disadvantageous to you and yet I could still be consistent with GAAP or IFRS.

EXAMPLE 13

Depreciation Affects You

You are paid 10% of my profits. I purchase a machine for $1,000,000. It has a ten-year life.

- If I expense it this year, my income is $1 million lower, and you receive $100,000 less.

- If I capitalize it and depreciate $100,000 per year for ten years, my income is only $100,000 lower each year—and you receive $10,000 less each year.

This affects the _timing_ of _your income_ and the _amount_ if you only work some of the years.

I purchase a machine for $1,000,000. Apparently, that is its historical cost and becomes its basis. But, as covered in LESSON ONE, what "costs" form the basis of a particular asset is often subject to judgement. Delivery costs, installation costs, employee training to use the machine, an extended warranty and insurance are all arguably part of the cost—and arguably not. Thus, you may not want to simply accept my statement that my cost was $1,000,000.

It has a useful life of 10 years. Says who? Perhaps that is clear or perhaps it is an estimate. For example, the average life of a dishwasher (not a million-dollar machine but bear with the example) is 10 years. But one can last a much shorter period while another can last longer. The same is true of most things. But, as you will see, the longer the useful life, the lower the depreciation per year and thus the higher the income. Hence, if I must pay you 10% of my income, I have an incentive to choose a shorter life for the machine. This is likely a judgment call: it might be 8 years or 9 or 12. I likely choose using good judgement, but my choice can substantially affect you in any event.

I may have an option to expense the machine, at least for tax purposes. If so, that could have a huge impact on my profits in the year of acquisition and thus your income. Of course, expensing it this year would result in no deduction in future years, which would increase my income for those years and increase yours; however, you and I may have a one-year contract, in which case, the future impact is irrelevant to you.

In contrast, if I capitalize the $1,000,000 cost and then depreciate it straight-line over ten years, it reduces my income by $100,000 per year and yours by $10,000. Hence, my choices affect both the _timing_ of your income as well as the _amount_. This impact can have substantial collateral legal consequences:

- If my business is publicly traded, my income will affect my stock price; hence, my choices regarding depreciation of valuable assets will have that effect. I thus might want a long life and a high capitalized historical cost to inflate my income.

- If either of us applies for a loan, our respective incomes will be important. Once again, I would want a long life for the asset and a higher capitalized cost.

- But one of us might be going through a divorce and be concerned about child support and alimony. If so, we would prefer to report lower income. As a result, we would prefer to expense as much of the cost as possible (and thus capitalize as little as possible) and then use as short a life as possible to deflate current income, deferring it to years which do not affect the legal matter.

Throughout this course, we consider many instances in which a legal result is the function of income. If that "income" is business-related, it likely involves depreciation or amortization, which may be very substantial. In the long run, the choices have zero impact: eventually all expenses appear as expenses. For example, whether I expense the machine in one year or ten or fifteen, it ultimately—over time—reduces my income by $1 million. No more and no less. But for many collateral legal consequences, the timing is what is most important. People do not apply for loans every year and they certainly do not get divorced every year. Thus, while the judgment calls regarding capitalization and depreciation may have no *ultimate* impact, they can have a material impact in individual years—which may be all that matters to you.

Consider the various uses of depreciation:

- Tax law.

- Financial accounting.

- Internal or cost accounting.

Tax Law: As we will cover, U.S. tax law (and that of other countries) have arbitrary rules regarding depreciation and amortization. These often differ substantially from GAAP or IFRS. Remember, the purpose of an income tax is to raise revenue (and sometimes to impact the economy) rather than to represent reality. As a result, income reported for tax purposes may be very different than income reported for financial purposes. Thus, in EXAMPLE 13, using tax income from the entity rather than financial income could have a large effect on you.

Financial Accounting: GAAP and IFRS will control this, if one of these applies (a large if, as we covered in LESSON TWO). Financial depreciation and amortization, at least under GAAP, differs materially from tax depreciation.

Internal and Cost Accounting: Internally, a business can prepare whatever information it wants. It may adjust depreciation and amortization or omit it entirely. As we cover in LESSON SEVEN, EBITDA is a commonly used measure. It refers to earnings before interest, tax, depreciation, and amortization. In EXAMPLE 13, you may want to see how management deals with depreciation for tax, financial, and internal purposes.

3. DEPRECIATION IN THE BOOKS

Next, consider EXAMPLE 14. It ignores salvage value and a convention, topics for LESSON FIVE-B. It assumes straight-line depreciation, which means we treat each year the same. LESSON FIVE-C covers other methods. It assumes a purchase date at the beginning of the year to make the problem simple; otherwise, we would need to allocate for the days the desk was used unless we adopted a convention.

EXAMPLE 14
Simple Depreciation Example
Paula purchased a desk for $5,000 cash. Assume straight-line depreciation, a life of five years, zero salvage value, no convention, and a purchase date of January 2d. <ul><li>Show the journal entries for the purchase and for depreciation for the first year.</li><li>Show the balance sheet item for the desk.</li></ul>

Initially, note EXAMPLE 14 does not provide all the needed information. The date of acquisition is not the critical date for depreciation; instead, the date the asset is placed into service is critical. In most cases, the dates will be the same or very close to the same to not matter. But conceivably, a business could purchase a desk on January 2, 2021, but not plan to use it until 2022 or even 2023. If so, the desk would not be depreciable until placed into service—when someone began to use it. The journal entries for depreciation appear in **Figure 50**.

General Journal for Paula			
Date	Account	Debit	Credit
1/2	**Desk**	**5,000**	
	Cash		**5,000**
	Purchase of desk.		
12/31	**Depreciation Expense**	**1,000**	
	Accumulated Depreciation		**1,000**
	SL depreciation on asset with 5-yr life.		

Figure 50: General Journal for EXAMPLE 14, Year 1

The first entry in **Figure 50** reflects the purchase of the desk, with a debit and a credit to asset accounts: increasing the account "desk" and decreasing cash. The second entry is an adjusting entry. It appears here at the end of the year. We could alternatively do this monthly. As you should recall, adjusting entries occur at the end of each period to reflect matters that occur continuously—things such as depreciation, amortization, and accrual of regular items such as interest income and expense. The amount involved is $1,000 because we allocated—using the straight-line method—the $5,000 cost basis (historical cost) over five years. It is "straight-line" because we choose to treat each year the same. If we were to graph it, the graph would be a straight line across the page.

Paula's Balance Sheet December 31, Year 1			
Assets		**Liabilities**	
Desk	5,000		
Accum. Depr.	(1,000)		
Net	4,000		
Total Assets		**Liabilities & Equity**	

Figure 51: Balance Sheet for EXAMPLE 14, Year 1

As shown in **Figure 51**, the balance sheet would list the tangible asset at its $5,000 historical but would then show the accumulated depreciation "contra asset" as a negative. Then it would show the net amount. In the second year, the adjusting entry would be the same $1,000 debit to depreciation expense and $1,000 credit to accumulated depreciation. At the end of the second year, the balance sheet would continue to show the desk at its $5,000 historical cost but then with accumulated depreciation "contra asset" of $2,000 and thus a net book value of $3,000. Eventually, after five years, the desk would have a book value of zero, as shown in **Figure 52**.

Paula's Balance Sheet December 31, Year 5			
Assets			**Liabilities**
Desk	5,000		
Accum. Depr.	(5,000)		
Net		00	
Total Assets			**Liabilities & Equity**

Figure 52: Balance Sheet for EXAMPLE 14, Year 5

Stop and consider the meaning of book value: it is the historical cost of an asset with upward adjustments for improvements (at cost) and downward adjustments for depreciation, amortization or other recorded losses and impairments. It is another term for the asset's adjusted basis. It does not, however, reflect the fair market value of the asset. Perhaps the desk is worth more than $5,000. That may be unlikely, but some assets do indeed appreciation—though the increase in real economic value would not normally be reflected in the balance sheet. We will see limited exceptions to this in LESSON EIGHT in relation to marketable securities under GAAP.

CAUTION   **Be Very Wary of Book Value**

As a lawyer, you should be very careful about using the book value of any asset. It may be accurate, but it likely is not and is not meant to be. Depreciation and amortization are arbitrary. They may approximate economic reality, particularly over the long-run, but never assume they reflect economic reality, especially in the short-run or when looking at only some assets. If someone were to offer to pay you "book value" for an asset, you should be wary. The conservatism principle suggests the asset is worth at least book value: if it is not and the loss is material, the CPA would likely consider it an impairment and would require recognition of an unrealized loss. But, except as covered in LESSON EIGHT, a business would not increase an asset over historical cost less adjustments. Thus, the book value of an asset could be modest while the actual economic value could be great.

Imagine a marriage dissolution case in which Wife owns a building used in her business with a book value of $100,000. It could have a fair market value of $3,000,000 but would still appear at its historical cost less depreciation. Thus, it would appear as $100,000. Husband would be very ill-advised to accept half the $100,000 book value. He should seek half the $3,000,000 fair market value.

LESSON FIVE-B

BASIS, SALVAGE VALUE, USEFUL LIFE, AND CONVENTIONS

■ ■ ■

LESSONS FIVE-B and C deal with the computation of depreciation, which comprises five elements:

- Basis, adjusted basis, and depreciable basis.

- Salvage value.

- Useful life.

- Conventions.

- Methods of depreciation.

LESSON FIVE-B deals with the first four issues. LESSON FIVE-C deals with methods. We focus on depreciation rather than amortization. Generally, the same issues arise in relation to amortization of intangibles; however, salvage value is less of a consideration, if at all.

Each issue is subject to choices and the exercise of judgment. Further, tax law, financial accounting, and internal/cost accounting also deal with each issue and can result in differing amounts or choices for each. As a result, considerable divergence can—though it may not—arise among the various purposes for which a business calculates depreciation.

1. BASIS, ADJUSTED BASIS, AND DEPRECIABLE BASIS

To review from prior discussions, all assets have a basis for tax law and for financial accounting, although the amount may (and often will) differ between the two. Basis starts with the historical cost of the asset, with adjustments made for capitalization of various related items such as delivery and set-up costs. Management can exercise some judgment regarding which costs to capitalize as part of the basis of a particular asset and which to expense separately or to define as a separate asset.

That raises the question of "what is the asset," which we discussed earlier in relation to cost segregation. To review an earlier example, management may consider a building to be a single asset, or it may segregate the ceiling tiles, windows, and other fixtures into a variety of assets with differing useful lives, conventions, and methods of depreciation. This can have a material impact on income as a result.

Once management determines what comprises the asset and its cost basis, it must then adjust that basis for future improvements, impairments, or depreciation/amortization. This results in the adjusted basis of the asset. That amount is critical for determination of gain or loss upon the disposition of the item. For example, if a desk has an adjusted basis of $3,000 but is sold for $2,300, the owner suffers a $700 loss. If instead it is sold for $3,600, the owner recognizes a $600 gain.

For U.S. tax law purposes, IRC section 1012[1] determines the cost basis and section 1016[2] the adjusted basis. Both GAAP and IFRS have detailed rules for these concepts, as well. The particulars are beyond this course. What you must know is that all assets have a basis of zero or a positive number. The concept of a negative basis is mostly forbidden (the exceptions, if any are far beyond this introductory course). Thus, the computer you use, the clothes you wear, your car, your furniture . . . indeed every asset you own—whether for personal use or business use—has a cost basis and an adjusted basis (though the two can be identical).

Below we consider salvage value. For now, understand that depreciable basis is the cost basis (or adjusted basis in some cases) less the salvage value. Only that portion of the basis is subject to depreciation.

For U.S. tax purposes, the adjusted basis of an asset follows the asset when it is distributed incident to a divorce.[3] As a result, the adjusted tax basis of an asset can be a very important number—perhaps as important or even more important than the fair market value of the item. A knowledge of both accounting and tax law is thus important for property division matters. Unfortunately, in at least some states, the information regarding basis is not readily available.

For example, in Florida, the standard financial affidavit requires both spouses to list assets and estimated value, but not cost basis or adjusted basis.[4] The Florida standard interrogatories,[5] amended in 2017, request

---

[1]   IRC § 1012.

[2]   IRC § 1016.

[3]   IRC § 1041 treats transfers incident to divorce or between spouses as if they were gifts. Per IRC § 1014, the recipient's basis of an asset received by gift is the basis of the donor.

[4]   Florida Family Law Rule of Procedure FORM 12.902(c). The form has space for "Current Fair Market Value" but no space for historical cost or adjusted basis.

[5]   Florida Family Law Rules of Procedure FL 12.930(b). Oddly, the form does not specify whether the depreciation "taken" regarding real property is for tax purposes or financial purposes. Likely it is for tax purposes, but that conclusion comes from experience and common sense, not

the cost and amount of depreciation "taken"[6] for real property, but fail to request any information other than cost for personal property, including intangible property. Similarly, the interrogatories fail to request basis information for items held in trust. Without information regarding the tax basis, parties cannot make informed decisions regarding the division of property—and neither can the court.

Consider EXAMPLE 15 to demonstrate the importance of basis information in a family law matter:

EXAMPLE 15

Family Law Divorce Game

You and your spouse seek a dissolution of your marriage. You have three marital assets. You agree one spouse will choose an asset to receive. The other spouse will receive the remaining two assets. The assets are:

- Cash of $100,000.

- An office building with a fair market value of $100,000 but a tax adjusted basis of $10,000.

- Securities with a fair market value of $100,000 but a tax basis of $3,000,000.

- Do you want to pick first? If yes, which do you pick?

For the example, ready willing and able purchasers are available to buy the building and securities for cash. The fair market value is the amount remaining after all transfer costs. To decide, you would need to know not merely the adjusted basis of each asset, but also the likely after-tax value.

The cash is worth $100,000. The office building has an after-tax value of about $77,500,[7] and the securities have an after-tax value ranging from $125,000 to $1,600,000.[8] To be more precise, one would need additional

---

from anything in the form or its instructions. Properly, the form should request both the depreciation allowed and the amount allowable for tax purposes. It should do so for both real and personal property, and it should also request amortization allowed or allowable for intangible property.

[6] Per IRC § 1016, the tax adjusted basis of an asset is a function of the depreciation taken (and from which the party benefitted), and the depreciation the party could have taken but failed to take. As a result, the interrogatory is poorly phrased.

[7] The building would have $90,000 built-in gain which would be taxed as unrecaptured § 1250 gain, subject to a maximum 25% rate. IRC § 1(h)(1)(E).

[8] The securities would almost certainly be long-term capital assets and would thus generate a $2,900,000 long-term capital loss. Per IRC §§ 1211–12, the loss would be deductible to the extent of capital gains, affecting long-term gains before short-term gains with a lifetime carryover. Further, the seller could deduct up to $3,000 of the loss annually against ordinary income. As a result, the seller would receive $100,000 plus at least the lifetime benefit of the $3,000 annual deduction. The present value of that approximates $125,000. More likely, someone with such

information, such as the financial well-being of each spouse and the tax knowledge of each spouse and his/her advisors. Gamesmanship would also come into play. One might, for example, prefer the securities and the built-in loss (a valuable "asset" in its own right); however, if one thought his/her spouse was ill-advised, he/she might choose second believing the other would choose the gain property rather than the loss property.

The point is not to train you to be a tax lawyer. Instead, it is to insure you know the critical importance of basis plus some accounting and tax knowledge for the practice of family law.

2. SALVAGE VALUE

Salvage value is the estimated value an asset will retain at the end of its expected useful life. Generally, the amount is small or zero, but that varies by asset and by who is making the estimate.

For example, a $5,000 desk may last twenty or more years in a law practice. At that point, it may be relatively invaluable, and the time of thing sold at a garage sale for perhaps $100. Or it could be a very nice mahogany desk and increase in value. Pianos tend to have a high salvage value while automobiles tend to have a low salvage value if used ten years.

For U.S. tax purposes, salvage value is presumed to be zero under section 168.[9] For financial accounting, management must determine a salvage value for each asset. It then subtracts that amount from the items cost basis to determine its depreciable basis. Because actual economic salvage value tends to be small, the room for manipulation or distortion in relation to this issue is also small.

3. USEFUL LIFE

The expected useful life of an asset is another item for management to estimate. This is the period over which a business expects to use an asset. This issue has room for judgment and thus manipulation particularly in tax law.

For U.S. tax purposes, section 168(c)[10] arbitrarily assigns a "recovery period" to depreciable assets used in a trade or business. Congress set these shorter than economic reality would typically suggest to effectively subsidize the purchase of business assets. Arguably, that stimulates the economy—the more equipment purchased, the more people are employed and the better off we all are. Whether the economics work is not the subject

---

assets would have future capital gains, including short-term gains which could result in substantially greater tax benefits. For example, if the seller married a person with $2.9 million of short-term gains, the benefit (including state and local taxes) could exceed $1,500,000, resulting in a present after-tax value of about $1.6 million.

[9]   IRC § 168(b)(4).

[10]   IRC § 168(c).

of the course. But, as a lawyer, you need to understand that U.S. tax depreciation recovery periods (effectively the useful life, but not exactly) are artificially short, which results in higher depreciation in the early years of an asset's life and thus lower income for the owner.

That result may be good economics and good tax policy, but it does purport to reflect economic reality. Thus, it necessarily results in artificially low reported income for tax purposes and artificially low adjusted tax basis (and thus book value) for depreciable property. Lawyers must be careful dealing with contracts, tort cases, family law matters and other cases in which the income of a party matters or in which the reported value of an item matters. Likely in all legal matters (other than tax law) the tax depreciation should mostly be irrelevant.

Determination of U.S. _tax_ useful life is complicated. It involves several steps.

1. **Determine the "class life".** Pursuant to IRC section 168(i)(1),[11] assets have a class life largely based on Revenue Procedure 87–56.[12]

2. **Determine how the property is "treated"** under section (e)(1) which provides:

Property shall be treated as:	If such property has a class life (in years) of:
3-year property	4 or less
5-year property	More than 4 but less than 10
7-year property	10 or more but less than 16
10-year property	16 or more but less than 20
15-year property	20 or more but less than 25
20-year property	25 or more.[13]

These are intentional reductions in the lives of assets. Congress enacted this to encourage businesses to purchase assets. By shortening the lives, Congress effectively subsidizes the purchase through the early allowance of depreciation expenses for tax purposes. Congress further enacted special treatment for particular assets, again with the intention of either favoring or disfavoring the acquisition of them. For example, section 168(c)(3)(D) provides:

---

[11] IRC § 168(i)(1). The "class life" is an evidence-based range. The 168(e)(1) treatment is arbitrarily shorter than the class life.

[12] Rev. Proc. 87–56, 1987–2 C.B. 674 (1987).

[13] IRC § 168(e)(1).

The term "10-year property" includes—

(i) any single purpose agricultural or horticultural structure (within the meaning of subsection (i)(13)),

(ii) any tree or vine bearing fruit or nuts, and

(iii) any qualified smart electric meter, and

(iv) any qualified smart electric grid system.[14]

Notice the favorable treatment for fruit and nut bearing trees as well as for "smart' " electrical systems. Whether such provisions are wise economic or tax policy is irrelevant to this course; instead, you should focus on the existence of the provisions and how they likely differ from economic reality. In a legal matter in which "income" is relevant, the economic reality of that income is arguably more relevant than the tax treatment. But the tax treatment will likely be the most easily obtainable information, however inaccurate it may be.

3. **Determine the "recovery period"** for the assets pursuant to section 168(c)(1):

In the case of:	The applicable recovery period is:
3-year property	3 years
5-year property	5 years
7-year property	7 years
10-year property	10 years
15-year property	15 years
20-year property	20 years
Water utility property	25 years
Resident rental property	27.5 years
Nonresidential real property	39 years
Any railroad grading or tunnel bore	50 years

Largely this step changes nothing—3, 5, 7, 10, 15, and 20-year property have a recovery period of those number of years; however, it illustrates the complexity of tax law. The recovery period is what a business would use for U.S. tax purposes as the "useful life" of the asset.

In contrast, for financial accounting purposes, a business would examine the real expected life of the asset, modified to a shorter period if the business intends to use it for only part of its expected life. The real life

---

[14] IRC § 168(c)(3)(D).

is likely comparable to the old "class life" system used in tax law. That system provided ranges for most assets.

Management, with the ultimately approval of the auditors, must select the useful life of assets. A 1987 New York Times article described a choice made by General Motors:

> General Motors. . . revised . . . accounting procedures, enabling it to avoid reporting a third-quarter operating loss . . . .
>
> With the accounting revision . . . G.M. reported . . . net income . . . more than doubled, to $812 million . . . compared with $345.1 million . . . in the comparable 1986 quarter.
>
> Under the revised accounting policy, G.M. will . . . assume longer depreciation periods to charge off its investments in plants and equipment. Without the revision, G.M. would have reported an operating loss of $537 million . . . .[15]

However valid, the change in the useful life affected quarterly earnings by more than $1.3 billion, which was over $5 billion annually, back in 1987. This change occurred for financial reporting purposes, not tax purposes. Over time, the change was irrelevant, as ultimately the plant and equipment would be fully depreciated; however, for the immediate years involved in the late 1980's, the change was remarkable.

Pay particular attention to that because it reflects the purpose of this course and what you should learn. Accounting changes and choices may not have any impact over a large period (one either deducts an expense now or later); however, the impact on a single year in isolation can be huge. Lawyers tend to look at isolated periods. For example, in a tort case measuring lost income, a court is likely to look at the few years prior to the injury, rather than the entire life of the earner. Similarly, in a divorce case, the court will likely determine child support and alimony obligations by examining the years near the date of separation, rather than all year, particularly future ones. Your job as a lawyer is to help the court put isolated years into perspective. You must understand that accounting choices can be distorting, especially when viewed in the short run. General Motors in 1987 did not suddenly have an economic profit rather than a loss; instead, it merely changed an assumption regarding the useful life of material assets.

4. CONVENTIONS

In both financial accounting and in tax law, a convention assumes a common purchase or disposition date for assets. This simplifies the

---

[15] New York Times 10/28/1987.

computation of depreciation. Over the life of the assets, it has little impact; however, in a particular year, it can have a large impact.

The most common convention is the mid-year convention. U.S. tax law requires it for most non-real property and financial accounting permits it. Under the convention, a business treats all purchases as occurring on July 1 and all dispositions as occurring on June 30 (assuming a calendar year). As a result, the business need not deal with actual purchase and disposition dates for depreciation calculations.

For example, if JOE'S BAR & GRILL were to purchase a new computer on January 12, 2022, it would record the purchase in its general journal on that date. But, if it adopted the mid-year depreciation convention, it would accrue depreciation expense attributable to the computer for only one-half year in 2022. Assuming a three-year useful life, it would then accrue a full year of depreciation expense in 2023 and 2024, and then a half-year in 2025. Hence, the item with a three-year life would be depreciated over four calendar years: two half years and two full years. If JOE'S were to sell the computer on October 22, 2024, it would accrue only a half-year of depreciation expense for 2024.

Notice the simplicity that results. JOE'S would use the computer for 344 days in 2022—94.24% of a year rather than 50% of the year. Similarly, it would use it for 80.82% of a year in 2024 rather than 50% of the year. In the life of a business, it likely purchases depreciable assets throughout the year; hence, assuming all are purchased on July 1st typically evens out with little real impact other than simplicity. However, the convention can have a significant impact in a single year, particularly if management so desires. For example, if either Scott or Adrian wanted the income for 2021 to be low—perhaps one is seeking a divorce and is concerned about child support or alimony—he/she could accelerate a planned purchase of a major asset from 2022 into late 2021. As a result, JOE'S would take a half-year of depreciation in 2021, even if the asset were placed into service late in December.

Other permissible (and sometimes required) conventions are the mid-quarter and mid-month. As their names suggest, they respectively presume all purchases and dispositions of depreciable assets occur on the mid-date of the quarter or month.

LESSON FIVE-C

METHODS OF DEPRECIATION AND AMORTIZATION

■ ■ ■

LESSON FIVE-C considers the three main methods of depreciation:

- Straight-line.

- Accelerated.

- Per unit or usage.

Amortization (for intangibles) is almost always straight-line.[16] For depreciation, management has considerable leeway in choosing the method.

Before we examine the methods, briefly consider two competing theories of depreciation. Both have some validity and some inaccuracies. Neither control fully. They are:

- Cost allocation.

- Loss in value.

Under the cost allocation theory, the purpose of depreciation is merely to allocate the cost of the asset over its useful life. This is generally consistent with the matching principle of accounting: match the costs of producing income with the income they produce. Assuming an asset roughly produces income evenly over its useful life, this theory is generally consistent with straight-line depreciation.

A competing theory focuses on loss in value. Accelerated depreciation is most consistent with this theory: assets tend to lose value more quickly in the early years of their lives and less in the latter years. This theory is more consistent with the economic reality of income—it attempts to recognize costs as they incur.

Assuming a business continually purchases assets, the two theories are not likely much at odds. Depreciation for some assets may be greater than cost allocation would desire, but depreciation for other assets is likely lesser. The same applies to the loss-in-value theory: some assets will lose value greater than the income they produce justifies, but other assets will lose less. Over time, the costs are the same. With sufficient assets, the differences probably average to zero. That consolation, however, ignores

---

[16]   An important exception appears in § 467(f) of the Internal Revenue Code, dealing with pre-paid rent. It effectively imposes an economically real, _upward_ sloping curve. Discussion of the provision is beyond this course.

the periodic assumption of accounting, which attempts to reflect income annually. To the extent one focuses on the long run, the periodic assumption matters little, but to the extent one focuses on the short run, it can matter a great deal. Lawyers and legal matters tend to focus on one year or a few years; hence, the theories and methods matter more from a lawyer's perspective than from an accountant's.

1. STRAIGHT-LINE DEPRECIATION

While simple to use, straight-line depreciation and amortization are unlikely to reflect economic reality. Life experience informs you that most assets do not lose value evenly over their useful lives. Nevertheless, because it is simple, it is also common.

For example, if JOE'S purchased a gas grill for $5,000 expecting to use it for 5 years, it would depreciate $1,000 per year for each year (assuming zero salvage, a January 1 purchase date, and no convention). If, instead, JOE'S expected to use the grill for 10 years, the depreciation would be $500 per year. Whatever the useful life, straight-line depreciation effectively—though probably not accurately—allocates the cost of an asset over its life. It very generally approximates the asset's probable loss in value. Likely, the grill lost more value in the first year of use and much less in the last 2 years. If JOE'S sells the grill after using it for 6 months of a 5-year life, JOE'S would have taken $500 depreciation; however, the used grill would probably sell for considerably less than its $4,500 adjusted basis. Your own life experience should tell you a grill used for 6 months is significantly less valuable than a brand new one. In contrast, a 5-year-old used grill probably is worth about the same as one 4-years old.

Theoretically, straight-line depreciation—ignoring the time value of money—properly allocates costs. In the example, the Grill undoubtedly loses significant value quickly in the first year and then much more slowly; however, its utility to JOE'S is probably equal over the years: JOE'S likely can grill the same amount of food in the last year of use as it did in the first. That illustrates the cost allocation theory of depreciation as opposed to the loss in value theory.

2. ACCELERATED DEPRECIATION

Accelerated depreciation emanates generally from the loss-in-value theory of depreciation. It assumes an asset loses more value in the early years of its life than in the latter years. The method does not attempt to measure the actual loss in value: annual appraisals of what could be thousands or millions of assets held by a business would be expensive and subject to inaccuracies inherent to appraisals. Instead, accelerated depreciation methods use various formulae to approximate value losses.

Two main accelerated depreciation methods exist:

- Declining balance.

- Sum of the year's digits [SYD].

The declining balance methods are more common, but both are acceptable. The most common form of a declining balance method is _double_ declining balance [DDB]. Under DDB, the entity depreciates an asset at twice the straight-line rate using a declining balance. The method ignores salvage value for allocation, but ultimately does not reduce the adjusted basis below salvage value. It switches to straight-line depreciation when that method produces a larger amount over the asset's remaining life. Although DDB sounds complicated, it actually is subject to mechanical algebraic formulae. EXAMPLE 16 illustrates the method.

EXAMPLE 16

DDB Depreciation Example

Assume JOE'S placed into service an asset with a 5-year life, a $10,0000 cost and no salvage value. Ignore any convention. Illustrate DDB depreciation.

For 5-year property, the straight-line rate would be 20% each year; hence, for DDB, deduct 40% of the depreciable basis in year 1. Then, in year 2, deduct 40% of the remaining depreciable basis, and do the same in years 3–5.

- Year 1 depreciation expense is $4,000: 40% of $10,000. The adjusted basis (AB) drops to $6,000.

- Year 2 expense is $2,400 (40% of $6,000). AB drops to $3,600.

- Year 3 is $1,440 (40% of $3,600). AB drops to $2,160.

- Years 4 and 5 are $1,080, half the AB each year. That illustrates the switch to straight-line. 50% of the AB is larger than 40%. In contrast, year 3 straight-line depreciation would have been 33% for each of the remaining years, which would have been less than 40%. Thus, the switch did not occur in year three.

U.S. tax law per section 168[17] imposes DDB for most assets. Occasionally for tax or for financial accounting purposes, management may elect a slower method, such as 150% declining balance. Under such a method, the annual depreciation expense is 1.5 times the straight-line rate. Thus, for 5-year property, as used in the example, depreciation in year 1 would be 30% (1.5 times 20%) in each year.

Sum-of-the-year's digits is even more arbitrary, at least in appearance; however, it has a long history of use. The method adds the digits of the

---

[17]   IRC § 168(b)(1).

asset's life expectancy and then annually multiplies the depreciable basis times a fraction. The numerator is the number of remaining years, and the denominator is the sum of the years.

For example, for 5-year property, the bookkeeper would add 5 plus 4 plus 3 plus 2 plus 1 to produce a sum of 15—the sum of the digits of the asset's life. For 7-year property, the sum would be 28: $7 + 6 + 5 + 4 + 3 + 2 + 1 = 28$. In the first year of 5-year property, the depreciation would be 5/15ths of the depreciable basis. The second year would be 4/15ths, the third years 3/15ths, the fourth year 2/15ths and the last year 1/15th. Hence, all 15/15ths of the depreciable basis would be expensed. Seven-year property would have a similar result but would start with 7/28ths in the first year, 6/28ths in the second year and so forth.

Both DDB and SYD methods are approximations: neither attempts to appraise the affected assets. But they are relatively easy to use, with DDB being the most common method.

As a lawyer, you should pay attention to depreciation methods. If the entity is consistent from year-to-year and asset-to-asset, the result is generally accurate. A change of method—other than the traditional DB switch to straight-line—should be alarming. Although it may be justifiable (information may have changed), you should look closely. For audited statements, it would likely result in a modified qualified opinion. For unaudited statements, a lawyer should inquire, seeking justification.

Also, lawyers will want to look closely at the purchase and placement into service dates of material assets. Typically, in the life of a business, such purchases are either level or increasing as the business increases. If an owner sought to manipulate short-run income, he/she could accelerate the purchase of assets from future years into current ones. Although unlikely to waste funds by purchasing unnecessary assets, an entity seeking manipulation may very well alter the timing of the purchase.

Consider EXAMPLE 17. If JOE'S decides to repair the existing freezer, Scott's income will be $197,500 for each of the next 2 years ($200,000 less his one-half share of the $5,000 maintenance expense).

EXAMPLE 17

JOE'S Needs a Freezer/Scott Wants His Ex to Pay

JOE'S BAR & GRILL is considering a new freezer at a cost of $90,000, a 15-year life and expected salvage value of $10,000. Scott and Adrian believe the existing freezer—which is fully depreciated—will last a couple more years with extra annual maintenance of $5,000.

Scott expects to file for divorce soon and expects his spouse to seek alimony and child support. Thus, Scott seeks to minimize short-run income, the years he expects the court to consider. His income—ignoring the freezer—would be $200,000 each year.

In the alternative, Scott (with Adrian's support) proposes to purchase the freezer in December of the current year and to forgo the $5,000 maintenance (hoping the current freezer lasts until the purchase). He thus accelerates the purchase by 13 months but saves $10,000 in maintenance during the two years. JOE'S year-1 GAAP depreciation will be $6,000,[18] even though JOE'S used it for only part of a month. Scott's income will be $197,000. Purchasing the freezer 13 months early is arguably a bad business decision, although it accelerates a tax deduction for both Scott and Adrian, which helps some. Scott will show $500 less income for family law purposes.[19] JOE'S year-2 GAAP depreciation will be $11,200,[20] Scott's income will be $194,400. If the family court focuses on year-2 income for alimony, child support, and property division, Scott may save $15,500 in present value terms, which is five times the drop in income.

Suppose, alternatively, Scott suggests JOE'S use a 10-year life for the new freezer rather than 15 (JOE'S is not audited, so the only person affected will be his soon-to-be ex-spouse), a mid-year convention, and DDB depreciation, which initially ignores salvage value. The book depreciation would then be the same as that for tax purposes, which likely makes his claim palatable to a family law judge (it should not, but I bet it does). This is EXAMPLE 18.

---

[18] $90,000 depreciable basis divided by 15 (the straight-line portion times two but also divided by two because of the mid-year convention) equals $6,000.

[19] But for the purchase, Scott would have $200,000 income less his $2,500 share of maintenance expense. With the purchase, he has $200,000 income less his $3000 share of depreciation.

[20] $84,000 depreciable basis divided by 7.5 (twice the straight-line rate) equals $11,200.

EXAMPLE 18

JOE'S Needs a Freezer/Scott Wants His Ex to Pay

Same facts as EXAMPLE 17 except Scott convinces Adrian to use a 10-year life for the freezer for financial reporting, rather than the more accurate 15-year life.

In the EXAMPLE 18 acquisition year depreciation is now $9,000[21] Scott's income drops by an additional $2,000 to $195,500.[22] In year 2, DDB depreciation will be $16,200 (20% of the $81,000 adjusted depreciable basis). Scott's income will be $191,900 rather than $197,500. He could thus show a downward trajectory in his income—it would fall from $195,500 in year 1 to $191,900 in year 2). A court might be persuaded that predicts further decreases. Scott would push this argument.[23]

As explained in prior lessons, child support and alimony are logically viewed as a tax on the payor's income—a tax that can range up to 500% or more of marginal income. As a result, Scott might logically project the purchase of the freezer 13 months early could save him approximately $28,000 in present value terms just looking at the family law consequences. As explained below, JOE'S would likely experience significant tax savings as well, making the purchase rather than repair even more economically viable. The economics are not "real" in the sense they result in Scott's ex-spouse (and children) as well as Uncle Sam (through lower tax revenues) paying for the savings. But from Scott's perspective, the plan is attractive.

As a lawyer, would you detect it? Would you be able to explain the consequences and that a court should impute income undoing the consequences if you represented Scott's ex-spouse? If you represented Scott, could you defend it? That is largely the point of this course. Representing Scott, you might emphasize the tax savings, the risk of repairs not working, the risk of a broken freezer, and that the shorter life and accelerated depreciation are permitted in tax law.

Representing his ex-spouse, you would seek to prove the purchase was economically unwise: that two years of repairs made more sense. But, without testimony from Adrian (Scott's brother) or any written and discoverable plans, the best you could probably hope for would be to attack

---

[21] Ten percent of $90,000 (twice the 10% straight-line rate, but for only one half year).

[22] Instead of a $2,500 share of repair expense, Scott would have a $4,500 share of depreciation. Without the new freezer, Scott has $197,500 income ($200,000 less $2,500 repair expense). With the freezer purchase and a 10-year life, his income is $195,500.

[23] For an interesting exercise, consider the GLOSSARY explanation of a slope. A graph of the downward trending income could be accurate but very misleading. A critical issue with graphing income over time involves how many inches are in a year or a dollar. As silly as that sounds, it is vital to the graph's appearance. Changing the x and y axes alters the income angle of descent, but it will not change the slope; thus, it remains accurate, albeit potentially misleading.

the useful life—and that might be a difficult battle itself. Without basic knowledge of tax and accounting, you likely would not even notice something was amiss. Without basic knowledge of finance, you likely would not notice the large present value savings Scott would have.

JOE'S would likely elect section 179 expensing for the freezer. Depending on the year, that could result in a $200,000 expense for tax purposes, reducing Scott's income by $100,000. If Scott uses his tax return as the basis for filing the required financial affidavit and if the court and parties focus on the year JOE'S acquires the freezer, the consequences are enormous. In present value terms, Scott might see a reduction in alimony, child support and property division of over $500,000.

In a bigger nightmare, JOE'S might be a partnership. If so, Scott and Adrian could specially allocate the entire $200,000 179 expense to Scott, reducing his income to zero, which could devastate his ex-spouse's alimony, child support, and property division claims. Per IRC section 704(b),[24] the allocation would be proper only if it had substantial economic effect, a complicated issue. Scott and Adrian could agree to offsetting future allocations which could provide needed effects. Such a plan seems horribly distorting and morally suspect. If understood by the family law judge, it likely would not succeed. But would you notice it? Would you understand sufficient accounting and tax law—including partnership tax law—to explain it to a judge? If not, the plan could work. Indeed, Scott and Adrian could have JOE'S as part of a tiered group of partnerships and S corporations, some of which were out of state or out of the U.S., making detection of the scheme more difficult and discovery of the records very difficult. Such additional steps may lack substance for tax purposes and thus may not work in that arena, but the scheme would be for divorce planning, not tax planning. For them not to work for family law, you as the attorney for Scott's ex-spouse would have to attack them.

3. UNITS OF PRODUCTION OR USAGE DEPRECIATION

When available, the units of production method is the most accurate. Most assets—such as tables and chairs—are not used for a particular number of "uses"; but some are. A delivery truck might last 200,000 miles; if so, an accurate way of depreciating it would be by mileage. If the truck cost $100,000, the owner would depreciate it at 50 cents per mile. A high-quality blender used for mixed drinks or milkshakes may have a 10,000

---

[24] IRC § 704(b) permits partnerships to make "special allocations" of income, deductions, gains, losses, and other items to a partner. One partner can have all the losses and another all the gains. They could reverse the allocations in a later year, but the off-setting allocations would have to have "substantial economic effect" to be acceptable for tax law. That is very technical; however, it can work. Detecting it would not be simple without expert tax advice.

"uses" rating. If so, that would provide a more accurate measure for cost allocation than would other depreciation methods.

4. IRC SECTION 179

For U.S. tax, many businesses elect to use IRC section 179[25] to expense assets rather than to capitalize and depreciate them. Although not permitted for audited financial reporting, section 179 expensing is likely to be the most common type of cost recovery lawyers will come across. Why? That is because most businesses are unaudited; hence, the likely statements they have are those prepared for tax purposes.

Congress has frequently changed the section 179 rules, so be careful. The maximum amount allowed for years starting in 2018 and later was $1,000,000, subject to an annual inflation adjustment. The property must be acquired by purchase[26] and must be used in the active conduct of a trade or business.[27] Section 179 applies to tangible personal property as well as some real property (in particular, restaurant property). The dollar limitation decreases by the amount of section 179 property placed into service in excess of $2,500,000; hence, large entities are unlikely to benefit.

Material Assets Should Be Capitalized

Assets with a material value and a life greater than one year should be capitalized. You should insist upon it (unless, of course, that hurts your client).

For example, if JOE'S were to spend $5,000 on a heavy-duty blender, it would likely elect to expense the full $5,000 under section 179 for U.S. tax purposes. It would thus not capitalize any cost and would not compute or deduct depreciation expense over the blender's useful life—at least not for tax purposes. If JOE'S were to prepare financial reports consistent with GAAP, it would have to capitalize the blender's cost and then depreciate it. As a result, the financial statements would differ for accounting purposes as compared to tax purposes. As a lawyer, you should be wary of relying on any tax returns as an accurate measure of income. You should insist (assuming it is to your client's benefit) that material assets be capitalized and depreciated.

---

[25] IRC § 179.

[26] IRC § 179(d)(1)(C).

[27] *Id.*

EXAMPLE 19

JOE'S Buys Machinery

JOE'S purchased machinery for $31,000, including set-up and delivery. Expected salvage value is $1,000 after a group 10-year life. They use the mid-year convention.

Prepare a depreciation schedule using, in the alternative, straight-line, double declining balance, and tax methods (ignoring section 179).

EXAMPLE 19 and **Figure 53** illustrate the differences among the various depreciation methods in a depreciation schedule which lists the annual depreciation and the adjusted basis for each asset/group. A "group" life means the business has grouped distinct but generally similar assets into a "group" for depreciation calculations. Some items may have an actual life close to 9 years and others up to 12, but they average ten years. Use of group depreciation would be common and acceptable.

Comparative Depreciation Amounts			
Year	**SL**	**DDB**	**U.S.**
1	1,500.00	3,100.00	4,429.90
2	3,000.00	5,580.00	7,591.90
3	3,000.00	4,464.00	5,421.90
4	3,000.00	3,571.20	3,871.90
5	3,000.00	2,856.96	2,768.30
6	3,000.00	2,285.57	2,768.30
7	3,000.00	1,828.45	2,768.30
8	3,000.00	1,803.95	1,379.50
9	3,000.00	1,803.95	
10	3,000.00	1,803.95	
11	1,500.00		

Figure 53: Comparative Depreciation

Notice how substantially different the dollar amounts are each year. In years 1 through 4, U.S. tax law produces the largest amount of depreciation; however, in years 5 through 11, the straight-line method produces the largest amount. Another useful exercise would be to compare the annual amount of depreciation under various methods.

As a lawyer, you are unlikely to compute depreciation schedules; however, you will need to understand the meaning (or lack thereof) of the term "income." You must understand the many choices and estimates that enter the calculation of income, with depreciation comprising one of the larger components of expense. Nevertheless, it does not hurt to look at a depreciation schedule. Using the DDB method, a depreciation schedule for the asset in EXAMPLE 19 appears in **Figure 54**.

DDB Depreciation Amounts			
Year	DDB	Accumulated Depreciation	Adjusted Basis
			31,000.00
1	3,100.00	3,100.00	27,900.00
2	5,580.00	8,680.00	22,320.00
3	4,464.00	13,144.00	17,856.00
4	3,571.20	16,715.20	14,284.80
5	2,856.96	19,572.16	11,427.84
6	2,285.57	21,857.73	9,142.27
7	1,828.45	23,686.18	7,313.82
8	1,803.95	25,490.13	5,509.87
9	1,803.95	27,294.08	3,705.92
10	1,803.95	29,098.03	1,901.97
11	901.97	30,000.00	1,000.00

Figure 54: Depreciation Schedule

LESSON FIVE-D

RECONCILIATION AND RECAPTURE

■ ■ ■

1. RECONCILIATION

Reconciliation of book and tax differences is a very complicated part of accounting. Depreciation differences are a substantial component of the differentials. The reconciliations will result in deferred tax assets or deferred liabilities. Fully understanding them is well beyond this course. But a simple overview is appropriate.

A deferred tax asset may appear on a balance sheet. It would exist because taxable income exceeded book income. As a result, the actual tax paid for the year would exceed the amount accrued and recognized as an expense for financial purposes.

EXAMPLE 20

Deferred Tax Asset

Suppose JOE'S has tax income of $40,000 but GAAP book income is only $28,000. Assume a tax rate of 25%.

JOE'S would owe $10,000 tax but would only have a book tax expense of $7,000. How would you reconcile this?

In EXAMPLE 20, tax paid exceeds the book tax expense by $3,000. For book purposes, JOE'S would credit cash for the $10,000 tax paid and debit tax expense for $7,000 (25% of the $28,000 book income). To balance, it would debit a *deferred tax asset* for $3,000. This would not be a real asset in the sense that it could be sold or could turn into cash. Instead, it would amortize the deferred tax asset as it recognized the extra $12,000[28] income for financial purposes. That would not involve typical straight-line amortization; instead, it would involve tracing the differential and amortizing the deferred tax asset as the differential disappeared.

A *deferred tax liability* is the opposite. It arises when tax income is less than financial income. Using the above figures, perhaps tax income is only $28,000 because of rapid tax depreciation or a section 179 election. Financial income could be $40,000 because DDB, while accelerated, is not nearly as rapid as U.S. tax depreciation, as illustrated in **Figure 53**. Thus, the tax paid would be $3,000 less than the book tax expense. The entity would credit cash for the $7,000 tax paid and would debit tax expense for the $10,000 tax owed using financial rather than tax income. The difference would result in a $3,000 credit to *deferred tax liability*. It is not a real liability because the entity would not owe the government anything; instead, it is an accounting concept used to reconcile the different measures of income and expense. In later years, book depreciation would be greater

---

[28] Possibly JOE'S book maintenance expense exceeded tax expense by $12,000 in the EXAMPLE 20 year. If so, in future years, book income would necessarily exceed tax income by the same $12,000, which would result from less future book maintenance expense. This might occur because of incurred-but-deferred maintenance has different treatment under GAAP versus tax law. For example, an airline must currently accrue a portion of expected maintenance attributable to aircraft usage even though the actual maintenance may be on an every-5-year schedule. Failure to accrue it annually as the planes flew and produced revenue would violate the matching principle. For tax law, however, IRC § 461(h)(2)(B) would defer deduction of the incurred but deferred costs until "economic performance" 5 years later. *See*, WILLIS III AND IV, *supra* note 18.

than tax depreciation. Rather than debit a deferred tax asset, as in EXAMPLE 19, the entity would debit the deferred tax liability.

For large entities, book and tax differences occur regularly regarding thousands of transactions. Reconciling them is an essential but a complex endeavor. Lawyers are unlikely to ever need to do the reconciliation; however, they will come across deferred tax assets and deferred tax liabilities. Lawyers must understand these are very important items, but they are neither real assets nor real liabilities.

2. RECAPTURE

Depreciation recapture reconciles depreciation expenses with economic results. If a business uses an asset for its entire useful life and if it also predicts the salvage value precisely, no recapture will result. However, those assumptions are often at odds with reality. Because depreciation (and amortization) uses a formula not tailored to the specific asset, it is rarely precise. Ultimately, the books must balance; hence, recapture—or sometimes extraordinary losses—appear.

Recapture results when an owner sells a depreciable asset for more than its adjusted basis. The owner must recognize gain; however, the gain—to the extent of prior depreciation—is not economic gain. Accountants and tax lawyers often refer to it as "phantom gain." Consider EXAMPLE 21. This simple example focuses only on the financial accounting consequences. We add tax consequences and book/tax discrepancies later.

EXAMPLE 21

JOE'S Has *Financial* Recapture Gain

JOE'S purchased the EXAMPLE 18 $31,000 machine with a 10-year life. JOE'S elected DDB depreciation and a mid-year convention for financial accounting.

In year five, JOE'S sold the machine for $19,000. What are the *financial accounting* consequences?

Per **Figure 54**, the machine would have a $14,284.80 financial-accounting adjusted basis at the end of year 4. Because of the convention, JOE'S would accrue one-half year of depreciation for the year 5, the year of sale. The convention assumes the sale occurred on July 1, regardless of when it occurred. Year 5 depreciation would thus be $1,428.48, which is half the $2,856.96 shown in the **Figure 54** depreciation schedule. The machine would thus have a $12,856.32 adjusted basis.[29]

---

[29] $14,284.80 adjusted basis at the beginning of year 5 less $1,428.48 depreciation expense.

The calculations could be more complicated. The above schedule computes depreciation on an annual basis. JOE'S would actually compute it monthly. It could allocate the annual amount evenly, or it could (and likely would) use the DDB method for 120 months rather than 10 years. As a result, the actual depreciation amounts would be slightly higher for the first half of year 5. But let's keep the calculations simple for now.

The sale for $19,000 would produce $6,143.68 of gain: the $19,000 sale price less the $12,856.32 adjusted basis. The gain, however, would almost certainly not be economically real. The machine likely did not gain any value whatsoever, let alone more than $6,000 in the fifth year. Instead, the machine did not lose value consistent with the DDB depreciation method, ten-year life, and mid-year convention: it apparently lost $12,000 in value during the 4.5 years of use rather than the $18,143.68 of depreciation JOE'S recognized. Such inconsistencies are routine, though perhaps not typically that large. **Figure 55** illustrates how JOE'S would record the sale for financial accounting purposes.

General Journal for JOE'S BAR & GRILL			
Date	Account	Debit	Credit
7/1/yr 5	Cash	19,000.00	
	Accumulated Depreciation	18,143.68	
	Machine		31,000.00
	Non-Operating Gain on Sale of Machine		6,143.68
	Sale of Machine/recognition of non-operating gain.		

Figure 55: Sale of Machine with Recapture Gain

The debit to cash reflects the receipt of payment. The debit to accumulated depreciation removes that account because JOE'S no longer owns the related asset. Remember: accumulated depreciation is a contra-asset and has a credit balance. The credit to machine removes the machine from JOE'S books at historical cost. The credit to gain (income) reflects the "phantom gain" or recapture gain resulting from the sale. This is the amount of excessive depreciation JOE'S accrued. A prior period adjustment would be inappropriate under GAAP, though JOE'S income for years 1 through 4 was artificially low because of the excessive depreciation.

JOE'S would classify the gain as non-operating on its income statement because the gain does not reflect income from operating a bar and grill; instead, the gain merely adjusts for prior depreciation inaccuracies. If, instead, JOE'S sold the machine for less than its adjusted basis of $12,856.32, it would recognize a non-operating loss on the sale.

Such non-operating gains and losses which correct for depreciation or amortization inaccuracies are routine. Over time, they tend to balance out and the net likely approaches zero. From the view of a lawyer, however, such items can be material and thus noteworthy. Lawyers, unlike accountants, tend to focus more on single years or merely a few years. Thus, a material recapture gain or a material loss on the sale of a depreciable asset can have significant legal effects. As a lawyer, you will seek an adjustment for such items if the amounts affect your client adversely. As we have seen, family law can magnify income/loss distortions by five or six hundred percent. Hence, a non-operating gain of approximately $3,000 (Scott's and Adrian's respective shares) could result in one of the paying more than $15,000 in excessive alimony, child support, or property distribution—unless his or her lawyer properly and convincingly adjusted income to reflect economic reality. But the opposite impact could affect Scott or Adrian's ex-spouse in such a case if the divorce proceeding considered the years of excessive depreciation and if no sale occurred. In such an instance, the ex-spouse's lawyer would need to adjust for a more economically real depreciation method.

The two scenarios are not equal. From Scott or Adrian's viewpoint, the non-operating income will have a proper label and the lawyer's job of convincing a court to ignore it should be relatively easy. But, from their respective ex-spouses' viewpoints, the lawyers are far less likely to recognize excessive depreciation and thus far less likely to seek any accommodation. Without a sale of the asset, how would they know the depreciation was excessive? Likely, they would not.

Also, consider the impact on Lamar. His annual bonus is a function of operating income. He would suffer from the excessive depreciation but would not benefit from the recapture gain (assuming the contract defined his bonus as a function of operating income). Thus, understanding the inherent inaccuracies of depreciation and amortization, as well as the accounting methods of recapture are an important part of contract negotiations which are a function of operating income. Lamar should consider asking for a better definition of his bonus. Rather than have it a function of operating income, it should be a function of operating income plus any recapture gain attributable to depreciation expense during his bonus-accruing employment.

EXAMPLE 22

JOE'S Has Tax Law Recapture Gain

JOE'S purchased the EXAMPLE 18 $31,000 machine with a 10-year life. JOE'S uses DDB depreciation for tax reporting.

In year 5, JOE'S sold the machine for $19,000. What are the *tax law* consequences?

Next, consider EXAMPLE 22 which changes the depreciation to a tax rather than financial computation. As explained earlier, U.S. tax law—under IRC section 168—would use a seven-year recovery period, zero salvage, a mid-year convention, and DDB depreciation. For EXAMPLE 21, ignore bonus depreciation and section 179. At the end of year 4, the machine would have a $10,116.40 adjusted tax basis.[30] Year 5 depreciation would be $1,384.15 (half the amount in **Figure 53**) producing an adjusted tax basis of $8,732.25. JOE'S would have $10,267.75 taxable gain—the difference between the $19,000 sale price and the adjusted basis. Per IRC section 1245,[31] this would be taxed at "ordinary income" rates and would be classified as depreciation recapture.

Notice the substantially higher *tax* phantom gain than *financial* phantom gain: $10,267.75 versus $6,143.68. The financial non-operating gain can create material legal distortions if not properly analyzed. Legal matters are all-too-often resolved as a function of tax income rather than financial income, however unwise that may be.

An additional problem arises in this simple problem: the book/tax discrepancy. At the end of year 4, earnings and profits[32] would be $4,168.40 lower than retained earnings. That results because the accumulated depreciation would be $4,268.40 higher for tax purposes. Assuming a 25% tax rate, JOE'S would have accrued $1,042.10 more tax expense than it would have paid because its financial income would have been higher by $4,168.40. That would appear as a deferred tax asset of $1,042.10 on JOE'S balance sheet. The sale of the asset and corresponding recognition of differing recapture amounts for book and tax purposes would ultimately result in the deferred tax asset disappearing: tax owed for the disposition year would exceed financial tax expense by $1,042.10. A full understanding of book/tax discrepancies is far beyond this basic course; however, a lawyer

---

[30] IRC § 1016.

[31] IRC § 1245.

[32] IRC § 312 deals with corporate "earnings and profits" for tax purposes. Financial reporting uses the similar term "retained earnings," though it can differ substantially because the underlying accounting rules differ. Corporate statutes often use a third term, earned surplus, which has its own varying state definitions.

should have a general knowledge of the great complexities the different accounting rules produce.

LESSON SIX

ACCRUAL ACCOUNTING

Methods of Accounting and Why Accrual is Essential

■ ■ ■

Lesson Objectives

1. Student will learn that both GAAP and IFRS require the accrual method of accounting.

2. Student will learn that U.S. tax law does not require accrual accounting for most taxpayers.

3. Student will learn that most entities and most individuals use the cash method of accounting, which does not clearly reflect income in most instances.

4. Under the accrual method, income is included when earned and deductions when all events show they are owed.

5. Under the cash method, income is included when received and deductions when paid.

Terminology Introduced

- Cash method.
- Accrual method.
- Inventory method.
- Hybrid method.
- Permanent accounts.
- Temporary accounts.
- Present value.
- Future value.
- EBIT.
- EBITDA.
- S Corporation status (for U.S. tax purposes).

_____

LESSON SIX-A

INTRODUCTION TO THE ACCRUAL METHOD

■ ■ ■

Multiple methods of accounting are available, but financial accounting mostly uses either the cash method or the accrual method. Both GAAP and IFRS require accrual accounting; however, most individuals use the cash method because they are not audited, and the method is far simpler to use. For U.S. tax purposes, other methods exist, such as the "inventory method,"[1] the "installment method,"[2] and "the completed contract method"[3]; however, those are hybrid/modified accrual methods.

1. ACCRUAL METHOD

Figure 56 illustrates the basic *financial* accounting differences between the cash and accrual methods.[4]

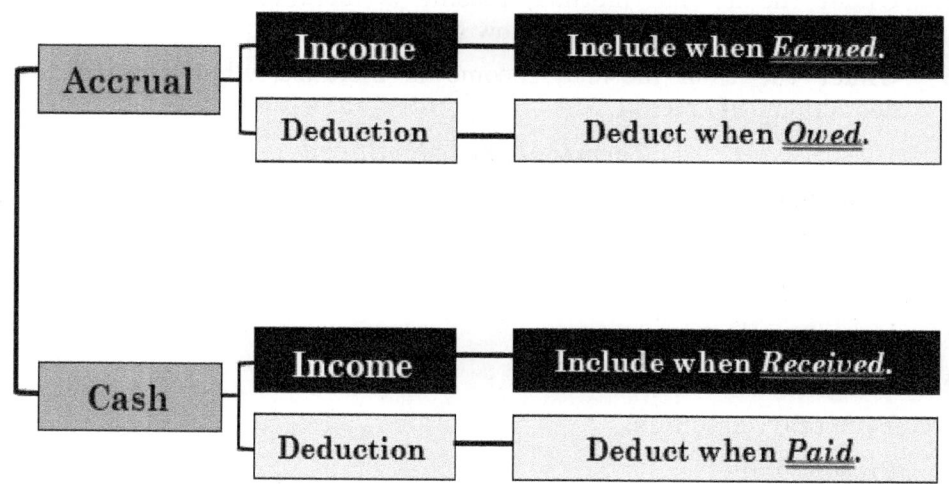

Figure 56: Accrual vs. Cash Method

The accrual method recognizes income when it is earned, while the cash method recognizes it upon receipt of payment. Similarly, the accrual

---

[1]   IRC § 471.

[2]   IRC § 453.

[3]   IRC § 460.

[4]   The cash versus accrual differences for U.S. tax law are substantially greater. See *supra* note 88.

method recognizes an expense when it is owed, while the cash method recognizes it upon payment.

The concepts of "earning" and "owing" in relation to accrual are not simple. In contrast, "receipt" and "payment"—the basics of cash accounting—are generally straightforward. We will cover each in more detail, but first you should understand and memorize some black-letter points about accounting methods:

- GAAP and IFRS require the accrual method.

- Most individuals and entities use the cash method for financial reporting.

- The cash method does not aim to clearly reflect income.

- For tax, most individuals and businesses use the cash method.

- The tax law accrual method is very different from the GAAP/IFRS accrual methods.

- Sometimes, the cash method is accurate: its results are close to what accrual would produce.

These points are essential because, as a lawyer, you should seek an accurate, clear reflection of income (at least if that benefits your client). Thus, you must understand you will often face cash method financial statements which are easily manipulated and often are economically inaccurate. Indeed, many statutes may define income using the cash method or, worse, with some items reflecting cash transactions and others reflecting accrual. Whether you can resolve any inequities resulting from the cash or mixed methods is not always clear; however, you certainly cannot address them unless you first understand the issues.

Just as one should be very careful when comparing GAAP-based statements with IFRS-based statements, one should be even more careful comparing cash-method statements with accrual-method statements. An analogy I use in the lesson is facially silly, but nevertheless apt. I could compare your age to the color of my client's hair, but the comparison would be both useless and ridiculous. But at least the silliness of the comparison would be obvious to all. Similarly, in many cases, comparing cash-method financial statements to accrual-method statements is just as useless; however, the ridiculousness of the comparison is not facially obvious to all. That may be the most important thing you learn in this lesson: be very careful comparing financial statements based on different methods of accounting.

Be Wary Comparing Cash to Accrual

For some moderate-income persons, the cash method and the accrual method produce similar results. For many persons, the differences are large.

That said, consider EXAMPLE 23 in which the cash method and the accrual method produce essentially the same result.

Someone such as the schoolteacher likely has little opportunity to manipulate income. He/she receives a salary and has little bargaining power to seek advanced or deferred income (other than in a well-established "qualified" retirement plan"). He/she also receives a regular paycheck and relatively small salary increases. The cash method would consider actual receipts as income. The accrual method, in contrast, would consider what the employee earned. The difference, however, is slight.

EXAMPLE 23

Cash vs. Accrual for Moderate Income

Posit a schoolteacher who earns $52,000 per year, who has no outside business operations and no significant investments.

Suppose the teacher is paid every two weeks and he/she receives a 2% raise in 2023.

The first paycheck in January likely reflects earnings from the prior year. Hence, the first paycheck will be for $2,000 while the remaining paychecks will be for $2,040, reflecting the 2% raise. Thus, the cash method will reflect $40 less income for 2022 than would the accrual method. Under the accrual method, the employee would recognize the December earnings in December when earned, while the cash method would recognize them in January when received. Other than for the first paycheck each year the two methods produce the same result.

What should you conclude from EXAMPLE 23? In many run-of-the-mill instances involving salaried, non-managerial employees, use of the cash method is fine. Thus, do not assume the cash method produces incorrect numbers. Nevertheless, you should always be cautious when using cash method financial statements.

In contrast, consider EXAMPLE 24, which reflects how many businesses operate. Lawyers, doctors, plumbers, electricians, and builders often operate small businesses. They have the option of demanding payment at the time of service, in advance of service, or at completion. They are likely consistent in what they do, and they base the timing of payment demands on individual cases. Some clients are not credit worthy. Some clients need time to pay. Some clients are willing to pay an amount at the beginning, but then insist upon satisfactory completion before final payment. If the mixture is consistent from year-to-year and no unusual clients exist, the cash method and the accrual method likely produce similar results. But lawyers tend not to deal in the "likely" case.

EXAMPLE 24

Cash vs. Accrual for Service Provider

Posit a dentist who operates his/her own practice. The office usually expects payment at the time of service, but it sometimes bills clients, particularly for extensive work.

The posited situation offers the dentist/plumber/electrician with a very tempting opportunity to manipulate income. Likely, most customer or clients would be willing to defer payment if given the opportunity. Few will pay unless asked. The dentist, plumber, or electrician could thus easily decide in 2023 to demand up-front payment from fewer customers. As a result, he/she could defer income under the cash method to 2024 upon receipt. In contrast, the accrual method would recognize the income when earned: upon performance of the services. The service provider also could control when the services are complete. Although clients may balk at long delays, they may not mind a delay of a few weeks or even a month. That could have a large impact under the cash method if a substantial portion of the price is due upon completion. Under the accrual method, such a delay would also have an impact, but perhaps less so if the service provider normally accrues as part of the job is completed, as opposed to all of it.

What should you conclude from EXAMPLE 24? The owner of a small business, particular a service provider, has a great deal of leeway when he/she recognizes cash method income. We will later see examples of how such a business can also easily alter the timing of expenses under the cash method. Thus, although you should not assume manipulation of income by a service business, you must fully understand how easily the owner can manipulate and how difficult it may be to detect.

As an aside, consider an example I heard from a student. He had one of those "Ah hah" moments of understanding. During the fall semester, his dentist's office manager called him and asked that he not pay his bill until January. As she explained, the dentist was going through a divorce and wanted his income to appear lower for the current year.

Most surprising was how honestly dishonest the office manager acted. She used a very simple technique to defer income under the cash method—openly asking patients to defer payment. She surely understood the dentist's alimony, child support, or property division obligations would be largely a function of the current year's income. Unfortunately, she likely understood little about discovery. Had she "misplaced" some billing, or had she not called late payers to collect (or called them less often), the result may have been the same, but detection of it would have been far more difficult. Under the chosen scheme, the dentist's ex-spouse's lawyer might easily discover the manipulation and inform the court. Likely, the court would agree to modify the reported income to undue the manipulation.

Do not conclude that I suggest you help clients cheat with greater subtlety; instead, conclude that many lawyers, accountants, or office managers will be tempted to do so. Some will succumb to temptation. Do not assume all small-business service providers using the cash method misrepresent and manipulate income; however, you must understand how simple it is for them to do so. Given the large legal consequences of even a small amount of manipulation, humans will often be tempted to behave in unethical ways.

2. INVENTORY AND GOVERNMENTAL METHODS

LESSON SEVEN covers the inventory method of accounting, which is a specialized type of accrual. Both GAAP and U.S. tax law require use of an inventory method for businesses that sell inventory. As explained in LESSON SEVEN, the GAAP and tax inventory methods differ in some significant respects.

Governments typically use specialized methods which are essentially the cash method. As a result, governmental accounting focuses on cash flows rather than on traditional accounting principles such as clear reflection of income. The use of cash accounting by governmental units is arguably necessary for many reasons. Governments do not seek profits. Their activities are very complex and subject to political constraints. As a lawyer, you may deal with governmental agencies and their budgets or long-term plans. While this course does not deal with those topics in depth, a brief analysis is appropriate.

Governmental budgets rarely reflect depreciation or amortization. As a result, building or re-surfacing a road is typically an expense. The state or county may separate its budgets into operating and capital budgets, but it will unlikely prepare an accrual-type income statement or balance sheet. As a result, if the entity reports a surplus, the reality may be very different than an accrual method business which shows a profit. The business will have capitalized long-term investments and then made an effort to spread the cost of the assets useful lives. It will also accrue as-yet un-repaired damage or losses. In contrast, typical governmental accounting does neither. A road is an expense, even if it lasts twenty years; and ignoring a pothole prompts no accounting entry until the hole is repaired.

As a result, a governmental "deficit" may reflect large capital improvements which will provide benefits for many years. Or the deficit could reflect wasted expenditures with short-term or no benefit. One simply does not know if all one knows is the reported governmental "surplus" or deficit. All-too-often, that is all the public sees. As a result, you should be very wary of accepting governmental accounting at face value. Avoid comparing it to financial accounting, as the comparison will almost certainly produce incorrect conclusions.

This course is not designed to give you the skills to analyze governmental budgets and accounts; however, it should provide you with the basic knowledge to understand that governmental accounting differs from financial accounting.

3. ALL EVENTS TEST

LESSON TWO-B discussed the all-events test, the revenue recognition principle, and the expense recognition principle. You should review them. They are essential for an understanding of accrual, governmental, and inventory accounting.

LESSON SIX-B

ACCRUALS FOR DECEMBER

■ ■ ■

LESSON SIX-B covers three sets of accruals:

- Account receivable and related revenue accruals for December. This illustrates important points from LESSON SIX-A.

- Seven additional accruals during December which complete a typical month of operations.

- Adjusting entries.

1. ACCOUNT RECEIVABLE AND RELATED REVENUE ACCRUALS

PROBLEM 2

JOE'S BAR & GRILL'S Special Customer

A good customer (Hans) starts a tab on December 15, planning three parties during the holiday period. He keeps the tab open, charging food and drinks amounting to $7,500 between 12/15 and 12/31. He pays with $7,500 cash on 1/5. The various parties involve:

- December 15: $1,000 of food and drink.

- December 24: $2,000.

- December 31: $4,500.

Prepare the accounting entries using—in the alternative—the accrual method and the cash method. Ultimately, use the accrual method entries for JOE'S journal and ledgers.

Unfortunately, JOE'S accounting system does not yet reflect inventories—a topic for LESSON SEVEN. As a result, the accrual method journal entries merely accrue the PROBLEM 2 receivables from Hans as well as the corresponding revenue, as shown in **Figure 57**.

Notice several important things regarding the accrual method reflection of the parties. _First_, the account receivable is an asset and thus results in a debit. It exists because JOE'S earned the amount due—it performed the services at a determinable price and has a reasonable expectation of collection. Thus, the lack of cash being transferred—Hans paid nothing as of December 31—is irrelevant.

Accrual General Journal for JOE'S BAR & GRILL			
Date	**Account**	**Debit**	**Credit**
12/15	**Accounts Receivable**	1,000	
	Revenue		1,000
	Accrual for Hans's Party.		
	Accounts Receivable	2,000	
	Revenue		2,000
	Accrual for Hans's Party.		
	Accounts Receivable	4,500	
	Revenue		4,500
	Accrual for Hans's Party.		

Figure 57: Accruals for Parties

Second, notice the revenue entry is a credit. It is not an asset. Income is *never* an asset; instead, it enters a temporary income account that JOE'S will ultimately close to retained earnings on the right side of the balance sheet. *Third*, notice JOE'S accrues no related expenses for the cost of the drinks, food, or wages for the services—at least not here and now. JOE'S will accrue those expenses separately (below) but will not relate them to the three parties. In general, the accrual method provides information for the period—such as for a month—as opposed to a transaction (Hans's parties). Thus, management will know whether December operations were profitable, but it will not—without additional accounting techniques—know whether these parties were profitable.

LESSON SEVEN covers both inventory and cost accounting in more depth. It discusses how to account for and to measure transactional profits or losses rather than periodic ones. Using those cost accounting techniques, management could determine how profitable (if at all) these functions were. The accrual method, however, focuses upon a period pursuant to the periodic assumption discussed in LESSON TWO-B. It does not typically account for individual functions.

In contrast, as shown in **Figure 58**, the cash method of accounting would result in no December journal entries related to the December parties. The page is blank. Why? Because Hans has not yet paid anything to JOE'S. Thus, under the cash method, the entire $7,500 of revenue will appear on the January income statement rather than on the December income statement. Ultimately, all the revenue appears. Thus, from a big-picture viewpoint, whether it appears in December under the accrual method or in January under the cash method does not matter. Lawyers, however, do not typically deal with the big picture; instead, they tend to be much more concerned with isolated parts.

Cash Method General Journal for JOE'S BAR & GRILL			
Date	Account	Debit	Credit

Figure 58: Cash Method Journal Entries for Parties

For example, Lamar's December bonus is a function of December profits. Without the $7,500 revenue, Lamar will receive less: indeed, $2,500 less. Perhaps he is the manager in January and perhaps he has the same contractual relationship. If so, his January bonus will reflect the $2,500. But perhaps Lamar is not the manager in January or perhaps he has a different contract. If so, JOE'S use of the cash method hurt Lamar.

Either Scott or Adrian may be involved in a divorce, as in EXAMPLES 19–20, or they may be seeking to borrow money from a bank. In each case, their respective December income may be a critical number and their January income may be irrelevant, or at least less relevant. Thus, accrual accounting matters—it attempts to place revenues and expense into the proper period. The cash method does not.

Even seemingly minor legal issues may be significantly impacted by the choice of accounting method for Hans's parties. For example, as law students, many of you seek financial aid. As a result, your parents may have to file a FAFSA report annually. Including—or not including—that $7,500 revenue may have a real impact on the ability of Scott or Ann's dependents to receive financial aid if they are currently in school. Similarly, whether Lamar receives the extra $2,500 bonus as a function of year one profits versus year two profits will affect any FAFSA he must file.

2. REMAINING DECEMBER ACCRUALS

PROBLEM 3 adds seven additional entries for December to complete a month of normal operations. Before we consider those, recall the ending balance sheet for November 30 in **Figure 31**. It became the beginning balance sheet for December 1 in **Figure 59**. As we covered in prior lessons: a balance sheet is the collection of permanent accounts. It carries over from month to month and from year to year. In contrast, the income statement is periodic: it re-starts at zero each period (which management might define as a month or a quarter or a year).

JOE'S BAR & GRILL Balance Sheet December 1				
Assets		**Liabilities**		
Cash	$308,000			
Inventory	30,000			
Machinery	31,000			
Liquor License	80,000			
Local Permit	1,000			
Pre-paid Rent	22,500	**Owner's Equity**		
Trademark	6,000	Scott	250,000	
Training	20,000	Adrian	250,000	
Signs	4,000	Retained Earnings	2,500	
Total Assets	**$502,500**	**Liabilities & Equity**	**$502,500**	

Figure 59: JOE'S Balance Sheet

At the beginning of December, JOE'S had no liabilities; however, that changes in December. For now, we list all assets together, but in LESSON SEVEN we split them between current (short-term) assets and fixed (long-term) assets. We maintain Scott and Adrian's capital accounts separately, which is non-typical for a corporation: it is more like a partnership or trust balance sheet equity section. However, because the entity has only two owners, keeping the balances separate is informative and permissible.

Recall from LESSON FOUR-A, each of the accounts—cash, inventory, etc.—has its own permanent ledger account. Those ledgers also carry over from period to period. In contrast, all the temporary ledgers reflecting income and expenses have a zero-balance beginning December 1 following the closing of the books November 30.

Let's examine the seven accruals individually. Each exists to demonstrate a particular point.

PROBLEM 3

JOE'S BAR & GRILL'S December Accruals

At JOE'S, we've seen the entries for customer Hans. Let's add these:

- On December 1, JOE'S distributes $100,000 to Adrian and the same to Scott because they "over-capitalized."

- On December 1, JOE'S borrows $50,000 from a bank at 6% nominal annual interest with monthly payments for 5 years. JOE'S plans to use the funds for additional improvements.

- JOE'S purchases $3,000 of supplies (napkins, coasters, soap) on December 1. It uses about one-third during the month.

- JOE'S pays wages of $10,000 to employees on the 1st and 15th of the month.

- JOE'S receives a utility invoice for $1,000 on December 15.

- JOE'S has monthly revenues of $40,000 in addition to Hans's parties.

- JOE'S owes Lamar, the manager, one-third of the monthly profits, using accrual accounting.

Prepare the accounting entries using—*in the alternative*—the accrual method and the cash method. Ultimately, use the accrual method entries for JOE'S journal and ledgers.

A. THE DISTRIBUTION

Accrual General Journal for JOE'S BAR & GRILL			
Date	Account	Debit	Credit
12/1	Owner's Equity Adrian	100,000	
	Owner's Equity Scott	100,000	
	Cash		200,000
	Repurchase of Stock / Partial Liquidation.		

Figure 60: PROBLEM 3 Distribution Journal Entry

On December 1, Scott and Adrian decide to distribute some of the capital they invested. **Figure 60** illustrates the journal entry. The amount to each is $100,000. LESSON TEN covers ratio analysis, so this issue foreshadows that lesson. Apparently, Scott and Adrian looked at their balance sheet and realized they had each contributed far more to the entity than was necessary. The business appears to have what it needs: adequate inventory, equipment, licenses, and training; but, it arguably has far too much cash. It is, in business parlance, heavily liquid. Any business needs significant liquidity—cash or assets easily turned into cash—so that it can meet its payroll and can pay regular expense; however, a business would not normally need nearly as much liquidity as JOE'S has.

A course on corporations will likely discuss the concept of "under-capitalization," which is the opposite of what JOE'S faces. That occurs when a business has too little equity when compared to debt and expected operating expenses (LESSON TEN covers ratio analysis, the comparison of one part of a statement to another). Under-capitalization may risk shareholder liability or the piercing of the corporate veil. That, however, is not JOE'S problem: it has cash that the owners could probably put to better use as they individually deem appropriate. JOE'S is a bar and grill, not an investment entity; hence, Scott and Adrian likely want to make their own investment decisions and not have them part of the business. Distributing $100,000 to each is probably too little, but for now, that is their decision.

LESSON NINE covers the corporate structure in more depth, including various types of dividends and distributions. Typically, a corporation does not distribute funds during its first month of operations; but Scott and Adrian have decided early in JOE'S operations to distribute a significant amount. Hence, you as it's lawyer would need to understand what laws restrict them when they seek your advice. Section 6.40 of the Model Business Corporations Act provides:

(a)   A board of directors may authorize and the corporation may make distributions to its shareholders subject to restriction by the articles of incorporation and the limitation in subsection § 6.40(c).

(b)   If the board of directors does not fix the record date for determining shareholders entitled to a distribution (other than one involving a purchase, redemption, or other acquisition of the corporation's shares), it is the date the board of directors authorizes the distribution.

(c)   No distribution may be made if, after giving it effect:

(1)   the corporation would not be able to pay its debts as they become due in the usual course of business; or

(2)   the corporation's total assets would be less than the sum of its total liabilities plus (unless the articles of incorporation permit otherwise) the amount that would be needed, if the corporation were to be dissolved at the time of the distribution, to satisfy the preferential rights upon dissolution of shareholders whose preferential rights are superior to those receiving the distribution.

(d) The board of directors may base a determination that a distribution is not prohibited under subsection § 6.40(c) either on financial statements prepared on the basis of accounting practices and principles that are reasonable in the circumstances or on a fair valuation or other method that is reasonable in the circumstances.[5]

Notice a few points:

- The Board of Directors may authorize a distribution to shareholders. Thus, the CPA would likely want to see the authorization before rendering a clean opinion on any financial statements reporting a distribution. The CPA may seek the opinion of counsel—your opinion—that the distribution was appropriate under state law.

You would pay attention to part (c) of the statute, which forbids a distribution that would impair the entity's ability to pay its debts "in the regular course of business." JOE'S is just starting its business; thus, as lawyer you might not be comfortable speculating on regular expenses that would need to be paid. But you could look at ratios (LESSON TEN) from similar businesses (similar in size and location) or you could seek the CPA's advice. Ultimately, at the end of December we know that JOE'S had operating expenses of about $45,000 (before Lamar's bonus), which you might have sufficient information to estimate. After the distribution, the entity will have $300,000 in contributed capital and $108,000 in cash ($308,000 currently less the $200,000 distribution). That is more than twice expected expenses even assuming zero revenue; hence, you could reasonably conclude the distribution would not impair JOE'S ability to pay its debts in the ordinary course of business.

You would also notice part (c) of the statute forbids a distribution if it would cause the entity's liabilities to exceed its assets. Because JOE'S has zero liabilities and plenty of assets, this would not be a problem. Hence you would approve the distribution, although you would likely re-style it as a stock re-purchase.[6] As such, you hope to avoid the issue of whether you must treat it as a dividend to the extent of retained earnings.

- If a distribution/dividend, it would be paid to shareholders of record. For JOE'S, that would be Scott and Ann.[7]

---

[5]   ABA MODEL BUSINESS CORPORATIONS ACT § 6.40 (2016).

[6]   Whether your advice is appropriate is best left to a course in corporations and state law.

[7]   Either of them may (unless the stock is restricted, as discussed in LESSON NINE) sell their shares to someone else. Suppose, for example, Adrian sold her shares to Lamar. He would have to "register" the shares with JOE'S (or its stock transfer agent). If he failed to do so, JOE'S would send future distributions to Adrian rather than to Lamar.

- A distribution must have a "record" date.[8] That is the date the entity determines who gets a particular distribution. If the Board of Directors does not set a date, the statute provides the record date is the authorization date. This date puts shareholders and prospective purchasers of shares on notice regarding who will receive a particular distribution. Thus, if the Board approved the $200,000 as a distribution/dividend on December 1, it could choose a later date—perhaps December 5—as the record date.[9]

B. THE BORROWING

General Journal for JOE'S BAR & GRILL			
Date	**Account**	**Debit**	**Credit**
12/1	**Cash**	50,000	
	Loan Payable		**50,000**
	To reflect borrowing $50,000 for 5 years at 6% NAI with monthly payments beginning Jan. 1. of $966.64.		

Figure 61: PROBLEM 3 Journal Entry to Record the Loan

As shown in **Figure 61**, on December 1, Scott and Adrian decide to borrow funds from a bank. The terms are for five years with level monthly payments and a nominal annual interest rate of 6%. They plan to use the funds for additional improvements. The borrowing immediately after the distribution is unusual, but the problem needs to demonstrate both a distribution and some debt.

A separate but related course—FINANCE FOR LAWYERS—covers how to amortize this loan. The payments would be $966.64 per month for 60 months, although the final payment would be for $966.65. A portion of each payment would be for accrued interest and the remainder would be a payment of principal.

This loan introduces a new use of the term "amortize" or "amortization." LESSON FIVE covered the amortization of intangibles, such as pre-paid rent. That process allocated the intangible's cost over its useful

---

[8] The day after the record date is also known as the "ex-dividend" date. Corporations announce a record date for dividends and other distributions. Shareholders of record receive a particular announced dividend. The process of recording transferred shares can take some time. Dividends thus have an "ex-dividend" date: as of that date, time no longer exists to record any transfer; hence, purchasers will not receive the next dividend. As a result, the trading price typically falls to reflect the loss of that dividend. Stock exchange rules determine the length of time involved. Typically, it is about two days prior to the record date.

[9] If Adrian sold his shares to Lamar on December 2, he would receive the distribution if he properly registered the shares by December 5; otherwise, Adrian would receive the distribution.

life. Loan amortization is a financial calculation which allocates principal payments over the life of the loan. Typically, payments are level—the same amount each month (with the final monthly payment being adjusted for any rounding issues). Because some of each loan payment is actually a principal payment, the principal amount of the loan drops each month. As a result, the amount of interest accruing each month decreases as well because it is a percentage of the outstanding principal owed. Thus, because the payment amount is level, the portion allocated to principal increases each month.

The loan interest allocable for December—the first month—is $250. That is 0.5% (one-twelfth of the 6% nominal rate) of the principal amount owed at the beginning of the month, $50,000. JOE'S will accrue the interest expense and record the interest payable on December 31 as an adjusting entry. The January 1 loan payment is $965.64, comprising the $250 of December interest plus a $716.64 principal payment of, leaving a principal balance due of $49,283.36 at the beginning of January. On January 31, JOE'S will accrue interest expense of 0.5% times $49,283.36, or $246.42. The February 1 payment will again be $965.64, comprising $246.42 of interest and $720.22 of principal. The loan is known as a "level self-amortizing installment obligation" because it has regular, equal payments which pay the interest accrued plus a portion of the principal.

C. THE PURCHASE OF SUPPLIES

On December 1st, JOE'S purchased $3,000 worth of supplies such as napkins, coasters, and soap. Scott, Adrian, and manager Lamar expect the supplies to last for about two months. Ultimately however—at the end of the month, they discover they have used about one-third of the supplies. Eventually, experience will help them more accurately predict their needs.

General Journal for JOE'S BAR & GRILL			
Date	Account	Debit	Credit
12/1	**Supplies**	3,000	
	Cash		3,000
	To reflect purchase of supplies expected to last three months.		

Figure 62: PROBLEM 3 Journal Entry to Record Purchase of Supplies

This common transaction presents two accounting issues. *First*, management must decide whether to capitalize the $3,000 with a debit to supplies and a credit to cash. The alternative would be to merely expense them as immaterial: a debit to supplies expense and a credit to cash. The dollar amount is small, but still sufficiently large in comparison to total assets and expected revenues such that capitalization is arguably the better choice. But this is a choice.

Expensing supplies would not be unusable, even with audited financial statements. Typically, a business will maintain sufficient items to last for weeks or a couple months, but likely not longer. They probably would have an arrangement with suppliers to continually purchase additional items so that the business will not deplete these consumables. Thus, the dollar amount will remain relatively small and generally constant, although it should grow as revenues and needs increase. Thus, expensing the $3,000 would distort income in the first month of operations; however, all future months would likely have a smaller and fairly constant amount of purchases.

On December 1st, JOE'S expects the items to last two months. Thus, its initial plan is to keep two months supplies on hand. It thus plans to consume $1,500 worth in December, but also to purchase an additional $1,500 in early January and then each month thereafter. If that plan works, expensing the items in December will distort December income by about $1,500; however, expensing of the regular purchases would be unlikely to have much impact in future months. As things turn out, the supplies last longer than predicted such that future monthly purchases should average about $1,000. The matching principle is very important; however, if JOE'S buys $1,000 of supplies in February but uses them in March and buys $1,050 in March but uses them in April, the matching principle is essentially satisfied. Because the dollar amounts are fairly constant, exact matching is arguably not worth the trouble and expense.

In the alternative, JOE'S could capitalize the supplies cost—as it chooses to do in the problem. This choice, which is certainly acceptable, presents the *second* issue. If JOE'S capitalizes the supplies, it will need an accounting mechanism to keep track of the items so that it can reasonably allocate usage to each period. LESSON SEVEN deals with inventory and the difficulties of tracking inventory usage. Inventory accounting is very important because inventory tends to be material in amount. In contrast, supplies such as pencils or napkins tend to be quite small in value and often not worth the cost of meticulous tracking. For example, management may need to watch every ounce of alcohol poured and every bottle of wine purchased and sold, but it is unlikely to be worth the trouble of tracking paper napkins. Nevertheless, employees can be tempted to steal supplies if given the opportunity. LESSON TWO dealt with internal controls. Control of inventory and supplies, as well as other assets, is something an auditor would look at.

Figure 62 shows the entry for capitalizing the supplies, with the expectation of amortizing them over three months. As a lawyer, you should realize a business may legitimately expense supplies as they are purchased. Distortions are unlikely and maintenance of a complex tracking system is often not cost effective. But those observations are valid *generally* and *over the long run.* As we frequently note, lawyers tend to deal in *specific periods* and the *short-run.* A divorce case will likely examine one to three years of financial information, not ten. That is also likely true in tort and even business valuation matters. Thus, one should at least look out for unusual transactions, particularly at the beginning and the end of a year or other relevant period. For example, if management seeks to inflate earning for 2023, it could end or slow down supplies purchases in late November and December (assuming it expenses supplies). That would risk the business running out or needing to pay a higher price for short-term needs; however, it would defer the expense to the following period and thus artificially inflate 2023 income.

Or, in the alternative, if management sought to decrease reported 2023 income, it could suddenly purchase a larger amount of supplies at the end of the year. While that would present storage issues, it would lower income and thus Lamar's bonus and whatever else is a function of that income. Such gamesmanship will have little impact over time because eventually the business purchases only what it needs. But the accounting method can change the year to which the items are allocated. Small matters tend to add up to large ones, as well. Thus, any distortion from altering supplies purchases may seem small, but management could also alter equipment (and thus depreciation expenses) as well as the timing of bonuses and many other expenses or even revenues. Together, such matters could be material. A lawyer will need to look for such behavior or have a forensic accountant do so. In any event, the lawyer will need to understand what can occur, how to determine whether it is unusual, and then whether it affects his or her client.

The ultimate discovery that JOE'S used only one-third of the supplies rather than the predicted one-half demonstrates the frequent inadequacy of predictions. Eventually, experience and accounting records will help management predict such things more accurately. JOE'S will fine-tune its supplies ordering and amortization as its gains information. Thus, the change from amortizing capitalized supplies over a two-month to a three-month period is not alarming, even though it is an accounting change.

D. THE PAYMENT OF WAGES

JOE'S pays employees on the 1st and 15th of each month. In a typical month—one other than the first month of operations—JOE'S would do three things:

- On the 1st of the month, it would pay accrued wages. This would involve a debit to wage liability and a credit to cash. It would not involve an expense because the related expense would have been recorded as an adjusting entry the day before.

- On the 15th of the month, it would debit wage expense and credit cash. This would be for wages from the first half of the month.

- On the last day of the month, it would debit wage expense and credit wages payable. This would accrue the wages for the second half of the month and recognize the liability.

Because December was the first month of operations, JOE'S would not have any operating wages to pay. Any wages during the start-up period would have been capitalized as start-up costs. The November 30 balance sheet and ledgers show no liability for wages, so it would have no payment on the first. **Figure 63** shows the general journal entries on December 15.

Date	Account	Debit	Credit
	General Journal for JOE'S BAR & GRILL		
12/15	**Wage Expense**	10,000	
	Loan Payable		10,000
	To reflect purchase of supplies expected to last three months.		
12/15	**Employment Tax Expense**	750	
	Cash		750
	To reflect social security and Medicare taxes on wages.		

Figure 63: PROBLEM 3 Journal Entry for Payment of Wages and Employment Taxes

The first entries recognize the expense for and the payment of wages. The second recognize the related employment taxes JOE'S would owe for social security and Medicare. The entries would be more complicated because JOE'S would likely have to accrue a small amount for worker's compensation and unemployment taxes along with each wage accrual. It would further withhold a portion of each employee's wages for the employee's share of both social security and Medicare as well as for the employee's personal federal (and possibly state) income tax liability. Also, JOE'S may have a deferred compensation or retirement plan to which either it or the employees (or both) would contribute in each wage period. Plus, JOE'S probably provides health insurance to its employees, who likely contribute a portion of the cost. Thus, each wage accrual would also involve other fringe benefit accruals for health insurance, life insurance, disability insurance, dental coverage and likely many more items.

For simplicity, the problem includes only the accrual for employment taxes. The point is to demonstrate the complexity of wages and employment law. Here, the wages are listed as $10,000 but the expense is actually $10,750—a 7.5% increase. The additional items for taxes, insurance, and other fringe benefits often add up to twenty or twenty-five percent of wages (or even more). Thus, as a lawyer, you should understand that stated wages typically understate the actual cost to the employer and the actual benefit to the employee by a large amount.

E. THE ACCRUAL OF UTILITY EXPENSES

JOE'S received a utility invoice on December 15 for $1,000. This presents a common, but easily resolvable matching problem. Undoubtedly, the bill reflects a meter-read date prior to the billing date and thus likely reflects electricity usage for several November weeks and about a week to ten days of December usage. The matching principle supports allocating the invoice between the months; however, that presents two problems:

- How much to allocate to each month.

- The need to accrue an estimated amount at the end of each month as an adjusting entry. Without that entry, JOE'S would not be able to close the books and then prepare a monthly set of financial statements.

General Journal for JOE'S BAR & GRILL				
Date	Account	Debit	Credit
12/15	**Utility Expense**	1,000	
	Utility Payable		1,000
	To reflect receipt of utility bill.		

Figure 64: PROBLEM 3 Journal Entry for Receipt of Utility Invoice

Assuming utility usage is stable from month-to-month, JOE'S would probably decide to ignore the matching principle. It would, instead, record the invoice amount as an expense upon receipt. Matching some November utility expenses with December income would not likely be a significant mismatch because the usage is likely consistent. JOE'S could read the meter itself at the end of each month, but whatever incremental accuracy that would result is likely is not worth the additional trouble. This should reinforce one of the first rules from LESSON ONE: accounting is not a science and does not aim for perfection. This part of the example illustrates how the matching principle can conflict with the materiality principle. We aim to match income with the costs of producing that income; however, if the item does not matter because it is small, we ignore it and can simply expense it. In this case, the consistency principle also is important: follow the same rule from month to month and from year to year. **Figure 64** shows the journal entry.

F. THE ACCRUAL OF REVENUES

General Journal for JOE'S BAR & GRILL			
Date	**Account**	**Debit**	**Credit**
12/31	**Cash**	40,000	
	Revenue		40,000
	To reflect revenue for the month.		

Figure 65: PROBLEM 3 Journal Entry to Record Monthly Revenue.

The final regular journal entry would be for general revenues of $40,000. PROBLEM 3 presents this information at the end of the month; hence, for bookkeeping we would have little choice but to record it then.[10] All the revenues are for December: we know that because we did not open the business for operations until December 1. The $40,000 amount is for all sales other than those for Hans's parties. We would, as shown in **Figure 65**, debit cash and credit revenue for $40,000.

This part of the example presents a common, but serious flaw in JOE'S operations: the failure to record cash and revenue regularly. The entity should have cash and credit card registers that record receipts continuously during business hours. For bookkeeping, this should be recorded as soon as possible: daily in most cases, if not more often. That way management can track all receipts and can judge which days and times produce the most revenue. All-too-often, however, a small business shows up to an accountant with receipts and records in the proverbial "shoebox." Such a process would be an egregious violation of internal controls. Indeed, management must have a system to watch all sales closely to ensure they are properly recorded.

Consider a few examples:

- Have you ever been to a fast-food restaurant that had a sign by the cash register that said, "If the amount on your receipt does not match the amount you paid, tell a manager and your meal is free!" That is a simple, but important, internal control. Employees who manage cash may be tempted to pocket some of the cash rather than to place it in the register. To do so successfully, however, the employee needs to charge the customer a different amount than is shown on the receipt because the cash register undoubtedly keeps a secure copy of

---

[10] The bookkeeper would unlikely be working on New Year's Eve. He or she would make this entry a few days later but would date it December 31.

the receipts. Hence, you may pay $12.50 for your burgers and fries, but receive a receipt (which you never look at) for $11.50. If so, almost certainly, the employee puts $11.50 in the register and surreptitiously puts $1.00 in his/her pocket. Those dollars add up. The sign and offer of free food make you the enforcer. Too many such "mistakes" and the employee will lose his/her job or worse.

- About six years ago, I sat in a typical beach bar in Jacksonville Beach. Unremarkable drinks with some interesting scenery. But most striking was the open cash register from which one bartender after another made change for over an hour. Perhaps they actually "rang up" a drink every 15 minutes or so, but mostly, it remained open and largely unattended. I could have easily reached it with my own hands (though I did not not). No responsible manager would have permitted this. Undoubtedly, the few bartenders colluded to steal most of the revenues during that hour. If they did not steal, then how would they justify the large amount of cash that inevitably would not agree with the register's internal records? Clearly, they could not. Thus, management may want cameras focused on all cash registers in addition to signs offering to reward "stool pigeon" customers. Naturally, I discussed the serious internal control and accounting issues the open cash register presented.[11]

- Thirty years ago, the manager of a local fabric store sought my advice. She said revenues were less than expected and the home office was concerned. I watched the operations for a short while. A customer entered with some fabric to return. She gave it to the manager who marked the receipt "returned," put the marked receipt into the cash drawer and withdrew money which she handed to the customer. I was aghast. The manager explained she and several employees had authority to handle returns and to refund cash. I said, "Well there is a big part of your problem. Your employees are stealing." "How," she asked. "Look at what you just did," I said. "How often do you ever keep or even examine a receipt for small purchases when you personally buy something?" The answer was "probably almost never." Exactly. With the poor internal controls in place, an unscrupulous employee could easily "forget" to hand the customer a receipt and, instead, pocket it. Then, when no customers or other employees were around, the employee could simply mark it

---

[11] Arguably not the best "over drinks" conversation. But it gave her a nice story to tell regarding how "fascinating" I am. Plus, it gave me a great story for my students.

"returned," put it into the cash drawer and remove the appropriate amount of cash. The cash register would then balance. Inventories—as covered in LESSON SEVEN—would be distorted, but unless the business had a perpetual inventory system (which it did not), then that would likely never be discovered. And, unless the number of returns were suddenly unusually high, the scheme would likely not be noticed, as well. Alas, a few months later I learned the manger had stolen many thousands of dollars in precisely the way I had just taught her to steal. I thought I was teaching about internal controls for cash, but actually I was teaching her how to be a thief (although apparently not a very good one: she was caught).

JOE'S was irresponsible for not recording all revenues daily. But now that Scott and Adrian and Lamar understand that (and so do you), we still must record the information they have,

3. ADJUSTING ENTRIES

JOE'S has one last regular journal entry for December—the accrual of Lamar's bonus, which equals one-third of the month's profits. To determine the bonus, we must first record adjusting entries for depreciation, amortization, interest, wages, and cost of goods sold.

A. DEPRECIATION EXPENSES

JOE'S has two depreciable assets: a sign and some equipment. The sign had a depreciable basis of $4,000, a five-year life. Management allocated zero to salvage value and chose double declining balance depreciation with no convention. Management also chose to allocate the declining balance depreciation evenly over each twelve-month period. The CPA determined each of these decisions was reasonable.

Thus, the 5-year life produces twice the straight-line depreciation rate in the first year. Straight-line is 20% per year for 5 years; hence, DDB would be 40%. Forty percent of $4,000 is $1,600. That divides by 12 to produce an even $133.33 per month for December through the following November. Then, the year 2 December depreciation would be $80, which would remain level for 11 months. Management could have chosen a more complicated method that treated each month differently. If so, the first month (December) would expense 2/60ths of $4,000 (twice the 1/60th straight line rate) for the same $133.33. January of year 2, however, would then expense 2/60ths of the reduced depreciable basis of $3,866.67 ($4,000 minus $133.33) or $128.89. The total for the first 12 months would be slightly lower under such a method than under the level-during-the-year method. The switch to straight-line, as discussed in LESSON FIVE-C, would occur earlier. Ultimately, JOE'S would expense the same amount, but a little less rapidly. What management chose is fine and is certainly simpler.

For the machinery and equipment, management also chose DDB, with zero salvage, but a ten-year life for the $31,000 depreciable basis. The December depreciation expense would thus be $516.67. That is 20% of $31,000, divided by 12 months—again, with level allocation during each 12-month period. The journal depreciation entries appear in **Figure 66**. Notice the credit to accumulated depreciation, a contra asset. JOE'S would repeat this same adjusting entry at the end of each month for twelve months, at which point the dollar amounts would decrease as the assets entered their second year of use.

General Journal for JOE'S BAR & GRILL			
Date	**Account**	**Debit**	**Credit**
12/31	**Cash**	133.33	
	Revenue		133.33
	Sign with 5-year life, DDB depreciation, zero salvage, no convention, and annual depreciation spread SL over the year.		
12/31	**Depreciation Expense**	516.67	
	Accumulated Depreciation		516.67
	Machinery with 10-year life, DDB depreciation, zero salvage, no convention, and annual depreciation spread SL over the year.		

Figure 66: Accrual of Depreciation

For U.S. tax purposes, the depreciation would likely be very different. As explained in LESSON FIVE-C, IRC section 168 would use a seven, rather than ten-year life for the machinery. In contrast, the sign would have a five-year recovery period for both purposes. Because JOE'S placed all its assets into service during the final quarter of the year, IRC section 168 would not allow use of the mid-year convention. Instead, it would permit a mid-quarter convention, which would result in JOE'S taking 1.5 months of depreciation in year one for tax purposes, as compared to the one month for financial accounting. Ignoring IRC section 179 and any "bonus depreciation," the year one tax depreciation would be $1,107.15 for the machinery and $200 for the sign. Thus, the year one total tax depreciation expense would be $1,307.15 as compared to the financial accounting depreciation total of $650. Notice the tax amount is more than double the financial amount. That would result in a deferred tax liability, as discussed in LESSON FIVE-D. Because such entries are mostly beyond this course, let's ignore that complication.

As a lawyer, you are unlikely to compute either type of depreciation (a bookkeeper will do so); however, you must understand a few things:

- Depreciation expense differs substantially between U.S. GAAP and U.S. tax law.

- Depreciation expense is arbitrary: it is a function of many choices, such as useful life, salvage value, deprecation method, and convention.

- Depreciation does not result in any cash flow: the journal entry has no impact on cash. As a result, depreciation can result in cash build-up. As a result, for some financial purposes, an analyst may ignore depreciation because it is not a typical expense. For example, we have discussed EBITDA— earnings before interest, taxes, depreciation, and amortization. LESSON TEN covers this issue in more depth. But, ignoring depreciation expense can also be risky: at some point, the related asset must be replaced, which will involve a significant cash expenditure.

B. AMORTIZATION EXPENSES

At the end of each month, JOE'S will also record various amortization expenses for rent, permits, the trademark, employee training, and the liquor license. These are adjusting entries which appear on the last day of the month because they are not only repetitive, but they also do not result from a transaction on any particular day. They each spread the cost of various "pre-paid" items over their projected useful lives. Both GAAP and U.S. tax law use straight-line amortization for most of these items.[12] U.S. GAAP will use the actual projected useful life; in contrast, IRC section 195 arbitrary requires a 15-year amortization period for many (but not all) intangibles. The journal entries appear in **Figure 67**.

---

[12] IRC § 467 effectively imposes an "upward sloping curve" amortization method for pre-paid rent if the dollar amounts exceed $250,000 over the life of the rental agreement. Application of this method is beyond this course. But, because the method imputes interest income in the pre-paid amount, it more closely reflects the actual economics of the transaction. GAAP in most cases, would be similar for large leases.

General Journal for JOE'S BAR & GRILL			
Date	Account	Debit	Credit
12/31	**Rent Expense**	2,500	
	Pre-Paid Rent		2,500
	To reflect SL amortization of pre-paid rent.		
12/31	**Permits Expense**	83.33	
	Permits		83.33
	SL amortization of 1000 permit fees paid in advance. Paid on 8/15 but runs from 12/1 to 11/30.		
12/31	**Amortization Expense**	50.00	
	TM		50.00
	SL amortization of TM over its 10-year legal life. We will capitalize and amortize any renewal costs when they occur. Management decided not to keep an accumulated amortization account.		
12/31	**Training Expense**	555.55	
	Employee Training		555.55
	SL amortization of employee training over management's determination of a 3-year life. We will expense future employee training as it occurs.		

Figure 67: Accrual of Amortization

Unlike depreciation, the corresponding credit for amortization is directly to the asset being amortized rather than to a contra-asset such as accumulated depreciation. No good explanation is readily apparent for this traditional difference.

Regarding the liquor license, JOE'S discovered an error in relation to the original journal entry. Initially, JOE'S paid $80,000 for the license and recorded it as an asset, with a debit to liquor license and a credit to cash. Later, the accountant discovered $1,750 of the initial cost was for the annual renewal fee. Under U.S. GAAP, the license—because it is perpetually renewable under state law—is non-amortizable. The $78,250 cost does not ever repeat if JOE'S pays the annual renewal fee. Thus, the cost is not amortizable. The annual fee, however, repeats annually; hence, it is amortizable under GAAP. As a result, JOE'S makes a correcting entry at the end of December to decrease the liquor license by $1,750 and to increase the liquor license lee by the same amount. It then amortizes the fee over its 12-month life. Such a "correcting entry" is not unusual, as people make mistakes.

The important point is to learn is that the correction is prospective only: JOE'S would not, under U.S. GAAP, restate any prior period financial statements to reflect the correction. As a result, new statements will not be comparable to older ones to the extent of the correcting entry. In this example, the accountant discovered the mistake during the first month of operations, so no disparity occurred. Had the discovery been later and had it been larger in amount, JOE'S might have prepared pro-forma prior statements for comparative purposes: what would have happened in prior periods had the mistake been discovered timelier. Such pro-forma statements, however, would not be the actual prior statements, which would remain uncorrected.

Figure 68 shows the correcting and adjusting journal entries.

General Journal for JOE'S BAR & GRILL			
Date	Account	Debit	Credit
12/31	**Annual Liquor License Fee**	1,750	
	Liquor License		1,750
	Correcting for over-capitalization of annual fee into liquor license.		
12/31	**Amortization Expense**	145.83	
	Liquor License Fee		145.83
	SL amortization of liquor license fee over 1-year legal life. We will capitalize and amortize renewal costs when they occur. We will <u>not</u> amortize the remaining liquor license costs, as the license is perpetually renewable under state law.		

Figure 68: Correcting Entries

In contrast, for tax books, the liquor license would be a section 197[13] intangible. As such, it would be amortizable over fifteen years. Thus, JOE'S would have an annual liquor license *tax-method* amortization expense of $5,216.67 ($434.72 per month). Its financial income would thus be greater than its taxable income by $5,216.67 merely from this one item. Recall, the tax depreciation for machinery and other items would also be greater. Together, these differences are material. As a lawyer, you must consider them in any matter involving a definition of income. For example, Lamar's December bonus of one-third the profits is $144.90 lower using tax amortization for the liquor license rather than GAAP rules.

---

[13] IRC § 197 includes "any license, permit, or other right granted by a governmental unit or an agency or instrumentality thereof."

C. INTEREST EXPENSE

Regarding the note payable, JOE'S has two important adjusting entries at the end of December.

- Accrual of interest expense.

- Classification of note payable.

Figure 69 shows the interest-related journal entries.

First, it accrues the $250 interest expense and interest payable. As explained earlier, the interest amount will decrease each month the loan is outstanding. For example, the January 31 accrual amount will be $248.42 because JOE'S will pay off part of the loan principal on January 1.

General Journal for JOE'S BAR & GRILL			
Date	**Account**	**Debit**	**Credit**
12/31	**Interest Expense**	250.00	
	Interest Payable		250.00
	Adjusting entry to recognize interest expense accrued on the note payable for December (the first payment is due January 1, 2016, in the amount of $966.64. It will comprise $250 of interest and 716.64 of principal.)		
12/31	**Note Payable**	8,840.15	
	Note Payable (current)		8,840.15
	Adjusting entry to reflect <u>current</u> (12 months) principal on note payable. The remaining 41,159.85 is classified as Note Payable (long term).		

Figure 69: Interest and Note Accruals

Second, JOE'S should allocate the note payable between a current liability and a long-term liability. Of the note principal liability, $8,840.15 belongs to "Note Payable (Current)" rather than merely to "Note Payable." This is the *principal* due during the following twelve months. JOE'S should adjust the amount each month, as it pays some of the principal. LESSON TEN covers ratio analysis, which explains the reasons for this detail in more depth. A useful balance sheet will distinguish between short-term (current) liabilities and long-term liabilities, just as it will distinguish short-term (current) assets from long-term assets.

If, for example, your client is a creditor of JOE'S, you may be more concerned with JOE'S ability to pay its debts over the next year as opposed to its ability to pay over the long-term of many years. That would be especially true if your client is a short-term lender. As covered in LESSON TEN, to measure JOE'S creditworthiness, one needs to know what liabilities are due in the near term as opposed to the long-term. Over the long-term, a business can re-finance debts or alter operations to resolve long-term cash-flow problems. Over the short-term, it may have fewer options; at the very least, the short-term options differ from the long-term ones. Thus, accountants list short and long-term assets and liabilities separately so that creditors can properly analyze the balance sheet.

D. WAGE ACCRUALS

General Journal for JOE'S BAR & GRILL			
Date	Account	Debit	Credit
12/31	Wages Expense	10,000	
	Wages Payable		10,000
	Adjusting entry to accrue wages payable on 1/1 of year two.		
12/31	Employment Tax Exp.	750	
	Employment Tax Payable		750
	Adjusting entry to reflect employment tax on wages payable.		

Figure 70: Wage and Related Accruals

On December 31, JOE'S would accrue the wages payable for the second half of the month—amounts which are due on January 1. It would also accrue the related employment tax liabilities and expenses. **Figure 70** shows the entries.

E. SUPPLIES EXPENSE ADJUSTMENT

At the end of the month, Scott and Adrian (or Lamar) notice the supply usage has been lower than expected. Originally, they purchased and capitalized $3,000 of supplies, expecting to use about half during December. Thus, their plan was to expense $1,500 of supplies and to replace that same amount, again capitalizing the purchase. Their discovery of lesser usage would not itself result in a journal entry; however, it would cause them to change the planned adjusting entry and likely to change the planned replacement purchases. **Figure 71** shows the adjusting entry.

General Journal for JOE'S BAR & GRILL			
Date	**Account**	**Debit**	**Credit**
12/31	**Supplies Expense**	1,000	
	Supplies		1,000
	Adjusting entry to show actual supplies usage of about 1/3d of supplies.		

Figure 71: Supplies Expense Adjusting Entry

F. COST OF GOODS SOLD

Before the *preliminary* closing of the books to determine Lamar's bonus, JOE'S would recognize an expense for cost of goods sold [COGS]. LESSON SEVEN covers inventory accounting and various ways of determining COGS. For now, apparently Scott, Ann, and Lamar counted the remaining inventory of liquor, wine, and food. On October 15, JOE'S purchased $30,000 of inventory, which it properly capitalized. At the end of the year, it discovered only $15,000 of inventory remained. As a result, it must recognize an expense of $15,000. **Figure 72** shows the entry.

General Journal for JOE'S BAR & GRILL			
Date	**Account**	**Debit**	**Credit**
12/31	**Cost of Goods Sold**	15,000	
	Inventory		15,000
	Adjusting entry for COGS.		

Figure 72: COGS Accrual

As covered in LESSON SEVEN, JOE'S could adopt various inventory accounting and valuation methods. Because this is the first month of operations, the valuation method is, for now, irrelevant. The count and resulting journal entry suggests JOE'S must be using a periodic inventory system, rather than a perpetual one. As a result, it knows only the total expense of $15,000, but it does not know whether it sold that amount or whether some of the inventory was stolen or lost due to spoilage. Because inventories are often a large aspect of a business and because accounting for them can result in inevitable distortions, we will devote an entire lesson series to them. As a lawyer, inventory costs are among the most important for you to examine.

For U.S. tax purposes, JOE'S would also need to adopt an inventory accounting and valuation method. It would, mostly, be the same method as used for financial accounting purposes; thus, COGS for tax purposes will likely be the same number as COGS for financial purposes.

4. LEDGERS

Before closing the books, JOE'S would post each journal entry into the appropriate ledger. This process simplifies the closing as well as the preparation of financial statements. At this point, you should begin to see the need for ledgers: all those journal entries are needed but visualizing them is difficult because they are chronological and not grouped.

A. EQUITY LEDGERS

Capital Stock Ann		
Date	Debit	Credit
8/1		250,00
12/1	100,000	
		150,000

Figure 73: Capital Stock: Adrian Ledger

Capital Stock Scott		
Date	Debit	Credit
8/1		250,000
12/1	100,000	
		150,000

Figure 74: Capital Stock: Scott Ledger

Retained Earnings		
Date	Debit	Credit
11/30		2,500

Figure 75: Retained Earnings Ledger

Figures 73 to **75** show the three equity ledgers prior to determination of Lamar's bonus and taxes and the closing of the books.

B. ASSET LEDGERS

Figure 76 shows the final cash ledger for the period. Notice it begins with the balance from 11/30. It would properly contain the prior postings which are omitted to save space. Several other things are immediately apparent.

General Journal for JOE'S BAR & GRILL		
Date	**Debit**	**Credit**
11/30	308,000	
12/1		200,000
12/1	50,000	
12/1		3,000
12/15		15,000
12/15		750
12/31	40,000	
12/31	184,250	

Figure 76: JOE'S Cash Ledger

First, $184,250 is a large amount of cash for such a small business. Unless JOE'S has expansion plans, it is overly liquid. *Second*, it really did not need that loan. It occurs to demonstrate how a loan affects the books and statements. *Third*, we cannot compute the average daily balance of cash because JOE'S failed to record revenues and receipts daily. That is a serious internal control over-sight: keeping very close track of cash is usually critical.

Figures 77 to **87** show 11 other permanent *asset* ledgers.

Account Receivable (Hans)		
Date	**Debit**	**Credit**
12/15	1,000	
12/24	2,000	
12/31	4,500	
	7,500	

Figure 77: Acc. Rec. (Hans) Ledger

Liquor License		
Date	Debit	Credit
11/30	80,000	
12/31		1,750
	78,250	

Figure 78: Liquor License Ledger

Liquor License Fee		
Date	Debit	Credit
12/31	1,750	
12/31		15.83
	1,604.17	

Figure 79: Liquor License Fee Ledger

Employee Training		
Date	Debit	Credit
11/1	20,000	
12/31		555.55
	19,444.45	

Figure 80: Employee Training Ledger

Inventory		
Date	Debit	Credit
10/15	30,000	
12/31		15,000
	15,000	

Figure 81: Inventory Ledger

Signs		
Date	Debit	Credit
11/15	4,000	

Figure 82: Signs Ledger

Machinery		
Date	Debit	Credit
10/1	31,000	

Figure 83: Machinery Ledger

Pre-Paid Rent		
Date	Debit	Credit
11/30	22,500	
12/31		2,500
	20,000	

Figure 84: Pre-Paid Rent Ledger

Trademark		
Date	Debit	Credit
11/30	6,000	
12/31		50
	5,950	

Figure 85: Trademark Ledger

Local Permit		
Date	Debit	Credit
8/15	1,000	
12/31		83.33
	916.67	

Figure 86: Local Permit Ledger

Supplies		
Date	Debit	Credit
11/30	3,000	
12/31		1,000
	2,000	

Figure 87: Supplies Ledger

Figures 88 and **89** show the accumulated depreciation ledgers for the machinery and the sign. Notice these *contra asset* accounts each have a credit balance, which means they are negative numbers. They will appear on the left side of the balance sheet as subtractions from the related historical cost amounts for machinery and sign.

Compare those with **Figures 78**, **79**, **80**, **84**, **85**, and **86** for the liquor license, liquor-license fee, employee training, local permit, pre-paid rent, and trademark. We recorded amortization expense for each (a debit) along with a credit directly to those asset ledgers. We did not create accumulated amortization accounts.

Acc. Depr. Machinery		
Date	Debit	Credit
12/31		516.67

Figure 88: Acc. Depr. Machinery

Acc. Depr. Sign		
Date	Debit	Credit
12/31		133.33

Figure 89: Acc. Depr. Sign Ledger

C. LIABILITY LEDGERS

Wages Payable		
Date	Debit	Credit
12/31		10,000

Figure 90: Wages Payable Ledger

Figures 90 to **94** are the permanent liability ledgers, which form the balance sheet.

Note Payable		
Date	Debit	Credit
12/1		50,000
12/31	8,840.15	
		41,159.85

Figure 91: Note Payable Ledger

Wage Taxes Payable		
Date	Debit	Credit
12/31		750
		147.61
		897.61

Figure 92: Wage Taxes Payable Ledger

Utilities Payable		
Date	Debit	Credit
12/1		1,000

Figure 93: Utilities Payable Ledger

Note Payable (Current)		
Date	Debit	Credit
12/31		8,840.15

Figure 94: Note Payable (Current) Ledger

D. REVENUE LEDGER

Revenue		
Date	Debit	Credit
12/15		1,000
12/24		2,500
12/31		4,500
12/31		40,000
		47,000

Figure 95: Revenue Ledger

Figure 95 shows the revenue ledger, a temporary account. JOE'S should have recorded the $40,000 of miscellaneous revenue (not from Hans's parties) daily. Recording it at the end of the month could result in many problems. It makes tracking sales difficult, which means the manager would not know which days were good days and which were not. It also makes tracking cash and evaluating employees or promotions very difficult.

E. EXPENSE LEDGERS

Figures 96 to **103** are the expense ledgers. We now appear to have four steps left before we can prepare financial statements:

Cost of Goods Sold		
Date	Debit	Credit
12/31	15,000	

Figure 96: COGS Ledger

Rent Expense		
Date	Debit	Credit
12/31	2,500	

Figure 97: Rent Expense Ledger

Depreciation Expenses		
Date	Debit	Credit
12/31	133.33	
	516.67	
	650.00	

Figure 98: Depreciation Expense Ledger

Amortization Expenses		
Date	Debit	Credit
12/31	83.33	
	50.00	
	555.55	
	145.83	
	834.71	

Figure 99: Amortization Expense Ledger

Supplies Expense		
Date	Debit	Credit
12/31	1,000	

Figure 100: Supplies Expense Ledger

Interest Expense		
Date	Debit	Credit
12/31	250	

Figure 101: Interest Expense Ledger

Wage Expenses		
Date	Debit	Credit
12/31	10,000	
	10,000	
	20,000	

Figure 102: Wage Expense Ledger

Wage Tax Expenses		
Date	Debit	Credit
12/31	750	
	750	
	1,500	

Figure 103: Wage Tax Expense Ledger

- We must close the books, at least so that we can preliminarily determine profits.

- Then we can accrue Lamar's bonus (1/3d of profits for the month).

- We also must accrue expected income taxes (state and federal) as well as expected other taxes (personal property).

- Then we can "close the books."

Then we can prepare financial statements. Not surprisingly, in the next part, we discover another item we forgot; hence, we have more steps.

———————

LESSON SIX-C

CLOSING OF THE BOOKS

■ ■ ■

"Closing the books" refers to closing all the income and expense ("temporary") accounts into a temporary Profit & Loss (*aka* Revenue and Expense) Summary account. From that account, we can determine Lamar's bonus, which we will need to accrue. We will also accrue an appropriate amount for expected federal, state, and local taxes which are a function of income.

Then we close the bonus expense and tax expense into the profit and loss summary account, which we then close into retained earnings. *Then* we can prepare the financial statements. The balance sheet will include all the permanent accounts, which carry over to the following period. The Income Statement will include all the temporary accounts, which will each then have a zero balance. They will start anew in the next period.

The closing is effective as of the last day of the period—in this case a month. That does not mean that JOE'S accountant/bookkeeper needs to spend his/her time on New Year's Eve recording journal entries and posting to ledgers. They will likely actually perform some of the work in advance and the remainder soon after the end of the period. That is also true of the inventory count: although it is supposed to be a count at the stroke of midnight on New Year's Eve, that is not practical. It, too, likely occurs several days or a week later.

Unfortunately, but not surprisingly, we discover both a mistake and some confusion in the process. We examine the revenue accounts and discover we forgot to accrue any interest income. We apparently do not have the bank records—an unrealistic problem, but a necessary one to demonstrate a particular forensic issue. In addition, we look at Lamar's contract—he is to receive one-third of the "profits"—but we are unable to locate a definition of "profits." As a result, we must resolve these two issues before we can close the books.

1. INTEREST INCOME ACCRUAL AND FORENSICS

When we pull up the cash ledger, we find the following a balance of $184,250, which continues to be far too much cash for a business this size. Scott and Adrian should hold some cash in demand deposits (such as a checking account) and the remainder should be in term deposits or other investments earning income. How much in each is more a topic for LESSON TEN. Or Scott and Adrian should consider another distribution.

In any event, surely, they did not deposit such a large amount in non-interest-bearing accounts. Because we have no record of regular deposits, we cannot be certain of our average daily balance of cash. Without that information, we cannot determine how much interest we earned, even if we know the interest rate. But we do have some relevant information:

- We know they earned $10,000 of interest income during the start-up period; hence, they opened interest-bearing accounts initially at least.

- We know the dates of most deposits and payments—all other than the $40,000 which was recorded late.

- We know the interest rates typically paid on similar amounts during the period involved.

With that information, we can estimate the amount of interest income that JOE'S likely earned. To be clear: this example is unrealistic because they would surely have access to bank records. Nevertheless, learning about forensic accounting is very important. Thus, suspend your knowledge of reality for a moment and join in some detective work.

As shown in **Figure 104**, JOE'S had $155,000 on deposit for 15 days. After paying wages and wages taxes on the 15th, it had $144,250 on deposit for the next 16 days. That averages to approximately $150,000 (ignoring the $40,000 in unrecorded revenue receipts). Using a mid-month convention for the $40,000 (we have no better information regarding it), the average daily cash balance is about $167,000.

Cash Ledger for JOE'S BAR & GRILL		
Date	Debit	Credit
11/30 12/1 12/1 12/1 12/15 12/15 12/31	308,000 50,000 40,000	200,000 ⎤ 3,000 ⎦ These net to 155,000 15,000 750
12/31	184,250	

Figure 104: JOE'S Cash Ledger

Using a similar analysis, JOE'S had an average cash balance of $370,000 during the start-up period. Although its accounting records were insufficient during that period, we can determine the monthly balances from the cash ledger:

- August: 460,000.
- September: 389,000.
- October: 325,000.
- November: 308,000.

Those average to approximately $370,000. Under the materiality principal, more accuracy would not be helpful. JOE'S accrued $10,000 of interest income during that four-month period. With that information, a forensic accountant could reasonably estimate a monthly periodic interest rate of 0.67%. A few points are noteworthy:

- Calculating the periodic interest rate for the start-up period is not part of ACCOUNTING FOR LAWYERS; however, it is a skill covered in the related course FINANCE FOR LAWYERS.

- The periodic rate is very high considering rates in recent years. JOE'S would likely have earned a great deal less; however, this is a hypothetical example. During many months over the past four decades, that interest rate would have been realistic. The point of the example is not the rate; instead, it is the forensic process of calculating the likely rate. Knowing the amount earned and the average cash balances, a forensic expert can easily estimate the likely rate.

- If JOE'S earned 0.67% periodic (monthly) interest during the start-up period, it likely earned a similar amount during December.

Applying the estimated interest rate to the estimated average daily cash balance of $167,000 produces an estimated $1,118.90 of estimated interest income during December. JOE'S CPA would likely round this number to $1,120 for the journal entry. Eventually, the bookkeeper will discover the actual numbers and will enter a correcting entry. For the December closing, precision is less important than having an approximate number. Although $1,120 is not a large amount of income, it is sufficiently material to report. Whether the correct amount is $1,120 or $1,118.90 or a few dollars more or a few dollars less is unimportant. Indeed, using $1,118.90, knowing it is an approximation, gives a false sense of precision and is thus arguably more misleading than a rounded number. Arguably, the CPA should have used $1,100 or even $1,000. Such a round, even number would obviously be an estimate, at least to the educated eye. LESSON TEN will cover more on forensic analysis tools used to reconstruct missing information.

2. DEFINITION OF "PROFITS" IN LAMAR'S CONTRACT

Before preliminarily closing the books to determine Lamar's bonus, we need to understand Lamar's employment contract. The information provided merely says that Lamar is to receive "one-third of the profits" during the period he is the manager. Perhaps, Scott and Adrian entered a detailed contract with Lamar specifying the definition of profits. Such a contract could have required the use of accrual accounting, consistent with U.S. GAAP, particular depreciation and amortization methods, conventions, and concepts of materiality. It could have specified the useful lives of various assets as well as rules regarding capitalization versus expensing of various items such as supplies. Likely, however, it did not.

Without such contractual specifics, whoever initially determined Lamar's bonus would have to exercise judgment regarding what the parties intended and what would be traditional in the particular industry. The various choices made so far in the problem all seem reasonable. Without question, the useful lives could have been shorter or longer, the supplies could have been expensed, and the business could have made many other accounting decisions. However, that is the nature of accounting: it is not a science. Thus, the bonus would almost certainly be a function of the choices made. If Lamar objected, he would likely have a heavy burden to show any of the choices and estimates were unreasonable.

But that is not the end of the inquiry. The word "profits" standing alone is not a term of art. From Scott and Adrian's viewpoint, "profits" are after all expenses, including taxes, interest, and Lamar's bonus. In contrast, from Lamar's viewpoint, his bonus is unlikely a function of itself: he likely would view the term "profits" as being a preliminary number prior to the determination of his bonus.

Accountants have developed various types of "profit" or "earnings." LESSON TEN covers these in more depth. For now, two are important to understand:

- EBIT.

- EBITDA.

EBIT stands for *E*arnings *B*efore *I*nterest and *T*axes. Roughly, this corresponds to operating income. Consider why Lamar receives the bonus. The point is to incentivize him to properly manage the Bar and Grill. How Scott and Adrian choose to capitalize the business—whether they use equity or debt and how much of each—is a decision for the owners to make, but not the non-owner manager. He would have less control over the amount of interest expense, or even interest income, at least considering the amounts involved in this example. As a result, those items arguably should not be part of his bonus determination. Similarly, he has no control (or at least very little control) over the amount of taxes owed. Additionally, his bonus is tax deductible by JOE'S. Thus, if the bonus is a function of taxes, it once again is a function of itself—a resolvable, but nevertheless complicated factor.

EBITDA stands for *E*arnings *B*efore *I*nterest, *T*axes, *D*epreciation, and *A*mortization. This commonly used measure of earnings generally corresponds to cash flows (assuming income and expense accruals are relatively stable). Although depreciation and amortization expenses are important for the matching principal, they do not reflect any out-flow of cash. Lamar might legitimately believe his intensification is to provide sufficient operating cash net income to keep the business going in the short to mid-term. His management duties may not include consideration of long-term investments and replacement of those assets. In particular, he might legitimately view the various start-up costs as "sunk costs"—items incurred prior to his employment. Amortization of them provides important information to Scott and Adrian as owners, but that information may not be relevant to judging Lamar's performance in each month.

Ultimately, as shown below, Scott and Adrian use EBIT to measure Lamar's bonus. Lamar would be unlikely to object. If he did, he would be unlikely to prevail as using EBIT is reasonable. It most closely represents operating income. Because Lamar is the manager, operating income is a function of his management skills. The interest is non-operating and is more a function of the owners' decisions. Lamar could have negotiated a more favorable contract, but he instead left the discretion to Scott and Ann, who exercised it reasonably.

3. CLOSING THE BOOKS

To close the books, JOE'S would proceed through several steps.

First, it would close all temporary accounts to an account called revenue and expense summary (or some similar name) as shown in **Figure 105**. These are not operational entries; instead, they merely transfer existing balances from the temporary accounts to another temporary account. As a result, each of the regular temporary accounts—such as rent expense and revenue—would have a zero balance. That way, they begin the following period with no entries, which allows the matching principal to work: December expenses and income matter only for December. January expenses and income will later appear alone, without December numbers. Notice the first twelve entries in **Figure 105** close expense accounts and the last two close income accounts.

General Journal for JOE'S BAR & GRILL			
Date	Account	Debit	Credit
12/31	R/E Summary	20,000	
	Wage Expense		20,000
	R/E Summary	250	
	Interest Expense		250
	R/E Summary	1,000	
	Supplies Expense		1,000
	R/E Summary	1,500	
	Wage Tax Expense		1,500
	R/E Summary	2,500	
	Rent Expense		2,500
	R/E Summary	145.83	
	License Amort. Exp.		145.83
	R/E Summary	15,000	
	Cost of Goods Sold		15,000
	R/E Summary	1,000	
	Utilities Expense		1,000
	R/E Summary	650	
	Depreciation Expense		650
	R/E Summary	83.33	
	Permit Amort. Exp.		83.33
	R/E Summary	50	
	Trademark Amort. Exp.		50
	R/E Summary	555.55	
	Training Amort. Exp.		555.55
	Interest Income	1,120	
	R/E Summary		1,120
	Revenue	47,500	
	R/E Summary		47,500

Figure 105: General Journal Closing Entries

Second, JOE'S would create the revenue and expense summary ledger, shown in **Figure 106** to contain all the expense debits and all the revenue credits. This facilitates preparation. As you see, we have all the relevant income statement items grouped together, which makes the statement preparation simple. For now, JOE'S can draw a single line and calculate a net figure. Recall: single lines indicate a netting process while double lines indicate a total. The December net income is $5,885.29, a credit. That credit will soon close to retained earnings, which is part of equity.

General Journal for JOE'S BAR & GRILL			
Date		**Debit**	**Credit**
	Wages	20,000	
	Interest	250	
	Supplies	1,000	
	Wage Taxes	1,500	
	Rent	2,500	
	License Amort.	145.83	
	CGS	15,000	
	Utilities	1,000	
	Depreciation	650	
	Permit Amort.	83.33	
	TM Amort.	50	
	Training Amort.	555.55	
	Interest Income		1,120
	Revenue		47,500
			5,885.29

Figure 106: JOE'S Revenue and Expense Summary Ledger

EBIT would be $5,015.29—the $5,885.29 reported income less the interest income of $1,120 and plus the interest expense of $250. EBITDA would be $6,500—EBIT plus $1,484.71 of various depreciation and amortization expenses.

Third, Scott and Adrian decide to use the EBIT figure to compute Lamar's bonus—the least favorable measure in this case. GAAP produces $5,885.29 income and thus a bonus of 1,961.76. EBITDA produces 6,500 income and thus a bonus of 2,166.67. EBIT produces income of $5,015.29 and thus a bonus of 1,671.76. The differences are not huge, but the EBITDA bonus is 494.91 larger than the EBIT bonus, which is almost 30%, a material difference in relative terms. Thus, the next accruals will be for the bonus and related employment taxes, plus the closing entries for those items, as shown in **Figure 107**.

General Journal for JOE'S BAR & GRILL			
Date	**Account**	**Debit**	**Credit**
12/31	Lamar Bonus Expense	1,671.76	
	Wage Tax Expense	125.38	
	Bonus Payable		1,671.76
	Wage Tax Payable		125.38
	To record Manager's year-end Bonus.		
12/31	R/E Summary	1,797.14	
	Bonus Expense		1,671.76
	Wage Tax Expense		125.38
	To close expenses to summary account.		

Figure 107: Bonus and Related Taxes Accrual and Closing Entries

Fourth, as a result, the net income figure appearing in the R & E summary ledger would be $4,088.15—the prior net of $5,885.29 less the $1,797.14 expenses for the bonus and related employment taxes.

Fifth, JOE'S would need to accrue its liability for federal, state, and local income taxes. This step creates some complications which are beyond the course. Nevertheless, all lawyers need to understand some basics:

- All entities (even tax exempt) are responsible for taxes at various levels—federal, state, and local.

- Some entities—such as S Corporations—are mostly not subject to federal income tax.

- Most small entities operate as a partnership, LLC or S corporation; thus, most tax liability falls on the owners rather than the entity.

Thus, to make the problem more realistic, we need additional facts:

- JOE'S BAR AND GRILL is actually Joe's Bar and Grill, Inc which, elected S corporation status under IRC section 1362.[14]

- The state of operation has no property tax on either real or personal property. *This is unrealistic*, but a complete problem is beyond this course.

As a *sixth* and final step, JOE'S would close the R & E summary to retained earnings. Then it can prepare the financial statements.

---

[14] IRC § 1362 permits some entities to elect S corporation status. An S corporation is generally (exceptions are beyond this course) not a taxpayer; instead, the shareholders report their share of taxable income.

LESSON SIX-D

FINANCIAL STATEMENT PREPARATION

■ ■ ■

1. FINAL CLOSING ENTRIES

Lamar objected to his bonus amount. He initially liked using EBIT because it typically produces a larger amount; however, because JOE'S has more interest income than interest expense, EBIT produces an anomalous result. After discussions, Scott and Adrian agreed the bonus would be a function of U.S. GAAP financial earnings. They probably should not have because it rewards Lamar for the interest income which resulted because Scott and Adrian over capitalized JOE'S. They then made new entries to reflect it as shown in **Figure 108** and erased the old!

General Journal for JOE'S BAR & GRILL			
Date	**Account**	**Debit**	**Credit**
12/31	**Lamar Bonus Expense**	1,961.76	
	Wage Tax Expense	147.61	
	Bonus Payable		1,961.76
	Wage Tax Payable		147.61
	To record Manager's year-end Bonus.		
12/31	**R/E Summary**	2,109.37	
	Bonus Expense		1,961.76
	Wage Tax Expense		147.61
	To close expenses to summary account.		

Figure 108: Bonus and Related Taxes Accrual and Closing Entries

They should not have corrected these items retroactively if the discussion about the amount of the bonus occurred in January; instead, they should have left the original entry the same and then recorded the difference as an extraordinary item in January. They could have prepared a *pro forma* set of statements to reflect what December results would have been had they agreed to this amount originally. But as often occurs, clients and businesses do not follow all the rules correctly. More importantly, they should never have erased the original entries: they should have reversed them and then recorded the **Figure 108** entries. Erasing **Figure 107** is a serious breach as it removes what could be an important record. Thus, we must proceed with what we have to prepare the financial statements.

General Journal for JOE'S BAR & GRILL			
Date	Account	Debit	Credit
12/31	Revenue & Exp. Summary	3,775.92	
	Retained Earnings		3,775.92
	Closing.		

Figure 109: Closing Entry

Retained Earnings		
Date	Debit	Credit
11/30		2,500
12/31		3,775.92
		6,275.92

Figure 110: Retained Earning Ledger

The final entry would be to close the R & E summary to retained earnings as shown in **Figure 109**. With the posting of this journal entry to the appropriate ledgers as shown in **Figure 110**, the books are closed for December.

2. FINANCIAL STATEMENTS

The December income statement appears in **Figure 111**. Notice how the statement separates income and expenses into operating and non-operating categories. JOE'S had no non-operating expenses, but it had interest income, which does not result from operations. Notice also that each of these items appears in the R/E summary ledger (although some have been combined, such as wages and wage taxes).

As shown in **Figure 112**, the December 31 balance sheet has similar classifications. It separates assets between current (short-term) assets and fixed (long-term) assets. It similarly separates liabilities between current and long-term liabilities. These classifications are critical in LESSON TEN when we deal with ratios.

JOE'S BAR & GRILL Income Statement Month Ending December 31		
Income:		
Operating Income:		$47,500.00
Expenses:		
Operating Expenses:		
Wages (including bonus/tax)	23,609.37	
Cost of Goods Sold	15,000.00	
Rent	2,500.00	
Utilities	1,000.00	
Depreciation and Amortization	1,484.71	
Supplies	1,000.00	
Interest	250.00	
Total Operating Expenses		**44,844.08**
Net Operating Income		**2,655.92**
Non-Operating Income		**1,120.00**
Net Income:		**$3,775.92**

Figure 111: Income Statement

A few observations are appropriate:

- The balance sheet classifications assume JOE'S is a going concern. If that assumption were invalid, the permits, license, trademark, training supplies, and the sign would likely have negligible value. They are each useful to JOE'S as long as it is operating, but they likely would not be easily transferable to a purchaser—at least not at book value.

JOE'S BAR & GRILL Balance Sheet December 31			
Assets		**Liabilities**	
Current		Current	
Cash	$185,370.00	Util. Payable	$1,000.00
Inventory	15,000.00	Note Payable	8,840.15
Supplies	2,000.00	Wages Payable	10,000.00
Accounts Rec.	7,500.00	Wage Tax Payable	897.61
Local Permit	916.67	Interest Payable	250.00
Liq. Lic. Fee	1,604.17	Bonus Payable	1,961.76
Pre-Paid Rent	20,000.00		
Total Current	**232,390.84**	**Total Current**	**22,949.52**
Fixed Assets		**Long-Term**	
Machinery	31,000.00	Note Payable	41,159.85
Acc. Depr.	(516,67)		
	30,483.33	**Total Liabilities**	**64,109.37**
Liquor License	78,250.00		
Trademark	5,950.00	**Owner's Equity**	
Emp. Train.	19,444.45	Scott	150,000.00
Signs	4,000.00	Adrian	150,000.00
Acc. Depr.	(133.33)	R/E	6,275.92
	3,866.67		
Total Fixed	**137,994.45**	**Total Equity**	**306,275.92**
Total Assets	**$370,385.29**	**Liabilities & Equity**	**$370,385.29**

Figure 112: Balance Sheet

- The machinery and pre-paid rent may have transferable value, but probably less than book value. If the business were to falter, the time needed for a transfer could consume the remaining rental period. Also, a purchaser would likely prefer new equipment and machinery. In contrast, the liabilities are correct: even if the business had trouble, they would continue.

- The current assets are about ten times the current liabilities. As covered in LESSON TEN, that is extreme. Typically, a 2:1 current ratio (current assets divided by current liabilities) is sufficient. Ten to one suggests the business likely has under-performing assets.

- JOE'S earned approximately 5.6 cents on each dollar of sales. To determine this, divide net operating income ($2,655.92) by operating income ($47,000). This return on sales seems quite low. Scott and Adrian would want to investigate industry standards to determine whether their operations are generally consistent with traditional industry benchmarks. LESSON TEN covers this in greater depth.

- If JOE'S were to increase its prices by a mere 5%, it would nearly double its profit. To determine this, multiply the $47,000 of revenue by 5% and assume no customers would object (*i.e.*, assume demand is inelastic at that level of price change). Five percent of $47,000 is $2,350 which is close to the operating profit of $2,655.92. Thus, a four-dollar beer would change to $4.20, and a $7.50 glass of wine would become about $7.90. Scott and Adrian may want to experiment with some items to assess customer sensitivity and price elasticity.

- Wages, including employment taxes, are about half of sales. This amount appears high. Industry benchmarks suggest the amount, including benefits (which we ignore) should be around 30 to 35% of sales. Thus, Lamar needs to motivate the staff to produce more sales.

- The return on investment [ROI] is a healthy 1.23% for the month. Compounded for a full year, that is the equivalent of a 15.8% effective interest rate return. Viewing one month in isolation provides too little information for Scott and Adrian to draw significant conclusions; however, it is all they have for now. They will want to watch their various ratios closely.

3. OTHER ANALYSIS AND POTENTIAL USE OF THE STATEMENTS

A. TAX CONSEQUENCES

Because Scott and Adrian elected S corporation status for Joe's Bar & Grill, Inc., the entity will not pay federal tax on the income. Instead, the income will—for federal tax purposes—flow through to the two shareholders. The total income through December—using U.S. GAAP—was $6,275.92, the amount of retained earnings. For U.S. tax purposes, the number would be different largely because depreciation and amortization would be subject to different rules. Determining the taxable income is beyond this course.

Assuming the taxable income amount were the same $6,275.92, Scott and Adrian would each report half on their personal U.S. tax returns: $3,137.96. JOE'S would file a Form 1120-S information return along with a Schedule K. Scott and Adrian would each receive a Schedule K-1, which would show their respective share of the income.

LESSON NINE will deal with the business structure of entities, including corporations. It will cover distributions and dividends. For now, you should understand JOE'S could—if the board of directors chose—distribute part or all the earnings to the shareholders, Scott, and Adrian. But, for federal tax purposes, Scott and Adrian must report their share regardless of whether JOE'S makes a distribution from earnings. That is the nature of an S Corporation.

B. FAMILY LAW

How Scott and Adrian must treat their respective $3,137.96 share of JOE'S earnings is also important in other legal matters. Because they did not actually receive the funds and because state laws routinely consider a corporation a separate entity from the shareholders, this is a serious issue. Analysis of it will vary from jurisdiction to jurisdiction, as well as by the matter involved.

For example, state laws regarding child support, alimony, and property division incident to divorce vary on what they count as either "income" or "assets" of the parties. Accounting, tax, and corporate issues play a role in measuring *what* is income and *when* something is income. In Florida, for example, the statute provides:

(a) Gross income shall include, but is not limited to, the following:

1. Salary or wages.

2. Bonuses, commissions, allowances, overtime, tips, and other similar payments.

3. Business income from sources such as self-employment, partnership, close corporations, and independent contracts. "Business income" means gross receipts minus ordinary and necessary expenses required to produce income.

4. Disability benefits.

5. All workers' compensation benefits and settlements.

6. Reemployment assistance or unemployment compensation.

7. Pension, retirement, or annuity payments.

8. Social security benefits.

9. Spousal support received from a previous marriage or court ordered in the marriage before the court.

10. Interest and dividends.

11. Rental income, which is gross receipts minus ordinary and necessary expenses required to produce the income.

12. Income from royalties, trusts, or estates.

13. Reimbursed expenses or in-kind payments to the extent that they reduce living expenses.

14. Gains derived from dealings in property unless the gain is nonrecurring.[15]

The statute is problematic both facially and as applied. First, we examine the statute. Then we will examine a Court decision applying it. Both are flawed.

1) Criticism of the Statute

The statute is faulty for at least 5 accounting-related reasons. As a result, the Court did not have much to work with in developing a rule.

a. No Clear Accounting Method

As is true of most states,[16] Florida family law statutes defining income, expenses, gains, losses, assets, and liabilities lack a clearly adopted method of accounting. Specifically, section 61.30(2)(a) not only fails to adopt an accounting method, but it also uses conflicting terms. The statute uses cash method terminology for some items—such as for bonus or tip *payments* in section 2, retirement and annuity *payments* in section 7, support *received* in section 9, and in-kind *payments* in section 13.

The use of *from* arguably suggests the cash method in relation to business, royalty, trust or estate income in sections 3 and 12. But, the section 9 use of *received from* suggests the legislature knew how to require receipt from a source, thus at least negating any inference for sections 3 and 12. Indeed, the contrasting "received from" and payment references more strongly suggests use of the accrual method when the word receipt or payment is lacking. Other sections lack even a hint as to the proper method of accounting: salary and wages (1), disability, worker's compensation, unemployment, and social security *benefits* (4, 5, 6, and 8) interest and dividends (10).

---

[15] F.S. 61.30(2)(a). For a discussion of this statute, see WILLIS I AND II, *supra* note 13, page 27.

[16] *E.g.,* NY Fam. Ct. § 413 (using federal tax law as an initial basis for income).

Without a defined method of accounting—or clear rules favoring one method over another—the statute leaves room for manipulation and confusion. Adoption of the cash method would present many opportunities for manipulation, though for many people, the opportunities would be small.[17] Adoption of the accrual method would create complexity for many people; however, for most the difference between cash and accrual would likely be immaterial. For business owners and large investors, the accrual method should not be problematic. Using the cash method for some items and accrual for others is probably the worst possible choice, as it presents extra opportunities for manipulation.

b. *No Accounting Principles and Assumptions*

Even if the statute adopted a method of accounting, it would not be sufficient absent the adoption of accounting principles and assumptions. At the very least, the statute should require matching of income and related expenses, as well as consistency from year-to-year. Without those principles, an accounting method is largely meaningless.

c. *Two Definitions*

Having two definitions for income—one for alimony and another for child support—is facially troubling. Litigants must file a financial affidavit, not two separate affidavits. While the standards for awarding alimony differ from those for child support, no apparent defensible reasons exist for defining income differently for the two awards. As a practical matter, litigants and the courts use the child support definition for both. Still, having two definitions at least creates some confusion, as noted by the *Zold* Court.

d. *Inconsistent Use of Gross and Net Numbers*

The child support statute *partially* uses net numbers to define gross income in section 3, 11, and 14, dealing with business income, rental income, and gains from property dealings. It uses gross numbers for all other items. It then permits "allowable deductions" for determining net income, which is the important number. Unfortunately, the term allowable deductions is far from clear. Section 61.30(3) provides:

> (3) Net income is obtained by subtracting allowable deductions from gross income. Allowable deductions shall include:
>
>   (a) Federal, state, and local income tax deductions, adjusted for actual filing status and allowable dependents and income tax liabilities.

---

[17] People who work for regular wages often have little opportunity to manipulate because they can neither accelerate nor postpone income. In addition, most people have no employee business expenses to deduct.

(b) Federal insurance contributions or self-employment tax.

(c) Mandatory union dues.

(d) Mandatory retirement payments.

(e) Health insurance payments, excluding payments for coverage of the minor child.

(f) Court-ordered support for other children which is actually paid.

(g) Spousal support paid pursuant to a court order from a previous marriage or the marriage before the court.[18]

Categories (b), (c), (e), and (f) are mostly clear, although (c) could use a reference either to "paid" or to "contributions," as appears in the other provisions. Each of these appears to use the cash method.

Category (a) facially is obscure. "Federal, state, and local income tax deductions, adjusted for actual filing status and allowable dependents and income tax liabilities." It surely allows a deduction for the actual tax owed, considering not only tax deposits but also payments. The reference to "deductions" appears to refer to tax withheld by an employer (or other payor) and deposited on behalf of the earning spouse. The adjustment likely requires a spouse to adjust the withheld amount for the actual liability. *When* a spouse makes the adjustment, however, is unclear. For example, if Adrian has 2023 tax deposits of $30,000 but owes only $28,000 (as determined on his return filed April 15, 2024), the statute is unclear whether the 2023 "allowable deduction" is $30,000 or $28,000. At least to a tax lawyer, "income tax deductions" refers to deductible items, not to regular tax deposits, which was apparently intended. Additionally, the reference to actual income tax liabilities necessarily encompasses actual filing status and actual allowable dependents and thus the phrase is internally redundant.

Category (g) is facially circular, as it is a function of itself, at least in part. Spousal support in the current matter is an allowable deduction; however, to the extent courts use the child support income definition for alimony determinations, the current support facially affects itself. Fixing the circularity is simple, but it requires two determinations of income: one for alimony and one for child support. Evidence that this occurs is lacking from appellate opinions.

Category (d) is oddly written—mandatory retirement *payments*. It surely refers to mandatory *contributions*. The category prompts another criticism of the gross income definition. For mandatory retirement contributions, the contribution plus any income it generates does not count as family-law income until received in some later period, perhaps years

---

later. For voluntary contributions, the original contribution does not generate an allowable deduction and thus counts as income in the year of the contribution; however, the ultimate future distribution (the section 61.30(2)(a)(7) pension or retirement payments) fully counts as income, including both the original contribution and the related earnings. As a result, the contributed amount counts twice. That seems unwise; however, it is very clear. A similar problem exists for annuity payments: nothing allows a deduction for the cost of the annuity, but the full payment received from the annuity counts as family-law income. As a result, the cost counts twice. Consider EXAMPLE 25.

EXAMPLE 25

Spouse Buys an Annuity

Spouse A purchased an annuity in year 1 for $100,000, using separate assets. It will pay $12,950.46 annually at the end of years 1 through 10.

Spouses A and B decide to divorce in year 5. Analyze the annuity.

The EXAMPLE 25 annuity does not involve a mandatory retirement contribution per category (d). As a result, the $100,000 year-1 cost is neither deductible nor excludible regardless of whether Spouse A plans to use the distributions for retirement or merely for annual cash flows. Yet, under section 61.30(a)(7), the entire annuity receipts count as income each year. For years 1 through 4, a determination of family-law income may not occur because the Spouses are in a seemingly happy marriage; however, it will occur for year 5 and probably year 6, the years surrounding the divorce. **Figure 113** shows an amortization of the 10-year annuity.

Annuity Schedule				
Year	Payment	Interest	Principal	Balance
				100,000.00
1	12,950.46	5,000.00	7,950.46	92,049.54
2	12,950.46	4,602.48	8,347.98	83,701.56
3	12,950.46	4,185.08	8,765.38	74,936.18
4	12,950.46	3,746.81	9,203.65	65,732.53
5	12,950.46	**3,286.63**	9,663.83	56,068.70
6	12,950.46	**2,803.44**	10,147.02	45,921.68
7	12,950.46	2,296.08	10,654.37	35,267.31
8	12,950.46	1,763.37	11,187.09	24,080.22
9	12,950.46	1,204.01	11,746.45	12,333.77
10	12,950.46	616.69	12,333.77	0.00

Figure 113: Annuity Amortization

Per section 61.30(a)(2), A will have $12,950.46 year-5 and year-6 income from the annuity payment received. The investment, however, earns 5% annual interest, at least internally.[19] Because the principal balance at the end of year 4 is only 65,732.53, the actual year-5 interest income is only $3,286.63. The year-6 interest is less: $2,803.44. Thus, for the 2 years likely examined for family law income determination, the economic income totals $6,090.07; however, the Florida[20] family law income totals $25,900.92. The difference occurs because the statute includes the year-5 $9,663.83 principal distribution, as well as the year-6 $10,147.02 principal distribution. Thus, the statute includes $19,810.85 as income for the 2 years even though that amount comprises assets and not income in any traditional accounting sense. If A, for whatever reason, had computed family law income in year 1, A would not have had a deduction or exclusion for the $100,000 used to purchase the annuity. Further, if A used earnings to purchase the annuity, those earning would have counted as family law income in the year earned, year-1 or earlier. Counting them again as principal in years 5–6 results in counting them twice.

---

[19] The posited annuity has a 5% nominal annual interest rate with annual payments. Because interest rates external to an instrument change frequently, we cannot be sure what economic interest the instrument actually yields—it changes with the market. The payment amount and term, however, remain the same, as they are contractual. Thus, using the initial 5% rate is useful.

[20] Florida is not alone in double counting annuity principal. *E.g.*, N.Y. Fam. Ct. Act. § 413(b)(5)(iii)(H).

e.   *Counts Both Income and Assets Unclearly*

For both alimony and child support, the statute begins with income as the primary touchstone. For both purposes, however, the court can consider the spouses' assets as well, albeit by way of an adjustment requiring court findings.[21] That creates two problems: one undercounts and one overcounts.

To understand the problem, one needs to understand two things: imputed income and economic value. *First*, for unemployed or underemployed spouses, a court can impute income.[22] In contrast, nothing statutorily permits a court to impute income on under-performing assets.[23] *Second*, an asset is worth the present value of its future utility.

EXAMPLE 26

Spouse Has Three Assets

Asset 1 is undeveloped land which produces zero cash flows. It has a fair market value of $100,000 after considering all costs of sale. A buyer is ready, willing, and able to purchase it for fair market value.

Asset 2 is a readily marketable bond that annually pays $5,000 interest at the end of the year and has a remaining life of 10 years. The bond has a present value of $100,000.

Asset 3 is high rated, marketable annuity paying $12,950.46 at the end of each year for 10 remaining years. It has a present value of $100,000.

Consider the three assets of EXAMPLE 26. Each asset has an undisputed fair market value of $100,000. In an initial income determination, Asset 1 produces zero income, Asset 2 produces $5,000 income, and Asset 3 produces $12,950.46 income. The example uses a 5% nominal annual interest rate comprising expected future inflation and liquidity interest components. It ignores the risk component of interest.[24]

Because each of the three assets has the same value, they are economically fungible (ignoring tax issues). Asset 1 underreports income and Asset 3 overreports income while Asset 2 disburses appropriate annual income.

---

[21] F.S. 61.30(11)(a)(7) (the court may consider "available assets"). *See also* 61.30(13). For a deviation from the guidelines greater than 5%, the court must make written findings explaining why the guideline amount is "unjust or inappropriate." F.S. 61.30(1)(a).

[22] F.S. 61.30(1)(b).

[23] Equity jurisdiction is an option for alimony. F.S. 61.08(j). For child support, a Florida court can consider non-recurring income and assets. F.S. 61.30(13). In contrast, a NY court can impute income for "non-income producing assets." NY Fam. Ct. § 413(b)(5)(iv)(A).

[24] For a discussion of why the example excludes the risk component *see id* at 129–46.

A court might be tempted to use its statutory power to consider the value of the assets as an additional factor in determining alimony or child support. For Asset 1, that seems appropriate as it underperforms on an annual basis. A court should impute $5,000 income to it because Spouse could (under the given facts) sell Asset 1 and purchase Asset 2, which would produce $5,000. Spouse's investment decision should not inure so heavily to Spouse's benefit. The court should consider the asset, not in an *ad hoc* non-mechanical manner, but by way of imputing an appropriate level of annual income to the asset. Thus economically, Asset 1 produces $5,000 annual income, considering its actual disbursements (zero) and its appropriate imputed income. To be sure, no Florida statutory authority exists for this imputation; however, it reflects economic reality. The same analysis would apply if Asset 1 produced merely $1,000 annually: a court should then impute the $4,000 of underperformance. Oddly, in some states—such as New York—courts can impute income only on non-income producing assets. If such statutes apply as written, a court could impute $5,000 for Asset 1 (which otherwise produces nothing) but impute nothing for a similarly valuable asset that produced merely $1,000. Such statutes reflect a misunderstanding of economic value: assets are worth the present value of their future utility. An asset with no utility (income being a common utility) is worth nothing; thus, the concept of "non-income producing" is itself odd if one considers use and enjoyment—in addition to monetary distributions—as utility and thus income. In any event, "underperforming" should be the standard, not "non-income producing."

For Asset 2, a consideration of assets should be irrelevant as the bond already produces an appropriate market rate of income. Spouse could sell the bond and purchase something else, but the new asset could at most produce $5,000 annually after adjusting for any change in risk. Thus, a court should not consider the Asset 2 value if it also considers the Asset 2 income, which it statutorily must. Because the value of an asset is the present value of its future cash flows (and other utility) including the $5,000 income is the same thing as considering the value of the asset. Considering the asset value under F.S. 61.30 would result in counting the income twice. States such as New York—which permit imputation for non-income producing assets—avoid this issue in part. As explained above, such rules should apply to "underperforming" assets, as opposed to "non-income producing" ones. Thus, Asset 2 produces $5,000 annual income, considering its disbursements ($5,000) and any potential imputed income (zero).

Asset 3 illustrates a serious flaw in the statute: it counts the entire "annuity payment" of $12,940.56 as income, which considers not only the interest but also the principal disbursed. EXAMPLE 25 illustrated this issue. Thus, the statute defining income already considers the asset value. Considering it again under the court authority to consider assets would effectively consider it more than *three* times. For example, if a court were to impute $5,000 income to the annuity based on a simplistic view of its $100,000 value, it would then count $17,940.56 income from the annuity. In reality, the annuity produces $5,000 economic income annually: $12,940.56 plus the imputed $5,000. Ideally, Asset 3 produces $5,000 annual income, considering its economic income disbursements ($5,000) plus the utility of its principal disbursement plus the utility of its retained principal.

With the EXAMPLE 26 parameters—each asset has the same risk and liquidity—Spouse should have $15,000 annual income considering actual disbursement and asset values. In contrast, using merely the Florida statutory definition of income, Spouse has $17,940.56 income, which is % too high. Potentially, using a plausible income imputation under the authority to consider asset values, Spouse risks having $32,940.56 income.

2) *Zold v. Zold* Applies the Income Statute

The Florida Supreme Court dealt with this statute in a case involving undistributed S Corporation earnings—such as the $3,137.96 allocated to both Scott and Ann. The relevant part of the statute is sub-paragraph 3, which includes "business income from sources such as ... close corporations. . . ." JOE'S BAR & GRILL, INC. is closely held—it only has two shareholders.[25]

The *Zold v. Zold* decision follows. Mr. Zold was one of two shareholders in an S Corporation. He owned 57% of the stock. His 2001 share of corporate profits was about $100,000, which he reported for tax purposes. The entity had retained earnings of $372,908 ($212,557 was Mr. Zold's share), including the 2001 earnings.

The Court reviewed the entity's status as an S Corporation and ultimately grounded its decision on two issues:

- The child support statute largely uses "cash method" language,

- The corporate entity is a separate entity from its shareholders, which is consistent with corporate law and the separate entity assumption of accounting. As such, the proceeds of earnings belong to the entity, rather than to the shareholders.

The Court held a shareholder-spouse in an S corporation need not include retained earnings as income for determining child support and alimony if he/she can prove the amounts were retained for a "corporate purpose" or a "legitimate business purpose". Unfortunately, the Court did

---

[25] The term "close corporations" connotes a "closely held" entity but is not the current term used in Florida corporate law.

not explain what constitutes a "corporate purpose" or what constitutes a "legitimate business purpose." Pay close attention to the bolded words as wells as the annotations. In depth analysis follows the decision.

ZOLD V. ZOLD

911 So. 2d 1222 (Fla. 2005)

(some footnotes omitted)

[* * * *] The [* * * *] issue is whether "pass-through" income[26] from an S corporation that is not actually distributed to the shareholder-spouse is to be considered income for the purposes of calculating alimony, child support, and attorney's fees.

FACTS AND PROCEDURAL HISTORY

[* * * *] The husband, who was sixty-five years old at the time of the trial, is the chief executive officer of Tri Tech Electronics, Inc., (Tri Tech), a close corporation[27] that elected to be taxed pursuant to Subchapter S of the Internal Revenue Code. The wife, who was fifty years old at the time of the trial, was a full-time housewife with one year of college education. The couple's minor child was fifteen years old at the time of the trial. The husband's only marital asset and **sole source of income** is his interest in Tri Tech. The husband and another shareholder, A.J. Stanton, own all of Tri Tech's capital stock.

> Did Mr. Zold receive wages for being the CEO? Would be helpful if the Court put that amount in perspective with his share of retained earnings.

The trial court found that the husband owned 57.1543 percent of Tri Tech stock (400 shares), and that his ownership interest was worth $890,000 based on an appraisal report that used the asset based approach to determine the fair market value of 400 shares of Tri Tech stock. The trial court also found that the husband had income exceeding $245,000 per year **as reflected on his individual federal income tax return for 2001.** The trial court based its determination of child support and alimony on the fair market value of the husband's interest in Tri Tech stock and the husband's income reported on his individual federal income tax return for 2001. In entering final judgment, the trial court ordered the husband to pay a lump sum amount, permanent periodic alimony, child support, premiums on a life insurance policy, and one-half of the child's expenses.

---

[26] "Pass-through" income refers to a small business corporation's income, deductions, losses, and credits that pass through to the shareholders of the corporation in accordance with each shareholder's pro rata share of ownership in the corporation and is reported on each shareholder's individual federal income tax return under the Subchapter S Revision Act of 1982. See 26 U.S.C.A. § 1366 (West Supp.2005).

[27] A close corporation is a corporation "whose stock is not freely traded and is held by only a few shareholders." Black's Law Dictionary 365 (8th ed.2004).

The husband was also required to pay for health and dental insurance for the couple's minor child. Thereafter, the trial court supplemented its previous order and required the husband to contribute to the wife's attorney's fees and costs. The entire amount of the husband's immediate obligations was in excess of $179,406.20.[28] [* * * *]

The issue before the Court is whether "pass-through" income of an S corporation that is not distributed to shareholders constitutes income within the meaning of chapter 61, Florida Statutes (2004), for purposes of calculating alimony, child support, and attorney's fees. Further, we must decide whether the resolution of this issue requires an exclusively legal determination that can be governed by a bright line rule, or whether it also requires factual findings to be made on a case-by-case basis. [* * * *]

I.   Subchapter S Revision Act of 1982 and Section 607.06401, Florida Statutes (2004)

The Subchapter S Revision Act of 1982 (the "Act") allows a small business corporation to elect to have all of the corporation's income, deductions, losses, and credits pass through to the shareholders of the corporation for income tax purposes in accordance with each shareholder's pro rata share of ownership in the corporation. See 26 U.S.C.A. § 1366 (West Supp. 2005). This "pass-through" income is then taxed to the shareholders directly on the shareholders' individual federal income tax returns. See 26 U.S.C.A. § 1363 (West Supp.2005). Corporations are generally treated as separate legal entities from their shareholders for tax purposes. [* * * *]

Although an S corporation's net income is taxed directly to the shareholders under the Act, the shareholders do not necessarily receive distributions in an amount equivalent to what is taxed pursuant to the Subchapter S election. In Florida, an S corporation's authority to make distributions to shareholders is limited by the corporation's articles of incorporation and section 607.06401, Florida Statutes (2004). Section 607.06401 prohibits a corporation from making distributions in certain circumstances and provides in pertinent part that

(3)   No distribution may be made if, after giving it effect:

    (a)   The corporation would not be able to pay its debts as they become due in the usual course of business; or

    (b)   The corporation's total assets would be less than the sum of its total liabilities plus (unless the articles of

---

[28] The husband's total immediate obligations consisted of $172,088.50 (a portion of the lump sum award payable within sixty days); $1,797.66 (monthly payment of remainder of lump sum award); $5,000 (monthly payment of permanent periodic alimony); and $520.04 (monthly payment of child support). This total does not include the husband's obligations to pay the premiums on a $500,000 life insurance policy, one-half of the child's expenses, and the wife's attorney's fees.

incorporation permit otherwise) the amount that would be needed, if the corporation were to be dissolved at the time of the distribution, to satisfy the preferential rights upon dissolution of shareholders whose preferential rights are superior to those receiving the distribution.

§ 607.06401(3), Fla. Stat. (2004). Thus, section 607.06401(3) prohibits distributions that would render the corporation unable to fulfill its corporate duties to its debtors and shareholders. In those circumstances, a corporation must retain its income and cannot make a distribution to shareholders without violating Florida law.

> Corporations are subject to distribution restrictions; however, these hardly apply in most cases involving material retained earnings. These involve the two types of insolvency.

II. Chapter 61, Florida Statutes (2004)

We next review the pertinent statutory provisions of chapter 61 to determine how the concept of "pass-through" income applicable to shareholders of an S corporation applies to the statutory definitions of income for calculating alimony, child support, and attorney's fees. Chapter 61 governs dissolution of marriage, support, and child custody proceedings. In evaluating the amount of alimony, where applicable, the trial court is instructed to consider and make findings regarding, inter alia, "[a]ll sources of income **available** to either party." § 61.08(2)(g), Fla. Stat. (2004).[29] In addition, the trial court must consider the "financial resources of each party," § 61.08(2)(d), Fla. Stat. (2004), and may

> Remarkably. Florida has two definitions of income for family law purposes As a practical matter, the child support definition applies for both alimony and child support.

consider "any other factor necessary to do equity and justice between the parties." § 61.08(2), Fla. Stat. (2004). Similarly, the child support guidelines establish that the presumptive amount of support is based on the parties' "combined monthly available income." § 61.30(6), Fla. Stat. (2004).[30] Lastly, in determining whether to award attorney's fees, the trial court must consider the "financial resources of both parties." § 61.16(1), Fla. Stat. (2004).[31]

---

[29] *See also* Canakaris v. Canakaris, 382 So.2d 1197, 1201 (Fla.1980) ("The two primary elements to be considered when determining permanent periodic alimony are the needs of one spouse for the funds and the ability of the other spouse to provide the necessary funds.").

[30] *See also* Finley v. Scott, 707 So.2d 1112, 1116 (Fla.1998) ("Consideration of both the bona fide needs of the child and the financial circumstances of each parent complies with [the child support guidelines enumerated in] section 61.30, Florida Statutes (1993).").

[31] *See also* Rosen v. Rosen, 696 So.2d 697, 699 (Fla.1997) (stating that in deciding whether attorney's fees are appropriate, "the trial court must look to each spouse's need for suit money versus each spouse's respective ability to pay").

Chapter 61 contains two separate definitions of income relevant to this case. First, section 61.046(7), Florida Statutes (2004), sets forth a general definition of the term "income" and provides that income as used within chapter 61 means

> any form of **payment** to an individual, regardless of source, including but not limited to: wages, salary, commissions and bonuses, compensation as an independent contractor, worker's compensation, disability benefits, annuity and retirement benefits, pensions, dividends, interest, royalties, trusts, and any other **payments**, made by any person, private entity, federal or state government, or any unit of local government. United States Department of Veteran Affairs disability benefits and unemployment compensation, as defined in chapter 443, are excluded from this definition of income except for purposes of establishing an amount of support.

(Emphasis supplied.) This definition applies to the determination of income attributable to a spouse for purposes of determining awards of alimony and attorney's fees. Second, section 61.30, Florida Statutes (2004), defines "gross income" for child support purposes in part as including:

> Business income from sources such as self-employment, partnership, close corporations, and independent contracts. "Business income" means gross receipts minus ordinary and necessary expenses required to produce income.

§ 61.30(2)(a)(3), Fla. Stat. (2004) (emphasis supplied). Although sections 61.046(7) and 61.30(2)(a)(3) utilize different language to define income, both statutory provisions focus on income that is **available** to a spouse.

> The Court focused on the word payment, which connotes "delivery."

The plain language of section 61.046(7) defines income in terms of **payment** to an individual. It is a rule of statutory construction that where the Legislature has chosen not to define a term, "the plain and ordinary meaning of [the] word can be ascertained by reference to a dictionary." [* * * *] The term "payment" has been defined to mean "the act of paying" or "something that is paid." Merriam Webster's Collegiate Dictionary 852 (10th ed.1999); *see also* Black's Law Dictionary 1165 (8th ed.2004) (defining "payment" to mean the "[p]erformance of an obligation by the **delivery** of money or some other valuable thing accepted in partial or full discharge of the obligation"). **Thus, the term "payment" connotes something that is given to or received by an individual and, hence, is available to the individual to satisfy financial obligations imposed by the trial court during dissolution proceedings.**

Similarly, in defining business income attributable to a spouse when computing child support, section 61.30(2)(a)(3) expressly excludes any portion of business income that is needed to satisfy the business's "ordinary and necessary expenses required to produce income." These funds are excluded because they are expected to be used by the business to cover its expenses and therefore are not available to the shareholder-spouse to satisfy court-ordered financial obligations upon dissolution of marriage.

> **This paragraph is faulty.** Expenses are *deductions* from gross income to determine net income or profit. They are *not exclusions* and do not refer to assets retained for future needs.
>
> The Court conflates expenses and assets. Retained assets can be available; in contrast, prior expenses cannot be "funds" and cannot be "used" in the future: they have already occurred!
>
> Most importantly, the issue involves retention of the net proceeds for future needs, not the expenses. Thus this critical paragraph makes no sense.

The doctrine of in pari materia requires that statutes relating to the same subject or object be construed together to harmonize the statutes and to give effect to the Legislature's intent. [* * * *] We conclude that construed together, sections 61.046(7), 61.30(2)(a)(3), 61.08(2)(g), 61.30(6), and 61.16(1), reflect legislative intent that trial courts consider only that portion of a spouse's **income that is available** to the spouse. In fact, both section 61.08(2)(g), which concerns alimony, and section 61.30(6), which concerns child support, expressly refer to income that is available to a spouse. See § 61.08(2)(g) (stating that the trial court is to consider "all sources of income available to either party") (emphasis supplied); § 61.30(6) (stating that the trial court is to consider the parties' "combined monthly available income") (emphasis supplied).[32]

III. Case Law Addressing Undistributed Business Income for Chapter 61 Purposes

In Zipperer, the First District Court of Appeal held that a spouse's undistributed business income fell within the general definition of income set forth in section 61.046 and thus was properly considered by the trial court in awarding alimony. See 567 So.2d at 917. The First District rejected the argument that undistributed business income should not be considered income under chapter 61 because it was reported only for tax purposes and was not actually received by the payor spouse. See *id.* The First District noted that income is broadly defined in section 61.046 to include "any form of payment to an individual, regardless of source." *id.* (quoting § 61.046(4),

---

[32] Of course, this includes imputed income under section 61.30(2)(b), Florida Statutes (2014), for those spouses found to be voluntarily "unemployed or underemployed."

Fla. Stat.). Deeming the source of funds irrelevant under this section, the First District concluded that undistributed business income constitutes income for alimony purposes. In effect, the First District adopted a bright line rule that automatically treats undistributed business income as income attributable to a spouse under chapter 61. [* * * *]

> The appellate courts were divided on the issue. The First DCA considered retained earnings to be available. The Third agreed, at least in one case. The Fourth and Fifth found the retained earnings not available if retained for corporate purposes.

The Third District has also considered whether undistributed "pass-through" income constitutes income for alimony and child support purposes. See Martinez, 761 So.2d at 434. [* * * *]

In McHugh v. McHugh, 702 So.2d 639, 642 (Fla. 4th DCA 1997), the Fourth District Court of Appeal concluded that undistributed "pass-through" income from an S corporation does not constitute income under chapter 61 where the shareholder-spouse was a minority shareholder, and the income was retained for corporate purposes. The uncontradicted testimony was that the corporation "retained the income for purposes of building the business and keeping it going." *id.* at 641. However, the Fourth District pointed out that if undistributed "pass-through" income has been retained for noncorporate purposes, such as to reduce a shareholder-spouse's amount of income during dissolution, the trial court could consider it as income under chapter 61. See *id.* at 642 n. 1.

Similarly, the Fifth District in the present case concluded that the determination whether undistributed "pass-through" income constitutes income under chapter 61 depends on the purpose for which the income has been retained. [* * * *]

IV. Whether Undistributed "Pass-Through" Income That Has Been Retained for Corporate Purposes Constitutes Income under Chapter 61

> The Court held: earnings retained for "corporate purposes" are not available to the owner spouse.

We conclude that undistributed "pass-through" income that has been retained by a corporation for **corporate purposes** does not constitute income within the meaning of chapter 61. Specifically, undistributed "pass-through" income that has been retained for corporate purposes is not available "income" under section 61.046(7) or "business income" under section 61.30(2)(a)(3). [* * * *] In contrast, where undistributed "pass-through" income has been retained for noncorporate purposes, such as to shield this income from the reach of the other spouse during dissolution, the improper motive for its retention makes it available "income" under section 61.046(7) or "business income" under section 61.30(2)(a)(3).

This conclusion is consistent with our observation in *Rosen v. Rosen,* 696 So.2d 697, 700 (Fla.1997), that "proceedings under chapter 61 are in equity and governed by basic rules of fairness." *See also* § 61.011, Fla. Stat. (2004) ("Proceedings under this chapter are in chancery."). In fact, section 61.08(2) expressly allows a trial court to "consider any factor necessary to do equity and justice between the parties" when determining whether alimony is appropriate. **Allowing a shareholder-spouse to reduce the amount of available income by manipulating the retention of "pass-through" income for his or her personal benefit is inconsistent with the stated legislative intent that dissolution proceedings under chapter 61 are equitable.**

The basic approach adopted by the Fifth District is consistent with the statutes applicable to S corporations and various sections of chapter 61, including the statutory definitions of income which focus on income that is available to a spouse. The income reported on an individual federal income tax return for a shareholder-spouse of an S corporation is not necessarily equivalent to the income available to the shareholder-spouse. [* * * *]

> The Court sought to avoid manipulation, but adopted a standard so easily met it invites manipulation.

We decline to establish a bright line rule in these circumstances. On the one hand, establishing a rule that undistributed "pass-through" income can never constitute income for purposes of computing alimony, child support, or attorney's fees, could encourage a shareholder-spouse to manipulate an S corporation's "pass-through" income in order to shield this income from the reach of the other spouse during dissolution proceedings. The potential for manipulation is greater if the spouse is a sole or majority shareholder of the corporation who, by virtue of his or her ownership, has more control than does a minority shareholder over whether income is retained or distributed by the corporation. [* * * *] Clearly, income retained for purposes of avoiding financial obligations related to dissolution proceedings would not be income retained for corporate purposes.

> The Court states the "corporate purposes" rule as "legitimate business reasons."

On the other hand, establishing a rule that undistributed "pass-through" income always constitutes income within the meaning of chapter 61 ignores the fact that an S corporation may have been prohibited by Florida law from making distributions or that **the corporation may have had legitimate business reasons for retaining its income**. See Brett R. Turner, Classifying the Retained Earnings of a Separate Property Business as Marital Property, 15 Divorce Litig. 141, 148 (2003) ("[T]he owner of a business should not be required to place protection of the marital estate above all other legitimate business concerns."). **Attributing to a shareholder-spouse income that has been retained by a corporation for corporate purposes does not provide a workable framework for trial courts to assess either the needs of a spouse or a spouse's ability to pay.** Moreover, ascertaining whether a corporation was prohibited

> Why is it not workable? How does it differ from a sole proprietorship? Or rental property, which may need funds for maintenance or improvement.

from making a distribution under section 607.06401(3) or whether undistributed "pass-through" income was retained for corporate purposes involves factual determinations that are properly made on a case-by-case basis.

We conclude that when the issue of whether undistributed "pass-through" income was retained for corporate purposes is contested, the shareholder-spouse should have the burden of proving that the undistributed "pass-through" income was properly retained for **corporate purposes** rather than impermissibly retained to avoid alimony, child support, or attorney's fees obligations by reducing the shareholder-spouse's amount of available income. **The burden is properly on the shareholder-spouse**

> The Court goes back to "corporate purposes" and places the burden of proof on the owner spouse.

because he or she has the ability to obtain information to establish the propriety of the corporation's actions.

In determining whether the shareholder-spouse has met his or her burden of proving that the undistributed "pass-through" income was retained for corporate purposes, the trial court should consider (1) the extent to which a shareholder-spouse has access to or control over "pass-through" income retained by the corporation, (2) the limitations set forth in section 607.06401(3) governing corporate distributions to shareholders, and (3) the purpose(s) for which the "pass-through" income has been retained by the corporation. **Although a shareholder-spouse's ownership interest should be considered, it is**

> Even a 100% shareholder can satisfy the test, though the degree of ownership is relevant.

not dispositive even where the spouse is a sole or majority shareholder in the corporation and has the ability to control the retention and distribution of the corporation's income. Ownership of capital stock does not entitle shareholders to income that has been retained by an S corporation because shareholders do not have a right to an interest in the corporation's income. See Anson, 772 So.2d at 57 (Peterson, J., concurring specially) ("A stockholder has certain rights in a corporation, but those rights do not include a direct interest in any corporate asset or income."). In addition, "where the decision to retain earnings was controlled **partly** by the desires of other shareholders or **partly** by economic forces requiring that earnings be retained, it seems questionable to assert that the marital estate is being injured merely because the [shareholder-spouse] had to some extent the raw ability to injure it." Brett R. Turner, Classifying the Retained Earnings of a Separate Property Business as Marital Property, 15 Divorce Litig. 141, 148 (2003). Thus, more important than the shareholder-spouse's ownership interest is the purpose for which the undistributed "pass-through" income has been retained by the corporation. [* * * *]

It is so ordered.

PARIENTE, C.J.

WELLS, ANSTEAD, LEWIS, QUINCE, CANTERO, AND BELL, JJ., concur.

The decision is disappointing for many reasons. Blame for the lack of clarity falls on both the legislature, as discussed earlier, and on the Court.

3) Criticism of the Court

Criticism of the Court also falls into seven points.

a. Zold Adopts a Weak Standard: "Corporate Purpose"

Requiring a "corporate purpose" for accumulations is a very low threshold, easily satisfied with modest planning. Similarly, requiring the purpose to be "legitimate"[33] adds very little as courts would presumably disregard illegitimate corporate purposes. As the *Zold* Court understandably explained, a decision to retain earnings to disadvantage a spouse or children is not a legitimate purpose.[34] What *would* be a legitimate and reasonable purpose? A list is not difficult to discern.

- To provide working capital, including for the procurement of inventory for an expanding business.

---

[33] *Zold*, 911 So. 2d at 1233.
[34] *Id.* at 1231–32.

- To expand the business or to acquire a subsidiary.

- To acquire new equipment or other fixed assets.

- To perform anticipated repairs, maintenance, or improvements.

- To provide for the retirement of debt.

- To accumulate a "rainy day" fund because of anticipated competition or a weakening economy.

- To provide for investments or loans for suppliers or customers so as to maintain the business.

- To provide for anticipated product liability or other litigation losses or costs.

A roadmap for such purposes even appears in treasury regulations dealing with the accumulated earnings tax.[35] While that tax does not apply to S corporations,[36] the government-sanctioned list on how to avoid it is instructive and includes many of the above purposes. Further help for accumulator/manipulators would flow from an understanding of the very similar "business purpose" doctrine generally applicable in tax law: transactions which reduce tax typically must satisfy a business purpose, as opposed to a tax avoidance purpose.

The tax doctrine has existed for many decades. Over time, it proved to be inadequate and thus morphed into several more extensive doctrines[37] and code sections,[38] which are arguably themselves inadequate to prevent tax manipulation. A taxpayer needing to establish a business purpose or economic substance (or to avoid the sham and step-transaction doctrines) faces a knowledgeable adversary in the IRS; nevertheless, such taxpayers are all-too-often successful. Whether a spouse seeking to establish a mere corporate purpose for S corporate accumulations would typically face such a sophisticated adversary is doubtful. Regardless, the family law adversary's arsenal of weapons would be far less than that of the IRS.

Particularly disturbing is the Court's apparent belief that it placed a material burden on a shareholder spouse. It did not.

---

[35] Treas. Reg. § 1.537–2.

[36] IRC § 1361(a) exempts S corporations from most chapter one taxes, including those imposed by section 531 (accumulated earnings) and 541 (personal holding company undistributed income).

[37] *E.g.*, Welch v. Helvering, 293 U.S. 465 (1935) (business purpose, substance versus form); Knetsch v. U.S., 364 U.S. 361 (1960) (sham transactions), Comm'r v. Gordon, 391 U.S. 83 (1968) (step transaction doctrine).

[38] *E.g.*, IRC §§ 267 (related party rules), 269 (acquisitions to avoid tax), 355 (controlled corporation distributions), 482 (income and deduction allocation among controlled trades or businesses), 531 (accumulated earnings tax), 541 (personal holding company tax), 465 (at-risk rules), 469 (passive activity rules), 704(b) (partnership allocations), 7701(o) (economic substance doctrine).

For example, for JOE'S, the business is very early in its operations; hence, it cannot know its capital needs and may require the retained $6,275.92. That argument would be far more convincing if the entity were not so over-capitalized; however, if either owner were expecting an upcoming divorce, they likely would already have reduced the over-capitalization with a larger initial distribution or a smaller initial contribution. Then, retention of future earnings proceeds would be wise. JOE'S may also have plans for expansion—such as the WINE SHOP that appears in LESSON SEVEN. Expansion plans are routinely thought to be a legitimate reason for retaining earnings.

b. Zold's "Availability" Discussion Is Unconvincing

The statute requires inclusion of "available" income. Thus, the meaning of availability was central to the *Zold* decision. The Court's determination of a lack of availability upon the showing of a corporate purpose is unconvincing. First, to the extent the owner spouse has a majority or otherwise controlling interest, the assets are "available" by definition except for the statutory insolvency exceptions. Yes, they are in a corporate form, which would require modest corporate formalities prior to a distribution; however, accessing any funds not stuffed-in-a-mattress requires at least some process.

Second, the Court did not explain why business or corporate needs—even assuming that is a significant standard—trump family needs causing the assets to be "unavailable." Consider EXAMPLE 27. A spouse operates a sole proprietorship plumbing, electrical, or dry-cleaning business. Such activities need working capital, funds for rainy days, funds for expansion plans and potential litigation losses. The needs do not change merely because Scott and Adrian choose a proprietorship rather than a corporation. The choice of entity—corporate versus sole proprietorship—has nothing to do with needs. The money and the accounting entries do not care whether about the legal formalities, at least not at the fundamental level involved. A business purpose is a business purpose regardless of legal niceties.

EXAMPLE 27

JOE'S Is a Sole Proprietorship

Rather than incorporate, Scott and Adrian operate the BAR AND GRILL as a sole proprietorship in Scott's name. It has the same activities, income and expenses except Scott pays Adrian her share as his employee.

If, however, we apply *Zold v. Zold* to the EXAMPLE 27 JOE'S PROPRIETORSHIP, suddenly the earnings belong directly to Scott. They thus count as income for family law purposes. Scott may "retain" the earnings through bookkeeping entries, just as JOE'S BAR & GRILL, INC. might; however, such retention would be irrelevant regardless of whatever business needs Scott might be able to show. Scott's choice of "entity"—a proprietorship rather than a corporation—may thus greatly affect his family law obligations.

c. Uses Tax Law Definition of Income

Zold earnings are facially those computed for federal tax purposes. Nowhere does the Court recognize the underlying artificiality of the earnings definition. The case deals with whether the corporation is an artifice to disadvantage a spouse and children. It failed, however, to recognize the nature of the income itself as artificial.

The Court fell into the all-too-common trap of using tax return information as a surrogate for income. Apparently, all of Mr. Zold's income was from the entity and the Court relied on what he reported for tax purposes. But his financial income for GAAP purposes—if it could be determined—would almost certainly be different from his tax income. Nothing in the decision suggests the Supreme Court, the various D.C.A.'s, or the trial court appreciated the difference, let alone that GAAP income would be more accurate than tax income.

d. Equates Past Expenses with Assets

Consider the paragraph annotated "**This paragraph is faulty**." The Court stated:

> [S]ection 61.30(2)(a)(3) expressly **excludes** any portion of business income that is needed to satisfy the business's "ordinary and necessary expenses required to produce income." These **funds** are **excluded** because they are expected to be used by the business to cover its expenses and therefore are not available to the shareholder-spouse . . . .[39]

Goodness. Those two sentences are packed with basic errors reflecting a fundamental misunderstanding of accounting.

First, expenses are *deductions* from gross income to determine net income or profit. They are *not exclusions*. They are not part of gross income, which one records as a credit; instead, they are debits for costs. One might argue that debits and credits do not really matter in law; however, one would be wrong. Mislabeling and misunderstanding basic accounting led to the next error, as it can lead to many other errors.

---

[39] *Zold*, 911 So. 2d at 1232 (emphasis added).

Second—and more significantly—the Court conflated expenses and assets. It called expenses "funds,"[40] and it suggested such "funds" might be "used" in the future! Funds, however, are assets. They appear on a balance sheet and certainly an owner of funds can use them in the future. Expenses, however, are also not assets: they exist in temporary accounts and appear on the income statement. They do not exist as "things" or "funds" or "assets" in any sense. They are not property: they are merely an accounting entry. Nothing more and nothing less. Ultimately, they reduce retained earnings, which is part of *equity*—again, *not assets*. Indeed, retained (undistributed) *assets* (*not* earnings) can be available for future expenses, acquisitions, or distributions; in contrast, *prior* expenses cannot be "funds" and cannot be "used" in the future "to cover expenses."[41] That statement makes no accounting or financial sense. Any *use* has already been incurred, which is why the items are expenses.

For example, suppose Tri-Tech incurred a $1,000 expense for utilities. It would debit utility expense for $1,000 and credit $1,000 to cash (if it paid the invoice) or to utility payable (if it has not yet paid the bill). The expense is in the past. The need $1,000 of funds required to satisfy the utilities obligation will either already have been expended or they will be subject to a creditor's claim for a $1,000 payable. The expense cannot be "available" for future expenses. That is accounting gobbledygook. Significantly, the $1,000 of cash also cannot be "available" for future expenses because the funds have either already been transferred to the utility company, or they soon will be to pay the debt.

The Court is correct that a business may need liquidity: for debts, for future operations, and for expansion. Those are legitimate reasons to "retain earnings" and thereby not distribute assets. But those are not remotely supported by the statutory language which clearly refers to prior expenses which match with prior earnings. Effectively, the Court thus counts those expenses—or at least the statutory support for the expense— twice: once in determining the amount of retained earnings and again in justifying the retention of the earnings. But past expenses cannot justify a need for liquidity. Whether the Court would reach the same conclusion had it properly understood the statute is unclear. Future liabilities can justify liquidity and the expectation of future expenses can justify it, but the past cannot.

e.   *Overstates Corporate Restrictions*

The Court emphasized corporate law distribution restrictions. It cited F. S. 607.06401, which precludes distributions that would render the corporation insolvent under either a liquidity or balance sheet insolvency

---

[40]   *Id. at* 1229.

[41]   *Id.*

definition. While correct, the concern appears overstated: nothing in *Zold* suggested the corporation was insolvent. Certainly, current profit might follow prior losses such that the entity either has near negative equity or very low liquidity; however, that is unlikely the typical scenario.

f.   Does Not Address Other Entities

The Court did not address how its holding would affect other forms of business: *e.g.*, partnerships, trusts, estates, and sole proprietorships. Admittedly, the Court did not have such entities before it. Nevertheless, practitioners should recognize the similar, but distinct, issues that will arise in relation to various business forms. Partnership tax accounting, for example, is quite different from corporate tax accounting, which itself differs from S Corporation tax accounting. Financial accounting for each type of entity should be approximately the same; however, the Court so heavily relied on tax return information, one must expect it would do the same for other entity forms.

g.   Does Not Address Risk of Double Counting and Under Counting

Double counting—or not counting—income is a real possibility following *Zold* because the case does not adopt any method for tracing or restricting retained earnings once counted. The fault lies more with the poorly drafted statute rather than with the Court; nevertheless, it necessarily follows from the decision. Consider two scenarios.

EXAMPLE 28
Current Retained Earnings _Are_ Income
JOE'S retains $10,000 2021 earnings but has no corporate purpose for doing so. In 2022, JOE'S has $15,000 earnings, but distributes $25,000.

In EXAMPLE 28, the 2021 retained earnings _do_ count as income for child support or alimony calculations because no corporate purpose for the retention exists. Thus, Scott has $5,000 of *Zold* earnings if he is then involved in a family law proceeding for which 2021 earnings matter. If he is not in current litigation, presumably the family law earnings still exist, despite the probable lack of any such determination. *Ideally*, JOE'S would reclassify the $10,000 as "retained earnings classified as 2021 income for Florida family law." A debit to retained earnings and a credit to the new classification would do the trick. Of course, that is non-traditional accounting[42] and would be a cumbersome determination, especially if

---

[42]   For U.S. tax law, an analogous entry is required for controlled foreign corporations [CFC]. IRC section 959 excludes from income, distributions of previously tax earnings and profits (PTEP) retained in a prior year but taxed to shareholders per sections 951 or 1248. Section 959 has a

neither owner were then involved in child support or dissolution proceedings. Similarly, because one can never be sure in which state owners will someday reside, JOE'S would need to make similar classifications for each state regarding each owner—a truly unrealistic set of entries.

In 2023 JOE'S distributes $25,000, including the previously retained earnings plus $15,000 of 2023 earnings. If Scott were then involved in a relevant family law matter, his $7,500 share of the distributed 2023 earnings would count as income. That is clear in the statute.[43] The extra $5,000 distribution to Scott—attributable to his share of the retained 2022 earnings—should *not* count as 2023 family law income because it previously counted in 2022 or *would have counted* had the year been relevant for family law calculations. Facially, the statute counts dividends as income.[44] Would practitioners or courts appreciate the previously "taxed" nature of the 2023 distributions of 2023 earnings as distinct from the 2022 distribution of 20223 earning? Perhaps so, but do you really believe that?

EXAMPLE 29

Current Retained Earnings *Are Not* Income

JOE'S retains $10,000 2021 earnings but has a corporate purpose for doing so. In 2022, JOE'S has $15,000 earnings, but distributes $25,000.

In EXAMPLE 29, the current retained earnings *do* count as income for child support or alimony calculations because the owner spouse cannot prove a corporate purpose for the retention. Suppose the following year the entity distributes the previously retained earnings. Although the second-year distribution in excess of second year earnings might be overlooked, as posited in EXAMPLE 29, it also might be counted as a dividend under F. S. 61.30. Or perhaps the original earning year was not considered by the court in fashioning a support award, but the distribution year was considered. In that instance, the non-owner spouse would have the burden of proving a corporate purpose existed for the prior year retention. How could that be? Logic explains.

The non-owner spouse discovers the distribution in excess of current earnings and asserts it is income. The owner spouse, having the general burden of proving a corporate purpose for retention, concedes the issue and

---

complex ordering provision detailing how to allocate current distributions among current or prior earnings, taxed or not. To work properly, the *Zold* scheme would require similar complex allocations. Expecting that to work in theory, let alone practice, seems laughingly naïve. Despite what the Court said, something much closer to a bright-line test appears the only realistic option.

[43] F.S. § 61.30(2)(a)10.

[44] *Id.*

readily admits no such purpose existed in the prior year. At that point, the retained earnings would constitute income for the prior year and thus logically not income for the current year being considered. To overcome this, the non-owner spouse would oddly have the burden of proving a corporate purpose for the prior retention—a very strange obligation, not easily met.

Also, if we impute the income in year one—the retention year, owner spouse has income, though the entity has the related asset. Then, in valuing assets (which is relevant for alimony and child support) we likely capitalize earnings, but we would also examine assets and liabilities.

This is not a course in family law; hence, the details of *Zold v. Zold* are not essential. But studying the case should illustrate how important accounting knowledge is to an understanding of corporate law, tax law, and family law.

LESSON SEVEN

INVENTORIES AND COST ACCOUNTING

■ ■ ■

Lesson Objectives

1. Student will learn that inventory accounting varies among GAAP, tax law, and internal accounting.

2. Student will learn why basic knowledge of inventory accounting is important to lawyers.

3. Student will learn about two basic inventory management methods: periodic and perpetual.

4. Student will learn about multiple inventory valuation methods, particularly LIFO and FIFO.

5. Student will learn basic cost accounting.

Terminology Introduced

- Stock in trade.
- Capital asset (mostly a tax law term).
- Property held primarily for sale to customers in the ordinary course of a trade or business (tax law).
- Property used in a trade or business.
- Dealer vs. investor status.
- Cost accounting.
- Categories of costs:
    - Direct versus indirect.
    - Variable versus fixed costs.
- Incremental cost.
- Cost-plus pricing.
- Opportunity cost.
- Cost segregation.
- Market segmentation.

LESSON SEVEN deals with two intertwined subjects: inventory accounting and cost accounting. Any business that sells a non-service product—particularly a tangible one—maintains inventory. That requires specialized accounting rules for financial reporting and for tax law. In addition, such businesses must price the product which involves cost accounting.

Fundamentally, inventory accounting involves tracking items and valuing them for purposes of the balance sheet as well as "cost of goods sold," an expense for the income statement. Cost accounting relates to these issues but focuses more on pricing the product in the marketplace. Logically, to set a proper price, management must know the cost of what it sells. That cost is not necessarily the cost reflected in COGS or on the balance sheet; hence, cost accounting differs from inventory accounting, though the two overlap. Budgets and planning operations also involve an accurate knowledge of costs, as allocated not only to a product but also to a service, a project, or a department. Traditional GAAP (or IFRS) rules exist mostly to provide a consistent disclosure of information to investors and creditors; in contrast, cost accounting's audience is more internal—management as it prices and plans. Because the purpose and the audience differ, the assumptions and rules differ as well.

LESSON SEVEN-A

INTRODUCTION TO INVENTORY ACCOUNTING

■ ■ ■

LESSON SEVEN-A covers two topics:

- Why lawyers need to understand inventories.
- Terminology.

Much of inventory accounting can seem tedious. The temptation for lawyers is often to be dismissive of it, thinking "that is for accountants to know." Fair enough, but for a business with inventories, the inevitable accounting judgements can have a large impact on valuation and costs. Particularly in the short run, both valuation and cost are easily manipulated, which can affect many areas of law.

Terminology is important because inventory and cost accounting involve many commonly used terms as well as some terms of art. A lawyer who does not understand at least the basic terminology will not understand valuation and cost issues and can be easily mislead.

1. WHY LAWYERS NEED TO UNDERSTAND INVENTORIES

This section covers five legal areas impacted by inventories. Others exist, but these provide a solid framework for understand the subject:

- Trust Law (including trust and estate planning).
- Family Law.
- Federal Tax Law.
- State Tax Law.
- Sale of a Business.

A. TRUST LAW

Courses in trust law, trust, and estate planning, as well as the income taxation of estates and trusts cover many topics. A central focus of each—and likely the central concern of clients—is who gets what. Ultimately, it's about the money and who gets it: the income beneficiary, the principal beneficiary, or the government through taxation.

"Trust accounting" commonly refers to the obligation of the trustee to account for trust assets and liabilities and to provide that "accounting"—effectively the financial statements—to the beneficiaries.[1] Accounting for trusts is not a separate field; however, it is subject to state statutes regarding how to allocate income, gains, expenses, and losses among the beneficiaries. Federal tax law also has rules regarding the allocation of income and thus the allocation of taxes.[2]

As a very general rule, profits from operations—including from the sale of inventory—belong to the income beneficiary rather than to principal. The government will take a share of profits; however, as discussed below, the government's share often depends on the character of the income—whether it is properly classified as ordinary (such as from inventory sales) or capital (generally sales not in the ordinary course of business). The importance of these general allocation rules is clear because they fundamentally affect who gets what.

No so obvious, however, are the rules, including many nuances, by which accountants (and necessarily lawyers) classify items between inventory and non-inventory, as well as ordinary business operations and extraordinary activities. Ultimately, that classification—rather than the

---

[1]   *E.g.* F.S. 736.0813, UFIPA §403.

[2]   IRC §§ 641, 651.

rule—is paramount. For example, a trust could own JOE'S BAR, with the income flowing to Scott but the principal flowing to Ann. If so, Scott would know he would receive the benefit of inventory sales; however, unless he clearly understood what constitutes inventory, as well as its cost and valuation, what he received could vary a great deal. The person classifying property, costing, and valuing it would have great control over the ultimate allocations between him and Ann. Both—and their lawyers—could challenge allocations only if they first understood them.

Section 403 of the Uniform Principal and Income Act—adopted in many states—provides a rule, albeit not fully clear:

> If a trustee sells assets of the business or other activity, other than in the ordinary course of the business or activity, the trustee shall account for the net amount received as principal in the trust's general accounting records to the extent the trustee determines that the amount received is no longer required in the conduct of the business.[3]

From an accounting perspective, that rule is partially clear, but leaves several open questions. Sales of inventory as inventory—as opposed to a liquidation or bulk sale—are by definition in the ordinary course of the business. For example, JOE'S is in the business of selling beer, wine, and food. Thus, when it sells beer, wine, and food to customers, that is in the "ordinary course" of its business. *Profits*[4] from such sales necessarily are *income* and should inure to the benefit of the income beneficiary. Bookkeeping for such ordinary income would involve closing the revenue and expense summary to the income beneficiary's equity account rather than to the principal beneficiary's equity. Otherwise, the journal and ledger records would have no important difference from what we have covered before. In contrast, profits from extraordinary sales would close to the principal beneficiary equity account.

Oddly, the statute refers to the "net amount received" rather than to *income* or *profit*. The words *net* and *received* are unclear, at least from an accounting perspective. Receipt suggests the cash method of accounting rather than accrual. The drafters likely did not intend to impose the cash method, but *receipt* suggests it. For example, when JOE'S sold drinks and food to Hans in PROBLEM 3, it received only his promise to pay. Surely trust law would consider that as a sufficient *receipt* and would value it consistent with accrual accounting; however, such a rule is not self-evident.

More broadly, the statute speaks of accounting for sale receipts as either principal or income (roughly, extraordinary being principal and

---

[3]   UPIA § 403.

[4]   Profits refers to a net figure, after expenses, typically including direct costs, depreciation, and overhead. Proceeds refers to a gross figure. The profits, not the proceeds, from inventory sales traditionally belongs to the income beneficiary.

ordinary being income). While that may superficially appear clear, from an accounting perspective, it is not clear. We account for receipts as assets, not equity. Recall **Figure 36** illustrating an accounting entry that affects only assets. We could purchase something or sell something for our adjusted basis. In both cases, we debit an asset and credit another asset. We do not have an entry to a temporary account or to equity. **Figure 37** illustrates a situation in which we sell an asset for more than basis. We debit an asset for the amount received, credit an asset for a lesser amount and then credit income or gain for the difference. That difference and the income credit is to a temporary account which ultimately closes to equity. But in no case would the *net amount received* be credited to a temporary account.

Treating assets as equity is fundamentally wrong. This is not merely about terminology because the receipts almost certainly differ a great deal from the resulting/related profit or loss.

The reference to the *net* amount suggests a reduction for costs; however, which costs it anticipates are unclear. A reference to income or profits in the ordinary course of business would be clear in accounting terms. As discussed below in relation to cost accounting the word *net* is confusing because it does not clearly elucidate whether it involves both direct and indirect costs. Having the word *net* modify the word *received* suggest costs directly related to the receipt; indeed, taken literally, it suggests costs directly related to the sale process, but not necessarily the cost of the thing sold.

In any event, the *net amount received* language specifically refers to receipts not in the ordinary course of business; hence, the language suggests the possibility of a different measure for ordinary sales. The most reasonable construction for ordinary sales would be U.S. GAAP or IFRS rules. That would accrue income and expenses, including depreciation and amortization as covered in prior lessons. Such rules, however, do not flow directly from the statute.[5]

Net proceeds of non-ordinary sales belong to the principal beneficiary unless the trustee determines the amount "is required in the conduct of the business." That rule is clear in part, unclear in part, and mostly troubling in substance. For example, if JOE'S were to sell its depreciated machinery and equipment—tables, chairs, refrigerators, stoves, and such—so that it could purchase new ones, the sales would not be in the "ordinary course" of the business. JOE'S is in the business of selling beer and wine, not used chairs and refrigerators. Application of the rule, however, is unclear on its face. Facially, the rule is clear: the net proceeds from the equipment sales belong to the principal beneficiary. That appears appropriate because the principal beneficiary should be allocated all the equity other than retained

---

[5]   *See* UPIA § 501.

earnings. The rule, however, confusingly refers to the net received, as opposed to any gain or loss.

Consider the language in accounting terms: the amount received will result in a debit to an asset, along with a credit for the basis of the thing sold, a debit for costs and ultimately a credit for any gain or a debit for any loss. That gain/loss credit or debit is what the trustee should allocate to the principal beneficiary's capital account with a credit. The amount received—the statutory reference—would result in the debit to an asset account, not an equity account. Thus, the statute's intent seems clear, but the literal words make no accounting sense.

To further complicate the issue, the statute strangely allocates the *net received* (again a bizarre reference) to the income beneficiary *if* the trustee determines it is required in the conduct of the business. The plain meaning of that is the opposite of what would appear to be sensible.

For example, had a trust established JOE'S rather than Scott and Adrian, as per EXAMPLE 30, the capital contributions would belong to the principal beneficiary, Ann, consistent with **Figure 36**: a debit to cash and a credit to Ann's equity. The purchase of tables and chairs would not alter the allocation—it would merely involve a debit to an asset (table) and a corresponding credit to an asset (cash), consistent with **Figure 37**. It would not affect equity—the allocation between Scott (income beneficiary) and Adrian (principal beneficiary). Sales to customers similarly would not themselves affect equity until the books were closed. Ordinary profits—including phantom recapture gain[6]—would properly inure to Scott, but extraordinary profits and losses would affect Adrian.

Thus, as the tables and chairs depreciated, the depreciation expense would reduce income and Scott's equity, thus increasing Adrian's. But non-phantom gain or loss on the sale of old tables and chairs would affect Adrian because those would be part of the trust capital—a synonym for principal. That would be sensible regardless of whether the trustee felt the need to retain the proceeds or to distribute them. Certainly, if the original tables inured to the principal beneficiary, then any replacement tables should as well; however, the statutory language suggests the net proceeds from sales of an old table to the extent needed to purchase new tables would belong to Scott the income beneficiary. That makes no sense; yet it appears to be the law. The journal entry to record that statutory provision is illusive.

---

[6] Because depreciation affects income, so should depreciation recapture which merely adjusts for prior excessive depreciation.

EXAMPLE 30

SCOTT AND ADRIAN TRUST

The SCOTT AND ADRIAN TRUST owns Joe's Bar & Grill, Inc. *This is a significant variation of* PROBLEM 3]. Scott is the income beneficiary.

Adrian is the principal beneficiary. The initial $500,000 capital contribution came from Steve and Vickey, their parents. Thus, the initial equity account would reflect Adrian with $500,000 and Scott with zero. All other facts of the problem remain the same, except for two matters:

- the $200,000 distribution from principal was entirely to Adrian, the principal beneficiary; and,

- the trustee (acting as the Board of Directors) decided to sell the machinery for $33,000 and then to replace it with machinery and equipment costing $50,000.

Consider EXAMPLE 30 in accounting and statutory terms. Prior to the sale, Adrian's capital account would reflect $300,000 and Scott's would have $6,275.92, the entire retained earnings. Scott probably would have a legitimate complaint against the trustee who distributed $200,000 to Adrian—the grantors intended for the income from that amount to inure to Scott's benefit, but the distribution precludes that from occurring.

As shown in the **Figure 108** balance sheet, the machinery had a historical cost of $31,000, accumulated depreciation of $516.67 and an adjusted basis of $30,483.33. The $33,000 sale in EXAMPLE 30 would produce $2,516.67 of non-operating income, including $516.67 of depreciation recapture (phantom) gain. Under traditional financial accounting principles, the $516.67 would inure to Scott because it represents excessive depreciation taken on the machinery, which lowered his prior allocation of earnings. The $2,000 of real gain on the machinery, however, would belong to Ann: it represents capital appreciation not associated with the ordinary course of the business. Then the purchase of new machinery and equipment for $50,000 would not affect capital (principal and income) allocations: it would merely result in a debit to assets and a credit to cash of $50,000.

The UPIA statute, however, *facially* behaves very differently. It would allocate the $33,000 *net receipt* to Adrian if the trustee decided the business did not need new machinery and equipment. But such an allocation makes little sense because it effectively treats an asset as equity. On the **Figure 108** balance sheet—prepared consistent with GAAP and IFRS—$30,483.33 of the equipment value would already be part of Ann's equity allocation. Allocating that amount to her a second time is redundant. It would also cause the books not to balance. Thus, it cannot be what the words means, though it is what they say. Also, allocating the $516.67 phantom gain to her would be inappropriate because it is so closely related to operations. Only the $2,000 *extraordinary* gain should appropriately be allocated to Adrian—and that should be the case regardless of whether the trustee believes the funds are needed for ordinary operations.

Because the trustee decided to retain the proceeds for use in the business, the statute appears to allocate the entire $33,000 to Scott. That, too, makes no sense. All but $516.67 of that amount was effectively part of principal prior to the sale, and no reason exists to change its character to income. The statutorily required allocation would also result in the books not balancing unless the trustee debited Ann's account by $32,484.33 and credited Scott's by the same amount. But the substance of selling some machinery and purchasing new machinery does not justify a re-allocation.

What courts and practitioners do with this statute is not the subject of this course. Undoubtedly, they impose some common sense; however, unless they use accounting terminology and principles, the guidance they provide is almost certainly unclear. You can study that in a course in trust law. But you should do it with an understanding that income/principal allocations necessarily involve accounting. You should also understand the statute's drafters failed to use accounting terminology to describe the allocations. They failed even to describe the allocations with traditional references to which accounts would be debited or credited. A well-drafted trust would eliminate the statutory presumptions and would adopt more traditional accounting rules and terminology.

B. FAMILY LAW

A key question in a dissolution of marriage involves "who gets the assets and liabilities?" That necessarily requires accounting rules. States vary in how they define, let alone allocate, income, gains, expenses, and losses. Generally—in both equitable distribution and community property states—income from a trade or business conducted during the marriage produces marital income and assets. Uniformly, if the "trade or business" is marital, the income, gains, expenses, and losses are also marital; in contrast, states vary regarding separately owned property and the income or losses it produces.

In a typical state, a separately owned "trade or business" (such as JOE'S BAR & GRILL) managed during a marriage produces marital income and resulting marital assets.[7] Thus profits from inventory sales likely inure to the "community" or "marital active mass,"[8] while profits from

---

[7]   Whether losses from separately owned property managed during a marriage are shared it often unclear. In any event, that topic is beyond this course.

[8]   In a typical equitable distribution state, the concept of marital property and liabilities does not legally exist during a valid marriage; instead, it becomes relevant upon the filing of a petition for dissolution. That presents accounting anomalies when measuring a separately owned business

casual sales typically insure to the owner spouse. The difference between inventory sales in the ordinary course of a trade or business (which typically produce marital income) and casual sales (which typically remain separate) is often clear. For example, if Scott's interest in JOE'S BAR & GRILL is separate property he brought into a marriage, profits from its operation clearly result from active services and sales of inventory and thus would typically inure to the "marriage." In contrast, if Scott had 1000 acres of land he inherited, the land would typically be his separate property. If he sold it all in a single transaction, any gain would likewise typically be separate. If, instead, he subdivided it and sold it in 1000 separate transactions, he likely converted the activity of managing the property to a "trade or business." The lots would be akin to inventory. Profits would likely inure to the marriage.

The difference, however, may not always be so clear. Perhaps Scott sold the property in two transactions, or five. At what point does he convert the activity from one which remains separate into one that becomes marital? The answer is not clear but is likely best understood in relation to U.S. tax law, an area which has litigated the topic many times. How an accountant or tax lawyer classified the sales is undoubtedly relevant but almost certainly not binding in a family court.

But consider the consequences. For each incremental dollar of profit, Husband will owe additional child support to Wife. The amount varies by state guidelines but can be up to 9.5 cents.[9] The present value is approximately $1.10.[10] Also, Husband might owe alimony under state law. While amounts vary, 20% of his income would not seem high. Thus, an increase of one dollar in his income would produce a 20-cent liability for perhaps thirty or more years. The present value is approximately $4.25.[11]

---

that has both good and bad years. Whether one must measure the net change over the term of the marriage, or instead account for the changes annually (potentially with increases becoming marital and decreases remaining separate) is not always clear. The likely treatment would involve measuring the net change over time, though finding appellate cases that say that is not easy.

[9]   F.S. 61.30.

[10]   Using an annual discount rate of 3%, a payment of 9.5 cents, and a term of 15 years produces a present value of $1.17. In reality, the amount owed would likely decrease as each child reached the age of majority.

[11]   Using an annual discount rate of 3%, a payment of 20 cents, and a term of 30 years produces a present value of $4.04. The lesson uses a figure of $4.25. Because the value is a function of the interest rate as well as the term (to say nothing of the amount), either number is realistic.

> ### EXAMPLE 31
>
> #### SCOTT AND ADRIAN TRUST
>
> Husband and Wife have three young children but are seeking a divorce after 17 years of marriage. Husband has substantial income but wife, who has primary residential responsibility of the children, does not.
>
> For now, assume the income comes from Husband's operation of JOE'S BAR & GRILL.

In addition, for each incremental dollar produced by JOE'S, the value of JOE'S rises. Valuing a small business is a topic for LESSON TEN. For now, a common method would involve a multiple of earnings—perhaps four or five times. Thus, if JOE'S has an additional dollar of income from the sale of inventory, the value may increase by up to $5.00. In either a community property or equitable distribution state, Wife would likely receive half the value, or an additional $2.50.

Together the child support, alimony, and equitable distribution consequences of that extra dollar of income realistically increase Husband's obligation to Wife by $7.85 in present value terms. That is the equivalent of a 785% tax rate: an incredible incentive to defer income, accelerate deductions or to classify something as inventory or not depending on which side is making the decisions.

C. FEDERAL TAX LAW

U.S. tax law treats income from inventory sales as "ordinary" and thus subjects it to regular tax rates. In contrast, gains from the sale of "capital assets" held more than one year result in capital gain treatment and a significantly lower tax rate than that on ordinary income. As with family law, the difference in classification is often clear: JOE'S BAR & GRILL would produce ordinary income from a trade or business. In contrast, if Scott owned 1,000 acres of land he sold in a single transaction, any resulting gain would almost certainly be capital.

But, if we posit Scott selling the acreage in many transactions, he may consequently convert it to "property held primarily for sale to customers in the ordinary course of a trade or business." Drawing the line between property held for investment (capital) and property held for sale to customers (ordinary) is highly factual. The more sales, the more likely it is ordinary, the more Scott participates (as opposed to using an agent), the more likely it is ordinary, and the more Scott improves the property (roads and utilities), the more likely it is ordinary.[12] Cases uniformly, however,

---

[12] *E.g.*, Malat v. Riddel, 383 U.S. 569 (1966); Suburban Realty v. U.S., 615 F.2d 171 (5th Cir. 1980); Biedenharn v. U.S., 526 F.2d 409 (5th Cir. 1976); Bynum v. Comm'r, 46 T.C. 295 (1966).

treat the result as either all capital or all ordinary. Thus, the line-drawing has substantial consequences. IRC section 1237 provides a "safe-harbor" for capital treatment.

Consider the consequences for tax law, as compared to family law. If Scott has an extra $1.00 of capital gain from the sale, he likely owes about 15–20 cents in tax. If, instead, he has $1.00 of ordinary income, he may owe 30 to 35 cents in tax—a large difference. But the family law consequences are much greater. Passive, non-recurring gains may be ignored for child support and alimony, and they likely do not result in marital consequences for property division. But, if Scott crosses the line such that his sales are "to customers," the proceeds (or perhaps just the profits) belong half to his wife. Each additional dollar, as shown above may result in a family tax of $5.35 for alimony and child support. Plus, at least half the profit amount likely results in an increased distribution to his wife.

Thus, the determination whether property is "investment" or "capital" versus whether it is "inventory" and "ordinary" has very large tax consequences, but also enormous family law consequences.

Another issue in U.S. tax law involves the impact of GAAP. As a rule, GAAP treatment is relevant in determining tax treatment; however, it is not controlling.[13]

D. STATE TAX LAW

Most states have an *"ad valorum"* tax on property. Most people are familiar with the real property tax, particularly as it applies to a primary residence. States also **typically** tax business assets which comprise tangible personal property (such as tables and chairs). At least 14 states also tax inventory held at the end of the year; but 36 states do not tax business inventory.[14] Thus the classification (to say nothing of the valuation) of inventory can have significant state tax consequences.

E. SALE OF A BUSINESS

Lawyers frequently deal with the sale of a "going concern." Sometimes, such a sale involves the sale of stock and other times it involves the sale of assets. In either case, the lawyer needs to understand how the state treats bulk sales of inventory.

For example, in Florida, the bulk sale of a business' inventory may cause the purchaser to be responsible for the seller's unpaid sales taxes on *prior* inventory sales to others. Per F.S. 213.758, the buyer can obtain a "clearance" or "transferee liability audit" to stop the liability. Failure to

---

[13] Although courts often *consider* GAAP in defining tax law terms and rules, GAAP *does not control* tax law. Thor Power Tool v. Comm'r, 439 U.S. 522 (1979) (the case dealt with inventory valuation and the "write-off" of excess inventory).

[14] https://taxfoundation.org/does-your-state-tax-business-inventory/

obtain the "clearance" risks an assessment for uncollected sales taxes (or collected but unpaid) on sales during the seller's ownership. At least in Florida, the liability applies regardless of whether the sale involved the sale of stock or merely assets.

Similar rules exist in many states, with varying methods of obtaining a "clearance."[15] In addition, most states have a "bulk sales" law involving sales of substantial amounts of inventory.[16] The results of a "bulk sale" can be complicated. While states typically apply a sales tax to inventory sales, they often exempt "bulk sales" from sales tax. However, a bulk sale can also trigger notice obligations to creditors[17] in addition to the sales tax state notification.

2. INVENTORY TERMINOLOGY

The main inventory accounting *general* terms lawyers should understand are:

- Stock in trade.

- Capital asset (mostly a tax law term).

- Property held primarily for sale to customers in the ordinary course of a trade or business (tax law).

- Property used in a trade or business.

- Dealer vs. investor status.

Stock in trade refers to manufacturing inventory, or more precisely inventory components. For example, for Ford Motor Company, a pick-up truck is inventory; in contrast, a fender or door not yet installed onto a truck is "stock in trade." U.S. tax law distinguishes stock in trade from inventory, but the two uniformly receive the same treatment. That may not be the same for state tax purposes; hence, a lawyer should carefully examine state law regarding taxation of inventory, as well as inventory components.

For U. S. tax purposes, "capital asset" is a term of art. IRC section 1221 defines it as including all property *other than* items on an *exclusive* list. Section 1221 lists:

(1) stock in trade of the taxpayer or other property of a kind which would properly be included in the inventory of the

---

[15]	See New York Sales Tax Bulletin, No. TB–ST–70, 06/24/2013N.Y. Tax Law § 1141(c).

[16]	https://content.next.westlaw.com/practical-law/document/I3a9a0f99ef1211e28578f7ccc 38dcbee/bulk-sales-laws?viewType=FullText&originationContext=document&transitionType= DocumentItem&ppcid=49bc377174f8481780c9cdab394cc79b&contextData=(sc.Default)&firstPag e=true#:~:text=Also%20knownäs%20bulk%20transfer,the%20seller's%20businessörässets.

[17]	U.C.C. article 6 applied to bulk sales and contained provisions to protect creditors. Most states have repealed the provision. https://www.uniformlaws.org/committees/community-home?CommunityKey=82c71a46-d1c9-44be-85f3-1d4138a51b4b

taxpayer if on hand at the close of the taxable year, or property held by the taxpayer primarily for sale to customers in the ordinary course of his trade or business;

(2) property, used in his trade or business, of a character which is subject to the allowance for depreciation provided in section 167, or real property used in his trade or business;

(3) a copyright, a literary, musical, or artistic composition, a letter or memorandum, or similar property, held by—

   (A) a taxpayer whose personal efforts created such property,

   (B) in the case of a letter, memorandum, or similar property, a taxpayer for whom such property was prepared or produced, or

   (C) a taxpayer in whose hands the basis of such property is determined, for purposes of determining gain from a sale or exchange, in whole or part by reference to the basis of such property in the hands of a taxpayer described in subparagraph (A) or (B);

(4) accounts or notes receivable acquired in the ordinary course of trade or business for services rendered or from the sale of property described in paragraph (1); [* * * *]

(8) supplies of a type regularly used or consumed by the taxpayer in the ordinary course of a trade or business of the taxpayer.[18]

Much litigation involves the category-one phrase: *property held primarily for sale to customers in the ordinary course of a trade or business.* Such items often involve investment property which a person held as a capital asset but which the owner later converted to *inventory.* The change in tax rate can be very significant.

For United States (and many other jurisdictions) *tax purposes,* long-term capital gains result in a materially lower tax rate than do short-term gains or ordinary income.[19] *Capital gains* result from the sale or exchange

---

[18]   IRC § 1221.

[19]   *For tax purposes,* IRC section 1222 defines a capital gain as gain resulting from the *sale or exchange* of a capital asset. *Long term* gain—generally entitled to preferential tax treatment—flows from assets held more than one year. The *sale or exchange* treatment is essential for capital gain or loss treatment. Some code sections, *e.g.,* § 1271, *impute* a sale or exchange for transaction which would not otherwise satisfy the definition of that phrase (which is not well-defined). Over the history of the Internal Revenue Code, the treatment of capital gains has varied. Often long-term (variously defined, but often a function of a holding period of more than one year) gains have triggered a substantially lower tax rate than ordinary income.

For family law and trust purposes, lawyers must play close attention to the character of gains and losses. While ordinary—non-*capital*—gains and losses (such as from sales of inventory) likely are marital (in the family law realm) and income (in the income versus principal beneficiary realm), the treatment of capital gains and losses is less clear. In family law, such gains on separate property may remain separate (depending on the jurisdiction and the level of management). For trust law, such gains typically belong to the principal beneficiary. The distinction, however,

of a capital asset. The long versus short distinction has traditionally been at one year; however, it has been as short as six months and longer.

IRC section 1221(2)—generally depreciable property—forms a category in between capital assets and ordinary assets, which generate ordinary income and losses. Those are *IRC section 1231 assets*, which very generally produce capital gains and ordinary losses—the best of both types.

For family law purposes, generally most states keep separate property brought into a marriage as separate. Many, however, consider such property converted to marital or community property status—either in whole or in part—to the extent marital labor and industry significantly impacts its value. The process of developing property—such as a tract of land—and thus converting it from a capital asset to *property held primarily for sale to customers in the ordinary course of a trade or business* is related to the <u>*family law*</u> status change. Indeed, the two separate legal consequences largely overlap: to the extent a person converts property for tax purposes, he likely also converts some or all of it for marital purposes. Of note, the tax consequences may result in an extra 20% of the value going to pay taxes. But, in contrast, the family law consequences may result in an extra 50% of the value going to the other spouse for property division, plus up to 10% going to child support and another significant percentage going to the other spouse for alimony. Hence, the classification of an asset as capital or not is very important for tax purposes; however, it is potentially profoundly important for family law purposes.

Similarly, <u>*trust law*</u> may be significantly impacted by an asset's classification. For the most part, capital gains and losses should belong to the principal beneficiary; however, ordinary gains and losses—such as those resulting from inventory or *property held primarily for sale to customers in the ordinary course of a trade or business*—should belong to the income beneficiary.

Another fuzzy distinction between capital gains and ordinary income involves *retained earnings*. Earnings belong to the common shareholders. If distributed, they result in dividends. For tax purposes those are taxable to the extent of earnings and profits. For other legal purposes, dividends are almost always—if not always—income. Whether they constitute income from labor and industry—and thus marital assets in most states even if derived from separate property—depends on the degree of management, a question of fact. But undistributed *retained earnings* economically result in share appreciation. This, in turn, results in capital appreciation or capital gains if the owner disposes of the shares. But, many jurisdictions consider such capital appreciation in separate property to retain its character as separate property, regardless of the degree of

---

between inventory and capital assets can be fuzzy, particularly when it involves subdivided property of the sale of assets formerly used in a trade or business.

management. This is widely true for C corporate investors and also commonly true of S corporate investors.[20]

For financial accounting purposes, one might use the term capital assets to distinguish them from inventory, supplies, and variously consumable assets, or more generally to refer to long-term investments such as plant and equipment. Such usage is not incorrect; however, it risks confusion with the important tax law terminology. Accountants would know this, but non-accountants may not. Also, one might refer to a "capital intensive" business which requires large investments in buildings or manufacturing equipment. This would contrast with a "labor intensive" business—such as a law firm—which has relatively little physical assets, but many human ones.

Property used in a trade or business is a U.S. tax term defined in section 1231. It mostly involves depreciable property. Losses from sales are ordinary, while gains may be capital (after a complex netting process). Generally, the distinction between inventory and property used in a business is clear: inventory is what is for sale to customers (perhaps milk or paper towels in a grocery store), while property used in the business includes the shelves, cash registers, and such. Sometimes, however, the distinction is less clear. Some businesses offer specific products both for sale and for lease. Items held primarily for sale to customers effectively[21] constitute inventory, while items primarily held for lease are "used in a trade or business" and thus depreciable. Much tax litigation exists focusing on the difference, which is sometimes slight.[22]

LESSON SEVEN-B

INVENTORY MANAGEMENT SYSTEMS

■ ■ ■

LESSON SEVEN-B covers two topics:

- Periodic inventory systems
- Perpetual inventory systems

---

[20] *See, e.g.*, Zold v. Zold, 911 So. 2d 1222 (Fla. 2005).

[21] For tax purposes, they are "property held primarily for sale to customers in the ordinary course of a trade or business" and are not inventory, but the differences are not large. IRC § 1221.

[22] *E.g.*, Malat v. Riddel, 383 U.S. 569 (1966); Suburban Realty v. U.S., 615 F.2d 171 (5th Cir. 1980); Biedenharn v. U.S., 526 F.2d 409 (5th Cir. 1976); Bynum v. Comm'r, 46 T.C. 295 (1966); International Shoe Machine Corp. v. U.S., 491 F.2d 157 (1st Cir. 1974); Hollywood Baseball, 423 F.2d 494 (9th Cir. 1970); Deltide Fishing Tools, 279 F. Supp. 661 (E.D. La. 1968).

Under a periodic inventory accounting system, the business physically counts inventory annually (or sometimes periodically). Cost of goods sold in such a system represents:

$$COGS = (BI + P - EI)$$

Where *COGS = Cost of Goods Sold, BI = Beginning Inventory, P = purchases,* and *EI = Ending Inventory.*

A *periodic inventory system*—as opposed to a *perpetual system*—requires little bookkeeping; thus, historically, it was very common. The system, however, does not distinguish between the cost of inventory sold and the cost of spoilage or theft: anything not included in ending inventory is part of *COGS* if it was available for sale (either part of *BI* or *P*).

In contrast, a *perpetual* system tracks each item of *inventory*. Users also physically count inventory annually; however, because of the tracking they can accurately determine theft and spoilage. The wide-spread use of bar codes, and more recently small, implanted IDs, has caused many businesses to move from a *periodic inventory system* to a *perpetual inventory system.*

1. PERIODIC INVENTORY SYSTEM

Consider seven significant points regarding a periodic system.

A. NO CURRENT ENTRIES FOR COST OF SALES OR TO INVENTORY

Because a periodic system does not track inventory as it is sold, no accounting entry occurs regarding inventory or cost of goods sold at the time of sale. As a result, current information about profit from the sale is not readily available. Consider EXAMPLE 32: JOE'S sold a bottle of wine for $100 that cost $60 and used a periodic inventory system. The journal entry appears in **Figure 114**. It records the revenue and the debit to cash, but it does not record anything to costs or to inventory.

EXAMPLE 32

JOE'S Sells Some Wine

JOE'S uses a periodic inventory system. It sold a bottle of wine for $100. The bottle cost $60. Record the journal entry.

Let that sink in: no entry would occur for an expense or for COGS: under a periodic system JOE'S would not *currently* (at the time of sale) track which bottle of wine it sold, let alone the cost of it. Thus, the wine inventory ledger would remain unchanged.

General Journal for JOE'S BAR & GRILL			
Date	Account	Debit	Credit
1/15	Cash	100	
	Revenue		100
	Adjusting entry for COGS.		

Figure 114: Periodic Inventory System Journal Entry for a Sale

B. PERIODIC COUNT OF INVENTORY

Periodically—at least annually, but perhaps more frequently—a business should count each item of inventory. This is true both for a periodic and a perpetual system. For an automobile dealer, the process is simple because the number of cars is likely a few hundred; in contrast, a business that sells many inexpensive items has a more daunting task counting each box of pencils or fishing lures or whatever it sells. In a periodic system, the count is essential because it helps determine cost of goods sold. In a perpetual system, the count is less critical but still important, as it identifies spoilage and theft.

C. DETERMINATION OF INVENTORY AVAILABLE FOR SALE

This simple process adds the beginning inventory (the result of the count at the beginning of the year) to the amount of inventory purchased during the year. Inventory purchases would be recorded on the date of purchase. The inventory ledger—a permanent account—would start the period with beginning inventory and would increase by purchases. The total, prior to the inventory count, would represent inventory available for sale. Because no inventory entries would occur with sales, the amount shown as available would not be accurate. Still, it would form a critical part of the next point.

D. DETERMINATION OF COST OF GOODS SOLD

EXAMPLE 33

JOE'S Cost of Goods Sold

JOE'S uses a periodic inventory system. It began the month with $4,000 of wine inventory. During the month it purchased an additional $3,000 of wine. An end-of-the month count showed $2,000 of wine remaining (using historical cost).

Record the appropriate journal entries and show the wine inventory ledger.

This involves subtracting the ending inventory—what remains at the end of the year—from the inventory available for sale. The difference is what left the business. The entity will have an adjusting entry at the end of the period to recognize cost of goods sold. As noted below, the actual count informs management of how much wine left; however, it does not distinguish sales from theft or spoilage.

Consider EXAMPLE 33. JOE'S beginning wine inventory had a $4,000 historical cost. JOE'S would know that from an actual inventory count at the end of the prior period. Purchases during the period cost $3,000 and would be recorded in the journal and ledger as shown in **Figures 115** and **116**. Inventory available for sale would be $7,000: $4,000 plus $3,000. JOE'S would not have a journal entry for this number. The end-of-the-month count determines $2,000 of wine remains. Thus, the cost of goods sold must be $5,000 ($7,000 available for sale less $2,000 remaining). That calculation would occur separate from the journal. JOE'S would then debit cost of goods sold for $5,000 and credit inventory for $5,000. As a result, beginning inventory on the balance sheet would be $2,000 for the following period. The wine inventory ledger would reflect the purchases and the cost; however, it would not reflect the timing of the sales. As a result, it would provide insufficient information for management.

General Journal for JOE'S BAR & GRILL			
Date	**Account**	**Debit**	**Credit**
2/15	**Wine Inventory**	3,000	
	Cash		**3,000**
	To reflect purchase of inventory.		
2/28	**Cost of Goods Sold**	5,000	
	Wine Inventory		**5,000**
	Wine Inventory count and CGS.		

Figure 115: Periodic Inventory System Journal Entries for Purchases and CGS

E. SIMPLE AND INEXPENSIVE

A periodic system is easy to manage and relatively inexpensive (except for the cost of the count, which is necessary for both periodic and perpetual systems). It has few entries and does not require RFID tags or bar codes and scanners. For very small retailers, it remains an acceptable system. Until the 1970's it was very common even for large retailers.

F. NO INFORMATION ON SPOILAGE OF THEFT

A periodic system, however, does not identify spoilage—broken bottles of wine—or theft. In EXAMPLE 33 above, COGS was $5,000 for wine. JOE'S, however, would not (under a periodic system) know whether it actually sold wine which cost $5,000. All it would know is that that amount left it possession. Perhaps all of it was sold. But perhaps some bottles were broken and perhaps an employee or customer stole some other bottles. Or perhaps Scott or Adrian took some wine home for personal consumption. A periodic inventory system would not detect that.

Wine Inventory		
Date	**Debit**	**Credit**
1/31	4,000	
2/15	3,000	
2/28		5,000
2/28	2,000	

Figure 116: Wine Inventory Ledger

Consider EXAMPLE 34. Scott and Adrian regularly supply themselves with food, alcohol, cleaning supplies, and similar items. Such personal "theft" would reduce JOE'S income. The supplies would be part of an expense and the food and alcohol would be part of COGS. As a result, Scott and Adrian would each have $1,000 less monthly income from JOE'S. The theft would not correspondingly increase Scott or Adrian's income attributable to the consumption in a readily determinable way. Collectively, that could distort their income significantly in a family law matter or for federal and state income tax liability. For tax purposes, reporting this as an expense for JOE'S would be tax fraud,[23] a serious crime. The IRS has experience detecting such schemes, but the smaller they are relative to the size of the business, the more difficult to detect. Family law practitioners likely have even less experience detecting such things. This is a significant flaw in a periodic system.

EXAMPLE 34

Scott and Adrian Steal from Themselves

JOE'S uses a periodic inventory system and has no significant internal controls for supplies. Monthly, Scott and Adrian take home $1,000 each of food, alcohol, and supplies. How does this affect their income?

G. LITTLE CURRENT INFORMATION

A periodic system provides very little current information regarding inventory amounts. Management would not know from examining the books, how much inventory exists, let alone which inventory. For example, a grocer using a periodic system would know the volume of sales because of the entries to revenue but would not know whether it sold lots of corn and few potatoes, or the opposite. That can hamper buying replacement inventory, as well as pricing: if one does not know what was sold recently, one does not know what to buy to replace it, let alone what to put "on sale" because few customers are buying it. Managers can "look around" and estimate or rely on the produce manager to inform them "we are running out of potatoes" or the meat manager to say, "we have too much hamburger."

2. PERPETUAL INVENTORY SYSTEM

In contrast, a perpetual system provides much better accounting information, albeit more complex. The creation of bar codes, scanners, and RFID tags have simplified the difficulties to a great extent. Consider the same seven issues in relation to a perpetual system.

A. CURRENT ENTRIES FOR COSTS AND INVENTORY

Because a perpetual system tracks inventory as it is sold, an accounting entry occurs regarding inventory and cost of goods sold at the time of sale. In EXAMPLE 35, JOE'S sold a bottle of wine for $100 that cost $60 and used a perpetual inventory system.

---

[23] IRC § 7206 provides for criminal fraud. Section 6663 provides for civil fraud.

EXAMPLE 35

JOE'S Sells Some Wine

JOE'S uses a perpetual inventory system. It sold a bottle of wine for $100. The bottle cost $60. Record the journal entry.

The journal entry for EXAMPLE 35 appears in **Figure 117**. Notice how it differs from **Figure 114**, the same entry in a periodic system. The perpetual entry has four parts, rather than the traditional two. One could call that quadruple entry, rather than double bookkeeping. It reflects both the balance sheet and income statement components. Notice also, while the four parts are essential in both periodic and perpetual systems, the last two occur in a periodic system at the end of the period as part of a conglomerate entry for all inventory costs, as shown in **Figure 114**.

B. PERIODIC COUNT OF INVENTORY

A perpetual system also has a periodic inventory count. In a perpetual system, the count is less critical but still important, as it identifies spoilage and theft.

C. DETERMINATION OF INVENTORY AVAILABLE FOR SALE

This simple process adds the beginning inventory (the result of the count at the beginning of the year) and adds to it the amount of inventory purchased during the year. A perpetual system computes this; however, management can also at any point, determine the current amount by subtracting sales. That is particularly useful because it allows management to replace things being sold and to "mark-down" things not being sold.

D. DETERMINATION OF COST OF GOODS SOLD

General Journal for JOE'S BAR & GRILL			
Date	Account	Debit	Credit
1/15	Cash	100	
	Revenue		100
1/15	Cost of Goods Sold	60	
	Wine Inventory		60
	To reflect sale of wine.		

Figure 117: Perpetual Inventory System Journal Entries for Sale of Wine

As with a Periodic System, this involves subtracting the ending inventory—what remains at the end of the year—from the inventory currently available for sale. The difference is what left the business other than through a sale: it was either spoiled or stolen. The entity will have an adjusting entry at the end of the year to recognize spoilage and theft.

E. MORE EXPENSIVE

A perpetual system is arguably more expensive than a period one; however, those costs have dropped dramatically. Bar codes, scanners and RFID tags are cheap enough they can be used for a very large number of items.

F. INFORMATION ON SPOILAGE OR THEFT

A Perpetual System provides helpful information regarding spoilage and theft. Further, management may require employees to track spoiled items, which is not difficult if they have a bar code or other tag.

G. BETTER CURRENT INFORMATION

A perpetual system provides current information. A small business such as JOE'S may effectively track inventory by the eye-ball method: management can look at the bar and the stock room to tell if customers are buying beer or wine or scotch. But a larger entity—such as Walmart—cannot eyeball inventory. But interconnected scanners can tell management—in real time—what items are popular, and which are not.

Why would a lawyer want to know about inventory systems? Several reasons exist. First, any business with inventories must use an inventory system. Lawyers typically need to understand their client's business; hence, a general understanding of inventory systems seems helpful.

Second, lawyers may ultimately need to deal with theft and fraud issues. Employee theft is better measurable with a perpetual system. As covered in LESSON TEN, information regarding common spoilage and theft rates is likely available for most types and sizes of business. If the numbers for a client are materially different from the norm, management, accountants, and lawyers should pay attention. For example, spoilage for restaurants generally hovers around six to eight percent—though that varies by the type of food sold (fresh fruit, for example spoils much faster than salted peanuts). If JOE'S were to have a spoilage rate of 15 or 20 percent, one might start to suspect theft or fraud. Perhaps employees are stealing food and beverages, or perhaps either Scott or Adrian is doing so. Certainly, an owner would be tempted to take home a steak or bottle of wine; however, doing so creates an expense unrelated to the business. It results in under-stated profits, which can affect employee compensation, taxes owed, and owners' shares. One steak and one bottle of wine are likely immaterial; however, such things can multiply with temptation. Lawyers and owners should be aware. They also need to know the government—as well as interested parties—can find reliable information regarding the typical magnitude of spoilage and theft.

LESSON SEVEN-C

INVENTORY VALUATION SYSTEMS

∎ ∎ ∎

LESSON SEVEN-B dealt with inventory *management* systems, which focus on how a business _counts_ the inventory, either periodically or perpetually. LESSON SEVEN-C deals with inventory *valuation* systems, which focus—as the name suggests—on inventory _valuation_. Regardless of whether a business uses a periodic or a perpetual system for counting inventory, it still must choose a valuation method. Four common methods are available:

- LIFO.
- FIFO.
- Average cost.
- Specific identification.

No method is perfect, although if realistic to use, the specific identification method would normally produce the most accurate information. The method, however, typically is useful for businesses with relatively few items of inventory, with each item being expensive. For example, an automobile, boat, airplane dealer, or a jewelry store would likely benefit from specific identification and would be able to absorb the cost of it. Other businesses most likely use one of the other systems, which each rely on assumptions.

Inventory valuation serves two purposes. It measures the cost of inventory sold and it values ending inventory. For example, with Joe's, it would tell us how much each glass of wine cost, which affects the income statement. It would also value the remaining wine, which affects the balance sheet.

Let's go through an overview of LIFO and FIFO. Then we will work an example involving JOE'S and the sale of wine.

1. LIFO: LAST-IN FIRST-OUT

This common inventory system assumes the last inventory purchased was the first inventory sold.

The word "assumes" is key—unless the company has a very sophisticated specific identification system tracking inventory, it will not know precisely which item it sells. Consider a very simple example.

In EXAMPLE 36, a furniture store bought two identical chairs, one for $100 and a second (more recently) for $125. A customer purchased a chair today for $200. Which chair did he buy? LIFO assumes he bought the second chair. As a result, profit is only $75 and remaining inventory is $100. In contrast, FIFO would assume he bought the first chair, which would produce profit of $100 and remaining inventory of $125.

In a more complex example, a hardware store may know it sold a hammer because the hammer had a bar code on it which the cashier scanned; however, the bar code likely merely identifies the hammer type, brand, and size, but not precisely which hammer. Picture yourself in a hardware store looking at hammers. The store has ten varieties and perhaps six of each on the shelf. Each different variety will have a different barcode, but all six identical hammers of a particular brand will have the same code. The store may have purchased those six at the same time, or it might have purchased them at different times. It also likely has additional hammers in a stock room. The bar-code scan by the cashier will tell management which brand and size of hammer you bought, but it will not tell them which one of the six you took off the shelf. The same is true in a grocery store. You may find 100 varieties of cereal, including ten brands of corn flakes. Each variety, brand and size has a different bar code. But, if you look at five 18-ounce boxes of Kellogg's Corn Flakes, they will each have the same code—even if the store purchased them in different shipments. In contrast, if a car dealer has four identical Dodge RAM pickup trucks for sale, it almost certainly tracks them individually. Individually tracking trucks and gold watches is cost-effective; in contrast, individually tracking fungible hammers and boxes of cereal is not. As a result, the seller inevitably must "assume" which of many identical items of inventory it sold. Perhaps someday, technology will permit unique tags on cans of corn, boxes of cereal, and hammers, but that day is not yet here.

EXAMPLE 36

Small Furniture Store

- We bought two chairs for sale:
  - One a few months ago for $100, and
  - A second today for $125.
- Then we sold a chair for $200.
- Which one did we sell?

LIFO provides a possible assumption: the last hammer or box of corn flakes was the one sold. The advantage is clear: LIFO—as opposed to FIFO—better reflects inventory "cost of goods sold" in times of inflation. For example, if JOE'S has six identical bottles of Merlot for sale and if all six cost the same amount, the inventory valuation method is irrelevant. But if three bottles cost $15 several months ago and three cost $17 more recently, which one JOE'S sold suddenly matters. The wine may be identical, and the customer may not care, but if the sale price is $30, JOE'S cares and Lamar, the manager who receives a bonus based on profits cares. And the IRS cares. That is because the sale of an older bottle results in $15 profit ($30 sale price less $15 cost) while the sale of a more recently purchased (but identical) bottle results in only $13 profit. Scott and Adrian—the owners of JOE'S—have mixed incentives. They want high profits to show to a bank if they are applying for a loan (which pushes them to FIFO), but they want low profits to show to the IRS and to determine Lamar's bonus (which pushes them to LIFO). They do not know which bottle they sold any more than the hardware store knows which hammer it sold or the grocer knows which box of corn flakes a customer bought. The customers do not care because the items are fungible—the same for all practical purposes.[24] But the accounting differs, the tax bill differs, the apparent profitability of the business differs, and Lamar's bonus differs. If Scott or Adrian is in the process of getting a divorce, the difference matters for computing child support, alimony, and property valuation.

For U.S. tax purposes, LIFO is permissible only if the taxpayer also uses LIFO for financial reporting purposes;[25] however, the computation of corporate "earnings and profits" effectively requires the use of FIFO.[26] Use

---

[24] The hypothetical does not suppose a change in quality because of age—either improvement or deterioration. It, instead, assumes significant price changes because of inflation over a short period of time.

[25] IRC § 472.

[26] IRC § 312(n)(4).

of LIFO by for U.S. publicly traded entities prompts additional reporting requirements.[27] GAAP permits LIFO.[28] IFRS does not.[29]

Inventories are an important part of many legal relationships. The use of LIFO versus FIFO inventory accounting can have a substantial impact on income and costs—particularly if the user changes from one method to another. While such a change of inventory method is an item that should always be reported or disclosed, life does not always work that way. Hence, inventory accounting is an area ripe for misleading statements. If JOE'S must pay Lamar a share of profits, JOE'S can affect its liability to Lamar by adoption of one inventory method as opposed to another. Of course, Lamar should be aware of this choice and should have some part in the choice; however, if Lamar's lawyer is unaware of the meaning and the impact of LIFO and FIFO, then he is unlikely to make a wise choice.

Similarly, in other areas of the law dependent upon a definition of income—such as family law (for alimony and child support) and trust law (for measuring an income beneficiary's share of a trust)—the choice of an inventory system can have a profound effect. If one party has significant accounting and finance knowledge, while the other does not, the one with knowledge can take unfair advantage over the ignorant party. Whether such behavior is actionable varies. More importantly, if the ignorant party is unaware of the deception, he is unlikely to seek any reparation even if he is entitled to it.

2. FIFO: FIRST-IN FIRST-OUT

This common inventory system assumes the first inventory purchased was the *first* inventory sold. FIFO, in times of inflation, will understate COGS and thus overstate income. LIFO—as opposed to FIFO—better reflects inventory and replacement costs in times of inflation. For tax purposes, *LIFO* is permissible only if the taxpayer also uses LIFO for financial reporting purposes. For purposes of computing corporate earnings and profits, IRC section 312 effectively requires the use of FIFO.

As explained later, a specific identification system would be ideal because it would (along with a perpetual counting system) specifically identify each item purchased and later sold. As a result, it would best reflect costs. For fungible items, management would continue to have room to distort costs by choosing which item it sold. The method, however, is

---

[27] Per SEC Rule S-X, listed companies using LIFO must report—at least in a footnote to the balance sheet—a "LIFO reserve": "(c) If the LIFO inventory method is used, the excess of replacement or current cost overstated LIFO value shall, if material, be stated parenthetically or in a note to the financial statements." 17 C.F.R. 210.5–02.6(c).

[28] Codification at 330-10-30-1.

[29] IAS 2.

more likely used by businesses with less inventory, each item of which is unique and expensive.

3. DETAILED EXAMPLE

EXAMPLE 37

- JOE'S opens the WINE SHOP.

  - In January, JOE'S buys a case of Willis Chardonnay for $10 per bottle. During the month JOE'S sells 7 bottles for $20 each. At the end of the month, it buys another case for $12 per bottle.

  - In February, JOE'S sells 12 bottles at $22 each. It purchases another case for $15 per bottle.

  - In March, JOE'S sells 15 bottles at $25 each. It purchases 18 new bottles for $20 per bottle.

  - In April JOE'S sells 20 bottles at $35 each and purchases 24 bottles for $25 per bottle.

In EXAMPLE 37, JOE'S has opened the WINE SHOP. From January through April, it bought and sold various amounts of a particular Chardonnay are ever changing costs and prices. Clearly, the wine is becoming more expensive as the cost increases from $10 per bottle to $25. JOE'S WINE SHOP increases the sale price, albeit at a different pace—from $20 per bottle to $35. JOE'S must determine its profit each month *and* must report its inventory on its balance sheet.

A. LIFO

Figure 118 is a LIFO chart for January through April. These are not bookkeeping entries; instead, they comprise a separate supporting document used to determine LIFO costs and valuation. Notice two keys numbers: profit for the four months is $456 and ending inventory is $256.

	Beginning Inventory	Purchases	Revenue	LIFO Cost	Ending Inventory	Profit
Jan.	12 at 10	12 at 12	7 at 20 = 140	7 at 12	12 at 10	140
					5 at 12	(84)
	Total 120			Total 84	Total 180	56
Feb.	12 at 10	12 at 15	12 at 22 = 264	12 at 15	12 at 10	264
	5 at 12				5 at 12	(180)
	Total 180			Total 180	Total 180	84
March	12 at 10	18 at 20	20 at 25 = 500	18 at 20	12 at 10	500
	5 at 12			2 at 12	3 at 12	(384)
	Total 180			Total 384	Total 156	116
April	12 at 10	24 at 25	20 at 25 = 700	20 at 25	12 at 10	700
	3 at 12				3 at 12	(500)
					4 at 25	
	Total 156			Total 500	Total 256	200
	Total Profit					**456**

Figure 118: LIFO Chart

Let's examine it one month at a time. Then we will prepare the same chart using FIFO. Examine January in **Figure 119**.

	Beginning Inventory	Purchases	Revenue	LIFO Cost	Ending Inventory	Profit
Jan.	12 at 10	12 at 12	7 at 20 = 140	7 at 12	12 at 10	140
					5 at 12	(84)
	Total 120			Total 84	Total 180	56

Figure 119: LIFO Chart for January

Beginning inventory comprises 12 bottles which cost $10 each. LIFO and FIFO produce the same number as this is the first month. JOE'S purchases 12 bottles for $12 each and sells 7 for $20 each. LIFO assumes JOE'S sold 7 of the last bottles purchased, which each cost $12. Because each of the 24 bottles available for sale were identical (including identical scanner codes) and because JOE'S does not track individual bottles, we are uncertain which bottles were sold. LIFO nevertheless produces a cost of $12 each. As a result, ending inventory must include the original 12 bottles ($10 each) and 5 of the more recent purchases ($12 each). Revenue was $140 (7 bottles at $20 each), COGS was $84, and profit was $56. Notice the WINE SHOP priced each bottle at twice the cost of beginning inventory and did not adjust for the increased inventory costs during the month.

The January ending inventory becomes beginning inventory for February. Examine February in **Figure 120**.

	Beginning Inventory	Purchases	Revenue	LIFO Cost	Ending Inventory	Profit
Feb.	12 at 10	12 at 15	12 at 22 = 264	12 at 15	12 at 10	264
	5 at 12				5 at 12	(180)
	Total 180			Total 180	Total 180	84

Figure 120: LIFO Chart for February

Beginning inventory is 12 at $10 and 5 at $12. JOE'S purchases 12 bottles for $15 each and sells 12 for $22 each. Pricing increased to $22 per bottle, which is twice the average cost of January beginning inventory and purchases. LIFO assumes JOE'S the last bottles purchased, which each cost $15. Apparently, the bookkeeper is using LIFO but the manager setting prices is using a method akin to average costs. As a result, the profit margin per bottle is dropping as compared to replacement costs.

The February ending inventory becomes beginning inventory for March. Examine March in **Figure 121**.

	Beginning Inventory	Purchases	Revenue	LIFO Cost	Ending Inventory	Profit
March	12 at 10	18 at 20	20 at 25 = 500	18 at 20	12 at 10	500
	5 at 12			2 at 12	3 at 12	(384)
	Total 180			Total 180	Total 156	116

Figure 121: LIFO Chart for March

Beginning inventory is 12 at $10 and 5 at $12, the same as in February, which is typical of LIFO. JOE'S purchases 18 bottles for $20 each and sells 20 for $25 each. LIFO assumes JOE'S the last bottles purchased, which each cost $20 plus two of the beginning inventory at $12 each. Pricing increased to $25 per bottle, which is about twice the cost of January purchases, but now significantly less than double the average cost ($15.43 each), the LIFO cost ($19.20 each) let alone the replacement cost of $20 each. The pricing manager is not keeping up with costs. Arguably, he should focus on replacement cost which exceeds LIFO.

The March ending inventory becomes beginning inventory for April. Examine April in **Figure 122**.

	Beginning Inventory	Purchases	Revenue	LIFO Cost	Ending Inventory	Profit
April	12 at 10	24 at 25	20 at 35 = 500	20 at 25	12 at 10	700
	3 at 12				3 at 12	(500)
					4 at 25	
	Total 156			Total 500	Total 256	200

Figure 122: LIFO Chart for April

Beginning inventory is 12 at $10 and 5 at $12, the same as in February and March. JOE'S purchases 24 bottles for $25 each and sells 20 for $35 each. LIFO assumes JOE'S the last bottles purchased, which each cost $25. Pricing increased to $35 per bottle, which still is not keeping pace with replacement costs. The manager should be pricing them at $50.

B. FIFO

Figure 123 is a FIFO chart for January through April. These are not bookkeeping entries; instead, they comprise a separate supporting document used to determine FIFO costs and valuation. Notice two keys numbers: profit for the four months is $675 and ending inventory is $375. That compares to $456 LIFO profit and $256 LIFO ending inventory. FIFO profit is almost 50% higher than LIFO.

Neither LIFO nor FIFO is perfect as both rely on arbitrary assumptions. In inflationary periods, FIFO produces higher profits because it assumes lower costs. The FIFO profits, however, are no more real than the LIFO amounts. As shown earlier, pricing is best a function of replacement cost which is akin to LIFO but not quite the same as it.

	Beginning Inventory	Purchases	Revenue	FIFO Cost	Ending Inventory	Profit
Jan.	12 at 10	12 at 12	7 at 20 = 140	7 at 10	5 at 10	140
					12 at 12	(70)
	Total 120			Total 70	Total 180	70
Feb.	5 at 10	12 at 15	12 at 22 = 264	5 at 10	5 at 12	264
	12 at 12			7 at 12	12 at 5	(134)
	Total 180			Total 134	Total 240	130
March	5 at 12	18 at 20	20 at 25 = 500	5 at 12	15 at 20	500
	12 at 15			12 at 15		(300)
				3 at 20		
	Total 240			Total 384	Total 300	200
April	15 at 20	24 at 25	20 at 35 = 700	15 at 20	19 at 25	700
				5 at 25		(425)
	Total 300			Total 500	Total 375	275
	Total Profit					675

Figure 123: FIFO Chart

4. FAMILY LAW EXAMPLE

EXAMPLE 38

- You represent wife in a dissolution case. She seeks an equitable portion (or half in a community property state) of the marital assets plus child support and alimony, which are each a function of spousal incomes.

- You discover that husband's business, for which inventory is a significant factor, recently changed from FIFO to LIFO. How do you respond?

A change in accounting method is always a red flag. That includes a change from FIFO to LIFO. Legitimate reasons may exist for the change; however, it raises suspicions in a matter being litigated such as in EXAMPLE 38.

You should be concerned, particularly about the _recent accounting_ change. It likely resulted in lower income and assets—possibly substantially lower. Even if the business had always used LIFO, you should consider the impact a FIFO valuation might have. With LIFO, the inventory assets are likely undervalued—perhaps very substantially. Husband's business will appear to have a lower value for book purposes. That could result in a materially lower award to Wife under the state equitable distribution or community property statute. Husband's business will appear to have lower income as well: the COGS will likely be higher with LIFO and thus lower than it otherwise would have been. That could result in a materially lower award to Wife under the state alimony or child support statute.

You should ask the court to impute additional income or to increase the value of the reported inventory.

5. PROFIT SHARING EXAMPLE

EXAMPLE 39

- Your client is negotiating a contract under which she will receive a percentage of profits earned by the person who sells an item of inventory your client designed.

- The other party has agreed to allow _you_ to draft the initial contract.

    – Should you include a definition of profits?

    – If so, should the contract specify an inventory method?

Yes, include a definition of profits. Without it, your client is at the mercy of the other party. Also, without a contractual definition of "profits," you will need to resort to general legal principles, which likely refer to GAAP. That, however, is too vague a concept, considering the many available choices—such as inventory method—which can have a substantial impact on profits. _Thus, you should contractually determine those choices._

You might also consider negotiating for a percentage of gross receipts rather than profits. The percentage would be lower, but the amount of gross receipts is more difficult to manipulate than the profits amount. If you continue with the profits percentage, you should consider requiring FIFO inventory valuation if you expect inflation. That will maximize profits and thus your client's share. If the other side is adequately represented, they will question this choice. Would you feel guilty if they failed to grasp the impact of the choice? Would you call it to their attention?

6. EMPLOYMENT CONTRACT EXAMPLE

EXAMPLE 40

- JOE'S BAR & GRILL pays Lamar a bonus based on profits. In the first month, we only had one purchase of inventory, so LIFO versus FIFO did not matter.

- But eventually, the business must purchase more inventory; hence it must choose a valuation system. That affects Lamar.

In EXAMPLE 37, FIFO profits for January through April were 50% higher than LIFO profits. Thus, this would have a material impact on Lamar's bonus. Because of the inflation, Lamar should have used replacement costs to price wine sales. JOE'S likely used LIFO to determine cost of goods sold. The employment contract, however, could have its own inventory valuation method. It probably would not; however, it could.

LESSON SEVEN-D

COST ACCOUNTING

■ ■ ■

Cost accounting refers to the study of and allocation of costs. This is essential in at least two ways:

1. By allocating costs to a division, department, or activity, management can determine whether the activity is profitable.

2. By allocating costs to a product, management can determine the appropriate price for the product.

For example, if a project/division is not sufficiently profitable, management can seek to control costs, increase revenues, seek new employees, or divert resources to a different project. Without useful information about costs, management decisions risk being arbitrary or misinformed.

Cost Allocation Is Not a Science

It can be subjective. As a result, the person allocating costs may be motivated by something other than accuracy:

•   He/she may benefit from a greater bonus if his division has lower costs.

•   He/she may have an agenda to end a project or activity. By allocating costs to it, he/she makes it appear to be overly expensive.

•   Contract/commercial litigation may be a function of the profitability of a particular activity; hence, the cost allocation is critical.

•   Some areas of law—such as partnership _taxation_—permit "special allocation" of costs with little basis in short-term reality (though the allocation may ultimately have to meet the "substantial economic effect" test.

LESSON SEVEN-D focuses on why you need to know something about cost accounting and then some important terminology.

1. EXAMPLES OF WHY THIS MATTERS

A. EMPLOYMENT EXAMPLE

In EXAMPLE 41, JOE'S opens a second venture: JOE'S WINE SHOP. Scott and Adrian negotiate a new contract with Lamar, the manager. He will manage both ventures; however, his profit-sharing bonus only applies to profits from JOE'S BAR & GRILL and not from the WINE SHOP. Unwisely, Scott and Adrian continue to delegate to Lamar authority for cost allocations and supervision of bookkeeping.

EXAMPLE 41

JOE'S BAR & GRILL opens JOE'S WINE SHOP as a second business.

- Lamar, as overall manager, receives a bonus for the BAR & GRILL profits, but not a bonus from the SHOP profits.

Lamar will quickly realize the benefits if he allocates costs shared by the two businesses more to the SHOP and less to the GRILL. For example, if the two activities are next to each other, they may share utilities, insurance, some supplies, bookkeeping, some employee, and janitorial services. Lamar will need a method to apportion such costs. Detailed records are not likely feasible: would you really want the cleaning staff to keep time records as they shift from one room to another? Square footage, foot traffic, or volume of business are each plausible methods, but each also leaves "wiggle" room.

Perhaps in March such shared costs are $4,500. Clearly Lamar could not allocate the entire $4,500 to the Shop and none to the Grill; Scott and Adrian would quickly notice and question that. If perchance, Lamar was successful in such a ruse, his monthly bonus (a one-third share of profits) would be $1,500 higher than if he apportioned the shared costs all to the Grill.[30] If, instead, Lamar apportioned the costs equally, his monthly bonus would decrease (compared to allocating all to the Shop) by $750. Indeed, each dollar he allocates to the Shop increases his bonus by 33 cents. Lamar may be very honest, but a mere 10% extra allocation to the Shop ($450) increases his bonus by $150, which would be tempting and difficult to detect.

---

[30] A $4,500 increase in Grill costs would reduce his bonus by $1,500 because profits would drop by $4,500.

B. LAW SCHOOL EXAMPLE

In EXAMPLE 42, a college of law has multiple programs and centers. The Dean reasonable wants to know the profit or loss of each. Although both governmental and not-for-profit accounting differs from GAAP, the differences are not material to this example.

> ### EXAMPLE 42
>
> A college of law has multiple programs and centers. The Provost directs the Dean to create separate budgets for each.

Allocations would involve tuition, endowment, and university income/receipts as well as numerous costs. Some of the shared costs would be administrative, building depreciation, maintenance, supplies, janitorial, and staff. Nearly all such allocations would likely be imprecise and have plenty of room for subjective judgment. For example, I teach both J.D. and LL.M. courses. At some point, someone must apportion my salary and my office costs between the J.D. program and the LL.M. program. Arguably, if that is not done, then no one can reasonably evaluate the finances of each program.

But how would one apportion my salary? The Dean could use credit hours taught, student conduct hours, timesheets prepared by me, or perhaps some other method. Each would produce precise numbers; however, the numbers produced would have significant arbitrariness to them. For example, a 100-student 2-credit course is not remotely the same as two 50-student 2-credit courses. Office time and individualized instruction differs depending on the level of student. Courses are not equal: new courses take substantially more time than ones taught for decades.

University administrators (at what level, I am unsure) allocate my time for me to a variety of boxes: to courses, research, committee work, service and some miscellaneous categories. I must "approve" the allocations in advance and later must "certify" them as accurate. But on a practical level, I merely sign what they prepare, as does almost everyone I suspect. I have no interest in keeping detailed records supporting an allocation of my time and productivity. Indeed, I'm unsure how I would do it. What is most amazing is that someone does this for me. Not once in 42 years has anyone spoken to me about the allocations as they pertain to me. I understand from general conversations/announcements at faculty meeting that the allocations affect the budget. The amounts allocated to "research," "service," "committee work," and courses seems to differ significantly over time. I suspect this is done to appease higher-level administrators or legislators who wish to see more (or less research), more (or less) administrative work, and more (or less) time spent teaching students. Of course, the numbers have almost zero correlation to what happens in a given semester.

The actual allocations, in my experience, do not seem horribly unreasonable. For example, they do not allocate all my time to my accounting course and nothing to anything else. But the allocations are certainly imprecise and inaccurate. They are easily manipulable depending on the agenda (if any) of the person allocating. They are never audited other than the cursory "certification" demanded of me. Collectively—considering the many faculty we have—the numbers are large. Are they manipulated? Almost certainly yes. Does such manipulation have budgetary consequences? Again, almost certainly yes. However, because the people doing the work are not materially involved in making the allocations, the resulting numbers are not trustworthy. Yet, from my experience, they have been trusted for 42 years. Amazing.

Cost accounting is very important, but if the allocations are untrustworthy, the resulting reports and analysis is equally untrustworthy no matter how precise they may appear.

C. HOLLYWOOD ACCOUNTING EXAMPLE

For many decades the film industry had a reputation for what was derisively called "Hollywood Accounting." It applied such that virtually no film made a profit, at least as "profit" was defined in employment contracts providing a percentage of profits to actors.

EXAMPLE 43

- A contract provides your client with a percentage of "profits" from a film. The movie grosses $1,000,000,000 world-wide but fails to make a "profit" according to the studio.

- How can this be?

In EXAMPLE 43 the contract may provide for a percentage of U.S. or North American profits. If so, substantial "shared costs" may be over-allocated to North American operations. Other costs, as covered in prior lessons, may be expensed when they should have been capitalized or they may be expensed over a short rather than longer period.

Such examples of "Hollywood Accounting" abound.[31] Supposedly the accounting industry has made significant strides in standardizing fair accounting rules for the creative arts. Whether it has been successful is unclear.

---

[31] Barnett, *Hollywood Deals: Soft Contracts for Hard Markets*, 64 DUKE L.J. 605; Barnett, *Hollywood Deals: Soft Contracts for Hard Markets*, 64 DUKE L.J. 605.

Film accounting is a specialty, fraught with intricacies specific to the industry.

2. TERMINOLOGY

Cost accounting—both for internal use and for pricing—uses terminology we have not yet covered. The terms are not universally used with the exact same meaning. The following discussion provides common usage.

- Categories of Costs:
    - Direct Versus Indirect.
    - Variable Versus Fixed Costs.
- Methods of Costing:
    - Full Absorption Costing.
    - Incremental Costing.
- Cost-Plus Pricing.
- Opportunity Cost.
- Cost Segregation.

A. CATEGORIES OF COSTS

Two broad cost categories exist. All costs fit into both categories but into one sub-category for each. That results in four groups: direct-variable, direct-fixed, indirect-variable, and indirect-fixed.

1) Direct Versus Indirect

All costs are either direct or indirect.

a. Direct Costs

Direct costs are those associated fully with a particular product or item. For example, the cost of lumber is a *direct* cost of furniture, as is the labor which produced it. Typically, all direct costs are allocated to the item to which they relate. This would be true for cost accounting as well as financial accounting: one would generally capitalize all direct costs into the basis of the related item.

b. Indirect Costs

Indirect costs are as their name suggests, not direct. They typically involve multiple items. For example, costs generally denominated as "overhead" are indirect. They are necessary for an entity's various products or activities, but they apply to multiple items. Examples include administrative employee costs, janitorial services, and utilities. Typically, all indirect costs are apportioned among the various items to which they relate.

2) Variable Versus Fixed Costs

a. Variable Costs

Variable costs do what their name suggests: they vary as a function of the activity or activities being measured. For example if management wants to produce an extra quantity of inventory, the *variable costs* will include:

- *Stock in trade* (inventory components).

- Additional labor.

- Additional energy (electricity or gas).

- Additional wear and tear on machinery.

Some variable costs are also direct costs. For example, in the production of inventory, the stock in trade or the lumber (in the furniture example) are both direct and variable: the more furniture we produce, the more lumber we use. Other variable costs are indirect. For example, if we produce extra inventory, we likely incur more utility costs; however, unless the utilities are metered to the inventory production, we cannot be certain how much is allocable to which inventory produced as opposed to some other activities.

b. Fixed Costs

Fixed costs are likewise what their name suggests: fixed. Building depreciation and salary for the chief officer are fixed. Whether we have a great many customers, or few, those costs exist. Insurance is typically fixed, as well. We may require additional insurance for a special activity, but mostly insurance does not vary by the amount of production or the numbers of customers.

Mostly, fixed costs are indirect. We must incur them, but they nevertheless are part of each activity. Thus, for cost accounting we would apportion fixed indirect costs. The apportionment cannot be exact, but for many purposes we must try.

B. METHODS OF COSTING

1) Full Absorption Costing

Full absorption costing involves allocating all direct and indirect costs to a relevant activity or product. It particularly involves indirect overhead costs. This provides important information; however, it can be misleading.

EXAMPLE 44

Suppose we want to compute the cost of offering this course you are taking, or the cost of teaching you.

The administration will want to know the total cost, which would include all "Direct Costs" *plus* a reasonable allocation of "Indirect Costs" such as administrative and facility overhead (including such things as maintaining the building and landscaping and parking lot, plus a portion of my salary and office).

This would be useful information, especially in the long-run evaluation of a program or course or in pricing tuition. Ultimately, all costs must be covered, so pricing must consider all costs of the total operation.

EXAMPLE 44 illustrates full absorption costing. It may, for example, determine the cost of each student is $1,000 per credit hour based on an average of 750 students. That is useful information in setting the amount of tuition.

2) Incremental Costing

Incremental costing focuses only on variable costs and mostly only on direct costs. Any cost that would exist without the activity is irrelevant. This is also referred to as the marginal cost—essentially, the cost of one more.

Consider EXAMPLE 44, but in the context of adding one additional student: 751 rather than 750. In this case, the total direct and allocable share of indirect costs would be very misleading. To add one more student has very minimal variable/marginal/incremental cost:

- Slightly more electricity (*email, computer time*), which is so small it is not measurable.

- Slight ink on the printed grade sheets.

- The registrar is paid regardless, so there is no added cost there, and Faculty are paid regardless, so there is no cost there either.

Thus, the variable "marginal/incremental" costs of adding you are close to zero. Adding 50 students may require additional staff or faculty, but would unlikely alter utilities, landscaping, parking lot maintenance, janitorial services, or depreciation on the building, tables, and chairs. It may also lower the full absorption cost because fixed overhead could be spread over more students.

If the full absorption cost of each of the 750 students is $10,000 each and tuition is $12,000 each, then the college is making a profit of $2,000 per student. But, if we add one more student, that student produces a profit of $12,000 because the marginal/incremental costs are so low.

EXAMPLE 45

Suppose we want to compute the cost of offering this course you are taking, or the cost of teaching you.

The administration will want to know the total cost, which would include all "Direct Costs" _plus_ a reasonable allocation of "Indirect Costs" such as administrative and facility overhead (including such things as maintaining the building and landscaping and parking lot, plus a portion of my salary and office).

This would be useful information, especially in the long-run evaluation of a program or course or in pricing tuition. Ultimately, all costs must be covered, so pricing must consider all costs of the total operation.

Your client has a business that makes 1000 widgets. Total costs of the operation are $100,000, so that amounts to $100 per widget.

- To make a profit, your client must sell the widgets for more than $100.

- Suppose a discount store offers to buy 100 widgets for $35 each. Should your client enter the contract?

- That depends on the marginal costs. Overhead, depreciation, management costs are all covered by the main customers for the 1000 widgets. If they can operate the machine and produce another 100 widgets for a marginal cost of $25, then the contract makes sense.

EXAMPLE 45 illustrates incremental costing in manufacturing. Each widget costs $100 using full absorption costing. That is essential information for management in setting the price for the typical sales of 1,000 widgets. But, as with the extra student in EXAMPLE 44, the opportunity to produce 100 additional widgets for a discount store is best evaluated using marginal or incremental costing. The overhead and many direct costs (special machinery and the product manager) are already covered. If the extra run requires no new machinery or management, the incremental costs can be far lower, and the manufacturer can earn substantial additional profits at a price significantly lower than its full absorption cost.

EXAMPLE 46

Tort Example

Your client is being sued for costs the plaintiff incurred in producing a product your client failed to purchase.

- The direct and indirect costs could be very large.

- The variable (incremental/marginal) costs could be very small.

EXAMPLE 46 illustrates incremental costing in a tort case. Your client ordered a manufactured product but failed to purchase it. Client is sued for the costs. State law will provide a measure of recovery, perhaps costs plus lost profits. Incremental/marginal costs should be the best measure of damages.

C. COST-PLUS PRICING

A contract—perhaps for supervising construction or remodeling—may provide for "costs plus 10%" as compensation for the contractor. If so, costs should be defined as direct variable costs. That would include actual costs for sub-contractors, appliances, flooring, and fixtures. The 10% (or maybe 15%) mark-up would cover the contractor's time, profit, and overhead. The contractor should have sufficient jobs to cover all overhead (office expenses and office employees) and produce sufficient profit for his time. A full-absorption contract risks having the contractor collect multiple times for the same overhead: how would the customer monitor/audit such costs?

D. OPPORTUNITY COST

Opportunity costs are universal. Proper evaluation of a project should consider them. They represent income or other activities which would have occurred but for the project being evaluated. For example, you are taking this course and likely are a law student. Your direct costs involve tuition, books, and other school-related expense. You have living costs; however, you would have those whether you were a law student or working in whatever field you would have worked but for being a law student. They are thus not particularly relevant in evaluating the cost of your education.

Your opportunity costs, however, are relevant. Perhaps you could have worked for three years as an engineer earning $50,000 per year after taxes. If so, your opportunity costs are $150,000. Perhaps you have the chance to take on extra work that will occupy weekends for two months. Your opportunity costs—admittedly difficult to quantify—would include less leisure time, less time with family and friends. Or, you could view your leisure/family time as having an opportunity cost equal to not taking on extra work.

E. COST SEGREGATION

Cost segregation involves defining assets and components. For example, you may have a building which cost $500,000. Generally, that would be depreciable over perhaps 40 years. The building, however, is not uniform. It comprises bricks, motor, beams, walls, and foundation which each may indeed last 40 years. But it also has a roof which may only last 25 years. It has windows which may last 15 and light fixtures which may last 10. Cost segregation involves defining such components as separate assets for maintenance and depreciation as well as for the balance sheet.

LESSON EIGHT

GOODWILL AND OTHER INTANGIBLES

Hidden Assets

■ ■ ■

Lesson Objectives

1. Student will learn about accounting for receivables.

2. Student will learn about accounting for securities held by an entity.

3. Student will learn about goodwill and covenants not to compete.

Terminology Introduced

- Confirming.

- Aging.

- Factoring.

- Allowance for bad debts.

- Mark to market.

- Liquidity.

- Treasury stock.

- Goodwill.

- Covenant not to compete.

LESSON EIGHT has three parts:

- Accounts Receivables.

- Securities, including Treasury Stock.

- Goodwill.

It groups important intangible assets most businesses will own. Accounting for intangibles differs from tangibles.

LESSON EIGHT-A

ACCOUNTS RECEIVABLE

■ ■ ■

Terminology for LESSON EIGHT-A involves aging, factoring, and an allowance for bad debts Account receivables are a "current" asset because collection is typically expected in the near term. Customers who plan to pay over longer periods will create a note receivable.

Accounts Receivable is an important—and often substantial—asset for many businesses. Unless a service provider (or inventory seller) demands payment in advance or at the time of service, it will have receivables. For example, Doctors and plumbers often insist on payment at the time of service, but other professions and businesses (*e.g.*, lawyers, lawn maintenance, utilities) often send invoices to customers.

As covered in prior lessons, accrual accounting requires the recognition of income when earned. If the customer pays, the debit is to cash and the credit to income/revenue. If, instead, the customer will pay later, the debit will be to an account receivable and the credit to income/revenue.

An important job of an auditor is to _confirm_ accounts receivable. That requires either contacting all or a representative sample of customers to _confirm_ the amount the company claims is owed. The auditor will send the confirmation request and will receive it: it will not pass through the business. Auditors know many customers will not respond to confirmation requests, but they also will have experience regarding typical response rates.

1. AGING RECEIVABLES

Aging receivable involves exactly what the term suggests: determining the age of each receivable. This process is important for valuing and factoring as well as managing receivables. The classification is simple and likely performed with a computer program. It involves grouping receivables into categories.

For example, a business may expect payment within 10 days. If so, it might group receivables into the following categories:

- 0–10 days.
- 11–30 days.
- 31–60 days.
- 61–90 days.

- More than 90 days.

The entity will have developed experience with its customers and should know the level of attention required for each group. Current receivables—those within the expected payment period—are likely collectible. Receivables which are modestly past-due require a reminder, but probably are collectible. Receivables more than a month old require more attention and perhaps an interest or late penalty. After two months, a business might begin to doubt collectability and may need even greater management involvement. After 90 days, serious doubt about collection probably arises (depending on the business and customer involved) and may require legal action.

A summary of the aging report should appear either on the balance sheet or in a footnote.

2. FACTORING RECEIVABLES

Although receivables are current assets and highly liquid, they are not cash. As a result, businesses with substantial receivables may experience cash-flow issues. One solution is to accept only cash upon performance or a third-party credit card. Although credit cards have fees, they reduce the need to account for and to manage receivables.

An alternative is factoring, which involves either selling or borrowing against the receivables. Selling them is typically without recourse: the purchaser buys the receivables for a discount, assuming the risk of non-collection. A factor may purchase all receivables or perhaps only older ones, which would naturally involve a larger discount.

As explained in earlier lessons, most business use the cash method for tax purposes. If so, uncollected receivables produce no income/revenue: the business would recognize income upon collection. Factoring receivables without recourse, however, would trigger taxable income equal to the amount received from the purchaser as the receivable would have a tax basis of zero. For accrual account, both under GAAP and tax, accrued receivables have a basis equal to the face value. If factored the business would recognize a factoring expense equal to the difference between the face amount owed and the amount received from the purchaser.

Factoring may also be with recourse. Essentially, the business is borrowing from the factor and putting up the receivables as collateral for the loan. Different arrangements exist for such agreements. The factor may style it as a typical loan, charging interest for the days each receivable is outstanding. Or the factor may nominally purchase the receivables at a discount but seek recourse against the business for all or a portion of uncollected receivables.

3. ALLOWANCE FOR BAD DEBTS

At some point, receivables are uncollectible. When to recognize them as uncollectible is a key judgment call. As with other subjective rules, it is subject to abuse. Under *GAAP*,[1] an entity may deal with bad debts (doubtful accounts) in two ways:

1. Specific Allowance method.

2. Allowance Experience method.

With *specific allowance*, the entity debits "expense for bad debts" (or "loss on uncollectible accounts" or some similarly named *temporary* account) and credits a *specific account receivable* known to be uncollectible in whole or in part. This requires management to determine which specific account is uncollectible. Aging helps with the determination but is not the only factor.

For U.S. tax purposes, specific allowance is the only method permitted for tax law and continues to apply for some taxpayers who used it prior to the repeal.[2]

Allowance experience—permitted by U.S. GAAP—allows an entity to write off a percentage of all receivables. This is a function of entity and industry experience. For example, perhaps 5% of all receivables are never collected. The entity is confident of the percentage but does not know in advance which accounts will be collected and which will not be. Common sense suggests that if management knew which customers would not pay, it will not do business with them in the first place.

Each period, the entity will record an adjusting entry equal to 5% of outstanding receivables less the existing allowance for bad debts. It will debit expense for bad debts and credit a contra asset called "allowance for bad debts." Whenever a specific account becomes uncollectible, the entity will debit the allowance for bad debts account and credit the receivable. It will then periodically make an adjusting entry to maintain the 5% allowance.

---

[1]   Under IAS 9 (effective 2023), *IFRS* mandates a more specific to the *asset impairment study*. It also includes a 12-month rule.

[2]   I.R.C. § 166(c) (repealed 1986); Treas. Reg. § 1.166–1(a)(2).

EXAMPLE 47

Bad Debt

- On January 31, JOE'S has accounts receivable of $15,000. Hans still owes $5,000 from December and the rest is current. JOE'S expects customers to pay within 20 days.

  - Management reviews Hans' receivable (which is starting to get old) and decides it remains fully collectible.

Consider EXAMPLE 47. Hans has apparently paid the $1 000 he owed from 12/15 and $1,500 of the $2,000 he owes from 12/24 but none of the $4,500 he owes from 12/31. $500 is 38 days old. Because JOE'S expects payment in 20 days, it is 18 days *past due*. $4,500 is 11 days *past due*. These are not alarmingly *past due*, but JOE'S needs to think about charging interest or a penalty for late payment.

If JOE'S uses a specific allowance method for accounts receivable, it will have no January entry related to doubtful accounts.

If, instead, JOE'S uses an allowance experience method with a 5% experience amount, it would have recognized an expense for bad debts of $375, which is five percent of the $7,500 receivables outstanding on December 31. This adjusting entry would occur even though management was confident then (and remains confident) that Hans would pay the receivable. The adjusting entry would have been a debit to expense for bad debts and a credit to allowance for bad debts. This would have changed the December profit and thus the bonus awarded to Lamar. **Figure 124** shows what would have been the general journal adjusting entry for the December bad debt accrual.

General Journal for JOE'S BAR & GRILL			
Date	**Account**	**Debit**	**Credit**
12/31	**Expense for Bad Debts**	375	
	Allowance for Bad Debts		375
	Adjusting Entry for Amortization		

Figure 124: Allowance for Bad Debts

Ignoring the collateral consequences to Lamar (perhaps his bonus contract ignores bad debt accruals), the modified December balance sheet appears in **Figure 125**. Notice the allowance for bad debts is a contra asset which reduces accounts receivable. Retained earnings dropped by $375 to account for the added bad debt expense.

JOE'S BAR & GRILL Balance Sheet December 31			
Assets		**Liabilities**	
Current		Current	
Cash	$185,370.00	Util. Payable	$1,000.00
Inventory	15,000.00	Note Payable	8,840.15
Supplies	2,000.00	Wages Payable	10,000.00
Acct. Rec.	7,500.00	Wage Tax Payable	897.61
Less Allowance	375.00	Interest Payable	250.00
	7,125.00	Bonus Payable	1,961.76
Local Permit	916.67		
Liq. Lic. Fee	1,604.17		
Pre-Paid Rent	20,000.00		
Total Current	**232,015.84**	**Total Current**	**22,949.52**
Fixed Assets		**Long-Term**	
Machinery	31,000.00	Note Payable	41,159.85
Acc. Depr.	(516.67)		
	30,483.33	**Total Liabilities**	**64,109.37**
Liquor License	78,250.00		
Trademark	5,950.00	**Owner's Equity**	
Emp. Train.	19,444.45	Scott	150,000.00
Signs	4,000.00	Adrian	150,000.00
Acc. Depr.	(133.33)	Retained Earnings	5,900.92
	3,866.67		
Total Fixed	**137,994.45**	**Total Equity**	**305,900.92**
Total Assets	**$370,010.29**	**Liabilities & Equity**	**$370,010.29**

Figure 125: Balance Sheet

Next consider EXAMPLE 48. A different customer has serious legal problems such that it becomes very clear he will not pay his $500 receivable. At this point—on January 31—total receivables are $15,000. Using the allowance experience method, Joe's will have the entries shown in **Figure 126**: a debit to bad debt expense for the $500, a credit to receivables for the $500, and another debit to bad debt expense for $350 with a corresponding credit to allowance for bad debts of $350. The allowance experience method includes an adjustment for accounts known to be uncollectible. The periodic allowance accrual is adjusted accordingly.

EXAMPLE 48

Bad Debt

- On January 31, a customer (John Doe) lost his job for embezzlement. He was arrested and confessed. He owes Joe's $500; but he owes his former employer $100,00 and has no money because he lost it at a casino. His lawyer insisted on receiving all of John's other assets as a retainer.

  – Management makes the reasonable decision to "write-off" the receivable.

For EXAMPLE 48, January ends with $14,500 of receivables after the specific write-off of the John Doe $500 account. The 5% allowance amount is appropriately $725. Because the account (which is a permanent account) has a credit balance of $375 (from December), JOE'S must accrue an additional $350 allowance for January.

General Journal for JOE'S BAR & GRILL			
Date	**Account**	**Debit**	**Credit**
1/31	**Expense for Bad Debts**	500	
	Allowance for Bad Debts		500
	Write-off of John Doe account.		
	Expense for Bad Debts	350	
	Allowance for Bad Debts		350
	To reflect a 5% allowance for bad debt.		

Figure 126: Allowance for Bad Debts

LESSON EIGHT-B

ACCOUNTING FOR SECURITIES

■ ■ ■

LESSON EIGHT-B has several important topics:

- Liquidity.

- Marketability.

- Bonds.

- Mark to market rules.

- Treasury stock.

Before we delve into the topics, let's explore the meaning of a "security.' The definition may vary by statute in various jurisdictions, but _generally_ the term "security" refers to a transferable (tradable) financial instrument, _including_ equities (common and preferred stock) and debt (bonds and debentures). For this purpose, distinguish the use of the term "security" in relation to secured debt. For example, if a home loan is secured by a mortgage, the house is "security" for the debt. That is a very different use of the word "security."

The UCC section 8–102 provides:

(15) "Security," except as otherwise provided in Section 8–103, means an obligation of an issuer or a share, participation, or other interest in an issuer or in property or an enterprise of an issuer:

> (i)   which is represented by a security certificate in bearer or registered form, or the transfer of which may be registered upon books maintained for that purpose by or on behalf of the issuer;
>
> (ii)   which is one of a class or series or by its terms is divisible into a class or series of shares, participations, interests, or obligations; and
>
> (iii) which:
>
> > (A) is, or is of a type, dealt in or traded on securities exchanges or securities markets; or
> >
> > (B) is a medium for investment and by its terms expressly provides that it is a security governed by this Article.

1. LIQUIDITY

Securities are often liquid assets, which means they can easily be turned into cash. For ratio analysis in LESSON TEN, they are also called "current" assets. Assets have varying degrees of liquidity. For example:

- Currency—particularly U.S. dollars and Euros—are very liquid: they are accepted in trade almost everywhere.

- Gold and silver—particularly coins or bullion—are also very liquid.

- Land and buildings, in contrast, are not liquid: they can take months or years to sell.

- Furniture and machinery are typically illiquid.

- Inventory is typically liquid, though that can vary: milk is more liquid than diamonds.

Not all securities are liquid. Some are "restricted" which means contractually they cannot be transfer other than as provided contractually. Even unrestricted securities can be illiquid because a market for them is small.

2. MARKETABILITY

Marketability is related to liquidity—the more marketable something is, the more liquid it is. The term "marketable" is not a term-of-art, but it generally refers to something which is readily tradeable and for which a significant "market" (buyers and sellers) exists.

The internal revenue code uses the term frequently but with differing definitions and, in some cases, with no meaningful definition. For example, section 453(f)(2) defines "marketable securities" as "any security for which, as of the date of the disposition, there was a market or an established securities market or otherwise."[3] In contrast, section 1296 has a far more-detailed definition.[4]

Stocks listed on the New York Stock Exchange (NYSE) tend to be the most marketable. The exchange has detailed rules about what can and cannot be listed. It also has "market makers" who stand ready to trade listed shares. Prices change frequently, as in seconds.

The NASDAQ[5] is another very large exchange in the United States; indeed, it is the largest exchange by volume. Many very large, highly liquid

---

[3] I.R.C. § 453(f)(2) (dealing with installment sales).

[4] I.R.C. § 1296(e) provides:

1296(e) Marketable stock. For purposes of this section—

(1) In general. The term "marketable stock" means—

(A) any stock which is regularly traded on—

(i) a national securities exchange which is registered with the Securities and Exchange Commission or the national market system established pursuant to section 11A of the Securities and Exchange Act of 1934, or

(ii) any exchange or other market which the Secretary determines has rules adequate to carry out the purposes of this part,

(B) to the extent provided in regulations, stock in any foreign corporation which is comparable to a regulated investment company and which offers for sale or has outstanding any stock of which it is the issuer and which is redeemable at its net asset value, and

(C) to the extent provided in regulations, any option on stock described in subparagraph (A) or (B).

[5] National Association of Securities Dealers Automated Quotations, founded in 1971 by the NADA, the precursor of FINRA.

shares are listed on the NASDAQ. It, too, provides market makers. In contrast, over the counter (OTC) markets are less liquid.

Two legal aspects of marketable securities are critical: transferability and negotiability. Unrestricted securities are transferable, which means the owner can sell it to a buyer. Negotiability is a sub-category of transferability. A negotiable security creates a "holder in due course" under the UCC. All negotiable instruments are transferable, but not all transferable instruments are negotiable.

3. BONDS

Bonds are debt instruments, as opposed to shares representing ownership equity. Terminology is important for an understanding of such instruments.

A. BONDS VERSUS DEBENTURES

Both bonds and debentures are debt instruments which bear interest. The terms are often inter-changed. Generally, bonds are secured, and debentures are unsecured. For some purposes, the term bond indicates a longer-term instrument. For example, U.S. Treasury obligations twenty and thirty-year terms are referred to as bonds. Shorter term obligations generally use the denomination "notes" and very short obligations are referred to as "bills."

B. REGISTERED VERSUS BEARER

Debt instruments are either registered or bearer. The owner of a registered bond is listed with the issuer as the owner. Interest payments are issued to the registered owner. The bond itself—the paper if a paper copy exists—is transferable only by the registered owner and only through the registration agent. In contrast, bearer bonds are akin to currency. They are freely transferable by merely handing them to another. They typically have coupons attached for the interest. The holder will clip the coupon and send it to the issuer to receive the interest payment. Coupon/bearer bonds are no longer used in the United States.[6]

---

[6]   IRC § 163(f) denies a deduction for interest on bearer bonds. § 4701 imposes an excise tax of 1% on the issuer. Until 2012, US corporations could issue bearer euro bonds, but that exception to 163(f) was repealed.

EXAMPLE 49

Registered Bond Example

- Suppose Ford issued registered bonds with a face value of $1,000 each paying 6% nominal annual interest quarterly. That would be $150 every three months. Lamar purchases one bond for its face amount of $1,000 (aka at par).

  - He would register the bond with Ford, which would pay the interest quarterly. If a year later he sold the bond to Paula, Lamar would continue to receive the interest until Paula registered the bond in her name with Ford (or the transfer agent).

  - If Paula did so, she would receive the interest. If she lost the certificate (the paper), she would continue to receive the interest. If someone stole the paper, it would be worthless to them (though Paula may have to pay a fee to replace it).

EXAMPLE 50

Bearer Bond Example

- Suppose DeBeers issued Bearer Bonds with a face value of €10,000, a term of 20 years and with 80 €1,500 coupons attached.

- Lamar purchases one bond at its face value. He must clip the coupon every three months and submit it through the transfer agent to receive the interest.

  - If he wants to sell the bond to Paula, he would merely hand her the paper with the coupons attached and she would hand him money.

  - If someone stole the bond, that person would have effective ownership in the same sense as if you were to find a $100 bill in the parking lot.

C. DISCOUNT AND PREMIUM BONDS

Bonds are issued (initially sold) at par, a discount, or at a premium. Similarly, they are traded in the secondary market (on an exchange, for example) also at par, a discount, or at a premium. Market interest rates affect the bond price for issuance and secondary trading.

1) Par

For debt instruments, par means the face amount of the bond. For example, a bond with a face value of $1,000 bearing 10% nominal annual interest[7] paid quarterly will typically be sold to the initial purchaser for $1,000—its par or face value—if the appropriate market interest rate is 10% NAI paid quarterly.

Issuance of a bond, however, takes time because of securities laws. Thus, the issuer may plan to issue the bond for $1,000 but may later sell it for a premium or a discount because market interest rates have changed between the original date in the indenture agreement and the actual initial sale. If interest rates have risen, the bond will issue at a discount. If rates have fallen, the bond will command a premium.

2) Discount

Some bonds are designed to be issued at a discount. For example, a ten-year bond priced to yield 10% effective[8] interest with all interest paid at maturity will initially sell for $385.54. The yield is 10% because $1,000 is the future value of $385.54 in ten years at that interest rate.

For both tax[9] and accounting purposes, the holder must accrue the interest on the bond.

3) Premium

Bonds frequently sell at a premium in the secondary market. This results if market interest rates have fallen since the first issue of the debt instrument. For accounting purposes, the holder will amortize the premium over the remaining life of the instrument. Taxpayers have two options for reporting such "acquisition premium."[10]

D. STRIPPED

The holder of a debt instrument can separate the interest obligation from the principal obligation. That process is called "stripping." The holder could then transfer one or both of the separated parts. The process also occurs with regard to shares of stock, particularly preferred stock.

---

[7]   See the Glossary at 505 for a definition of nominal annual interest.

[8]   See the Glossary at 439 for a definition of effective interest rate.

[9]   IRC § 1272 requires accrual of interest on a bond with original issue discount—discount existing from the first issue. IRC §§ 1275–76 provide taxpayers with four alternative ways of reporting market discount—that which results from a sale in a secondary market.

[10]   IRC § 1272 permits an arithmetic amortization of acquisition premium for tax purposes. In the early years, it results in taxable income lower than what is economically real. In later years, it overstates income. The accompanying treasury regulation permits taxpayers to amortize premium based on economic reality. Most will not because they tend to prefer income deferral.

Significant tax consequences flow from the stripping of bonds.[11] Very different consequences flow from the stripping of preferred stock.[12]

4. MARK TO MARKET RULES

Despite the U.S. GAAP historical cost assumption, some securities must be reported at fair market value. Per GAAP, securities will also be listed by tiers:

- Tier I, which are publicly traded and must be marked to market. These include instruments held for trading or for available for sale.

- Tier II, which have a more limited market (this is a judgment call for the CPA) and may be marked to market.

- Tier III, which are non-marketable and are thus held at book value and are not marked-to-market.

The summary of FAS 115 describes the rule as:

> This Statement addresses the accounting and reporting for investments in equity securities that have readily determinable fair values and for all investments in debt securities. Those investments are to be classified in three categories and accounted for as follows:

> Debt securities that the enterprise has the positive intent and ability to hold to maturity are classified as *held-to-maturity securities* and reported at amortized cost.

> Debt and equity securities that are bought and held principally for the purpose of selling them in the near term are classified as *trading securities* and reported at fair value, with unrealized gains and losses included in earnings.

> Debt and equity securities not classified as either held-to-maturity securities or trading securities are classified as *available-for-sale securities* and reported at fair value, with unrealized gains and losses excluded from earnings and reported in a separate component of shareholders' equity.[13]

The process of marking shares to market requires an accounting entry. If the shares increased in value, it would involve a debit to the asset

---

[11] IRC § 1286 requires the holder to apportion his/her basis to the various components, with each interest obligation and the ultimate principal obligation having a separate basis. This basis allocation affects the tax consequences to both the person who strips and then transfers one or more parts as well as the consequences for the person who receives the part.

[12] IRC § 305 governs stripped preferred stock. For implications, see Steven J. Willis *Naked Stripping for Alimony and Child Support Tax Benefits,* 73 TAX LAWYER 861 (2020)

[13] https://www.fasb.org/page/PageContent?pageId=/reference-library/superseded-standards/summary-of-statement-no-115.html&bcpath=tff.

account and a credit to gain on marketable securities marked to market. If the shares decreased in value, the entry would be the opposite: a credit to the asset and a debit to loss due to mark-to-market securities.

LESSON EIGHT-C

ACCOUNTING FOR GOODWILL

■ ■ ■

LESSON 8-C focuses on goodwill and covenants not to compete. It also covers cost allocation in the sale/purchase of a going concern.

1. GOODWILL

A. SELF-CREATED GOODWILL

Goodwill is an intangible asset comprised of a business's reputation, customer base, advantageous location, and similar qualities that cause the total value to be greater than the sum of the individual parts. If goodwill appears on the balance sheet for GAAP or for U.S. tax law purposes, it was _almost certainly_ purchased or acquired in a merger. Only a rare entry would occur involving a debit to goodwill other than through a purchase or other acquisition.

Of course, a business self-creates goodwill in an economic sense by doing a good job, by treating customers well, and through advertising. Nevertheless, self-created goodwill _does not_ appear on GAAP-based or U.S. tax-based balance sheets. Whatever costs/expenditures created the goodwill results in an expense and not in a capitalized asset.

EXAMPLE 51

Self-Created Goodwill Example

- Suppose Lamar does a particularly good job as manager at JOE'S BAR & GRILL. As a result, he helps develop a large and loyal customer base who consistently return to what they view as their favorite neighborhood tavern.

- JOE'S will debit salary expense and credit cash (or salary payable). It will make **no entry** to an asset called goodwill—not for accounting purposes and not for U.S. tax purposes.

As a result, goodwill is often a hidden asset: it exists and it may have considerable value, but it its absence from the balance sheet may cause it to be over-looked. Suppose in EXAMPLE 51 Lamar did two noteworthy projects in March:

- He built a table and the portion of his salary applicable to the table was $3,000.

- He also worked on developing a larger customer base. The allocable salary was $5,000.

Both projects result in a credit to cash for the amount paid to Lamar. The first project will prompt a debit to table for $3,000. In contrast, the second project will prompt a debit to salary expense for $5,000. The table may have an estimate useful life of three years and thus result in depreciation. The goodwill (the newly expanded customer base) may also have a useful life of multiple years; however, it results in no capitalization and thus no amortization. Instead, the entire expense is allocated to the period in which the goodwill is created.

Likely, JOE'S would not separately state the entry for salary expense from all other salary expenses; instead, all of Lamar's salary would be lumped together. JOE'S economic value would increase because of Lamar's customer building efforts; however, the book value would decrease.

General Journal for JOE'S BAR & GRILL			
Date	Account	Debit	Credit
3/31	**Table**	**3,000**	
	Cash		**3,000**
	Employee-built table/capitalized wage.		
	Salary Expense	**5,000**	
	Cash		**5,000**
	Wage expense (customer base).		

Figure 127: Assets Created by an Employee

In 1971 Coca-Cola launched an advertising campaign including perhaps the most memorable commercial in television history:

I'd like to buy the world a home
And furnish it with love
Grow apple trees and honey bees
And snow white turtle doves

I'd like to teach the world to sing
In perfect harmony
I'd like to buy the world a Coke
And keep it company
That's the real thing

The long-lasting goodwill created by the commercial certainly dwarfed its costs. Likely anyone alive during the early 1970's can sing the song and, as a result, at least subliminally associates Coke with good feeling. That self-created goodwill may have been worth billions of dollars and may have cost a million; however, it resulted in an expense and no asset on the balance sheet.

Goodwill can be very valuable; indeed, it may be the most valuable asset a person or business has. But *if* it does not show up on a balance sheet for accounting or for tax purposes, you need to know to look for it anyway. Your client may be:

- Involved in a divorce.
- Involved in a tort in which a business was damaged.
- Selling or purchasing a business.

LESSON TEN (which deals with ratios) covers more on valuation and detection of things such as goodwill.

B. TREATMENT OF PURCHASED GOODWILL

How we treat goodwill that _does_ appear on the balance sheet differs for tax law and GAAP. _Generally_, GAAP does not permit amortization of goodwill; thus, it perpetually remains on the balance sheet at historical cost. Closely held entities and not-for-profit entities may elect to amortize goodwill over a ten-year period. For public companies, management must annually examine goodwill for possible "impairment" or loss of value. If it is materially impaired, the entity must recognize a resulting loss. Impairment of goodwill is a serious matter. A business or celebrity may be caught in a scandal which can quickly destroy its goodwill

In contrast, U.S. tax law requires[14] the straight-line amortization of goodwill over fifteen years.

C. ENTERPRISE VERSUS PERSONAL GOODWILL

Many states distinguish enterprise goodwill from personal goodwill, at least for family-law. Enterprise goodwill is tied to an entity, name, location, process, method of operation or similar intangible. It is transferable because it does not require a specific human for it to exist. As a result, it is typically recognized as an asset at its economic value.

In contrast, many jurisdictions ignore personal goodwill. This is tied to an individual, such as a popular chef, doctor, lawyer, or designer. This is _not_ easily transferable because without the person, the goodwill evaporates. Both types of goodwill have value and both receive the same accounting and tax treatment. They both produce future income. But they often receive different family-law treatment, which can be material.[15]

---

[14] IRC § 197. If a taxpayer fails to amortize goodwill (or depreciate assets), its basis will decrease, nevertheless. IRC § 1016.

[15] _E.g._, Thompson v. Thompson, 576 So. 2d 267 (Fla. 1991).

EXAMPLE 52

Enterprise Versus Personal Goodwill

- Spouse A (Pete) a well-known lawyer, attracts considerable clientele because of a reputation as a "fighter" or a "showman." This results in Pete having substantially higher annual income compared to lawyers with similar training and experience.

- Spouse B (Kendall) is a partner in a law firm with a strong reputation for success. This reputation results in Kendall (and other firm partners) having substantially higher annual income compared to lawyers with similar training and experience.

- In both cases, the increased earning capacity produces increased annual earnings of $175,000 over what comparable lawyers earn. In both cases, experts for the lawyer and his/her spouse agree on the increased earning capacity and on the value of the goodwill as $2.5 million.

In EXAMPLE 52, Pete creates substantial goodwill through his personality and individuality. Whatever it is about him that draws clients is part of him and not easily transferable to another. Honing his skills is an accounting expense and a tax expense. The same is essentially true for family law, as this "personal" goodwill is not typically an asset, at least not for property division. Nothing exists to divide.

In contrast, Kendall creates substantial goodwill through her skills, experience, and high standards. This reputation also draws clients, but it is more likely enterprise goodwill. It is something that "goes with the firm" and can be taught and transferred. For accounting and tax law, whatever costs are associated with it result in expenses. But for family law, it the enterprise goodwill is an asset measured at its economic value.

The differences between the two types of goodwill are not always clear. The consequences, however, can be profound.

2. COVENANTS NOT TO COMPETE

When purchasing goodwill, an entity will likely consider a covenant not to compete from the seller. States vary regarding permissible durations of covenants.[16]

---

[16] For example, Florida statute § 542.335 provides:

Valid restraints of trade or commerce.—

A CNC must have a reasonable duration.

- For former employees or independent contractors (not sellers of a business), 6 months is reasonable, and 2 years is presumed unreasonable.

For financial accounting a covenant (non-compete agreement in accounting terminology) should be valued and treated as an asset separate from acquired goodwill. Generally, it is non-amortizable, but instead subject to an impairment test. Private companies and NFP can elect to amortize over ten years by combining NCA with goodwill.

For U.S. tax law, a taxpayer must capitalize the cost of a covenant not to compete.[17] The cost is amortizable over 15 years, beginning with the month of acquisition.[18] If a CNC becomes worthless, the taxpayer cannot deduct a loss unless it has disposed of the entire interest in the acquired business.[19]

An alternative is to hire the person as an employee for a few years. That results in a faster deduction for tax law and also a deduction for accounting. Both treatments are subject to whether the "employment" relationship is respected as such, or whether it has "substantially the same effect as a covenant."[20]

3. SALE/PURCHASE OF A GOING CONCERN

If the transaction involves the sale of stock, the seller will have an amount realized equal to the price and gain or loss as a function of basis, both for tax and financial accounting. The purchaser will have a basis in the stock equal to the cost. A later merger of the entities will raise substantial accounting and tax issues which are beyond the scope of this course.

If, instead, the transaction involves the sale of asset, both the seller and the purchase must allocate the price among the assets sold and acquired. This will affect the seller who will have gain or loss on individual asset sales, rather than the bulk transaction treatment which results from the sale of stock. The purchaser will have total basis in the various assets equal to the sale price; however, individual assets will have differing future accounting and tax treatment. For example, some will consumables subject to expensing, others will have short or long lives for depreciation and amortization, and some, such as land will be non-depreciable.

- For a seller of a business, 3 years is reasonable, and more than 7 years is presumed unreasonable.

[17] IRC § 197(f)(3). This applies to "any covenant not to compete (or other arrangement to the extent such arrangement has substantially the same effect as a covenant not to compete) entered into in connection with an acquisition (directly or indirectly) of an interest in a trade or business or substantial portion thereof . . . ." IRC § 197(d)(1)(E).

[18] IRC § 197(a).

[19] IRC § 197(f).

[20] See, IRC § 197(d)(1)(E).

For tax law, section 1060[21] applies:

(a) General rule

In the case of any applicable asset acquisition, for purposes of determining both—

(1) the transferee's basis in such assets, **and**

(2) the gain or loss of the transferor with respect to such acquisition,

the consideration received for such assets shall be allocated among such assets acquired in such acquisition in the same manner as amounts are allocated to assets under section 338(b)(5). If in connection with an applicable asset acquisition, the transferee and transferor agree in writing as to the allocation of any consideration, or as to the fair market value of any of the assets, such agreement shall be binding on both the transferee and transferor unless the Secretary determines that such allocation (or fair market value) is not appropriate.

EXAMPLE 53

Sale/Purchase of JOE'S

- You want to purchase JOE'S BAR for $500,000. You are purchasing the assets and assuming the liabilities.
  - How do you want to allocate the purchase price?
  - How would JOE'S want to allocate the purchase price?

For EXAMPLE 53, consider JOE'S balance sheet from December 31 in **Figure 128**. This is a purchase of assets with assumption of liabilities. The price is $500,000. Liabilities of $61,109.37 would reduce the payment to $438,890.63. Purchasing cash of $185,370 makes little sense, but that is the EXAMPLE; thus, that would reduce the payment to $253,520.63, which is the amount you (the purchaser) must apportion among the assets other than cash. JOE'S must apportion the same amount to properly determine gains/losses for tax purposes. Although the parties need not agree on the apportionment, if they do, the government will respect it per section 1060, assuming the government deems the apportionments appropriate. The ability of the government to disregard inappropriate allocations forces the parties to be reasonable, but within substantial area to negotiate.

Consider what you would want, ignoring the constraint of being reasonable or appropriate. You cannot allocate more to cash than the

---

[21] IRC § 1060, enacted in 1986. Prior to 1986, Williams v. McGowan, 152 F.2d 570 (2d Cir. 1945) controlled. Essentially, section 1060 enacted the Second Circuit test.

amount of cash; hence, we reduced the amount by that. You also cannot alter the allocation to debt, at least not under the constraints of the example which suggest a verification of liabilities. Pre-paid rent, accounts receivable, and the remaining amortizable portions of the permit and license fee are not good candidates for apportionments greater than book value.

JOE'S BAR & GRILL Balance Sheet December 31				
Assets			**Liabilities**	
Current			**Current**	
Cash	$185,370.00		Util. Payable	$1,000.00
Inventory	15,000.00		Note Payable	8,840.15
Supplies	2,000.00		Wages Payable	10,000.00
Accounts Rec.	7,500.00		Wage Tax Payable	897.61
Less Allowance	375.00		Interest Payable	250.00
	7,125.00		Bonus Payable	1,961.76
Local Permit	916.67			
Liq. Lic. Fee	1,604.17			
Pre-Paid Rent	20,000.00			
Total Current	**232,015.84**		**Total Current**	**22,949.52**
Fixed Assets			**Long-Term**	
Machinery	31,000.00		Note Payable	41,159.85
Acc. Depr.	(516,67)			
	30,483.33		**Total Liabilities**	**64,109.37**
Liquor License	78,250.00			
Trademark	5,950.00		**Owner's Equity**	
Emp. Train.	19,444.45		Scott	150,000.00
Signs	4,000.00		Adrian	150,000.00
Acc. Depr.	(133.33)		R/E	5,900.92
	3,866.67			
Total Fixed	**137,994.45**		**Total Equity**	**305,900.92**
Total Assets	**$370,010.29**		**Liabilities & Equity**	**$370,010.29**

Figure 128: Balance Sheet

You notice the total asset book values are $370,010.29. Removing the $185,370 cash (which cannot change) you have $184,640.29 book value of the remaining assets. Because you are unlikely to alter the rent, receivable, permit, and fee (which add to $29,645.84) you are left with $154,994.45 of book value assets subject to adjustment. Of the $253,520.63 you have to allocate, $29,645.84 goes to assets you cannot reasonably alter, leaving $223,874.79 to allocate. If you accept book value for the remaining assets ($154,994.45), you must allocate $68,880.34 to goodwill. That is the excess you paid over book value. You paid $438,890.63 (net of liabilities) for assets (including cash) of $370,010.29, for an excess of $68,880.34.

Allocating $68,880.34 to goodwill, however, results in an asset with a 15-year life for tax purposes, which spreads the amortization tax benefit over a long period, reducing its present value. You would prefer to allocate as much of the $68,880.34 to short-term assets as possible. Ignoring the constraint of being reasonable, you would allocate all to supplies, which you will likely use and thus expense within the next few months. Of course, that would be grossly unreasonable. Allocating to inventory would have a similar effect, though perhaps over a slightly longer period. It would result in high bases and thus losses upon sale. Once again, allocating a large portion of the $68,880.34 would be unreasonable, but you would at least allocate enough to bring it all to fair market value, especially if you use LIFO. Because the signs have a shorter depreciable life than the machinery, you would prefer to allocate to them. The same is true of employee training, which is not only very subjective but also is arguably the reason for the goodwill.[22]

JOE'S will have a very different outlook. It will seek to allocate the excess to assets which produce long-term capital gain. Because the holding period in this example is so short (less than one year), none of the assets would be long-term. If they were, that would materially affect JOE'S allocations, which would be to goodwill or the liquor license first and then to other fixed assets. Because of the short-term and the dearth of assets reasonable to adjust (again the newness of the business affects that), the negotiations would likely favor you, with JOE'S largely being indifferent. Because of the "appropriate" standard, you would likely allocate a substantial portion to goodwill. A larger business, with a greater variety of assets, however, would present considerable opportunities for negotiation.

---

[22] Because the training overlaps with the goodwill, a substantial allocation to the training would likely trigger a negative response from the government. But a little might work.

LESSON NINE

CAPITAL STRUCTURE

The Fundamental Structure of an Entity

■ ■ ■

Lesson Objectives

1. Student will learn the basic capital structure of a corporation.
2. Student will be able to define and distinguish bonds from debentures.
3. Student will be able to distinguish debt from equity.
4. Student will be able to distinguish common from preferred stock.

Terminology Introduced

- Debenture.
- Convertible debt.
- Subordination.
- Common stock.
- Preferred stock.
- Convertible stock.
- Participation rights.
- Cumulative dividend rights.

———————

This brief LESSON divides into two parts: debt and equity. Part A (debt) also includes a general discussion regarding capital. This is not a substitute for a course in Corporations; instead, it covers basic corporate terminology only.

———————

LESSON NINE-A

CAPITAL STRUCTURE: DEBT

■ ■ ■

1. CAPITAL

The term *capital* has several meanings, so be careful using the term. For LESSON NINE, it refers to the right side of the balance sheet—both debt and equity. A common phrase refers to the cost of capital. This would compare common stock (which requires price support through the maintenance of an adequate rate of return on *equity* and dividends which are not deductible for tax purposes), *preferred stock* (which requires dividends that are not tax deductible) with debt (which pays interest which is tax deductible.

Capital often refers, however, merely to the equity: common and preferred stock plus excesses and retained earnings. I use the broader meaning (debt plus equity) merely as an educational tool: this is an appropriate LESSON to cover debt and equity together because both are used to "fund" the entity.

Equity, as used in this LESSON, refers to owner's equity. As covered in earlier LESSONS, equity can also refer to the value of an asset net of encumbrances. For example, people often refer to their "equity" in a home, which equals its value less debt obligations secured by the asset.

Capital can also refer to fixed assets, such as plant and equipment as opposed to inventory or receivables. Some entities, especially those involved in heavy manufacturing (such as steel or automobiles), are notoriously "capital intensive." That usage of "capital" refers to their need for large investment in fixed assets. In contrast, other entities may be "labor intensive." That refers generally to their need for lots of employees, but perhaps few fixed assets. A software company is likely to be more "labor intensive" than "capital intensive."

In tax law, one would often distinguish capital income from ordinary income. Capital income flows from the sale or exchange of "capital assets" as defined in IRC section 1221. That is an important use of the term "capital"; however, it is not the one used in this LESSON.

The word "capital" standing alone is vague. For example, if someone were to ask "how much "capital" do you have or does your business have, you would need them to define "capital" so you could answer the question.

2. DEBT

Debt comes in two broad categories: secured and unsecured. You will cover these in more depth in courses on security devices and bankruptcy.

A. SECURED DEBT

Secured debt is secured with an encumbrance on an assets. The encumbrance is typically a mortgage, but it could also be a pledge, a pawn, or some other state-law device. For financial accounting we list secured debt separately from unsecured debt. That can be critical information for both creditors and owner's. As explained in LESSON EIGHT-B, the word "bond" often refers to secured debt.

Secured debt can have "levels" of security, also known as subordination. For example, one might grant a first and then a second or third mortgage on property. If the debt were foreclosed, the first mortgage holder would be paid in full, with the second mortgage holder being paid second, and then the third. If any amount remained unpaid, the remained would typically become an unsecured debt as to all other entity assets. In that example the first mortgage is "superior" to the second and third, which are each "subordinate" to the ones above.

Because debt is debt—and not equity—it has no voting rights, at least not under normal circumstances. Debt, however, can be convertible to equity—in part or in whole. The indenture agreement (the contract governing the issuance of the debt) will describe any conversion rights. In some cases—perhaps triggered by low-performing ratios (covered in LESSON TEN)—holders of particular debt may gain voting rights and a right to representation on the board of directors. In other defined circumstances, the holders of particular debt may have to right to convert the debt into shares of stock. You will cover such issues in greater depth in courses on corporations, corporate finance, security devices, and bankruptcy.

B. UNSECURED DEBT

Unsecured debt is subordinate to secured debt as to the asset securing the debt. Routine unsecured debt is typically an account payable. Other (typically short-term) debt is commonly called "commercial paper."

Unsecured paper with longer terms is often called a debenture or a debenture bond. It would typically look and act just like a bond, but it would be unsecured. Debentures could also have conversion right similar to those available to bonds.

C. CURRENT VERSUS FIXED

For financial accounting, we separate debt—both secured and unsecured—into current or fixed. Current liabilities (debt) are those due within one year. Fixed are all other debt. The distinction is important for several financial ratios, as discussed in LESSON TEN.

D. DEBT VERSUS EQUITY

Although the classifications described above may appear distinct from equity (other than as to conversion rights), the legal distinction between debt and equity is not always clear. Mostly a discussion of this is beyond this course; however, some understanding is important. Because debt has tax benefits to the entity (interest is deductible while dividends are not), owners have some incentive to disguise equity as debt. This would also help if the entity were bankrupt, as debt holders have preference over equity owners.

LESSON NINE-B

CAPITAL STRUCTURE: EQUITY

■ ■ ■

1. COMMON STOCK

A. GENERAL RULES

Common stock comprises most of the equity in a typical corporation. It typically has voting rights, which means it controls the entity. The GLOSSARY definition is:

> This is a type of security (a term which includes stock, bonds, and *debentures*) which has voting rights. Although a corporation may issue various classes of *common stock* with various voting rights and liquidation rights, generally *common stock* is at the bottom in terms of preference upon liquidation. As a result, all other obligations—secured and unsecured—plus *preferred stock* would normally receive full payment on liquidation before common stockholders received anything.

But, *common stock*, in case of liquidation, would also have no cap on what it received on liquidation; hence, common shareholders would receive everything left after senior debts and securities received satisfaction. Thus, *common stock* is riskier than *preferred stock* or *debentures*; however, it also has greater opportunity for gain.

The key points are the voting rights and liquidation status. Creditors and preferred stockholders typically lack voting rights. Also, they are each paid upon liquidation prior to common shareholders. Typically, common stock has all the control—it selects the board of directors and thus has direct control over management. It also has the greatest risk of loss. Upon liquidation, it is paid last—after debt and after preferred stock. But common stock also has all—or almost all—opportunity for gain. Retained earnings are part of the coon stock equity. Upon liquidation, an entity would pay credits (by ranking), then preferred stock. Whatever is left belongs to common.

Because the retained earnings are part of common shareholder equity, common dividends go to common shareholders. Sometimes, preferred shareholders can participate in common dividends.

A corporation—per state laws which vary—can issue various classes of common stock. The classes will have defined voting rights. For example, Class A might elect 7 directors, and Class B might elect 5. The classes may also have rankings for liquidation and for dividends. You will cover such matters in a course on corporations.

B. ACCOUNTING FOR PAR OR NO PAR

Par value is largely an *antiquated* term denoting the original stated issue price of corporate shares. Historically, if an entity issued shares for less than par value, they were assessable for the under-paid amount. As a result, many companies issued stock with a par value of $1 per share but charged an appropriate market price. The excess would be accounted for as "APIC" (additional paid-in capital) or "EPIC" (excess paid-in capital). Many states changed laws to permit a "stated value" rather than a 'par value"; however, that change in terminology had no real meaning. States now vary regarding whether they require a stated/par value or permit it.

The difference between the Par and the No Par value examples involves a journal entry. Later we see how it affects a stock dividend; the economic differences, however, are probably non-existent.

EXAMPLE 54

Par Value

- Scott & Adrian each contributed $250,000 to start JOE'S BAR & GRILL, INC.
- Suppose they issue 1,000 shares to each with a $10 *par* or stated value.

In EXAMPLE 54, JOE'S issues 1,000 shares to each Scott and Adrian with a $10 par value but a $250 per share price. As illustrated in **Figure 129**, JOE'S debits cash for the $250,000, credits par value for $10,000, and credits excess paid-in capital for $240,000. The equity portion of the balance sheet will list the par value of $20,000 (total) and the EPIC of $480,000 (total). The existence of EPIC is insignificant. Historically, some jurisdictions allowed distributions to be paid to the extent of EPIC.

Date	General Journal for JOE'S BAR & GRILL	Debit	Credit
	Account		
8/1	**Cash**	250,000	
	Capital Stock Par		10,000
	Excess Paid-in Capital		240,000
	Issue Stock to Scott.		
	Cash	250,000	
	Capital Stock Par		10,000
	Excess Paid-in Capital		240,000
	Issue Stock to Adrian.		

Figure 129: Issue Stock with Par Value

In EXAMPLE 55, JOE'S issues 1,000 shares to each Scott and Adrian with no par value. As illustrated in **Figure 130**, JOE'S debits cash for the $250,000 and credits capital stock for $250,000. The equity portion of the

EXAMPLE 55

No Par

- Scott & Adrian each contributed $250,000 to start JOE'S BAR & GRILL, INC.
- Suppose they issue 1,000 shares to each with no par or stated value.

balance sheet will list the capital stock of $500,000. In earlier LESSONS, we separated the capital accounts of Scott and Adrian for illustration.

General Journal for JOE'S BAR & GRILL			
Date	Account	Debit	Credit
8/1	Cash	250,000	
	Capital Stock		250,000
	Issue Stock to Scott.		
	Cash	250,000	
	Capital Stock Par		250,000
	Issue Stock to Adrian.		

Figure 130: Issue Stock with No Par Value

2. PREFERRED STOCK

Preferred stock is part of equity, but it has some attributes of debt. The GLOSSARY definition is:

This is a type of security (a term which includes stock, bonds, and *debentures*) which typically has no voting rights. The name preferred does not indicate anything about value or the wisdom of preferred stock ownership. Instead, it merely refers to the legal preference the stock has for dividends and liquidation over common stock. Normally, all other obligations—secured and unsecured—would receive full payment on liquidation before *preferred stockholders* received anything. Then *preferred stockholders* would receive full payment (including generally for accrued but unpaid *dividends*) before *common stockholders* received anything.

The rights of *preferred* stockholders appear in the indenture agreement that accompanied their issue, or in the corporation's articles. Preferred stock dividends _may accumulate_—which means they carry over if unpaid to future years. In such cases, common stockholders may not receive dividends until accumulated preferred dividends are paid.

Preferred Stock typically has a _right_ to a fixed _dividend_, which is similar to interest on a debenture. However, preferred *stock dividends* are not interest and thus are not deductible for tax or financial reporting purposes. Often the differences between *preferred stock*—which is a type of *equity*—and an unsecured, *subordinated debenture*—which is debt—are slight. But, for tax and accounting purposes, the differences are substantial.

Preferred Stock may also have limited *participating* rights—which means it can partially or fully participate in common stock dividends. Often, *participating preferred stock* does not receive a common dividend until the *common stock* dividend equals the *preferred stock* dividend. This is, however, a matter of contract.

An entity may list a class of security as preferred stock; however, litigation may re-classify it as subordinated debt if that is its substance.

Or subordinated debt may effectively/substantively be preferred stock. The differences are not always legally clear though the consequences can be large.

3. STATUTORY REQUIREMENTS

A. GENERAL RULES

States vary, but many follow the Model Business Corporation Act. Section 6.07 of that Act appears (with small modifications) in Florida Statute 607.0601 (with emphasis added):

607.0601   Authorized shares.—

(1) The articles of incorporation <u>must prescribe the classes of shares</u> and the number of shares of each class that the corporation is authorized to issue. If more than one class of shares is authorized, the articles of incorporation <u>must prescribe a distinguishing designation</u> for each class, and prior to the issuance of shares of a class the preferences, limitations, and relative rights of that class must be described in the articles of incorporation. All shares of a class must have preferences, limitations, and relative rights identical with those of other shares of the same class except to the extent otherwise permitted by s. 607.0602 or s. 607.0624.

(2) The articles of incorporation <u>must authorize</u>:

(a) One or more classes of shares that together <u>have unlimited voting rights</u>, and

(b) One or more classes of shares (which may be the same class or classes as those with voting rights) that together are entitled to receive the net assets of the corporation upon dissolution.

(3) The articles of incorporation may authorize one or more classes of shares that:

(a) Have special, conditional, or limited voting rights, or no right to vote, except to the extent prohibited by this act;

(b)   Are redeemable or convertible as specified in the articles of incorporation:

>   1.   At the option of the corporation, the shareholder, or another person or upon the occurrence of a designated event;

>   2.   For cash, indebtedness, securities, or other property; or

>   3.   In a designated amount or in an amount determined in accordance with a designated formula or by reference to extrinsic data or events;

(c)   Entitle the holders to distributions calculated in any manner, including dividends that may be cumulative, noncumulative, or partially cumulative;

(d)   Have preference over any other class of shares with respect to distributions, including dividends and distributions upon the dissolution of the corporation.

(4)   The description of the designations, preferences, limitations, and relative rights of share classes in subsection (3) is not exhaustive.

(5)   Shares which are entitled to preference in the distribution of dividends or assets shall not be designated as common shares. Shares which are not entitled to preference in the distribution of dividends or assets shall be common shares and shall not be designated as preferred shares.

Some important points to take from the statute:

*   The *articles of incorporation* must set out the rights of the various classes of stock.

*   Some class of stock must have *unlimited voting rights* (though multiple classes can have voting rights).

*   Some class of stock must receive the *remainder* upon dissolution.

*   Stock can be *convertible* into debt or other stock or property.

*   Stock can have *cumulative* dividends rights.

*   If a class of stock has a *preference* on dividends or assets, it cannot be called common stock.

B.   SHARE DIVIDENDS

Florida Statute 607.0623, modelling section 6.23 of the Model Act, covers share dividends:

607.0623   Share dividends.—

(1) Unless the articles of incorporation provide otherwise, shares may be issued pro rata and without consideration to the corporation's shareholders or to the shareholders of one or more classes or series. An issuance of shares under this subsection is a share dividend.

(2) *Shares of one class or series may not be issued as a share dividend in respect of shares of another class or series unless*:

> (a) The articles of incorporation so authorize,
>
> (b) a majority of the votes entitled to be cast by the class or series to be issued approves the issue, or
>
> (c) there are no outstanding shares of the class or series to be issued.

(3) If the board of directors does not fix the record date for determining shareholders entitled to a share dividend, it is the date the board of directors authorizes the share dividend.

The main point to take away from that is:

- Typically, common stock can be issued to common, but not to preferred and *vice versa*; hence, it does not affect relative ownership.

Stock dividends (*aka* share dividends) have three types:

- Split.
- Small.
- Large.

1) Stock Split

A stock split is a very large *stock dividend*, often involving two shares in exchange for one, or even more. Typically, a *stock split* results in a price drop comparable to the increased number of shares outstanding. As a result, the market capitalization (stock price times the number of shares outstanding) does not change materially. For both tax and financial accounting purposes, this does not involve any book entry; instead, it merely requires a notation of the change in number of shares outstanding.

Corporations *split* their stock to provide greater market *liquidity*. For example, if a company has 1 million outstanding shares selling for $100 each, it could split the stock five for one, resulting in 5 million outstanding shares selling for roughly $20 each. Investors will arguably have an easier time buying and selling shares priced at $20 rather than shares priced at $100.

As a result, with a publicly traded company, a split may result in a small increase in the total value of the shares outstanding: perhaps each of the shares in the example would trade for $20.50 instead of exactly $20. That is because the "market" arguably perceives a split as a good sign. It also increases the liquidity because the shares are more affordable in "blocks" (usually 100 shares).

EXAMPLE 56

Stock Split

- Scott & Adrian each contributed $250,000 to start JOE'S BAR & GRILL, INC.
- They would like to split the stock so that each has 2,000 shares.

Consider EXAMPLE 56: a routine 2 for 1 split. nothing economically happened: Scott and Adrian were equal owners before and equal owners afterwards. Whatever was the value of the business remains the value of the business and whatever was the value of their shares likely dropped in half; however, because they have twice as many, nothing materially changed.

No accounting entry would be appropriate in the journals, although we could make a notation of it. We might list the number of shares on the balance sheet or in a footnote to the balance sheet. Before the 2 for 1 split, each owned 1,000 shares valued at $250 per share (total $250,000). *After* the split, each owns 2,000 shares valued at $125 per share (total $250,000).

2) Small Stock Dividend

A "*small stock dividend*" typically increases the number of shares by less than 20 to 25%. Thus, in EXAMPLE 57, if JOE'S increased Scott's and Adrian's shares from 1,000 to 1,100 each, we would call it a small stock dividend rather than a stock split.

Had they done this, nothing economically vis a vis the corporation would have happened: they were equal owners before and equal owners afterwards.

EXAMPLE 57

Small Stock Dividend

- Scott & Adrian each contributed $250,000 to start JOE'S BAR & GRILL, INC. Each started with 1,000 shares.
- They would like to issue a small stock dividend the stock so that each has 1,100 shares.

Per GAAP, we would "capitalize" a portion of retained earnings into either "capital stock" or both "capital stock" and APIC/EPIC (if we use that account). We would use the "fair market value" of the stock for the entry. For financial accounting, this makes the distribution appear as if we distributed a cash dividend and the recipients re-contributed it for additional stock.

State laws historically varied on whether an entry was required. Some required a journal entry to "capitalize" earned surplus into capital stock and APIC/EPIC. Other states were silent, or more likely would follow GAAP. For some historical state laws, the payment of a cash dividend required either "earned surplus" or "current earnings". If so, the stock dividend accounting entry would affect the ability to pay future cash dividends: it reduced "earned surplus."

3) Large Stock Dividend

A "*large stock dividend*" typically increases the number of shares by more than 25%. Thus, in EXAMPLE 58, if JOE'S increased Scott's and Adrian's shares from 1,000 to 1,300 each, we would call it a large stock dividend rather than a stock split.

The line between a large stock dividend (more than 25% of outstanding shares) and a stock split is *fuzzy*. Management determines the line. The journal entries differ, which may create an appearance of reality, even if the economic value is unchanged.

EXAMPLE 58

Large Stock Dividend

- Scott & Adrian each contributed $250,000 to start JOE'S BAR & GRILL, INC. Each started with 1,000 shares.

- They would like to issue a large stock dividend the stock so that each has 1,300 shares.

Per GAAP, we would "capitalize" a portion of retained earnings into either "capital stock" or both "capital stock" and APIC/EPIC (if we use that account). We would use the par value or stated value of the stock for the entry.

The differing accounting treatment for small and large stock dividends is often confusing and arguably not justifiable. Some authorities argue the accounting world should reconsider the issue to provide more unity.[1]

---

[1]   *See, Sheldon R. Smith, Student Confusion about Small and Large Stock Dividends*, 17 J. HIGHER ED. THEORY AND PRAC. 101 (2017).

How various levels of share dividends differ, however, is important for lawyers to understand. Consider a practical example.

EXAMPLE 59

Stock Split by a Large Entity

- XYZ, Inc. has one billion shares outstanding. Shares currently trade at $400 per share, resulting in total market capitalization of $400,000,000,000.
- XYZ, Inc. splits the stock ten for one.
- What happens to the market price?

In EXAMPLE 59, a ten for one stock split will result in each shareholder having ten times as many shares. For example, if prior to the split, John had 100,000 shares and Mary had 30,000, then post-split John would have 1,000,000 and Mary would have 300,000. Their proportional ownership would not change. The value per share, however, would certainly change.

Prior to the split each share was worth $400; hence, John's shares were worth $40,000,000 and Mary's were worth $12,000,000. Post-split, each share would be worth approximately $40 (one-tenth the pre-split value). The total market capitalization would not necessarily change; thus, John's new shares would continue to have a market value of $40,000,000 and Mary's a value of $12,000,000. In reality, market values change constantly and for many reasons, including liquidity and investor perceptions and expectations. One reason for the split might be to make the shares more easily tradeable. Share often trade in blocks of 100 shares. Smaller blocks can result in higher trading fees. A pre-split block of 100 would have had a value of $40,000—a substantial trade for most investors. In contrast, a post-split trade of a 100-share block would have a value of only $4,000. That might find more potential buyers, as well as sellers. As a result, the post-split value per share may be slightly greater than $40 per share— perhaps $41 or $42. Thus, a stock split can have some economic reality, although the increase in market capitalization is not likely large.

In contrast, a small stock dividend may have material economic consequences. Consider EXAMPLE 60.

EXAMPLE 60

Small Stock Dividend by a Large Entity

- XYZ, Inc. has one billion shares outstanding. Shares currently trade at $400 per share, resulting in total market capitalization of $400,000,000,000.

- XYZ, Inc. issues a 5% stock dividend.

- What happens to the market price?

Suppose that prior to the dividend, Mark had 1,000 shares worth $400,000. After the split he has 1,050 shares. Probably, the market value will not decrease proportionately with the dividend. If it did drop proportionately, the post-dividend price would be $380.95. With 1,050,000,000, the total market capitalization would remain at $400,000,000,000. Empirical studies, however, suggest the price will drop, if at all, by significantly less than $19.05 per share.[2] Apparently, investors view a small stock dividend as a very positive sign of growth. Many recipients may sell the new shares, viewing them more like a cash dividend rather than a share dividend. Arguably that market reaction justifies the differing accounting treatment.

4)   Legal Treatment of Stock Dividends

As lawyers, we must contemplate the legal treatment of stock dividends. A very large stock dividend—at the level one would call it a split—should not no legal significance. After all, it merely exchanges two shares for one (or perhaps ten for one). It does not even result in a bookkeeping entry. If pre-split, the shares were separate property in a marriage or considered principal in a trust, they should retain that character post-split.

A small stock dividend, however, is not so easily dismissed as non-substantive. Arguably, it should receive legal treatment comparable to a cash dividend: as if the recipient received cash and immediately purchased additional shares. As such—depending on state law—it may become a marital asset even if the original stock were separate, or it may belong to the income beneficiary, rather than to the principal.

Tax law provides a clear answer regarding stock dividends. In 1920, the Supreme Court held a stock dividend does _not_ produce gross income for U.S. tax law.[3] This applies regardless of whether the dividend is small,

---

[2]   _Id._

[3]   Eisner v. Macomber, 252 U.S. 189 (1920).

large, or a split. Both the Constitution[4] and the Internal Revenue Code[5] require income to be "derived" "from" a source.

In 1916, the Standard Oil Company of California had substantial retained earnings (then called earned surplus) of $45 million, of which $20 million was earned prior to ratification of the Sixteenth Amendment. The Board of Directors issued a 50% stock dividend. On its books, it capitalized earned surplus. As explained by the Court, "Congress in the Revenue Act of 1916 declared (39 Stat. 757) that a "stock dividend shall be considered income, to the amount of its cash value.' "[6] As a result, the government asserted a tax on a recipient to the extent his new shares represented capitalized income since March 1, 1913. The *Macomber* Court, however, found the statute unconstitutional because the stock dividend was not "derived."

> A "stock dividend" shows that the company's accumulated profits have been capitalized, instead of distributed to the stockholders or retained as surplus available for distribution in money or in kind should opportunity offer. Far from being a realization of profits of the stockholder, it tends rather to postpone such realization, in that the fund represented by the new stock has been transferred from surplus to capital, and no longer is available for actual distribution.

> The essential and controlling fact is that the stockholder has received nothing out of the company's assets for his separate use and benefit; on the contrary, every dollar of his original investment, together with whatever accretions and accumulations have resulted from employment of his money and that of the other stockholders in the business of the company, still remains the property of the company, and subject to business risks which may result in wiping out the entire investment. Having regard to the very truth of the matter, to substance and not to form, he has received nothing that answers the definition of income within the meaning of the Sixteenth Amendment.[7]

4. TREASURY STOCK

Entities often purchase their own shares. If the entity intends to become smaller, this would be a stock redemption or partial liquidation. That involves a credit to cash and a debit to capital stock. In other cases,

---

4   U.S. Constitution, Amendment 16: The Congress shall have power to lay and collect taxes on incomes, from whatever source derived, without apportionment among the several States, and without regard to any census or enumeration.

5   IRC § 61: [G]ross income means all income from whatever source derived . . . "

6   *Macomber* at 226.

7   *Id.* at 211.

the entity purchases its own shares with the intention of holding the shares for a short period and then re-selling them. This creates treasury stock.

EXAMPLE 61

Treasury Stock

- ABC, Inc. has one million shares outstanding. Shares currently trade at $100 per share.

- ABC, Inc. purchases 10,000 shares for $100 each, intending to hold them for a short period.

- A month later, ABC sells the 10,000 shares for $110 each.

- How must ABC account for these transactions?

Because an entity cannot own itself, special accounting rules are necessary to deal with treasury stock. In EXAMPLE 61, ABC, Inc. paid $1,000,000 for the shares, which necessitates a credit to cash of $1,000,000. Because debits must equal credits, ABC must debit something regarding the shares for the same $1,000,000. But the debit cannot be to an asset because ABC, Inc. cannot own itself. It did not acquire an asset; instead, it got smaller, at least temporarily. Thus, the debit must be a reduction in equity.

If this were a permanent equity reduction—a partial liquidation—that is what would occur. It would be a debit to capital stock of $1,000,000 with the corresponding $1,000,000 cash credit. If the stock had a par or stated value, the debit would be partially to par value and partially to excess paid in capital. The transaction would not affect the income statement and would signal to balance sheet users that the entity partially liquidated.

That, however, is inconsistent with the facts of EXAMPLE 61 in which ABC, Inc. intended to hold its own shares for a short period and then to re-sell them. GAAP requires such shares—called treasury stock—to be recorded in a contra-equity account. Just as accumulated depreciation is a contra-asset (a negative on the left side of the balance sheet), treasury stock is a *negative on the right side of the balance sheet*, as illustrated in **Figure 131**. This treatment avoids showing the treasury shares as an asset, but instead shows them on the balance sheet as a temporary equity _reduction_.

ABC. Inc. Balance Sheet	
Assets	Liabilities
	Equity
	Capital Stock
	Less Treasury Stock
	Net Stock
	Retained Earnings
	Total Equity
Total Assets	Liabilities & Equity

Figure 131: Balance Sheet

When ABC, Inc. sells the 10,000 shares treasury stock for $110 per share, it would debit cash for $1,100,000, credit treasury stock for $1,000,000 and credit excess paid in capital or some other capital account for $100,000. It would *not* credit income for the $100,000 "profit" and it would *not* credit retained earnings.

General Journal for ABC, INC.			
Date	Account	Debit	Credit
8/1	**Treasury Stock**	1,000,000	
	Capital Stock		1,000,000
	Purchase of 10,000 shares of Treasury Stock.		
9/1	**Cash**	1,100,000	
	Treasury Stock		1,000,000
	Excess Paid-in Capital		100,000
	Sale of 10,000 shares of Treasury Stock for cost plus $100,000.		

Figure 132: Journal for Purchase and Later Sale of Treasury Stock

LESSON TEN

RATIO ANALYSIS

Applied Accounting

■ ■ ■

Lesson Objectives

1. Student will learn about the basic five types of financial ratios.

2. Student will be able to apply many ratios to a set of financial statements.

3. Student will be able to analyze basic financial ratios in relation to a legal matter.

4. Student will be able to determine ranges for common financial ratios.

Terminology Introduced

*   Liquidity ratio.

*   Solvency ratio.

*   Profitability ratio.

*   Turnover ratio.

*   Earnings ratio.

*   Quick ratio.

*   Current ratio.

*   P/E ratio.

*   Earnings per share.

*   Inventory turnover.

*   Fixed asset turnover.

*   Debt/equity ratio.

*   Gross profit ratio.

This LESSON involves applied accounting: how we use and analyze financial statements. We do this by using ratios. A ratio takes one number from a financial statement and divides it by another. For example, the Debt/Assets ratio divides debt by total assets. This tells us how leveraged an entity is. In some industries high leverage is normal, while in others it is not. The degree of leverage—be it 10% or 90%—will help us understand whether an entity is solvent, whether it is likely to remain solvent, and whether it fits within a normal range for similar entities.

Lawyers need to understand the basics of ratios for several reasons. *First*, a lawyer needs to be able to interpret financial statements at a fundamental level. This is helpful not only when dealing with expert witnesses (the second reason) but also when the client lacks the funds for an expert.

Second, a lawyer needs to be able to deal with experts who can provide more sophisticated analyses of financial statements. Ratios put financial statements into perspective. They tell us how to use the numbers, to compare them sensibly to other periods and to other entities. They also help make predictions about the future. For example, ratio analysis will help predict whether an entity will remain solvent, whether it is becoming more or less successful, and how it compares to similar entities.

Third, a lawyer needs to understand forensic accounting. Comparing an entities ratios to industry and geographical standards or traditions, one can determine what the financial statements should look like. If they look worse, perhaps that reflect poor management or poor economic conditions; however, it could also involve an owner hiding or mis-labeling assets, liabilities, and cash flows.

Perhaps the legal matter involves family law. A lawyer needs to understand not only the current and past financial information, but also what the situation is likely to be in the foreseeable future. This helps value an entity and to predict likely earnings or losses. The same is true in a tort matter. Perhaps the owner or key employee was injured. A lawyer needs to evaluation the entity damage from the injury, which requires valuation and predictions.

Five main _types_ of ratios are common:

1.   Liquidity Ratios.

2.   Leverage/Solvency Ratios.

3.   Profitability Ratios.

4.   Earnings Ratios.

5.   Turnover Ratios.

Accountants and financial analysts may have other categories, but these are the main ones a lawyer should be familiar with. Each involves multiple separate ratios.

1. LIQUIDITY RATIOS

Liquidity involves the ability of a person/entity to pay its obligations in the short term—typically one year or less. As discussed in various Lessons, liquid assets are those easily converted into cash. They form the working capital of a business—the assets used for day-to-day operations to pay expenses, service debts, and to acquire inventory and to maintain assets. Too much liquidity suggests a person is not wisely investing assets. Too little suggests the person may not be able to operate as it may lack sufficient cash to pay what is due.

Accountants commonly use three liquidity ratios

- Current Ratio.
- Quick Ratio.
- Cash Ratio.

A. CURRENT RATIO

A balance sheet should separate assets into categories—mostly current and fixed. Current assets are liquid and might be understood as short-term. Cash, marketable financial instruments, accounts receivable, and inventory are the most common current assets. They are either cash, something easily converted to cash, or something likely to be turned into cash (sold) within one year. Pre-paid expenses and supplies are also current assets as they typically will be consumed within one year.

Marketable securities which, per FAS 115, are classified as *held-to-maturity* securities are not listed as current assets. As explained in LESSON 8B, they are also listed at historical cost and are not marked to market. The management/accounting judgment regarding whether to classify marketable securities as *held for trading, available for sale,* or *held to maturity* affects important ratios. As learned in the SVB bank collapse in March 2023, the consequences can be disastrous.

A balance sheet should similarly separate liabilities into categories—mostly current and long-term or fixed. Current liabilities are those due within the next twelve months. Fixed liabilities are all others.

The current ratio is:

$$\frac{(Current\ Assets)}{Current\ Liabilities}$$

Although generally all ratios are best analyzed in relation to specific industry standards and common ranges, a rule-of-thumb for the current ratio is for it to be 2:1, which presents a very strong position. A 1:1 ratio may be acceptable, but less probably raises some concerns. Thus, current assets should be approximately twice current liabilities. In such a situation, the entity would expect to be able to service all expected obligations within the next year.

Figure 133 shows the JOE'S BAR & GRILL balance sheet for December 31. It has a ludicrously high current ratio of about ten to one. Including pre-paid rent as a current asset distorts the ratio because it does not have any rent liability. Joe's may need to replenish the pre-paid amount annually, as it will also need to annually renew the permit and annual license fee.

Without examining any other ratios, one could reasonably (initially) posit that JOE'S has far too much cash. One might start thinking the entity should reduce its cash by about $150,000, perhaps through a distribution or an expansion. The business is quite young; hence, expansion might be pre-mature. JOE'S might also consider longer term investments if it wants to remain highly liquid. Of course, it would not be wise to make any decision based on a single financial ratio.

JOE'S BAR & GRILL Balance Sheet December 31			
Assets		**Liabilities**	
Current		Current	
Cash	$185,370.00	Util. Payable	$1,000.00
Inventory	15,000.00	Note Payable	8,840.13
Supplies	2,000.00	Wages Payable	10,000.00
Accounts Rec.	7,500.00	Wage Tax Payable	897.61
Less Allowance	375.00	Interest Payable	250.00
	7,125.00	Bonus Payable	1,961.73
Local Permit	916.67		
Liq. Lic. Fee	1,604.17		
Pre-Paid Rent	20,000.00		
Total Current	**232,015.84**	**Total Current**	**22,949.52**
Fixed Assets		**Long-Term**	
Machinery	31,000.00	Note Payable	41,159.85
Acc. Depr.	(516,67)		
	30,483.33	**Total Liabilities**	**64,109.37**
Liquor License	78,250.00		
Trademark	5,950.00	**Owner's Equity**	
Emp. Train.	19,444.45	Scott	150,000.00
Signs	4,000.00	Adrian	150,000.00
Acc. Depr.	(133.33)	R/E	5,900.92
	3,866.67		
Total Fixed	**137,994.45**	**Total Equity**	**305,900.92**
Total Assets	**$370,010.29**	**Liabilities & Equity**	**$370,010.29**

Figure 133: Balance Sheet

B. QUICK RATIO

The Quick Ratio is a more conservative view of liquidity. It is also known as the Acid Test Ratio. While the denominator remains as current liabilities, the numerator includes only cash and cash equivalents, plus receivables and short-term investments. It pointedly eliminates inventory. Pre-paid expenses are also excluded, as they likely are not refundable and thus cannot provide liquidity for immediate needs. Essentially, the ratio examines how well the entity can operate if sales end. The formula is:

$$\frac{(Cash + Cash\ Equivalents + Receivables + Short\ term\ Investments)}{(Current\ Liabilities)}$$

A quick ratio of 1:1 is generally considered strong, although 0.5:1 might be acceptable. If an entity has a quick ratio under 1:1, it should closely examine the timing of receivable and payables. Perhaps receivables are due on average in 30 days while payables are due in 180. If so, sufficient cash would seem likely to become available. In contrast, if payables are due within 30 days and receivables mostly due in 180, the entity may run out of cash quite soon.

Creditors—particularly large ones—may include references to current and quick ratios in the lending agreement. For example, one might agree to lend funds for a term (perhaps one year or three) but make the entire loan callable (due immediately) if the current ratio falls below 1:1 or the quick ratio falls below 0.5:1. Such low ratios indicate liquidity problems and possible insolvency, creditors will want to be paid sooner rather than to risk entity bankruptcy.

Similar analytic tools exist for humans. Many people seek to have at least savings equals at least to six months of living expenses. With that, they could survive six months if all income suddenly stopped, or longer if there were to economize. Far too many people live paycheck-to-paycheck: if they do not get paid Friday, they may not have food soon thereafter. Or, if they lose their job, they may be on the street in a month. For entities, a strong current and quick ratio will eliminate that level of stress: they provide time to handle unfortunate/unexpected situations.

C. CASH RATIO

The Cash Ratio reduces the numerator merely to cash and cash equivalents, eliminating receivables and anything but the most liquid of investments. The formula is:

$$\frac{(Cash + Cash\ Equivalents)}{(Current\ Liabilities)}$$

Banks must be particularly aware of the cash ratio because demand deposits are the most current of current assets. Marking cash equivalents to market is essential—at least in footnotes—for a proper analysis of the cash and other liquidity ratios. Whether an entity recognizes otherwise unrealized losses is less important than whether they properly admit them for the balance sheet.

For example, consider **Figure 134**—the December 31, 2022, consolidated balance sheet for Silicon Valley Bank, which closed on March 7, 2023.

The cash ratio was generally acceptable:

$$\frac{39,872,000,000}{80,753,000,000}$$

That includes only demand deposits in the denominator. But look at the equity. It was reported at $16,004,000,000, down slightly from a year earlier when it was $16,236,000,000. But on 12/31/21, unrealized losses on *held-to-maturity* securities were about $968,000,000 or about 6% of equity. On 12/31/22, unrealized losses were $15,152,000,000 or almost 95% of equity. Goodwill and other illiquid intangibles were $511,000,000, which comprised 60% of the $852 million equity if *held-to-maturity* securities were marked to market. Going concern doubt was huge and obvious, *but undiscussed in the auditor's report.*[1] The report was issued on 2/24/23, eleven days before the collapse. Interest rates had risen since 12/31/22, which meant the $91 billion *held-to-maturity* (and the $26 billion *available-for-sale*) securities had certainly lost value. The entity was facially insolvent but received an almost clean audit report (it included an unrelated audit concern[2]).

---

[1]   SVB 10K (filed 2/24/23) at 91–94.

[2]   *Id.*

(Dollars in millions, except par value and share data)	December 31, 2022	December 31, 2021
Assets		
Cash and cash equivalents	$ 13,803	$ 14,586
Available-for-sale securities, at fair value (cost of $28,602 and $27,370, respectively, including $530 and $61 pledged as collateral, respectively)	26,069	27,221
Held-to-maturity securities, at amortized cost and net of allowance for credit losses of $6 and $7 (fair value of $76,169 and $97,227, respectively)	91,321	98,195
Non-marketable and other equity securities	2,664	2,543
Total investment securities	120,054	127,959
Loans, amortized cost	74,250	66,276
Allowance for credit losses: loans	(636)	(422)
Net loans	73,614	65,854
Premises and equipment, net of accumulated depreciation and amortization	394	270
Goodwill	375	375
Other intangible assets, net	136	160
Lease right-of-use assets	335	313
Accrued interest receivable and other assets	3,082	1,791
Total assets	$ 211,793	$ 211,308
Liabilities and total equity		
Liabilities:		
Noninterest-bearing demand deposits	$ 80,753	$ 125,851
Interest-bearing deposits	92,356	63,352
Total deposits	173,109	189,203
Short-term borrowings	13,565	71
Lease liabilities	413	388
Other liabilities	3,041	2,467
Long-term debt	5,370	2,570
Total liabilities	195,498	194,699
Commitments and contingencies (Note 21 and Note 26)		
SVBFG stockholders' equity:		
Preferred stock, $0.001 par value, 20,000,000 shares authorized; 383,500 and 383,500 shares issued and outstanding, respectively	3,646	3,646
Common stock, $0.001 par value, 150,000,000 shares authorized; 59,171,883 and 58,748,469 shares issued and outstanding, respectively	—	—
Additional paid-in capital	5,318	5,157
Retained earnings	8,951	7,442
Accumulated other comprehensive income (loss)	(1,911)	(9)
Total SVBFG stockholders' equity	16,004	16,236
Noncontrolling interests	291	373
Total equity	16,295	16,609
Total liabilities and total equity	$ 211,793	$ 211,308

Figure 134: SVB Balance Sheet

The SVB collapse was remarkable, but not surprising to anyone who glanced at page 95 of the 193-page 10-K.[3] One wonders why it took large depositors eleven days before they precipitated a run on the bank. Discovering the problems did not require sophisticated accounting knowledge or investigation. The bank was surely insolvent when the **Figure 129** balance sheet was issued. That practically leaps off the page. That the auditors neglected to emphasize it (or issue a qualified or adverse opinion) is disturbing.

2. LEVERAGE/SOLVENCY RATIOS

Solvency—or better *insolvency*—has two forms. One focuses on cash-flows and liquidity: can you pay what is due? Under this view, an entity may be solvent in that its assets exceed liabilities; however, it may be insolvent because its liquidity is low. That results from having large short-term liabilities but large long-term investments which cannot easily be liquidated. Liquidity ratios—current, acid-test, and cash—focus on this view of solvency.

---

[3] *Id.* At 95.

A second view of solvency focuses on the balance sheet. Essentially, do you have any equity and is it sufficient? Accountant commonly use several:

- Debt/Equity Ratio (D/E).
- Debt/Assets Ratio (D/A).
- Equity/Assets Ratio (E/A) (Equity Ratio).
- Interest Coverage Ratio.

The first three provide the exact same information because of the basic accounting equation:

$$Assets = Liabilities + Equity$$

For example, if assets = 5, liabilities = 3, then equity = 2. D/E = 3/2. D/A = 3/5 and E/A = 2/5. In other words, if you know one of the three ratios, you also know the other two. The numbers will differ, but the conclusion will be identical.

A. DEBT/EQUITY RATIO (D/E)[4]

The formula is:

$$\frac{(Total\ Debt)}{(Total\ Equity)}$$

Industries vary greatly regarding the traditional or appropriate amount of leverage (debt) as compared to assets or equity. In some cases, 50% leverage, which is a 1:1 D/E ratio, would be acceptable. That would mean assets are twice liabilities. It would equate to a 1:2 A/D ratio, and a 1:1 Equity ratio. Other industries might view 80% leverage traditional. That equates to a 4:1 D/E ratio, a 4:5 D/A ratio, and a 1:4 Equity ratio.

A very general rule-of-thumb suggests a D/E ratio greater than 1 is cause for concern. Banks, however, have their own ratio standards, as do most industries. For banks, a D/E ratio greater than 33 is generally unacceptable.[5] The ratio is high considering the type of business: all deposits are debts. In 2022, most large U.S. banks had a D/E ratio of 12 to 15, which was generally thought to be healthy. In **Figure 134**, the SVB D/E ratio was 8.186, compared to 8.531 at the end of 2021. however, with the *held-to-maturity* securities marked to market (which they were not), the 2022 ratio was only .004. Interest rates rose between 12/31/22 (the date of the balance sheet and auditor's report) and 2/24/23 (the date the

---

[4]   The debt/asset ratio and the equity/debt ratio will produce different numbers than the D/E; however, they provide the same information.

[5]   Basel III. Banks use more complicated ratios than the D/E to evaluate solvency in what is commonly called a stress test. An SLR Ratio of at least 3% is required internationally. Full discussion of this is beyond this text/course. The D/E is good rough substitute, but it likely exceeds the SLR.

statement and report were issued); as a result, the held-to-maturity securities were surely lower in value, causing the true amount of equity to be negative.[6]

For individuals, a D/E ratio of 4 is typically required for a home loan. That equates to a 20% down payment. Buyers who lack that level of down payments typically must provide a co-signatory or mortgage insurance.

B. INTEREST COVERAGE RATIO

Debtors must pay interest to creditors; thus, high amounts of debt correlate with high interest costs. How easily an entity services debt is an important factor in evaluating leverage levels and solvency. The commonly used interest coverage ratio is:

$$\frac{EBIT}{(Interest\ Expense)}$$

This is an income statement ratio. As such, it applies for a period—perhaps a year, quarter, or month. The numerator is typically earnings before interest and taxes (EBIT). The numerator eliminates interest so that interest is not a function of itself. It typically eliminates taxes because interest is typically deductible for tax purposes.

The denominator can be either interest expense, which is an accrual method of accounting term, or it could be interest paid during the period. The two numbers may be very similar or identical; however, if they are not, interest paid is more useful in the short run. To obtain a longer-term picture of financial health, accrued interest expense will paint a more accurate picture. One should look at both.

The numerator could also be EBITDA (earnings before interest, taxes, depreciation, and amortization). Although depreciation and amortization are real economic expenses (however imprecise they may be), they are not cash flows (at least not in the near term); hence, eliminating depreciation and amortization is useful in determining *near-term* financial health.

3. PROFITABILITY RATIOS

Many profitability ratios exist. The two most well-known are:

- Return on assets (ROA).
- Return on equity (ROE).

---

[6] Publicly available information is insufficient to measure the amount of the likely deficiency. SVB had non-marketable fixed assets with historical costs of several billion dollars. In the midst of a bank run, they would likely be worth far less. Thus, by the date the financial statements were issued, SVB almost certainly had negative equity of 3 to 5 billion dollars. That depositors neglected to precipitate a bank run for 11 days is remarkable.

A. RETURN ON ASSETS RATIO (ROA)

$$\frac{(Net\ Income)}{(Total\ Assets)}$$

By itself, the ratio says little, although it is appropriately compared to market interest rates or returns on similar assets. In the context of the specific industry and specific mix of assets, it informs whether the entity is as profitable (and productive) as comparable entities. Comparisons are best within the same line of business. Geographical comparisons are also important. For example, the return on an auto parts store in the rural mid-west may traditionally differ from a similar store in a large city on the west coast.

An entity should also compare this and other ratios to those of prior periods: is the return on assets stable, or it is increasing or decreasing? The answer can be very informative, especially in the context of other ratios. Forensically, this ratio can be useful. Consider EXAMPLE 62.

EXAMPLE 62

Forensic Example

- Father owns and operates a pharmacy in a small city. Former spouse/Mother seeks increased child support. Father's reported income does not justify a significant increase; however, Mother suspects Father is hiding income by not reporting significant sales.

- How might one forensically examine Father's financial statements?

Owner/operated small businesses with significant "small amount" cash flows can tempt an owner to "pocket" some sales. For example, a pharmacy likely sells, in addition to medications, shampoo, face creams, and other sundry items, few of which sell for large amounts. The owner should have sufficient internal controls to protect against employee theft— either inventory theft or embezzlement through the non-reporting of sales and pocketing of receipts. Those internal controls, however, would not apply to the owner. Assuming the statements are unaudited (which is almost certain for a small business), the owner could easily supply him/herself with many items and never be detected. Moreover, the owner could pocket cash from sales and not run them through a cash register. That is criminal behavior if it affects sales tax or income tax; however, it is not easy to detect.

To detect such shenanigans, one would look at a variety of ratios. Statistics regarding the average return on assets for a pharmacy are easily available, as would be the average return for a pharmacy of a similar size in a similar sized city. Likely state government has such information specific to the state.

Suppose in EXAMPLE 62, the ROA is 3%, meaning the business reports profits equal to 3% of assets. One would look to see if the number is comparable to prior periods. Someone planning a divorce and hoping to hide income might start to pocket sales proceeds a year or two prior to the divorce or suddenly in the year of the divorce. The pattern would be informative.

Nationally, the 2022 ROA for retail pharmacies was about 7.5%. Father's business is 450 basis points below that average. If total assets equal $1,000,000, then about $45,000 of profit is missing. It may be because he is a poor manager, or perhaps the economy in the area or neighborhood is unusually bad. Or he might be hiding it. A forensic analysis would also examine the return on square footage in the store, return per employee or return as a function of wages. Profit margins and inventory turn-over ratios could also help distinguish income hiding from poor management.

Parallel, the forensic analyst would also do a life-style audit. Is Father's apparent lifestyle—size of home, automobiles, expenditures for clothing, travel, and eating out—are they consistent with his reported income. Information regarding average spending habits is easily obtainable both nationally and by state. Perhaps Father's lifestyle is about $50,000 greater annually than justified by his reported income. That could indicate he is wasteful, not thrifty, or perhaps he had some emergency needs this year. Or perhaps he is spending currency for many items rather than charging expenses or paying by check. If one suspects significant use of cash, then one would inquire about the source: were there bank withdrawals or gifts, or did he have a large stash of cash buried in the backyard? If he has no plausible explanation, he is probably pocketing many small sales and not using the cash register. An owner can easily do that, and customers often do not check receipts, especially if they are only paying $10 or $20. Bars, restaurants, laundromats, and personal care businesses often deal in substantial amounts of currency, which can be tempting and easily hidden.

B. RETURN ON EQUITY RATIO (ROE)

$$\frac{(Net\ Income)}{(Equity)}$$

The return on equity ratio provides information on equity returns and thus is directly affected by debt. It represents the return owners earn on *their* investment—the equity. That makes it an important number from their perspective. Large amounts of debt, however, can cause the ratio to be less helpful to others, such as creditors. If the entity has a typical debt/equity ratio, the return on equity is similar in its usefulness as the ROA. But if the entity is highly leveraged, the ROE may be fleeting as well as misleading.

EXAMPLE 63

Return on Equity Example

- A and B each have $1,000,000 in assets with a return on assets of $100,000.
- A has 250,000 of liabilities. B has $750,000 of liabilities.
- Compare the Return on Equity for A and B.

In EXAMPLE 63, Both A and B have a return on assets of 10% $\left(\frac{100,000}{1,000,000}\right)$. A's return on equity would be 13.3% $\left(\frac{100,000}{750,000}\right)$. B's return on equity would be much higher at 40% $\left(\frac{100,000}{250,000}\right)$. The example demonstrates how significant leverage can increase the return on equity. The example is flawed because it assumes the same return on assets. B's additional debt, however, would not free. As a result, B's income would be lower by the cost of servicing that debt. Making the example more realistic produces a noteworthy result.

EXAMPLE 64

Return on Equity Example Modified

- A and B each have $1,000,000 in assets with a return on assets of $100,000.
- A has 250,000 of liabilities. B has $750,000 of liabilities.
- Both A and B pay 5% interest annually on debt.
- A and B each have $112,000 income before interest.
- Compare the Return on Equity for A and B.

In EXAMPLE 64, A's income after $12,500 interest expense is $100,000 but B's is only $75,000, following $37,500 of interest expense. A's return on assets is 10% $\left(\frac{100,000}{1,000,000}\right)$ and A's return on equity is 13.3%. In contrast, B's return on assets would be 7.5% $\left(\frac{75,000}{1,000,000}\right)$, and B's return on equity would be at 30% $\left(\frac{75,000}{250,000}\right)$. The debt thus increased B's return on equity substantially, although not by as large an amount as the flawed EXAMPLE 63.

Change B's leverage in EXAMPLE 64 $\left(\frac{62,500}{1,000,000}\right)$ to 90%. B's interest expense would be $45,000 per year and B's income after interest would be only $62,500. B's return on assets would drop to 6.25% but B's return on equity would balloon to 62.5% $\left(\frac{62,500}{100,000}\right)$.

EXAMPLE 64, especially with its modification, illustrates how leverage will significantly increase the return on equity assuming the interest on the debt is lower than the return on assets. One must not, however, draw hasty conclusions from the modified example. In Example 64, A's leverage ratio is only 25%. A has sufficient equity to withstand an economic downturn in which income drops or asset values drop. For example, if A's return on assets dropped to 4%, A would still have income after interest of $27,500. A's return on assets would be 2.75% and A's return on equity would be 5%.

In contrast, if B's return on assets dropped to 4%, B's income after interest would be 2,500. B's return on assets would be only 0.25% and B's leverage return on equity would be 5%. At 90% leverage, B's return on assets would be *negative* 0.5%, although the return on equity would remain at 5%. This occurs because interest rates on debt are traditionally fixed, while return on assets fluctuates.

Look more closely at EXAMPLE 64, exploring why the return on assets might have decreased and what else might have occurred. Perhaps a general economic downturn caused demand for products generally to drop, reducing sales across the economy. A could much more easily weather such an economic storm than could B, particularly modified B. Perhaps interest rates rose precipitating the economic downturn. If so, asset values would tend to decrease. A has sufficient equity to withstand significant decreases in asset values. B has much less equity and thus less room for asset drops. Modified B has almost no room for decreases in asset values.

To make the potential situation more dire, if the hypothesized economic downturn results from interest rate increases, both A and B will likely need to re-finance their respective debt at some point, and at higher rates. A might consider selling assets, albeit at probably losses, to reduce the need for new financing. A would have room to consider that option because of A's high equity ratio. B, in contrast, would have far fewer options to reduce its size or to move to a different line of business: B's leverage ratio (particularly with decreased asset values) would likely preclude new financing. Creditors would focus on the leverage ratio and likely demand much higher interest rates because of increased risk for them.

To summarize, the return on equity ratio is important, but viewed in isolation it can present a very incomplete picture. High leverage can produce high returns on equity, but high leverage can also rely economic assumptions that can quickly become invalid.

4. EARNINGS RATIOS

Earnings analysis is very important with two ratios being particularly significant:

- Earnings per share (EPS).
- Price to Earnings Ratio (P/E).

A. EARNINGS PER SHARE (EPS)

Earnings per share (EPS) is one of the most well-known ratios. It is:

$$\frac{(Net\ Income)}{(Number\ of\ Shares\ Outstanding)}$$

In isolation, it means very little because the number of outstanding shares can be arbitrary. For example, an entity with $10,000,000 equity and $1,000,000 of net income may have one owner and a single share outstanding; or, it may have 100 owners with a million shares outstanding. When compared to prior periods, the number becomes more useful. When compared to the price or value of the shares, it becomes paramount.

Within the ratio, both the numerator and the denominator can vary; hence users must be certain they are comparing the same ratios using the same definitions. Net income can be net income. Often, an entity will modify net earnings to eliminate preferred stock dividends and extraordinary (non-recurring) items.

The denominator will often vary. It may be reported using three formats: regular, diluted, and fully diluted. Regular earnings per share would be the ratio shown above with the shares outstanding either being the end of the period number of common shares, or a weighted average of outstanding shares during the year. Diluted EPS would increase the number of "outstanding shares" by the predicted number of shares which will result from likely conversions. These may be commonly referred to as those "in the money." Examples are convertible preferred stock, convertible bonds, and stock options. Those "in the money" would be ones which have not been converted or exercised, but for which conversion or exercise is economically sensible. Fully diluted EPS includes all possible conversions and options, including those which are not currently viable.

B. PRICE TO EARNINGS RATIO (P/E)

An entity's P/E ratio is essential to its valuation. Indeed, it is the valuation. Although various methods exist to value an entity,[7] by far the

---

[7] Valuing small businesses is complex and beyond this article's scope. Experts use multiple methods and various earnings measures, such as EBIT (earnings before interest and taxes) or EBITDA (earnings before interest, taxes, depreciation, and amortization). Some use revenue

most common is a multiple of earnings. P/E ratios for publicly traded companies are often in the mid-teens up to the mid-twenties, with significant variations by industry. Over the past 75 years, the S & P 500 average P/E ratio has been as low as 5.9 in June 1949, and as high as 122.41 in June 2009. In February 2023, it was 22.53.[8] On May 3, 2023, Apple traded at a P/E ratio of 28.43, Tesla at 47.26, GM at 5.105, and ATT at 6.72. Standing alone, the P/E ratio merely informs the price of the stock at that moment. Very generally, a high ratio suggests investors expect earnings to increase, while a low P/E suggests investors expect decreasing earnings.

Closely held entities typically have lower P/E ratios than do publicly traded ones. Industries and locals vary, but very generally a closely held entity might sell for 3–4 times earnings.

5. TURNOVER RATIOS

Turnover ratios also provide useful information regarding the health and efficiency of an entity. Common ones are:

- Accounts Receivable Turnover Ratio.
- Inventory Turnover Ratio.
- Asset Turnover Ratio.

---

multiples and most use multi-year averages. The multiple varies by business size with larger businesses having higher multiples. Very-small businesses may result in a multiple of merely 1.5. Multiples vary, as well, by industry and business age. New businesses often fail, justifying a lower multiple than a more established firm. See, *e.g.*, Hammond, *What's the Value of My Business? The Ins and Outs of EBITDA Multiples* (2019). https://www.cronkhitecapital.com/articles/2019/4/1/business-valuation.

Courts typically choose among three valuation methods. A 2020 Nebraska appellate court explained:

> There's asset approach, and what you're doing there is you're looking at the hard assets of the company, you're looking at the liabilities of the company and you're really just subtracting off those liabilities from the assets and coming up with what the value is. That's kind of the asset approach.

> There's a market approach. Most people would be familiar with that from a real estate perspective. It's—you know, when you're do [sic] real estate you look at a house—if you can find a house across the street that sold and it's the same as your house, it's a good indication of what your house is. The same thing with business valuation. If you can find the sale of another business like your business that you're valuing, it's a good indication of what your business is worth. So that's kind of the market approach.

> And then the last approach is the income approach. Again, you're looking at the financial benefits of the company, the income of the company and you're translating that into a value. You're converting that income stream to a value and that's the income approach.

Bornhorst v. Bornhorst, 941 N.W.2d 769, 783 (Neb. App. 2020).

8   https://www.macrotrends.net/2577/sp-500-pe-ratio-price-to-earnings-chart

A. ACCOUNTS RECEIVABLE TURNOVER RATIO

Accounts receivable turnover measures how quickly an entity collects its receivable. It is related to the aging process discussed in LESSON EIGHT-A. The ratio is:

$$\frac{(Net\ Credit\ Sales)}{(Average\ Accounts\ Receivable)}$$

The numerator excludes cash sales. As with other ratios, this one standing by itself may not be informative. Compared to other periods, however, it can explain or predict increasing or decreasing liquidity. A number of one results if the entity collects it's full amount of receivables once per period. The period could be a month, a quarter, or a year.

Generally, a high number suggests effective collection practices; however, it could result from very conservative credit approval rates. Thus, management may see a high number and initially believe the entity is highly efficient at collection procedures. But a closer look may show lower management was overly conservative in granting credit and thus missed the opportunity for greater sales.

B. INVENTORY TURNOVER RATIO

Inventory turnover is also called an activity ratio. It measures how frequently an entity sells its average inventory. Naturally, this varies greatly by the type of business as well as individual products. For example, a grocery store will have a high inventory turnover because food spoils and thus must be sold quickly. A hardware store, in contrast, will still want frequent sales, but will be less concerned with the turnover rate because its inventory—such as hammers and nails—have a far longer shelf life than bread or milk. The ratio is:

$$\frac{(Cost\ of\ Goods\ Sold)}{(Average\ Inventory)}$$

A higher than normal for the industry and product at least superficially appears good because it indicates strong sales. However, it also suggests the entity may have insufficient inventory on hand to meet demand and thus it risks running out of items and thus losing sales and customers. A high inventory ratio may also suggest the entity consider raising prices, which would lower the ratio but with greater profits.

In contrast a low ratio suggests sluggish sales and too much inventory. Items sitting on a shelf do not produce income until they are sold, and they risk deterioration or obsolescence. Thus, a low ratio would suggest management should slow down acquisitions of new inventory and also consider lowering prices to "move the merchandise."

C. ASSET TURNOVER RATIO

Asset turnover is an efficiency or productivity ratio that varies tremendously by industry. Thus, one uses it to compare current results to prior periods or to industry standards. The ratio is:

$$\frac{Sales}{(Average\ Assets)}$$

An alternative ratio would focus on fixed assets, rather than total assets. This eliminates current assets, such as cash, receivables, and inventory from the ratio. It may be referred to as *FAT* for fixed asset turnover.

$$\frac{Sales}{(Average\ Fixed\ Assets)}$$

This tells management how efficiently an entity is using its assets to produce revenue. Unlike inventory turnover, it does not directly say anything about how quickly the entity replaces anything. This is related to the concept of an entity being "capital intensive," or not, discussed in LESSONS SEVEN and NINE. For example, a retail business may seek a FAT of perhaps 3. It would have relatively low investment in fixed assets with perhaps a building, shelving, and cash registers. In contrast, an electric utility company would typically have massive investments in fixed assets which have a very long life and thus produce a low asset turnover ratio.

GLOSSARY OF FINANCIAL, TAX, ACCOUNTING, AND ECONOMIC TERMS *PLUS* RELATED ACRONYMS

Much of Finance, Accounting, and Economics involve definitions, as does much of law. If a reader fails to understand the proper meaning of a term, that reader will not understand the contract, obligation, agreement, statute, or instrument. As every lawyer knows, confusion[1] in financial and legal matters is a dangerous situation.

But, in an even *worse* scenario, a reader may "think" he or she understands the terms, but actually does not. Remember this moral:

> *T'is best to know.*
> *T'is second best to know what you do not know.*
> *T'is worst to know what is not so.*

Some financial terms are *terms of art*, *i.e.*, everyone agrees on their definition. Many other terms, however, are *not* terms of art; as a result, people—including lawyers—frequently disagree regarding them. An attorney may view this phenomenon from three angles:

1. *Avoid Litigation* (the *moral* angle): define all terms and ensure the other parties agree with your definitions, which should be prominent and clear. If your definition is unconventional, be clear about that, as well. If all parties do not agree on the definitions, you lack a meeting of the minds and you do not have a valid contract.

2. *Take Advantage* (the risky/zealous/*amoral* angle): use terms to your advantage. Use terms of art correctly. In particular, if you perceive another party misunderstands the term to his disadvantage, use the term and later insist on the proper meaning—even if that risks litigation. You should win, as a term of art, if clearly used in writing, is not subject to debate. For other terms, be precise, but not so clearly precise. For example, slyly alter compounding terms or periods or stated nominal rates when apparent small change actually result in large differences. If you do so openly—or if you are detected—concede another factor (which may appear large to the uninformed, but which is actually insignificant relative to your proposed change). The other party will believe

---

[1]   Except, perhaps, for the Civil Law Doctrine of Confusion. In Civil Law, confusion refers to the financial situation in which debtor and creditor become the same; as a result, the debt is confused.

he has won, when he actually has lost. Or, when using a non term-of-art, either slyly insert a definition which supports you, or—if you are in the stronger position—line up experts to testify to your definition and bully your way through the ultimate conflict.

To be very clear: I do not recommend this second approach; however, despite its moral deficiencies, it is probably acceptable under most state bar rules. At the very least, lawyers should be aware that others may use this approach.

3. ***Be Wary*** (the *smart* angle): if you ever detect a lawyer/banker/investment advisor using Angle B, never, ever trust him again and never do business with him again. If he will cheat you on one issue, he is likely cheating you on many others. Then practice Angle A.

The following are some common terms used in this course. This is by no means a complete—*or even nearly complete*—list of important terminology. Several good Financial Dictionaries are available.[2] You should have one available. You should, however, be familiar with at least the following terms.

> Many free Finance, Tax Law, Accounting, and Economics dictionaries are available over the internet. Use them with *caution*. Most—probably all—define *non*-terms-of-art as if they have a fixed meaning. This is dangerous for lawyers. Also, many provide incorrect definitions for terms-of-art. That, too, is dangerous. Even the United States *Federal Reserve* website contains several erroneous or dangerously imprecise definitions.

In addition, Finance, Tax Law, Accounting, and Economics use many **ACRONYMS**. Lawyers should be familiar with these for several reasons.

1. Expert witnesses will use them. Lawyers need to be able to speak with their own expert, to cross examine an opponent's expert, and to translate to a judge or jury the terminology (including acronyms) used by an expert.

2. Financial, economic, and accounting reports may use these terms and acronyms. Lawyers need to understand them.

---

[2] Two examples are: John Downes and Jordan Elliot Goodman, DICTIONARY OF FINANCE AND INVESTMENT TERMS (BARRON'S 1995); John Downes and Jordan Elliot Goodman, FINANCE & INVESTMENT HANDBOOK (BARRON'S 1995).

3. Contracts will sometimes use these acronyms, with or
    without a clear reference. Lawyers need to be able to
    understand the terms, especially if the reference is unclear
    (which is an unfortunate situation, but a real possibility).

---

1. **Acid Test Ratio:** A commonly used accounting/financial ratio, this
    measures very short-term liquidity. Generally, the following formula
    represents it:

$$\left(\frac{cash + marketable\ securities}{current\ liabilities} \right)$$

In a very general rule, a one-to-one acid test ratio is good. A ratio much
higher indicates the entity may be overly liquid; it should therefore
consider more investment in operations. A ratio much below one-to-
one indicates *liquidity* problems in the near term; the entity should
therefore focus on raising more *working capital* so that it can satisfy
obligations as they come due.

One important point to remember about the *Acid Test Ratio* and the
Current Ratio: liabilities are fixed but assets other than cash are not.
Inventory can become worthless quickly as competitors produce a new
product. Accounts Receivable can become uncollectable as customers
become *insolvent*. Marketable Securities can quickly drop in value in
a *Bear Market*.

By itself, the *Acid Test*—or *Quick*—*Ratio* does not tell an analyst
much. But, in context of other *ratios* covering multiple years, as well
as quarters (so as to show trends) plus the *Statement of Cash Flows*,
an analyst can confidently predict short-term solvency.

2. **Accelerated Cost Recovery System:** *ACRS* [pronounced **ak**-ris].
    Under *IRC* section 168, taxpayers may use rapid (accelerated)
    depreciation for various assets. Since 1986, this system has also been
    known as **MACRS** for *Modified Accelerated Cost Recovery System*
    [pronounced **mac**-ris].

Accelerated Depreciation for tax purposes is generally much more
rapid than permitted by *GAAP* for *financial accounting*; hence, it
results in a book/tax disparity. This is one reason tax returns are a
poor measure of income for legal purposes. Rapid depreciation through
MACRS—or even more rapid write-offs under *IRC* section 179—will
cause income to be significantly lower than justified. For tax purposes,
this is exactly what Congress intended; however, when lawyers use tax
returns for other legal purposes, the low income (and if the
depreciating assets were recently acquired, lower trending income)
will predict even lower income for the future. In reality, the person or

entity's ability to invest in productive assets predicts higher economic income—the opposite of what the numbers suggests.

Congress first adopted accelerated tax depreciation in the 1960s under the Kennedy Administration. The intention was to stimulate investment in assets and thus stimulate the economy. The policy was successful. This is an example of *fiscal policy*.

Lawyers should be wary of statutes and contracts which use income tax returns as measures of income. In some cases—such as for wage earners with few deductions, such returns may provide a good measure of income. In contrast, however, as suggested above, tax returns are often a very poor measure of income for small businesses. The use of accelerated depreciation is only one reason for this—it lowers income artificially fast. Other tax provisions are similarly distorting. That is not to say they are unreasonable: Congress can legitimately use the tax system to foster fiscal and social policy—at least in the eyes of many. However, the more Congress uses the tax system as a tool, the less accurate it becomes in measuring income for other purposes. Tax lawyers and accountants are often skilled at using such policy provision to manipulate income—particularly over the short run.

For example, suppose B's income is a function of A's income. If A controls the definition of income (*e.g.,* by choosing depreciation, inventory, and capitalization methods), A also has the legal ability to distort B's income. This can be very disadvantageous for B. Practical examples include:

- A and B are partners with A being the managing partner.

- A and B are married (but soon to be divorced) and A controls the family business and finances.

- A hires B in a recording/publishing/producing contract whereby B's income is a percentage of the total income from the activity.

- In each example, A has the power to manipulate B's results. While using such power may be abusive and amoral, it is probably not illegal. Indeed, many persons, including many lawyers may view such manipulation as appropriate, if not admirable and "cutting edge." Hence, B's counsel must be aware of tax and accounting tools which facilitate A and then be prepared to oppose them or to shed light upon them.

3. **Accounting Principles and Assumptions:** *GAAP* has eleven fundamental principles and assumptions. Lawyers, legislators, regulators, and judges should heed these fundamental principles and assumptions and should note the following:

*Any accounting system—such as legal or contractual
definitions of income or profit—without such
fundamental rules is inherently flawed.*

For example, lawyers often refer to income or profits in a contract or other legal document. Unfortunately, many fail to define those words adequately or by reference to adequate standards. Similarly, many statutes or court decisions use the terms—including income, assets, profit, losses, expenses, and liabilities—and also provide a definition for them. Almost always, however, they do so without reference to any fundamental standards, rules, principles, or assumptions. State family law references to income and assets for alimony, child support, or property division are a common and unfortunate example. The results are often unfair, subject to manipulation, wasteful in terms of unnecessary litigation, and distorting in terms of the economic impact they have on decision making.

Each principle, test, and assumption has its own definition herein.

- The *Matching Principle*.
- The *Historical Cost Assumption*.
- The *Going Concern Assumption*.
- The *Monetary Unit Assumption*.
- The *Consistency Principle*.
- The *Revenue Recognition Principle*.
- The *Expense Recognition Principle*.
- The *All Events Test* (*this formerly comprised the revenue recognition and expense recognition principles*).
- The *Materiality Principle*.
- The *Separate Entity Assumption*.
- The *Time Period Assumption*.
- The *Full Disclosure Principle*.
- The *Conservatism Principle*.

4. **Accredited Investor:** As explained by the *SEC*:

Under the Securities Act of 1933, a company that offers or sells its securities must register the securities with the SEC or find an exemption from the registration requirements. The Act provides companies with a number of exemptions. For some of the exemptions, such as rules 505 and 506 of Regulation D, a company may sell its securities to what are known as "accredited investors."

The federal securities laws define the term accredited investor in <u>Rule 501 of Regulation D</u> as:

1. a bank, insurance company, registered investment company, business development company, or small business investment company;

2. an employee benefit plan, within the meaning of the Employee Retirement Income Security Act, if a bank, insurance company, or registered investment adviser makes the investment decisions, or if the plan has total assets in excess of $5 million;

3. a charitable organization, corporation, or partnership with assets exceeding $5 million;

4. a director, executive officer, or general partner of the company selling the securities;

5. a business in which all the equity owners are accredited investors;

6. a natural person who has individual net worth, or joint net worth with the person's spouse, that exceeds $1 million at the time of the purchase, excluding the value of the primary residence of such person;

7. a natural person with income exceeding $200,000 in each of the two most recent years or joint income with a spouse exceeding $300,000 for those years and a reasonable expectation of the same income level in the current year; or

8. a trust with assets in excess of $5 million, not formed to acquire the securities offered, whose purchases a sophisticated person makes.

http://www.sec.gov/answers/accred.htm.

5. **Accrual Method:** This has *two* distinct meanings, with four subparts and effectively three fundamental rules:

- For *Financial Accounting* purposes:

  - *Income recognition* is appropriate when *all events* have occurred such that the earner has a right to the item and the amount thereof can be determined with reasonable accuracy.

  - *Deductions* are appropriate when *all events* have occurred such the obligor must incur the item and the amount thereof can be determined with reasonable accuracy.

- For *Tax Accounting* purposes:
  - ○ *Income recognition* is appropriate at the earliest of three events:
    - ▪ When *all events* have occurred such that the earner has a right to the item and the amount thereof can be determined with reasonable accuracy.
    - ▪ When the item is due.
    - ▪ When the taxpayer has *received payment* of the item.
  - ○ *Deductions* are *normally* appropriate at the later of two events:
    - ▪ When *all events* have occurred such the obligor must incur the item and the amount thereof can be determined with reasonable accuracy.
    - ▪ When *economic performance* of the item has occurred.

For *Financial Accounting*, both the *income* and the *deduction* rules are essentially identical: they require satisfaction of the *all events* test, which is fundamental to the *Matching Principal*.

For United States *Tax Accounting*, the *income* and the *deduction* rules differ dramatically in definition, but have essentially the same impact:

- The *income rule* often requires recognition *before* satisfaction of the *all events* test; as a result, it *materially* *increases* the effective tax rate on the affected items and it distorts the meaning of income.

- The *deduction rule* often requires recognition *after* satisfaction of the *all events* test; as a result, it also materially *increases* the effective tax rate on the affected items (by materially decreasing the effective tax benefit) and it, distorts the meaning of *net income*.

6. **Acquisition Premium:** *AP:* This is the amount by which a financial instrument's market price exceeds its stated or face value. A basic law of economics and finance is:

   As interest rates <u>fall</u>, bond values <u>rise</u>.

Similarly:

As interest rates rise, bond values fall.

Bond values and interest rates are thus inversely related.

Generally, *bonds*, *debentures* and other financial instruments have fixed, stated or coupon rates; hence, their internal or stated interest rates do not float or adjust as market interest rates change. Such market rates change continuously during trading hours. If the market rate for a particular instrument falls below the instrument's stated rate, the price of the instrument will naturally rise. Purchasers must therefore pay an *acquisition premium* for the instrument.

IRC section 1272(a)(7) provides a modified straight-line method for *amortizing acquisition* premium for tax purposes; as a result, taxpayers report—and pay tax upon—a more accurate amount of interest than the instrument itself will reflect. Treasury Regulation section 1.1272–2 provides an alternate—and even more accurate—method of amortizing *acquisition premium*. The Regulation method relies on a *constant yield to maturity* assumption and thus closely reflects the correct economic interest rate. The Code method, in contrast, permits taxpayers to defer recognition of some interest income because it relies on an arguably simpler formula. Well-advised taxpayers will typically adopt the less accurate Code method over the more accurate Regulation method because it defers income—and thus the taxes on that income.

Although the tax deferral of income possible though the purchase of bonds at a premium is small, it can be significant, particularly in conjunction with other tax deferral devices. Hence, lawyers should be wary of using tax return information as presumptive of economic income for legal purposes.

For *Financial Accounting*, the owner should amortize any acquisition premium using a *constant yield to maturity* (*CYM*) assumption.

7. **Active Foreign Business Income:** *AFBI*: *IRC* section 861(c)(1)(B) defines *AFBI* as:

> gross income which—
>
> > (i)　is derived from sources outside the United States (as determined under this subchapter) or, in the case of a corporation, is attributable to income so derived by a subsidiary of such corporation, and
> >
> > (ii)　is attributable to the *active conduct of a trade or business* in a foreign country or possession of the United

> States by the individual or corporation (or by a
> subsidiary.)

Emphasis added.

Active foreign business income results in different consequences than does other types of foreign income, such as passive or investment income.

8. **Active Conduct of a Trade or Business:** *See Passive Activity.* The phrase "active conduct of a trade or business" appears in twenty-six separate section of the Internal Revenue Code (as of 2011). The phrase's meaning is inconsistent and *not* clearly defined. For example, *IRC* section 167(j)(5) provides:

> For purposes of this subsection, the rental to others of real property located within an Indian reservation shall be treated as the *active conduct of a trade or business* within an Indian reservation.

IRC section 335(b)(2) defines the term [titling itself a Definition] (albeit not particularly helpfully) as:

> For purposes of paragraph (1), a corporation shall be treated as engaged in the active conduct of a trade or business if and only if—
>
> (A) it is engaged in the active conduct of a trade or business
>
> . . . .

One wonders what the term means for purposes other than paragraph (1) of subsection 335(b).

The term "trade or business" appears frequently in the *IRC*; however, it has no consistent definition, although it generally connotes something involving "activity" rather than "passivity." As a result, the term "active conduct of a trade or business" may appear facially redundant, though in practical terms it certainly has meaning even if one cannot quite define it. In one provision, an entity is engaged in the active conduct of a trade or business if it merely reasonably expects to generate revenues within three years. Treas. Reg. § 1.45D–1(d)(4)(iv)(A).

9. **Additional Paid-In Capital:** *APIC*: This finance and accounting term has little meaning. It refers to the excess paid for shares over par or stated value. Par value has long lost most of its meaning. At one time, shareholders were liable for corporate debts to the extent they had not paid par value for their stock. For many years, however, companies have issues no-par stock or stock with an extremely low par value in states that retain the notion of par. The accounting line for *APIC* is part of owner's equity.

Some accountants refer to this as *EPIC* or *excess* paid-in capital.

10. **Adjustable Rate:** This is a contractual interest rate that changes over time, generally as a result of market changes. Often used for home mortgage loans—referred to as *Adjustable Rate* Mortgages (*ARMs*)—an initial *adjustable rate* may be artificially low such that the borrower may more easily qualify for the loan, based on outside conditions (such as those imposed by government programs). Contracts with *adjustable rates* require a reference rate. Many use a function of the *prime rate*, or the federal funds rate, or the *LIBOR* rate.

Consumers—and the lawyers who represent them—should be cautious of *ARMs*. They are useful for persons with reliably predictable income increases; however, they can be dangerous for persons with stable income. Adjustments can be large if market rates increase; as a result, the debtors may have great difficulty making the resulting high loan payments.

ARMs make sense when one can reliably predict falling interest rates; however, if one can reliably predict falling interest rate, one need not take this course, or even practice law for a living, as one must have a crystal ball. Reliably predicting income increases is more feasible. For example, college graduates often see substantial increases in pay in the early years of working. Others have contractual arrangements or trust arrangements which provide for secure increases. In contrast, the interest rate market can be very fickle.

11. **Adjusted Basis:** In general, for accounting purposes (after capitalization, amortization and depreciation), the historical cost basis of property can be increased or decreased.

For tax purposes, *IRC* section 1016 outlines the circumstances when basis adjusts. For example, depreciation reduces an asset's basis. Deprecation, which is a function both of what one did and what one should have done, will result in an adjusted basis that is lower than the cost basis for an asset. For all other purposes tax adjustments are a function of what one should have done.

For accounting purposes, basis adjustments should always be a function of what one should have recorded—shown by an extraordinary item on the financial statements if it is inconsistent with what one actually recorded. The adjusted basis is the basis upon which gains and losses are calculated at the time an asset is sold or disposed of.

A very simplified formula for adjusted basis is:

Adjusted Basis = Cost Basis + Capitalized
Expenditures − Depreciation (or amortization)

12. **Adjusted Gross Income:** *AGI:* This is a tax term or art defined by *IRC* section 62. In includes *Gross Income* (a tax term of art define by *IRC* Section 61), minus a list of *"above the line"* deductions. Most of the deductions are for ordinary and necessary *trade or business* expenses allowed by *IRC* section 162; however, the list also includes alimony deductible under *IRC* section 71 and moving expenses.

Of significant importance, *AGI* does not include most employee business expenses, which are not only *"below-the-line"* deductions, but which are also subject to the 2% floor limitations of *IRC* section 64.

Above-the-line refers to deductions allowable for purposes of *IRC* section 62 and *AGI*. *Below the line* refers to all other deductions. With few exceptions, above the line deductions appear on a tax return and benefit the taxpayer. *Below-the-line* deductions, however, are subject to several limitations and restrictions before they reach a tax return. Hence, whether a deduction is *above* or *below-the-line* can be very significant.

Although taxpayers pay tax at their respective brackets on taxable income, the correct computation of *AGI* is important. Many deductions are a function of *AGI*: *e.g.,* medical expenses and charitable contribution deductions. Also, the statute of limitations, per *IRC* section 6501(e) can be a function of omissions from *AGI*.

The *line* referred to in both *above* and *below-the-line* references is a line on a United States Form 1040—INDIVIDUAL TAX RETURN—which denominates the computation of *AGI* by requiring the addition and subtraction of the numbers above it. In accounting and financial reports, a *single line* indicates the need for addition and subtraction, while a *double line* indicates the net result of addition and subtraction.

13. **Adjusting Entry:** At the end of each period (which may be a month, a quarter, or a year) an accountant or bookkeeper makes a series of entries for non-transactional items. These include *depreciation* and *amortization*. In accounting parlance, they are *adjusting entries*, as they adjust for items which are not the result of events or transactions. Regular entries appear chronologically in the journal, but *adjusting entries* and *closing entries* appear at the end of a period.

14. **Affinity:** Relationship by Marriage. See *consanguinity*, which refers to relationship through a common ancestor. Spouses are related by *affinity*, as are in-laws. Blood relatives are related by *consanguinity*. Tax law has significant rules for related party transactions. Such transactions may result in imputed income, deduction disallowance, or even a collapse of the transactional steps into a single event or result. In some cases, accounting rules incorporate relationships, as well. Other legal areas—such as agency law, trust law, and family law—

also impute or define legal consequences at least partially from a consideration of the parties' relationships.

Hence, lawyers should have a clear understand of human relationships.

15. **After-Tax Interest Rate:** See LESSON EIGHT, which explains the concept of an *after-tax interest rate*. This is the appropriate statement of interest (*nominal, periodic,* or *effective*) computed after reduction for the income tax benefits resulting from deduction of the interest. For United States tax purposes, most business interest is deductible (although some must be capitalized); as is investment interest (subject to limitations) and some home mortgage interest. The tax benefits under *IRC* Section 163 can be substantial; hence, to reflect the true economic interest cost, planners should convert the *stated interest rate* to the equivalent *after-tax interest rate*. One must understand, however, that tax consequences often change over time, resulting in an *after-tax interest rate* being an *adjustable rate*.

The formula for an *after-tax interest rate* is:

$$atir = sir(1 - tr)$$

Where tr = marginal tax rate, $atir$ = after-tax interest rate and sir = stated interest rate.

A related concept is an ***after-tax cost***. In turn, this is related to the *True Cost of Ownership (TCO)*. Algebraically, the *after tax cost* is:

$$ATC = (1 - mtr) \times sp$$

Where ATC = after-tax cost, mtr = marginal tax rate, and sp = stated price.

Depreciable and deductible assets thus do not cost their *stated price*. For example, a $5,000 desk subject to *IRC* section 179 expensing at a 40% *marginal tax rate* (which is realistic considering federal and state income and employment taxes) has an *after-tax cost* of only $3,000.

$$\$3,000 = (1 - .4)(\$5,000)$$

or

$$\$3,000 = (.6)(\$5,000)$$

Another related concept is an ***after-tax value***. This one is more subtle than the other two and significantly less precise; nevertheless, it can be profoundly important. Far too often, lawyers and courts ignore the concept to the unfair detriment of some (and unfair benefit) of others.

To understand *after-tax value*, one must first understand *Fair Market Value (FMV), Basis,* and *Minority Discount (MD),* as well as other discounting. All property has a *FMV* as well as a tax *basis* (generally cost). The difference between the two numbers is the potential or inherent taxable gain or loss in the property. Under the United States income tax system (which is also the case with most countries), the inherent gain or loss is not subject to tax recognition until the occurrence of a taxable event, generally a sale or exchange. Upon such an event, the owner must pay income tax on the gain (or he may deduct the loss subject to many deferral and disallowance provisions). The margin tax rate on the gain will vary depending not only on the owner's tax bracket, but also on the character of the property sold or exchanged. In many income tax systems, including that of the United States, *capital gain income* is subject to a lower set of tax rates than other types of income. The exact rate has varied substantially over the past nine decades of the U.S. income tax system.

But, if one owns property which one must value, one must consider the potential tax consequences of a disposition of the property. For example, if the *marginal tax rate* is 20% and the basis is zero, the property has an after-tax value of only 80% of the stated or nominal *FMV*, assuming an imminent sale. If the marginal tax rate is 40% and the basis is zero, the property has an *after-tax value* of only 60% of the nominal *FMV*, again assuming an imminent sale.

Dissolution of marriage—divorce in some jurisdictions—often involves the division of property. This can occur under a community property or equitable division statute, or as a result of the settlement of alimony rights. In any of these cases, for tax purposes, *IRC* section 1041 treats the transaction as a gift (hence no income or loss results from the transfer itself). But, section 1041 also transfers the property's tax *adjusted basis* (under *IRC* section 1016) to the recipient. High basis assets—and capital assets—potentially have a dramatically different after-tax value than low basis assets and ordinary assets.

For example, posit a soon-to-be divorced couple who together own four assets:

- Cash of $100,000.
- Securities with an undisputed *FMV* (after transaction costs) of $100,000 and with a *tax adjusted basis* of $1,000.
- Securities with an undisputed *FMB* (after transaction costs) of $100,000 and with a *tax adjusted basis* of $1,000,000.
- Inventory with an undisputed *FMV* (after transaction costs) of $100,000 and with a *tax adjusted basis* of $1,000.

Nominally, each asset has the same *FMV*: $100,000. Most state statutes and financial disclosure forms related to marriage dissolution do not require disclosure of tax adjusted bases or of the tax character of property. Hence, legally, each asset may have identical *FMV*s. But, assuming each would be sold immediately by the recipient, their relative after-tax values differ substantially. Assuming a 40% marginal tax rate (20% on capital gains), the after tax values would be:

- $100,000 for the cash.

- $80,800 for the appreciated securities.

- Up to $280,000 for the depreciated securities.

- $60,600 for the inventory.

The cash would have no potential tax consequences. The appreciated securities would likely generate long-term capital gains taxed at an assumed 20% rate. The depreciated securities would likely generate *long-term capital losses*, limited in deductibility by *IRC* sections 1211–1212, but potentially benefiting the owner/seller 20% (and possibly as much as 40%) of the loss. The inventory would likely generate *ordinary income* taxed at 40%.

With an *after-tax interest rate*, the computation is simple and reliable—the only variable being the deductibility of the interest and the rate of the payer—each of which could change, but each of which is nevertheless predictable with a high degree of certainty. Similarly, the computation of an *after-tax cost* is also simple and reliable because the transaction is current and thus subject to the current variable of the buyer's tax rate, which, again, is highly predictable (though it can change during the year).

But, computing an *after-tax value* requires information regarding the timing of the property disposition. If a sale is imminent, the computation is simple and highly reliable. If, instead, no sale is currently contemplated, the computation introduces a new variable—the likelihood and timing of a potential disposition. Eventually, an owner will dispose of all his property: at some point, he will die (remember we are considering humans in the process of a divorce). Statistical information is available regarding the typical ownership period of other property, be it securities or inventory or buildings. This requires informed speculation based on historical information regarding macro trends, as well as particular information regarding the particular property and the particular owner. With an assumed disposition date (be it imminent or postponed until death), an expert witness can compute an **after-tax present value**. The information will not be perfect, as it is subject to the speculative variable; however, the resulting computation is arguably more reliable than ignoring the inherent tax consequences altogether, as do most state statutes and courts.

Understanding that most property divisions result from *marital settlement agreements*, one should realize: clients with lawyers who understand the concept of *after-tax value* have a substantial advantage over clients with lawyers who do not.

16. **All Events Test:** This is one of the thirteen fundamental *accounting principles and assumptions*. It applies to the *accrual method* of accounting and is the cornerstone of the *Matching Principle*. See also the Revenue Recognition Principle and the Expense Recognition Principle.

    - *Income recognition* is appropriate when *all events* have occurred such that the earner has a right to the item and the amount thereof can be determined with reasonable accuracy.

    - *Deductions* are appropriate when *all events* have occurred such the obligor must incur the item and the amount thereof can be determined with reasonable accuracy.

    The *all events test* is irrelevant for the *cash method* of accounting.

17. **Alternative Minimum Tax:** *AMT:* Under *IRC* section 55, the *AMT* system is an alternative tax system to the general U.S. *income* tax system. Enacted in 1969, it originally targeted a small number of high income taxpayers who largely escaped income taxes because of investments in tax exempt securities. It now reaches many households with more modest income levels. For tax purposes, an inclusion in *AMT* is not the same as an inclusion in *gross income*, which affects some significant procedural rules.

    As more and more households have entered the reach of the *AMT*, the system has become *politically* controversial. Arguably, it raises significant revenue; however, arguably it also places too heavy a burden on households which are more middle class than upper class. When one computes an *after-tax interest* rate, an *after-tax cost*, or an *after-tax value*, one must consider the potential *AMT* consequences, which can be complicated.

    Lawyers who consider *Taxable Income* as relevant to the legal concept of *income* should pay heed to the *AMT* rules. In part, these rules add items to income which are otherwise excluded, such as tax exempt interest (*e.g.,* interest on state and local bonds). To be clear, *AMT* income is not necessarily a better measure of income than is *Taxable Income*, but it is certainly different and thus provides a different perspective.

18. **American Institute of Certified Public Accountants:** *AICPA:* According to the organization's mission statement:

The American Institute of Certified Public Accountants is the national, professional organization for all Certified Public Accountants. Its mission is to provide members with the resources, information, and leadership that enable them to provide valuable services in the highest professional manner to benefit the public as well as employers and clients.

In fulfilling its mission, the AICPA works with state CPA organizations and gives priority to those areas where public reliance on CPA skills is most significant.

http://www.aicpa.org.

Among other activities, it establishes ethical rules for public accountants. It also provides technical support to the *FASB*, which is responsible for *GAAP*. Further, it grants the *PFS* certification.

19. **American Stock Exchange: AMEX:** [pronounced *am*-eks]. This was one of the main stock exchanges in the United States from the 1920s until the late 1990s. Generally, it listed companies with capitalized values less than those on the *New York Stock Exchange*. In 1998, it merged with *NASDAQ*.

20. **Amortization:** This is the process of allocating a cost or a principal amount over time. An **AMORTIZATION CALCULATOR**—as explained in FINANCE FOR LAWYERS **LESSON THIRTEEN**—performs two important functions. First, it determines the amount of level payment required to reduce the principal amount of a loan to zero over a stated period, at a given periodic interest rate. Second, it determines—in an *amortization* schedule—the portion of each payment properly allocable to interest and the portion properly allocable to principal. For contracts with actual payments less than the determined interest component of each payment, *negative amortization* will occur: the principal amount will thus increase.

An *amortization* is either in *end mode* (payments occur at the end of each period) or *begin mode* (payments occur at the beginning of each period).

The **AMORTIZATION** calculation is one of the six basic calculations performed by a *Financial Calculator*. The formula for an *amortization* is:

$$PMT = \left[\frac{\left(PV \left(\frac{i}{100} \right) \right)}{1 - \left(1 + \frac{i}{100} \right)^{-n}} \right]$$

where i = nominal annual interest rate, n = number of periods per year, and FV = the future value.

Amortization has another important meaning. For accounting and tax law purposes, it involves the process of allocating *intangible* costs over time. Similarly, *depreciation* involves the allocation of *tangible* costs over time. Interestingly, for U.S. tax purposes, amortization generally follows a straight-line approach. *See, e.g., IRC* sections 195, 197, and 263 (with accompanying regulations). Occasionally, however, tax *amortization* properly follows an up-ward sloping curve. In contrast, tax and accounting *depreciation* generally follows a downward sloping curve per *IRC* sections 167 and 168. For real property, U.S. tax depreciation is straight-line—a graph of zero slope. Economically, the downward sloping curve would be most appropriate.

21. **Annual Percentage Rate: APR:** See LESSON FIVE-C: *Annual Percentage Rate.* In credit transactions not involving *points* or some other fees, the *annual percentage rate* equals the *nominal annual interest rate.* However, transactions involving *points* and some other fees have an *annual percentage rate* which reflects both the *nominal* rate and the *compounded* amortized effect of the points or other fees. United States Federal Law requires disclosure of this rate law for most credit transactions. "*APR*" is the typical abbreviation. The legal definition appears in federal statute, **15 U.S.C. § 1606.** LESSON FIVE-C explains the *APR.* Arguably the Truth in Lending Law requirement that lenders disclose the *APR* actually favors banks and mis-leads borrowers.

    In credit parlance, a "point" is equal to one percent of the principal amount loaned. Thus on a $100,000 loan, one point equals $1,000 and two points equals $2,000. On a $200,000 loan, one point equals $2,000 and two points equals $4,000.

    Of critical importance, the *APR* does not equal the *EFF* (*effective interest rate*) unless the obligation *compounds* annually. Financial Calculators always have an *EFF* function; however, they rarely have an *APR* function, as it is a legal rather than a financial term.

    Other nations also use the term *Annual Percentage Rate* and abbreviate it as *APR.* Several of them define it differently than does U.S. law. Lawyers must therefore be careful when using the term contractually. They must define the meaning in relation to the law of a particular jurisdiction.

22. **Annual Percentage Yield: APY:** The term *Annual Percentage Yield* (*APY*) and its legal consequences appear in federal statute. **12 U.S.C. § 4302.** Specifically, the statute defines it as "the total amount of interest that would be received on a $100 deposit, based on the annual rate of simple interest and the frequency of compounding for a 365-day period. . . ." Advertisements for deposits generally must include a statement of the *APY.* The definition assumes re-investment of

periodic interest at the stated interest rate and a maturity of at least one-year. For deposits for which those assumptions do not apply, the *APY* is not accurate; nevertheless, federal law generally requires its disclosure.

23. **Annuity:** A series of payments. A fixed *annuity* is a series of payments for a fixed period. A life *annuity* is a series of payments for the remainder of a person's life. A joint life *annuity* is a series of payments for the remainder of the longer of two persons' lives.

    For tax purposes, an *annuity* issued by an insurance company receives special benefits: internal accumulations in value are not taxable until disbursed.

    Be careful when using the term *annuity*: to some people it inherently refers to an insurance product. While that is correct under one definition, it is not correct under the more general definition: an *annuity* is merely a series of payments.

    For some legal purposes *annuities* receive preferential treatment. Examples include federal tax law (accumulations are tax deferred) and some state laws regarding garnishment (*annuities* are sometimes not subject to garnishment). In other cases, *annuities* receive detrimental legal consequences. An example commonly includes the determination of income for alimony or child support purposes. Many state statutes include "*annuity* payments" as income for these purposes. Such statutes are unfair to the *annuity* investor because—in most cases—the *annuity* is self-amortizing and thus the payments are part principal and part interest. Because family law definitions of income rarely define principal withdrawals as income, when they do so in relation to *annuities*, they are unfair.

24. **Annuity Due:** This is a reference to the *Mode*. Payments on an *annuity due* begin today, in contrast to an *annuity in arrears* for which payments begin one period in the future. Loan amortizations almost always use end mode to create an annuity of payments, because the first loan payment—for new loans—is typically one period in the future. Sinking funds—which are also annuities—use the begin mode, or annuity due format, if the creator wants to begin saving immediately.

25. **Annuity in Arrears:** This is a reference to the *Mode*. Payments on an *annuity in arrears* begin one period from now, in contrast to an *annuity due* for which payments begin today. Loans are almost always *annuities in arrears*: the first payment is due one period in the future; otherwise, the borrower would make the first payment simultaneously with borrowing the money. In such a case, he would merely be borrowing less. In contrast, loans with deferred payments—such as student loans—can effectively be annuities due. At the moment of

amortizing the loan, the first payment can indeed be due currently, as opposed to one period in the future.

26. **Annuity Trust:** This is a shortened reference to a *CRAT, or Charitable Remainder Annuity Trust*. It provides an annuity to the grantor for either a single or joint life with the remainder benefiting a charity. United States tax law provides significant tax benefits for annuity trusts—with the magnitude of the benefits a function of the grantor's income and asset levels. See the discussion on *CRAT* for more information.

27. **Applicable Federal Rate:** *AFR*: Internal Revenue Code section 1274(d) defines the *Applicable Federal Rate*—the *AFR*. Announced monthly, this rate forms the basis for many tax calculations, including *original issue discount* loan interest (OID per *IRC* sections 1272–74), *below market loans* (per *IRC* section 7872), and advanced or deferred payments for rent (per *IRC* section 467).

    Under *Treasury Regulation* section 1.7872–13(a)(1)(i), the *IRS* annually announces a blended short-term rate for short-term obligations outstanding for the entire year, or a substantial part thereof. Some *IRC* provisions—e.g., section 467—use a higher rate which is 110% or 120% of the *AFR*. These various rates are important for imputing current interest and other tax events for loans with deferred or understated interest.

    IRC section 1274(d) provides:

    (1) Applicable Federal rate

    (A) In general

In the case of a debt instrument with a term of:	The applicable Federal rate is
Not over 3 years	The Federal short-term rate.
Over 3 years but not over 9 years	The Federal mid-term rate.
Over 9 years	The Federal long-term rate.

    (B) Determination of rates

    During each calendar month, the Secretary shall determine the Federal short-term rate, mid-term rate, and long-term rate which shall apply during the following calendar month.

(C) Federal rate for any calendar month

For purposes of this paragraph—

(i)   Federal short-term rate

The Federal short-term rate shall be the rate determined by the Secretary based on the average market yield (during any 1-month period selected by the Secretary and ending in the calendar month in which the determination is made) on outstanding marketable obligations of the United States with remaining periods to maturity of 3 years or less.

(ii) Federal mid-term and long-term rates

The Federal mid-term and long-term rate shall be determined in accordance with the principles of clause (i).

(D) Lower rate permitted in certain cases

The Secretary may by regulations permit a rate to be used with respect to any debt instrument which is lower than the applicable Federal rate if the taxpayer establishes to the satisfaction of the Secretary that such lower rate is based on the same principles as the applicable Federal rate and is appropriate for the term of such instrument.

The *AFR* is typically lower than market interest rates for comparable periods. That fact is particularly noteworthy. Taxpayers enter transactions with below market rates, or with deferred interest, because they want to escape, defer, or accelerate the tax consequences of market rates. By requiring use of the *AFR* in many situations, the *IRC* effectively precludes much of the intended manipulation: the escape, the deferral, or the acceleration. However, because the *AFR* is lower than market rates, it does not eliminate all the benefits of the affected transactions.

28. **Ask Price:** The ask price is the offer to sell price for items without a highly liquid market—*e.g.,* many stocks, bonds, debentures, or commodities. It contrasts with the bid price which is the offer to buy price. For securities listed on a major exchange, a "market maker" ensures the bid and the ask price come together. For other exchanges, the spread between the bid and ask prices exists until it does not, *i.e.,* until it "closes."

29. **Audit:** A *CPA* audits the financial statements of an entity or person. The audit consists of a plan, a management letter describing the audit, random sampling of various bookkeeping entries, and verification of

cash, receivables, liabilities, and other material items. It also includes an evaluation of the entity's *internal controls*. The auditor will suggest to management changes in *internal control* or in bookkeeping procedures and policies, as appropriate. Ultimately, management prepares the *financial statements* and either follows the *CPA* auditor's advice or rejects it. Then the auditor expresses an opinion on the *financial statements*: whether they conform to *GAAP* and whether they present fairly the financial condition and operations of the entity for the period and as of the date stated.

Audit procedures follow *GAAS*. An auditor must make a variety of assumptions, including whether the entity is a going concern. If these assumptions are invalid, the auditor must so state and explain why.

Of significance, an audit does not certify or guarantee anything other than the fairness of the statements with the assumptions made and consistent with *GAAP*. If an auditor suspects fraud, he will conduct a more intensive fraud audit; or, he may withdraw from the engagement.

30. **Audit Committee:** Large, especially publicly traded entities, typically have an audit committee formed from the Board of Directors. This committee meets with the independent auditors, receives their recommendations, and reports to the general Board of Directors. The major purpose of an audit committee is independence from management. Along with management, they often have responsibility for ensuring proper *internal controls*.

31. **Auditor's Report:** This is the opinion of a *Certified Public Accountant* attesting to audit results. It follows a standard form under *Generally Accepted Auditing Standards (GAAS)*. It takes one of four common forms:

    - Unqualified Opinion
    - Qualified Opinion
    - Adverse Opinion
    - Disclaimer of Opinion

An unqualified opinion reflects the *CPA's* conclusion that the financial statements, including footnotes, fairly present the issuer's operations and condition for a particular period and at a particular time.

A ***Qualified Opinion*** follows the standard unqualified format; however, it conditions the opinion because of some irregularity. It does so in an "except for" paragraph explaining the condition. The irregularity is not one such that the auditor finds the statements to be unfair: that would result in an ***Adverse Opinion***. Instead, the qualification may result from such things as:

- the inability of the auditor to examine a particular asset

- the necessity of the auditor's reliance on the opinion of another auditor not legally associated with the primary auditor

- a single deviation from *GAAP*, which does not affect the overall fairness of the statements.

A standard ***Unqualified Opinion*** follows the following format—and does not deviate from it significantly:

INDEPENDENT AUDITOR'S REPORT

Board of Directors, Stockholders, Owners, and/or
Management of ABC Company, Inc.
123 Main St.
Anytown, Anystate

We have audited the accompanying Balance Sheet of ABC Company, Inc. (the "Company") as of December 31, 20XX and the related statements of Income, Retained Earnings, and Cash Flows for the year then ended. These Financial Statements are the responsibility of the Company's management. Our responsibility is to express an opinion on these financial statements based on our audit.

We conducted our audit in accordance with generally accepted auditing standards. Those standards require that we plan and perform the audit to obtain reasonable assurance about whether the financial statements are free of material misstatement. An audit includes examining, on a test basis, evidence supporting the amounts and disclosures in the financial statements. An audit also includes assessing the accounting principles used and significant estimates made by management, as well as evaluating the overall financial statement presentation. We believe that our audit provides a reasonable basis for our opinion.

In our opinion, the financial statements referred to above present fairly, in all material respects, the financial position of the Company as of December 31, 20XX, and the results of its operations and its cash flows for the year then ended in accordance with generally accepted accounting principles.

Signature
Auditor's name and address
Date

A ***Disclaimer of Opinion*** is also the possible result of an audit or the engagement of a *CPA*. A disclaimer is appropriate if the limitations placed on the auditor were so significant that the *CPA* could not render an opinion.

Lawyers should never rely on statements accompanied by an *Adverse Opinion* or a *Disclaimer of Opinion*. They should be wary of a *Qualified Opinion* and should pay close attention to the "*except-for*" paragraph. Even an *Unqualified Opinion* will have many footnotes and explanations outside the actual opinion letter. Lawyer should be wary about relying on any *Financial Statements*—including those with an *Unqualified Opinion*—unless they are conversant with accounting terminology, financial ratios, and have comparative data.

32. **Balance of Payments:** This is an often-misunderstood measure of the payments between nations, generally on an annual basis. By definition, it must balance—just as a balance sheet must balance. Components of the measure, however, may be out-of-balance, depending on how one defines them.

    For example, Country A can have an annual *trade imbalance* with Country B because Country A sold more goods and services to Country B than Country B purchased. Hence, the Trade measures between the two countries—as defined in terms of goods and services—will reflect a deficit for Country B and a surplus for Country A.

    In terms of the *Balance of Payments*, however, a balance will result in every instance—although it may flow through multiple countries. For the above example, eventually the surplus country or countries—here Country A—will acquire currency, coin, government obligations, or assets in Country B (though with multiple countries, Country A may actually acquire surplus assets in Country C, which acquires surplus assets in Country B).

    Hence no nation can have a *Balance of Payments* deficit or surplus, any more than a company's books can be out of balance. Imbalances, if they occur, are inevitably the result of recording or math errors, *e.g.,* a bookkeeper forgetting to enter a number or adding 2 plus 2 and getting 7. These things happen, but one should not place any greater significance on them other than people make mistakes.

    Even in terms of <u>alleged</u> *Trade Deficits*, the numbers can be misleading for many reasons:

    - The numbers may reflect <u>definitions</u> of trade which exclude material accounts. For example, if the United States buys 100,000 automobiles from Japan and sells the equivalent value of lumber and bricks to Japan, many *experts* suggest the trade accounts balance. However, if, instead, the United States exports nothing to Japan, but Japan instead purchasing a building in

Seattle comprised of those same bricks and lumber, many experts suggest the United States would have a *Trade Deficit* with Japan. Such a conclusion would be accurate, but only by defining the sale of lumber and bricks in Seattle as something other than Trade. Indeed, it is not an export—but only if one defines exports in terms of tangibles goods physically moving out of a nation.

- The numbers may reflect inter-company transactions which, partially because of the *Separate Entity Assumption*, reflect misleading numbers.

For example, X Corporation—a multi-national entity (but with substantial United States shareholders)—may sell a beverage at a fast food establishment in Gainesville, Florida. The $1.99 sale of a large Coke® comprises many components: the cup (which includes all the manufacturing parts of that cup), the ice, the carbonated water, the syrup, the service of someone filling the cup and accepting payment and printing/providing a receipt, the provision of the building or drive-thru window at the *POS*, and the use of the name of the fast-food establishment. Probably, all the manufacturing of the cup, ice, receipt, straw, napkin, syrup, and window occurred within the United States. Probably, none of it occurred in the Cayman Islands. But, the trademark and trade name for the fast food company may belong to an entity other than X Corporation; indeed, that is very likely.

Under the Separate Entity Assumption, X Corporation and Trademark Corporation have separate accounting records. Trademark Corporation will charge X Corporation for the use of the name, logo, and emblem on cups, napkins, signs, sales personnel uniforms and other such places. If the United States is a high tax jurisdiction (which it tends to be in relative terms) and the Cayman Islands is a low tax jurisdiction (which it tends to be), then X Corporation has a strong incentive to place a high *FMV* on the use of the trademark. This is particularly true if the shareholders of X Corporation and Trademark Corporation are identical, or if they overlap substantially.

In the above example, perhaps $.25 of the transaction involves trademark costs. If so, then the micro economic accounting for the transaction will involve a *Trade Deficit* between the United States and the Cayman Islands—even though neither the customer nor the beverage has ever been in the Cayman Islands and no money (other than through an electronic transfer) ever appeared in the Cayman Islands. The alleged *Trade Deficit* is thus a *fiction* resulting from accounting assumptions and allocations. It has some reality in terms of tax consequences and share values and financial statements; however, is has no other economic value or reality.

If users of Trade Statements draw the wrong conclusions from the alleged resulting deficit, they risk making bad decisions. Similarly, if users of Financial Statements misunderstand their meaning—as lawyers often do—they, too risk making bad decisions.

- Many people assume *Trade Deficits* are bad and *Trade Surpluses* are good. While such assumptions have some validity, they also require a broader view.

First, numbers reflecting deficits and surplus are no better than the assumptions underlying the definitions of those terms. Because terminology is easily manipulation through misleading definitions, one should be wary of the numbers unless one fully understands the definitions—and, under the *Consistency Principle*—uses the identical definitions for any comparisons with other periods or nations.

Second, to the extent a *Trade Deficit* excludes the sale of currency, financial instruments, and domestic investments (*e.g.*, the building in Seattle posited above), the alleged *Trade Deficit* is actually positive for the nation incurring it—at least in the short or mid-term. Think pragmatically: the deficit country has additional automobiles, computers, trinkets, oil, or whatever it imported. The surplus country, however, has additional paper currency and coin (neither of which has any intrinsic value) plus intangible obligations and some tangible property located in the deficit nation. Demand in the deficit nation is offset by increased supply (at no current cost other than paper) from the surplus country; hence, the deficit nation will have less inflationary pressures. The surplus nation, however, has increased demand (because of the sales and resulting profits) but decreased supply (which it exported); hence, the surplus nation will have increased inflationary pressure. Overall, the deficit nation has exported its inflation.

Admittedly, such *Trade Deficits* have a turning point: eventually—in the long run—the surplus nation will spend the excess currency reserves. It will thus export its own inflation to the deficit nation, which will suffer the unpleasant macro economic consequences of an *alleged* *Trade Surplus* (alleged because the definitions are so imprecise).

The United States has experienced annual, continuous *Trade Deficits* (as that term is traditionally defined by excluding paper, coin, and domestic investments) for many decades. Whether—and when—those turn into *Trade Surpluses* (using the same misleading definition as used for Trade Deficits) is unclear. In the long run, it is inevitable; however, as famed economist John Maynard Keynes once said, "Long run is a misleading guide to current affairs. In the long run we are all dead."

For an excellent discussion of trade and balance of payments, see commentary by Martin Feldstein, a former Chairman of the Council of Economic Advisors.

http://www.econlib.org/library/Enc/BalanceofPayments.html.

33. **Balance Sheet:** This is one of three important *Financial Statements*, the other two being the *Income Statement* and the *Statement of Cash Flows*. It presents a financial picture as of a particular date. Many users refer to it as a snapshot: it says a great deal about conditions at one moment.

The *Balance Sheet* lists assets on the left side and liabilities plus owner's equity on the right side. The two sides necessarily balance, as owner's equity results from the basic accounting equation:

$$(Assets - Liabilities) = Owners' Equity$$

or

$$Assets = (Liabilities + Owners' Equity)$$

Balance Sheet

Assets	Liabilities
	Owners' Equity
Total Assets	Total Liabilities plus Equity

A *single underline* on a *Financial Statement* indicates the column above it is being added or subtracted. A *double underline* indicates a sum.

34. **Balloon Payment:** Some loans provide for short-term partial *amortization* of the principal with the remaining principal due in a lump sum. This remainder is a *Balloon Payment* The word arises from the notion of the payment amount suddenly ballooning or inflating to a large amount. Usually a balloon payment is a lump sum payment due at the maturity of a loan.

35. **Bankers Acceptance:** According to the *Fed,*

> *Bankers acceptances* are negotiable time *drafts,* or bills of exchange, that have been accepted by a bank which, by accepting, assumes the obligation to pay the holder of the *draft* the face amount of the instrument on the maturity date specified. They are used primarily to finance the export, import, shipment or storage of goods.

See the definitions of *negotiable instrument* and *draft* for fuller information.

36. **Basis:** In accounting and tax parlance, basis is the *historic cost* of an item, adjusted for subsequent events. Every asset has a *basis*, even if the amount is zero. A negative *basis* is impossible. Currency has, by definition, a basis equal to its face value.

The *basis* is essential for the determination of gain or loss on disposition of the thing. For example, if a chair has a cost basis of $500 and the entity sells it for $700, the gain is $200. Without knowledge of the *basis*, one could not measure the gain or loss.

For tax purposes, *IRC* section 1012 provides for a *cost basis* in all property. *IRC* section 1016 then provides for adjustments to *basis*. *Depreciation* and *amortization* result in downward adjustments. Similarly, improvements result in basis increases in the process called *capitalization*.

Because tax gains are taxable and tax losses are often deductible, an item's tax *basis* is a critical number in determining the item's **after-tax value**. For example, a tract of land with a *FMV* of $1,000,000 and a *basis* of $1,000,000 has no potential tax gain. It therefore has an *after-tax* value of $1,000,000. But another tract with a similar *FMV* but a basis of $1,000 has a built-in gain of $999,000. The owner of the second tract will be subject to income tax (at either ordinary or capital gains rates) upon the sale or other taxable disposition of the tract. Because that built-in tax gain may result in income taxes due in the amount of $150,000 or more, the *after-tax FMV* of the tract is significantly lower than the stated $1,000,000. Similarly, a third tract with a *basis* of $3,000,000 has a build-in loss of $2,000,000.

The owner may benefit from a substantial tax deduction upon a taxable disposition of that third tract; as a result, the *after-tax FMV* of the tract is significantly higher than the stated amount of $1,000,000.

Mostly, the legal system ignores tax *basis* for Family Law and other purposes. This refusal to consider important information results in some persons having substantial advantage over others. Lawyers need to be aware of this phenomenon. For example, in dividing property incident to marriage dissolution, the tax *basis* of a thing may be as important as the stated *FMV*. Too often, however, the parties ignore the tax *basis*.

A famous—and initially counter-intuitive—tax case defines tax *basis* in an arm's length taxable transaction as:

The Fair Market Value Received.

Philadelphia Park Amusement Company v. United States, 126 F. Supp. 184 (Cl. Ct. 1954).

See also the definition of *Adjusted Basis*.

37. **Basis Point:** One one-hundredth of one percent. Thus 100 *basis points* comprise 1 percent. If a bond yield changes from 10% to 11% that is a change of 100 *basis points*, but also a change of 10% (1% is 10% of 10%). Lawyers need to be familiar with the terminology in stating *interest* rates as a function of an index.

For example the *prime rate* may be 5%. A loan 150 *basis points* above *prime* would be 6.5%. That phraseology is clearer than referring to a loan 1.5% above *prime*: some readers may mistakenly view the 1.5% as a function of the underlying *prime rate* rather than a fixed addition to it.

38. **Bear Market:** This is a colloquial description of a period during which various stock market indexes are lower than during the immediately prior period. Generally, a *Bear Market* exists when an index is down 10% or more from his previous high. In contrast, a *Bull Market* is one in which stock indexes are generally higher and rising. To be *bearish* or a *bear* is to believe stocks will fall. In contrast, to be bullish or a bull is to believe stocks will rise.

Investors who are *bearish* often *short* stocks or use *put options* to benefit from expected declines. Investors who are *bullish* tend to have *long* positions or use *call options*. An old saying worth noting is:

> One can make money as a Bull and one can make money
> as a Bear, but one cannot make money as a Pig.

Another version states:

> Bulls make money. Bears make money. Pigs get slaughtered.

39. **Begin Mode: BM:** In *Begin Mode*, the first *payment* of an *annuity* (or for the *amortization* of a loan or for a *sinking fund*) is due today. In contrast, for *End Mode*, the first *payment* is due one period in the future.

Lawyers should be careful with the *mode* function. Mode mistakes are one of the more common errors in financial calculations. Unlike *P/YR* errors, *mode* mistakes do not result in profound consequences; hence, they are not obvious to most users. In contrast, compounding errors may result in large consequences; as a result, even the most inexperienced user should notice a problem. *Mode* mistakes are more subtle; nevertheless, they can be material.

The *Mode* is irrelevant in FUTURE VALUE and PRESENT VALUE computations. It is relevant for computations involving the FUTURE VALUE OF AN ANNUITY, the PRESENT VALUE OF AN ANNUITY, a SINKING FUND, or an AMORTIZATION.

40. **Below-Market Loan: BML:** For tax purposes, *IRC* section 7872 defines a *below-market loan* in two ways:

- For demand loans, a *BML* is one for which interest is payable at less than the *Applicable Federal Rate (AFR)*.

- For term loans, a *BML* is one for which the present value of all loan payments, *discounted* at the appropriate *AFR* is less than the stated *principal* amount of the loan.

Generally, *IRC* section 7872 imputes interest on *below-market loans* such that they reflect the *AFR*.

Employers often use *BMLs* as a form of disguised compensation to employees, particularly highly paid employees. *IRC* section 7872 forces the parties to recognize the economic reality of such loans, at least to the extent of the *AFR*. Corporations—particularly closely held ones— have also used *BMLs* as disguised distributions. Again, *IRC* section 7872 forces the parties to recognize the economic reality of such loans, at least to the extent of the *AFR*. Similarly, parents often use *BMLs* as disguised gifts to their children. Once again, *IRC* section 7872 removes most tax benefits from such transactions.

Below-market loans are common-place in many other types of transactions. For example, over the past several decades car companies have often offered low or zero-interest loans to buyers. Inevitably, these are in the alternative to a price reduction. Indeed, for tax purposes, such loans would have the consequence of a price reduction along with market interest. For financial accounting purposes, the same result should follow.

Accounting for such loans becomes difficult when the lender and the seller are different entities. Typically, however, they are substantially related entities, with common ownership. Hence the economic impact of the loan is that of a distribution from the lender to the seller of the present value of the discount, plus a rebate from the seller to the buyer of the *present value* of the discount (*i.e.*, a price reduction).

Marketing departments know that some consumers react to (are motivated by) lower prices, while others react to lower stated interest rates. Because money is fungible, the seller is indifferent whether it drops the price or the state interest rate, as the *IRR*—the *present value* of the cash flows—is the same. But, if offering two economically identical, but nominal different, prices helps to sell cars, then car companies are more than willing to join the charade.

Taxpayers enter transactions with below market rates, or with deferred interest, because they want to escape, defer, or accelerate the tax consequences of market rates. By requiring use of the *AFR* in many situations, the *IRC* effectively precludes much of the intended manipulation: the escape, the deferral, or the acceleration. However, because the *AFR* is lower than market rates, it does not eliminate all the benefits of the affected transactions.

41. **BEPS:** Base erosion and profit shifting. This is an international tax term which refers to a business shifting the "location" of income to a lower-tax jurisdiction through various accounting schemes. The "tax base" for the jurisdiction shifted from decreases, which results in loss of revenue.

42. **Beta:** In finance terms, an investment's beta indicates how volatile it is. A beta of 1 equals the general market. A beta greater than one suggests the investment has more volatile price swings.

43. **Bid Price:** The bid price is the offer to buy price for items without a highly liquid market—*e.g.*, many stocks, bonds, debentures, or commodities. It contrasts with the *Ask Price* which is the offer to sell price. For securities listed on a major exchange, a "market maker" ensures the bid and the ask price come together. For other exchanges, the spread between the bid and ask prices exists until it does not, *i.e.*, until it "closes."

44. **Blue Book:** This term has three very different meanings for lawyers. To most, it refers to THE BLUEBOOK: A UNIFORM SYSTEM OF CITATION (compiled by the editors of the Columbia, Harvard, and University of Pennsylvania Law Reviews and the Yale Law Journal). It provides a commonly-used (not universal, but close to it) system of authority citations for law articles. It contrasts with the APA (American Psychological Association) format used by most social scientists.

The term also, however, has special meaning in tax law. It commonly refers to the report prepared by the staff of the Joint Committee on Taxation. The "Bluebook" appears after the enactment of tax legislation and thus is not "legislative history" however, it provides contemporaneous information regarding the legislation. Some people suggest the point of view may be slanted by the party in power or by staff members subjected to lobbying; hence, the Bluebook may contain interpretations and constructions at odds with the legislation. Whether that cynical viewpoint is valid is unclear; however, it exists. In any case, the Bluebook is important in the study of U.S. tax law.

Further, the term often refers to the NADA Blue Book, which reports the value of used automobiles.

45. **Blue Book Value:** The value of a car in the *Blue Book*. This will vary based on the condition of the automobile and thus is not an absolute. It also varies depending on whether one is looking for a trade-in value or a used-car-dealer sales price or a consumer-to-consumer used car sales price. See *National Automobile Dealers Association* and *NADA*. The *Blue Book Value* of a car is not necessarily the *Fair Market Value* (*FMV*) of the automobile. Often one can purchase a car for less than *Blue Book Value*.

Be careful not to confuse the acronym *NADA* with the acronym *NASD*.

46. **Bond:** A *Bond* is a corporate or government obligation to pay money in the future. The term *bond* is **not** a term of art. Generally, it refers to long-term obligations (more than ten years, as opposed to notes (generally mid-term of approximately five to ten years) and commercial paper or bills (generally short-term obligations of less than five years). Often, people refer to secured obligations as *bonds* and unsecured obligations as *debentures*. Others, however, use the term *secured bonds* and then inter-change the terms *bond* and *debenture*. Almost always the term *debenture* refers, however, to an unsecured obligation.

Bonds may be registered or bearer (coupon). With registered *bonds*, the obligor remits interest to the registered owner; hence, the paper evidence of the *bond* does not by itself indicate ownership. In contrast, with *coupon bonds*, the obligor remits interest to whoever presents the interest coupon. For such bearer instruments, the paper itself reflects ownership. In recent years, almost all *bonds* have been in registered form because *coupon bonds* were commonly used to evade taxes.

The term bond also appears in relation to various obligations. For example, the issuer of a *Bail Bond* guarantees the presence of a criminal defendant. The issuer of a *Performance Bond* guarantees the obligation or contractual performance of another.

47. **Books:** In *financial accounting*, a set of books refers to:

- *Journals*: These are chronological entries of transactions. An entity may have a single journal. More likely, it will have multiple journals, including ones for cash receipts and disbursements, one for sales, one for inventory, and one for closing entries.

- *Ledgers*: These are topical entries of transactions. They include all journal entries, but in a different format. Often called *T-accounts*, ledgers group a period's transactions by type. For example, all debits and *credits* affecting cash will appear in the cash ledger. All *debits* and *credits* affecting supplies will appear in the supplies ledger.

Accountants maintain *journals* daily, as transactions occur. They then transfer the *debits* and *credits* separately to the appropriate *ledgers*. Both *journals* and *ledgers* provide important information. *Journals* show the timing of transactions while *ledgers* show the impact. *Journals* are continuous, although accountants separate them by periods. Some *ledgers* are continuous—those which are *balance sheet* items, such as assets, liabilities and equity. Accountants net them periodically, but the *ledgers* and their balances continue from period to period. In contrast, some *ledgers* are temporary—confined to a particular period. These are the income and expense, profit and loss *ledgers*, which are *Income Statement* items.

At the end of each period, accountants *close temporary ledgers* to a single *ledger* which produces the *Income Statement*. Accountants then close this *ledger* into *Retained Earnings*. A periodic *profit* will have a *credit* balance in the *income statement* ledger. The final *closing entry* will be a *debit* to the *ledger* and a credit to *Retained Earnings*, a permanent ledger (account). A periodic loss will have a *debit* balance in the *income statement* ledger. The final *closing entry* will be a *credit* to the ledger and a *debit* to *Retained Earnings*.

Management is responsible for keeping an entity's books. Internal accountants supervising bookkeepers perform this task. From the books, management will prepare the entity's *Financial Statements*: the

Income Statement, the *Balance Sheet*, and the *Statement of Cash Flows*.

The external auditor—a *CPA*—will audit (check and verify, often using statistical samples), the *financial statements*. He will then issue an *auditor's opinion* regarding whether they are fair and consistent with *GAAP*. He will base his audit on *GAAS*. The auditor neither prepares the books nor the statements.

Most entities will have multiple sets of books. Contrary to popular wisdom, not only is this appropriate, but it is required:

- *Financial Books*, consistent with *GAAP* for external reporting.

- *Tax Books*, consistent with the *IRC* for tax reporting.

- *Internal Books* for managerial and *cost accounting*.

- *Pro Forma Books*, for special circumstances which require adjustments to account for changed methods or assumptions. For example, a Bank may require special assumptions or depreciation or inventory methods. If so, the entity will re-state its accounts to conform to such contractual requirements.

Accountants must be able to reconcile the different sets of books. As one might suppose, this is not a simple process. Lawyers should be aware of the multiple sets of books and the multiple sets of *Financial Statements* which flow from them. In particular, lawyers who need to know an entity's income or *equity* must realize that these are not terms of art. Accountants have many ways of presenting income, expenses, assets, liabilities, and *equity*. Lawyers who request information about these terms should expect multiple answers—which may appear to conflict and which may be very different.

Also, too often lawyers accept a single set of *Financial Statements*, as if they are correct. An unfortunate example involves the common acceptance of tax returns as evidence of *income* for Family Law and other legal matters. Hence, lawyers who request, through discovery, financial information should request all of it, including tax statements, external accounting statement, internal accounting statements, and any *pro forma* statements used in loan or other applications or disclosures.

48. **Book Value:** This represents the value of an entity for financial reporting purposes. Because accounting uses several significant and conservative reporting principles, *book value* is not generally representative of *fair market value*. For example, accountants generally record items at historical cost and do not change that

number unless the item has clearly lost value. Rarely would an accountant increase the value. Hence, *book value* is generally much lower than *fair market value.*

Lawyers need to pay special heed to *book value.* While *Financial Statements* are an important tool, they are not easily interpreted by non-accountants. Lawyers should not take numbers on *Financial Statements* literally without understanding the context of the numbers, the methods of accounting used, and the various assumptions made, as well as the *auditor's opinion.*

49. **Bretton-Woods:** In 1944, 44 allied nations met at the Mount Washington Hotel in Bretton-Woods, New Hampshire. They signed a monetary and economic agreement which eventually established the *International Monetary Fund (IMF)* and the *World Bank.* The agreement pegged the price of gold at $35 per ounce. The United States took itself off the gold standard in 1971, which resulted in undermining much of the *Bretton-Woods* agreement. Since that date, the U.S. dollar has effectively been the world's reserve currency and other currencies have floated exchange rates in relation to the dollar.

50. **Brokerage Accounts:** Brokerage investment accounts have three basic formats:

- **Cash Management.** For this account, the customer deposits cash or securities. The broker-dealer executes trades as directed by the customer. The broker, however, exercises no discretion over the account; hence, he or she has a substantially lower duty owed to the investor than in relation to a discretionary account.

- **Margin.** For this account, the customer may borrow funds (generally not more than 50% of the value) from the broker-dealer.

- **Discretionary.** For this account, the customer grants authority to the investment advisor to execute trades on his behalf.

See: http://www.sec.gov/answers/openaccount.htm.

51. **Broker/dealer:** Generally, a broker executes trades for a customer. A dealer executes trades on his or its own behalf.

The *SEC* regulates brokers and dealers under the Exchange Act and requires them to register. According to the *SEC*:

Section 3(a)(4)(A) of the Act generally defines a "broker" broadly as

any person engaged in the business of effecting transactions in securities for the account of others.

Sometimes you can easily determine if someone is a broker. For instance, a person who executes transactions for others on a securities exchange clearly is a broker. However, other situations are less clear. For example, each of the following individuals and businesses may need to register as a broker, depending on a number of factors:

- "finders," "business brokers," and other individuals or entities that engage in the following activities . . .

- investment advisers and financial consultants;

- . . .

- persons that operate or control electronic or other platforms to trade securities;

- persons that market real-estate investment interests, such as tenancy-in-common interests, that are securities;

- persons that act as "placement agents" for private placements of securities;

- persons that market or effect transactions in insurance products that are securities, such as variable annuities, or other investment products that are securities;

- persons that effect securities transactions for the account of others for a fee, even when those other people are friends or family members;

- persons that provide support services to registered broker-dealers; and . . .

https://www.sec.gov/reportspubs/investor-publications/divisions marketregbdguidehtm.html#II.

52. **Bridge Loan:** This is a temporary loan intended to "bridge" between two other loans—perhaps a construction period loan and more permanent financing.

53. **Bull Market:** This is a colloquial description of a period during which various stock market indexes are higher than during the immediately prior period. Generally, a *Bull Market* exists when an index is up 10% or more from his previous low. In contrast, a *Bear Market* is one in which stock indexes are generally lower and falling. To be bearish or a bear is to believe stocks will fall. In contrast, to be *bullish* or a *bull* is to believe stocks will rise.

54. **By-Pass Trust:** This is a United States *Estate Planning* tool used to minimize estate taxes. Typically, it involves joint planning by a

husband and wife. Each leaves substantial assets to a trust which can benefit the survivor during the survivor's life, but which leaves the principal to others (often children at the survivor's death). The corpus of the trust should maximize the *Unified Credit* to reduce or eliminate estate taxes.

55. **Calendar Year:** A year ending on December 31st. *Income Statements* are periodic (as opposed to *Balance Sheets* which focus as a snapshot of one point in time) and thus focus on operations over a defined period. Because the earth revolves around the Sun in a period we call a year, humans have customarily reported operations, life events, and many activities based on an annual calendar. The same is true of finance and accounting. This, naturally, requires a beginning point and an ending point. For most individuals (humans), the calendar year is ideal— beginning on January 1 and ending on December 31. For non-human persons, *fiscal years* are often useful—particularly for cyclical business which have lots of operations for part of the year and little for others. In such cases, a fiscal year ending during the slow season is sensible; indeed, splitting a normal business cycle between two years could be misleading. For example, many retail businesses have their dominant sales period between the U.S. Thanksgiving (the fourth Thursday of November) through Christmas, and then after-New Year's sales. Because such a business cycle fits together, the use of a *Calendar Year* for financial reporting would split the year in ways that generate distortions. Last year's after New Year's sales would join with this year's before Christmas sales, generating less than optimal information. A *fiscal year* ending in February or March would make more sense in terms of presenting annual operations.

Thus, lawyers should realize: every person must have an annual reporting period because of custom. The *Calendar Year* makes sense in most cases, but can be distorting in others. But, lawyers should heed the discussion in relation to the definition of a *Fiscal Year (FY)*— because the option of having multiple entities with differing years presents opportunities for manipulation of financial information.

56. **Callable:** This refers to a common feature of an obligation: one party— or both—can *call* the obligation due. If the obligor has this power, it has the right to pay off the obligation—such as a *bond*—early. Investors should be aware of whether *bonds* and other investments are *callable*. If indeed they are, then they cannot rely on earning the interest rate prevailing at purchase should general market rates decline. In such a case, the issuer might *call* the obligation, pay it off, and then issue new obligations at a lower fixed rate. Often, people refer to this as the "call risk" of the instrument. The *bond indenture* will describe the call rights, if any. They may be restricted to certain dates, periods, or circumstances.

If the lender has this power, it can *call* the obligation due and thus insist on current rather than deferred payment. From the lender's standpoint, this makes the obligation a *demand loan.* Contractually, the power may be conditional. For example, a lender may retain a *call option* triggered by the borrower's *insolvency* or some other defined economic condition. Contracts frequently have call provisions triggered by defined financial circumstances, such as an entity's *current ratio* falling below 1.5 or its *acid-test ratio* falling below 0.75.

57. **Call Option:** This refers to a contractual right to force another to sell something or to pay some amount otherwise owed in the future. For example, if A owns a *call option* on stock in XYZ Corp., issued by B with a call price of $50, A can force B to sell him the stock for $50. A will have paid for this option. He will exercise it if the price of XYZ exceeds $50 at the time the option is exercisable.

Call options—as well as *put options*—are often traded on public exchanges.

Options have three flavors:

- At the Money: the right to purchase the item at the current market price. This option has no current value other than that equal to fixing the price, *i.e.,* the opportunity to gain without the opportunity of loss.

- In the Money: the right to purchase the item for a price below the current market price. This option has a measurable value separate from the opportunity for gain.

- Out of the Money: the right to purchase the item for a price greater than the current market price. This option has no value other than the gain opportunity minus the required price increase.

58. **Carry-Over Basis:** This is a tax term with no significant financial accounting meaning. Generally, it refers to a tax basis in property carried over to another at the time of death. A similar term—*transfer basis*—generally refers to the transfer of a tax basis in property to the recipient of a gift. *IRC* section 1014 generally provides for a transfer basis for gifts, as does *IRC* section 1041 for transactions between spouses or incident to divorce.

The concept of a *Carry-over Basis* appeared briefly in the *Internal Revenue Code* in section 1023. Enacted in 1976, the provision was repealed in 1977 because of its alleged complexity.

Currently, the United States uses a *Stepped-up Basis* for most property received from a decedent. While very popular with many taxpayers, this provision—*IRC* section 1015—substantially distorts economic decisions by many property owners.

59. **Capital:** This term has many meanings:

In finance it may mean:

- *Equity.*

- *Debt* plus *equity* to equal *total capital investment*. A common phrase refers to the cost of capital. This would compare common stock (which requires price support through the maintenance of an adequate rate of return on *equity* and dividends which are not deductible for tax purposes), *preferred stock* (which requires dividends which are not deductible for tax purposes) with debt (which pays interest which is deductible for tax purposes).

- Fixed assets and producing assets such as plant, land, and equipment, as opposed to inventory and consumables.

Many people also refer to *human capital*—referring to an entity's trained labor force—or *intellectual capital*, which might refer to highly trained persons or intellectual property.

A capital intensive industry is one which requires large investment in fixed assets for production. In contrast, a *labor intensive industry* may require little *capital* but a large labor force.

In tax law, one might refer to *capital income* as opposed to *ordinary income*. This would be short-hand for *capital gain* income.

In other areas of the law, one might refer to *capital income* as opposed to income from labor and industry. Such a reference would include passive investment income such as interest, dividends, and *capital gains*. This usage is vague; hence, lawyers should avoid it without a more complete definition.

60. **Capital Asset:** *For tax purposes*, this is a United States tax term of art. *IRC* section 1221 defines it as including all property *other than* items on an *exclusive* list. Section 1221 lists:

(1) stock in trade of the taxpayer or other property of a kind which would properly be included in the inventory of the taxpayer if on hand at the close of the taxable year, or property held by the taxpayer primarily for sale to customers in the ordinary course of his trade or business;

(2) property, used in his trade or business, of a character which is subject to the allowance for depreciation provided in section 167, or real property used in his trade or business;

(3) a copyright, a literary, musical, or artistic composition, a letter or memorandum, or similar property, held by—

(A) a taxpayer whose personal efforts created such property,

(B) in the case of a letter, memorandum, or similar property, a taxpayer for whom such property was prepared or produced, or

(C) a taxpayer in whose hands the basis of such property is determined, for purposes of determining gain from a sale or exchange, in whole or part by reference to the basis of such property in the hands of a taxpayer described in subparagraph (A) or (B);

(4) accounts or notes receivable acquired in the ordinary course of trade or business for services rendered or from the sale of property described in paragraph (1);

(5) a publication of the United States Government (including the Congressional Record) which is received from the United States Government or any agency thereof, other than by purchase at the price at which it is offered for sale to the public, and which is held by—

(A) a taxpayer who so received such publication, or

(B) a taxpayer in whose hands the basis of such publication is determined, for purposes of determining gain from a sale or exchange, in whole or in part by reference to the basis of such publication in the hands of a taxpayer described in subparagraph (A)

(6) any commodities derivative financial instrument held by a commodities derivatives dealer, unless—

(A) it is established to the satisfaction of the Secretary that such instrument has no connection to the activities of such dealer as a dealer, and

(B) such instrument is clearly identified in such dealer's records as being described in subparagraph (A) before the close of the day on which it was acquired, originated, or entered into (or such other time as the Secretary may by regulations prescribe);

(7) any hedging transaction which is clearly identified as such before the close of the day on which it was acquired, originated, or entered into (or such other time as the Secretary may by regulations prescribe); or

(8) supplies of a type regularly used or consumed by the taxpayer in the ordinary course of a trade or business of the taxpayer.

Much litigation involves the category one phrase: *property held primarily for sale to customers in the ordinary course of a trade or business*. Such items often involve investment property which a person held as a capital asset but which the owner later converted to *inventory*. The change in tax rate can be very significant.

For United States (and many other jurisdictions) *tax purposes*, long-term capital gains result in a materially lower tax rate than do short-term gains or ordinary income. *Capital gains* result from the sale or exchange of a capital asset. The long versus short distinction has traditionally been at one year; however, it has been as short as six months and also longer.

IRC section 1221(2)—generally depreciable property—forms a category in between capital assets and ordinary assets, which generate ordinary income and losses. Those are *IRC* section 1231 assets, which very generally produce capital gains and ordinary losses—the best of both types.

For family law purposes, generally most states keep separate property brought into a marriage as separate. Many, however, consider such property converted to marital or community property status—either in whole or in part—to the extent marital labor and industry significantly impacts its value. The process of developing property—such as a tract of land—and thus converting it from a capital asset to *property held primarily for sale to customers in the ordinary course of a trade or business* is related to the *family law* status change. Indeed, the two separate legal consequences largely overlap: to the extent a person converts property for tax purposes, he likely also converts some or all of it for marital purposes. Of note, the tax consequences may result in an extra 20% of the value going to pay taxes. But, in contrast, the family law consequences may result in an extra 50% of the value going to the other spouse for property division, plus up to 10% going to child support and another significant percentage going to the other spouse for alimony. Hence, the classification of an asset as capital or not is very important for tax purposes; however, it is potentially profoundly important for family law purposes.

Similarly, *trust law* may be significantly impacted by an asset's classification. For the most part, capital gains and losses should belong to the principal beneficiary; however, ordinary gains and losses—such as those resulting from inventory or *property held primarily for sale to customers in the ordinary course of a trade or business*—should belong to the income beneficiary.

Another fuzzy distinction between capital gains and ordinary income involves *Retained Earnings*. Earning belong to the common shareholders. If distributed, they result in dividends. For tax purposes those are taxable to the extent of earnings and profits. For other legal purposes, dividends are almost always—if not always—income. Whether they constitute income from labor and industry—and thus marital assets in most states even if derived from separate property—depends on the degree of management, a question of fact. But, undistributed *Retained Earnings* economically result in share appreciation. This, in turn, results in capital appreciation or capital gains if the owner disposes of the shares. But, many jurisdictions consider such capital appreciation in separate property to retain its character as separate property, regardless of the degree of management. This is widely true for C corporate investors and also commonly true of S corporate investors. *See, e.g., Zold v. Zold*, 911 So. 2d 1222 (Fla. 2005).

For accounting purposes, one might use the term capital assets to distinguish them from inventory, supplies, and variously consumable assets. Such usage is not incorrect; however, it risks confusion with the important tax law terminology.

61. **Capital Gain:** *For tax purposes*, IRC section 1222 defines a capital gain as gain resulting from the <u>sale or exchange</u> of a capital asset. *Long term* gain—generally entitled to preferential tax treatment—flows from assets held more than one year. The <u>sale or exchange</u> treatment is essential for capital gain or loss treatment. Some code sections *impute* a sale or exchange for transaction which would not otherwise satisfy the definition of that phrase (which is not well-defined). Over the history of the Internal Revenue Code, the treatment of capital gains has varied. Often long-term (variously defined, but often a function of a holding period of more than one year) gains have triggered a substantially lower tax rate than ordinary income.

For family law and trust purposes, lawyers must play close attention to the character of gains and losses. While ordinary—non *capital*—gains and losses likely are marital (in the family law realm) and income (in the income versus principal beneficiary realm), the treatment of capital gains and losses is less clear. In family law, such gains on separate property may remain separate (depending on the jurisdiction and the level of management). For trust law, such gains typically belong to the principal beneficiary.

62. **Capital Lease:** For accounting purposes, both under U.S. *GAAP* and IFRS, a capital lease (also known as a finance lease) receives treatment as ownership. Thus the nominal lessee must record the property as an asset and must record all associated liabilities for the balance sheet. Also, the substantive owner recognizes related expenses such as depreciation.

     IAS17 and ASU2016–02 deal with this. One should compare capital leases to IRC section 461(h), to sale-leaseback and gift-leaseback transactions, as well as the substance over form and economic substance doctrines. Also, one should distinguish a capital lease from an operating lease.

63. **Capital Loss:** *For tax purposes*, *IRC* section 1222 defines a capital loss as loss resulting from the *sale or exchange* of a capital asset. *Long term loss*—generally entitled to detrimental tax treatment—flows from assets held more than one year. The *sale or exchange* treatment is essential for capital gain or loss treatment. *IRC* sections 1211 and 1212 deal with capital loss limitations and carryovers.

     A capital loss carryover—which exists for the remainder of the holder's life—can be a valuable asset. While that statement may appear counter-intuitive, it is not. The loss carryover represents a loss which already occurred, but which has not yet appeared on a tax return because of limitations. It thus is a positive tax attribute which may result in positive tax benefits in the future. It is thus a valuable asset.

     One of the more difficult oddities for non-tax law experts to understand is:

     > *Losses, including built-in losses, are attributes.*
     > *Gains, including built-in gains, are detriments.*

     Of course, one does not want to lose money and one wants to gain money. Hence, overall, losses are bad and profits are good. However, if I get the money and you get the tax consequences, losses are good and profits are bad. Lawyers need to understand:

     > *Tax consequences and the money related to those consequences do not necessarily flow together.*

     To the extent they do not, much room for manipulation or advantage (and disadvantage) exists. The horribly complex rules involving partnership taxation provide enormous room for separating income, gains, deductions, losses, and credits from the money or assets associated with them. See *IRC* section 704(b). While treasury regulations defining whether special allocations of such items have substantial economic effect sharply limit the ability of persons to allocate them for tax purposes, they say nothing about the ability of persons to allocate them for non-tax legal purposes, if only for the short-term. Lawyers unfamiliar with the intricacies of partnership allocations risk respecting them in non-tax legal areas without understanding the likely future tax implications, which may be years away—outside the time period being considered in the non-tax legal matter.

64. **Capitalization of Earnings:** This is a common method of valuing a business. It is quite similar to a *DCF* (Discounted Cash Flow) analysis.

The formula is:

$$FMV = \frac{projected\ future\ earnings}{discount\ rate}$$

Projected Future Earnings are typically a function of past earnings; although, information regarding new products or activities could involve non-historically based earnings. For many legal purposes, however—such as torts and family law—most jurisdictions will likely limit projected earnings to those which have an historical basis

The discount rate includes an evaluation of the interest rate risk the investor is willing to accept, adjusted for projected earnings increases and inflation or deflation.

An alternate way of computing the FMV is to multiply the expected earnings by a factor, which is the inverse of the discount rate. For example, if the appropriate discount rate is 20% or 1/5, then the multiplier would be 5.

In a simple example, an appraiser would first determine average net earnings during a base period—perhaps the prior three years. He would then multiply that number by 5 (or whatever the inverse of the appropriate discount rate happened to be) to obtain the current business value. Hence, if a business had average net earnings of $100,000, it would (using 5 as the multiplier) have a fair market value of $500,000.

For publicly traded companies, P/E ratios (price to earnings ratios) are often in the 12 to 20 range (though they can certainly be as low as 4 or 5 and as high as 100). For smaller, more closely held companies, however, an earnings multiplier of 12 to 20 would historically be excessive.

65. **Capitalization of Interest:** For finance purposes, the process of *capitalizing interest* involves adding it to principal. This is also known as *negative amortization*. It occurs because periodic payments on a loan are less than the periodic interest accrued

For tax purposes, it can have the same meaning as it does for finance, but it also has a separate meaning. It refers to the process of adding construction period interest to the basis (cost) of a project. Under this definition, the process of capitalization is distinguishable from the process of expensing or deducting an item or cost.

66. **Capitalize:** For both tax law and accounting purposes, "to capitalize" an expenditure means to add it to an asset account. For example, if expenditure is for an asset or service with a life greater than one year—and if it is material—one would typically add the cost to an asset account via a debit. The corresponding credit would be to cash or a liability. The resulting asset would be "amortized" over its useful life (typically straight-line) or "depreciated" over its useful life. Capitalization furthers the **Matching Principal of Accounting** by ensuring costs properly match with the income they produce. One would "expense" short-term or immaterial expenditures.

67. **Carrying Charges: Cost of Carry:** Holding an asset costs money—directly in terms of storage and insurance, as well as indirectly in terms of opportunity costs. When computing the rate of return on investments in physical assets—such as precious metals—one should include the cost of carry.

68. **Cash:** Generally this refers to currency, coin, and demand deposits (mostly checking accounts). The term mostly has meaning in relation to a *payment*. Whether the use of a credit card as *payment* is considered a "cash payment" is up to the parties. Lawyers should be careful in using the term *cash* in a contract: they should define the meaning, as it is _not_ a term of art.

69. **Cash Flows:** For *financial calculation* purposes, the term *"cash flows"* refers to the direction of *payments*. For example, cash may flow from A to B as a loan and then back from B to A as a *payment* to amortize the loan. For some *financial calculators*, one of these *cash flows* must be a positive number and the other a negative number; indeed, the mathematical formula for computing the loan amortization requires that opposite direction *cash flows* have opposite signs (positive versus negative). *Financial Calculators* manufactured by HEWLETT-PACKARD® typically have this feature. Many *financial calculators*, however, have built-in computer software which eliminates the need for the user to state the various opposing flows with opposite signs.

If two *cash flows* occur simultaneously, _all_ *financial calculators* will collapse them into a single net flow. Hence, mathematically, the *pre-payment* of interest is impossible, as it would be simultaneous with the borrowing of *principal* (or at least with the obligation to continue to owe *principal*). The interest and the *principal* necessarily would have opposite signs as they are opposing *cash flows*. Thus they necessarily collapse and the attempted pre-payment of interest becomes a *principal* payment—or more simply, a lessening of the amount loaned.

Despite the economic and financial impossibility of *pre-paid interest*, tax law oddly contemplates such an event. See *IRC* section 461(g):

> (g) Prepaid interest
>
>> (1) In general
>>
>>> If the taxable income of the taxpayer is computed under the cash receipts and disbursements method of accounting, interest paid by the taxpayer which, under regulations prescribed by the Secretary, is properly allocable to any period—
>>>
>>>> (A) with respect to which the interest represents a charge for the use or forbearance of money, and
>>>>
>>>> (B) which is after the close of the taxable year in which paid,
>>>
>>> shall be charged to capital account and shall be treated as paid in the period to which so allocable.
>>
>> (2) Exception
>>
>>> This subsection shall not apply to points paid in respect of any indebtedness incurred in connection with the purchase or improvement of, and secured by, the principal residence of the taxpayer to the extent that, under regulations prescribed by the Secretary, such payment of points is an established business practice in the area in which such indebtedness is incurred, and the amount of such payment does not exceed the amount generally charged in such area.

See the discussion of *pre-payments* for more information.

One of the three main *Financial Statements* is the *Statement of Cash Flows*.

70. **Cash Method:** This is a commonly used *Method of Accounting*. *GAAP* does not recognize it, as it does not normally clearly reflect income.

Under the *Cash Method*, a person has income when he receives *payment* for the item. He has a deduction when he *pays* an item. Naturally, those definitions are a function of the definition of the term *payment*, which is often imprecise. A significant issue in U.S. tax law concerns the definition of the term payment. The litigation centers on three important, controversial issues:

- How does a *payment* differ from a mere *deposit?*

- May one pay an amount using borrowed money?

- If one uses money borrowed from the creditor, can one pay the creditor?

Most United States taxpayers may use the *Cash Method* for reporting income and deductions—as opposed to the *Accrual Method*, or a hybrid method. See *IRC* section 446. As a result, for many people, tax return information does _not_ clearly reflect income; hence, lawyers should be wary of federal tax return numbers.

Use of the *Cash Method* is common because of its simplicity. A basic check book register use the cash method: one does not record deposits until one deposits the money and one does not record checks until one writes the check. Most people can use the method with a high level of accuracy (to the extent the method is accurate). If a tax system required everyone to use the *Accrual Method*, the result would likely be hugely complex.

71. **C Corporation:** A corporation subject to Subchapter C of Subtitle A of the Internal Revenue Code of the United States. C Corporations are themselves taxpayers. They pay taxes on income generally at a rate of 34%. Dividends and Distributions from them are not deductible; however, taxpayers who receive dividends are subject to preferential treatment. Nevertheless, *C Corporation* income is subject to double taxation in the U.S.: once at the corporate level and once at the shareholder level. This is as opposed to income of an *S Corporation*, which is a *pass-through entity*.

As a general rule, large corporations and widely-held (generally publicly traded) corporations are C's. Most other corporations elect *S* status or they are LLCs (limited liability companies).

72. **Charting: Chartist:** Some investors pay close attention to the graphic images presented by investment price changes. A chartist is a trader/investor who concentrates on chart theory. Under chart theory, prices form common (sometimes very complex) patterns. A common example involves a consistent floor or ceiling: the graphed price keeps reaching a particular level, followed by a rise or drop. That level is a ceiling or floor. If the price ever breaks through that level, it tends to keep going until it reaches another floor or ceiling. Often, even numbers simplistically become floors and ceilings, *e.g.*, $100, or $75, or $25.

73. **Chicago Mercantile Exchange: CME:** Now part of the CME Group, a publicly traded company, the *Chicago Mercantile Exchange* has existed since 1898. Originally it primarily traded or facilitated trades of commodities, such as metals and grains. It now also trades currencies, as well as futures, options, and derivatives.

74. **Churning:** In a discretionary account, the investment manager may be tempted to trade excessively so at to increase commissions for himself. This is an inherent conflict of interest with the owner/investor.

75. **Circuit Breaker:** This is a system for halting trading in particular securities—or for an entire market—upon the occurrence of defined events. Triggers include substantial price drops, which might cause a trading halt for a short period, or, in some cases, a much longer period. The intention is to prevent or to slow down panic and rumors and to create a "cooling off" time for investors and traders.

76. **Certificate of Deposit: CD:** A *CD* is a time deposit with a financial institution. They often have terms as short as 30 days or up to five years. Longer term *CDs* generally bear higher interest rates. The *FDIC* insures bank *CDs*. Interest may accumulate or it may be paid to the holder. Typically, a penalty applies for early withdrawal of funds.

77. **Certified Financial Planner: CFP®:** According to the Certified Financial Planner Board of Standards, Inc.:

> CFP® certificants must pass the comprehensive CFP® Certification Examination, pass CFP Board's *Candidate Fitness Standards*, agree to abide by CFP Board's *Code of Ethics and Professional Responsibility* which puts clients' interests first and comply with the *Financial Planning Practice Standards* which spell out what clients should be able to reasonably expect from the financial planning engagement. These are just some of the reasons why the CFP® certification is becoming increasingly recognized.

Since 1993, to become a *CFP®*, one must pass the *CFP®* exam which lasts about 10 hours. This is not a state issued license; however, the designation carries some evidence of expertise.

78. **Certified Forensic Accountant: Cr. FA®:** This is a designation sought by some *Forensic Accountants*. It is not a state license. See the discussion of *Forensic Accountant* and *Forensic Economist* for more information.

79. **Certified Fraud Examiner: CFE:** This is a designation sought by some *Forensic Accountants*. It is not a state license. See the discussion of *Forensic Accountant* and *Forensic Economist* for more information.

80. **Certified Internal Auditor®: CIA®:** According to the Institute of Internal Auditors:

> The Certified Internal Auditor® (CIA®) designation is the only globally accepted certification for internal auditors and remains the standard by which individuals demonstrate their

competency and professionalism in the internal auditing field. Candidates leave the program enriched with educational experience, information, and business tools that can be applied immediately in any organization or business environment.

http://www.theiia.org/certification/certified-internal-auditor/.

81. **Certified Public Accountant: CPA:** To use the designation *CPA* or (in most states) public accountant, one must have passed the *Uniform Certified Public Accountant Examination*. One must also satisfy state imposed education and continuing education requirements to earn a *license* to practice public accounting.

    Certified Public Accountants may express an opinion on audited financial statements.

    An Independent *CPA* is one who is not employed by the client. He expresses an independent opinion on financial statements prepared by management. His duties are to the public, investors, and creditors, rather to the client who seeks his opinion. In most states, conversations between a client and a CPA are *not* subject to an evidentiary privilege.

    The first-time pass rate on the *CPA* exam is historically low— sometimes in the single digits and often less than 25%. Many states require 150 credits hours of study (essentially a Master's Degree) as well as substantial work-experience before one can obtain a license as a *CPA*. *In some states*, being certified is separate from being licensed: all licensees must have a *Certificate*, but some persons with a *CPA* Certificate do not have a license or have an inactive license. Although CPAs cannot generally handle litigation, they are allowed to represent taxpayers before the United States Tax Court.

    Contrary to popular wisdom, *CPA*s often have little special expertise in tax law. While most—if not all—accounting schools offer courses in tax law and tax return preparation, they are not the equivalent of a law degree or an LL.M. in tax law. While many *CPA*s are knowledgeable about many aspects of tax law, they are not lawyers (unless they also have a law degree or Bar membership). CPAs, however, may enroll to practice before the *IRS* and may appear before the Tax Court.

    *CPA*s, as well as attorneys who are *CPA*s, may properly identify themselves with the designation *PFS* or *CFP*, if they have earned the designation. *See Ibanez v. Florida*, 512 U.S. 136 (1994) [majority approving the use of *CPA*, *CFA* designation by an attorney in advertising over the objection of the regulatory bodies for *CPA*s in Florida].

In most other countries, a licensed accountant is called a Chartered Accountant or something similar. The designation varies significant but "chartered" and "accountant" are often part of the terminology.

82. **Certified Security:** This is a security for which the issuer has issued a certificate—such as for a stock or bond. Uncertified security have no certificate, but are instead merely noted on the issuer's or transfer agent's records. The UCC refers to certificated securities and uncertificated securities.

83. **Charity:** This is _not_ a term of art. Generally, the term refers to an organization exempt from United States income tax under _IRC_ section 501(c)(3). Contributions to such organizations are generally deductible by the donor for income tax purposes under _IRC_ section 170(c)(2). In this sense, the term _Charity_ includes organizations benefiting the arts, religion, the under-privileged, education, public safety, and many other endeavors not traditionally considered "charitable."

The term is _not_ synonymous with the term _non profit organization_. Nothing in _IRC_ section 501(c)(3) requires an approved entity to be _non-profit;_ indeed, many charities make substantial profits (of course, depending on how one defines the term _profits_). Many state corporation statutes have provisions for Non-profit Corporations (or Not-for-profit Corporations); however, seldom (= ever) do such acts forbid profits, at least as one might typically define that term.

The term _Charity_ is also not synonymous with _Tax Exempt Organization_ (_TEO_), a United States tax term of art (and also a term or art in many countries). _IRC_ section 501(c) lists more than two dozen ways an entity can be exempt from United States income tax; however, only those described in paragraph 501(c)(3) fit the common usage for the term _Charity_.

Two sub-categories of charities exist in the United States:

- Public Charities, which are subject to few federal tax law restrictions.

- Private Foundations, which are subject to extensive federal tax law restrictions.

The _Private Foundation_ category has several sub categories, as well.

84. **Check:** A _check_ is a kind of _draft_, drawn on a financial institution account. It is a directive to the institution to pay a stated amount of money to the order of a person or the bearer. The "to the order of" language is critical and is part of what makes a check a negotiable instrument under the Uniform Commercial Code. Not all _drafts_ are _checks_, but all _checks_ are _drafts_. See the definition of _Negotiable Instrument_ for more information.

In some countries—particularly the U.K.—the spelling is *cheque*. In many countries—particularly in Europe—*checks* are largely a thing of the past, having been replaced by *ATM*s, electronic transfers or *giros*. In the United States, on-line banking, *ATM*s, direct deposits, and direct debits have substantially reduced the usage of paper *checks*.

For tax purposes, the transfer of a *check* has the same effect as the transfer of cash: it reflects payment and receipt. This rule is subject to the *check* not being dishonored. *E.g., Kahler v. Commissioner*, 18 T.C. 31 (1952).

85. **Closing Costs:** These are costs, other than interest, associated with a loan. They include an application fee, an appraisal fee, a notary fee, a title insurance premium, and a private mortgage insurance fee. They often amount to one to three percent of the amount loaned. They may include *points*—which are a separate charge denominated as *pre-paid interest*. *Points* and some other closing costs receive interest treatment under federal law. As such, they form part of the *Annual Percentage Rate (APR)* disclosed in relation to the loan.

86. **Charitable Lead Trust:** *CLT*: This is a tax term of art. Generally, such trusts fit into two types:

- *CLAT*: **Charitable Lead Annuity Trust:** This must pay a fixed dollar amount at least annually to a charitable beneficiary. It then pays the remainder to the grantor. This would be a *Qualified Grantor Charitable Lead Annuity Trust (QGCLAT)*. *IRC* section 170(f)(2)(B) provides:

    (B) Income interests, etc.

    No deduction shall be allowed under this section for the value of any interest in property (other than a remainder interest) transferred in trust unless the interest is in the form of a guaranteed annuity or the trust instrument specifies that the interest is a fixed percentage distributed yearly of the fair market value of the trust property (to be determined yearly) and the grantor is treated as the owner of such interest for purposes of applying section 671. If the donor ceases to be treated as the owner of such an interest for purposes of applying section 671, at the time the donor ceases to be so treated, the donor shall for purposes of this chapter be considered as having received an amount of income equal to the amount of any deduction he received under this section for the contribution reduced by the discounted value of all amounts of income earned by the trust and taxable to him before the time at which he ceases to be treated as the owner of the interest. Such amounts of income shall be discounted to the date of the contribution. The Secretary shall prescribe such regulations as may be necessary to carry out the purposes of this subparagraph.

- *CLUT*: **Charitable Lead Unitrust**: This must pay a fixed percentage of trust FMV at least annually to a charitable beneficiary. It then pays the remainder to the grantor. This would be a *Qualified Grantor Charitable Lead Unitrust* (*QGCLUT*).

Under *IRC* section 170(a), the grantor receives a charitable contribution deduction (subject to section 170(b) limitations) for the **PRESENT VALUE OF AN ANNUITY**: the income interest benefitting a *Charity* (or some other permitted beneficiaries described in *IRC* section 170(c)). The term for this non-fixed annuity would be the life expectancy of the grantor.

The grantor, however, must *include* the trust income annually. Some people may view that as a disadvantage: the grantor will have annual income, but no receipts. An evaluation of whether such a trust is beneficial would compare the *after-tax* **PRESENT VALUE OF A SUM**: the current income tax deduction to the *after-tax* **PRESENT VALUE OF AN ANNUITY**: the annual income inclusion minus the *after-tax* **PRESENT VALUE OF AN ANNUITY**: the annual deductible charitable contribution of the income amounts. Important factors in the analysis include:

- The donor's expectation that he will live less than his life expectancy as determined by relevant actuarial tables.

- The donor's expectation of decreasing tax rates in general, or for him individually.

Charitable Lead Trusts may also be *non-grantor trusts*, which in turn, may either be *qualified* or *non-qualified*. See the discussion of *Grantor Trusts* for a more complete explanation.

- A *Qualified Non-Grantor CLT* may fit either the *annuity trust* or the *unitrust* formula. Hence, they would be either a *QNGCLAT* or a *QNGCLUT*. Such a trust does not generate a charitable contribution deduction for the grantor; however, the trust may deduct the annual charitable contributions. Also, the donor will receive a partial gift tax deduction. Because the charitable deductions belong to the trust rather than to the grantor, they avoid the percentage limitations of *IRC* section 170(b). Also, because the trust is not itself a charity under *IRC* section 501(c)(3), it avoids *Private Foundation* status.

- A *Non-Qualified Non-Grantor CLT* need not fit either the annuity trust or the unitrust formula; hence, it may pay a percentage of trust income to charity. One may describe such entities as *NQNGCLT*. The trust will annually deduct charitable contributions; hence, the grantor avoids the section 170(b) percentage limitations. Also, *IRC* section 642(c) permits contributions to foreign charities, while *IRC* section 170(c) limits them; hence, the grantor also avoids those restrictions.

87. **Charitable Remainder Trust: *CRT*:** This is a tax term of art. Generally, such trusts fit into two types:

- **CRAT: Charitable Remainder Annuity Trust:** This must pay a fixed dollar amount at least annually to the income beneficiary. It then pays the remainder to a *Charity*. *IRC* section 664(d) provides:

  (1) Charitable remainder annuity trust

  For purposes of this section, a charitable remainder annuity trust is a trust—

  (A) from which a sum certain (which is not less than 5 percent nor more than 50 percent of the initial net fair market value of all property placed in trust) is to be paid, not less often than annually, to one or more persons (at least one of which is not an organization described in section 170(c) and, in the case of individuals, only to an individual who is living at the time of the creation of the trust) for a term of years (not in excess of 20 years) or for the life or lives of such individual or individuals,

  (B) from which no amount other than the payments described in subparagraph (A) and other than qualified gratuitous transfers described in subparagraph (C) may be paid to or for the use of any person other than an organization described in section 170(c),

  (C) following the termination of the payments described in subparagraph (A), the remainder interest in the trust is to be transferred to, or for the use of, an organization described in section 170(c) or is to be retained by the trust for such a use or, to the extent the remainder interest is in qualified employer securities (as defined in subsection (g)(4)), all or part of such securities are to be transferred to an employee stock ownership plan (as defined in section 4975(e)(7) in a qualified gratuitous transfer (as defined by subsection (g)), and

(D) the value (determined under section 7520 of such remainder interest is at least 10 percent of the initial net fair market value of all property placed in the trust.

- *CRUT*: **Charitable Remainder Unitrust:** This must pay a fixed percentage amount at least annually to the income beneficiary. It then pays the remainder to a *Charity*. *IRC* section 664(d) provides:

  (2)   Charitable remainder unitrust

  For purposes of this section, a charitable remainder unitrust is a trust—

  (A) from which a fixed percentage (which is not less than 5 percent nor more than 50 percent) of the net fair market value of its assets, valued annually, is to be paid, not less often than annually, to one or more persons (at least one of which is not an organization described in section 170(c) and, in the case of individuals, only to an individual who is living at the time of the creation of the trust) for a term of years (not in excess of 20 years) or for the life or lives of such individual or individuals,

  (B) from which no amount other than the payments described in subparagraph (A) and other than qualified gratuitous transfers described in subparagraph (C) may be paid to or for the use of any person other than an organization described in section 170(c),

  (C) following the termination of the payments described in subparagraph (A) the remainder interest in the trust is to be transferred to, or for the use of, an organization described in section 170(c) or is to be retained by the trust for such a use or, to the extent the remainder interest is in qualified employer securities (as defined in subsection (g)(4)), all or part of such securities are to be transferred to an employee stock ownership plan (as defined in section 4975(e)(7) in a qualified gratuitous transfer (as defined by subsection (g)), and

(D) with respect to each contribution of property to the trust, the value (determined under section 7520 of such remainder interest in such property is at least 10 percent of the net fair market value of such property as of the date such property is contributed to the trust.

Under *IRC* section 170(a), the grantor receives a charitable contribution deduction (subject to section 170(f) limitations) for the **PRESENT VALUE** of the remainder interest benefitting a *Charity* (or some other permitted beneficiaries described in *IRC* section 170(c)). The term for the **PRESENT VALUE OF A SUM** computation would be the life expectancy of the income beneficiary.

88. **Chartered Financial Analyst: CFA:** This is a designation granted by the *CFA* Institute. It is _not_ a state license. According to the Institute:

> To earn the CFA charter, you must successfully pass through the CFA Program, a graduate-level self-study program that combines a broad curriculum with professional conduct requirements, culminating in a series of three sequential exams. Level I exams are held in June and December. Levels II and III are only held in June.

The designation *CFA* is multi-national. The Institute and its predecessors have granted it since 1963. The three required examinations total 18 hours.

89. **Chartered Life Underwriter: CLU®:** This is a designation granted by the *American College*. It is _not_ a state license. According to the College:

> The Chartered Life Underwriter (CLU®) is the world's most respected designation of insurance expertise, helping you gain a significant advantage in a competitive market. This prestigious course of study helps advance your career by providing in-depth knowledge on the insurance needs of individuals, business owners, and professional clients.

http://www.theamericancollege.edu.

90. **Chief Executive Officer: CEO:** This is the head of a corporation or group of related corporations. He may also serve with the title of President.

91. **Chief Financial Officer: CFO:** This is the person in charge of a corporation's financial operations. He would oversee bookkeeping,

records, internal and external audits, and the management of investments and working capital.

92. **Class Life:** This is a tax law term of art (with often modified statutory definitions) without a clear statutory definition. *IRC* section 168(i) provides:

> (i) Definitions and special rules
>
> For purposes of this section—
>
>> (1) Class Life
>>
>> Except as provided in this section the term "class life" means the class life (if any) which would be applicable with respect to any property as of January 1, 1986, under subsection (m) of section 167 (determined without regard to paragraph (4) and as if the taxpayer had made an election under such subsection). The Secretary, through an office established in the Treasury, shall monitor and analyze actual experience with respect to all depreciable assets. The reference in this paragraph to subsection (m) of section 167 shall be treated as a reference to such subsection as in effect on the day before the date of the enactment of the Revenue Reconciliation Act of 1990.

IRC section 167(m), referred to in the definition, no longer exists, having been repealed in 1990.

For *depreciation*—either tax or financial—an asset must have a useful life—the period over which the owner allocates the depreciation expense. For tax purposes, *Rev. Proc. 87–56 (1987)* includes the old *class life* system numbers, which set a range of acceptable class lives for a great many types of property.

For current United States tax *depreciation* under *IRC* section 168 (*MACRS*), the taxpayer must know the *Applicable Recovery Period* for the asset under IRC section 168(c). *Applicable Recovery Period* is a function of the asset's *Classification*, as defined by *IRC* section 168(e). *Classification* is a function of the asset's *class life*, if any.

Because current *IRC* section 168 *Applicable Recovery Periods* are typically much shorter than the more economically realistic *class lives*, the tax *depreciation* deduction is accelerated faster than the more economically justifiable (but often still accelerated) financial accounting depreciation deduction. The differences result in complicated book/tax disparities, which provide room for manipulation of financial information by educated, but less than scrupulous persons, including lawyers. Congress permits the super-*accelerated depreciation* as a form of *fiscal* policy: accelerated deductions lower tax obligations for affected taxpayers, who—because they are price elastic regarding the subject property—invest more or spend more. The resulting increased consumption results in increased economic activity, which results in a stronger economy (at least in theory).

93. **Closing Entry:** At the end of each period, accountants and bookkeepers *close* the books. More specifically, they close all *temporary accounts*, which are the income and loss or expense accounts.

An income account would normally have a *credit* balance. To *close* it, the bookkeeper *debits* the account for the amount of the periodic balance and credits another temporary account called profit and loss summary (or some similar name). The income *ledger*—or *T-account*—will then have a zero balance; hence, it has *closed*.

After similarly *closing* all income and expense *ledgers* to the profit and loss summary *ledger*, the bookkeeper will then close that *temporary account*. If it has a credit balance, the entity had a profit for the period. If the account has a *debit* balance, the entity had a loss for the period. In either event, the bookkeeper will *debit* or *credit* the balance so as to cause the resulting balance to be zero. He will correspondingly *debit* or *credit* retained earnings for the profit or loss. As a result, all *temporary accounts* effectively transfer to the *Balance Sheet* in the form of an increase or decrease to *retained earnings*. From the profit and loss summary *ledger*, the bookkeeper and accountant can easily prepare the periodic *Income Statement*.

Remember: *Balance Sheet* accounts are permanent accounts, and *Income Statement* accounts are temporary accounts.

By *closing* the books with such *closing* entries, the accountant keeps each period's operations separate. He also, by transferring those operations to *Retained Earnings*—either as an increase or decrease—maintains a proper snapshot of the entity's cumulative operations.

94. **COBRA: The Consolidated Omnibus Budget Reconciliation Act of 1986:** [pronounced **koh**-br*uh*]. It primarily affects health care plans of employees.

According to the U.S. Department of Labor:

> The Consolidated Omnibus Budget Reconciliation Act (COBRA) gives workers and their families who lose their health benefits the right to choose to continue group health benefits provided by their group health plan for limited periods of time under certain circumstances such as voluntary or involuntary job loss, reduction in the hours worked, transition between jobs, death, divorce, and other life

events. Qualified individuals may be required to pay the entire premium for coverage up to 102 percent of the cost to the plan.

COBRA generally requires that group health plans sponsored by employers with 20 or more employees in the prior year offer employees and their families the opportunity for a temporary extension of health coverage (called continuation coverage) in certain instances where coverage under the plan would otherwise end.

COBRA outlines how employees and family members may elect continuation coverage. It also requires employers and plans to provide notice.

http://www.dol.gov/dol/topic/health-plans/cobra.htm.

95. **Codification:** The Financial Accounting Standards Board (the *FASB*) began codifying *FASB* statements (later called FASs or Financial Accounting Standards) into a code in 2009. It is now the official statement of U.S. *GAAP*.

96. **COLA: Cost of Living Adjustment: Cost of Living Allowance:** The cost of living adjustment generally refers to an automatic increase in Social Security Benefits. Since 1973, it does not require legislation by Congress. Since its enactment, the reference measure for the increase has changed. Currently the Social Security Administration uses the *CPI*-W, or the core inflation rate for urban wage earners.

The term *COLA* also refers to a *Cost of Living Allowance* granted by the United States military to service personnel stationed in high cost areas.

97. **COLI: Corporate Owned Life Insurance:** This describes insurance owned by a corporate employer on the life of an employee—often, but not necessarily a highly valued or *key employee.*

98. **Comfort Letter:** This term has many usages.

For accounting purposes, it can refer to a letter written by an independent *CPA* (not one employed by the entity) reflecting the opinion that current, not-yet-audited, financial information appears to conform to *GAAP*. This may accompany an entity's prospectus for an *Initial Public Offering* (*IPO*).

It can also refer to a *CPA's* letter to potential lenders or investors regarding the continuing solvency of the entity. Rules Regulating the Professional Conduct of *CPAs* have some impact on the propriety of comfort letters in varying situations. *CPAs* should heed those rules carefully.

For tax purposes, it can refer to a letter written by a charity's counsel to a donor reflecting the opinion that a proposed donation will not adversely affect the charity's tax status. Or, it may more generally refer to an opinion letter from counsel regarding the expected or projected tax consequences of a stated transaction.

99. **Commercial Paper:** These are notes—typically short-term (less than one year and as short as a few days)—issued by various entities. A well-developed market exists for issuing and trading paper. Some *paper* provides for regular interest payments, while most defers interest to maturity. Often, paper is in bearer format and typically has a term of 5 to 270 days.

100. **Commodity:** According to the CFTC, the term means:

> (1) A commodity, as defined in the <u>Commodity Exchange Act</u>, includes the agricultural commodities enumerated in Section 1a(4) of the Commodity Exchange Act, 7 USC 1a(4), and all other goods and articles, except onions as provided in Public Law 85–839 (7 USC 13–1), a 1958 law that banned futures trading in onions, and all services, rights, and interests in which contracts for future delivery are presently or in the future dealt in; (2). A physical commodity such as an agricultural product or a natural resource as opposed to a financial instrument such as a currency or interest rate.

101. **Commodity Futures Trading Commission: CFTC:** The U.S. Commodity Futures Trading Commission, created by Congress in 1974, is an independent agency headed by five commissioners appointed by the President and subject to Senate Confirmation. Initially, it regulated trading in commodities; however, over the years, its authority has broadened to include futures in other items, including government bonds, and derivatives. In some areas, *CFTC* authority overlaps with that of the *SEC*.

http://www.cftc.gov/index.htm.

102. **Common Stock:** This is a type of security (a term which includes stock, bonds and *debentures*) which has voting rights. Although a corporation may issues various classes of *common stock* with various voting rights and liquidation rights, generally *common stock* is at the bottom in terms of preference upon liquidation. As a result, all other obligations—secured and unsecured—plus *preferred stock* would normally receive full payment on liquidation before common stockholders received anything.

But, *common stock* in case of liquidation, would also have no cap on what it received on liquidation; hence, common shareholders would receive everything left after senior debts and securities received satisfaction. Thus *Common Stock* is riskier than *preferred stock* or *debentures*; however, it also has greater opportunity for gain.

103. **Community Property:** This refers to property held in a Marital Property Regime used in most nations and in nine U.S. states plus Puerto Rico:

- Louisiana
- Texas
- New Mexico
- Arizona
- California
- Nevada
- Washington
- Idaho
- Wisconsin

Community property regimes vary regarding how they define terms. Generally, income from labor and industry during a marriage creates community property. Similarly, liabilities incurred during a marriage create community liabilities. In some jurisdictions, income attributable to separate property remains separate, while in other jurisdictions it becomes community.

The regimes apply for all legal purposes—ownership during marriage, ownership in case of divorce (each party receives one-half), or ownership in case of the death of one party.

In contrast, most separate property states have adopted *equitable distribution* regimes which define marital assets and liabilities, as opposed to community assets and liabilities. Three significant differences between the regimes exist:

- While *community property* regimes apply during a marriage, *equitable distribution* regimes do not—they keep property separate unless the parties' behavior (through gifts or commingling) provide otherwise.
- While *community property* regimes apply if one party dies, *equitable distribution* regimes do not. Spouses in such jurisdictions may have an elective share in the property of the other, but it is typically not an issue of family law; instead, that is an issue of probate law.
- While *community property* regimes provide for equal division of community assets and liabilities, *equitable distribution* regimes provides for equitable division of

assets and liabilities in case of marriage dissolution or divorce.

Alaska has an opt-in system for *community property*. Other jurisdictions permit parties to enter pre-marital (*ante* nuptial) agreements, which can include the adoption of a *community property* regime at least for family law purposes. Jurisdictions vary regarding their rules for post nuptial agreements.

Community property regimes historically fit into two major categories:

- A community of movables. Historically, such regimes descended from the French system. Movable property—personal property in common law terms—owned by the parties formed the community. Real property did not.

- A community of gains. Historically, such regimes descended from the Spanish system. Gains—*aka* income or profits—during the marriage formed the community.

104. **Comparative Financial Statements:** Generally, *Financial Statements*—the *Balance Sheet*, the *Income Statement*, and the *Statement of Cash Flows*—appear in comparison with prior years, often three. Standing alone, *Financial Statements* provide useful, but incomplete information. Standing alongside prior periods, the statements provide information regarding trends. Trend analysis, along with *ratio analysis*, helps financial analysts predict the future.

Predicting the future is the fundamental purpose of financial statements. Users certainly are interested in knowing an entity's current situation, as well as what it has done. But, they primarily want to know how the entity will perform in the future: whether it will be profitable and whether it can pay its obligations. *Financial Statements*, with the use of *Ratio Analysis* and *Trend Analysis* help predict the *micro economic* future of the relevant entity.

105. **Complex Trust:** This is a tax term of art, although the Internal Revenue Code does not use the term. Such trusts may accumulate income. Under *IRC* section 661, the trust is a taxpayer for accumulated income. It receives a deduction for distributions up to the amount of *DNI* and the beneficiary is then taxed on the distributions.

Complex trusts have many characteristics common to *pass-thru entities*; however, they also have differences in that they are themselves taxpayers, at least until they distribute accumulated *DNI*.

The family law impact of undistributed *DNI* in a *complex trust* is unclear in most jurisdictions. To the extent accumulated income must eventually be distributed to a particular beneficiary (and possibly to the extent it likely will be), the amount arguably is income for the determination of alimony and child support obligations, as well as for the determination of marital assets. But, a contrary view is also reasonable. To the extent a trust accumulates income, the beneficiary may *never* receive it. Distribution may be discretionary or the deferral period may be substantial.

The notion of *payment* then becomes important. To the extent a legal definition—such as the family law or contractual definition of income—is a function of trust *distributions* or *payments*, it may have a legal meaning different from the tax definition of income or *DNI*. Risk of double inclusion is possible: in one year the parties (or court) may include accumulated income and then in a later year, they may include distributions. One of the fundamental *Principles and Assumptions of Accounting* is the *Consistency Principle*. Whether it applies, either in theory or in practice, to family law and other legal matters is unclear. Lawyers should be aware of the possibility of such inconsistencies.

Readers may want to contemplate the prior paragraph. Inconsistencies in accounting methods are not permissible for financial accounting. Typically, they are also not permissible for tax accounting, although the rules involving inconsistencies are very complex. One can imagine an educated—but unscrupulous—person taking advantage of the complexities. Such a person might create difficult-to-detect inconsistencies with the knowledge that feigned ignorance of the rules will pass muster in the unlikely event of detection.

To the extent, accumulated *DNI* does not comprise income for family law purposes, much room for manipulation and divorce planning (both pre and post marriage) exist. Unlike marriage contracts—which both parties sign and which typically involve full or fair disclosure—non-contractual divorce planning may be apparent only to the party involved in the planning. Whether that is good or bad depends on one's perspective.

106. **Compound Annual Growth Rate: *CAGR*:** This is a financial term which represents the average compounded return on an asset. It does not represent any one year in particular; instead, it averages—or smoothes—a return over time. One formula for is is:

$$CAGR = \left[\left(\frac{Current\ Value}{Beginning\ Value} \right)^{\left(\frac{1}{n}\right)} - 1 \right]$$

Where *CAGR* = Compound Annual Growth Rate, *Current Value* = FMV at the time of measurement or computation, *Beginning Value* = the initial investment, and *n* = number of years.

This formula differs from an arithmetic mean average of annual growth rates; hence, the reference to *compound*.

107. **Compounding:** This is the process of paying or charging interest on interest. For example, if interest compounds monthly at 1%, then after one-month a $100.00 deposit would be worth $101.00. After two months, it would be worth $102.01. In the second month, the deposit would earn 1% interest on the original $100.00 deposit plus 1% interest on the first month's $1.00 of interest. All interest compounds, which helps explain the term effective interest rate. The *EFF* reflects the result of compounding the periodic rate for one year.

Arguably, interest on an *amortizing* loan does not compound because the borrower pays it regularly (typically monthly). This is correct when viewed solely as it affects the borrower and lender together. Individually, however, the interest necessarily compounds because it either goes somewhere or came from somewhere. The lender who receives the $1.00 interest at the end of the first month does not later receive any additional interest on the $1.00 of interest from that particularly borrower because the borrower has paid his debt of the $1.00 interest. The lender, however, may then lend the $1.00 to someone else—and thus effectively earn compounded interest; or, the lender will spend the $1.00. In the latter case, the lender receives no compounded interest; however, he reduces what would otherwise be borrowing costs or reduces what would otherwise be income from his *capital* and thus experiences the same effect.

The same analysis applies to the borrower who pays his $1.00 interest obligation at the end of the first month. He does not owe or pay any additional compounded interest on that interest to that lender; however, the $1.00 he paid came from somewhere. If he took it from a deposit, he earns less interest. If he borrowed it from someone else, he pays additional interest. Thus, his effective cost expressed in terms of a year necessarily involves compounded interest.

108. **Compounding Period:** This refers to the frequency of compounding for interest. For example, the period may be a month, which would result in twelve instances of compounding per year. Or, the period could be a day, which would result in 365/66 compounds per year.

A critical rule of finance is: the compounding period and the payment period must be the same or it must be annual. The mathematical formulae for determining present and future values for sums and annuities require this rule. Of course, if the two are not the same, one can easily adjust the compounding period—and the resulting nominal interest rate—to reflect compounding consistent with the payment period.

109. **Consanguinity:** Relationship though a common ancestor. See *Degrees of Relationship* for a fuller explanation. *See also, affinity,* which refers to relationship by marriage.

110. **Conservatism Principle of Accounting:** Under this principle, when given reasonable choices, an accountant will tend to choose the more conservative: the lower valuation for assets and receipts, and the higher valuation for obligations and expenses. Properly applied, this principle results in financial information such as income and net worth being more likely understated than overstated.

    The mere existence of this principle illustrates an important point often missed by non-accountants:

    > *Accounting is not a science. It is more art. Financial Accounting is filled with many legitimate but materially different choices, methods, assumptions, and rules.*

111. **Consistency Principle of Accounting:** Under this principle, accounting statements must rest on consistent principles and assumptions from period to period. Such assumptions may include depreciation methods, inventory methods and valuation techniques, cost segregation rules, capitalization rules, timing of income recognition rules, and similar decisions. As explained in relation to the *Conservatism Principle,* Accounting is not a science. Lawyers who view it as a guarantee of precision do so at their peril.

    Comparative Financial Statements are essential for financial analysis. If those statements do not rest on consistent principles, any comparison of them risks being misleading.

    Because most people and most entities do not have an annual audit, they are free to be inconsistent in their accounting choices. Viewed in isolation, such inconsistency is unwise as it impairs the validity of year-to-year comparisons.

    While such inconsistency-created comparisons may be *useless* for internal purposes, they may be *beneficial* for illicit external uses: they may materially distort income and equity, particularly in terms of how those items appear on a trend graph. Most people would view the presentation of such distortions in legal matters as dishonest; nevertheless, such inconsistencies may not be illegal or unethical or even a breach of contract. Lawyers should thus be very careful in viewing multi-period un-audited financial statements.

112. **Consolidated Financial Statements:** For both accounting and tax purposes, related entities may report consolidated Financial Statements. In these, the entities combine their statements—income, expenses, assets, liabilities, and such.

For accounting purposes, creating *consolidated statements* is a difficult process. Why? Because of the elimination of inter-company activities. For example, if Corporation A owns shares in corporation B, that value already appears on A's *Balance Sheet*. If A and B were to file consolidated statements, the investment of A in B would need to disappear, as it is implicit when B's Balance Sheet combines with A's. Similarly, if B owes money to A, B separately reports a liability and A reports an asset. Combined, neither an asset nor a liability exists because one cannot owe money to oneself. In a third example, if A sells inventory to B, the sale as well as any resulting gain must disappear. Viewed as separate entities, the transactions between A and B are real; however, viewed as one entity, the transactions have no meaning. Reporting them would inflate the affected *Income Statement* or *Balance Sheet* accounts.

Failure to report consolidated statements can be very misleading. In many cases, *GAAP* or *SEC* regulations will require such reporting. For unaudited companies, however, such reporting is voluntary or contractual. Lawyers should heed this carefully. If your compensation is a function of an entity's financial statements—either in terms of income or ratios—you must define the entity carefully and you must anticipate related party transactions. If you do not, the entity could easily manipulate its numbers by entering transactions with an affiliate. Those transactions can artificially inflate or deflate numbers to the entity's advantage and to your disadvantage. An expert viewing the related entities in isolation could truthfully testify as to their accuracy, even though many of the numbers lack real economic meaning. Lawyers should also be careful of the *cliff effect* used in deciding whether consolidated statements are appropriate. For example, clearly a wholly-owned subsidiary should combine with its parent for clear financial reporting. In contrast, an entity should not combine statements with another entity in which it has a negligible ownership interest. Somewhere between negligible and 100%, consolidated statements become important. Tax law has specific guidelines for this. For example, one part of *IRC* section 1504 becomes applicable at 80% ownership; however, if one wanted to avoid this application, one could decrease ownership to 79%: the difference would be slight in reality, but substantial in reporting.

For United States tax purposes, *IRC* section 1501 grants groups of *affiliated corporations* the privilege of filing consolidated returns:

> An affiliated group of corporations shall, subject to the provisions of this chapter, have the privilege of making a consolidated return with respect to the income tax imposed by chapter 1 for the taxable year in lieu of separate returns. The making of a consolidated return shall be upon the

condition that all corporations which at any time during the taxable year have been members of the affiliated group consent to all the consolidated return regulations prescribed under section 1502 prior to the last day prescribed by law for the filing of such return. The making of a consolidated return shall be considered as such consent. In the case of a corporation which is a member of the affiliated group for a fractional part of the year, the consolidated return shall include the income of such corporation for such part of the year as it is a member of the affiliated group.

IRC section 1504 defines the very complicated term *affiliated group*.

113. **Constant Yield to Maturity: CYM:** This term assumes a constant interest rate on a loan, as opposed to a variable rate. Internally, such a constant interest rate is common. Externally, however, interest rates vary frequently; hence, they affect the present value of the payments due under the obligation. Federal tax law uses a *Constant Yield to Maturity* (*CYM*) assumption for purposes of *Original Issue Discount* computations. *See, IRC* sections 1272 and 7872(b)

114. **Consumer Price Index: CPI:** According to the United States Bureau of Labor Statistics (*BLS*):

> The Consumer Price Indexes (CPI) program produces monthly data on changes in the prices paid by urban consumers for a representative basket of goods and services.

http://www.bls.gov/cpi/home.htm.

Many government programs and benefits, as well as many contracts have provisions which are partially functions of changes in the *CPI*. For example, a compensation agreement may provide for automatic wages increase to match the *CPI*—or perhaps the *CPI* plus or minus a stated amount (preferably stated in terms of basis points).

As further explained by the *BLS*:

> The BLS publishes thousands of CPI indexes each month, including the headline All Items CPI for All Urban Consumers (CPI-U) and the CPI-U for All Items Less Food and Energy. The latter series, widely referred to as the "core" CPI, is closely watched by many economic analysts and policymakers under the belief that food and energy prices are volatile and are subject to price shocks that cannot be damped through monetary policy. However, all consumer goods and services, including food and energy, are represented in the headline CPI.

Most importantly, none of the prominent legislated uses of the CPI excludes food and energy. Social security and federal retirement benefits are updated each year for inflation by the All Items CPI for Urban Wage Earners and Clerical Workers (CPI-W). Individual income tax parameters and Treasury Inflation-Protected Securities (TIPS) returns are based on the All Items CPI-U.

115. **Contra Account:** This is an account used to reduce another account. It carries a balance opposite to what would normally be seen for its type. It is an accounting term for what amounts to a negative asset or negative *equity* account in Balance Sheet terms, or negative income in Income Statement terms. For example, *accumulated depreciation* will have a *credit* balance; however, instead of appearing on the right side of the balance sheet as a positive number, it appears on the left side as a negative number. Similarly, *Treasury Stock* will have a debit balance; however, it cannot appear on the *Balance Sheet* left side, as it is not an asset. Because *Treasury Stock* is part of *Owner's Equity*, it appears on the *Balance Sheet* right side as a negative number reducing the *Capital Stock* account. On an Income Statement, Returns would have a negative balance and would appear as a reduction to Sales or Revenue. Consider the two illustrations in the *Balance Sheet* below:

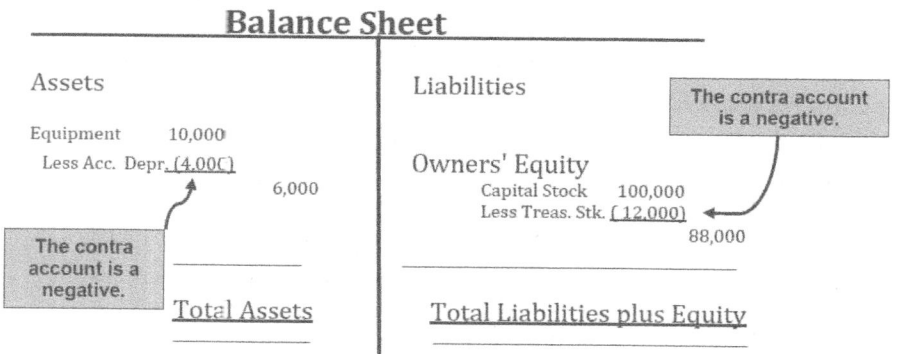

Equipment would appear at its *historical cost* of $10,000. Over time, the entity would have depreciated the equipment—in this example in the amount of $4,000. The depreciation journal entry—an *adjusting entry*—would have appeared as:

Depreciation Expense	$4,000	
Accumulated Depreciation		$4,000

No entry would affect the Equipment *ledger*, which would continue to appear as follows, along with the Accumulated Depreciation *ledger* (also a *permanent account*):

Equipment	Accumulated Depreciation
$10,000	$4,000

Both would then appear on the left side of the *Balance Sheet*—the equipment *historical cost* as a positive number and the *Accumulated Depreciation* as a negative number—as a *Contra Account*. The *temporary* account, Depreciation Expense, would have a $4,000 debit balance. Ultimately, the journal would have a closing entry crediting the depreciation expense for $4,000 and debiting a *Profit and Loss* account for $4,000. This would reduce *Retained Earnings*.

Similarly, if the entity purchased its own shares with the intention of holding them and later re-selling them, it would record the purchase as:

Treasury Stock	$12,000
Cash	$12,000

If, instead, the entity intended to cancel the shares—thereby permanently reducing shareholder capital—the entry would be:

Capital Stock	$12,000
Cash	$12,000

For Treasury Stock, the entity would maintain a *Permanent Account Treasury Stock ledger* with a *debit* balance. This ledger debit balance would not appear on the Balance Sheet left side, as do other permanent account debit balances. Instead, the Treasury Stock debit balance would appear as a negative number—a *Contra Account*—on the right side of the *Balance Sheet*.

Showing *Accumulated Depreciation* and *Treasury Stock* as negative numbers—*Contra Accounts*—provides useful information For example, if the entity replaced the *Accumulated Depreciation* credit with an Equipment *credit*, the *Balance Sheet* would list Equipment with a $6,000 balance. While that number would be correct—and indeed, it is the same ultimate number shown above—it would fail to disclose the Equipment historical cost and the account of prior depreciation. Considering the potential, if not probable, inaccuracy of depreciation expense and accumulated depreciation, showing the accumulated depreciation number on the Balance Sheet reveals important information about potential inaccuracies. That Depreciation Expense appears annually on the *Income Statement* is insufficient: the accumulated number is also important.

Similarly, showing Treasury Stock on the Balance Sheet as a negative number reveals the expected temporary nature of the capital reduction.

116. **Contra Positive:** This is generally a math term, but can be useful in law and logic. It involves negating both the hypothesis and conclusion of a conditional statement and then reversing them. For example, consider the following statement: "If the moon is full, then the tides are high." The contrapositive would be "If the tides are not high, then the moon must not be full."

117. **Converse:** This is a math or logic term. It involves switching the hypothesis and the conclusion in relation to a conditional statement. For example, "If the moon is full, then the tides are high." The converse would be "If the tides are high, then the moon is full."

118. **Controlled Foreign Corporation: CFC:** *IRC* section 957(a) defines a *CFC* as:

> any foreign corporation if more than 50 percent of—
>
>> (1) the total combined voting power of all classes of stock of such corporation entitled to vote, or
>>
>> (2) the total value of the stock of such corporation,
>
> is owned (within the meaning of section 958(a)), or is considered as owned by applying the rules of ownership of section 958(b), by United States shareholders on any day during the taxable year of such foreign corporation.

119. **Corpus:** This is generally a term for Trust Law. It refers to the principal of the trust. Derived from Latin, the word translates as *the body*.

120. **Correction:** *aka Market Correction*: This is not a term of art. Generally, it refers to a short-term drop in price of 5% to about 20%. At the upper range, some might refer to the trend as a *bear market,* or one trending downward. Corrections are common following sustained rallies or *bull markets.*

121. **COSO Opinion: Council on Sponsoring Organizations:** An auditor's opinion regarding the merits of internal controls.

122. **Cost/Benefit Analysis:** This is an accounting technique which weighs a project's costs with its benefits. If costs exceed benefits, the project is uneconomical. If benefits exceed costs, the project should proceed. *IRR* analysis and *TCO* analysis is similar.

Although the technique may appear simple—even common sensible—it is actually complex and fraught with room for manipulation.

For example, consider the term *cost*. Standing alone, the term has little meaning. It might include *direct costs, variable costs,* and *indirect costs*. It might rely on *full absorption costing*, or it might focus instead on *marginal costing*. Clearly, if one supports the project, one has a

strong incentive—see *moral hazard*—to define costs narrowly. If one
opposes the project, one would be tempted to do the opposite.

The term benefits are even more *elastic*. Some benefits are
quantifiable—such as reduced expenses, and higher revenues. Other
benefits are less clear and direct, such as longer life spans, which
result in higher costs and are also less directly traceable to any
particular project. For example, anti-smoking programs reduce
expenditures for lung cancer, but they increase expenditures for Social
Security and Alzheimer's treatments. Still other benefits are entirely
non-quantifiable—such as a more beautiful landscape or more peace
and quiet or more wolves or lizards or snail darters . . . or even more
bald eagles which eat more black cormorant chicks. Species extinction
is generally considered a cost; however, what if the species is HIV or
Ebola or cockroaches or love-bugs? Do we add that to the cost or to the
benefit column?

Cost benefit studies tend to make great headlines and wonderful
fodder for politicians, but realist lawyers should remember:

The devil is in the details.

Or even better,

The devil is in the definitions.

123. **Cost of Capital:** See *WACC: Weighted Average Cost of Capital*.
Capital generally includes both debt and equity. Each has a cost: debt
costs the after-tax interest rate, and equity "costs" the expected
dividend or return rate.

124. **Cost of Goods Sold: COGS:** This is an important function in
inventory accounting. *Gross Profit* refers to:

$$Sales - COGS$$

In turn, *COGS* (in a periodic inventory system) refers to:

$$COGS = (BI + P - EI)$$

Where *COGS* = Cost of Goods Sold, *BI* = Beginning Inventory,
P = Purchases, and *EI* = Ending Inventory.

Accounting for inventory costs is not as simple as the above equation
appears. The term *"purchases"* includes *direct costs* of newly acquired
inventory plus some *capitalized indirect* costs. Accountants and
entities differ on which costs they capitalize into inventory; hence, the
number is open to interpretation and manipulation.

Similarly, the numbers for Beginning and Ending Inventory require
not only an annual physical count, but also an inventory method:
LIFO, FIFO, average cost, or specific identification. The choice of
method can have a substantial impact on the *BI* and *EI* numbers;

hence, it can also have a substantial impact on *COGS* and *Gross Profit*. Such impacts are particularly significant in times of price instability, be it inflation or deflation.

Lawyers analyzing financial statements for businesses which maintain inventories should carefully scrutinize the numbers for *COGS*. They should ensure consistency of capitalization choices and inventory valuation (LIFO, FIFO, average cost, or specific identification). They may also want to question the choices, even if they are consistently made. While consistent treatment of inventory provides useful and generally dependable information for comparison of many periods, it may nevertheless provide distorted information for a single period or a few consecutive periods. For example, for the determination of compensation bonuses, valuation of a business through capitalization of earnings, or determination of alimony or child support obligations, inventory decisions can result in misleading numbers for the short run. LIFO can seriously understate income and asset valuations, which FIFO can do the opposite.

For United States tax purposes, *COGS* is not a deductible amount; instead, it is a reduction in Sales for purposes of determining Gross Income under *IRC* section 61.

125. **Cost-Plus Pricing:** This refers to various methods a producer may use to set his price to the customer. *CPP* is most common for activities with large variable costs which are difficult to predict. For example, it may be used in construction: rather than agree to an absolute fixed cost (which can be risky for the builder), the parties may agree to cost plus. Understandably, the builder is entitled to a profit. He may want to earn 30%, for example, as his mark-up. He would then contractually agree to charge his costs for all items or labor plus 30% of those costs.

As is true of many financial and accounting terms, however, the details are important. Lawyers must be very careful to define the term *costs*. Clearly *variable* costs are relevant; however, some or all fixed costs may be relevant as well—that is a matter of negotiation. One could legitimately argue that the 30% mark-up compensates the builder for its time and expertise plus a fair share of fixed or overhead costs. Under such an argument, no fixed costs should enter the equation. Or, the parties may agree the builder is entitled to allocate a portion of his fixed costs to the contract: as long as which costs are involved is clear, the parties may contract as they please.

Another issue involves the definition of a *variable* cost. Clearly, lumber used solely on the particular project is a *variable* cost of the project. However, transportation costs for the lumber—including depreciation on trucks and labor costs for the driver—also may vary by the project; or, they may not. Plus, the builder may legitimately combine transportation for various projects. That would be efficient, but it would also raise the accounting question of how to apportion the costs among projects. With regard to the *variable* nature of transportation, the fuel used is surely *variable*; however, the builder may maintain a fleet of trucks and drivers at a fixed cost (or partially fixed cost). Fairly, some of that cost should be allocated to the project, even if it does not vary by the project. These are fixed but direct costs, as opposed to fixed and indirect costs—such as electricity at the home office, which does not apply to any particular project.

The key message for lawyers is two-fold:

- Cost-Plus Pricing is common.

- Defining costs is difficult, subjective, and easily manipulated.

126. **Cost Recovery:** Cost Recovery has two basic meanings:

- The *accounting* method of allocating costs over time.

- A *tax law* rule affecting the timing of gain recognition.

For accounting purposes, one must allocate capitalized costs to the proper period under the matching principal of accounting. Three main terms encompass various methods:

- Depreciation: for tangibles.

- Amortization: for intangibles.

- Depletion: for minerals.

Some property—in particular, land—does not depreciate (at least not in traditional accounting and tax theory). For it, the owner recovers cost upon disposition by subtracting the land's adjusted basis from the amount realized.

For *tax law*, "cost recovery" sometimes refers to an accounting method for gain under which the seller recognizes no gain until he has recovered his "cost"—adjusted basis. This method, also known as an "open transaction" was more commonly used prior to *IRC* amendments in 1980 to section 453, which deals with installment sales. *See, Burnet v. Logan,* 283 U.S. 404 (1931).

127. **Cost Segregation:** *Cost Segregation* is an important—and controversial—accounting and tax law technique. It goes to the issue of what is an asset. For example, a building may comprise many separate assets: light fixtures, ceiling tiles, elevators, doors, windows and frames, wiring, and plumbing fixtures. The process of cost segregation does not change the total cost of a purchase; however, it places the cost in different assets subject to different depreciation or amortization rules. This can have a *material* impact on income.

128. **Coupon Bond:** Bonds are either registered or bearer. Bearer bonds which pay current interest have coupons attached to them. The bearer must clip the coupon (cut it off with scissors) and submit it to the issuer to receive the interest earned. Traditionally, banks handle the submission for depositors.

Coupon Bonds are not common in the U.S. because of government restrictions. People have often used them to evade tax—which their bearer status facilitates.

Internal Revenue Code Section 1286 deals with the tax consequences of Stripped *Coupon Bonds*. A stripped bond is one for which the non-accrued coupons (those due in the future) are separated from the bond itself (the principal). The code apportions the owner's basis among the component parts based on their relative present values.

One of the most famous of all U.S. tax cases—*Helvering v. Horst*, 311 U.S. 112 (1940)—dealt with a stripped coupon bond. The owner gave the coupons to another but retained the principal. The Supreme Court found this act to be an unsuccessful assignment of income; as a result, while the donee received the interest payments, the donor had to pay the tax on the resulting income.

129. **Coupon Rate:** The *coupon rate* is the stated interest rate on a transferable instrument. Because interest rates change continuously with market forces, the coupon rate differs from the *current yield* on the instrument—which is traditionally a function of the instrument's current value. The issuer will pay the instrument owner interest based on the *coupon rate* times the face value, adjusted for the payment period. This is not a term of art, but it is a commonly used term. Compare to the *notional rate*.

130. **Credit:** This term has two very different, but equally important (and related) meanings:

   - A *credit* is a bookkeeping entry on the right. It increases liabilities and owners' equity on the balance sheet and income on the income statement. It decreases assets and owners' equity on the balance sheet and expenses on the income statement.

   - *Credit* also refers to one's ability to borrow money. A person with good *credit* can borrow at a lower interest rate than can a person with poor *credit*. A person's ability to borrow is generally a function of their "credit score."

The terms are related: for bookkeeping, a *credit* increases debt and in finance *credit* refers to debt. See the term *debit* for a fuller explanation.

131. **Credit Default Swap: CDS:** This is a *derivative* contract similar to insurance. It also has similarity to a <u>*gamble*</u> or bet. The holder pays a fee to the issuer in exchange for the issuers promise to pay in the event a financial instrument defaults. But, the holder need not own the referenced financial instrument, which causes it to differ from insurance. Also, United States and various state laws do not consider the issuer to be writing insurance for purposes of the swap; hence, the issue need not maintain any reserves (assets set aside) in case it must satisfy the promise.

    Generally, *CDSs* are subject to *Mark to Market* Accounting. During the credit crisis of 2008–09, many holders of *CDSs* found their paper guarantees to lack much value. As a result, they had to right down the swaps. This, in turn, raised serious concerns about their own solvency, which caused swaps on their obligation to lose value, which impaired the capital of still other entities. Also, the issuers of *CDSs* suddenly found themselves obligated to pay far more than they anticipated, which resulted in defaults or expected defaults which also led to a downward spiral in valuations.

132. **Crummey Trust Doctrine:** An important tax doctrine, this arose from a famous case: *Crummey v. Commissioner* 397 F2d 82 (9th Cir. 1968). A *Crummey Power* grants a trust beneficiary the right to demand ownership of deposited property for a limited period. As a result, it is a <u>present</u> interest and thus excludable for gift tax purposes. It applies even if the beneficiary is a minor.

    Five years after *Crummey*, the Internal Revenue Service promulgated Revenue Ruling 73–405 which essentially restated the case's holding:

    > [A] gift in trust for the benefit of a minor should not be classified as a future interest merely because no guardian was in fact appointed. Accordingly, if there is no impediment under the trust or local law to the appointment of a guardian and the minor donee has a right to demand distribution, the transfer is a gift of a present interest that qualifies for the annual exclusion allowable under section 2503(b) of the Code.

    The Ruling revoked a contrary 1954 ruling.

    Eight years later, the Service again reviewed the *Crummey Power* factors. Specifically it found some donee rights illusory, resulting in non-excludable <u>*future interests*</u>. Revenue Ruling 81–7 hypothesized a donee who lacks a reasonable opportunity to learn of and to exercise a demand right before it lapses. The ruling grantor created the *Crummey Power* on December 29, did not inform the beneficiary, and provided for the demand right to lapse two days later According to the Ruling:

A trust provision giving a legally competent adult beneficiary the power to demand corpus does not qualify a transfer to the trust as a present interest eligible for the gift tax annual exclusion under section 2503(b), if the donor's conduct makes the demand right illusory and effectively deprives the donee of the power.

In 1991, the Tax Court added further gloss to the *Crummey Power*. In *Cristofani v. Comm'r*, 97 TC 74 (1991), the court reaffirmed its support for the *Crummey* holding; however, it also addressed whether a demand power possessed by an individual with merely a contingent remainder trust interest qualifies as a *present interest* for purposes of the annual gift tax exclusion.

The taxpayer excluded trust gifts to her children and also to her grandchildren as secondary beneficiaries. The trust contained demand powers exercisable by the grandchildren who would benefit from the trust only if a child of decedent's died before decedent or failed to survive decedent by more than 120 days. The grandchildren ranged from three to thirteen years old. The demand power existed for merely fifteen days after the contribution.

According to the Commissioner, the only reason decedent gave her grandchildren the demand rights to withdraw was to obtain the benefit of the associated annual exclusion. The court disagreed with the Commissioner and held the decedent intended to benefit her grandchildren, if only remotely. Although the grandchildren never exercised the demand rights, they had a legal right to do so which satisfied the primary *Crummey* test. The court also found irrelevant the grantor's intention to obtain a tax benefit. Significantly, the entire Tax Court reviewed the opinion, with all 16 participating judges joining.

133. **Currency:** This comprises paper money issued by a government. A payment in "cash" would include a payment in currency or coin; however, a cash payment might also include use of a check, draft, or credit card. Currency and coin are thus only a small part of an economy's money supply.

134. **Current Assets:** Cash plus other assets easily converted to cash. It includes accounts receivable and similar items expected to be collected within one year. On a *Balance Sheet*, *Current Assets* appear separately from *Fixed Assets*. See the definition of *Working Capital* for a fuller explanation.

135. **Current Liabilities:** Liabilities which are due within one year. This includes the *current* portion of long-term liabilities. On a *Balance Sheet*, *Current Liabilities* appear separately from *Long-term Liabilities*.

136. **Current Ratio:** A commonly used accounting financial ratio, this measures short-term liquidity. Generally, the following formula represents it:

$$\left(\frac{current\ assets}{current\ liabilities} \right)$$

The *current ratio* differs primarily from the *acid test ratio* in that it eliminates accounts receivable. Generally, a *current ratio* of two to one is ideal. Much less than that indicates near-term liquidity problems and much more than that indicates excess liquidity.

137. **Debenture:** An unsecured obligation. Some people refer to these as *debenture bonds*. Others inter-change the terms *bond* and *debenture*. As explained in reference to the definition of *Bond*, still others distinguish between a *debenture* (which is an unsecured obligation) and a *bond* (which, under their definition, is a secured obligation).

138. **Debit:** A *debit* is a bookkeeping entry on the left. It decreases liabilities and owners' equity on the *Balance Sheet* and income on the *Income Statement*. It increases assets on the *Balance Sheet* and expenses on the *Income Statement*.

Why *debits* are on the left and *credits* are on the right confuses many beginning accounting students. The answer is simple: that is how we define them. They have no other meaning. If one pictures a *Balance Sheet* (which is merely a complete *ledger*) as a T-account, one can see how the two sides should balance. Hence, for every entry on the left (a *debit*), one must have an entry on the right (a *credit*).

Balance Sheet	
Debit	Credit

Often, the actual number of *debit* and *credit* entries does not balance because the bookkeeper uses summations for one or the other. For example, one could *debit* cash deposits $10,000 (which increases cash) and correspondingly *credit* ten different customer accounts for $1,000 each, reflecting payments from each of them. The single *debit* of $10,000 would balance the ten *credits* of $1,000 each: the totals are what are important.

From the business's point of view, it would *credit* each customer account to reduce the respective asset accounts called *Accounts Receivable*. From the customer's point of view, they would each—on their own books (in their own journals and on their own ledgers)—*debit* their respective liabilities called *Accounts Payable*.

139. **Debt to Assets Ratio:** This is a commonly used leverage ratio:

$$\left(\frac{total\ liabilities}{total\ assets} \right)$$

The appropriate number varies considerably by industry. For example, historically, some capital intensive industries were highly leveraged, often posting ratios of 80%. Other industries are not highly leveraged; however, debt is itself not a bad thing. A 50% ratio—in very general terms—is typically acceptable.

To the extent the ratio is a function of historical cost less depreciation—rather than *FMV*—it can be misleading. But, *FMV* is itself a soft number in that it depends on opinion and on the recent pricing and sale of things other than the thing being measured. If the thing being valued were the thing recently sold (so as to indicate market value), then the value stated would be cost value rather than fair market value.

140. **Debt to Equity Ratio:** This is a commonly used leverage ratio:

$$\left(\frac{total\ liabilities}{total\ equity} \right)$$

It will track the *Debt to Assets Ratio* because of the basic Accounting Equation:

$$assets = liabilities + equity$$

Clearly, creditors like to see a low debt to equity ratio, as it provides them with a larger cushion.

141. **Defined Benefit Plan:** This is a type of deferred compensation plan which defines the benefit to be received. Many people refer to this as a pension plan, although such plans need not involve retirement.

Defined Benefit Plans became very popular in the United States, particularly with larger employers and particularly after the adoption of *ERISA*. In more recent years, they have largely fallen into disfavor. Such plans must—for tax, regulatory, and financial accounting purposes—be actuarially sound. In other words, the *FMV* of their assets must equal or exceed the **PRESENT VALUE** of the expected pay-outs. Computation of the soundness involves the **PRESENT VALUE OF AN ANNUITY** or multiple annuities with indeterminate lives.

If a Plan is unsound, the creator—the employer in most cases—must make it sound. In a *bear market*, this can be very expensive. But, in a bull market, such a Plan may have such an excess of soundness, the employer may skip contributions. Temptation to raid such plans can be enormous. A less risky alternative is a *Defined Contribution Plan*.

Employers which offer Defined Benefit Plans typically also offer a plan through which employees may contribute funds as well. Such plans would immediately vest.

142. **Defined Contribution Plan:** This is a type of deferred compensation plan which defines the contribution to be made. It is not a traditional pension plan.

For example, a plan may provide for an employer to contribute the equivalent of 15% of each employee's wages or salary to the plan. Many plans provide for employee direction of investments. If the Plan performs well—as in a *bull market*—the employee benefits. In such a case, the employer must continue with contractually agreed to contributions. If, instead, the Plan performs poorly—as in a *bear market*—the employee suffers. In such a case, the employer has no obligation to provide extra contributions.

Most deferred compensation plans adopted in recent years have been *Defined Contribution Plans*. In addition, many employers have dissolved or discontinued *Defined Benefit Plans* in favor of *Defined Contribution Plans*. Employers that offer Defined Contribution Plans typically also offer a plan through which employees may contribute funds as well. Such contributions immediately vest. The two plans may merge as one or they may remain separate and be subject to different rules, *e.g.*, with regard to withdrawals and borrowing.

143. **Deflation:** This is an uncommon economic situation in which general price levels decrease. The opposite of *inflation*, it can seriously distort economic decisions. When consumers anticipate deflation, they will tend to postpone purchases, believing prices will fall. Collectively, such decisions depress demand, which further depresses prices, resulting in a downward cycle. One of the three main components of *interest* rates is inflationary expectation. In times of deflation, this component is negative.

144. **Degrees of Relationship:** This refers to relationships between and among persons. First *degree* is the closest relationship—it exists between parent and child. A second degree relationship is also close. It exists between grandparents and their grandchildren and also between brothers and sisters.

To count degrees, one can draw a family tree of descendants from a common set of relatives. Each step—from a parent to a child or the reverse—counts as one *degree*. Hence, for siblings, one travels one step up to the common parent and one step down to the sibling, for a total of two steps or *degrees*. First cousins are fourth degree relatives. One would count up two steps to the common grandparent and down two steps to the first cousin. The child of one's first cousin—a first cousin once removed—is a fifth degree relationship: two up to one's grandparents and three down to one's cousin's child.

Relationships are important in many areas. For inheritance, closer relatives typically inherit before more distant ones. Also, many jurisdictions prohibit marriage by persons related more closely than fifth (sometimes fourth) degree.

The following chart illustrates relationship degrees up to the tenth degree.

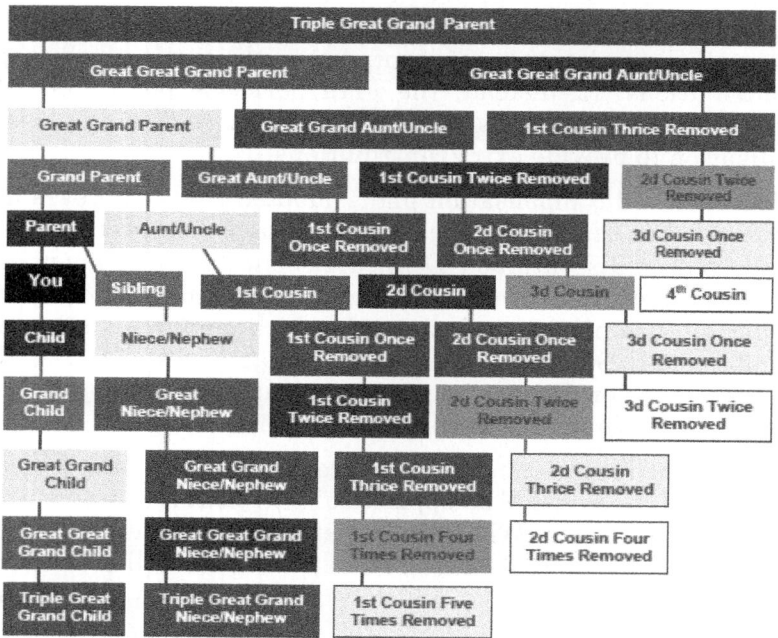

Red = 1 degree. Orange = 2 degrees. Yellow = 3 degrees. Green = 4 degrees. Blue = 5 degrees. Purple = 6 degrees. Brown = 7 degrees. Grey = 8 degrees. Light grey = 9 degrees. White = 10 degrees.

Common folklore often claims Franklin Roosevelt and Eleanor Roosevelt were cousins. People tend to be shocked by this revelation. Actually, according to the Franklin D. Roosevelt Presidential Library and Museum, they were fifth cousins. That would mean they had a common Quadruple Great Grandparent and were related in the twelfth degree—a quite distant relationship.

http://www.fdrlibrary.marist.edu/.

145. **De-Leverage:** This term refers to the process of reducing debt in absolute terms, or at least in terms of the *Debt to Assets Ratio*. An entity—or person—will want to de-lever when it has trouble satisfying obligations as they come due: debt payments are significant cash out-

flows. During the credit crisis of fall 2008, many persons—individuals
and businesses—quickly began to de-lever as they feared a weakening
economy. Generally, in times of expected deflation, one will want to de-
lever. In times of expected inflation, one will seek leverage at fixed
rates.

146. **Deposit:** This word has two significant legal meanings. The first is
simple: it is merely the initial positive cash flow in a present or future
value computation. Or, it represents the regular positive cash flow in
an annuity computation. In that sense, it carries the same meaning as
a payment.

In other legal arenas—particularly tax law—the distinction between a
deposit and a payment is profound. Deposits create assets in the view
of the depositor and debt in the view of the holder. In contrast,
payments reduce debt in the eyes of both the payor and the recipient.
Also, payments of obligations involved in income producing
transaction result in gross income to the recipient and possible
deductions to the transferor.

Many judicial opinions distinguish deposits from payments for tax
purposes. Most of it is inconclusive and provides little predictive value.
See, e.g., Commissioner v. Indianapolis Power and Light, 493 U.S. 203
(1990).

147. **Depreciation:** This refers to various cost recovery methods for
tangible assets. Common methods include:

- Straight-line.

- Accelerated.

- Units of production or use.

Straight-line Depreciation allocates the asset's depreciable basis
evenly over the recovery period, which is typically the asset's useful
life.

Accelerated Depreciation allocates more of the asset's basis in the early
years of its recovery period and less to the later years. Common
methods of *Accelerated Depreciation* include:

- Double Declining Balance Method.

- 150% Declining Balance Method.

- Sum-of-the-Year's Digits Method.

- *MACRS* (for U.S. tax purposes).

Units of Production or *Use Depreciation* allocates an asset's
depreciable basis as a function of the use of the asset. This is useful for
assets which have a useful life which is a function of hours used, miles

drives, or units produced. It is arguably the most accurate method of depreciation; however, most assets—such as a desk or chair—are not conducive to this method.

For financial accounting purposes, depreciation results in an *Adjusting Entry*:

Depreciation Expense $xxxxx

    Accumulated Depreciation $xxxxx

The Depreciation Expense debit affects a *Temporary Account* which closes ultimately to *Retained Earnings* and directly affects the *Income Statement*.

The Accumulated Depreciation credit affects a *Permanent Account* which appears on the *Balance Sheet* as a *Contra Asset*.

For both tax and accounting purposes, an asset's basis drops by the amount of depreciation expense. In addition, per *IRC* section 1016(1)(2), an asset's adjusted basis drops for tax purposes essentially by the greater of the amount allowed or the amount allowable; hence, if a taxpayer neglects to deduct depreciation expense on depreciable property, his basis drops anyway.

Lawyers analyzing financial statements for businesses which have depreciable should carefully scrutinize the numbers for depreciation expense. They should ensure consistency of capitalization choices, useful lives, salvage value, and depreciation method. They may also want to question the choices, even if they are consistently made. While consistent treatment of depreciation provides useful and generally dependable information for comparison of many periods, it may nevertheless provide distorted information for a single period or a few consecutive periods. For example, for the determination of compensation bonuses, valuation of a business through capitalization of earnings, or determination of alimony or child support obligations, d depreciation decisions can result in misleading numbers for the short run.

For United States tax purposes, taxpayers may choose to expense some purchased assets under *IRC* section 179. While the 179 expense is not technically depreciation, it has the same effects as depreciation—only it concentrates them into a single year. While appropriate for determining taxable income, section 179 expenses do not clearly reflect income and should not be used for non-tax legal definitions of income and expense.

148. **Depression:** An economic *depression* is a severe, prolonged downturn in a nation's or region's economy. Economists define it differently.

Some consider a 10% *GDP* decline as indicative of a *depression*, while others use a different measure.

In the 1930s, the United States experienced "The Great Depression," which resulted in unemployment rates as high as 25% and more than a 33% drop in *GDP* over several years.

Causes and cures for an *economic depression* are controversial. Conventional wisdom suggests increasing tax rates and restricting the supply of money will exacerbate rather than help an economic depression. Large increases in the money supply, however, risk causing inflation, which can be difficult to control. *Fiscal policy*— through government spending—is a typical governmental response.

It can result in rapid job creation and resulting consumer spending, each of which tends to improve economic measures. Arguably, such government action helps in the short run, but hurts in the long run as it distorts private economic activity by diverting resources.

President Reagan famously said, in 1980 while campaigning for office:

> *A recession is when your neighbor loses his*
> *job. A depression is when you lose yours.*

More directly, the difference between a bad *recession* and a *depression* is one of perception rather than one of definition or precision.

149. **Derivatives:** This is a broad class of assets whose value is a function of the value or cash flow of another asset. Futures contracts are common derivatives—their value is a function of the future value of some commodity or financial instrument. **Credit Default Swaps** (*CDS*) are a more recent type of derivative contract. In general, the use of derivatives transfers some underlying risk from an asset owner to another. For example, if a cereal manufacturer uses a substantial amount of corn and wants to avoid the risk of price changes in the value of corn, it can purchase corn futures contracts, essentially guaranteeing the price for the period involved. If the underlying corn price increases, the manufacturer can accept delivery of the corn purchased in advance, and the futures contract seller suffers the price increase. In contrast, if the price falls, the seller benefits either by delivering the corn at an above-market price or by settling the contract (essentially a bet) for the amount of the price drop. Complex derivative contracts can be highly volatile: they can produce large gains on small investments because the purchaser need not purchase the asset; instead, he merely purchases the right to the profit or part thereof. Also, such contracts can produce huge losses. For example, if A were to purchase a bushel of corn for $5.00 and the price dropped to $4.50, A would lose merely 10% of his investment. In contrast, if A were to

purchase a derivative which was a function of increased corn prices, A would lose his entire investment if the price dropped.

150. **Direct Cost:** *Direct costs* are those associated fully with a particular product or item. For example, the cost of lumber is a *direct* cost of furniture. *Direct costs* are also often *variable* costs in that they vary with more production. *Variable* costs, however, are either *direct* or *indirect*. The lumber cost of furniture is a *direct variable* cost. The electricity used in operating a manufacturing plant is an *indirect* cost that might be variable or fixed. it varies with production, but it is typically not traceable to a particular product; however, some portion is also likely fixed in that it occurs even if production is zero.

151. **Direct Tax:** Generally, this refers to a Capitation tax or to a direct tax on land. Per Article I, Section 9 of the U.S. Constitution, such taxes must be apportioned among the states by population. The Supreme Court invalidated an early income tax on individuals because it was not properly apportioned. *Pollock v. Farmers' Loan & Trust Co.,* 157 U.S. 429 (1895); *Pollock v. Farmers' Loan & Trust Co.,* 158 U.S. 601, 637 (1895). Later, in 1913, the 16th Amendment became part of the U.S. Constitution, permitting an un-apportioned income tax on income "from whatever source derived."

In contrast, *Indirect* taxes need not be apportioned under the Constitution; instead, they must be uniform. Examples include Excise Taxes, Duties, and Imposts.

Apportionment requires that the per capita amount of the tax be the same in each state. It does not require, however, that each person actually pay the same amount. States may decide themselves how to apportion a tax among its citizens.

152. **Discounted Cash Flow Analysis: DCF:** This is a method of valuing a project. It discounts the projected *cash flows* to the *present value.*

For investors, if the *present value* of projected cash flows exceeds the cost of investment, the project makes sense. Of course, the *discount interest rate* in such an evaluation is chosen by the prospective investor based on his desired return.

The model has many problems. First, it depends on projected cash flows. For investments such as bonds, that may not be problematic; however, for other investments, future cash flows from sales or rentals may be difficult to predict. Also, the model is highly affected by the choice of the discount rate: the higher the rate, the lower the present value.

If cash flows include everything—income, expenses, needed improvement costs, repairs, and residual value, then the *DCF* model is the same as the discounted value of profits.

Providing a formula for *DCF* analysis is not a simple matter because cash flows can vary in terms of amount, frequency and direction. If all cash flows are in level, regular, and in the same direction, the formula is essential the sum of the **PRESENT VALUE OF AN ANNUITY** plus the **PRESENT VALUE OF A SUM**.

$$DCF = \left[FV\left(1+\frac{i}{100}\right)^{-n} \right] + \left[\frac{\left[PMT\left(1-\left(1+\frac{i}{100}\right)^{-n}\right)\right]}{\frac{i}{100}} \right]$$

where i = nominal annual interest rate, n = number of periods per year, FV = the future value, and PMT = payment.

But, if cash flow amounts, frequency, and direction vary (as would be true of most businesses), the formula becomes essentially a series of *PV* computations, with each cash flow, time, and direction being entered separately.

153. **Discount Rate:** This term has three useful meanings:

- *Discount Rate* refers to the interest rate the *Federal Reserve Bank* or other Central Banks charge members banks for short-term loans.

- *Discount Rate* refers to the interest rate used in computing the present value of a sum or the present value of an annuity. In this sense, it has the same meaning as interest rate and requires a reference to a compounding frequency. For example, one might properly refer to a nominal annual discount rate compounded quarterly.

- *Discount Rate*, in reference to government bills and some instruments, refers specifically to the nominal annual discount interest rate on the instrument, without including any reference to compounding. For example, a Treasury Bill may sell for $950 and return $1,000 in one year. It would have a nominal discount rate of 5%, but an effective discount rate of 5.26316%. In this case, the 5% is a function of the principal plus the interest, rather than merely being a function of the principal, as is the typical case with statements of interest rates.

Because of the three different—actually, substantially different—meanings, a lawyer should be very careful in using the term *discount rate* and thus should always provide a clear definition.

154. **Distributable Net Income: *DNI*:** This is a tax law term under *IRC* section 643. It essentially reflects the taxable portion of a beneficiary's

share of a simple trust's distributions. For tax purposes, a simple trust (as opposed to a complex trust) is a pass-through entity. As such, the trust is not a taxpayer; instead, the income beneficiaries pay tax on the trust income, regardless of whether the trust distributes the proceeds.

155. **Domestic International Sales Corporation: DISC:** IRC section 992(a) defines a DISC as:

> a corporation which is incorporated under the laws of any State and satisfies the following conditions for the taxable year:

> > (A) 95 percent or more of the gross receipts (as defined in section 993(f)) of such corporation consist of qualified export receipts (as defined in section 993(a)),

> > (B) the adjusted basis of the qualified export assets (as defined in section 993(b)) of the corporation at the close of the taxable year equals or exceeds 95 percent of the sum of the adjusted basis of all assets of the corporation at the close of the taxable year,

> > (C) such corporation does not have more than one class of stock and the par or stated value of its outstanding stock is at least $2,500 on each day of the taxable year, and

> > (D) the corporation has made an election pursuant to subsection (b) to be treated as a DISC and such election is in effect for the taxable year.

156. **Double-Entry Bookkeeping:** This is an accounting system of *debits* and *credits*. All bookkeeping entries have both a *debit* and a *credit*; hence, books always balance absent recording errors.

Fundamentally, a *Balance Sheet*—which comprises all financial information (including the *Income Statement* closed to *Retained Earnings*)—is one large T-account. On the left are assets. On the right are claims on those assets—either creditors or owners. *Fundamentally*, that explains double entry bookkeeping: each entry ultimately affects property and the claim on that property. Of course, the actual entries are more complex that this fundamental model, but nevertheless the model is correct.

157. **Double Declining Balance Depreciation: DDB:** This is an arbitrary, but common method of allocating tangible asset costs over time. It allows a depreciation expense equal to twice the straight-line percentage as a function of the declining asset basis. Because the

system relies on a fixed life for the asset, it switches to straight-line depreciation in the year in which that produces a higher number.

Most U.S. tax law depreciation under *IRC* section 168 uses *DDB* depreciation.

158. **Dow Jones Industrial Average: DOW:** [pronounced dou]. This is a stock index which is a function (but not simply an additive composition) of 30 large industrial companies traded on the New York Stock Exchange. Charles Dow, the founder of the Wall Street Journal and Dow Jones Company, originally created the index. From time-to-time, the index drops a company and adds a new one. Probably the most famous stock index, the *DOW* is not the best indicator of the state of the economy. Broader indexes, such as the *S & P 500* or the *NASDAQ* arguably provide better current information.

159. **Durable Power of Attorney:** A power of attorney (contractual grant of authority to act on another's behalf) which survives the incapacity of the grantor. In many jurisdictions—and at common law—a general or specific power of attorney ends on the mental incapacity of the grantor. Most jurisdictions now recognize a durable power through which the grantor specifically provides for some or all powers to survive the grantor's mental incapacity. In all events, however, such powers end on the death of the grantor.

A *Durable Power of Attorney* is an important tool for the elderly. It can grant authority to adult descendants to act on the grantor's behalf. Such powers typically include the authority to pay bills, provide for repairs, invest property, collect income, and often to sell property.

160. **Dutch Auction:** This is a special type of auction often used by the Treasury. The lowest bid price necessary to sell the entire amount of product offered becomes the price for all bidders.

161. **Draft:** A draft is an order to pay. Under Article 3–104 of the UCC it becomes a check under some circumstances and an instrument under others. See the definition of *Negotiable Instrument* for a fuller explanation.

An important rule to remember is:

> *All checks are drafts, but not all drafts are checks.*

162. **Due on Sale: DOS:** This is a special—and common—*call option* pursuant to which the lender can *call* a loan due if the borrower sells the property securing the loan. In contrast, some loans are assumable; hence, the purchaser of the security can assume the obligation and the lender will release the original obligor. At one time, many home mortgage loans in the United States were assumable. More recently, almost all have a *due on sale* clause.

The almost universal existence of *DOS* clauses in residential mortgage loans is fundamental to the reason the disclosure of an *APR* is misleading for loans which have *points*.

163. **DSO: Days Sales Outstanding:** This is ratio which helps evaluate solvency and operations. It computes the average number of days between a sale and collection. Companies which sell for cash only, would have a *DSO* of zero. A higher ratio indicates credit sales.

$$DSO = \left(\frac{average\ accounts\ receivable}{sales} \right) n$$

Where n = number of days in the period (*e.g.*, 30, 90, or 365), and *sales* = total sales for the period.

Other presentations include:

$$DSO = \left(\frac{ending\ accounts\ receivable}{sales} \right) n$$

Where n = number of days in the period (*e.g.*, 30, 90, or 365), and *sales* = total sales for the period.

$$DSO = \left(\frac{ending\ accounts\ receivable}{credit\ sales} \right) n$$

Where n = number of days in the period (*e.g.*, 30, 90, or 365).

$$DSO = \left(\frac{average\ accounts\ receivable}{credit\ sales} \right) n$$

Where n = number of days in the period (*e.g.*, 30, 90, or 365).

164. **Earnings and Profits: E & P:** This is a United States tax term roughly equivalent to *Retained Earnings* for *Financial Accounting* purposes and *Earned Surplus* for Corporate Law purposes. It has significant differences from those other two terms, however, and thus is _not_ interchangeable with them. A C corporate distribution is taxable to the recipient as a dividend to the extent of the corporation's *E & P*.

For a legal definition of *Earnings and Profits*, see generally *IRC* section 312. Generally, *E & P* includes taxable income (or losses) with several significant modifications, including:

- *IRC* section 453 installment sales deferrals are ignored.

- *IRC* section 179 expensing is instead amortized over five years.

- *IRC* section 168 *MACRS* depreciation is replaced with a modified system per *IRC* section 168(g)(2).

- Intangible drilling costs must be capitalized.

- The LIFO inventory method is effectively disallowed.

165. **Earnings before Interest and Taxes:** *EBIT:* [pronounced e-bit]. Used in financial analysis, this number provides useful information about a business' profitability. Essentially, it includes operating income by excluding interest and taxes. In some cases, users also exclude non-cash items such as depreciation and amortization. Because it is a function of earnings, it does not include (or, better, should not include) extraordinary items. Because the definition of extraordinary item—as well as the definition of interest—can be subject to some variation, lawyers should be careful with this term.

As is true of many financial analysis terms, *EBIT* can be useful in a contract. For example, a contract provision may trigger specified consequences (acceleration of a loan, the change of an interest rate, more frequent disclosure or oversight) if *EBIT* falls below a pre-determined level.

A related term is EBITDA: earnings before interest, taxes, depreciation, and amortization. Arguably this is a more useful number to measure current changes in liquidity in relation to loans because it excludes the artificial (non-cash flow) elements of depreciation and amortization.

See IRC section 163(j)(6)(A) for a definition of "adjusted taxable income" which is comparable to EBITDA. Section 163(j) limits the deductibility of interest between related companies as a partial function of "adjusted taxable income." Many EU countries have similar rules which are a function of EBITDA.

166. **Earnings per Share:** *EPS:* While facially simple to compute, *EPS* can be a complex computation. At its simplest, *EPS* comprises a companies:

$$\left(\frac{earnings}{number\ of\ shares\ outstanding} \right)$$

The term *earnings*, however, is open to definition. It may include all earnings; however, it may also exclude extraordinary items. Or, it may be *EBIT*.

The number of shares outstanding is also open to definition. It may be as of a particular date, or it may be a weighted average over a period of time. Or, for partially diluted *EPS*, it may include convertible securities, options, and warrants, which—because of current conditions—are expected to be converted or exercised. Or, for fully diluted *EPS*, it would include all convertible securities plus all options and warrants regardless of the likelihood of exercise or conversion.

A *PE* ratio—price divided by earnings—notes the relationship between a stock's market price and its *EPS*.

167. **Economic Benefit Doctrine: also, Secular Trust:** This is a United States tax law doctrine created by the judiciary. The *Secular Trust* name grew out of the *Rabbi Trust Doctrine*, which involved a successful deferred compensation arrangement which did not trigger the adverse consequences of the *Economic Benefit Doctrine*. The *Rabbi Trust* matter involved compensation to the Rabbi of a Synagogue. A *Secular Trust* is an unsuccessful attempted tax deferral for *non-qualified deferred compensation*.

Under the Doctrine, a *cash method* taxpayer has income when he receives the *economic benefit* of the proceeds. This occurs even if he lacks actual receipt, *constructive receipt*, or receipt of a *cash equivalent*. It results when the payor irrevocably places funds for the benefit of the taxpayer beyond the reach of the payor's creditors. *Sproull v. Commissioner,* 194 F.2d 541 (6th Cir. 1952). According to most authorities, the *Doctrine* applies only to service income and contest winnings; it does not apply to transactions involving the sale of property. The government has consistently, but unsuccessfully, disagreed with this limitation on the *Doctrine*.

168. **EDGAR: Electronic Data Gathering Analysis and Retrieval:** [pronounced **ed**-ger]. According to the Securities and Exchange Commission:

> EDGAR, the Electronic Data Gathering, Analysis, and Retrieval system, performs automated collection, validation, indexing, acceptance, and forwarding of submissions by companies and others who are required by law to file forms with the U.S. Securities and Exchange Commission (SEC). Its primary purpose is to increase the efficiency and fairness of the securities market for the benefit of investors, corporations, and the economy by accelerating the receipt, acceptance, dissemination, and analysis of time-sensitive corporate information filed with the agency.

> Not all documents filed with the Commission by public companies will be available on EDGAR. Companies were phased in to EDGAR filing over a three-year period, ending May 6, 1996. As of that date, all public domestic companies were required to make their filings on EDGAR, except for filings made in paper because of a hardship exemption. Third-party filings with respect to these companies, such as tender offers and Schedules 13D, are also filed on EDGAR.

> However, some documents are not yet permitted to be filed electronically, and consequently will not be available on

EDGAR. Other documents may be filed on EDGAR voluntarily, and consequently may or may not be available on EDGAR.

http://www.sec.gov/edgar/aboutedgar.htm.

169. **Effective Interest Rate: *EFF*:** Sometimes labeled an *EIR*, this is a compounded rate of interest. It is the *periodic* rate compounded for one year. It differs from the *nominal annual interest rate* (*NAI*) in that the *effective* rate is compounded while the nominal rate is not. All financial calculators have an *effective rate* function, as well as a nominal rate function. For financial calculations, a calculator uses the periodic rate; hence, the nominal rate—which is the *periodic rate* times the numbers of periods in one year—is useful. Given an *effective rate*, one can convert it to the equivalent nominal annual rate for a given compounding frequency; then, one can divide by the frequency to produce the needed periodic rate.

An effective rate (*EFF*) differs substantially from an *Annual Percentage Rate* (*APR*), which is mostly a non-compounded rate. Federal law defines the *APR*, which generally is the nominal annual rate plus points and some other closing costs amortized for the stated life of the loan. In contrast, the *EFF* treats points as principal rather than interest and then produces a number different from the *APR* (assuming the loan includes points).

An *EFF* is arguably inapplicable to most consumer loans, which require current periodic interest payments. As such, they do not internally compound interest because the borrower pays all interest currently to the lender. But, externally, the funds for interest payments come from somewhere and end up somewhere. Hence, from the borrower's perspective, interest compounds to the extent the funds used to pay current interest are no longer available for other uses. Similarly, from the perspective of the lender, interest compounds to the extent the funds received in payment of current interest are either deposited elsewhere or expended (whereby they free-up other funds which are deposited or they relieve the need for other borrowing).

The formula for the *effective* interest rate:

$$eff = \left[\ 100\ \left(\ \left(\ 1+\frac{pr}{100}\ \right)^{py} - 1\ \right)\ \right]$$

where *eff* = effective interest rate, *pr* = the periodic rate and *py* = the number of periods per year.

170. **Efficient Market Hypothesis:** Arguably, the stock market is efficient: all relevant information is fully and immediately reflected in a marketable security's price. Variations on the theory range from inclusion of past information, to inclusion of public information, to

inclusion of all information—public or private. The middle category is probably the most common. Under this theory, an investor cannot obtain an extra or abnormal return because the price of all traded securities is correct. While no such perfect market exists, the theory provides a reference or basis point. Over long periods of time and including large numbers of investors, the hypothesis tends to be correct. Over short periods, or involving few investors, the hypothesis can be very wrong. In other words, the theory holds true in a macro-economic sense, but not true in a micro-economic sense.

171. **Elasticity:** This is an economic term that relates to the propensity for one item to vary as a function of another. High variance indicates high elasticity, while low variance—or stability—indicates inelasticity.

Price is often the variable. For example, many luxury goods—such as visits to a spa or filet mignon are highly elastic to price. If the price goes up, the quantity demanded will drop. Other items, however, tend to be price inelastic. For example, basic staples such as bread and milk are less price elastic than highly discretionary items because people need them regardless of price.

A manager setting the price of an item will tend to set it at the point just below where the demand becomes highly elastic. That way, he will tend to maximize revenue.

A basic economics graph illustrates the relationship of supply and demand. Both vary as to price. As price increases, supply will increase but demand will drop. At some point, they reach equilibrium. That will be the market price for the item.

An important related concept concerns government budgeting. Often government bases tax and other legislation on *static models*: consequences of a tax rate increase are a function of past economic activity. Such models, however, are seriously flawed. They assume inelastic behavior: that people will not alter their investments and consumption as tax rates change. The essence of Keynesian fiscal policy, however, is the ability of the government to influence behavior through spending and taxing policy changes. A superior budget model is *dynamic*: it attempts to predict behavioral changes which result from tax and spending changes.

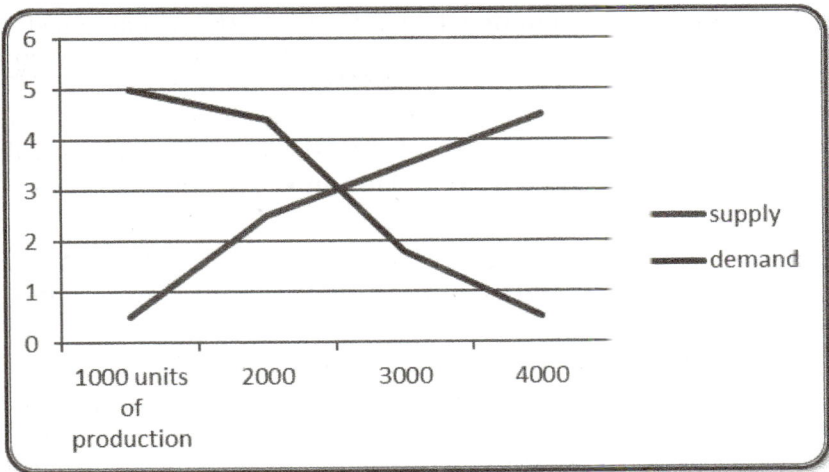

172. **Employee:** An employee—distinguished from an independent contractor—is a person whom an employer directs in terms of hours worked and manner of work. Largely, the distinctions appear in statutes, rules, and litigation under Subtitle C of the Internal Revenue Code: *Employment Taxes.*

Many areas of the law are functions of *employment* status or the lack thereof. These include:

- Social Security rules and taxes.
- Self employment tax.
- Unemployment compensation.
- Labor laws.
- Workers' compensation.
- Agency law.
- State and local laws requiring occupational licenses and work permits.
- Zoning rules regarding operating a business with employees in a particular location.
- Personal injury and tort laws regarding an employer's liability for acts of his employees.
- Deferred Compensation laws affecting qualified plans.
- Minimum wage laws.
- Employee benefits law.
- Insurance law regarding coverage of employees.

173. **Employee Stock Ownership Plan:** *ESOP:* [pronounced **ee**-sop]. This is a type of qualified deferred compensation plan permitted by *ERISA*. The plan invests in stock of the founding company on behalf of the employees. *ESOP*s have been popular with management because they provide a source of capital. They have been popular with employees because they provide an ownership interest in the employer.

174. **Employee's Retirement Income Security Act:** *ERISA:* [pronounced *uh*-**ris**-*uh*]. According to the United States Department of Labor:

> The Employee Retirement Income Security Act of 1974 (ERISA) is a federal law that sets minimum standards for most voluntarily established pension and health plans in private industry to provide protection for individuals in these plans.

> ERISA requires plans to provide participants with plan information including important information about plan features and funding; provides fiduciary responsibilities for those who manage and control plan assets; requires plans to establish a grievance and appeals process for participants to get benefits from their plans; and gives participants the right to sue for benefits and breaches of fiduciary duty.

> There have been a number of amendments to ERISA, expanding the protections available to health benefit plan participants and beneficiaries. One important amendment, the Consolidated Omnibus Budget Reconciliation Act (COBRA), provides some workers and their families with the right to continue their health coverage for a limited time after certain events, such as the loss of a job. Another amendment to ERISA is the Health Insurance Portability and Accountability Act (HIPAA) which provides important new protections for working Americans and their families who have preexisting medical conditions or might otherwise suffer discrimination in health coverage based on factors that relate to an individual's health. Other important amendments include the Newborns' and Mothers' Health Protection Act, the Mental Health Parity Act, and the Women's Health and Cancer Rights Act.

> In general, ERISA does not cover group health plans established or maintained by governmental entities, churches for their employees, or plans which are maintained solely to comply with applicable workers compensation, unemployment, or disability laws. ERISA also does not cover

plans maintained outside the United States primarily for the benefit of nonresident aliens or unfunded excess benefit plans.

http://www.dol.gov/dol/topic/health-plans/erisa.htm.

When spoken, the term *ERISA* is sometimes confused with the acronym *URESA*, which refers to the Uniform Reciprocal Enforcement of Support Act—an important family law measure. Clearly, they have nothing to do with each other. Hence, lawyers must be careful when pronouncing the two acronyms.

175. **End Mode: EM:** In *End Mode*, the first payment of an annuity (or for the amortization of a loan) is due one period in the future. In contrast, for *Begin Mode*, the first payment is due today.

Lawyers should be careful with the *mode* function. *Mode* mistakes are one of the more common errors in financial calculations. Unlike *P/YR* errors, *mode* mistakes do not result in profound consequences; hence, they are not obvious to most users. In contrast compounding errors may result in large consequences; as a result, even the most inexperienced user should notice a problem. *Mode* mistakes are more subtle; nevertheless, they can be significant.

The *Mode* is irrelevant in FUTURE VALUE and PRESENT VALUE computations. It is relevant for computations involving the FUTURE VALUE OF AN ANNUITY, the PRESENT VALUE OF AN ANNUITY, a SINKING FUND, or an AMORTIZATION.

176. **Errors and Omissions Insurance: E & O:** Generally known as *E & O* Insurance, this covers members of a Board of Directors for mistakes they may make in their capacity as board members. Generally it will not cover fraud or other criminal activity. A Notary Public may also purchase E & O insurance; indeed, state law may require it.

One would be very ill-advised to serve on a Board of Directors—including as a volunteer for a charity—that does not provide *E & O* insurance.

177. **Equitable Distribution (*ED*):** In contrast to a marital *Community Property* regime used by most nations, most United States jurisdictions have adopted a system of *Equitable Distribution* of Marital Assets and Liabilities upon dissolution of marriage. Ten States plus Puerto Rico use various forms of *Community Property*.

Typically, a states' *Equitable Distribution* statue applies for purposes of marital dissolution, but not for purposes of inheritance or even ownership during a valid marriage. In contrast, *Community Property* regimes typically apply for all three purposes, although they may have small varying rules within the three legal areas.

In an *ED* state, upon the filing of a petition for dissolution of marriage, the law fixes the status of assets and liabilities as either marital or separate (or mixed). State law definitions determine the reach of each category by using common financial and accounting terminology. Often, however, the family law usage differs from common financial or accounting usage. Also often, state law provides no definitions, leaving to courts the job of defining financial and accounting terms, some of which are terms of art and some of which are not.

Anecdotal evidence, as well as numerous reported court decisions, suggests parties often use United States federal tax returns as the basis for determining *income*, which is a component of any asset determination.

Some state statutes border on the ridiculous—*e.g.*, the Florida provision defining some *income* as an asset. *F.S. section 61.075(5)(b)(3)*. Of course, *income results* in assets and rights to *future income constitute* assets; however, income itself is not an asset. *Debits* to income go to a *temporary account*, not a *permanent* asset *account*. Income is a matter for an *Income Statement* and assets are a matter for *Balance Sheets*.

The term *income* itself has little meaning in terms of a *Balance Sheet*. The *Balance Sheet* includes *Retained Earnings*, which result from *income*, but include only the portion *retained*. Without a reference to expenditures, consumption, and losses, the word *income* is undefined for *Balance Sheet* purposes. Nevertheless, lawyers dealing with *ED* must resolve such difficult-to-resolve issues. Because *ED* necessarily deals with assets and liabilities, it has a *Balance Sheet* perspective. In contrast, alimony and child support deal specifically with *income* and thus have an *Income Statement* perspective. With regard to the Florida statute's use of the word *income*, courts have yet to provide any clear guidance.

Another important financial criticism of *ED* statutes involves their relationship to alimony and child support. Most fail to explain the relationship clearly. For example, they typically fail to provide whether the *Present Value* of future alimony and child support obligations constitute a liability in terms of deciding whether the distribution and division of marital assets and liabilities has been equitable.

178. **Equity:** In finance and accounting terms, this is a net figure reflecting ownership. For example, on a balance sheet, owner's equity is the difference between Assets and Liabilities. It appears on the right-side of the *balance sheet*. It can be a negative number (which indicates balance sheet insolvency).

With regard to a particular asset, one might properly describe the owner's *equity* as being the difference between the fair market value of the asset less the liabilities encumbering it. In this sense, equity is not itself an asset and does not represent ownership. The owner owns 100% of the asset and the creditor owns nothing but a security interest in it (a preference right on liquidation or sale). The distinction is important in many legal areas. For example, for family law purposes, posit a person who has a house worth $300,000 subject to a mortgage securing $200,000 of debt. The person has an asset of $300,000 and a liability of $200,000. He does not have an asset of $100,000. In other words, his equity is not his asset and does not reflect his property interest. This matters in two ways. First, in a divorce, the court may allocate assets and liabilities differently; hence, the parties should ensure they denominate the categories correctly. Second, payment of the liability securing the asset increases the equity in the asset (assuming the asset retains its value or appreciates); however, payment of the debt does not enhance or increase the asset. Payment of the debt merely reduces the debt. In some jurisdictions, the enhancement of an asset has different legal consequences than does the payment of a liability. Hence, lawyers must clearly understand what *is* an asset and what *is not*. Equity—in finance or accounting terms—is not an asset.

The term *equity*, however, is a type of asset in corporate parlance. It refers to stock, both common and preferred, as opposed to debt, such as bonds or notes. Whether a particular instrument represents *equity* or debt is occasionally controversial. For example, the difference between non-participating, non-convertible preferred stock and unsecured notes may not be substantial.

179. **Estate Tax:** This is a tax imposed on the *Gross Estate*, less deductions, of a decedent. Subtitle B of the United States Internal Revenue Code imposes an estate tax. Under U.S. tax laws, an estate is a person and a taxpayer. The estate is primarily responsible for the tax; however, if the estate fails to pay the tax, the recipient heirs and legatees bear some liability, as well.

Many jurisdictions, including many states, impose *Inheritance Taxes*. These differ from an estate tax in that they apply to the heir or legatee, as opposed to the estate. Nevertheless, most *Inheritance Tax* regimes require the estate to collect and to pay over the tax prior to distribution.

The vast majority of estates in the U.S. are not liable for any *Estate Tax*. The actual percentage of estates liable for tax has varied over the past several decades, but has typically been less than 10% and often less than 3%.

The United States also imposes a *Gift Tax* under Subtitle B of the Internal Revenue Code. *Gift Tax* rule and rates effectively merge with *Estate Tax* rules. Each person has a *Unified Credit* against the transfer taxes. He may use it during his life, reducing liability for *Gift Tax*; or, his estate may use it to reduce its liability for *Estate Tax*.

For 2009, the Unified Credit was mathematically approximately the equivalent of either a $3,500,000 *exclusion* or *zero-bracket amount* (two other tax law terms used from time to time). Hence, persons with a net worth of under approximately $3,500,000 did not then need concern themselves with either a Gift or Estate Tax. Their heirs and legatees, however, may have been responsible for state *Inheritance Tax*.

For persons dying in calendar year 2010, the United States Estate Tax did not exist; hence, the Unified Credit did not exist. For years post 2011, the Unified Credit equals $5,000,000 in equivalent exclusion.

Estate Planning has many functions. Primary among them is the reduction—or *apparent* reduction—in the value of one's *Gross Estate* so as to reduce or eliminate liability for Estate Taxes. The word *apparent* in the prior sentence is critical: people reduce their worth in many ways:

- They give it away, which requires consideration of Gift Taxes.
- They consume it.
- They destroy or waste it.
- They define its value as less than its true value.

Rational self interest generally prevents the third option of destruction and waste. Consumption is something everyone does; however, consuming huge sums of value can be difficult. Investment is not consumption; thus the purchase of a valuable painting, expensive jewelry, or an obscenely large residence does not consume any value (unless one pays too much, which is waste). In contrast, travel, entertainment, eating, gambling, fancy cars and fancy clothing are forms of consumption which can reduce one's net worth.

Gifts are common estate planning tools—tempered by the Gift Tax. Gifts to Charities help, as well.

Probably, however, the most useful *Estate Planning Techniques* involve financial and accounting tools which cause an asset to lose *apparent* value without it losing *actual* value. See the discussion on *Family Limited Partnerships (FPL)*. Because accounting is more art than science, such techniques abound, particularly in a self reporting system filled with *moral hazard*. Many people view such techniques as cutting edge. Others view them as magic tricks. Still others see them as abuse.

These *Estate Planning Techniques* have impact far beyond mere *Estate Planning*. Were they limited to that are, one might have little concern for them as they reduce revenues from a tax that generates a fairly insignificant amount of revenue in any event. But life is not so simple. Such techniques impact other areas of the law. For example, a technique which successfully reduces one's apparent worth for *Estate Tax* purposes likely also reduces one's apparent worth for *Equitable Distribution* or *Community Property* division incident to marriage dissolution. *Divorce Planning*—and *Bankruptcy Planning*—are arguably both outgrowths of *Estate Planning*. They generally use the same methods and techniques. Instead of avoiding *Estate* or *Gift Tax*, uses avoid liabilities to creditors or to former spouses and children.

The Supreme Court found the pre-cursor of the Estate Tax and Gift Tax valid in 1900, as an excise under Article I, Section 8 of the Constitution, in *Knowlton v. Moore,* 178 U.S. 41 (1900).

180. **Estate Tax Freeze:** This is an estate planning technique by which the planner attempts to "freeze" the value of the estate assets.

For example, a wealthy person with several children may place his appreciating assets into a family limited partnership. His children may receive interests which will likely appreciate in value while he retains an interest in assets which will likely maintain a fixed value. As a result, the value of the estate freezes with all appreciation avoiding the U.S. estate tax. Other techniques involve placing appreciating assets into a trust such that the donor has made a "completed gift" for estate tax purposes—a term of art. He will then owe a current gift tax; however, the trust income and appreciation will avoid estate taxes. The donor may retain some incidents of ownership, but not much.

181. **European Central Bank: ECB:** According to the website for the "bank":

> The ECB is the central bank for Europe's single currency, the euro. The ECB's main task is to maintain the euro's purchasing power and thus price stability in the euro area. The euro area comprises the 17 European Union countries that have introduced the euro since 1999.

http://www.ecb.int/home/html/index.en.html.

Because the *EU* members retain substantial sovereignty, the "bank" cannot act with the same powers as the *FED*, which operates with the authority of the U.S. By late 2011, considerable doubt existed regarding whether the euro could continue as a common currency for

so many sovereign nations and whether the *ECB* had the power and
resources to keep the currency stable.

182. **European Community: EC:** Under the 2007 Lisbon Treaty, this will
cease to exist and will officially merge into the European Union (*EU*).
Until the treaty is fully in force, the *EC* is one of three pillars forming
the *EU*: The *EC*, the Common Foreign and Security Policy, and the
Police and Judicial Cooperation in Criminal Matters.

183. **European Union: EU:** This is an organization of 27 member states
created by the 1993 Maastricht Treaty. Sixteen members have adopted
the Euro as their single currency (**listed below in bold**). Others
merely participate in a common market regarding trade, laws affecting
commerce, and the movement of people, goods, services, and capital.
The countries include:

- **Republic of Austria**
- **Kingdom of Belgium**
- Republic of Bulgaria
- **Republic of Cyprus**
- Czech Republic
- Kingdom of Denmark
- Republic of Estonia
- **Republic of Finland**
- **French Republic**
- **Federal Republic of Germany**
- **Hellenic Republic (Greece)**
- Republic of Hungary
- **Ireland**
- **Italian Republic**
- Republic of Latvia
- Republic of Lithuania
- **Grand Duchy of Luxembourg**
- **Republic of Malta**
- **the Netherlands**
- Republic of Poland
- **Portuguese Republic**
- Romania

- **Slovak Republic**
- **Republic of Slovenia**
- **Kingdom of Spain**
- Kingdom of Sweden

184. **Economic Value Added: EVA:** NOPAT minus capital times the cost of capital. See the definitions of NOPAT, capital, cost of capital, and weighted average cost of capital.

185. **Excess Paid-In Capital: EPIC:** This finance and accounting term has little meaning. It refers to the excess paid for shares over par or stated value. Par value has long lost most of its meaning. At one time, shareholders were liable for corporate debts to the extent they had not paid par value for their stock. For many years, however, companies have issues no-par stock or stock with an extremely low par value in states that retain the notion of par. The accounting line for *EPIC* is part of owner's equity.

    Most accountants refer to this as *APIC* or Additional Paid-in Capital.

186. **Excise Tax:** Generally, this term refers to taxes on activities, transactions, or the use of property. Typically, they are "pass on" taxes in that the obligor can pass on the tax to the consumer or user. Per Article I, Section 8 of the U.S. Constitution, Congress may impose excises, duties and imposts; however, each of these *Indirect* Taxes must be uniform throughout the country. The estate and gift tax systems are excises, as are the employer's share of FICA taxes, plus various levies on alcohol, tobacco, firearms, tires, telephone services, and many other items. In contrast, Direct taxes in the United States must be apportioned among the states by population per Article I, Section 9 of the Constitution.

187. **Exchange Traded Funds: ETF:** Available in the United States since 1993, *ETF*s have traditionally been index funds As such, they were mutual funds which tracked the value of a popular index such as the S & P 500 or the Russell 2000. Investors typically like the diversification offered by *ETF*s. They also like the ease of tracking the value.

    Since 2008, the U.S. has permitted managed *ETF*s.

188. **Expense Recognition Principle:** Per *GAAP*, an entity recognizes expense when incurred. Payment is irrelevant. Expenses break into three types:

    - Expenses recognized when revenue is recognized because the two are directly associated. An example would be the cost of goods sold.

- Expenses that will benefit the business over a period of multiple years. These must be capitalized and amortized over the relevant years. Depreciation is an example of the annual expense.

- Expenses that will benefit the business over a short period or which that provide no discernable future benefit. Research and development expenditures are often a good example. If management discerns a specific future benefit with regard to specific elements (such as a building or equipment) capitalization is appropriate. Otherwise, research expenditures are expensed. This is a substantial deviation from IFRS.

189. **Factoring:** This is the process of selling accounts receivable—often at a substantial discount—to a bank or other investor. Businesses factor *AR* to raise working capital and liquidity.

    Factoring is also an important algebraic tool for solving equations.

190. **Fair Market Value: FMV:** What a willing buyer would pay to a willing seller, neither under any special compulsion to buy or to sell at that particular time. For tax purposes, the amount realized in a taxable transaction includes the *Fair Market Value* (FMV) of any property or services received. At least a few lower court opinions have defined *FMV* in a personal sense, *i.e.*, at least partially as a function of the individual recipient's circumstances. For example, a person who won a first class trip to Brazil—but who seldom travelled and never first class—might have a *FMV* in the trip which is significantly less than would a more worldly winner. While authorities supporting such a viewpoint are few, lawyers should be aware of the potential "personal" nature of *Fair Market Value. See Turner v. Commissioner,* 13 T.C.M. (CCH) 462 (1954).

    See the definition of *Mark to Market* (*MTM*) and the *FASB* reference to *fair value* as opposed to *fair market value.*

191. **Family Limited Partnership: FLP:** This is a non-term-of art referring to a partnership owned by related parties—generally close family members. It would have some general partners and some limited partners. FLPs are useful in Estate Planning, as they can involve various allocations of risk, as well as gain potential. For example, a wealthy business owner may transfer his business to an FLP, allocating future gains to his children, but retaining substantial value for himself. With wise planning, the scheme can reduce or eliminate both gift and estate taxes in two ways:

- The future gain would not be part of the creator's estate for estate tax purposes and it may have minimal current value.

- The sum of the values of the various FLP interest will generally be substantially less than the value of the business when held by a single person. This value decrease results from valuation discounts attributable to minority interests.

192. **FDAP: Fixed or Determinable, Annual or Periodical:** This includes all income except: gains derived from the sale of real personal property and items of income excluded from gross income, without regard to the U.S. or foreign status of the owner of the income, such as tax-exempt municipal bond interest and qualified scholarship income. See, IRC sections 871a and 881a.

193. **Federal Deposit Insurance Corporation: *FDIC*:** According to the entity's website and mission statement:

> The *Federal Deposit Insurance Corporation* (*FDIC*) is an independent agency created by the Congress that maintains the stability and public confidence in the nation's financial system by insuring deposits, examining and supervising financial institutions, and managing receiverships.

Founded in 1933, the *FDIC* insures deposits at Banks. The limit is $250,000 per person per institution. Many entities such as insurance companies offer financial products similar to demand deposits at Banks or *CDs* at Banks. Such alternative instruments, however, are not insured by the *FDIC*.

194. **Federal Home Loan Mortgage Corporation: FHLMC: Freddie Mac:** According to the entity's website, its mission (which one should try to read without laughing) is (or was):

> Freddie Mac's mission is to provide liquidity, stability and affordability to the housing market.

> Congress defined this mission in our 1970 charter, which lays the foundation of our business and the ideals that power our goals.

> Our mission forms the framework for our business lines, shapes the products we bring to market and drives the services we provide to the nation's housing and mortgage industry. Everything we do comes back to making America's mortgage markets liquid and stable and increasing opportunities for homeownership and affordable rental housing across the nation.

Our mission strives to create:

- **Stability:** Freddie Mac's retained portfolio plays an important role in making sure there's a stable supply of money for lenders to make the home loans new homebuyers need and an available supply of workforce housing in our communities.

- **Affordability:** Financing housing for low- and moderate-income families has been a key part of Freddie Mac's business since we opened our doors. Freddie Mac's vision is that families must be able both to afford to purchase a home and to keep that home.

- **Liquidity:** Freddie Mac makes sure there's a stable supply of money for lenders to make the loans new homebuyers need. This gives everyone better access to home financing, raising the roof on homeownership opportunity in America.

Freddie Mac is an example of a *Government Sponsored Entity (GSE)*. Unlike *Ginnie Mae*, it lacks the full faith and credit of the Treasury for its obligations. Serious financial problems from the late 1990s until the fall of 2008 have raised substantial doubt about the continued viability of *Freddie Mac*.

195. **Federal Funds Rate:** This is generally an over-night interest rate at which banks lend to each other. Typically they do so through the *Fed* to maintain required reserves. The *Fed* sets the rate through the *FOMC*, which is one of its monetary policy tools.

196. **Federal National Mortgage Association: FNMA: Fannie Mae:** According to the entity's website (please read with a straight face):

Fannie Mae is a government-sponsored enterprise (GSE) chartered by Congress with a mission to provide liquidity and stability to the U.S. housing and mortgage markets.

Fannie Mae operates in the U.S. secondary mortgage market. Rather than making home loans directly with consumers, we work with mortgage bankers, brokers, and other primary mortgage market partners to help ensure they have funds to lend to home buyers at affordable rates. We fund our mortgage investments primarily by issuing debt securities in the domestic and international capital markets.

Fannie Mae was established as a federal agency in 1938, and in 1968 we were chartered by Congress as a private shareholder-owned company. On September 6, 2008, Director

James Lockhart of the Federal Housing Finance Agency
(FHFA) appointed FHFA as conservator of Fannie Mae. In
addition, the U.S. Department of the Treasury agreed to
provide up to $100 billion of capital as needed to ensure the
company continues to provide liquidity to the housing and
mortgage markets.

Fannie Mae has three businesses—Single-Family, Housing
and Community Development, and Capital Markets—that
work together to provide services, products, and solutions to
lender partners and a broad range of housing partners.
Together, these businesses contribute to the company's
chartered mission objectives, helping to increase the total
amount of funds available in America to make
homeownership and rental housing more available and
affordable.

http://www.fanniemae.com.

Fannie Mae is an example of a *Government Sponsored Entity (GSE)*.
Unlike *Ginnie Mae*, it lacks the full faith and credit of the Treasury for
its obligations. Serious financial problems from the late 1990s until
the fall of 2008 have raised substantial doubt about the continued
viability of *Fannie Mae.*

197. **Federal Open Market Committee: FOMC:** The Banking Act of
1935 created the Federal Open Market Committee (*FOMC*) to conduct
open market operations OMO, which various Federal Reserve Banks
had conducted without specific statutory authorization since 1923. As
defined by the *Federal Reserve, open market operations involve.*

> Purchases and sales of government securities and certain
> other securities in the open market, through the Domestic
> Trading Desk at the Federal Reserve Bank of New York as
> directed by the Federal Open Market Committee (FOMC), to
> influence the volume of money and credit in the economy.
> Purchases inject reserves into the banking system and
> stimulate growth of money and credit; sales do the opposite.

Such *OMOs,* are one tool of the Federal Reserve by its it can affect
("influence" in its words and "control" in the words of others) interest
rates and the money supply (or vice versa). Lawyers should
understand these functions, as they—despite controversy regarding
their effectiveness and wisdom—clearly have short-term, if not long-
term, impacts on interest rate.

LESSON SIX covers *Why People Charge Interest.* It discusses three
main factors of interest, including risk. Although much of 'risk" is
personal to the borrower, at least some of the factor is a function of *Fed*

behavior, including *FOMC* behavior. As a result, the measurement of risk is less a scientific study of the borrower than a well-educated evaluation of the borrower and a political and economic guess of future *Fed* and *FOMC* actions.

198. **Federal Reserve Bank: Fed:** [pronounced fed]. According to the Federal Reserve (Fed) website:

> The Federal Reserve, the Central Bank of the United States, provides the nation with a safe, flexible, and stable monetary and financial system.

In 1791, Congress created the first Bank of the United States under a twenty-year charter, which expired in 1811. In 1816, Congress created the Second Bank of the United States, again under a twenty-year charter, which expired in 1836.

In 1863, the National Banking Act effectively created the first national currency of the United States. Prior to then, various state bank notes were common. Because the 1863 Act taxed state, but not national, bank notes, the state notes became less common.

After a series of financial crises and much political debate, President Wilson signed the Federal Reserve Act in 1913. By late 1914, the nation had twelve regional Federal Reserve Banks.

The 1933 Banking Act, also known as the *Glass-Stegall Act*, created the *Federal Deposit Insurance Corporation (FDIC)*. The 1936, separate open market operations from direct *Fed* control by created the *Federal Open Market Committee* as a separate legal entity. It also created 14-year terms for *Fed* governors and removed the Treasury Secretary and Comptroller of the Currency as members. This further removed the *Fed* from government control—or at least gave that appearance.

The 1956 *Bank Holding Act* gave the *Fed* authority to regulate Bank Holding Companies (entities who own more than one bank). The 1977 *Community Reinvestment Act* (CRA) "encourages banks to help meet the credit needs of their communities for housing and other purposes, particularly in neighborhoods with low or moderate incomes, while maintaining safe and sound operations." Arguably, this act and later actions consistent with it helped cause the *sub-prime* mortgage loan crisis of 2008.

The *Monetary Control Act* of 1980 further changed the role of the Fed and introduced a more modern banking system for the U.S. The 1999 *Gramm-Leach-Bliley Act* effectively overturned the *Glass-Stegall Act* and permitted banks to offers a variety of investment banking services.

For a more complete discussion, see the **FEDERAL RESERVE SYSTEM,
PURPOSES & FUNCTIONS.**

199. **Federal Unemployment Tax Act: FUTA:** [pronounced **fyoo**-tə].
According to the *IRS*:

> The Federal Unemployment Tax Act (FUTA), with state
> unemployment systems, provides for payments of
> unemployment compensation to workers who have lost their
> jobs. Most employers pay both a Federal and a state
> unemployment tax. A list of state unemployment tax
> agencies, including addresses and phone numbers, is
> available in Publication 926, Household Employer's Tax
> Guide.

Only employers "pay" the tax. Unlike, *FICA*, no portion is deducted
from wages. The tax is currently 6.2% of *FUTA* wages, which are
$7,000. Employers receive a large credit of up to 5.4% for amounts paid
to state unemployment funds, resulting in a federal tax rate of .3%.

The definition of an *employee* and *employer* can be complex.
Essentially, an *employer* directs the activities of an *employee* but not
those of an independent contractor.

When calculating the cost of an employee—or that which he
produces—one must include not only his wages, but also any relevant
FICA or *FUTA* tax as well as fringe benefits, contributions to deferred
compensation and insurance plans, and other such items.

200. **Fiat Currency:** *Currency* printed or coined by a sovereign nation but
not backed by valuable property such as gold or silver. Fiat *currency* is
distinguishable from *commodity money*—such as actual gold or
silver—or *representative money*—such as silver or gold certificates
formerly issued by the U.S. Such certificates were redeemable in a
stated amount of a commodity.

Some economists believe fiat currency is worthless and the United
States should return to the gold standard: a system of representative
currency. Others consider such views as folly.

The United States mostly ended its gold standard system in 1934. For
several decades following that action, Americans could not legally own
gold bullion. In 1973, the U.S. devalued the dollar and fully ended its
agreement to redeem dollars for bullion.

201. **FIFO: First in First out:** [pronounced **fahy**-foh]. This is a common
inventory system under which the user assumes the first inventory
purchased was the first inventory sold. FIFO, in times of inflation, will
understate *COGS* and thus overstate income. LIFO—as opposed to
FIFO—better reflects inventory and replacement costs in times of

inflation. For tax purposes, LIFO is permissible only if the taxpayer also uses LIFO for financial reporting purposes. For purposes of computing corporate Earnings and Profits, IRC section 312 effectively requires the use of FIFO.

Inventories are an important part of many legal relationships. The use of LIFO versus FIFO inventory accounting can have a substantial impact on income and costs—particularly if the user changes from one method to another. While such a change of inventory method is an item that should always be reported or disclosed, life does not always work that way. Hence, inventory accounting is an area ripe for misleading statements. For example, if A must pay B a share of profits, A can affect his liability to B by adoption of one inventory method as opposed to another. Of course, B should be aware of this choice and should have some part in the choice; however, if B's lawyer is unaware of the meaning and the impact of LIFO and FIFO, then he is unlikely to make a wise choice.

Changing inventory methods violates the Accounting Principal of Consistency. As a result, if an audited entity were to change, it would need full disclosure in its statements, a notation in the *audit opinion*, and a clear reconciliation regarding the impact of the change.

Similarly, in other areas of the law dependent upon a definition of income—such as *family law* (for alimony and child support) and *trust law* (for measuring an income beneficiary's share of a trust)—the choice of an inventory method can have a profound effect. If one party has significant accounting and finance knowledge, while the other does not, the one with knowledge can take unfair advantage over the ignorant party. Whether such behavior is actionable varies. More importantly, if the ignorant party is unaware of the deception, he is unlikely to seek any reparation even if he is entitled to it.

202. **Financial Accounting Standards Board:** *FASB*: [pronounced **faz-bee**]. This is the entity that issues opinions or rules—called *FASB* opinions—on United States accounting issues and *GAAP*. These have also been called FASs (Financial Accounting Standards). Since 2015, they are part of the Codification.

203. **Financial Calculator:** This is a calculator which computes PRESENT and FUTURE values of either a sum or of an *annuity*. Necessarily, it will also have functions which AMORTIZE amounts over time and which compute SINKING FUNDS. These latter functions mirror the present and future value computations of annuities.

One must distinguish a *Financial Calculator* from a *scientific calculator*, which has functions more useful for engineering. Some calculators have both types of function; however, most commercially available calculators are simple, financial, or scientific.

204. **FINRA: Financial Industry Regulatory Authority:** According to the FINRA website:

> The Financial Industry Regulatory Authority (FINRA) is the largest independent regulator for all securities firms doing business in the United States. FINRA's mission is to protect America's investors by making sure the securities industry operates fairly and honestly. All told, FINRA oversees nearly 4,500 brokerage firms, about 163,470 branch offices and approximately 634,385 registered securities representatives.
>
> FINRA touches virtually every aspect of the securities business—from registering and educating industry participants to examining securities firms; writing rules; enforcing those rules and the federal securities laws; informing and educating the investing public; providing trade reporting and other industry utilities; and administering the largest dispute resolution forum for investors and registered firms. We also perform market regulation under contract for the major U.S. stock markets, including the New York Stock Exchange, NYSE Arca, NYSE Amex, The NASDAQ Stock Market and the International Securities Exchange.

http://www.finra.org/AboutFINRA/.

Typical broker/dealer or investment advisor accounts have clauses providing for mandatory arbitration under FINRA rules. Those rules also govern mediation involving such accounts.

205. **Fiscal Policy:** This involves government use of tax and spending to affect the economy. In contrast, *monetary policy* generally refers to government or Central Bank control of the *money supply* to affect the economy.

ACRS and *MACRS* are examples of fiscal policy

206. **Fiscal Year: FY:** This refers to a tax or accounting year which ends on the last day of a month other than December. Generally, taxpayers who use a financial *fiscal year* must use the same year for tax purposes. An alternative is the use of a *calendar year*.

Cases in which a person controls multiple entities with different fiscal years are ripe for manipulation. For example, consider one entity using a January 31, 2011 *FY* and another using a February 28, 2011 *FY*. One entity might pay the other in February. The payor, if on the February 28 *FY*, would deduct the cost for the year ending a few weeks later. However, the entity receiving the item of income would not include the income until the year ending January 31, 2012—eleven months later. Further manipulation could occur if the first entity were itself a reporting entity, but the second were a pass-thru entity such that it distributed the income item to the owner during January, 2012. The owner—who would likely use a calendar year—would include the income for the year ending December 31, 2012, and the payor would report a net of zero for the *FY* ending January 31, 2012.

Ultimately, all income and all deductions would appear; however, they would appear in differing years. Often, legal consequences flow from income reported for a particular period, which might span a single year or several years. Manipulation with *FYs* would aim toward moving income and deduction items either into or out of the relevant period.

Depending on the types of entities involved and the degree of control the owner possessed, both United States tax laws and *GAAP* may require a restatement or consolidation either to prevent, or with the impact of preventing, the manipulation. However, most financial statements are not subject to *GAAP* because they are unaudited, and tax laws are themselves open to varying interpretation and manipulation.

Lawyers should be wary if their client's rights are a function of group of persons' income, particularly if those persons have common control and use different *fiscal years*.

207. **FTSE 100:** [pronounced **foot**-see]. This "acronym" actually no longer officially stands for anything other than the name of a widely followed stock index of companies traded on the London Exchange. FTSE International, Lmt.—the FTSE Group—is a joint venture of the Financial Times of London (hence the FT) and the London Stock Exchange (hence the SE).

208. **Forensic Accountant:** This is an accountant trained to reconstruct realistic financial statements. For example, a forensic accountant might work in marriage dissolution as an expert for a spouse who believes the other spouse has manipulated or wasted assets or income. Or, he might work in a labor law case for a union which believes management has understated its ability to pay higher wages. Just as forensic medicine focuses on the cause of death, forensic accounting focuses on the cause or reasons why a situation is what it appears to be.

According to the **American College of Forensic Examiners (*ACFE*):**

> Forensic accountants are professionals who use a unique blend of education and experience to apply accounting, auditing, and investigative skills to uncover truth, form legal opinions, and assist in investigations. Forensic accountants may be involved in both litigation support (providing assistance on a given case, primarily related to the

calculation or estimation of economic damages and related issues) and investigative accounting (looking into illegal activities).

http://www.acfei.com/forensic_certifications/crfa/.

The *ACFE* offers certification for *Forensic Accountants* through a program leading to a designation called Cr. FA®. This is not a state granted license.

Some Forensic Accountants specialize in fraud detection. Some seek the designation of **Certified Fraud Examiner (CFE)**. This is a designation offered through the Association of Certified Fraud Examiners (*ACFE*). It is not a state granted license. According to the *ACFE*:

> Globally preferred by employers, the Certified Fraud Examiner (*CFE*) credential denotes proven expertise in fraud prevention, detection, and deterrence. Members with the *CFE* credential experience professional growth and quickly position themselves as leaders in the global anti-fraud community.

http://www.acfe.com.

209. **Forensic Economist:** This is an economist trained to reconstruct realistic financial information. Such an economist performs tasks similar to those of a forensic accountant. Considerable debate exists whether economists or accountants are better trained for these endeavors.

According to the National Association of Forensic Economics (*NAFE*):

> Forensic economics is the scientific discipline that applies economic theories and methods to the issue of pecuniary damages as specified by case law and legislative codes. Topics within forensic economics include (1) the analysis of claims involving persons, workers, firms, or markets for evidence concerning damage liability; (2) the calculation of damages in personal and commercial litigation; and, (3) the development and use of generally accepted forensic economic methodologies and principles.

> NAFE's peer reviewed academic journal, the *Journal of Forensic Economics* (JFE), publishes articles of interest to economists, accountants, finance and business professionals, vocational counselors, lawyers, and actuaries engaged in such fields as business valuation, commercial litigation, employment litigation, and personal injury and wrongful

death torts. The JFE is indexed by major economic and social science indexing services . . . .

http://nafe.net.

210. **Free on Board: FOB:** This is a term relating to ownership of an item which is the subject of a sales contract. *Free on Board* suggests that ownership transfers when the seller places the item with a common carrier. *FOB* Destination refers to ownership transferring when the item reaches its destination.

Ownership of the item determines risk of loss and the duty to insure the thing.

211. **Full Absorption Cost:** This is a type of *cost accounting* which includes a portion of all costs—including *indirect* and fixed costs such as overhead—in the defined cost of an item produced. The resulting information is useful for some internal purposes; however, it is also potentially very misleading.

For example, a car dealer may say "we sell below cost"; however, that statement, without a definition of cost, in meaningless. One type of costing is incremental or marginal cost. Under such a system, the cost of the car sold would include the price the dealer paid plus any *direct costs* associated with it, such as incremental and variable transportation costs associated with that particular car. In contrast, under a *full absorption* system, the cost of the car would include a portion of fixed overhead—such as rent on the land and building, depreciation on office desk, annual tax preparation fees, and such. In reality, those extra costs exist regardless of whether the dealer buys and sells the particularly referenced car; hence, they are not fairly included in its cost. Also, management is unwise to include them fully in a pricing system. At some point, a business must cover all *fixed* and *variable costs*; however, with regard to a particular sale, it need only cover *variable costs*—anything extra received is profit on that item which helps cover fixed costs.

Cost accounting is an important and complex area of accounting. Lawyers who use the term cost should understand the term has little meaning standing alone. See the discussion of *TCO* for a fuller explanation.

212. **Full Disclosure Principle of Accounting:** This financial accounting principle—part of *GAAP*—requires *Financial Statements* to disclose all material information, particularly negative information.

For example, an *auditor* will traditionally request a statement from an entity's counsel regarding pending or possible litigation or liabilities. Counsel may be reluctant to provide such information, as it can be damaging from a litigator's perspective. Nevertheless, a *CPA* cannot say the *Financial Statements* fairly present the entity's financial condition if undisclosed liabilities exist. In many cases, such liabilities may be contingent or difficult to assess; nevertheless, proper and *Full Disclosure* requires the release of as much information as is fairly and reasonably available.

213. **Fungibles:** These are items which are identical, or essentially so; hence, one is as good or bad as another. For example, bushels of wheat are fungible—one is as good as another (yes, we know about the possibility of rye in the wheat, but stay with the point). Electricity is *fungible*. Arguably, to large law firms, associates are *fungible*.

For finance and accounting, an important rule is:

Money is fungible.

Thus, one dollar or euro is the same as another. Whether one pays with equity or debt, one has paid and the dollar does not care. Whether one pays from one bank account or another also is irrelevant (other than transaction costs and re-investment costs). Saving money and paying off debt are also essentially fungible: neither has an impact on equity, although the two transactions will impact several ratios differently (which tells you something about the validity of those ratios if they are so easily manipulated).

Interesting tax issues arise upon the exchange of *fungibles*, especially if time is a factor. Also interesting is the definition of *fungible* for tax purposes. *See, Cottage Savings v. Commissioner,* 499 U.S. 554 (1991).

214. **Future Interest:** Anyone who has studied law in a common law system has studied future interests. These are remainder interests in property following the expiration of a term of years or a life estate.

Civil law jurisdictions recognize no concept of future interests; indeed for them, all interests are present interests. The right to use property for a period—and to obtain its fruits—is a *usufruct*. That is a present interest in property. The remainder interest which exists at the end of the *usufructuary's* rights is a *naked ownership* interest.

In financial and economic terms, *future interests* are impossible. Everything is measurable in terms of present value Anything subject to transfer is property. All property has a *Fair Market Value*, which is the *Present Value* of its future utility. The remainder interest following a life estate is itself a property right capable of being bought or sold or transferred by gift or inheritance. It is every bit a present interest as the current use of the underlying thing.

To illustrate what some common law lawyers might view as paradoxical, consider the following. Posit A who hires B to perform services for three years. In fulfillment of his obligations, A transfers a remainder interest in Blackacre to B at the beginning of the contract. Arguably, A has deferred payment to B. Or, has he? Just as arguably, A has currently transferred a property right—which B can sell or give away—in advance of B's performance. Thus A has pre-paid B. But, which is it—a pre-payment or a post-payment. It cannot be both . . . or can it be?

Consider the formulas for the **PRESENT VALUE OF A SUM** and *THE FUTURE VALUE OF A SUM*. Also compare the formulas for the **PRESENT VALUE OF AN ANNUITY** with the formula for the **FUTURE VALUE OF AN ANNUITY**. In each case, the formulas are algebraic equivalents. Of course they are the same. By definition, they are the identical. This is also true for pre-payments, post-payments, and current payments: they are all the same. *Accrual* accounting demands that this be so. Again, it is definitional. The numbers differ because the pre-payment is actually a loan from A to B and the post payment is a loan from B to A. Loans bear interest, which merely adds another transaction to the mix. But, the present values are identical to the *future values*. The *amortization* of the *present value* must equal the *sinking fund* of the *future value*. Both of these must equal the current payments. All of this is correct at any given, consistent rate of interest.

Once again, consider: does the Property 101 concept of a future interest make any sense?

215. **Futures Market:** A *futures market* trades *futures contracts*. These are agreements to purchase a specified quantity of a commodity at a set price at a specified time in the future.

The *Chicago Board of Trade* (*CBOT*) was the first real futures market in the United States. It opened in approximately 1820. It is now part of the CME Group, which include *CBOT*, the Chicago Mercantile Exchange, and the New York Mercantile Exchange (*NYMEX*). Most have standardized contracts for regular periods. For example, one can purchase a futures contract for 5,000 ounces of silver to be delivered on stated date in the future. Other contracts involve metals, grains, electricity and similar fungibles.

Typically, the holder of the contract does not actually take delivery; instead, he settles with the maker for a sum of money. Depending on the ultimate spot price, the money may flow from maker to holder or in the opposite direction.

Many companies use *futures* to hedge against unexpected price changes in essential commodities. For example, a maker of corn flakes may regularly purchase corn futures so as to ensure a stable, predictable price for corn. If the spot price increases, the company will accept delivery. If the price drops, the company will pay the difference, or will simply lose money. But, in so doing, it will have capped or limited its risk.

A famous tax decision—*Corn Products Refining Company v. Commissioner,* 350 U.S. 46 (1955)—dealt with the tax consequence of a company dealing in futures of an essential commodity. The Court held: *The IRC section 1221 list of non-capital assets is illustrative rather than exclusive.* Of mostly historical importance this decision found that property "integrally related" to a trade or business was not a capital asset. Common scenarios involving the Corn Products Doctrine involved investment in the securities of a critical supplier or customer. As "integrally related" to the business, any resulting gains were ordinary rather than capital. Losses, too, resulted in ordinary treatment and proved to be the most common application of the decision. As a result, the government regretted winning this decision. The Court subsequently severely limited the case in *Arkansas Best v. Commissioner,* 485 U.S. 212 (1988).

216. **Future Value of an Annuity:** *FVA:* This calculation computes the future value of a series of equal payments made at regular intervals, earning a constant interest rate. For example, $1,000 deposited at the end of each year for ten years earning 10% interest compounded annually, has a future value in ten years of $15,937.42. This calculation is particularly helpful in planning for retirement or saving for a child's education.

Such an annuity is either in end mode (payments occur at the end of each period) or begin mode (payments occur at the beginning of each period).

LESSON TWELVE explains the use of a FUTURE VALUE OF AN ANNUITY CALCULATOR.

The FUTURE VALUE OF AN ANNUITY calculation is one of the six basic calculations performed by a *Financial Calculator.* The formula for the *FVA* is:

$$FVA = \left[\frac{\left[PMT \left(1 + \frac{i}{100} \right)^n - 1 \right]}{\frac{i}{100}} \right]$$

where i = nominal annual interest rate, n = number of periods per year, and *PMT* = the periodic payment or deposit.

217. **Future Value of a Sum:** *FVS:* This calculation computes the future amount or value of a current deposit. For example, $1,000 deposited today, earning 10% interest compounded annually, will increase to $1,100 in one year. In two years it will increase to $1,210. In five years, it will be $1,610.51 and in 100 years it will be $13,780,612.34.

The **FUTURE VALUE OF A SUM** calculation is one of the six basic calculations performed by a *Financial Calculator*. The formula for the *FV* is:

$$FV = PV \left(1 + \frac{i}{100} \right)^n$$

where PV = present value, i = nominal annual interest rate, and n = number of periods per year.

218. *GAAP*: **Generally Accepted Accounting Principles:** [pronounced gap]. These rules form the basis of public accounting. In the United States, audited financial statements must conform to *GAAP* for them to receive an unqualified opinion of the auditors. Departure from *GAAP* is sometimes permissible—or even advisable; however, it will always raise a red flag of concern and thus necessitate a convincing justification.

Unaudited financial statements need not conform to *GAAP*. Publicly traded companies must issue financial statements consistent with *SEC* (the *Securities and Exchange Commission*) accounting rules, which differ from *GAAP* in some instances. They must also issue *GAAP* conforming statements.

Most nations other than the United States follow *IFRS* (International Financial Reporting Standards). The United States is considering the adoption of IFRS.

219. *GAAS*: **Generally Accepted Auditing Standards:** [pronounced gas]. Generally similar to *GAAP*, these are standards public accounting firms follow in conducting an audit. Part of the standard audit opinion refers to the audit having been conducted in accordance with *GAAS*. Since 2002, *GAAS* only applies for audits of non-publicly traded entities. For publicly traded entities, an auditor must follow standards issued by the Public Company Accounting Oversight Board (PCAOB). Prior to 3013, *GAAS* statements were called SAS's or Statements on Auditing Standards. Beginning in 2014, they are part of the Clarification (similar to the *GAAP/FASB* Codification) are have the designation AU (which stands for nothing). The PCAOB has, on an interim basis, adopted most of *GAAS*, but refers to it as PCAOB standards. It has issued some of its own standards with the designation AS.

220. **Generation Skipping Tax:** *GST*: This is a tax imposed by Chapter 13 of Subtitle B of the United States Internal Revenue Code. IRC section 2601 imposes the tax on Generation Skipping Transfers as defined in IRC section 2611.

With the *GST*, Congress aimed to tax transfers which skip a generation. For example, a wealthy Grandparent may have a similarly wealthy son. If Grandparent devises his property to son, Grandparent's estate must pay an *Estate Tax*. Then, when son dies and leaves the property to grandson, son's estate must again pay an *Estate Tax* on the value included in the *Gross Estate*. To avoid this, Grandparent may use various devices to skip son and to devise or to give the property directly to grandson. A successful skip avoids the second *Estate Tax* on son's estate.

221. **Gift Tax:** This is a tax imposed by Subtitle B of the United States Internal Revenue Code. See the discussion of *Estate Tax* for a fuller discussion.

222. **Giro:** Akin to a direct debit, a *giro* is the opposite of a *check*. The creditor sends the *giro* to the debtor who presents it to his financial institution for payment. With a *check*, the debtor sends the instrument to the creditor who presents it to his financial institution for collection. *Giros* are commonly used in the *EU* and Japan.

A *giro* payment system has the advantage of eliminating bounced *checks*: if the debtor has insufficient funds, his financial institution will not process the giro. As a result nothing bounces. With *checks*, the creditor deposits the instrument with his institution which then sends it to the creditor institution, which may dishonor it for insufficient funds.

223. **Going Concern:** The *Going Concern Assumption* is one of thirteen important principals and assumptions of financial accounting: it assumes the business will continue operating for the foreseeable future. With that assumption, the book numbers on the *Balance Sheet* and *Income Statement* have predictive meaning. It that assumption, however, is invalid, the validity of the numbers change. Asset values likely drop as a non-going concern will need to sell them to liquidate obligations. Income, likewise, will drop as sale losses mount and customers become concerned about future service. Supplies will be wary to provide inventory except on a cash basis, so working capital will evaporate.

For tax purposes, the asset sale of a *going concern* is an important transaction: it is also a common transaction for commercial law. Generally, a buyer is uninterested in purchasing a small corporation: with such a purchase comes contingent, difficult-to-detect and possibly undisclosed liabilities (recent slip and fall accidents are but one common example). Hence, buyers tend to prefer asset purchases. But, with asset purchases of a going concern, a critical issue—perhaps the most important factor—involves allocation of the purchase price among the component parts. Generally, the *IRS* will respect an allocation agreed upon by the parties at arm's length: what it gains from one it loses from the other, so it is effectively a zero-sum for the government. *See, Williams v. McGowan*, 152 F.2d 570 (2d Cir. 1945).

For the parties, however, the allocation is all-important. Sellers will want to place large value on assets that generate no taxable gain or long-term gain, such as land and goodwill. Buyers, in contrast, will want to place high value on quickly recoverable assets such as inventory, or fast depreciating assets such as supplies or furniture. Buyers will want to place little value on non-deductible and non- or slowly depreciating assets such as land, buildings, goodwill, and *IRC* section 197 intangible (which take fifteen years to recover on a straight-line basis).

Lawyers who understand accounting, finance, and tax law—especially the concept of *basis* and the *character* of gains and losses—will prevail over lawyers who do not. The allocation of purchase price to the asset sale of a *going concern* is but one situation example.

224. **Goodwill:** *Goodwill* is an intangible asset comprised of a business' reputation, customer base, advantageous location, and similar qualities that cause the total value to be greater than the sum of the values of the individual parts.

Generally, *goodwill* is property in a 6th Amendment sense and thus is compensable if taken by the government. Similarly, generally it is property in a tort law sense and thus compensable. In family law, state and jurisdictions vary widely. Most consider business *goodwill* to be property, but personal *goodwill* not to be property. The difference can be slight. For example, a law firm partner in a very large firm may own substantial *"goodwill."* Because, for the most part, the value of the good will is not tied to the individual partner, it is relatively easy to value and widely considered an asset. But, a partner in a small firm may have goodwill of similar value; however, the process of valuing it is more tied to the individual. As a result, transfer of the *goodwill* is more difficult. Some jurisdictions do not consider it property for family law equitable distribution or community property purposes.

For tax purposes, *goodwill* is an intangible asset *amortizable* over 15 years per *IRC* section 197.

One of the more important issues in the sale of a going concern regards the allocation of purchase price to *goodwill*. From the view of the seller, a high allocation is generally preferable as the character of any gain is likely long-term capital for tax purposes. From the point of view of the purchaser, a lower allocation is generally preferable because of the long-term, ratable *amortization* required by section 197.

For financial accounting purposes, self-created *goodwill* is carried on the books at historic cost, which may be negligible. Until 2001, *GAAP* required purchased *goodwill* amortization over 40 years. Under FAS 142, purchased goodwill is no longer amortizable in the United States. Goodwill, however, is subject to an "impairment test." If, in the opinion of the CPA (who will have applied the complicated tests) the intangible asset's value is materially "impaired," the loss in value must be reported. As a result, in most cases, the present of Goodwill on a company's Balance Sheet will have no impact on its Income Statement; however, if the Goodwill becomes impaired, it can have a sudden negative impact.

Some European countries require the preparation of an Intellectual Capital Statement, which includes employee training, customer base changes, and similar items.

225. **Government National Mortgage Association: GNMA: Ginnie Mae®:** According to the entity's website:

> At Ginnie Mae, we help make affordable housing a reality for millions of low- and moderate-income households across America by channeling global capital into the nation's housing markets. Specifically, the Ginnie Mae guaranty allows mortgage lenders to obtain a better price for their mortgage loans in the secondary market. The lenders can then use the proceeds to make new mortgage loans available.

> Ginnie Mae does not buy or sell loans or issue mortgage-backed securities (MBS). Therefore, Ginnie Mae's balance sheet doesn't use derivatives to hedge or carry long term debt.

> What Ginnie Mae does is guarantee investors the timely payment of principal and interest on MBS backed by federally insured or guaranteed loans—mainly loans insured by the Federal Housing Administration (FHA) or guaranteed by the Department of Veterans Affairs (VA). Other guarantors or issuers of loans eligible as collateral for Ginnie Mae MBS include the Department of Agriculture's Rural Housing Service (RHS) and the Department of Housing and Urban Development's Office of Public and Indian Housing (PIH).

> Ginnie Mae securities are the *only* MBS to carry the full faith and credit guaranty of the United States government, which means that even in difficult times an investment in Ginnie Mae MBS is one of the safest an investor can make.

http://www.ginniemae.gov/.

Ginnie Mae® is an example of a *Government Sponsored Entity* (GSE).

226. **Government Sponsored Entity: *GSE*:** This includes organizations chartered by Congress to conduct a particular activity. They *generally*

do not have the financial backing of the Treasury in that the Treasury does not owe full faith and credit for their obligations. *Fannie Mae, Freddie Mac, Ginnie Mae®,* the *FDIC,* and the *Fed* are examples. *Sallie Mae®* is a former *GSE.*

227. **Grantor Trust:** This refers to a trust in which the grantor retains a beneficial interest. In some cases, such grantors must report the trust income as their own. *IRC* Section 671 taxes grantors who are "substantial owners" of the trust. Section 678 provides instances in which a person other than the grantor is treated as a substantial owner.

Subpart E of Part I of Subchapter J of Chapter 1 of Subtitle A of the Internal Revenue Code deals with Grantor Trusts.

228. **GRAT: Grantor Retained Annuity Trust:** This is a device commonly used to avoid United States gift taxes. A grantor creates a trust in which he or she retains the right to income for a stated term. At the end, the remaining principle passed to a named beneficiary. A goal of the device is to use federal valuation methods such that the remainder has a zero value for gift tax purposes at the time of creation, thus resulting in no gift tax. A corresponding goal is for the remainder to have substantial value at the end of the fixed term, but to pass without subjecting the donor to a gift tax (because the gift occurred at creation and the gift value was "zero," no tax was owed then and no tax is owed at the end, because no "gift" occurs at that point, it having been made earlier).

229. **Gross Domestic Product:** *GDP*: This is the total amount of goods and services produced in an economy during a specified period.

$$GDP = MV$$

where GDP = Gross Domestic Product, M = money supply, and V = the velocity of money.

230. **Gross Estate:** *IRC* section 2031 defines this term for purposes of Subtitle B of the United States Internal Revenue Code:

> The value of the gross estate of the decedent shall be determined by including to the extent provided for in this part, the value at the time of his death of all property, real or personal, tangible or intangible, wherever situated.

Per *IRC* section 2032, valuation occurs on the date of death or within six months of the date of death, if the executor elects the later date.

231. **Gross Income:** This is a United States tax term of art defined by *IRC* section 61. It comprises "all income from whatever source derived . . . ." The code definition of Gross Income mirrors the words of the

Sixteenth Amendment which permits Congress to tax "all income from whatever source derived."

232. **Gross Margin:** Usually stated as a percentage, this sales ratio indicates the percentage of each sale that is *gross profit*:

$$\left(\frac{sales - COGS}{sales} \right)$$

where *sales* = revenue from sales and *COGS* = cost of goods sold.

Some users refer to this as *gross profit margin*. Others interchange the term with *gross profit*.

233. **Gross Profit:** Gross Profit refers to:

$$sales - COGS$$

Where *COGS* = cost of goods sold.

234. **Hedge Fund:** This is not a term of art. It generally refers to unregulated, or lightly regulated, investment groups which focus on a particular investment strategy. The concept of hedging involves taking an economic or financial position opposite to another position, so as to minimize risk. For example, a fund might generally be long (own) specific investments, but also be short (short sell) other investments. What the fund gains on one, it may partially lose on the other, hence the notion of hedging or minimizing risk.

The term *Hedge Fund* has become almost generic in referring to management private unregulated funds. Many funds limit the number of investors and many require substantial contributions. Some do not involve significant hedging in a traditional sense.

Typically, a Hedge Fund will form as a limited partnership, an LLC, or a combination of the two. It will be exempt from *SEC* registration under the *Securities Exchange Act of 1934* if it has fewer than 500 investors.

Under the *Investment Company Act of 1940*, many *hedge funds* escape significant regulation if they have 100 or fewer accredited investors— those with a specified substantial net worth. Under the act, funds fit generally under section 3(c)(1) or 3(c)(7). *15 U.S.C. § 80a–3(c)(1), (7).*

For tax purposes, hedge funds are typically taxed under Subchapter K of the Internal Revenue Code as a partnership, which means they are *flow-thru entities.*

235. **Historical Cost Assumption:** This is one of the *Fundamental Accounting Principles and Assumptions.* For financial accounting consistent with *GAAP*, financial statements list assets at their original

or historic cost. Some modification is permissible for depreciation and amortization; however, those changes appear in *contra accounts* rather than as actual reductions of the affected asset. *Mark to Market (MTM)* and *Lower of Cost or Market (LCM)* rules permit limited changes in *Historic Cost.*

The definition of *cost* is subject to debate and manipulation, as it is not a term of art. Some assets include only *direct costs*, while others *capitalize* a portion of *indirect costs*. Valuation Methods—such as LIFO and FIFO—also affect the meaning of *cost.*

Cost Segregation is another important issue. It goes to the issue of what is an asset. For example, a building may comprise many separate assets: light fixtures, ceiling tiles, elevators, doors, windows and frames, wiring, and plumbing fixtures. The process of cost segregation does not change the total cost of a purchase; however, it places the cost in different assets subject to different depreciation or amortization rules. This can have a *material* impact on income.

236. **IASB: International Accounting Standards Board:** Run by the IFRS Foundation, this Board is responsible for creating and updating International Financial Reporting Standards.

237. **Income:** This is not a term of art; hence, it must be defined. For tax purposes, the Internal Revenue Code, Subtitle A defines Income. For external financial reporting purposes, *GAAP* defines Income. For internal accounting purposes, cost accounting systems define income. Various statutes also define Income. For example, all 50 states have adopted Child Support Guidelines which are a function of the parents' combined income. Such statutes themselves define income for these purposes. Similarly, most states have provisions for alimony post dissolution of marriage (divorce in some cases). Those statutes also define Income, although many of them do so very briefly.

Contracts frequently refer to *Income* or *Profit* in general terms or in specific terms relating to a particular venture or sale. Without a precise definition, the terms *Income* and *Profit* have little meaning.

238. **Income in Respect of a Decedent:** *IRD:* *IRC* section 691 defines *IRD.* It includes gross income items which, if received by the decedent, would have been includible in his gross income. For tax purposes, *IRD* is part of the gross estate for computing the estate tax. It also becomes gross income when the estate, heir, or legatee receives the item. Under section 691(c), the recipient who includes the *IRD* for income tax purposes is entitled to a deduction which is a function of the estate tax on the item.

Section 691(b) has provisions for *DID*, or *Deductions in Respect of a Decedent.*

IRD-type items have significant consequences in family law. For example, they may easily be forgotten on a financial statement filed incident to dissolution of marriage. Also, if disclosed, they probably constitute marital assets or community property. Per *IRC* section 1041 (as interpreted by the *IRS*), such items have a zero basis, but are nevertheless subject to the imputed gift provisions of section 1041. As a result, a spouse who receives *IRD*-type items incident to dissolution should value them in an after-tax sense. The later impact of the items on alimony and child-support obligations is also important.

239. **Income Statement:** This is one of three important Financial Statements, the other two being the *Balance Sheet* and the *Statement of Cash Flows*. It reflects a business' operation for a defined period—often a year or a quarter or month. The *Income Statement* first lists income from operations. It deducts expenses attributable to those operations, as well as overhead. It nets the items to determine the current net operational income. The statement then lists extraordinary (unusual) income and expense items, as well as taxes. The bottom line figure reflects the period's net earnings.

A closing entry then adds the net to (or subtracts it from) *Retained Earnings* on the *Balance Sheet*.

A traditional *Income Statement*, consistent with *GAAP*, uses the accrual method of accounting. The accompanying *Statement of Cash Flows (fka, the Statement of Changes in Financial Position)* essentially converts the *Income Statement* to the cash method of accounting by eliminating non-cash items.

240. **Indirect Cost:** These are costs not clearly associated with a particular product or project. Often called overhead, they include management fees, general office maintenance, many utilities, insurance, and security. Indirect costs can be *fixed* or *variable*.

241. **Inheritance Tax:** This is a common state-imposed tax on inheritance. Such tax systems differ from the United States Estate Tax, which applies to the estate itself primarily, and to heirs and legatees secondarily. An inheritance tax applies to the act of inheriting.

242. **IFRS: International Financial Reporting Standards:** Generally, they are less specific and more open to the judgment of the auditor than are U.S. *GAAP*. They were developed by the IASB, the International Accounting Standards Board.

243. **Imputed Interest:** *Money has value over time*. That is a basic principal of finance. Except in rare circumstances involving deflation, interest rates are positive. Nevertheless, some transactions label what is economically interest as principal: they do so to gain tax or other advantage. Imputed Interest rules restate such transactions to reflect

economic reality. They do so by "imputing" interest—by reclassifying a portion of a transaction as interest rather than principal. Section 7872 of the Internal Revenue Code includes such rules. It "imputes" interest on many "below-market" loans. Sections 483 and 1274 contain similar provisions. State trust laws also often "impute" income to underperforming assets so as to properly and fairly treat income and principal beneficiaries. State family law statutes—particularly for alimony and child support determinations—often provide for imputed income for under-employed spouses; oddly, however, such provisions rarely impute income on underperforming assets.

244. **Incremental Cost:** The increased cost from an action as compared to the costs which would occur without the specific action. This is as opposed to "cost" or full absorption cost. These terms are important in cost accounting, which is an arm of accounting aimed toward management and the setting of prices. The term cost by itself is misleading.

245. **Independent Contractor:** An independent contractor is a status in contrast to an employee. For U.S. tax purposes, employees and their employers must generally pay Social Security and Medicare taxes. Employers must also often pay unemployment and worker's compensation taxes or premiums with regard to employee wages.

Generally, an independent contractor directs himself with regard to the time and manner of performance. In contrast, an employer directs an employee as to time and manner of performance.

An important benefit to entities or persons utilizing independent contractor services involves tort liability: generally, an independent contractor is liable for his or her own torts and such liability does not transfer to the person paying for the services.

246. **Individual Retirement Account: IRA:** *IRC* section 408 creates and defines IRAs. Contributions to them—within specific and changing limitations—are tax deductible. Withdrawals constitute taxable income. Employees and self-employed individuals who actively participate in an employer-maintained retirement plan cannot make deductible IRA contributions unless their adjusted gross income is within specified dollar limits.

Some persons are eligible for a Savings Incentive Match Plan (SIMPLE) under which they can contribute—and deduct—contributions of up to $11,500 annually (2010) which they employer may match (without tax consequences to the employee).

247. **Industrial Revenue Bond: IRB:** Bonds issued pursuant to *IRC* section 103, insistent with *Treasury Regulation* section 1.103–7. For

tax purposes, these are Industrial Development Bonds. The interest on them *may* be excludible for income tax purposes.

248. **Inflation:** In economic or financial terms, inflation refers to a general increase in the level of prices for goods and services in a nation's economy. Expected inflation is one of three important factors in determining interest rates.

The existence of *inflation* frequently becomes central to legal issues. For example, it is, as stated, one factor in interest rates. It may also be a factor in determining changes in legal obligations such as alimony or child support: significant inflation erodes the purchasing power of pre-determined obligations. As a result, substantial inflation may be sufficient to justify a modification of such obligations.

Further, *inflation* distorts most income tax systems, which are not indexed for inflation. This occurs in two ways. One, the value of property may rise over time. To the extent it rises because of inflation, the increase is illusory—it is exactly off-set by the drop in the purchasing power of the underlying currency. Nevertheless most income tax systems consider such inflation induced value to be gross income and thus taxable upon the occurrence of a taxable event. Similarly, interest income and to an extent dividend income includes an inflation component, which is, again, illusory wealth. Nevertheless, most income tax systems impose a tax on it. As a result, the property holder or interest income earner is worse off.

Another legal impact concerns the use of and definition of the term income for legal purposes. In family law, one's income is an important factor in determining one's obligation for or entitlement to alimony and child support. Similarly, in trust law, income belongs to an income beneficiary while principal belongs to a principal beneficiary. But, as indicated above, to the extent income includes compensation for *inflation*, it is illusory and it more accurately represents principal.

249. **Initial Public Offering: IPO:** Generally called an *IPO*, this refers to the first sale of a corporation's stock to the public.

250. **Insider Trading:** This refers to illegal activities by which people with "inside" information (information not yet public) trade a corporation's securities.

251. **Insolvent:** This term is dangerous because it has two distinct meanings.

- In one sense, the term *insolvent* refers to one whose liabilities exceed his assets. Such a person or entity has negative equity. This is the *Balance Sheet* definition.

- In another sense, the term *insolvent* refers to one's inability to pay what is currently due. Such a person or entity may have substantial positive equity, but little liquidity: his assets could be not easily marketable or his borrowing power may be limited. This is a *Cash Flow*— or in a loose sense—an *Income Statement* definition.

Both definitions are useful. Lawyers must be clear about which one they mean.

252. **Installment Sale:** This is a sale in exchange for a promise of *payments* over time. Such *payments* comprise an annuity. The stated sale price is the *present value of the annuity*. Also, the annuity reflects an *amortization* of the sale price.

For United States tax purposes, *IRC* section 453 provides for deferral of gain recognition by most taxpayers who sell non-inventoriable items on an installment basis. *IRC* section 483 provides for *imputed interest* on some installment sales with "unstated interest."

IRC section 453A(c) requires some taxpayers to pay what amounts to interest on the tax deferral. This *fascinating* provision is inconsistent with *IRC* section 461(h) which *fails* to compensate taxpayers for deduction deferrals and the **Schlude** case which fails to compensate taxpayers for early income accruals.

253. **Insurance Company:** What constitutes an insurance company and an insurance contract is mostly a matter of state law. Currently, states provide most regulation of insurance companies.

Subchapter L of the United States Internal Revenue Code provides the income tax consequences affecting income company income. Generally, insurance premiums are includible in an insurance company's gross income; however, the company may generally accrue a deduction for an amount equal to its expected liabilities under the contract. This treatment is very favorable when compared to the treatment given deferred liabilities of other entities by IRC section 461(h).

Holders of many insurance financial products receive favorable U.S. income tax treatment. In general, they may defer recognition of interest income until receipt; in contrast, holders of non-insurance financial products must often accrue interest income not yet received.

Thus, Lawyers need to understand the definition of an insurance company and an insurance contract for two main reasons:

- Insurance companies and their contracts are subject to significant state regulation.

- Insurance companies and their contracts receive substantial federal income and estate tax advantages.

254. **Interest:** The price charged for the use of money over time. LESSON SIX explains *Why People Charge Interest.* The components are liquidity, expected inflation or deflation, and risk

   For tax purposes, some *interest* is deductible, subject to limitations. Because (for tax purposes) the character of *interest* income differs from that of capital gain or service income, measuring what portion of a payment is *interest* as opposed to *principal* or service income can be very important.

   At least one famous Ninth Circuit opinion defined—for some tax purposes—compensation for the use of money over time as something other than interest. The decision was both widely applauded and widely ridiculed. Those who ridicule it have the better argument. *See, Albertson's v. Commissioner, 42 F.3d 537 (1994).*

255. **Interest-Only Loan:** This is a loan which does not *amortize*; instead, the borrower pays only *interest* for the term of the loan. He is then responsible for a *balloon payment* at maturity.

   A person might borrow money on an *interest-only* basis if he cannot afford the payments on an *amortizing* loan, but he expects both to be able to re-finance the loan at maturity and to be able then to *amortize* the *principal.*

256. **Interest Rate:** This term has no meaning.

   To describe interest correctly, one must state it in one of three ways:

   1)   as a *periodic rate* for a stated period;

   2)   as a *nominal annual interest rate* to be compounded at a stated frequency; or

   3)   as an *effective rate.*

   All three are identical ways of saying the same thing and are interchangeable (subject to rounding). Each of these methods includes the effect of compounding and the frequency of compounding. The term interest rate standing alone, however, does not; hence it is inherently non-specific and thus meaningless (or at least dangerous because of vagueness). Using the term interest rate without modifiers reflecting the compounding frequency is malpractice (or it should be).

257. **Internal Control:** This is a very important aspect of an entity's operations. It refers to methods and procedures used to monitor financial and accounting operations so as to minimize mistakes and fraud. Some very simple examples include:

   •   The person who orders inventory should not be the same person who pays for the inventory and who also accepts delivery of the inventory.

- Employees must provide a printed cash register receipt for each transaction to the customer.

- Employees cannot accept returns in exchange for cash except under closely monitored conditions.

One of the first steps in an audit includes the *CPA's* evaluation of the client's internal controls. The *CPA* will discuss *Reportable Conditions* (apparent weaknesses in internal controls) with the audit committee and with management. Unless the entity corrects such deficiencies, the *CPA* may decide not to issue an *unqualified opinion*.

258. **Internal Rate of Return: *IRR*:** In *internal rate of return* calculation can be very complex. It represents the *discount rate* at which the *net present value* of all cash flows (inward and outward) equals zero. If an investment has cash flows in only one direction (other than the initial deposit or final withdrawal), the computation of an *IRR* is the same as the computation of the **PRESENT VALUE OF AN ANNUITY**, the **FUTURE VALUE OF AN ANNUITY** an **AMORTIZATION**, or a **SINKING FUND**, none of which is particularly difficult.

However, if the direction of cash flows varies—and particularly if the periods and amounts vary substantially, the computation is difficult. Most calculators which compute an *IRR*, do so through an iteration method: they guess at the answer, test it, re-guess, and continue until an answer of acceptable precision is achieved.

The formula for an *IRR* is:

$$NPV = \left[\sum_{t=0}^{n} \frac{C_t}{(1+r)^t} \right] = 0$$

where NPV = net present value, n = number of periods, C = cash flow, t = time or a particular period, and r = periodic interest rate.

Most lawyers will never need to compute an *IRR* other than the basic annuities, amortization, and sinking fund. Those involved with *M & A*, however, will need to understand the computation of an *IRR*.

259. **Internal Revenue Code: IRC:** Title 26 of the United States Code. It comprises nine subtitles, including Subtitle A for Income Taxes, Subtitle B for Estate and Gift Taxes, Subtitle C for Employment Taxes and Subtitle F for Procedural Rules. Referring to it as the *IRS Code* is incorrect.

Depending on the font size, the *IRC* is either very long or obscenely long. Traditional publications put it at well over 5000 pages. Treasury Regulations accompanying the *IRC* add an additional 15,000 to 20,000 pages, again depending on font and margin size.

Much of the *IRC* contains obscure cross references. A famous sentence appears in the flush language to IRC section 509(a):

> For purposes of paragraph (3), an organization described in paragraph (2) shall be deemed to include an organization described in sections 501(c)(4), (5), or (6), which would be described in paragraph (2) if they were organizations described in section 501(c)(3).

At some level, one must admire the conciseness of that sentence. At another level, one might want to injure the drafter.

Another famous sentence—one closely related to financial calculations—appears in IRC section 467, dealing with pre-paid and post-paid rent as well as the interest component of *non-qualified deferred compensation*. *IRC* clause 467(e)(1), defining a constant rental amount describes it as one with:

> *an aggregate present value equal to the
> present value of the aggregate payments.*

To a trained finance ear, that is sheer poetry. To others, it is typical tax nonsense.

260.**Internal Revenue Service: IRS:** A division of the Treasury Department responsible for assessing and collecting U.S. taxes. The person in charge is the Commissioner of Internal Revenue (*CIR*). Much tax litigation is styled as *Commissioner* versus *Taxpayer*.

261.**International Monetary Fund: IMF:** According to the *IMF* website:

> The International Monetary Fund (IMF) is an organization of 185 countries, working to foster global monetary cooperation, secure financial stability, facilitate international trade, promote high employment and sustainable economic growth, and reduce poverty around the world.

> The work of the IMF is of three main types. Surveillance involves the monitoring of economic and financial developments, and the provision of policy advice, aimed especially at crisis-prevention. The IMF also lends to countries with balance of payments difficulties, to provide temporary financing and to support policies aimed at correcting the underlying problems; loans to low-income countries are also aimed especially at poverty reduction. Third, the IMF provides countries with technical assistance and training in its areas of expertise. Supporting all three of these activities is IMF work in economic research and statistics.

In recent years, as part of its efforts to strengthen the international financial system, and to enhance its effectiveness at preventing and resolving crises, the IMF has applied both its surveillance and technical assistance work to the development of standards and codes of good practice in its areas of responsibility, and to the strengthening of financial sectors.

The IMF also plays an important role in the fight against money-laundering and terrorism

http://www.imf.org/external/about.htm.

262. **Inventory:** Inventory refers to merchandise held for sale to customers. Businesses that hold inventories must follow "inventory accounting" methods or systems. This involves deciding when to count inventory as well as how to value inventory.

For example, for financial accounting, a business with inventories must count the items either periodically or perpetually to keep track of them. See the discussion of Periodic Inventory System and the discussion of a Perpetual Inventory System. Generally, a periodic system counts inventory once per period (generally a year). In contrast, a perpetual system keeps track of each item sold (often with a bar code or UFID tag).

Businesses must also determine how to value inventory—both that which was sold and that which remains unsold. See the discussions of LIFO and FIFO inventory systems. Often, inventory is fungible; for example, a grocery store may have 100 cans of green beans, each of which is the same, but which it purchased at different times and with different costs. Deciding which can was sold and which remain involves LIFO versus FIFO systems. That affects the entity's cost of goods sold (COGS) and can have a large impact on income for a particular period.

Inventory Accounting for United States tax purposes is a specialized field. The internal revenue code distinguishes between "stock in trade," "inventory," and "property held primarily for sale to customers in the ordinary course of a trade or business." See IRC sections 1221, 1231.

State law also may tax inventory differently from other property. For example, a state may impose a tangible personal property tax on business assets, but exclude "goods" held for sale.

263. **Inverted Yield Curve:** This refers to a yields graph for instruments of varying maturities (but similar rating/risk/quality). Normally, shorter term instruments yield less than longer term instruments; hence, the yield-curve has a positive slope. In an inverted situation,

longer term instruments yield less than those of shorter terms. Most investors view this with some alarm, as it tends to predict lower economic activity or recession.

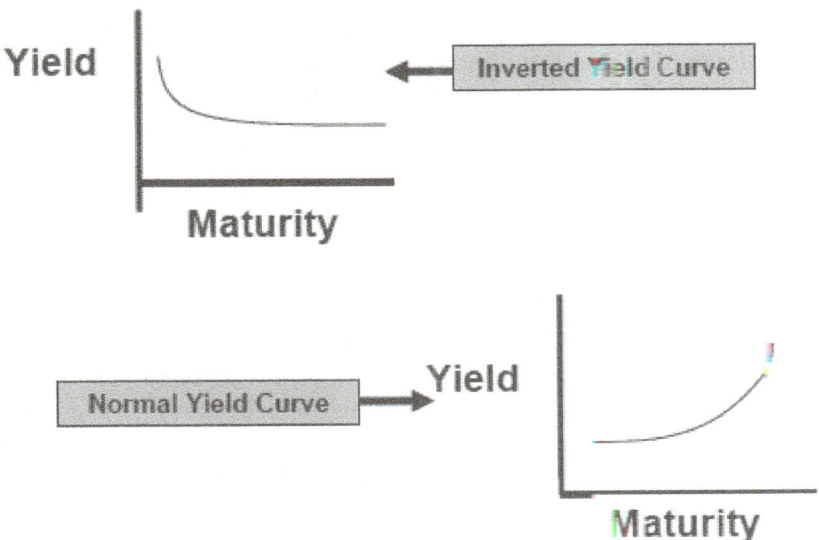

264. **Inverse:** Containing terms of which an increase in one results in a decrease of another. The **Multiplicative Inverse** (*aka* reciprocal) for a number x, denoted a 1/x, is a number which when multiplied by x yields the multiplicative identity. For example the multiplicative inverse of the number 5 is 1/5 and the multiplicative inverse of 1/4 is 4. Multiplied by each other, they produce the result of 1.

In contrast, the **Additive Inverse** of a number a is the number that when added to a yields zero. For example, the additive inverse of 5 is negative 5: added together they result in zero.

Lawyers should be careful in using the term "*inverse.*" They should specify whether they refer to the Multiplicative or the Additive Inverse, or perhaps some other usage. They must also be careful not to confuse the term with the similar-sounding term "*converse.*"

265. **Investment Advisor:** Defined in the Investment Advisors Act of 1940, any person or group that makes investment recommendations or conducts securities analysis in return for a fee, whether through direct management of client assets or written publications. In contrast, a Broker Dealer is a person or entity that is in the business of buying and selling securities for itself or on behalf of clients. Often, an investment advisor is also a broker dealer.

266. **Junk Bond:** This is a popular name for a lower grade, speculative bond. Because they carry significant risk of default, they have higher yields than investment grade bonds. Major ratings agencies consider bonds of BB and lower to be speculative, or *junk*.

267. **Keogh Plan:** This is a type of qualified retirement plan for self-employed and small business. Created in 1962, the plans derived their name from their main sponsor, Brooklyn Congressman Eugene Keogh. They are also known as HR 10 plans—after the House of Representatives Bill which created them. The plans take either the form of a *Defined Contribution Plan* or a *Defined Benefit Plan.*

More recent legislation has created SEP and SIMPLE plans for the self-employed or small businesses. In the opinion of many advisors, the new plans offer significant advantages over the older Keoghs.

268. **Key Employee: Key Employee Insurance:** Many small businesses have one or more employees who are very important to the business, if not essential. They may be the business founder or the creator of an important product. Generally, their name and presence contribute substantial *Goodwill* for the company. Without them, the company's continuation as a *going concern* may be in doubt.

If an entity has an employee who meets the above description, it may want to have *key employee insurance*. This would provide substantial benefits on the death of the employee, such that the company could locate a similar person or perhaps even liquidate. Valuation of a small business must account for *key employees* and whether any transfer of ownership would affect their continued employment and loyalty.

One insurance company which sells key employee insurance has a very good explanation of the term:

The untimely death of a key employee or business owner who is also a key employee can have a disastrous effect on a business. Some of the costs of such an event might include:

- A weakening of the company's credit rating.

- The financial cost (in time and dollars) to find, hire and train a replacement.

- The distraction of other employees, resulting in deadlines not met, deteriorating morale, or a higher level of personality conflicts.

- A need for cash to fulfill promises made to the deceased employee's spouse or family, such as salary continuation or deferred compensation.

- The inability to seize a business opportunity because cash reserves are being used to recruit and train the new employee.

- A loss of confidence among both suppliers and customers.

Additional problems (if key employee is an owner) might include:

- Disagreement between heirs and surviving business owners or key employees.

- Lack of cash to buy the interest of the deceased owner, requiring a sale of the business to an unknown "outside third party."

- Surviving owners may be forced to work with someone who is either not competent, or not motivated enough to make the business thrive.

- The business may have to be sold to pay estate taxes.

http://www.transamerica.com.

A *CPA* auditing a small business should inquire regarding the importance of various employees. While the definition of the term is often subjective, the *CPA* must exercise his or her judgment regarding whether disclosure of such information is necessary.

269. **Labor and Industry:** This is a commonly used term in family law regarding the type of efforts which generally create marital assets in Equitable Distribution states or Community property in other states. It connotes activity and efforts as opposed to passivity. For example, building a house by cutting the lumber and laying bricks is clearly labor and industry. Appreciation in value results more from the efforts at brick laying than from inflation affecting the bricks. Sitting back while undeveloped and used land appreciates is generally not labor and industry.

270. **Laffer Curve:** Named after economist Arthur Laffer, this graph illustrates the relationship of income tax receipts to income tax rates. At some tax levels—for example, a zero tax rate—revenue would be zero. Similarly, at a 100% tax rate, revenues would be zero as productivity would cease. In contrast, at other tax rates, revenues are positive. Rates higher than zero will produce increasing revenues to a point, at which further rate increases will result in decreasing revenues. The phenomenon occurs because income taxes discourage productivity. At low levels of tax, the economic discouragement is small and thus the increase in revenues is large. However, at high rates of tax, the economic disincentives become so large they outweigh any increases in revenue resulting from continued productivity. The

location of curve's zenith is debatable, but its existence is widely accepted. A common, simple depiction of a *Laffer Curve* is:

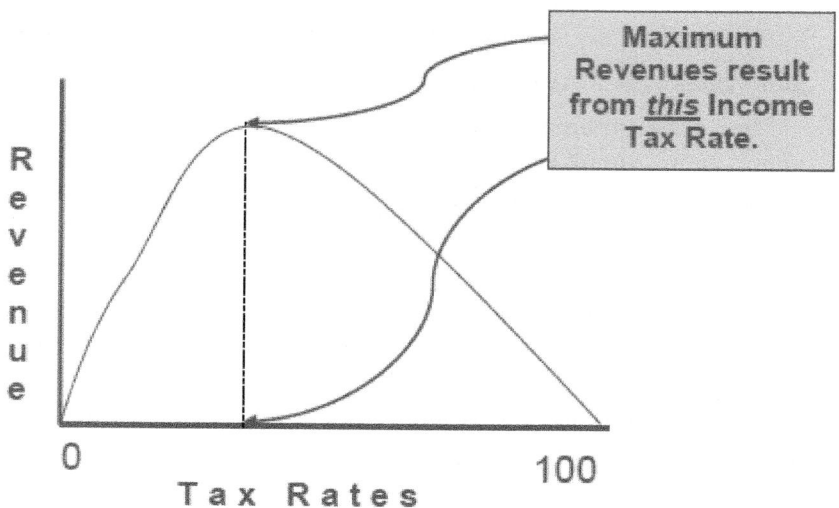

Clearly the zenith is greater than zero and less than 100%. Historically, total U.S. taxes have averaged within a few percentage points of 20%, although marginal rates have been as high as 94% as recently as the 1960s and as high as 70% as recently as the 1980s.

271. **Leverage:** This is a synonym for debt. See the various leverage ratios, such as *Debt to Assets*, *Debt to Equity*, and *LTV*.

272. **Leveraged Buy out: LBO:** This is a type of entity acquisition which is highly leveraged—financed. Often, the assets of the target secure the debt, which may be without recourse against the acquiring entity.

273. *LIBOR*: **London Interbank Offered Rate:** [pronounced **lahy**-bohr]. This is an interest rate generally comparable to the *Federal Funds Rate*. Contracts which have an adjustable or floating interest rate usually have a benchmark. Many contracts use the prime rate plus or minus a stated number of points. Similarly, many other contracts use the *LIBOR* plus or minus a stated number of points.

274. **LIFO: Last in First out:** [pronounced **lahy**-foh]. This is a common inventory system under which the user assumes the last inventory purchased was the first inventory sold. LIFO—as opposed to FIFO—better reflects inventory and replacement costs in times of inflation. For tax purposes, LIFO is permissible only if the taxpayer also uses LIFO for financial reporting purposes. Use of LIFO, however, is not permitted for publicly traded entities.

Inventories are an important part of many legal relationships. The use of LIFO versus FIFO inventory accounting can have a substantial impact on income and costs—particularly if the user changes from one method to another. While such a change of inventory method is an item that should always be reported or disclosed, life does not always work that way. Hence, inventory accounting is an area ripe for misleading statements. For example, if A must pay B a share of profits, A can affect his liability to B by adoption of one inventory method as opposed to another. Of course, B should be aware of this choice and should have some part in the choice; however, if B's lawyer is unaware of the meaning and the impact of LIFO and FIFO, then he is unlikely to make a wise choice.

Similarly, in other areas of the law dependent upon a definition of income—such as family law (for alimony and child support) and trust law (for measuring an income beneficiary's share of a trust)—the choice of an inventory system can have a profound effect. If one party has significant accounting and finance knowledge while the other does not, the one with knowledge can take unfair advantage over the ignorant party. Whether such behavior is actionable varies. More importantly, if the ignorant party is unaware of the deception, he is unlikely to seek any reparation even if he is entitled to it.

275. **Limited Liability Company: LLC:** An LLC is a type of state recognized entity. It operates much like a corporation in that it has shareholders and state granted limited liability. It is a person for purposes of bringing suit or being sued. For federal tax purposes, however, it is a partnership.

Such entities became very popular starting in the late 1980s.

An LLC operates essentially as a hybrid of a corporation and a partnership. An LLC is similar to a corporation because it has limited liability. It is similar to a partnership because it is a disregarded entity for U.S. federal tax purposes. LLC owners are called members; in contrast corporate owners are shareholders and partnership owners are partners and trust owners are called beneficiaries. Member-managed LLCs are those run by the member/owners; while manager managed LLCs are those run by a person selected by the owners. These distinctions have real legal consequences for issues such as liability, tax, and the determination of "income from labor and industry" for family law.

276. **Limited Partner:** All partnerships must have at least one General Partner, who is liable for partnership obligations. In most, if not all, jurisdictions, a partnership may also have many Limited Partners whose liability for partnership obligations does not exceed their investment in the partnership.

277. **Line of Credit:** An agreement between a bank and a customer under which the banks agrees the customer may maintain an outstanding loan up to the amount of the line of credit. Generally, the customer is responsible for paying current interest, but no principal on the loan. Such loans may be secured by a primary residence, in which case they are home-equity loans. Generally, such loans are callable, which places the borrower in a risky position. Credit cards are common examples of a line of credit.

278. **Liquidity:** This term has several important finance and accounting meanings:

- The most common usage refers to the degree a person has available cash. For example a person who is very *liquid* would have substantial resources either in the form of cash or easily converted into cash.

- *"Liquid Assets"* is an important category on a balance sheet. It includes cash deposits and other items readily convertible to cash. More generally, *"current assets"* includes not only items which are very *liquid*, but also inventory and accounts receivable, which generally turn into cash through sales and collections within one year.

- *Liquidity* ratios are important tools for analyzing financial statements. The *current ratio* and the *acid test ratio* are commonly used liquidity ratios. Inventory turnover also provides information regarding liquidity.

- As an element of interest rates, liquidity is a positive state for which people will pay money. A lender loses liquidity by exchanging cash for a promise to pay. In exchange, the lender will charge interest of approximately 2.5 to 3.5%. In addition, the lender will charge for risk and expected inflation.

279. **Living Trust:** This generally refers to a trust created during the life of the grantor with the grantor as the income beneficiary and others are the principal beneficiaries. Planned properly it will avoid the need for an estate or succession administration, as well as the need for a will regarding trust assets.

280. **Living Will:** This generally refers to a document pursuant to state law which provides instructions regarding the medical treatment wishes of the maker. It may provide, for example, that the maker does not want extraordinary measures taken to preserve his life in cases involving major injury or disease. Some people prefer a *Health Care Surrogate (or proxy)*, to whom they grant to power to make such decisions.

281. **Loan:** A *loan* is the lending of a valuable thing for a period of time. Typically, it involves money, but it need not. For example, one can loan the use of property. This is distinguishable from a gift of the use of a thing; while, that, too, would have value, it would not be a "loan" in the sense of this definition. Instead, that would comprise a gift of the use of property. A loan of the use of property essentially involves deferred rent.

One should also an exchange of the use of property for the use of other property. Two views of such a transaction are possible. From one perspective, each party lends or rents the use of one asset for another and each has rental income and a possible rent deduction. From another perspective, however, the use of a thing over time is a current property right. From that perspective, future interests in things do not exist—only present interests are possible. Hence, a transaction involving the use of property for the use of property or money is a current transaction or exchange rather than one over time. The difference may appear immaterial; however, it is not. The issue asks whether interest is a necessary component of time. If it is, then all transactions over time must involve interest, including the use of property . . . perhaps even the use of one's own property.

282. **Loan to Value Ratio:** *LTV*: This is a simple financial ratio used by lenders:

$$\left(\frac{loan\ principal}{fair\ market\ value} \right)$$

For example, a bank may offer a particular loan program and interest rate if the *LTV* is no more than 60%. In such a case the owner would have 40% equity in the property.

Compare the *LTV* with the *Debt to Assets Ratio*.

283. **Long Sale:** This is the sale of a thing owned by the seller. It contrasts with a short sale, which involves the sale of a thing not owned by the seller, but instead borrowed from another. One should also carve out from the concept of *long sales*, those which involve *wash sales*—which are really not sales at all.

A *long sale* results from the disposition of a *long position*, or ownership of a thing. *Long* positions are distinguishable from short positions in which the party involved has sold a thing borrowed and thus has an existing obligation to *cover*, *i.e.*, to return the thing borrowed but sold. One completes such an obligation—*covers* it—by purchasing a similar (fungible) thing and then transferring it to the lender. One might refer to a person who holds a long position as having *gone long* with regard to the things involved, typically securities or commodities.

284. **Macro Economics:** This is the study of large groups, trends, their behavior and their consequences. It may be at a national or world level. What holds true in a *macro* sense, however, does not necessarily hold true in a *micro* sense.

285. **Matching Principle:** The most important principle of accounting, the *matching principle* provides:

> *An income statement must match income with the costs of producing that income.*

Without proper matching, an income statement would provide misleading information. For example, management needs to know whether a particular division is worth keeping, expanding, reducing, or eliminating. To evaluate the division, the manager would want to know how much income it produces. For that to be a meaningful number, the periodic revenue must match with (be reduced by) the direct and indirect costs of producing that particular revenue. Similarly, costs must match with the income they produce; otherwise, management could not evaluate whether the costs were justifiable.

The *accrual method* of accounting rests on the *matching principle*: income is recognized when *all events* occur such that the item has been earned and the amount can be determined with reasonable accuracy. The conditions of the all events test temper the *matching principle* of accounting with the conservatism principle of accounting: do not recognize income before it is earned and reasonably determinable. Thus an entity will accrue income in a period even if it has received nothing. Similarly it will defer advance receipts to the proper period in which they are earned. Also, an accrual entity will accrue expenses (costs) when they are incurred, regardless of whether they have been paid.

In contrast, the *cash method* of account does not follow the matching principle. Instead, a cash method user recognizes income upon receipt and expenses upon payment. This risks matching income from one operation with expenses from another. *GAAP* does not recognize the *cash method* because it violates the *matching principle*.

A reasonable criticism of statutory accounting in many legal areas is that it fails to provide basic principles, including the matching principle. For example, in Family Law, both alimony and child support are functions of income; however, most (perhaps all) state statutes defining income for alimony or child support fail to require adherence to the matching principle. Unless the parties or the court imposes matching—which would tend not to be the case—the resulting numbers risk being inaccurate, perhaps to a very large degree. Of course, a person who works for a regular salary, paid frequently, and who has few employee expenses or other accessions to wealth would provide similar numbers under both the cash and accrual methods of accounting. But, that scenario is probably a small percentage of the populace. For example, many salaried employees accrue deferred compensation, bonuses, overtime, and various fringe benefits which may be irregular or easily advanced or deferred. They also typically have a variety of employee and other business expenses, which are also subject to timing choices.

286. **Micro Economics:** This is the study of small groups or individuals and their behavior in an economy. What holds true in a *micro* sense, does not necessarily hold true in a *Macro* sense.

287. **Mark to Market:** *MTM:* This important term has varying meaning and significance:

A. In ***financial accounting***, consistent with *GAAP*, audited entities must follow *MTM* rules of *FASB* 115 and 157.

FASB 115 provides:

- If an entity has the positive intent and ability to hold debt securities to maturity, it must classify them as held-to-maturity securities and report them at amortized cost less impairment.

- If an entity buys and holds debt or equity securities for the principal purpose of selling them in the near term, it must classify as trading securities and report them at fair value. It must include unrealized gains and losses included in earnings.

- If an entity holds debt or equity securities not classified as either held-to-maturity securities or trading securities, it must classify them as available-for-sale securities and report them at fair value. It must exclude unrealized gains and losses from operating earnings; however, it must report such gains and losses in a separate component of shareholders' equity as other income.

FASB 157 adds definitions and some other rules. Fair value is:

the price that would be received to sell an asset or paid to transfer a liability in an *orderly transaction* between *market participants* at the measurement date.

Much criticism of these rules—and their application—appeared during the financial crisis of fall 2008. Banks and other financial institutions suddenly marked various sub-prime loans and other financial products to a rapidly decreasing market. This prompted serious concerns regarding the liquidity, solvency, and viability of the institutions. Arguably, no fair market existed for many of the financial instruments, as few *market participants* were available and *orderly transactions* were not occurring. Arguably, banks and other financial institutions over-reacted, *marking* many assets at fire sale prices far below their worth as *held-to-maturity* securities. Also, *FASB* 115 requires marking to *fair value* as opposed to *fair market value*, a more generally understood term.

B.   For ***tax purposes***, *IRC* sections 475 and 1259 cover *MTM* rules.

Under *IRC* section 475, securities *dealers* must use *Mark to Market* accounting for tax purposes. Under subsection (e), commodities *dealers* may elect *Mark to Market* Accounting. Under subsection (f), securities traders and commodities *traders* may also elect *Mark to Market* Accounting. Subsection (a) requires *MTM* users to report affected property at *fair market value*. Nothing in the section, however, defines *fair market value*.

Under *IRC* section 1259, a taxpayer must recognize gain on the constructive sale of some property. Paragraph (c)(1) defines a constructive sale:

> A taxpayer shall be treated as having made a constructive sale of an appreciated financial position if the taxpayer (or a related person)—
>
> > (A) enters into a short sale of the same or substantially identical property,
> >
> > (B) enters into an offsetting notional principal contract with respect to the same or substantially identical property,
> >
> > (C) enters into a futures or forward contract to deliver the same or substantially identical property,
> >
> > (D) in the case of an appreciated financial position that is a short sale or a contract described in subparagraph (B) or (C) with respect to any property, acquires the same or substantially identical property, or
> >
> > (E) to the extent prescribed by the Secretary in regulations, enters into 1 or more other transactions (or acquires 1 or more positions) that have substantially the same effect as a transaction described in any of the preceding subparagraphs.

288. **Margin:** This term has many important usages:

   - In financial terms, *margin* refers to debt. More specifically, assets bought "on *margin*" are assets purchased with borrowed money, at least in part. Generally, a lender will require a specific *Loan to Value* ratio for such debt. If the *LTV* drops below the pre-determined level, the lender issues a "*margin call.*"

- In broader terms, *margin* refers to the difference between two numbers, either in relative or absolute terms. For example, a *profit margin* is an important financial ratio. It is:

$$(sales\ price - basis)$$

in *absolute* terms. Thus an item sold for $100 but with a basis (cost) of $60 would have an absolute margin of $40.

In *relative* terms, the *profit margin* is a percentage—either of the sales price or the basis (cost). The general formula, which is a function of sales price would be:

$$\left(\frac{sales\ price - basis}{sales\ price} \right)$$

For example, if an item with a basis of $60 sold for $100, the profit margin would be 40%. Of course, an important factor in this formula involves the term *cost* or basis. *Cost* is itself a fuzzy term: it can refer to *marginal cost* or it can include many other items under a *partial* or *full absorption method of costing.*

Another view of *profit margin* involves *mark-up*—the percentage by which the sales price exceeds the basis, as a percentage of the basis:

$$\left(\frac{sales\ price - basis}{basis} \right)$$

For example, if an item with a basis of $60 sold for $100, the *mark-up* would be 66.67%.

- The *marginal cost* of an item is also an essential finance, accounting, and economic term. This refers to the direct cost of one additional item. Under a common view of cost accounting, an entity should produce more items until the marginal cost equals the expected sales price. Such a policy would work well, however, only under conditions in which the seller can segment the market: sell some items at a high price so as to cover considerable overhead and other fixed, indirect costs. The seller could then produce more, but sell it at a lower price to other persons (perhaps under a different brand) as long as the marginal cost is less than the sales price.

- A *marginal tax rate* is also important. It refers to the tax rate imposed on the last dollar of income, considering not only the tax bracket but also collateral consequences such as deduction phase-outs or limitations triggered by the extra dollar.

289. **Margin Call:** A demand to a customer to deposit more money because his *Loan to Value (LTV)* ratio on securities has risen above a pre-determined level. *Margin Calls* are common in *Bear Markets*: many investors used borrowed money to purchase securities. In a *Bear Market*, those securities lose value, but the principal on the loan remains stable; hence, the *LTV* ratio deteriorates.

   Margin Calls can be self-reinforcing. A *Bear Market* occurs when demand for stocks is less than supply of stocks: the stock prices fall until a point of equilibrium—demand equals supply. But, a *Bear Market* triggers *Margin Calls*, which require investors to deposit money. But, in a *Bear Market*, investors may be *illiquid*; hence, they must often sell stocks to raise the money to cover *Margin Calls* on remaining investment. That increases the supply of stocks, but not the demand; hence, the prices fall further, resulting in even more *Margin Calls*.

290. **Market Discount: *MD*:** *Market Discount* results from increases in interest rates following the issuance of a debt instrument with a fixed interest rate. Because such a debt instrument is a series of cash flows—both the interest payments and principal payments—it has an easily computed present value. That *PV* drops as the relevant periodic interest rate rises. The *PV* drop is the *Market Discount*—the market, rather than the original issuer, has discounted the instrument.

   For tax purposes, holders of *MD* debt instruments have four options regarding the timing of interest income due to the discount. *IRC* section 1275 and 1276 explain the options.

   MD is the opposite of *Acquisition Premium*, which results from decreases in interest rates. *IRC* Section 1272 and the Treasury Regulations there under provide two methods regarding the timing of the negative interest income impact due to *AP*.

291. **Market Marker:** A Broker Dealer firm that accepts the risk of holding a certain number of shares of a particular security in order to facilitate trading in that security. Once an order is received, the Market Maker immediately sells from its own inventory or seeks an offsetting order.

292. **Market Risk:** This is the *risk*—danger—that an asset's value will change due to external factors such as:

   - General changes in securities markets.

- Changes in inflation different from expectations.

- Changes in currency exchange rates.

293. **Materiality Principal:** An important principle of accounting, this requires the reporting of material items only. Immaterial items may be expensed directly or even misstated without prompting a qualified opinion. Essentially, if something does not matter, it does not matter. Exactly what is material is situational. For example, for a small business, $1,000 may be a material amount, while it may be irrelevant for a large inter-national firm.

294. **Mean:** The word mean refers to a type of average. Traditionally, it contrasts with a Median (the mid-point on a list of numbers) and a Mode (the most common number or value in a group). A mean, however, has at least four significant forms:

- **Arithmetic Mean:** This is the sum of a group of numbers divided by the number of numbers. For example, 10, 15, 20 has an arithmetic mean of 15: 45 divided by 3. The arithmetic mean is the one we all learned in grammar school: add the numbers and divide by the number of numbers. A problem with it is that outliers (really large or very small numbers) distort it. That relates to life expectancies: the man who is expected at age 25 to live to 80, but dies at 26, has a big impact on the average, while the guy who lives to 81 or 82 has a very small impact (even though more of the latter exist). Each data point deserves (arguably) equal validity; however, the arithmetic mean over-weights the very short-lived person.

- **Geometric Mean:** A geometric mean multiplies the numbers (rather than adds them) and then takes the nth root of those numbers (if you have five numbers, take the 5th root). In finance, it makes sense because some years can have extraordinarily high or very low negative returns that can distort the "average." The geometric mean will be lower than the arithmetic mean if any of the numbers have a negative value.

- **Harmonic Mean:** The harmonic mean is the reciprocal of the arithmetic mean of the reciprocals of the various numbers. As I understand, it will underweight the highs and overweight the lows. It can, for example be used to compute average speeds (which may involve very high speeds, but low speeds cannot go below zero, thus lows deserve special attention because there is a limit to how low a low can be). It is also often used in finance, although I admit I cannot quite explain why it is sometimes thought to be more accurate than the geometric mean. In any event, it will likely be more conservative (lower) than the other two means.

- **Quadratic Mean:** Also called the root mean square (RMS) this is the square root of the arithmetic mean of the squares of a number set. It is used in electrical engineering.

295. **Merger:** Generally, a *merger* is the combining of two entities. Often, one entity acquires the other by issuing its stock to the shareholders of the target entity in exchange for their stock of the target. At that point, a parent-subsidiary relationship would exist. For an actual merger to occur, the parent would need to liquidate the subsidiary by transferring its assets and liabilities to the parent and by then cancelling the subsidiary's stock.

The term *merger* is not consistently defined; hence, lawyers should be careful about its use without a definition. For example, some people may define a *merger* in the truest sense: a combing of assets and liabilities from two formerly separate entities. Others may use the term more broadly, to include the *acquisition* of a subsidiary by a parent.

For United States tax purposes, *IRC* section 368 defines corporate reorganizations as including seven types. One—a Type A Reorganization—involves a "statutory *merger*" or traditional consolidation of two formerly separate entities into one new entity. A Type C Reorganization also involves a consolidation; however, it involves a continuing entity acquiring all the assets of another entity by the issuance of stock. A Type B Reorganization is better called an *acquisition*: a Parent acquires the stock of a subsidiary.

296. **Mergers and Acquisitions:** *M & A*: This is a term for the legal, accounting, and investment banking practice of handling both traditional mergers (usually consolidations) and parent-sub acquisitions.

297. **Method of Accounting:** This refers to various methods of allocating income and deductions among periods.

- For <u>audited</u> *Financial Statements*, only the *Accrual Method* is consistent with U.S. *GAAP*.

- For <u>unaudited</u> *Financial Statements*, most people use the *Cash Method*, which does not *clearly reflect income*.

- For *United States tax purposes*, taxpayers generally may use one of several methods—or even a combination of them—which include:

  o *Cash Method* (as specially defined for tax purposes).

  o *Accrual Method* (as specially defined for tax purposes, which is radically different from its definition for *Financial Accounting* purposes and *GAAP*).

  o *Installment Method*, to the extent permitted by *IRC* section 453.

  o Other special methods under *IRC* section 451.

Lawyers who refer to the term income for legal purposes need to be cognizant of the method of accounting used to measure that income. The various methods sometimes produce similar numbers; however, often they produce *materially* different numbers.

Lawyers should also be familiar with the *Consistency Principle of Accounting*, which requires an entity to use the same method of accounting from period to period. *Changes of Accounting Method* require complex adjusting entries and *pro forma Financial Statements* to ensure fairness and clarity. Lawyers must also recall the numerous intricacies of accounting methods: referring to the accrual method may sound clear, but it is not, as the Accrual Method prompts numerous choices and elections for matters such as capitalization, cost allocation, depreciation, and amortization. Hence, even one *Accrual Method* set of *Financial Statements* may not be consistent with—and therefore comparable to—another set of *Accrual Method* Statements from a separate entity. To a limited extent, *GAAP* requires specific rules which are at least comparable and consistent within industries, but even then it allows for many choices.

For United States tax purposes, a taxpayer cannot change from one method of accounting to another without permission from the Secretary of the Treasury. For many standard changes, permission is automatic; however, for others, it is not. Method Changes also necessitate *IRC* section 481 adjustments, which essentially subject the taxpayer to tax as if he had used the new method consistently since 1954 (the year of enactment for section 481).

What constitutes a Method of Accounting for tax purposes is a matter of significant controversy. Courts are divided on the issue. In particular, they disagree regarding whether an improper method of accounting is a method of accounting. According to the Treasury Department, consistent mistakes in multiple years may constitute a method of accounting; as a result, a taxpayer cannot, without permission, change to a proper method. With permission, he will be subject to *IRC* section 481 adjustments.

298. **Mill:** One-thousandth of a currency unit, as in one-tenth of a cent in the United States. Property taxes in the U.S. are often expressed in terms of millage, or the mill rate per dollar of value. For example, a tax of 10 mills would be one percent. On property with a value of $100,000, the tax would be $1,000. Often, property taxes are levied in fractions of a mill sometimes to several decimal places.

299. **Minimum Gain Chargeback:** This is a United States partnership tax provision required to be in a partnership agreement in some circumstances. Such a provision would effectively reverse a special allocation of gain to a non-contributing partner in order to ensure substantial economic effect for the allocation.

Non-tax lawyers probably need not worry about the technicalities of a *MGC* provision; however, they should be generally aware of what necessitates one and of the consequences resulting from one. With a *MGC* provision, a partnership could allocate gains on property to non-contributing partners in some years. It would later need to allocate other gains to the contributing partner to make up for the non-economically real original allocation. As a result, the tax benefits would mostly evaporate. But, non-tax legal consequences from such an allocation could nevertheless be substantial. The original allocation would inflate the income of some partners and suppress the income of others. The chargeback would later reverse these consequences. However, if legal consequences flow as a function of the early years' income and not as a result of the later years' income, distortions are possible. Naturally, a non-tax law measurement of income should not rely on tax law provisions for its definition of income; however, in many instances that is precisely what occurs.

300. **Minority Discount:** A minority interest in a business—generally less than 50% of the voting power, is not as valuable as a controlling interest. Common sense would indicate this is correct. As a result, the *Fair Market Value* of a minority interest must include a *discount* factor—a percentage reduction—to reflect the lack of control and the existence of control in the hands of others.

But, that which common sense says is true is not always true: appearance can deceive. This concept forms the basis for much chicanery—legal, but of questionable morality (assuming that is a relevant inquiry for legal actions).

For example, much of estate planning practice involves breaking closely held entities into various ownership interests. This may include different classes of stock or merely the transfer of ownership to various family members. The person whose estate is the subject of the plan would traditionally retain only a minority interest. As such, his or her estate would traditionally value the retained interest at a substantial *discount* for federal estate tax purposes. Because the *marginal rate* on estate is 45%, this can result in significant savings.

The *minority discount* estate plan scheme, however, rests on the questionable notion that people intentionally destroy value in their property. For many observers, that proposition is not credible. More likely, in their opinion, the only persons who would use such a plan have families who will likely cooperate and who will likely put the pieces back together—at least in practical terms. Hence, the minority discount is arguably unwarranted. The discount, instead, would be appropriate for families with considerable hostility among the various factions; however, rational planners would not divide valuable property into competing hostile factions.

Despite much concern in the eyes of the government and many others, estate planning which rests on *minority discounts* tends to be successful.

301. **Mode:** The *mode* reflects the timing of the first payment in an annuity, an amortization, or a sinking fund. In *Begin Mode*, a calculator treats the first payment or deposit as occurring today—at the time of the calculation. In *End Mode*, it treats the first payment or deposit as occurring at the end of the first period (*e.g.*, month, quarter, or year).

Most *financial calculators* default to *end mode* because that is the most common feature of loans. One of the most common mistakes people make in using financial calculators involves forgetting to set the mode correctly. The consequences may be significant; however, they may not be noticeable. For example, setting the payment period or the term incorrectly can produce an obviously wrong—even ridiculous—answer. Setting the *mode* incorrectly, however, will not produce an answer which is clearly and obviously wrong to most users. Hence, the *mode* function is a dangerous one in that it results in many errors.

302. **Monetary Policy:** This involves government or Central Bank control of the money supply to affect the economy. In contrast, *fiscal policy* generally refers to government use of tax and spending to affect the economy.

303. **Monetary Unit Assumption of Accounting:** This important principle or assumption of accounting requires the use of a monetary unit—such as the dollar—to represent assets, liabilities, and equity. The assumption has two important consequences:

- Non-quantifiable items—such as emotional value—may be disclosed in footnotes; however, they cannot be disclosed directly on financial statements.

- The monetary unit has a constant meaning; hence, a dollar in 1950 is the same—for financial reporting purposes—as a dollar in 2010. Inflation and deflation are generally irrelevant for financial reporting, although their impacts may be discussed in footnotes and *pro forma* statements.

304. **Money Supply:** The money supply in the United States has several definitions, each of which has multiple components.

M1 includes:

- Currency
- Travelers' checks
- Demand deposits
- Other checkable deposits at banks
- Other checkable deposits at thrift institutions

M1 has ranged from a total of $138.8 Billion (of which $28.5 Billion was currency) in January, 1959, to $1,884.6 Billion (of which $844.9 Billion was currency) in March, 2009.

M2 (without M1) includes:

- Savings Deposits at Banks
- Savings Deposits at Thrift Institutions
- Small Denomination Time Deposits at Banks
- Small Denomination Time Deposits at Thrift Institutions
- Retail Money Funds

Non-M1 M2 has ranged from a total of $147.7 Billion in January, 1959, to $6,754.3 Billion in March, 2009. In addition, institutional money funds—which are not a component of M1 or M2, ranged from zero in January, 1959, to $2,492.4 Billion in March, 2009.

The Fed issues notices regarding the United States Money Supply weekly:

The H.6 release, published weekly, provides measures of the monetary aggregates (M1 and M2) and their components.

M1 and M2 are progressively more inclusive measures of money: M1 is included in M2.

M1, the more narrowly defined measure, consists of the most liquid forms of money, namely currency and checkable deposits.

The non-M1 components of M2 are primarily household holdings of savings deposits, small time deposits, and retail money market mutual funds.

Monthly data are available back to January 1959; for most series, weekly data are available back to January 1975.

The Money Stock Measure, which is the broadest Fed measure of money, including M1, M2, and money market mutual funds has ranged from a seasonally adjusted $286.6 Billion in January, 1959, to a seasonally adjusted $8,316.6 Billion in March, 2009.

The nominal *GDP* for the economy is the velocity of money times the money supply:

$$GDP = MV$$

where *GDP* = Gross Domestic Product, M = money supply, and V = the velocity of money.

305. **Money Market:** This is not an actual physical or even electronic market. Instead, it is a general term referring to the borrowing, lending, and trading related to short-term debt world-wide. Many *money market* funds exist—they are *mutual funds* which invest in *money market*-type obligations. Such obligations includes:

- Commercial Paper
- Certificates of Deposit
- T-Bills
- Bankers Acceptances
- Short-Term Municipal Notes Issued In Anticipation of Tax Receipts.

306. **Moral Hazard:** This is the consequence of risk insulation. If a person does not bear the risks of his actions, he will tend to behave with less concern for the risk. OPM—Other People's Money—is a more colloquial way of describing the phenomena.

Law, economics, and finance produce myriad examples. In insurance law, an insured with a very low deductible may take insufficient precautions to protect his property. In agency, an agent may succumb to temptation to cheat his principal who may not have sufficient information to prevent such behavior. In family law, a spouse with substantial knowledge of finance and accounting will be tempted to act to his own advantage—if he views any significant risk of marital failure—even if the action is to the collective disadvantage of the couple. In law school, mandatory grade curves and minimal risk of failure heap *moral hazard* onto students who lack the self-discipline to seek knowledge for its own sake: they shun work because the

difference between a high score and a modest score is small and the
risk of failure is essentially non-existent.

A capitalist economy works because of reward and risk—more crudely
self interest and greed, tempered by a healthy dose of risk aversion.
But, if government takes the risk away from the equation by providing
too large a safety-net or too many bail-outs, greed may longer be
controlled by risk and thus may (will?) expand out of control. The
resulting economic distortions inevitably end badly. If government
responds with greater regulation of greed—rather than with lesser
protection from risk—additional distortions are inevitable.

A *Fed* definition of moral hazard is:

> The risk that a party to a transaction has not entered into a
> contract in good faith, has provided misleading information
> about its assets, liabilities or credit capacity, or has an
> incentive to take unusual risks in a desperate attempt to earn
> a profit before the contract settles.

307. **Mortgage:** This frequently mis-used term serves either as a verb or a
noun.

- The verb form stems from the infinitive to *mortgage*,
  which means to grant or sign a *mortgage* on particular
  property to secure an obligation.

- The noun form refers to the security interest in the thing
  secured.

A *mortgage* is just a security device—and nothing more. It is not an
asset and it (at least in most, if not all, jurisdictions) is not an
ownership interest in the thing *mortgaged*. Instead, the holder of a
mortgage has preference in bankruptcy over the proceeds of the sale of
the thing *mortgaged*. This preference is for an amount up to the
amount of the secured loan, but not more (except for foreclosure costs).
One cannot "pay a *mortgage*." One can pay a debt secured by a
mortgage. Similarly one does not owe a mortgage and one does not own
a *mortgage*. Persons owe debts and own promises to pay—which may
or may not be secured. The difference has substantial legal
significance. For example, in family law, if one spouse improves
separate property using marital funds, most jurisdictions would grant
the other spouse an interest in the improvement to the extent of the
marital funds used. What constitutes an improvement, however, is not
always easy to discern. If one spouse uses marital funds to add a room
onto a separately owned building, the addition is almost certainly an
improvement. However, if one spouse uses marital funds to pay part
of a loan (separate or marital) secured by the separate property, that
does not necessarily improve or enhance the value of the property.

Courts differ widely on this issue, probably because they often misunderstand the fundamental nature of a *mortgage*.

Related to this definition is the definition of equity. *Equity*, in one sense, equals the *Fair Market Value (FMV)* of the property minus the principal on a loan secured by the property. While that definition is correct, it does not make equity an asset. It is not. *Equity*—in that sense—is just a net figure . . . a number. The property is the asset and it appears on the left side of the balance sheet. The debt is a liability and it appears on the right side of the balance sheet. The two do not net for accounting purposes and they should not net for legal purposes.

308. **Mutual Fund:** This refers to an investment company regulated by the SEC. *See, 15 U.S.C. § 80a–3(a),* which codifies the *Investment Act of 1940.* It is a management company under 15 U.S.C. § 80a–4(3). Per section 80a–5, management companies further divide into sub-categories:

(a) Open-end and closed-end companies. For the purposes of this title, management companies are divided into open-end and closed-end companies, defined as follows:

(1) "Open-end company" means a management company which is offering for sale or has outstanding any redeemable security of which it is the issuer.

(2) "Closed-end company" means any management company other than an open-end company.

(b) Diversified and non-diversified companies. Management companies are further divided into diversified companies and non-diversified companies, defined as follows:

(1) "Diversified company" means a management company which meets the following requirements: At least 75 per centum of the value of its total assets is represented by cash and cash items (including receivables), Government securities, securities of other investment companies, and other securities for the purposes of this calculation limited in respect of any one issuer to an amount not greater in value than 5 per centum of the value of the total assets of such management company and to not more than 10 per centum of the outstanding voting securities of such issuer.

(2) "Non-diversified company" means any management company other than a diversified company.

In more layman's terms, an *open-end mutual fund* issues new shares daily as investors purchase share. The fund also redeems shares daily as investors sell shares. A *closed-end mutual fund* has a limited number of shares which the share owners may themselves trade.

309. **NAFTA: North American Free Trade Agreement:** This is a trilateral treaty among the United States, Canada, and Mexico. It went into effect on January 1, 1994.

310. **National Automobile Dealers Association: NADA: Blue Book:** According to the organization's website:

> The National Automobile Dealers Association, founded in 1917, represents more than 19,700 new car and truck dealers, both domestic and international, with more than 43,000 separate franchises.

> NADA membership is open to any new-automobile or new-truck dealership holding a new automobile or truck sales and service franchise.

> **NADA:**

> - Provides counsel on legal and regulatory matters
> - Represents dealers on Capitol Hill
> - Develops research data on the automobile industry
> - Operates training and service programs to improve dealership business operations, sales and service practices

The organization publishes a variety of pricing and value guides for new and used cars, motorcycles, recreation vehicles, and boats. These guides are available through nadaguides.com. Historically, they were known as the "Blue Book." Consumers and lenders often refer to blue-book value when referring to a used car.

311. **NASD: National Association of Securities Dealers:** See *NASDAQ*. Be careful not to confuse the acronym *NASD* with the acronym *NADA*.

312. **National Association of Securities Dealers Automated Quotations: NASDAQ:** [pronounced **naz**-dak]. According to the company website:

> NASDAQ is the largest U.S. electronic stock market. With approximately 3,200 companies, it lists more companies and, on average, trades more shares per day than any other U.S. market. It is home to companies that are leaders across all areas of business, including technology, retail, communications, financial services, transportation, media and

biotechnology. NASDAQ is the primary market for trading NASDAQ-listed stocks.

313. **Negative Amortization:** This occurs when *payments* on a loan are insufficient to cover current *periodic interest*. In such cases, the parties capitalize unpaid interest into *principal*. Thus, contrary to the traditional **AMORTIZATION** of a loan under which the principal drops over time, with negative amortization, the principal amount increases over time.

314. **Negative Interest Rate:** A negative interest rate is highly unusual. Prior to 2015, one might have thought it would impossible. In theory, it exists when expected deflation exceeds risk plus liquidity. For example, a particular borrower may have a personal risk factor of zero (generally the U.S. government or the *Federal Reserve Bank*). If expected deflation exceeds the traditional *liquidity* factor of 2.5 to 3.5 percent, then interest rates on government paper would be negative.

In practice, however, the theory initially seems to make little sense. Why would someone lend money to the U.S. government and demand less money in return after a period of time? Why would such a lender not simply maintain possession of the money? The answer involves a *liquidity risk*.

Generally, *liquidity* has value because the liquid person can spend the money while the illiquid person (the lender) cannot. This is why, as explain in **LESSON SIX:** *Why People Charge Interest,* the liquidity factor of interest typically ranges from 2.5% to 3.5%.

But *liquidity* also carries risk. Usually, this is tiny because someone who is liquid can park the funds in U.S. Treasury Securities or in insured demand deposits (such as a checking account or a *CD*). However, in times of considerable economic turmoil, such as faced in the United States and many countries during the Fall of 2008 through the Spring of 2009, many investors lost faith in many financial institutions, including banks. Hence, the risk associated with such deposits rose—sometimes beyond the inherent value of the liquidity. Other forms of liquid assets—such as gold, silver, and other commodities—also involve risk. Silver is bulky and thus expensive to store. One cannot typically store a great deal of silver at his home without increasing his risk of burglary. Similarly, gold—while less bulky than silver—has to be stored someplace. Storing it with a financial institution prompts both a fee and risk: what if the institution becomes insolvent?

For a short period—a few hours—some short-term interest rates on U.S. T-bills fell below zero during early November, 2008. For that time, one had to pay as much as $1,025,000 to purchase government securities that paid $1,000,000 thirty days later. While the notion of the lender paying interest to the borrower is strange, when viewed as a storage fee, it can seem rational. For that few hours at least, all other available options for those lenders carried so much risk, the lenders were willing to pay the Treasury to hold their money. Beginning in January 2015, many sovereign obligations in the EU began bearing or being issued at negative rates. By October 2015, some short-term U.S. obligations were selling at negative rates in secondary markets.

315. **Negotiable Instrument:** A negotiable instrument is a statutorily defined type of financial instrument. Under the Uniform Commercial Code, it creates a holder in due course. A negotiable instrument is necessarily transferable; however, a transferable instrument is not necessarily negotiable. Article 3–104 of the UCC provides:

(a) Except as provided in subsections (c) and (d), "negotiable instrument" means an unconditional promise or order to pay a fixed amount of money, with or without interest or other charges described in the promise or order, if it:

(1) is payable to bearer or to order at the time it is issued or first comes into possession of a holder;

(2) is payable on demand or at a definite time; and

(3) does not state any other undertaking or instruction by the person promising or ordering payment to do any act in addition to the payment of money, but the promise or order may contain (i) an undertaking or power to give, maintain, or protect collateral to secure payment, (ii) an authorization or power to the holder to confess judgment or realize on or dispose of collateral, or (iii) a waiver of the benefit of any law intended for the advantage or protection of an obligor.

(b) "Instrument" means a negotiable instrument.

(c) An order that meets all of the requirements of subsection (a), except paragraph (1), and otherwise falls within the definition of "check" in subsection (f) is a negotiable instrument and a check.

(d) A promise or order other than a check is not an instrument if, at the time it is issued or first comes into possession of a holder, it contains a conspicuous statement, however expressed, to the effect that the promise or order is not negotiable or is not an instrument governed by this Article.

(e) An instrument is a "note" if it is a promise and is a "draft" if it is an order. If an instrument falls within the definition of both "note" and "draft," a person entitled to enforce the instrument may treat it as either.

(f) "Check" means (i) a draft, other than a documentary draft, payable on demand and drawn on a bank or (ii) a cashier's check or teller's check. An instrument may be a check even though it is described on its face by another term, such as "money order."

(g) "Cashier's check" means a draft with respect to which the drawer and drawee are the same bank or branches of the same bank.

(h) "Teller's check" means a draft drawn by a bank (i) on another bank, or (ii) payable at or through a bank.

(i) "Traveler's check" means an instrument that (i) is payable on demand, (ii) is drawn on or payable at or through a bank, (iii) is designated by the term "traveler's check" or by a substantially similar term, and (iv) requires, as a condition to payment, a countersignature by a person whose specimen signature appears on the instrument.

(j) "Certificate of deposit" means an instrument containing an acknowledgment by a bank that a sum of money has been received by the bank and a promise by the bank to repay the sum of money. A certificate of deposit is a note of the bank.

316. **Net Operating Income: *NOI*:** Also known as *NOP* or net operating profit, this is generally another term for *EBIT*—earnings before interest and taxes; however, some users define it as earnings before interest but after taxes (some refer to this as NOPAT). It also represents an amount before *extraordinary* items. Some authorities interchange this term with "operating profit."

While finance and accounting authorities may quibble about whether *NOI* is a figure before or after taxes, lawyers should be more careful with the bigger picture. They must understand the distinction between "operating" income and "non-operating" income. Income from operations is an appropriate touchstone for managerial bonuses, valuation of business, and predictions of future income for child support and alimony. Non-operating items, however, generally should not figure into such calculations.

317. **Net Operating Loss: *NOL*:** For U.S. tax purposes, *IRC* section 172 defines an *NOL*. Taxpayers may carry-back an *NOL* for up to two years and carry forward an *NOL* for 18 years. Transferring an *NOL* to another person is complicated: a simple merger will not generally suffice. Hence, this is the subject of advanced tax courses.

A *NOL* has value, which may be non-intuitive to some: losses have value. To the extent a person can deduct the *NOL* for tax purposes; he will save his marginal tax rate, which may be upwards of 40%. Lawyers need to view such losses as assets, just as accountants would. For example, in relation to dissolution of marriage, an *NOL* can be quite valuable to the spouse entitled to use it. Similarly, a person with an *NOL* may be more attractive as a marriage prospect in the same sense that a person of wealth may be more attractive than a person who is poor.

For non-tax purposes, the term net operating loss refers to the same calculation as net operating income—it merely is a negative rather than a positive amount.

318. **Net Operating Profit After Taxes: NOPAT:** This is a realistic measure of income because it emphasizes *operating* profits, as opposed to profits (which include extraordinary gains and losses) and is *after* taxes. Whether it is after actual taxes paid or taxes accrued is important. A formula is:

$$(NOI)(1 - tr)$$

where *NOI* = net operating income and *tr* = the tax rate.

Whether "tax rate" is the "marginal rate" or the "effective rate" or the "average rate" depends on the user. Whether users consider all federal, state, local, and foreign income, excise, value added, and *ad valorem* taxes also varies. Be careful.

319. *NPV*: **Net Present Value:** This is the *present value* of all *cash flows* minus the initial investment. The number should be positive. If it is negative, the investment does not generate the assumed return.

320. **New York Stock Exchange: *NYSE*:** Also known as the *Big Board*, this is the major stock exchange in the United States.

321. **Non-Qualified Deferred Compensation:** For United States tax purposes, Deferred Compensation Plans and arrangements come in two basic formats: qualified and unqualified. Each format has subcategories, as well.

Under Internal Revenue Code section 404, the payor of non-qualified deferred compensation may not deduct the amount of compensation until the year the recipient—whether an employee or an independent contractor—must include it in income. As a result, non-qualified plans do not have the substantial tax subsidy given qualified plans.

IRC section 467(g) arguably provides for current inclusion of any non-qualified deferred compensation plan earnings in the income of the beneficiary, *i.e.*, the interest component of the deferral. This section, however, has not been operative since its enactment in 1986.

See the definition below of "Qualified Deferred Compensation."

322. **Non-Recourse Debt:** This refers to debt for which the borrower is not personally responsible. In contrast, the borrower is personally responsible for recourse debt. Banks and other institutions have, at times, been willing to lend on a non-recourse basis because they are then able to charge a higher interest rate. A mortgage on substantial property typically secures non-recourse debt; otherwise, no one would be willing to lend in such a way. If the borrower defaults, the lender may foreclose on the security interest. If the security sells for a sufficient amount to satisfy the obligation, any excess belongs to the borrower. If, instead, the security is insufficient to satisfy the obligation, the lender suffers the loss and it cannot seek a deficiency judgment against the borrower.

Two of the most important United States tax cases involve the impact of non-recourse debt. According to the Supreme Court in *Crane v. Commissioner,* 331 U.S. 1 (1947), if a buyer acquires property subject to a mortgage securing non-recourse debt, the seller must include the amount of the debt in his amount realized regardless whether the buyer assumes the debt, agrees to pay it, or merely takes the property subject to it. In a critical exception, the Court (in the famous footnote 21) declined to apply its rule if the amount of the debt exceeded the fair market value of the security. Several decades later, however, the Court applied the *Crane Rule* to debt exceeding the security value. *Commissioner v. Tufts,* 461 U.S. 300 (1983).

Another important legal issue involving non-recourse debt focuses on the meaning of ownership. The owner of property has legal rights which differ from the rights of a secured creditor. The existence of non-recourse debt, however, blurs the economic distinctions between ownership and creditor status. An important factor in ownership involves the risk of loss; however, in non-recourse situations the risk of loss falls on the creditor. Another important factor involves the opportunity for gain. In typical non-recourse debt situations, the nominal owner has the opportunity for gain. However, in some situations—such as complicate sale-leaseback transactions—the nominal owner lacks the opportunity for gain but retains the risk of loss. Whether such a nominal owner is legally the owner for tax law and other legal purposes varies from case to case. *See, e.g., Frank Lyon Co. v. United States,* 435 U.S. 561 (1978).

323. **Nominal Annual Interest Rate:** *NAI:* This is the *periodic interest* rate times the number of periods in one year. It is an uncompounded rate. Abbreviated as *NAI,* the nominal rate is an important key on all

financial calculators. The rate itself serves no purpose in computations; however, because humans tend to think in terms of one year, they typically multiply periodic rates times the number of periods in one year. The resulting *NAI* is a useful, albeit misleading, term for comparing financial instruments.

The formula for converting an *effective interest* rate to an *NAI* is:

$$\left[\ 100py\left(\left(1+\frac{eff}{100}\right)^{\frac{1}{py}}-1\right)\right]$$

where *eff* = the *effective interest rate* and *py* = the number of periods per year.

324. **Notional Debt:** The stated nominal principal debt amount of which interest payments or accruals are a function.

325. **Opportunity Cost:** This measures what would have happened had a particular decision or choice not been made. It is the lost opportunity. For example, when one spends money to purchase a pair of shoes, one no longer has the opportunity to spend that money on a shirt or to invest the money. That analysis measures the *opportunity cost*.

326. **Option:** Options have three basic types:

- American Option. Holders may exercise the option at any time prior to the expiration.

- European Option. Holders may exercise the option on a particular date (the expiration date).

- Exotic (including Asian) Option. Holders may exercise the option based on a variety of factors, which sometimes include the average price of the underlying asset during a defined period.

Options also divide into Put Options (contracts to force someone to buy) and Call Options (contracts to force someone to sell).

327. **Order of Magnitude:** Ten times. Thus the difference between one and ten is one order of magnitude. The difference between one and one hundred is two orders of magnitude.

328. **Original Issue Discount: OID:** Discount on a bond or similar instrument occurs in two ways:

- On original issue discount.

- As market discount.

For *original issue* discount, the maker defers payment of interest until maturity (which may include serial maturity—payments over time). For tax purposes, both holders and issuers of OID instruments must use the accrual method for reporting interest income or deductions. Internal Revenue Code (*IRC*) Sections 1271 through 1276 generally provide the needed rules, along with subsection 163(e).

In contrast, *Market Discount* (*MD*) results from increases in market rates of interest. *Acquisition Premium* (*AP*) results from decreases in market rates of interest. Both of these affect the value of debt instruments after original issue and prior to maturity. They affect the instrument holder, but not the issuers.

The United States tax timing rules for OID, *MD*, and *AP* differ; hence, investment strategies must differ regarding the three interest effects, which are themselves mathematically the same.

329. **Organization for Economic Co-operation and Development: OECD:** An international organization which seeks to promote policies that will improve the economic and social well-being of people around the world. It focuses primarily on helping governments tackle economic, social, and governance challenges of a globalized economy.

330. **Other People's Money: OPM:** This is a slang term in financial circles. It generally refers to leverage, *i.e.*, borrowed amounts. It can also refer to government spending or expense account spending: arguably people are more conservative and more responsible when they spend their own money than when they spend OPM.

331. **Over the Counter: OTC:** Over the Counter trades refer to securities transactions which do not involve an established market, such as the *NYSE*, the *AMEX*, or the *NASDAQ*. Often these are very small issues which may trade for low amounts. Individual dealers—such as investment banks—handle the trades either themselves or through networks they join or create.

332. **Par Value:** This is largely an antiquated term denoting the original stated issue price of corporate shares. Historically, if an entity issued shares for less than par value, they were assessable for the under-paid amount. As a result, many companies issued stock with a par value of $1 per share, but charged an appropriate market price. The excess would be accounted for as "*APIC*" (additional paid-in capital) or "EPIC" (excess paid-in capital). Many states changes laws to permit a "stated value" rather than a "par value"; however, that change in terminology had no real meaning. States now vary regarding whether they require a stated/par value or permit it.

A bond issue for "par value" would be one issued for its "face value"—the stated amount on the bond, which is the amount due on maturity. Interest on a bond (the coupon rate) is a function of the "par value" of the bond. Bonds issued for more than par have "acquisition premium." Bonds issued below "par" have "original issue discount" (OID).

333. **Partner Capital Account:** Partnerships maintain capital accounts for each partner. Accounting for these is very complicated.

For United States tax purposes, proper maintenance of partner capital accounts is controlled by Treas. Reg. section 1.704–1(b)(2)(iv). For a partnership allocation to have substantial economic effect and thus be respected for tax purposes, the partnership must generally maintain capital accounts consistent with this treasury regulation. The rules are among the more complicated provisions in U.S. tax law.

The partner's capital account balance does not by itself reflect the value of the partner's interest in the partnership. To determine the value of a partnership interest, an expert would want to know the balance in the partner's capital account, whether the accounts are maintained consistent with the treasury regulations, the partner's inside basis in partnership assets, the partner's share of partnership liabilities, and the partner's outside basis. Such information would not be sufficient, as the expert would also want to examine all financial statements of the partnership.

334. **Partner Inside Basis:** A partner not only has an outside basis in his partnership interest, but he also has an inside basis in various partnership assets. One partner's basis in an asset may or may not equal another equal partner's basis in the same asset. Differences occur for many reasons, including the effect of asset contributions to the partnership as well as special allocations of various partnership items (*e.g.*, income, gains, losses, deductions, and credits).

Because U.S. partnership tax law is so very complicated, non-tax lawyers should be cautious when dealing with valuation issues involving partnership interests. While some such interests may be uncomplicated and simple to value, others may involve astonishingly complicated rules and allocations which can effectively hide substantial income and value.

335. **Partner Outside Basis:** Internal Revenue Code section 705 defines a partner's basis in his partnership interest. In tax parlance, this refers to the partner's outside basis. Section 705 provides:

(a) General rule

The adjusted basis of a partner's interest in a partnership shall, except as provided in subsection (b), be the basis of such interest determined under section 722 (relating to contributions to a partnership) or section 742 (relating to transfers of partnership interests)—

(1) increased by the sum of his distributive share for the taxable year and prior taxable years of—

(A) taxable income of the partnership as determined under section 703(a),

(B) income of the partnership exempt from tax under this title, and

(C) the excess of the deductions for depletion over the basis of the property subject to depletion;

(2) decreased (but not below zero) by distributions by the partnership as provided in section 733 and by the sum of his distributive share for the taxable year and prior taxable years of—

(A) losses of the partnership, and

(B) expenditures of the partnership not deductible in computing its taxable income and not properly chargeable to capital account; and

(3) decreased (but not below zero) by the amount of the partner's deduction for depletion for any partnership oil and gas property to the extent such deduction does not exceed the proportionate share of the adjusted basis of such property allocated to such partner under section 613A(c)(7)(D).

Per section 752, a partner's share of liability increases is generally treated as a contribution to capital which thus affects his outside basis.

336. **Passive Activity:** A federal tax term where generally an individual or entity will not be considered to have materially participated in the management or operation of a activity when the entity spends less than 500 hours per year on that activity. Passive activity losses can only be used to offset passive activity gains. An example would be a partnership that owns and leases out a beach house where one partner manages the property while the passive activity partner merely contributed money towards the purchase of the beach house but engages in no further activity in its management. *See* IRC section 469.

337. **Passive Foreign Investment Company: PFIC:** A federal tax term found IRC section 1297a. This is a foreign-based company that has one of the following attributes: 75% of its income derived from income that is deemed passive (dividends from stock ownership, income from rental property with a third party manager); at least 50% of the company's assets are investments that produce interest, dividends, and/or capital gains.

338. **Pass-Thru Entity:** For United States tax purposes, several types of *pass-thru entities* exist:

- *S Corporations* under Subchapter S.

- Partnerships under Subchapter K.
- *Simple Trusts* under Subchapter J.
- *REMIC* under Subchapter M.

An LLC under state law is a partnership for tax purposes and thus is also a *pass-thru entity*. In some senses, a cooperative under Subchapter T is quite similar to a pass-thru entity. Also, a *REIT* under Subchapter M has many similarities to a complex trust under Subchapter J and to *pass-thru entities* as a result. A defective or failure *Grantor Trust* collapses into a pass-thru entity. A common *Estate Planning* tool involves an intentionally defective *Grantor Trust*.

One might more generally speak of *pass through entities*, as well. The broader term refers to the following:

> Such entities are not taxpayers themselves (with some minor exceptions); instead, the owners must include their share of the entity income, distributed or not. Each *pass through entity* has its own set of rules defining income, shares of income, the consequences of contributions, distributions, the incurrence of debt and other issues.

The more narrow term, *pass-thru entity* appears in the Internal Revenue Code many times. Typically, the section using the term does not define it. No section defines the term for the code as a whole. Also, various sections which define the term do so inconsistently. For example, sections 170 (dealing with charitable contribution deductions) and 267 (dealing with related party transactions) both use the term *pass-thru entity*. Each defines it as including a partnership or an S corporation. In contrast, section 1281 (dealing with OID accrual on short-term obligations) has special rules for *pass-thru entities*. This section defines them as including not only partnerships and S corporations, but also trusts (not just simple trusts). A third example appears in *IRC* section 461 (dealing with the timing of deductions). A provision applicable for years following 2009 specifically targets partnerships and S corporations. The provision also grants the Secretary of the Treasury authority to extend the rule to "other *pass-thru entities*" by way of regulations. It does not define which other "*pass-thru*" entities it has in mind and no such regulations yet exist.

Lawyers need to heed the great complexities inherent in these various forms, as well as the frequent (annoying?) inconsistencies. While each is similar to the others in many respects, they also have substantial differences. State laws also differ on how they treat them. For example, an individual may have gross income from a trust or partnership, but may receive nothing in terms of a distribution. For tax purposes, the individual has income. But, does he have income for purposes of computing an alimony or child support obligation? For purposes of determining what is and what is not a marital asset or community property? That depends on state law, which is often inconsistent within the various states—which often treat different types of income differently—as well as from state to state. Does he have income for purposes of determining a contractual provision? That depends on how the contract defined *income*—or even whether it defined *income*.

339. **Patent Box (*aka* IP Regime):** This is a common international tax "colloquial term" referring to an entity existing to hold intellectual property (IP) such as a patent, copyright or trademark. Placed in a "tax haven" it can charge significant fees for licensing of its property and thus lower the taxable income of the user (almost certainly a related entity) without suffering significant tax itself.

340. **Payable on Death: *POD*:** This is a common way of holding a bank account: it is owned by one person, but payable on death of that person to another or others. For *FDIC* purposes, the account is insured as if it has multiple owners.

The acronym *POD* can also mean *Payable on Demand*.

341. **Payment: *PMT*:** The word *payment* has two very different meanings:

- For *financial calculations*, the *PMT* button or function denotes the amount of the periodic cash flow for an *annuity, sinking fund*, or *amortization*.

- For *tax purposes*, a *payment* is distinguishable from a *deposit*. Cash method taxpayers have income when they receive *payment* of an income item; also, they may take a deduction when they *pay* a deductible item. Similarly, *accrual* method taxpayers have income at the earlier of the date they earn an income item, receive *payment* of it, or when *payment* is due. For *accrual* method deductions, *payment* is a significant factor in determining whether a transaction satisfies economic performance under *IRC* section 461(h).

Exactly when *payment* occurs for tax purposes is not clear. At least three important tax ramifications of payment are important:

- The Supreme Court considered the issue in *Commissioner v. Indianapolis Power and Light*, 493 U.S. 203 (1990); however, the decision arguably created more confusion than it resolved. The case involved the important distinction between a payment and a deposit. The same distinction—with different analysis—exists for financial accounting. A payment affects an asset account and a liability or expense account; however, a deposit merely affects two asset accounts.

- Another important tax decision held that the transfer of a check constitutes a *payment* for tax purposes. *Kahler v. Commissioner*, 18 T.C. 31 (1952).

- A third important tax analysis of the term *payment* involves the use of borrowed money. Typically for either tax or accounting purposes, the source of the funds used to satisfy an obligation is irrelevant. For example, A can borrow money from C to satisfy an obligation to B. For most United States tax purposes, A has paid B. If payment is significant, then A has whatever tax consequences flow from payment. Similarly, for financial accounting purposes, A would have the following bookkeeping entries:

Cash	1000	
Payable to C		1000

(to reflect a loan from C to A at x% *NAI* with y periodic payments and a term of n years).

Payable to B	1000	
Cash		1000

(to reflect satisfaction of an obligation to B).

These two transactions would not impact A's *Income Statement*, because payment is not an important factor in the accrual of an expense; hence, if the obligation to B involved an expense, the item would have been the subject of an accrual entry earlier in the Journal.

Similarly, the two transactions would not significantly impact A's *Balance Sheet* because both cash and payables would have a net effect of zero (although the term of the payable may change from current to a longer term, which would affect A's ratios).

Also, the two transactions would not significantly impact A's *Statement of Cash Flows*, although it would increase both in-flows and out-flows.

But, the above analysis changes if A is related to either B or C, or B and C are related.

If, for example, B and C are related, then A may not have paid anything for United States tax purposes. Borrowing from B to pay B is not a real transaction; hence, to the extent payment is an important taxable event, such a transaction has no tax significance. Similarly, borrowing from C to pay B may lack reality if B and C are closely related. Just how closely related is too closely related is a difficult issue, beyond the scope of this dictionary. See, *Battlestein v. Commissioner*, 631 F.2d 1182 (5th Cir. 1980) (*en banc*); *Burgess v. Commissioner*, 8 T.C. 47 (1947).

For *Financial Accounting*, borrowing from B to pay B or borrowing from C, who is related to B, to pay B is simply a re-financing arrangement. It typically has little or no real impact on the *Financial Statements* except to the extent the debt changes from a current liability to a longer-term liability, or vice versa.

If, instead, A is related to one of the other parties, then the economic reality of the transaction also changes from a true three-party transaction. One cannot truly owe money to oneself or pay oneself or borrow from oneself. Doing so may appear to inflate economic transaction which lack reality. As explained in relation to *Fiscal* and *Calendar* years and also in relation to *Consolidated Returns*, such related party transactions are a ripe area for misleading information and manipulation. Lawyers must be wary of them.

342. **Payments Per Year: *P/YR*:** This is the number of payments per year on a particular loan. Abbreviated as *P/YR*, it often serves the same purpose as the number of Periods Per Year. A basic rule of finance teaches us that the number of periods per year, also known as the compounding frequency, must equal the number of payments per year or it must be one.

   LESSON FOUR: *Calculator Terminology* covers the term *P/YR*.

343. **PCAOB: Public Company Accounting Oversight Board:** Created in 2002, this non-government entity has authority to oversee audits of publicly traded companies in the U.S.

344. **P/E Ratio:** Price to Earnings Ratio: this is current market price of one share divided by the *EPS*:

$$\left[\frac{current\ market\ price}{\left(\frac{earnings}{number\ of\ shares\ outstanding}\right)}\right]$$

or

$$\left(\frac{CMP}{EPS}\right)$$

where *EPS* = earnings per share and *CMP* = current market price.

345. **PEG Ratio:** Price to Earnings Growth: a financial ratio that takes the price/earnings ratio divided by the growth rate. This ratio helps determine a stock's value while taking the company's earnings growth into account. This is generally considered to provide a more complete picture than the P/E ratio. The ratio is the P/E ratio divided by the annual earnings per share (EPS) growth rate.

346. **Periodic Inventory System:** This is an inventory accounting system under which the business physically counts inventory annually (or sometimes periodically). Cost of goods sold in such a system represents:

$$COGS = (BI + P - EI)$$

Where $COGS$ = Cost of Goods Sold, BI = Beginning Inventory, P = purchases, and EI = Ending Inventory.

A Periodic Inventory System—as opposed to a perpetual system—requires little bookkeeping; thus, historically, it was very common. The system, however, does not distinguish between the cost of inventory sold and the cost of spoilage or theft: anything not included in ending inventory is part of COGS if it was available for sale (either part of BI or P).

In contrast, a *perpetual* system tracks each item of *inventory*. Users also physically count inventory annually; however, because of the tracking they can accurately determine theft and spoilage. The widespread use of bar codes, and more recently small implanted IDs, has caused many businesses to move from a *Periodic Inventory System* to a *Perpetual Inventory System*.

347. **Periodic Interest Rate:** This is the rate of interest earned in one period. The periodic rate is critical in all financial calculations. For simplicity, we often multiply the *Periodic Rate* times the number of periods per year—the *P/YR*—to produce the *Nominal Annual Interest Rate (NAI)*:

$$pr = \left(\frac{NAI}{P/YR} \right)$$

where pr = period interest rate, NAI = nominal annual interest rate, and P/YR = number of periods per year.

348. **Periods Per Year: *P/YR:*** This is the number of periods per year on a particular loan. Abbreviated as *P/YR*, it often serves the same purpose as the number of Payments Per Year. A basic rule of finance teaches us that the number of periods per year, also known as the compounding frequency, must equal the number of payments per year or it must be one.

349. **PFS: Personal Financial Specialist:** This is a designation awarded to *CPAs* who satisfy requirements defined by the *AICPA*. As explained by the *AICPA*:

> CPAs who specialize in personal financial planning can earn a specialist's designation, the Personal Financial Specialist (PFS). This designation can only be acquired by CPAs who are AICPA members (binding them to the Code of Professional Conduct), have a minimum of 3,000 hours of financial planning business experience, in addition to continuing education within the last five years and a comprehensive and rigorous personal financial planning exam.

CPAs, as well as attorneys who are *CPAs*, may properly identify themselves with the designation *PFS* or *CFP*, if they have earned the designation. See, *Ibanez v. Florida*, 512 U.S. 136 (1994) [majority approving the use of *CPA*, *CFA* designation by an attorney in advertising over the objection of the regulatory bodies for CFAs in Florida].

350. **PITI: Principal, Interest, Taxes, and Insurance:** These are the four main components of *payments* on a home loan secured by a *mortgage*. The lender naturally expects interest plus *amortization* of the loan principal. Often, the lender also expects a regular *deposit* into an escrow account which will pay insurance premiums on the property plus property taxes when due. That way, the lender ensures the property is insured and the property taxes are *paid*.

351. **Points:** A *point* is one percent of the stated amount loaned. Borrowers "pay" points as "pre-paid" interest. For tax purposes, points "paid" on loans to purchase or improve a principal residence are deductible in the year "paid." As a result, taxpayer/borrowers have an incentive to "pay" points. Banks typically advertise the Nominal Annual Interest (*NAI*) on a loan, with the points stated separately. Federal truth in lending law requires banks to amortize the points over the stated loan term, resulting in an Annual Percentage Rate (*APR*) higher than the stated *NAI*. Banks thus like points because they can advertise an *NAI* lower than the later and lesser disclosed, but higher, *APR*. The *APR*, however, is itself a misleading figure for two reasons. One, it is an uncompounded rate (other than with regard to the impact of the points). Second, it assumes the loan will be outstanding for its stated term, which is generally unlikely. Because most people pay off home loans when they sell their house—typically in about seven years—and because *points* are actually a pre-payment penalty, banks are particularly fond of them. A more accurate rate on a loan is the *Effective Interest Rate* (*EFF*), which reflects the reality of

compounding. The most significant and useful rate would be the *EFF* modified for the *expected*—rather than *stated*—life of the loan.

For example, if a loan has a stated principal amount of $300,000, one point would be $3,000, and two points would be $6,000.

352. **Point of Sale: *POS*:** This specifically refers to the place where a transaction occurs—a check-out line cash register is a common example. *POS* software allows companies to track sales continuously. Cash registers feed information about inventory to home offices and warehouses. Such *POS* operations substantially improve efficiency.

353. **Preferred Stock:** This is a type of security (a term which includes stock, bonds, and *debentures*) which typically has no voting rights. The name Preferred does not indicate anything about value or the wisdom of preferred stock ownership. Instead, it merely refers to the legal preference the stock has for dividends and liquidation over common stock. Normally, all other obligations—secured and unsecured—would receive full payment on liquidation before *preferred stockholders* received anything. Then *preferred stockholders* would receive full payment (including generally for accrued but unpaid *dividends*) before *common stockholders* received anything.

Preferred Stock typically has a right to a fixed *dividend*, which is similar to interest on a debenture. However, preferred *stock dividends* are not interest and thus are not deductible for tax or financial reporting purposes.

Often the differences between *Preferred Stock*—which is a type of *equity*—and an unsecured, *subordinated debenture*—which is debt—are slight. But, for tax and accounting purposes, the differences are substantial.

The rights of *preferred* stockholders appear in the indenture agreement that accompanied their issue, or in the corporation's articles. Preferred stock dividends may accumulate—which means they carry over if unpaid to future years. In such cases, common stockholders may not receive dividends until accumulated preferred dividends are paid.

Preferred Stock may also have limited *participating* rights—which means it can partially or fully participate in common stock dividends. Often, *participating preferred stock* does not receive a common dividend until the *common stock* dividend equal the *preferred stock* dividend. This is, however, a matter of contract.

Preferred Stock—and for that matter, bonds and debentures—may be convertible to common stock on the occurrence of a stated event. The existence of such conversion features has a significant impact on partially and fully *diluted Earnings Per Share* (*EPS*).

354. **Present Value of a Sum:** *PV:* This calculation computes the present value of a future amount. For example, $1,100 in one year, discounted at 10% interest compounded annually has a present value of $1,000.00 today. Thus, if one owes $1,100 one year from now, he should be able to pay off the obligation with only $1,000, assuming the appropriate interest rate is 10% nominal annual interest compounded annually.

The **PRESENT VALUE OF A SUM** calculation is one of the six basic calculations performed by a *Financial Calculator.* The formula for the *PV* is:

$$PV = \left(FV \left(1 + \frac{i}{100} \right)^{-n} \right)$$

where i = nominal annual interest rate, n = number of periods per year, and FV = the future value.

355. **Present Value of an Annuity:** *PVA:* This calculation computes the present value of a series of equal payments made at regular intervals, earning a constant interest rate. For example, $1,000 deposited at the end of each year for ten years, earning 10% interest compounded annually, has a present value today of $6,144.57. Similarly, $6,144.57 deposited today, earning 10% interest compounded annually will produce a fund from which $1,000 could be withdrawn for ten consecutive years, beginning one year from today. This might be used to compute the payoff amount for a loan or to value lottery winnings.

Such an annuity is either in end mode (payments occur at the end of each period) or begin mode (payments occur at the beginning of each period).

The **PRESENT VALUE OF AN ANNUITY** calculation is one of the six basic calculations performed by a *Financial Calculator.* The formula for the *PVA* is:

$$PVA = \left[\frac{\left[PMT \left(1 - \left(1 + \frac{i}{100} \right)^{-n} \right) \right]}{\frac{i}{100}} \right]$$

where i = nominal annual interest rate, n = number of periods per year, and PMT = the periodic payment or deposit.

356. **Pre-Payment:** This refers to a *payment* in advance of the due date.

- For *accounting purposes*, a *pre-payment* actually constitutes a *deposit*. It creates an asset which the owner must *amortize* over the appropriate period. For example, if one were to pre-pay an insurance premium for three years, it would debit *pre-paid* insurance and credit cash. Then, over the three years, the entity would *amortize* the asset by debiting insurance expense and crediting the intangible "pre-paid insurance."

Whether the appropriate financial amortization should be straight-line, accelerated, or decelerated is open to debate. Generally, entities use a ratable (straight-line) method.

- For *tax purposes*, a *pre-payment* has a variety of consequences. For the recipient, it constitutes income if indeed the receipt constitutes a *payment* rather than a *deposit*. Few exceptions to this rule exist—even for accrual method taxpayers. *Schlude v. Commissioner,* 372 U.S. 128 (1963). For the transferor, the transaction generally results in treatment comparable to that of *financial accounting—capitalization* and amortization under *IRC* section 263 and the regulations there under.

  Under *IRC* section 467, however, a *pre-payment* of rent receives loan or deposit treatment if the total amount involves more than $250,000. This rule applies both to the lessor and the lessee. Both must impute interest on the "loan" from the lessor to the lessee and then annual rent with an opposite cash flow.

  For *tax purposes*, *points* on a home loan receive *pre-paid* interest treatment and are thus generally deductible when "*paid*" under *IRC* section 461(d). See the discussion on cash flows for more information.

- For *financial and economic purposes*, interest cannot be pre-paid. Any attempt to do so constitutes a principal payment by definition. All financial calculators deal with cash flows and interest accruing over time. Thus an attempted *prepayment* of *interest* cannot occur: it will always collapse into a *principal* reduction.

357. **Pre-Payment Penalty:** Loans are contracts. As do most contracts, they *may* contain penalty provisions which apply to those who fail to satisfy the contractual terms. Generally, loans do <u>not</u> have *pre-payment* penalty provisions; hence, a debtor may pay the *principal* to the creditor in advance of the contracted due date. In such a case, interest accrual stops.

Under some loan contracts, however, *payment* of *principal* in advance of the contracted due date triggers a defined penalty. This may amount to all or some of the interest which would have accrued under the loan had the advance *payment* not occurred.

Points on a home mortgage loan are essentially a contracted-for *prepayment* penalty. For *tax purposes*, they receive treatment as *prepaid interest*. For federal *truth-in-lending* purposes, they receive *interest* treatment amortized over the contracted life of the loan. In reality, however, they constitute a penalty if the debtor pays off the loan early. Whether the preferable tax treatment outweighs the adverse economic effect of paying off a loan with *points* early depends on the tax bracket and on how early the pay off occurs.

358. **Prime Rate:** This is the base rate posted by 70% of the nation's largest banks.

> Effective December 16, 2008, the *WSJ* determines the Prime Rate by polling the 10 largest banks in the United States. When at least 7 out of the top 10 banks have changed their *Prime*, the *WSJ* will update its published *Prime Rate*.

http://www.wsjprimerate.us/.

The *prime rate* is a popular short-term rate. Many contracts reference it and float as the *prime* changes. For example, contracts may provide for an *interest rate* equivalent to the *prime* or *prime* plus or minus a specified number of *basis points*.

359. **Principal:** As is true of many terms, *principal* has varying meanings. It is not a term of art; hence, lawyers should always define it.

- *In relation to loans*, this is the amount borrowed or loaned. Interest accrues as a function of *principal*. In a **PRESENT VALUE OF A SUM** calculation, the *PV* is the *principal*. Similarly, in a **FUTURE VALUE OF A SUM** calculation, the *PV* is the *principal*. For an **AMORTIZATION**, the *PV* is the *principal*, as is a portion of each *payment*. For a **SINKING FUND** computation, each payment or deposit constitutes *principal*. The *FV* is the sum of *principal* plus capitalized interest.

  Unpaid accrued interest *capitalizes* into *principal*. This process involves *Negative Amortization* of the loan.

- *In relation to trusts*, the *principal* beneficiary effectively owns the underlying trust assets, while the *income* beneficiary owns the right to *income* from the *principal*.

  Much of trust law involves the proper allocation of items between *income* and *principal*. Lawyers should be familiar with state trust laws which define these terms. They should be aware of statutes and judicial doctrines which sometimes *impute* income on underperforming principal. Effectively, such income *imputation* moves items from the *principal* beneficiary to the *income* beneficiary.

Because the definition of *income* is imprecise—both for financial accounting and for tax accounting—lawyers should be careful with any legal relationship dependent upon income. Of necessity, a contract provision referring to *principal* also refers to *income*.

360. **Private Foundation:** This is a disfavored status for United States tax purposes. In other words, *Private Foundation* status is not generally preferred.

IRC section 509 presumes all charities (organizations described in IRC section 501(c)(3) to be Private Foundations. The organizations have the burden of proving *public charity* status.

For U.S. tax purposes, charitable contributions to Private Foundations are subject to greater reductions than comparable contributions to Public Charities. Also, the contributions are subject to stricter limitations. The Foundations themselves are subject to potentially onerous excise taxes under *IRC* sections 4940 through 4945.

Donors should consider alternatives to Private Foundation creation if the entity corpus is small—under U.S. $1 million. Donor-directed funds as elements of a Public Charity are one alternative, albeit with its own drawbacks.

361. **Private Placement:** The "opposite" of an Initial Public Offering (IPO), a private placement is a stock sale made to a relatively small number of select investors instead of the general public. The primary reason to do this is to raise money through equity without having to pay the expensive costs associated with an IPO.

362. **Private Placement Offering Memorandum: PPOM:** Whenever a Private Placement is made a company must include a PPOM with the offering. This document discloses the known risks that management is aware of an serves as a warning to investors that not all investments pan out and could result in a risk of loss up to the amount of the investor's investment.

363. **Producer Price Index: PPI:** This is a commonly watched index, used as a predictor of inflation or deflation. According to the Bureau of Labor Statistics, which compiles the index in the United States:

The **Producer Price Index (PPI)** program measures the average change over time in the selling prices received by domestic producers for their output. The prices included in the PPI are from the first commercial transaction for many products and some services.

http://www.bls.gov/ppi/.

364. **Prospectus:** This is a legal document filed with the *SEC* in relation to the issuance of new *registered* securities. Unregistered securities may, consistent with Regulation D, need to file either a state-required registration document or a Private Offering Memorandum.

365. **Put Option:** This is an option contract under which the holder has the right to sell an item at a particular price to the issuer. Generally called a *"put,"* the contract might colloquially be understood as my right to "put it to you." If I am the holder and you are the issuer, I can make you buy at the *strike price*.

Essentially, the holder expects the price to drop while the issuer expects the price to rise. The holder of a *put* is in a similar position to the seller in a *short sale*; however, the difference is significant. In a short sale, the seller hopes the price will drop. If it rises, his exposure is unlimited. With a *put option*, the holder also expects the price to drop. If it does not, his risk is limited to the price he paid for the *put*.

A *put* is the opposite of a *call option*. Generally, most *put* and *call* options involve publicly traded equities; however, they can also involve other securities or commodities.

With a *naked put*, the holder does not own the underlying item. With a *married put*, he does.

366. **Q-TIP: Qualified Terminal Interest Property:** This is a trust commonly used by married persons to reduce potential estate taxes. The trust supports the surviving spouse during his or her life. Remaining property then passes to named beneficiaries.

Under *IRC* section 2056, the value of property passing to a surviving spouse escapes estate tax; however, generally, terminal interests do not qualify for the marital deduction. Section 2056(b)(7) provides an exception for Q-TIP trusts, the value of which indeed escape estate taxation when created (upon the death of the first spouse). The remaining property then becomes part of the survivor's estate for tax purposes.

367. **Qualified Deferred Compensation Plan:** For United States tax purposes, Deferred Compensation Plans and arrangements come in two basic formats: qualified and unqualified. Each format has sub-categories, as well.

A qualified plan must satisfy rules found in Subchapter D of the Internal Revenue Code. Generally, it must not discriminate in favor of highly compensated employees, it must provide for vesting within specified time periods, it must satisfy funding requirements, and it is subject to significant caps on the amount and percentage of income permitted to enter the plan.

In general, qualified plans are either Defined Benefit Plans or Defined Contribution Plans.

Per *IRC* section 404, contributions to a qualified plan are not included in the gross income of the plan beneficiary for United States income tax purposes. In addition, employer contributions to such plans are deductible by the employer for U.S. income tax purposes. This disparate treatment amounts to a substantial federal subsidy. Also, plan earnings are not taxable to the beneficiary until the beneficiary withdraws funds. This income tax deferral also amounts to a substantial federal subsidy in most cases.

Generally, a plan beneficiary may not withdraw funds without penalty before he or she reaches the age of 59 ½. Also, generally a plan beneficiary must begin withdrawals no later than the time he or she reaches the age of 70 ½.

368. **Rabbi Trust:** A transfer of funds for the benefit of a taxpayer which remain subject to the claims of the transferor's creditors does not trigger the *Economic Benefit Doctrine*. As a result, the taxpayer does not have taxable income—in the United States—from the transfer of funds to a *Rabbi Trust*. The doctrine arose from a fact pattern involving a synagogue and a rabbi. *See, Private Letter Ruling 8113107.*

369. **Random Walk:** Burton Malkiel coined this term in his book "A Random Walk Down Wall Street." According to the theory, stocks take a random and unpredictable path and that the past is no indication of the future.

370. **Ratings:** Various agencies rate bonds and similar debt instruments. Moody's, Corporation, Standard & Poor's (a Division of McGraw-Hill, Inc.) and Fitch, Inc. are common rating agencies.

Generally, they rate instruments as either *Investment Grade* or *Speculative Grade*. Within the two main categories, each rating agency has many sub-categories. Generally, the higher the rating on an instrument, the lower the instrument's risk (or vice versa); therefore, the lower the interest rate the instrument will command.

For *S & P* and Fitch, the highest grade is AAA. *Investment grade* ranges from AAA, AA+, AA, AA−, A+, A, A−, BBB+, BBB, and down to BBB−. Moody's has similar grades, but labels them Aaa, Aa1, Aa2, Aa3, A1, A2, A3, Baa1, Baa2, and Baa3.

Ratings from each agency similarly proceed downward through the B and C range, which are highly speculative. The D range is for instruments in default.

Lawyers should be familiar with the rating systems as many contracts are a function of the ratings. For example, a particular fund or foundation may limit its investments to a particular grade or higher. Or, a loan may have a provision under which the lender can accelerate (call the loan due) if the *rating* falls below a pre-determined level.

371. **Real Estate Investment Trust: *REIT*:** [pronounced reet or rīt]. In the United States, a *REIT* is a corporation, trust or even a mere association which invests in real estate and which distributes 95% or more of its income. *REIT*s often trade publicly. To qualify for U.S. tax purposes, a *REIT* must have 100 or more investors.

IRC section 856 defines a *REIT* as:

> For purposes of this title, the term "real estate investment trust" means a corporation, trust, or association—
>
>> (1) which is managed by one or more trustees or directors;
>>
>> (2) the beneficial ownership of which is evidenced by transferable shares, or by transferable certificates of beneficial interest;
>>
>> (3) which (but for the provisions of this part) would be taxable as a domestic corporation;
>>
>> (4) which is neither (A) a financial institution referred to in section 582(c)(2), nor (B) an insurance company to which subchapter L applies;
>>
>> (5) the beneficial ownership of which is held by 100 or more persons;
>>
>> (6) subject to the provisions of subsection (k), which is not closely held (as determined under subsection (h)); and
>>
>> (7) which meets the requirements of subsection (c).

The subsection (c) requirements are themselves complex.

372. **Real Rate of Return:** This is <u>not</u> a term of art, so lawyers should be careful with it. Generally, a *real rate of return* refers to the actual return on an investment adjusted for actual *inflation*. One should also adjust for taxes.

Even that definition is imprecise because the definition of *inflation* is itself imprecise. The *CPI* and other *inflation* measures represent broad segments of the economy, but they may not represent the individual.

The following formula is an acceptable representation of a *RRR*; however, it is not the only acceptable formula.

$$RRR = \left[\left(\frac{1 + eff}{1 + inf} \right) - 1 \right]$$

where *RRR* = real rate of return, *eff* = effective interest rate, and *inf* = actual past inflation.

373. **Recession:** This term describes a declining economy. Generally, most economists define a recession as occurring after two consecutive quarters of negative economic growth. The National Bureau of Economic Research (*NBER*), however, states:

> The NBER does not define a recession in terms of two consecutive quarters of decline in real GDP. Rather, a recession is a significant decline in economic activity spread across the economy, lasting more than a few months, normally visible in real GDP, real income, employment, industrial production, and wholesale-retail sales.

http://www.nber.org/cycles/.

374. **Registered Bond:** This is a *bond* (or *debenture*) registered with the issuer. It is transferable only on the books of the issuer; hence, it is not bearer paper. The issuer will pay interest on the instrument to the registered owner. As a result, if a person purchases a *registered bond*, he must act to change the registration. In contrast, some bonds are in bearer form with coupons attached. While not used often in the United States, coupon bonds remain elsewhere. The issuer will pay interest on them upon presentation of the coupons. A transfer of ownership occurs upon the transfer of the paper evidencing the obligation.

375. **Registered Investment Advisor: RIA:** *See* Investment Advisor for a full definition. An RIA manages the assets of high net worth individuals and institutional investors. An RIA handles the buy side of the transaction.

376. **Regulation D:** According to the SEC:

> Under the Securities Act of 1933, any offer to sell securities must either be registered with the SEC or meet an exemption. Regulation D (or Reg D) contains three rules providing exemptions from the registration requirements, allowing some companies to offer and sell their securities without having to register the securities with the SEC.

While companies using a Reg D (17 CFR § 230.501 et sec.) exemption do not have to register their securities and usually do not have to file reports with the SEC, they must file what's known as a "Form D" after they first sell their securities. Form D is a brief notice that includes the names and addresses of the company's executive officers and stock promoters, but contains little other information about the company.

http://www.sec.gov/answers/regd.htm.

Regulation D has three broad exceptions:

- 504: Generally this applies if the offering is either registered in a State which requires an offering disclosure or if it is limited to "accredited investors." See http://www.sec.gov/answers/rule504.htm.

- 505: Generally this applies to the offering of "restricted securities" mostly sold to "accredited investors." It permits only very small offerings.

- 506: Generally this permits unlimited (in size) offerings mostly to "accredited investors" of "restricted securities." The restrictions and other requirements in this safe harbor rule are greater than under the 505 exception. See http://www.sec.gov/answers/rule506.htm.

377. **REMIC: Real Estate Mortgage Investment Conduit:** [pronounced **re**-mik]. This is a trust, partnership or even a corporation which holds notes backed by real estate mortgages. Typically, they pool instruments with similar grades and similar terms. The *REMIC* then issues securities to investors in what, for tax purposes, is a sale of assets rather than an issuance of debt. The *REMIC* is exempt from U.S. income taxes: it is a pass-thru entity, similar in that sense to an *S Corporation*, a partnership, or a simple trust. For tax purposes, *REMIC* rules appear in Sub Chapter M, Regulated Investment Companies and Real Estate Investment Trusts. The *REMIC* Rules appear in Part IV.

IRC Section 860D defines a *REMIC* as:

For purposes of this title, the terms "real estate mortgage investment conduit" and "*REMIC*" mean any entity—

(1) to which an election to be treated as a *REMIC* applies for the taxable year and all prior taxable years,

(2) all of the interests in which are regular interests or residual interests,

(3) which has 1 (and only 1) class of residual interests (and all distributions, if any, with respect to such interests are pro rata),

(4) as of the close of the 3rd month beginning after the startup day and at all times thereafter, substantially all of the assets of which consist of qualified mortgages and permitted investments,

(5) which has a taxable year which is a calendar year, and

(6) with respect to which there are reasonable arrangements designed to ensure that—

> (A) residual interests in such entity are not held by disqualified organizations (as defined in section 860E(e)(5)), and

> (B) information necessary for the application of section 860E(e) will be made available by the entity.

378. **Research & Development: R & D:** This commonly used term is not clearly defined. Generally, it includes an entity's expenditures which do not contribute to current products and sales, but which, instead, may lead to future products. Much expenditure can involve both current and future products; hence, accounting for *R & D* expenditures can be subjective. Generally, *GAAP* requires the expensing of R & D, while *IFRS* tends more toward capitalization.

Generally, an entity with significant *R & D* relative to revenues, earnings, assets or equity is forward-looking.

$$\left(\frac{R\,\&\,D}{revenues}\right) or \left(\frac{R\,\&\,D}{assets}\right) or \left(\frac{R\,\&\,D}{earnings}\right) or \left(\frac{R\,\&\,D}{equity}\right)$$

Investors may be willing to forgo current revenues in exchange for future revenues from yet-to-be developed products. Pharmaceutical companies often have very large *R & D*. These and other industries or companies with high *R & D* ratio are risky investment because the results of *R & D* are speculative.

379. **Reserve Currency:** For many decades, the United States dollar has been the major *Reserve Currency* for the world. As a result, many commodities—such as oil—are priced in terms of dollars. Also, investors seeking a safe haven in times of economic or political instability tend to place their investments in dollar denominated accounts or instruments. The *Euro* also acts as a major reserve currency for many purposes, as does the Japanese Yen. Whether the U.S. dollar will continue as the primary *Reserve Currency* for the world is an important issue.

As the primary world *Reserve Currency*, the dollar—and thus the United States—obtains substantial benefits. Because many countries hold dollars in reserve to back their own currencies, to provide liquidity for themselves, or as investments, the U.S. money supply is effectively larger than it otherwise would be at the resulting price levels. If other countries moved dollar accounts into another currency, they would sell dollars, which would increase the supply of dollars and thus depress the value. The result would be inflationary for the United States.

380. **Responsible Party:** *AICPA* definition—the person who has a level of control over, or entitlement to, the funds or assets in the entity that, as a practical matter, enables the individual, directly or indirectly, to control, manage, or direct the entity and the disposition of its funds.

381. **Retained Earnings: RE:** This is an accounting term for the sum of an entity's net earnings minus its cumulative *cash dividends* paid and minus any capitalized *retained earnings* pursuant to the recordation of a *stock dividend*.

The term is generally comparable to *Earned Surplus*, which some corporate statutes use to reflect accumulated earnings minus cash dividends and capitalized *earned surplus*. Both terms are generally comparable to *Earnings and Profits*, a tax term also reflecting generally cumulative income minus cumulative dividends. See *IRC* section 312 for the computation of *E & P*.

Lawyers must be very careful not to inter-change the three terms, which have similar but significantly different meanings. While the differences may sometimes be small, they can be large.

A fuzzy distinction between capital gains and ordinary income involves *Retained Earnings*. Earnings belong to the common shareholders. If distributed, they result in dividends. For tax purposes these are taxable to the extent of earnings and profits. For other legal purposes, dividends are almost always—if not always—income. Whether they constitute income from labor and industry—and thus marital assets in most states even if derived from separate property—depends on the degree of management, a question of fact. But, undistributed *Retained Earnings* economically result in share appreciation. This, in turn, results in capital appreciation or capital gains if the owner disposes of the shares. But, many jurisdictions consider such capital appreciation in separate property to retain its character as separate property, regardless of the degree of management. This is widely true for C corporate investors and also commonly true of S corporate investors. *See, e.g., Zold v. Zold*, 911 So. 2d 1222 (Fla. 2005).

382. **Return on Assets:** *ROA:* This is a commonly used profitability *ratio*. It helps investors and creditors interpret an entity's financial

statements. It combines analysis of the *income statement* and the *balance sheet*. While analysts define it differently, a common definition is:

$$\left(\frac{net\ profit\ after\ tax}{total\ assets} \right)$$

If the *ROA* is less than the general cost of capital, the firm will want to consider expanding: it can borrow money at a lower rate than it can return through operations. For this analysis to be effective, the net profit figure should not include extraordinary items. One should not consider an *ROA* figure for a single year in isolation. It will provide more useful information in the context of multiple years and multiple ratios.

383. **Return on Equity: *ROE*:** This is a commonly used profitability *ratio*. It helps investors and creditors interpret an entity's financial statements. It combines analysis of the *income statement* and the *balance sheet*. While analysts define it differently, a common definition is:

$$\left(\frac{net\ profit\ after\ tax}{total\ equity} \right)$$

If the *ROE* is higher than the return on alternative investments, then equity holders should generally continue to hold their investment and may want to consider increasing it. If the *ROE* is less than alternative investment, then equity holders should consider selling their investment and choosing alternatives. One should not consider an *ROE* figure for a single year in isolation. It will provide more useful information in the context of multiple years and multiple ratios.

384. **Return on Investment: ROI:** This is another term for *ROE*.

385. **Revenue Recognition Principle:** This is the current terminology for was once the "all events test for income." It has four elements:

- Has delivery (per the contract) occurred or the service been rendered?

- Is the price fixed or determinable? [Arguably this has a "reasonable" element to it].

- Is collection reasonably assured?

- Is there persuasive evidence of an arrangement, *i.e.,* that a transaction has taken place?

386. **Reverse Polish Notation: *RPN*:** In *reverse polish notation,* the mathematical operation follows the operands. For example, to add the numbers 3 and 5 in normal notation, one computes:

$$(3 + 5) = 8$$

But in *reverse polish notation*, one would perform

$$3,5 +$$

The comma represents the ENTER function. The calculator would have no equal sign, so one would not have that extra function. Early computers and calculators used this format. The HP 12C calculator still uses it and continues to be popular. Because the format does not require parenthesis and similar symbols, it can calculate some very complex functions more efficiently than standard notation.

Simple *polish notation* is the opposite: the operator appears first:

$$+ 3,5$$

The comma represents the ENTER function.

The term *Polish* dates from the creation of *Polish notation* by a famous Polish mathematician, Jan Lukasiewicz. The reverse method first appeared commonly in the 1960s.

Typically, lawyers have little use for *RPN*. They should be generally familiar with it because they will encounter many people—economists, real estate agents, and others—who use the HP 12C or similar calculators. As these people may be expert witnesses, a lawyer needs to understand their terminology and methodology.

387. **Risk:** This is a measure of the likelihood or probability that an investment's results will differ from the holder's expectations. *Risk* is one of three main interest components.

In terms of individual interest rates, *risk* assesses the probability of default in whole or in part (such as through payment deferral). Properly assessed, risk compensates for default. For example, a diversified investor might accept moderate *risks*, expecting some of his investments will fail, but most will succeed. If measured precisely, the *risk* premium would exactly compensate and the investor would earn no excess over risk-free investment.

In reality, investors cannot measure *risk* precisely because it is a prediction of future events. Hence, investors hope they are better at evaluating *risk* than their competitors. If so, they can earn an excess return.

388. **Roth IRA:** Under United States Internal Revenue Code section 408A, Roth IRAs are treated as IRAs in that the accounts are not taxable on their income. Contributions to such accounts however, are not deductible—in contrast to contributions to IRA accounts.

389. **Rule of 72:** This is a simple method of calculating the time needed for money to double at a given *EFF*:

$$FV = 2PV \text{ in } y \text{ years when } y = \frac{EFF}{72}$$

For example, with an *EFF* of 8%, a deposit will approximately double in 9 years, which is 8 divided by 72. At an *EFF* of 9%, doubling will take approximately 8 years. At an *EFF* of 4%, doubling will take approximately 18 years. The short-cut formula is most accurate for interest rates less than about 20%.

390. **Sales Tax Clearance:** a government-issued certificate that verifies an entity has paid all its tax liabilities at the time that the entity ceases to exist or is transferred to a new owner. The use of such certificates varies from state-to-state. In jurisdictions where they are available, a purchaser of a business with inventories risks responsibility for unpaid sales taxes if the purchaser fails to obtain a **Clearance**.

391. **Salvage Value:** This is the residual value of a thing at the expected end of its useful life. The figure is useful in computing depreciation for financial accounting purposes. Typically, the depreciable basis of an asset is the cost of the assets minus its salvage value. For United States tax purposes, salvage value is usually irrelevant per *IRC* section 168.

392. **S & P 500:** A popular stock index, the *S & P 500* is:

> Widely regarded as the best single gauge of the U.S. equities market, this world-renowned index includes 500 leading companies in leading industries of the U.S. economy. S&P 500 is a core component of the U.S. indices that could be used as building blocks for portfolio construction. It is also the U.S. component of S&P Global 1200.

393. **Scientific Calculator:** A *Scientific Calculator* is one generally used to calculator trigonometric functions, such as sine, cosine, tangent, secant, cosecant and cotangent. They also typically compute logarithms. These functions are very useful in engineering and architecture; however, they are largely unimportant in the practice of law.

Most *scientific calculators* do not compute *financial calculations*, such as *present* and *future values*, *amortizations* and *sinking funds*—at least they do not do so conveniently. Similarly, most *financial calculators* either do not compute trigonometric functions, or they do so inconveniently. The reasons for this have less to do with memory chips than with button design. By itself, a financial calculator has many confusing and overlapping buttons—most of which serve two purposes. A typical *scientific calculator* is similar, often with buttons serving one main function and two shift functions. Adding financial functions to the interface is possible, but not convenient. Because the audience—scientists versus accountants and lawyers—does not overlap for the most part, the better part of wisdom suggests separate calculators for separate functions: scientific and financial.

394. **S Corporation:** A corporation subject to Subchapter C or Subtitle A of the Internal Revenue Code of the United States. C Corporations are themselves taxpayers. They pay taxes on income generally at a rate of 34%. *Dividends* and Distributions from them are not deductible; however, taxpayers who receive dividends are subject to preferential treatment. Nevertheless, *C Corporation* income is subject to double taxation in the U.S.: once at the corporate level and once at the shareholder level. This is as opposed to income of an *S Corporation*, which is a *pass-through entity*.

As a general rule, large corporations and widely-held (generally publicly traded) corporations are C's. Most other corporations elect *S* status or they are LLCs (limited liability companies).

An S Corporation is a type of *pass-thru entity*.

395. **Secular Trust:** *also,* **Economic Benefit Rule** See the discussion of the *Economic Benefit Rule* and also the discussion of the *Rabbi Trust Doctrine.*

396. **Security:** This term has two broad but different meanings.

- Security for an obligation: This refers to the property that is the object of a security device such as a mortgage or pledge. For example, a mortgage on a house commonly secures a loan to purchase the house. The same is true of an automobile standing as security—through a mortgage—for a loan.

- A type of investment instrument: This typically refers either to equities—such as common or preferred stock (or options and warrants to purchase them—or to debt— such as bonds and debentures. The term may, depending on the jurisdiction or contract, refer to any transferable (tradable) financial instrument.

397. **Self Amortizing Obligation:** This is a traditional loan with regular *payments* of all current *periodic interest* plus a portion of *principal.* Typically, the *payments* are level; hence, the largest portion of the early *payments* are interest with very little being *principal*, and the largest portion of later *payments* being *principal* with very little being *interest.*

398. **Self Employment Tax:** United States Internal Revenue Code Section 1401—part of Chapter 2 of Subtitle A—imposes an income tax on self-employment income. This tax is generally equivalent to the social security and Medicare taxes imposed on employment income by Subtitle C. Self-employment refers to circumstances in which a taxpayer is not an *employee*. Generally, an employee is one who is subject to the direction and control of his employer. While the tax rate generally does not differ between the employment tax and the self-employment tax, other issues are critical. Employment taxes fall half upon the employer and half upon the *employee*, while self-employment falls entirely upon the earner. Also, the self-employment tax is an "income tax" imposed by Subtitle A and subject to all procedural rules applied to income taxes. In contrast, Subtitle C employment taxes are subject to different procedural rules.

399. **Separate Entity Assumption of Accounting:** One of the fundamental principles of accounting, this assumes an entity is separate from its owner. Hence, the entity has a set of books and financial statements, as does the owner.

400. **Shared Appreciation Mortgage Loan: SAM:** [pronounced sam]. This is a loan under which some or all of the interest is conditioned on appreciation in the property securing the loan. Arguably, it is more akin to equity rather than debt; however, for both banking and tax purposes, *SAM*s have generally received debt and interest treatment.

For example, in times of high inflation and high interest rates, some people may have difficulty qualifying for a home loan. The lender may also want to share in the expected appreciation of the property being financed. If so, the parties may contract for a relatively small fixed interest rate. In addition, they may contract that if the debtor sells the property within a specified period, the lender will receive a specified percentage of the increased value (which the contract should define with consideration given to the costs of sale). The contract may provide for appraisal of the property—and a payment of interest equal to a specified percentage of the increased value—if the debtor does not sell the property within a specified period.

The tax and other legal consequences of such an arrangement can be complex—and controversial. One must determine the period to which to allocate the conditional interest. One must determine whether the "conditional" interest truly represents interest or whether it represents a transfer of an ownership interest. One must determine whether the loan under which the debtor borrowed money was merely a loan with fixed and conditional interest, or whether it was a joint venture for the purchase of property, or even the sale of an interest in property.

For other legal purposes, one can sell appreciation rights in property separate from the property—at least in many jurisdictions. Stock appreciation Rights (*SARs*) are commonly bought and sold. Arguable, a SAM is more comparable to the sale of *SARs* than it is to a loan with conditional interest. The legal consequences of such a classification are substantial.

401. **Short Sale:** A transaction used by *bearish* investors, a *short sale* historically involved the sale of borrowed securities. The *bear* would borrow the securities from someone less bearish (someone who has a *long* position) and then sell them. The seller hopes the price will drop and he will then be able to cover (pay or satisfy) his obligation to return the borrowed stock by buying new stock at a lower price. The *short seller* would pay a small fee to the lender and would keep the remainder of the profit resulting from a price drop. Of course, if the price rises, the *short seller* loses money because he must purchase the securities at a higher price to cover his obligation.

Substantial *short selling* is mostly a *bearish* indicator because large numbers of investors expect prices to fall. However, it can also be a *bullish* indicator because it means the *short sellers* will have to cover their positions at some point, which will increase demand and thus prices.

402. **Simple Interest:** This term requires explanation in isolation as well as in the contextual usage of "simple interest rate," "simple-interest transaction" or "simple-interest obligation."

The term "simple interest" is not a financial or accounting term. Lawyers should understand no financial formulae or traditional financial calculators use the term; hence, it is undefined in the financial world.

The term "simple interest" is a legal term, used in federal and state statutes as well as regulations. Loan or deferred payment contracts also often use the term; hence, lawyers must understand its legal meaning. Further, they must understand how the term relates to similar financial terms of art.

As is true of many legal terms, this one is not defined uniformly by law and practical applications are not uniformly consistent. In contrast, the similar term "nominal annual interest rate" is a financial term with a specific meaning which forms part of the fundamental algebraic finance formulas. Definitions which different from that traditional meaning are wrong: they exist, but they are incorrect. 'Simple interest" is not a term about which one can be so certain.

In most cases—perhaps close to all—one should be able confidently to substitute the term "nominal annual interest rate" for the term "simple interest rate." In that sense, the simple interest rate equals the periodic interest rate times the number of periods in one year. In some cases, one may find a reference; however, that equates the "simple interest rate" to the periodic rate. While that would not be common, it would also not be surprising. Thus lawyers should insist on clarity whenever the term appears.

For example, *12 U.S.C. § 4313* refers to:

> (3) ANNUAL RATE OF SIMPLE INTEREST.—The term "annual rate of simple interest"—
>
> (A) means the annualized rate of interest paid with respect to each compounding period, expressed as a percentage; and
>
> (B) may be referred to as the "annual percentage rate".

That statutory usage suggests the term "simple interest" or "simple interest rate" might be a periodic rate.

Section 226.17 of the Federal Truth in Lending Act provides:

> 2. *Simple or periodic rates.* The advertisement may not simultaneously state any other rate, except that a simple annual rate or periodic rate applicable to an unpaid balance may appear along with (but not more conspicuously than) the annual percentage rate. An advertisement for credit secured by a dwelling may not state a periodic rate, other than a simple annual rate, that is applied to an unpaid balance. For example, in an advertisement for credit secured by a dwelling, a simple annual interest rate may be shown in the same type size as the annual percentage rate for the advertised credit, subject to the requirements of section 226.24(f). A simple annual rate or periodic rate that is applied to an unpaid balance is the rate at which interest is accruing; those terms do not include a rate lower than the rate at which interest is accruing, such as an effective rate, payment rate, or qualifying rate.

This provision distinguishes the simple rate from the effective rate and the annual percentage rate (*APR*).

403. **Simple Trust:** This describes a *pass-thru entity* trust under *IRC* section 641. Such a trust is not a taxpayer; instead, the income beneficiaries must report their share of the trust income, whether distributed or not.

404. **Simple Yield:** The term *Simple Yield* is not a term of art; hence, lawyers should use it only with an accompanying definition. Most often it represents the following formula:

$$\left(\frac{NAI}{market\ value}\right)$$

> where *NAI* = the nominal annual interest rate. This results in a variable yield.

Some users interchange the term *yield* with the term *simple yield*. Both usages are common and neither is correct or incorrect.

LESSON FIVE-E: *Yield* covers the term simple yield.

405. **Simplified Employee Pension: SEP:** Under *IRC* section 408(k), an employer may contribute to individual or group IRAs of its employees. These form a Simplified Employee Pension Plan (SEP). Because the creation of such a plan is "simple," administrative costs tend to be low.

According to IRS Publication 4333:

> Simplified Employee Pension plans (SEPs) can provide a significant source of income at retirement by allowing employers to set aside money in retirement accounts for themselves and their employees. Under a SEP, an employer contributes directly to traditional individual retirement accounts (SEP-IRAs) for all employees (including the employer). A SEP does not have the start-up and operating costs of a conventional retirement plan and allows for a contribution of up to 25 percent of each employee's pay.

Also according to Publication 4333, advantages of a SEP include:

> ❏ Contributions to a SEP are tax deductible and your business pays no taxes on the earnings on the investments

> ❏ You are not locked into making contributions every year. In fact, you decide each year whether, and how much, to contribute to your employees' SEP-IRAs.

> ❏ Generally, you do not have to file any documents with the government.

> ❏ Sole proprietors, partnerships, and corporations, including S corporations, can set up SEPs.

> ❏ You may be eligible for a tax credit of up to $500 per year for each of the first 3 years for the cost of starting the plan.

> ❏ Administrative costs are low.

406. **Sinking Fund: SF:** This calculation solves for the amount of the regular deposit needed, at a *stated interest rate* and period, to

accumulate a *future value*. This is the opposite of the calculation involving the *FUTURE VALUE OF AN ANNUITY*. For example, if you wanted to accumulate $25,000 in ten years and were willing to make ten equal annual deposits, beginning today, at an annual interest rate of ten percent, each deposit would need to be $1,426.03. Beginning one year from now, the necessary *deposits* would be $1,568.63. *Sinking Fund* schedules often involve the *begin mode* because savings plan deposits often begin at the inception of the plan, which would be the beginning of the first period. The *end mode* calculation, however, may also be used.

LESSON FOURTEEN explains the use of a SINKING FUND CALCULATOR.

The SINKING FUND calculation is one of the six basic calculations performed by a *Financial Calculator*. The formula for the *SF* is:

$$ SF = \left[\frac{\left(FV\left(\frac{i}{100}\right) \right)}{\left(1 + \frac{i}{100} \right)^n} - 1 \right] $$

where i = nominal annual interest rate, n = number of periods per year, and FV = the future value.

407. **Slope:** The formula for the slope of a line is:

$$ s = \frac{rise}{run} $$

The rise is the increase (or decrease) on the y-axis. The run is the increase in the x-axis. This is an important term for many areas of mathematics, as well as economics.

Lawyers must pay close attention to the difference between the slope of a line and its angle of change, which is a very different, but also important, factor. By altering the scale of either the x or y-axis, a graph user can dramatically alter the angle of change without affecting the slope. As a result, the user could "truthfully"—though misleadingly—testify that the graphed line presented the correct slope. While such testimony might sound impressive, honest, and helpful (and it might be), it could easily be misleading, distorting, and dishonest.

For example, lawyers often use income figures over a period of years to predict future income. In a tort case, this is useful to predict and thus value lost income for a victim. In business, a manager would use such information to analyze whether it should continue or cancel a particular project. In family law, such predictions of future income are useful in determining child support and alimony obligations. In the area of mergers and acquisitions, a potential purchaser will use such information to predict future income in deciding whether to purchase a target. In environmental law, a regulator would use such information in analyzing the predicted impact of rules and regulations.

Consider the following:

A's net annual income was:

2008	$500,000
2009	495,000
2010	485,000
2011	455,000

In this simple example, one can easily see—without a graph—the fairly gradual decline in income. Over the four-year period, income has fallen 9% and the rate of fall has increased. But, all four amounts are quite high and the change likely has little real impact on A's financial stability. Consider, however, three graphs of this information each of which presents a line with the same slope, but a different angle of descent.

The first uses a truncated y-axis with an arithmetic scale crossing the x-axis at 450,000. The truncated axis amplifies the angle of descent. A casual observer might conclude that A's income is dropping at an alarming rate. To further mislead, albeit with "truthful information," the x-axis labels appear in large, bold type while the y-axis labels appear in smaller, less visible type.

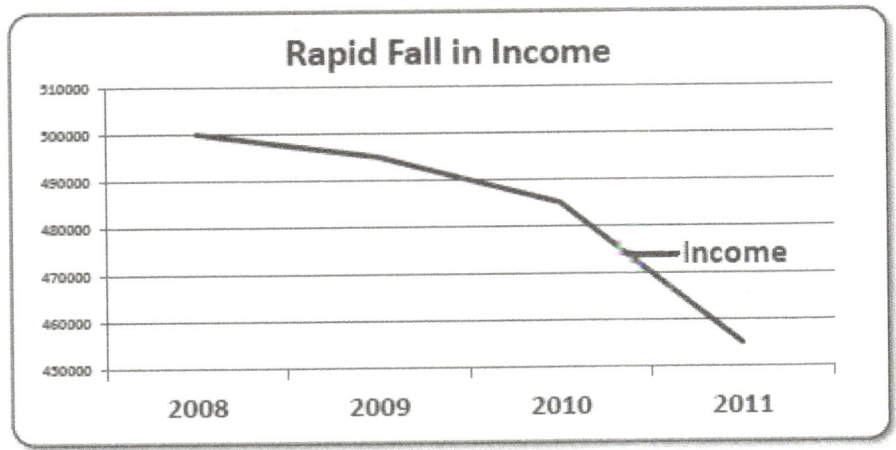

The second graph uses a non-truncated y-axis with an arithmetic scale crossing the x-axis at zero. It, however, uses a more elongated x-axis, which causes the income descent to appear even flatter. For the information provided, this is probably the most "honest" presentation in that it will likely lead a casual observer to the most accurate conclusions: A's income is falling, the rate is increasing, but over-all it is relatively stable.

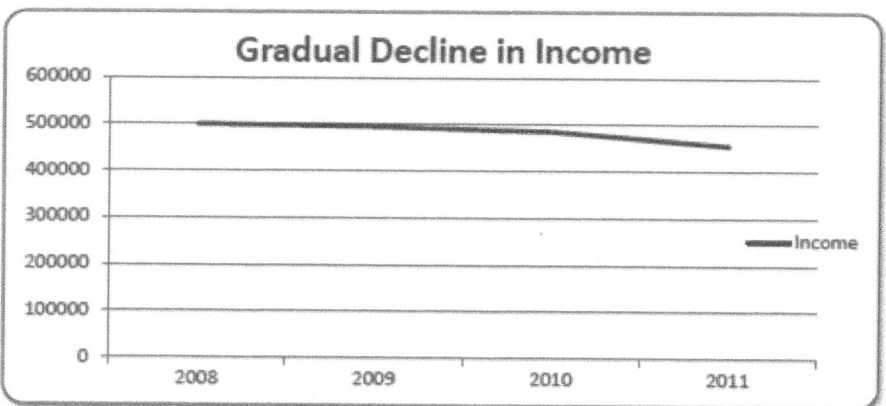

The third uses a non-truncated y-axis with a logarithmic scale crossing the x-axis at zero. The logarithmic scale minimizes the angle of descent, making the line appear very flat. While a logarithmic scale is often useful (*e.g.*, the Richter scale for measuring earthquake intensity), such a scale can present information in a way that would cause a casual observer to draw incorrect conclusions. In this graph, A's income appears very stable.

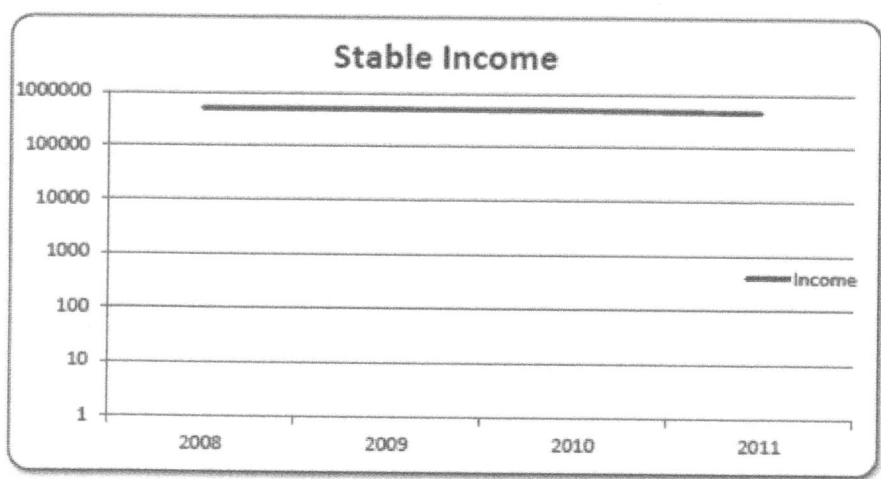

408. **Sovereign Wealth Fund:** A state owned investment fund investing in real and financial assets. SWFs are funded by revenues from commodity exports or from foreign-exchange reserves held by the central bank.

409. **Special Allocation:** This is a United States partnership law tax term
under section 704(b) of the Internal Revenue Code. See the discussion
of "substantial economic effect" for more information.

410. **Specie:** Coins, bullion, and commodity metals. This includes national
coinage, as well as silver, gold, and platinum bullion. Not all national
coins are struck from precious metals; indeed, since the 1930s, most
are not.

   The word *specie* is generally unspecific by itself. When using the term,
   lawyers should specify whether they refer to items in the form of
   specific metals, and if so, the level of purity.

411. **Spot Price:** This refers to the current price of a commodity. In
contrast, many quoted commodity prices refer to futures contracts for
delivery in a month or six months or some other period. The spot price
will sometimes vary substantially as a result of political, international
unrest, or similar factors. Most commodity users however, purchase
supplies through the futures market and are therefore less subject to
the volatility of the spot market.

412. **Substantial Economic Effect:** Under United States tax law,
partnership may "specially allocate" items of income, gain, deduction,
loss, or credit to particular partners. As a result one partner may be
allocated more capital gains, while another is allocated ordinary
income. Or, one partner may be allocated gains while another is
allocated losses. Naturally, the partners agree to such allocations
because their relative financial and tax situations make them
desirable, at least in the short term. For such "special allocations" to
be respect for tax law purposes, they must have "substantial economic
effect." *IRC* section 704(b) uses these three words. Treasury
regulations spend approximately 100 pages defining the three words—
which comprise perhaps the most complicated area of U.S. tax law.

   Of importance to lawyers is the impact of a special allocation which
   lacks substantial economic effect for non-tax purposes. Because the
   allocations result from contracts, they should be respected for other
   legal purposes, despite the lack of tax effect if they lack substantial
   economic effect. Lawyers dealing with definitions of income and loss
   for contractual, tort, or family law purposes should be wary of
   partnership allocations: in the short to midterm, such allocations may
   be contrary to economic reality and thus distorting. Even if they have
   substantial economic effect for tax purposes (because, for example,
   they result in an opposite future allocation through a minimum gain
   chargeback provision), they still may distort reality for non-tax
   purposes over a period of several years.

413. **Standard & Poor's Depository Receipt: SPDR: Spider:** These are Special Exchange Traded Funds (*ETFs*) which divide the S & P 500 into 9 sectors.

414. **Stated Interest Rate:** This refers to the given or *stated interest rate* on an instrument or financial obligation. While it may reflect the true interest rate—such as the current *effective rate* (*EFF*), it also may not. For example, it may fail to account for points or compounding. It also, by definition, does not adjust for external market forces which result in *market discount* or *acquisition premium*.

The term *stated interest rate* is thus not a term of art. Lawyers should use it only with a clear definition.

415. **Statement of Cash Flows:** Along with the *Income Statement* and the *Balance Sheet*, this forms a triad of fundamental *Financial Statements*. Essentially, the statement of cash flows is a cash method Income Statement. It eliminates accruals on un-paid expenses and receivables, as well as non-cash items such as depreciation, amortization, and bad debt write-offs. The statement does not comport to show accurate income; however, it does give a picture of an entity's liquidity or solvency and the direction or trend of liquidity.

416. **Statement of Changes in Financial Position:** Now known as the *Statement of Cash Flows*, this is one of the three principal *Financial Statements*.

417. **Statement on Financial Accounting Standards:** Issued by the *FASB* (Financial Accounting Standards Board), these are the actual opinions. They are also referred to as FAS number X.

418. **Stepped-Up Basis:** *IRC* section 1014 provides for a stepped-up basis for most property acquired from a decedent. Regardless of the decedent's tax basis, the heir or legatee will have a basis equal to the property's *FMV* at the date of death (or up to six months thereafter if the executor elects to use an alternate valuation date). Thus if a person owns Blackacre with a basis of $1,000 and a *FMV* of $1,000,000, his heir or legatee could receive the property upon his death and claim a basis of $1,000,0000.

In contrast, *IRC* section 1015 provides for a **Transferred Basis** for most property acquired by *inter vivos* gift. In the above example, if the property owner were to give Blackacre to his son, the owner's $1,000 *basis* would transfer to the son.

This important provision substantially distorts the economic behavior of many property owners. Elderly property owners have a strong disincentive to selling or otherwise developing their property, or to giving it away to the younger generation. If they were to sell it, they would suffer income tax on the resulting gain. If they were to give it to

their children, the basis would transfer; hence the children would
have taxable gain when they sold the property. If, instead, the owner
were to hold the property until his death, the heirs and legatees will
receive a stepped-up basis to *FMV*. They can then sell the property
without suffering any taxable gain.

For a brief period in 1977, the United States experimented with a
Carry-over Basis system. Congress repealed the provisions within
one year because of alleged complexities.

Be careful to distinguish this from the very different term: ***Adjusted
Basis***.

419. **Sterling:** This has two main definitions:

- The British Pound Sterling, denoted by £. Originally, 240
  British pennies weighed one troy pound. The British
  Pound equaled 240 pennies. The term pennyweight came
  from the old British penny.

- A level of purity in silver. Generally, *sterling silver* is an
  alloy of 92.5% silver and 7.5% copper (hence the tendency
  to tarnish). Most manufacturers stamp *sterling* products
  with the notation 925 or .925, indicating the level of
  purity.

Silver is a commonly traded commodity. Pure—fine—silver typically
has a purity of .999 and is widely available in 100 *troy ounce* bars.
Absolute purity is not possible with current metallurgy techniques.
Coin Silver—which has nothing to do with coinage—has a purity of .9.
Some older European silver had purity levels of from .800 to .875.
Investors should be careful when valuing silver flatware or hollowware
(trays and other non-utensil serving pieces). Silver coinage has
traditionally had a fineness of .800, although the United States issued
half-dollars from 1965 to 1970 with a fineness of .400, and silver
nickels from 1942 to 1945 with a fineness of .350.

420. **Stock Appreciation Rights (SARS):** Stock appreciation rights are a
portion of the bundle of rights which comprise the ownership of
corporate shares.

The holder of the stock sells to another the right to all or a portion of
the appreciation in the share value which will occur in the future. This
can be the basis of a contract between individuals or companies; or, it
may be a form of compensation to an employee.

The obligor would pay to the owner of the right the difference between
the value of a share on the target date and the value of a share on the
issue date.

The income tax consequences of a person issuing stock appreciation rights are complicated. Generally, it would result in an acceleration of ordinary income. Similarly, the income tax consequences of a person receiving SARS as compensation are also complicated. Generally, such a receipt results in ordinary income per IRC sections 409A and 83.

421. **Stock Dividend:** This refers to the distribution of additional shares to existing shareholders. Generally, it involves an increase in the number of outstanding shares by 20% or less. For (some) state and for financial accounting purposes, such a *small stock dividend* requires a bookkeeping entry to capitalize a portion of retained earnings (for financial purposes) or *eared surplus* (often for legal purposes). Such an entry debits contributed capital and credits *surplus* or *RE*. A *large stock dividend*—greater than 25% may not require such entries: that is open to the opinion of the *CPA* and attorney. A very *large stock dividend* is called a *stock split* and requires no bookkeeping entry.

For U.S. tax purposes, the receipt of a *stock dividend* does not result in income. *Eisner v. Macomber,* 252 U.S. 189 (1920). For tax purposes, the recipient of a *stock dividend* would apportion his basis among the pre-existing shares and the newly received shares by their relative *FMV*.

Whether a *stock dividend* represents income for <u>other</u> legal purposes is a matter of state law (which is often unclear if not conflicting) or contract. The issue can be significant in family law matters involving alimony, child support, and the division of marital or community property. If a *stock dividend* is income for those purposes, it will affect alimony and child support obligations. Similarly, if a spouse receives a stock dividend on separate property, the *dividend* portion may constitute income in the eyes of some courts—particularly if the spouse managed the separate property during the marriage.

The financial accounting treatment of *stock dividends*—requiring the capitalization of *Retained Earnings (RE)*—is consistent with the view that they constitute income. Effectively, financial accounting treats a *stock dividend* as a cash distribution of retained earnings following by a re-contribution of the distribution in exchange for more stock. Often, the effective income is a reality: the price of the stock either does not drop or drops to an extent disproportionately small when compared to the value of the stock.

According to at least some state courts, an increase in *Retained Earnings (RE)* does not produce income to the shareholder for purposes of alimony, child support, and apparently the determination of marital or community assets. This is true because the stockholder—unless he controls a majority of the shares—cannot force a distribution of the earnings. Whether that analysis holds for purposes of stock dividends is mostly an open question. In accounting terms, a stock dividend results in an entry changing the corporate capital structure. Under some state laws, it also results in such a change that effectively reduces the ability of the company to pay a *cash dividend* (which must come from *earned surplus* or *current earnings* in some states). In that sense, the stock dividend is an income item. But, an opposing view would recognize that despite the accounting entry, the total amount of stockholder equity does not change; instead, the entry merely moves it from one category to another. Hence a shareholder in a company with no stock dividend, but increased *RE*, is not in a substantially different position than a shareholder of a company that issues a *stock dividend* and then capitalizes some *RE*.

Lawyers must be familiar with *stock dividends*—small and large—as well as stock splits. They must understand the differences and the similarities. They must understand the financial and legal accounting issues and entries, as well. Failure to do so will result in adverse contractual or legal consequences from the incorrect or incomplete analysis of and definition of *income*.

422. **Stock Option:** Stock options, rights, and warrants are similar contractual rights. Generally, each grants the holder (owner) the right to purchase a fixed number of shares at a fixed price, often for a fixed period of time.

Generally, stock options are granted by an employer to an employee as a form of compensation. The U.S. income consequences of stock options granted to employees are covered, in part, by IRC section 83.

423. **Stock Rights:** Stock options, rights, and warrants are similar contractual rights. Generally, each grants the holder (owner) the right to purchase a fixed number of shares at a fixed price, often for a fixed period of time.

Generally, stock rights are granted by a corporation to its shareholders, who then have either the right to purchase additional shares at a fixed price or the right of first refusal on future share issues.

424. **Stock Split:** This is a very large *stock dividend*, often involving two shares in exchange for one, or even more. Typically, a *stock split* results in a price drop comparable to the increased number of shares outstanding. As a result, the market capitalization (stock price times the number of shares outstanding)

(stock price) times (number of outstanding shares)

does not change materially. For both tax and financial accounting purposes, this does not involve any book entry; instead, it merely requires a notation of the change in number of shares outstanding.

Corporations *split* their stock so as to provide greater market *liquidity*. For example, if a company has 1 million outstanding shares selling for $100 each, it could split the stock five for one, resulting in 5 million outstanding shares selling for roughly $20 each. Investors will arguably have an easier time buying and selling shares priced at $20 rather than shares priced at $100.

For legal purposes that are a function of *income*, a *stock split* should <u>not</u> be considered *income*; instead, it is merely an exchange of *principal* for *principal*. This could affect Trust allocations of income and principal, a joint venture or partnership allocation of *"income"* from an asset, or the definition of a marital asset versus separate property in family law. Lawyers should be careful with this as the line between a stock split and a stock dividend is not bright; indeed, in the 20 to 25% range, it is quite fuzzy. Mostly, an increase of more than 25% is a split, and less than 20% is a dividend.

425. **Stock Warrant:** Stock options, rights, and warrants are similar contractual rights. Generally, each grants the holder (owner) the right to purchase a fixed number of shares at a fixed price, often for a fixed period of time.

Generally, stock warrants are granted to debt holders or preferred stock holders. They receive the right to purchase common share at a fixed price.

426. **Stripped Bond:** This refers to a *coupon bond* with the *coupons* detached prior to their maturities. The underlying bond represents the *principal* obligation while the *coupons* represent the *interest* obligation. The phrase also refers to U.S. treasury securities which have been severed among their component parts: the various promises to pay interest and the underlying bond.

IRC Section 1286 deals with stripped and severed bonds. It requires the holder to apportion the basis among the various components according to their relative *FMV*s.

One of the most famous tax cases dealing with the Assignment of Income Doctrine arose from a stripped bond. *Helvering v. Horst*, 311 U.S. 112 (1940).

427. **STRIPS:** This refers to the division of U.S. Treasury obligations into separate instruments representing principal and the various promised interest payments. They then trade separately as zero-coupon obligations. The stripped principal becomes one security and each of the separate interest obligations becomes other separately traded securities, as well.

IRC section 1286 requires the "stripper" to apportion the original cost basis among the various components. Each instrument then becomes subject to sections 1271 through 1277 for determination of the tax consequences for accrued interest, market discount, and acquisition premium.

428. **Student Loan Marketing Association: SLMA: Sallie Mae®:** According to the company's website:

> Sallie Mae®, the nation's leading provider of student loans and administrator of college savings plans, has helped millions of Americans achieve their dream of a higher education. The company primarily provides federal and private student loans for undergraduate and graduate students and their parents.

> In addition, Sallie Mae offers comprehensive information and resources to assist students, parents, and guidance professionals with the financial aid process. Sallie Mae owns or manages student loans for 10 million customers and through its Upromise affiliates, the company also manages more than $17.5 billion in 529 college-savings plans, and is a major, private source of college funding contributions in America with 10 million members and $450 million in member rewards. Sallie Mae employs approximately 8,000 individuals at offices nationwide.

> Sallie Mae was originally created in 1972 as a government-sponsored entity (GSE). The company began privatizing its operations in 1997, a process it completed at the end of 2004 when the company terminated its ties to the federal government.

http://www.salliemae.com/about/.

Note that *Fannie Mae, Sallie Mae®,* and *Freddie Mac* all began as government sponsored entities (*GSEs*); however, *Sallie Mae®* no longer fits that category.

429. **Supplemental Security Income:** *SSI*: According to the Social Security Administration website:

> SSI stands for Supplemental Security Income. The Social Security Administration (SSA) administers this program. SSA pays monthly benefits to people with limited income and resources who are disabled, blind, or age 65 or older. Blind or disabled children, as well as adults, can get SSI benefits.

http://www.ssa.gov.

SSI differs from general Social Security Benefits in several ways. The SSA lists some of them:

- Social Security benefits, SSI benefits are not based on your prior work or a family member's prior work.

- SSI is financed by general funds of the U.S. Treasury—personal income taxes corporate and other taxes. Social Security taxes withheld under the Federal Insurance Contributions Act (FICA) or the Self Employment Contributions Act (SECA) do not fund the SSI program.

- In most States, SSI beneficiaries also can get Medicaid (medical assistance) to pay for hospital stays, doctor bills, prescription drugs, and other health costs.

- SSI beneficiaries may also be eligible for food stamps in every State except California. In some States, an application for SSI benefits also serves as an application for food assistance.

- SSI benefits are paid on the first of the month.

- To get SSI, you must be disabled, blind, or at least 65 years old and have "limited" income and resources.

- In addition, to get SSI, you must:

  o be a resident of the United States, and

  o not be absent from the country for more than 30 days; and

  o be either a U.S. citizen or national, or in one of certain categories of eligible

430. **Supply/Demand Curve:** This is a basic graph in economics. It illustrates the convergence of two principles. First, as supply of a product increase, price will fall. Second, as the demand for a product increases, the price will rise. A graph of the supply curve superimposed onto a graph of the demand curve will have an intersection point, which is the optimum supply and the optimum price.

The following graph also appears in relation to the discussion involving elasticity. As price—the y-axis (left side) rises, demand (red) drops, as reflected in the units demanded because customers will buy less for a higher price. Also, as price rises, supply (blue) rises because produces will produce more for a higher price. At some point, the two cross, which reflects the optimum level.

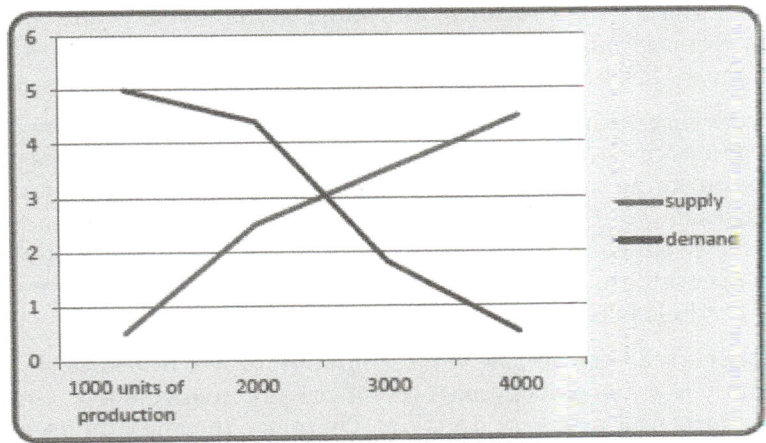

431. **TARP:** The *Troubled Asset Relief Program,* this was enacted by
Congress during the fall of 2008. Initially, it involved plans for the
Treasury to purchase sub-prime loans and other impaired (difficult to
value) assets from banks. Later, the Treasury used substantial funds
to purchase Preferred Stock in banks so as to infuse capital quickly.
The bill was part of the Emergency Economic Stabilization Act of 2008,
Public Law 110–343.

432. **T-Account:** Another term for a *ledger. See books/ledger.* These are
called T accounts because they look like the capital letter T. *Debit*
entries are on the left side and *credit* entries are on the right.

Asset and expense accounts/ledgers will normally have *debit* balances.
Liability, equity, and income accounts will normally have *credit*
balances. The aggregate *debits* will always equal the aggregate *credits*.

A *Balance Sheet* is actually one large *T-account* for all permanent
accounts (plus all temporary accounts closed to *Retained Earnings*).

433. **Tax Account Transcript:** Shows basic data from an individual's tax
return including marital status, type of return filed, adjusted gross
income and taxable income. Also shows adjustments that were made
after the return was filed. In contrast, a Tax Return Transcript shows
the amounts on each line of a return. Neither constitutes the actual
return.

434. **Tax Bracket:** The United States income tax system (and also most
other systems), uses a graduated method of brackets. The first dollars
of taxable income are subject to a low rate—recently 10%. Below that
level, the rate is zero percent. Income above another level is subject to
a higher rate—recently 15%, with the first dollars still subject to zero
percent and 10%. Hence the 15% rate is a marginal rather than flat
rate. Higher U.S. bracket in recent years have been 25%, 28%, 31%,

33%, and 35%. As recently as 1986, the highest U.S. bracket was 50%. As recently as 1982, the highest U.S. bracket was 70%. In 1961, the highest U.S. bracket was 94%.

According to many economists, a graduated tax system discourages productivity. Clearly, the higher the marginal rates, the more discouraging the system becomes. Other economists claim—in contrast—that high brackets actually encourage productivity: they leave producers with so little money, the producers will work harder to accumulate more. Little evidence supports the latter view which nevertheless is commonplace.

Other areas of the law work similarly to tax brackets. For example, family law dissolution matters effectively involve a tax: alimony, child support, and property division. The more income and assets one has, the more he must share with his former spouse on dissolution. Indeed, often the family law definition of income and assets parallel those of tax law. Often, the share percentage increases much like tax brackets. Indeed, one can view family law as just another tax system—only one with higher marginal rates and one in which the client has greater incentives. For example, consider how much a client will pay or do to pay less in tax to the government. Now consider how much a client might pay or do to pay less to a former spouse.

435. **10-K:** According to the *Securities and Exchange Commission*:

> The federal securities laws require publicly traded companies to disclose information on an ongoing basis. For example, domestic issuers (other than small business issuers) must submit annual reports on Form 10-K, quarterly reports on Form 10-Q, and current reports on Form 8-K for a number of specified events and must comply with a variety of other disclosure requirements.

> The annual report on Form 10-K provides a comprehensive overview of the company's business and financial condition and includes audited financial statements. Although similarly named, the annual report on Form 10-K is distinct from the "annual report to shareholders," which a company must send to its shareholders when it holds an annual meeting to elect directors.

> Historically, Form 10-K had to be filed with the SEC within 90 days after the end of the company's fiscal year. However, in September 2002, the SEC approved a Final Rule that changed the deadlines for Form 10-K and Form 10-Q for "accelerated filers"—meaning issuers that have a public float of at least $75 million, that have been subject to the Exchange Act's reporting requirements for at least 12 calendar months,

that previously have filed at least one annual report, and that are not eligible to file their quarterly and annual reports on Forms 10-QSB and 10-KSB. These shortened deadlines will be phased in over time.

http://www.sec.gov/answers/form10k.htm.

EDGAR publishes Forms 10-K along with other important information.

436. **TIN: Taxpayer ID Number:** This is a number assigned to all United States taxpayers. For individuals, it is the social security number. For others, as well as for sole proprietorships, it is an Employer Identification number, sometimes called an *EIN*.

437. **Time Period Assumption of Accounting:** Financial accounting, as well as *income* tax accounting, functions based on time. The arbitrary period used is one year, although many interim statements appear based on quarters or months.

See the discussion of a *Fiscal Year* and of a *Calendar Year* for a fuller discussion.

An alternative to the time period would involve transactional accounting. In such a system, one would report income, expenses, gains, and losses per transaction rather than per period. Many such systems exist:

- For *tax purposes*—at least from the consumer's perspective—excise taxes, sales taxes, VATs, gift taxes, estate taxes, and inheritance taxes are all transactional.

- For *financial accounting*, *GAAP* requires the time period assumption for regular Financial Statements; however, cost accounting—particularly for internal reporting—often functions on a transactional basis, or at least for groups of similar transactions.

- For *legal purposes*, many instances of transactional accounting exist. For example, a joint venture is often a single project or transaction. It would report financial operations for the venture, separate from activities and project involving other ventures. Similarly, partnership accounting has elements of transactional accounting, although it almost always is based on an annual period. Nevertheless, a partnership—which is not a legal entity—will prepare financial reports on a mixed annual and transactional basis.

  Family law also has elements of transactional accounting. While income for purposes of child support and alimony is typically based on a time period, financial reports for determinations of Community Property rules and Equitable Distribution rules are more transactional. That occurs because—in most jurisdictions—some transactions produce community or marital income while other transactions produce separate income. Oddly, under at least some regimes, some transactions which result in income from separate property affect marital property while those which produce losses from separate property do not.

Thus lawyers should be aware of the *Time Period Assumption*; however, they should also be aware that it is not universal.

438. **Total Cost of Ownership: TCO:** This is an element or method of *cost accounting* which reflects all costs associated with owning an asset. For example, if one were to purchase an automobile, the *TCO* would include all licenses, insurance, routine maintenance, parking, and similar costs. The analysis should help consumers and businesses evaluate a proposed purchase as it helps them understand the many necessary—or sometimes discretionary, but common—cost of having something. A very simple example would involve a dog. The animal itself may be free; however, it requires food, vaccinations, a license or tag, medications, check-ups, a bed, a dish, someone to watch it when the owner is away, and many other significant costs. When one budgets for a dog, or a car, or a college education, one should consider not just the direct costs associated with acquiring the thing, but also the *TCO*.

A complete *TCO* analysis is comparable to the calculation of an *IRR*: it would include the *present value* of all cash flows connected to the asset, from the original acquisition to the ultimate disposal.

439. **Trade or Business:** This important phrase appears in 271 separate sections of the Internal Revenue Code (as of 2011). It lacks a clear definition. Generally, it connotes business activity as opposed to investment activity. Trade or business expenses (per *IRC* section 162) receive more favorable treatment than do expenses for the "production of income" (per *IRC* section 212) or expenses in a "transaction for profit." More than two dozen sections further limit tax consequences to the *active conduct of a trade or business*. None, however, define that term, either.

440. **Transferable Instrument:** This is an *instrument* which can be transferred from one owner to another. It is distinguishable from a *negotiable instrument*, which creates a holder in due course.

A maker of a promise may destroy its transferability by providing merely a promise to pay a particular person but not his assignees.

Under the UCC, a non-transferable *instrument* would not actually be an *instrument*; instead it would merely be a promise.

441. **Transfer Pricing:** This is a profit allocation method used to attribute a multinational corporation's net profit (or loss) before tax to countries where it does business. It is the practice of setting prices among divisions within an enterprise. For example, Exxon owns an oil rig in Iraq, a refinery in Turkey, a shipping company in Greece, and is headquartered in the U.S. These subsidiaries act independently from each other except they are all subsidiaries of Exxon. The oil rig sells the oil it extracted to the refinery, the refinery then sells the oil to the shipping company and then the shipping company sells it to the headquarters. Transfer pricing determines at what price each of the subsidiaries sell the oil to each other.

Transfer pricing is also an important aspect of determining an entity's income or loss in a state within the U.S.

Often, transfer pricing results in significant distortions. For example, an entity will have a strong motivation to set a high price in low tax countries or states, which results in lower income or even losses in high tax jurisdictions.

442. **Treasury Inflation-Protected Securities: TIPS:** [pronounced tips]. Commonly known as *TIPS*, these are obligations of the U.S. Treasury. They earn a fixed rate of interest; however, the principal amount adjusts regularly as a function of changes in the *Consumer Price Index* (*CPI*). As a result, the coupon interest—which is based on a fixed rate—increases because it is a function of a greater principal amount. For U.S. tax purposes, both the interest and the inflation adjustment to principal are includible as gross income.

443. **Treasury Stock:** Corporations often purchase shares in themselves with the intention of selling the shares in the near future. Such shares are held as "Treasury Stock." They are never an asset; instead, they are a contra-equity account. Any "profit" or "loss" on the later sale must be closed to equity and does not appear on the income statement.

444. **Troy Ounce:** Most precious metal (*e.g.*, gold, silver, platinum) weights appear in *troy ounces*, rather than the more commonly used avoirdupois ounce. One troy ounce equals approximately 31.1034768 grams. Twelve troy ounces equal one troy pound.

One standard U.S. pound contains approximately 14.58 troy ounces as compared to 16.00 avoirdupois ounces. Hence, an ounce of gold weighs more than an ounce of feathers—the ounce of gold, whether noted or not—refers to a troy ounce. One troy ounce equals approximately 1.097 avoirdupois ounces.

One troy ounce also equals 120 carats or 155 metric carats, which is a commonly used weight for gems.

Lawyers and investors should be very careful in matters involving the weight of precious metals: while custom uses troy ounces, unscrupulous sellers may denote avoirdupois ounces or merely "ounces." For example, 16 ounces of gold—measured on a postal scale—would equal only 14.58 troy ounces. If the purchaser used the market value of gold (expressed in terms of troy ounces) but multiplied it by stated number of 16 ounces, he would pay approximately 10% too much for the metal.

445. *UBIT*: **Unrelated Business Income Tax:** This is a tax on exempt organizations imposed by *IRC* section 511. The highest corporate rate applies. Organizations exempt under *IRC* section 501—plus state colleges and universities—pay United States income tax on their *Unrelated Business Taxable Income (UBTI)*. The rules apply to all exempt organizations, not just *charities*.

Charities—and some other exempt organizations—with more than an *insubstantial* amount of *UBTI* risk losing their exempt status. The definition of insubstantial is not clear; however, many authorities place it at somewhere between 5% and 15% of the entity's operations or cash flow or activities. Most courts reject a percentage test; instead, they apply unclear subjective rules.

446. *UBTI*: **Unrelated Business Taxable Income:** This is the amount of income subject to the *IRC* section 511 tax. Several factors are significant:

- The activity producing the income must be unrelated to the reason the organization is exempt.

- The activity must constitute a trade or business.

- The activity must be regularly carried on.

- The income must not be within an *IRC* section 512(b) modification.

- The income must not be from an *IRC* section 513(a) excluded activity.

Generally, the *IRC* section 512(b) modifications include passive activities such as the collection of interest, dividends, rents, and royalties, as well as capital gains.

447. **Unified Credit:** This refers to a tax credit under *IRC* section 2010. It applies against either the United States Gift Tax or the U.S. Estate Tax.

448. **Uniform Gift to Minors Act:** *UGMA:* This is a uniform law adopted in some states to control non-trust gifts to minors. Drafted in 1956, most states adopted it, albeit with some variations. The act permits a custodian (typically a parent) to hold title to the property and to act on the minor's behalf until the child reaches the age of majority. While most states once adopted the *UGMA*, most have since replaced it with the *UTMA*.

449. **Uniform Reciprocal Enforcement of Support Act:** *URESA:* This is a uniform law adopted by all states to facilitate interstate collection of child support and alimony. The pronunciation of the acronym is easily confused with the pronunciation of *ERISA*, a wholly different act altogether.

450. **Uniform Transfer to Minors Act:** *UTMA:* This is a uniform law adopted (with modifications) in most states to control non-trust gifts to minors. It permits a custodian (typically a parent) to hold title to the property and to act on the minor's behalf until the child reaches the age of majority.

The *UTMA* has replaced the *UGMA* in most states since 1986. Under the *UTMA*, contractual references to *UGMA* accounts are treated as references to the *UTMA*.

451. **Unitrust:** This is a shortened term for a *Charitable Remainder Unitrust (CRUT)*.

452. **Usufruct:** This is a civil law term. It refers to an ownership interest in the use and fruits of a thing. The usufruct term may be specified or it may be for the life of a person. The remaining ownership interest is the naked ownership.

A usufruct is a present interest generally comparable to a term of years or a life estate in common law jurisdictions.

453. **U.S. Government Long Bond:** These are long-term obligations of the U.S. Treasury, also called *Treasury Bonds.* They earn a fixed rate of interest compounded semi-annually and typically have a maturity of thirty years.

454. **U.S. Government Note:** These are mid-term obligations of the U.S. Treasury (sometimes called *T-notes*). Typically, they earn a fixed rate of interest compounded semi-annually. Typically, they have maturities ranging from two to ten years.

455. **U.S. Government Series EE Bond:** According to the U.S. Treasury Website:

> Series EE savings bonds are safe, low-risk savings products that pay interest based on current market rates for up to 30 years for bonds purchased May 1997 through April 30, 2005*.

You may purchase EE Bonds via TreasuryDirect or at almost any financial institution or through your employer's payroll deduction plan, if available. As a TreasuryDirect account holder, you can purchase, manage, and redeem EE Bonds directly from your Web browser.

*Series EE bonds purchased May 2005 and after will earn a fixed rate of return.

Under *IRC* section 454(c), a holder may elect to include Series EE bond interest as it accrues; or, a holder may elect to defer recognition of the interest until disposition.

456. **United States Real Property Interest: USRPI:** IRC section 897c. Ownership of property located in the U.S. and its disposition. This is a tax term that determines the treatment of a purchase or sale depending on whether the buyer/seller is a domestic or foreign entity.

457. **U.S. Government T-Bill:** These are short-term (less than one-year) obligations of the U.S. Treasury (hence the T in *T-bill*). Typically they have terms of 4, 13, or 26 weeks, roughly corresponding with one-month, three months, and six months. They are distinguishable from *Treasury Notes* and *Treasury Bonds*, which have longer terms.

458. **Value Added Tax: VAT:** [pronounced vat]. This is a widely-used consumption tax system. It is similar to a sales tax; however, it is also critically different.

Under a sales tax, the consumer pays the tax to the seller at the point of sale. The seller then remits the tax to the government. Such a tax is relatively easy to cheat, if both the seller and consumer are willing.

Under a *VAT*, each level in the manufacturing/distribution process pays a tax to the government on the value added to the product at that stage. Each stage charges the full *VAT* rate on the sales price, but remits only that portion attributable to the added value. Hence, ultimately the consumer bears the entire tax and the last seller has a strong incentive to collect it: because he paid a similar tax to his seller, he will want reimbursement from his seller for that amount.

For example, if a painter paints a painting, he will have paid *VAT* on his materials. When he sells the painting to a distributor, he would collect *VAT* on the entire price, retain the amount of *VAT* he paid for the materials, and remit the *VAT* attributable to his addition to the value of the painting. When the distributor sells the painting to a gallery, it collects VAT on the entire painting, retains the amount it paid to the painter, and remits the portion on its price *profit margin*. Lastly, the gallery will collect *VAT* on the entire sales price to a consumer. The gallery will retain the amount of *VAT* it paid to the distributor, and will remit to the government the portion of the *VAT* collected on its profit margin. Ultimately, therefore, the consumer pays the entire *VAT*. At each stage the seller has an incentive to collect the *VAT*, as it will retain a significant portion.

Consistent with *WTO* rules, a county may refund *VAT* on exports. A country may not, however, refund the portion of an export's value attributable to capitalized income taxes—such as corporate taxes. Hence, a system which relies more on *VAT* and less on corporate tax has a trade advantage over a system without a *VAT*. The United States stands alone among industrialized nations in not having a *VAT*. The various sales taxes charged by state and local government, however, generally receive *VAT* treatment from the *WTO*.

459. **Variable Cost:** As explained in relation to *Cost*, *cost accounting* is a very important—generally internal—function. It helps management understand whether a particular activity is profitable. For cost accounting to be effective, however, one must pay close attention not only to *costs*, but also to the meaning and classification of *costs*.

Variable costs do what their name suggests: they vary. They vary as a function of the activity being measured. For example, if management wants to produce an extra quantify of inventory, the *variable costs* would include:

- *Stock in trade* (inventory components)
- Additional labor
- Additional energy (electricity or gas)
- Additional wear and tear on machinery

Variable costs, however, would not include *fixed costs* such as management salaries (unless they include an extra bonus for production), insurance (unless extra is needed for the activity), interest on loans (unless extra borrowing occurs because of the activity), *depreciation* on fixed assets, and customary accounting or legal costs.

The total of *variable costs* would generally equal the *incremental cost* of the inventory or the *marginal cost* of the inventory.

460. **Velocity of Money:** This represents the frequency a given quantity of money changes hands in a given period of time, usually one year. The *velocity of money* is a factor affecting *inflation*. Generally, if the *money supply* increases without a general increase in productivity, *inflation* results because, as was said by Milton Friedman, more money is chasing fewer goods.

But, the *velocity of money* must also fit into the equation to determine *inflation* or *deflation*. If the *money supply* increases, but the *velocity of money* decreases, *inflation* will not result.

$$V_t = \left(\frac{nT}{M} \right)$$

where V_t = the velocity of money in all transactions for the economy, nT = the aggregate value of all transactions in the economy, and M = the total supply of money in the economy. The definition of M is not a static concept, but is open to interpretation and multiples methods of measurement. *GDP* (nT) likewise does not have a uniformly fixed definition.

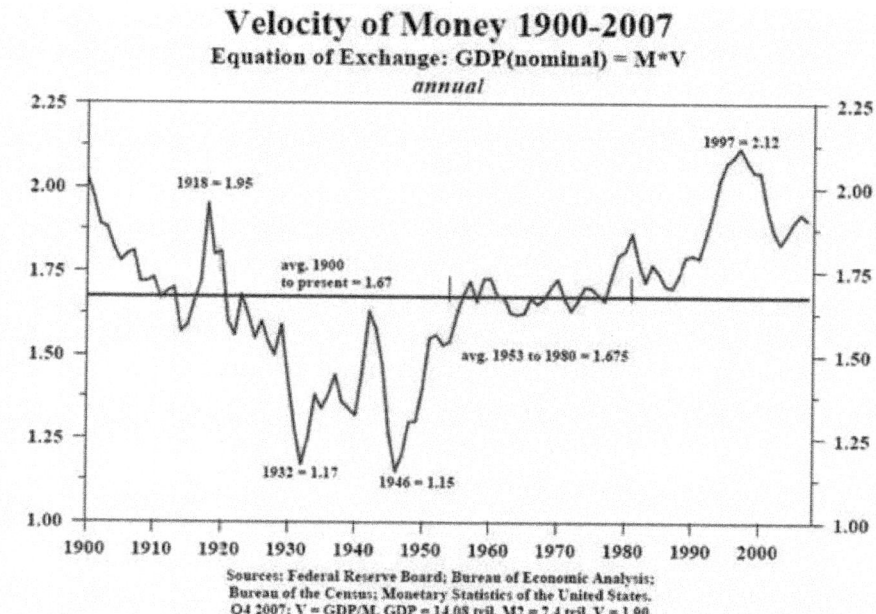

Velocity of Money 1900-2007
Equation of Exchange: GDP(nominal) = M*V
annual

Sources: Federal Reserve Board; Bureau of Economic Analysis; Bureau of the Census; Monetary Statistics of the United States. Q4 2007; V = GDP/M, GDP = 14.08 tril, M2 = 7.4 tril, V = 1.90

As the chart demonstrates, the United States' velocity of money has long hovered around 1.675. During the *Depression* years in the 1930s, the velocity dropped significantly, as it also did during the World War II years of rationing.

461. **Venture Fund:** An investment fund that manages money for investors seeking private equity stakes in startup of small and medium sized companies with prospects of strong growth. The fund is usually comprised of contributions from high net worth individuals that are looking to pool their resources in order to achieve high returns.

462. **Venture Capital:** A generic term that would include venture funds. Essentially any money contributed to a start-up company would be considered venture capital. There is a venture debt or equity but the characteristics of the recipient company would be the same. An early to mid-stage start up with an uncertain time horizon and a high risk of loss.

463. **Vesting:** This is the process by which rights become nonforfeitable. Vested rights are legal ownership of a thing or the right to a thing. Unvested rights are contingent or conditional. With Qualified Defined Benefit Deferred Compensation Plans, unvested interests are conditional on the passage of time and the employee continuing his employment for a specified period. IRC section 411 covers Minimum Vesting Standards for employer contributions. Generally, the section requires either full vesting in five years or a graduated vesting over a three to seven year period.

For several legal purposes, the existence of unvested rights is important. Such legal areas include the rights of creditors, contractual agreements concerning employment, contractual agreements concerning debt obligations, and family law. In a sense, an unvested right has no value; however, that view is simplistic. Certainly, while unvested, the right is valueless; however, many other legal rights accompany an unvested right. For example, an employee who is days short of vesting and who is then dismissed may have good cause to suspect improper treatment and the breach of good faith. Whether such causes are actionable depends on the specific facts; however, clearly the existence of unvested rights carries reasonable expectations of vesting absent misbehavior by the employee or unforeseen and unusual circumstances.

In family law, unvested rights constitute marital assets or community property in some jurisdictions, if earned during the marriage. Valuation of them is difficult. One must consider the absence of immediate value, coupled with difficult to determine expectancy value. One must also consider the cliff effect contribution. The last day of work prior to vesting is arguably the most important: without it, vesting will not occur. In a sense, therefore, all the value of the resulting vested rights belongs in the last day. Such a view is extreme, but not without some justification. An alternate view would place an equal amount of value in each of the days during the five year period (assuming five year vesting). But, that view, too, is unrealistic: many employees work for short periods and therefore never vest. One of the reasons deferred compensation plans require a vesting period is that it helps create loyalty by employees. Evidence of such loyalty—and arguably loyalty itself—increases during the five year period. Under that view, each day may legitimately receive some portion of the ultimate vested value, but in ever increasing amounts.

The financial calculations needed to apportion vesting value among various periods are not complex; however, they require some accounting principle to operate—straight-line value allocation, accelerated value allocation, or a cliff-effect (all at the end) value allocation are a few possibilities. Unfortunately, state laws provide little guidance.

464. **Vulture Fund:** A fund that invests in distressed and underpriced assets in hopes of making a large return on the investment. These funds had gone out of vogue for a while but cropped back up in 2009 when funds were put together to start snapping up homes that had gone into foreclosure.

465. **Wash Sale:** This is the loss sale and repurchase of substantially the same securities within 30 days. For United States tax purposes, the two transactions—if they occur within 30 days of each other—collapse into "no transaction" as if nothing happened. *IRC* section 1091 disallows the loss:

> In the case of any loss claimed to have been sustained from any sale or other disposition of shares of stock or securities where it appears that, within a period beginning 30 days before the date of such sale or disposition and ending 30 days after such date, the taxpayer has acquired (by purchase or by an exchange on which the entire amount of gain or loss was recognized by law), or has entered into a contract or option so to acquire, substantially identical stock or securities, then no deduction shall be allowed under section 165 unless the taxpayer is a dealer in stock or securities and the loss is sustained in a transaction made in the ordinary course of such business. For purposes of this section, the term "stock or securities" shall, except as provided in regulations, include contracts or options to acquire or sell stock or securities.

466. **Weighted-Average Cost of Capital:** *WACC:* *WACC* is the average of the costs of using debt and equity financing for a company. Debt and equity are weighted by their respective use in the given allocation. By taking a weighted average, a company can determine how much interest is paid for every dollar the company finances. The *WACC* computation also allows a company's managers to evaluate the economic feasibility of projects by determining whether the expected Rate of Return exceeds the *WACC* needed to fund the project.

WACC is computed using the following formula:

$$WACC = \left(\frac{(E)(Cost\ of\ Equity)}{V} \right) + \left(\frac{(D)(Cost\ of\ Debt)(1 - tax\ rate)}{V} \right)$$

E = fair market value of the company's equity; D = fair market value of the company's debt; $V = E + D$; E/V = percentage of financing that is equity; D/V = percentage of financing that is debt

A company uses all sources of capital in the computation of *WACC*. A company's goal is to maximize its Return on Assets (*ROA*) while minimizing the *WACC*. The goal of computing a company's *WACC* is to demonstrate the balance that maximizes of debt and equity that will maximize the return to stakeholders.

Many companies discount cash flows at *WACC* to determine the Net Present Value (*NPV*) of a project. Others may use a chosen *IRR* for the discount rate.

467. **Working Capital:** An important figure in the analysis of financial statements, *working capital* is:

$$working\ capital = (current\ assets - current\ liabilities)$$

This information—a *liquidity* "ratio"—indicates the ability of an entity to operate in the near term. Most businesses have regular needs for working capital to meet payroll, utilities, and similar obligations. They would likely maintain adequate amounts in highly liquid accounts. A sudden increase in the *DSO* ratio (days sales outstanding) could rapidly impair available working capital and liquidity. A localized or more general economic recession may occur when a substantial business faces a working capital shortage. It will be slow in paying bills, which results in increasing *DSO* ratios for its supplies, who in turn suffer *working capital* impairment, rising *DSO* ratios, and the cycle continues.

Cyclical businesses require a working capital budget that varies during the year. At some points, they may have large cash needs, while at other times, their needs are low. For example a resort during the off-season does not need the same cash flow it requires during the high season. Similarly, a hospital in the resort community may experience substantial seasonal working capital variations.

468. **World Trade Organization: WTO:** Following World War II, the United Nations attempted to create the *ITO*, or International Trade Organization. This movement grew, in part, from the *Bretton Woods* conference. The attempt generally failed. It resulted, however, in *GAAT*, the *General Agreement on Tariffs and Trade*. This widely respected treaty attempted to reduce trade barriers for international transactions.

In 1995, the *WTO* replaced *GAAT*. It currently has over 150 members and several dozen observers. Organization headquarters are in Geneva, Switzerland. It began with the *Marrakech Agreement*, a conference and treaty signed in Marrakech, Morocco. Earlier, another series of international negotiations—called the Uruguay Round (started, not surprisingly, in Uruguay) set the parameters for the *WTO* and the *Marrakech Agreement*. More recently, the Doha Round of negotiations (begun in Doha, Qatar) has focused attention on third-world (very poor) nations.

469. **Yield:** The term *Yield* is <u>not</u> a term of art; hence, lawyers should use it only with an accompanying definition. Often it represents the following formula:

$$\left(\frac{EFF}{purchase\ price}\right)$$

where *EFF* = the effective interest rate. Others define it as:

$$\left(\frac{EFF}{market\ value}\right)$$

which results in a variable yield. Some users call this alternative definition the *"current yield."* Both usages are common and neither is correct or incorrect.

Still other users impose the *NAI* as the numerator in one or the other above formulas:

$$\left(\frac{NAI}{purchase\ price}\right)\quad\left(\frac{NAI}{market\ value}\right)$$

Such usage interchanges the term *yield* with the term *simple yield.* Again, neither is correct nor incorrect, although the latter two are less common. In each of the formulas using "market price" in the denominator, one must determine whether the user considers the "asked" or the "bid" price to be the "market price" if firmer quotations are unavailable.

The *Fed* website has defined *yield* as:

> **Yield**—The return on a loan or investment, stated as a percentage of price.

The *Fed* defines *return* as:

> **Return**—The profit made on an investment.

Further, the *Fed* defines *profit* as:

> **Profit**—The return received on a business undertaking after all operating expenses have been met.

These three definitions are themselves <u>*disturbing*</u>—together they illustrate the dangers lawyers face with financial and accounting terminology. From the bottom up, the *Fed* defines *Profit* as a return *received* after operating expenses are *met.* The concepts of *received* and *met* suggest *cash method* of accounting, which is a <u>*bizarre*</u> assumption for the *Fed*: *GAAP* does not recognize the *cash method,* which does not clearly reflect income. Then the *Fed* defines *return* in relation to the term *profit,* which renders the two definitions circular. It then defines *yield* in relation to return, which is itself inadequately defined. Probably, the definition writer had *NAI* in mind for return, which would be consistent with one of the four common definitions of *yield*. But, even that definition fails to distinguish between the *yield* on a *discount* instrument from the *yield* on an instrument with current interest *payments*. It also fails to account for what the holder does with the interest paid. Ultimately, for the *Fed* to suggest that the term *yield* even has a firm definition is itself incorrect, as the term is unarguably imprecise.

470. **Yield to Maturity:** The term *Yield to Maturity (YTM)* is <u>not</u> a term of art; hence, lawyers should not use it without an accompanying definition. One statutory definition defines it in terms of a *yield*:

> *Definitions* (4) The <u>*yield to maturity*</u>, or *yield*, is the annualized rate of return to maturity on a fixed principal security expressed as a percentage.

70 FR 57437 (discussing 31 CFR Parts 356, 357, and 363, sale of T-bills, bonds etc.).

This particular definition has two problems. First, it assumes all interest received is re-invested at the stated rate. Second, it is a *nominal* rather than a *compounded* rate. Other users define the term *Yield to Maturity* using an *effective* or compounded rate.

471. **ZBB: Zero Based Budget:** This is a budgeting system under which the applicant for funds must regularly justify all items. In contrast, most budget systems work on additional fund requests: only increases necessitate intensive justification.

472. **Zero Coupon Bond:** This refers to a financial instrument with deferred interest. Also known as a Discount Bond, it would pay no current interest; instead, the issuer pays principal plus all the capitalized interest at maturity.

Financial, Tax Law, Acccunting, and Economic Acronyms

The financial arena is replete with acronyms. Lawyers avoid familiarity with them at their peril. To be conversant in accounting and finance circles, lawyers should be familiar with the following acronyms for several reasons:

1. Expert witnesses will use them. Lawyers need to be able to speak with their own expert, to cross examine an opponent's expert, and to translate to a judge or jury the terminology (including acronyms) used by an expert.

2. Financial, economic, and accounting reports may use these terms. Lawyers need to understand them.

3. Contracts will sometimes use these acronyms, with or without a clear reference. Lawyers need to be able to understand the terms, especially if the reference is unclear (which is an unfortunate situation, but a real possibility).

Definitions of most terms appear in the **GLOSSARY**.

1. **ACRS:** Accelerated Cost Recovery System.
2. **AFBI:** Active Foreign Business Income.
3. **AFR:** Applicable Federal Rate.
4. **AGI:** Adjusted Gross Income.
5. **AICPA:** Association of Independent Certified Public Accountants.
6. **Aka:** Also Known As.
7. **ALF:** Assisted Living Facility.
8. **ALP:** Arm's Length Principal.
9. **ALS:** Arm's Length Standard.
10. **AMEX:** American Stock Exchange.
11. **AMT:** Alternative Minimum Tax.
12. **AP:** Acquisition Premium.
13. **APIC:** Additional Paid-In Capital.
14. **APR:** Annual Percentage Rate.
15. **APY:** Annual Percentage Yield.
16. **ARM:** Adjustable Rate Mortgage.

17. **ATAD:** Anti-Tax Avoidance Directive.

18. **B2B:** Business to Business.

19. **B2C:** Business to Consumer.

20. **BEPS:** Base Erosion and Profit Shifting (important in international tax or multi-state tax).

21. **BI:** Beginning Inventory.

22. **BIS:** Bank of International Settlements.

23. **BLS:** Bureau of Labor Statistics.

24. **BM:** No this is not what you are thinking. It stands for *Begin Mode* or *Below Market*, as in Below Market Loan (also, **BML**). It can also stand for *Bull Market*.

25. **BRICS:** Brazil, Russia, India, China, South Africa.

26. **CAFE:** Corporate Average Fuel Economy.

27. **CAGR:** Compound Annual Growth Rate.

28. **CbC:** Country by Country.

29. **CCCTB:** Common Consolidated Corporate Tax Base (or **CCTB** without the consolidated).

30. **CD:** Certificate of Deposit.

31. **CDS:** Credit Default Swap.

32. **CEO:** Chief Executive Officer.

33. **CFA:** Chartered Financial Analyst.

34. **CFC:** Controlled Foreign Corporation; or Chlorofluorocarbon.

35. **CFE:** Certified Fraud Examiner.

36. **CFO:** Chief Financial Officer.

37. **CFP:** Certified Financial Planner.

38. **CFTC:** Commodity Futures Trading Commission.

39. **CIA®:** Certified Internal Auditor; or, Central Intelligence Agency.

40. **CIF:** Cost, Insurance, and Freight.

41. **CLT:** Charitable Lead Trust.

42. **CLU®:** Chartered Life Underwriter.

43. **CME:** Chicago Mercantile Exchange.

44. **COBRA:** Consolidated Omnibus Budget Reconciliation Act.

45. **COD:** Cash on Delivery.

46. **COGS:** Cost of Goods Sold.

47. **COLA:** Cost of Living Adjustment.

48. **COLI:** Corporate Owned Life Insurance.

49. **CPA:** Certified Public Accountant.

50. **CPI:** Consumer Price Index.

51. **Cr. FA®:** Certified Forensic Accountant.

52. **CRAT:** Charitable Remainder Annuity Trust.

53. **CRT:** Charitable Remainder Trust.

54. **CRUT:** Charitable Remainder Unitrust.

55. **CTB:** Check the Box.

56. **DBA:** Doing Business As.

57. **DCF:** Discounted Cash Flow.

58. **DDB:** Double Declining Balance Depreciation.

59. **DJIA:** Dow Jones Industrial Average.

60. **DNI:** Distributable Net Income. Also, Director of National Intelligence, Director of Naval Intelligence, and Do Not Intubate. The first use is the financial use.

61. **DOS:** Due on Sale.

62. **DOW:** Dow Jones Industrial Average.

63. **DRT:** Dis-regard Tape.

64. **DSO:** Days Sales Outstanding.

65. **E & O:** Errors and Omissions Insurance.

66. **E & P:** Earnings and Profits.

67. **EBIT:** Earnings Before Interest and Taxes.

68. **EBITA:** Earnings Before Interest, Taxes and Amortization.

69. **EC:** European Community.

70. **ECJ:** European Court of Justice.

71. **EDGAR:** Electronic Data Gathering and Retrieval.

72. **EEOC:** Equal Employment Opportunity Commission.

73. **EFF:** Effective Interest Rate.

74. **EI:** Ending Inventory.

75. **EM:** End Mode.

76. **ENE:** Early Neutral Evaluation: proposed in BEPS.

77. **EPIC:** Excess Paid in Capital.

78. **EPS:** Earning per Share.

79. **ERISA:** Employee's Retirement Income Security Act.

80. **ESOP:** Employee Stock Ownership Plan.

81. **ETF:** Exchange Traded Funds.

82. **EU:** European Union.

83. **FAS:** Financial Accounting Standard.

84. **FASB:** Financial Accounting Standards Board.

85. **FATCA:** Foreign Account Tax Compliance Act.

86. **FBO:** For the Benefit of.

87. **FDAP:** Fixed or Determinable, Annual or Periodical.

88. **FDIC:** Federal Deposit Insurance Corporation.

89. **Fed:** Federal Reserve Bank.

90. **FERC:** Federal Energy Regulatory Commission.

91. **FHLMC:** Federal Home Loan Mortgage Corporation: **Freddie Mac**.

92. **FICA:** Federal Income Contributions Act.

93. **FIFO:** First in First out.

94. **FINRA:** Financial Industry Regulatory Authority.

95. **Fka:** Formerly Known As.

96. **FLP:** Family Limited Partnership.

97. **FMV:** Fair Market Value.

98. **FNMA:** Federal National Mortgage Association: **Fannie Mae**.

99. **FOB:** Free on Board.

100. **FOMC:** Federal Open Market Committee.

101. **401(k):** A qualified deferred compensation plan under IRC section 401(k).

102. **403(b):** A qualified deferred compensation plan under IRC section 403(b).

103. **FSA:** Financial Securities Authority (U.K.); also, the Farm Service Agency; Flexible Spending Account; Foreign Student Aid; Federal Student Aid; Full Speed Ahead.

104. **FTA:** Forum on Tax Administration.

105. **FTSE:** Financial Times Stock Exchange.

106. **FUTA:** Federal Unemployment Tax Act.

107. **FV:** Future Value (also **FVS** for Future Value of a Sum).

108. **FVA:** Future Value of an Annuity.

109. **FY:** Fiscal Year.

110. **GAAP:** Generally Accepted Accounting Principles.

111. **GAAR:** General Anti-Abuse Rule (international tax, but not in U.S.).

112. **GAAS:** Generally Accepted Auditing Standards.

113. **GAAT:** General Agreement on Tariffs and Trade.

114. **GDP:** Gross Domestic Product.

115. **GNMA:** Government National Mortgage Association: **Ginnie Mae.**

116. **GNP:** Gross National Product.

117. **GRAT:** Grantor Retained Annuity Trust.

118. **GSE:** Government Sponsored Entity.

119. **GST:** Generation Skipping Tax.

120. **HELOC:** Home Equity Line of Credit.

121. **IFRS:** International Financial Reporting Standards.

122. **IMF:** International Monetary Fund.

123. **INTL:** International.

124. **IOSCO:** International Organization of Securities Commissions.

125. **IPO:** Initial Public Offering.

126. **IRA:** Individual Retirement Account.

127. **IRB:** Industrial Revenue Bond; or Internal Revenue Bulletin.

128. **IRC:** Internal Revenue Code; *never* IRS Code.

129. **IRD:** Income in Respect of a Decedent.

130. **IRR:** Internal Rate of Return.

131. **IRS:** Internal Revenue Service.

132. **LBO:** Leveraged Buy out.

133. **LCM:** Lower of Cost or Market.

134. **LDC:** Lesser Developed Countries.

135. **LIBOR:** London Interbank Offered Rate.

136. **LIFO:** Last in First out.

137. **LLC:** Limited Liability Company.

138. **Lmt:** Limited.

139. **LOB:** Limitation of Benefits.

140. **LTV:** Loan to Value Ratio.

141. **M & A:** Mergers and Acquisitions.

142. **MD&A:** Management Discussion and Analysis.

143. **MD:** Minority Discount; or Market Discount.

144. **MLE:** Multiple Location Entity.

145. **MNE:** Multi-National Enterprise.

146. **MTD:** Month to Date.

147. **MTM:** Mark to Market.

148. **NADA:** National Automobile Dealers Association.

149. **NAFTA:** North American Free Trade Agreement.

150. **NAI:** Nominal Annual Interest Rate.

151. **NASAA:** North American Securities Administrators Association.

152. **NASD:** National Association of Securities Dealers.

153. **NASDAQ:** National Association of Securities Dealers Automated Quotations.

154. **NOI:** Net Operating Income.

155. **NOL:** Net Operating Loss.

156. **NOPAT:** Net Operating Profit After Taxes.

157. **NPV:** Net Present Value.

158. **NSF:** Not Sufficient Funds.

159. **NYSE:** New York Stock Exchange.

160. **OBO:** Or Best Offer.

161. **OECD:** Organization for Economic Co-Operation and Development.

162. **OID:** Original Issue Discount.

163. **OPM:** Other People's Money.

164. **OTC:** Over the Counter.

165. **PCAOB:** Public Company Accounting Oversight Board.

166. **PE:** Permanent Establishment (important in international tax).

167. **P/E Ratio:** Price to Earnings Ratio.

168. **PFIC:** Passive Foreign Investment Company.

169. **PFS:** Personal Financial Specialist.

170. **π:** Principal.

171. **PITI:** Principal, Interest, Taxes, and Insurance.

172. **PMT:** Payment.

173. **PO:** Purchase Order.

174. **POD:** Payable on Death.

175. **POEM:** Place of Effective Management (international tax term).

176. **POS:** Point of Sale.

177. **PPI:** Producer Price Index.

178. **PPOM:** Private Placement Offering Memorandum.

179. **PPT:** Principal Purpose Test (international tax).

180. **PV:** Present Value (also **PVS** for Present Value of a Sum).

181. **PVA:** Present Value of an Annuity.

182. **P/YR:** Payments or Periods per Year.

183. **Q-TIP:** Qualified Terminal Interest Property.

184. **R & D:** Research and Development.

185. **REIT:** Real Estate Investment Trust.

186. **REMIC:** Real Estate Mortgage Investment Conduit.

187. **RIA:** Registered Investment Advisor.

188. **ROA:** Return on Assets.

189. **ROE:** Return on Equity.

190. **ROI:** Return on Investment.

191. **ROTH IRA:** A Special IRA Under IRC Section 403.

192. **RPN:** Reverse Polish Notation.

193. **S & P 500:** Standard & Poor's 500 Stock Index.

194. **SAAR:** Special Anti-Abuse Rule.

195. **SAM:** Shared Appreciation Mortgage Loan.

196. **SARs:** Stock Appreciation Rights. This also refers to Severe Acute Respiratory Syndrome, so be careful.

197. **SEC:** Securities and Exchange Commission.

198. **SEP:** Simplified Employee Pension.

199. **SF:** Sinking Fund.

200. **SFAS:** Statement on Financial Accounting Standards.

201. **SIMPLE:** Savings Incentive Match Plan.

202. **SLE:** Single Location Entity.

203. **SLMA:** Student Loan Marketing Association: **Sallie Mae**.

204. **SPDR:** Standard & Poor's Depository Receipt: **Spider**.

205. **SSI:** Supplemental Security Income.

206. **T-Bill:** Treasury Bill.

207. **TCO:** Total Cost of Ownership.

208. **10-K:** SEC Form 10-K.

209. **TEO:** Tax Exempt Organization.

210. **TIN:** Taxpayer Identification Number.

211. **TIPS:** Treasury Inflation Protected Securities.

212. **TVA:** Tennessee Valley Authority.

213. **TVM:** Time Value of Money.

214. **UBTI: UBIT:** Unrelated Business Taxable Income or Unrelated Business Income Tax.

215. **UGMA:** Uniform Gift to Minors Act.

216. **URESA:** Uniform Reciprocal Enforcement of Child Support Act. Do not confuse with ERISA, which—when spoken—sounds similar.

217. **USRPI:** United States Real Property Interest.

218. **UTMA:** Uniform Transfer to Minors Act.

219. **VAT:** Value Added Tax.

220. **WACC:** Weighted-Average Cost of Capital.

221. **WTO:** World Trade Organization.

222. *y*: Income (generally an economic reference).

223. **YTD:** Year to Date.

224. **YTM:** Yield to Maturity.

225. **ZBB:** Zero Base Budget.